What the Bible teaches

JEREMIAH

and

LAMENTATIONS

RITCHIE OLD TESTAMENT COMMENTARIES

What the Bible teaches

JEREMIAH

J. M. Riddle

EDITOR   **D. E. WEST**

LAMENTATIONS

J. M. Riddle

EDITOR   **D. E. WEST**

SERIES EDITORS
W. S. STEVELY   **D. E. WEST**

JOHN RITCHIE LTD
CHRISTIAN PUBLICATIONS

ISBN-13: 978 1 907731 66 2

WHAT THE BIBLE TEACHES
© 2012 John Ritchie Ltd.
40 Beansburn, Kilmarnock, Scotland

www.ritchiechristianmedia.co.uk

Typeset by John Ritchie Ltd.
Printed in China.

PREFACE

The publishers have commissioned this Old Testament series of commentaries to complement the completed set of New Testament commentaries issued under the general title "What the Bible Teaches". Together they seek to provide an accessible and useful tool for the study of, and meditation on, Scripture.

While there is no shortage of commentaries currently available on the various books of the Old Testament it was felt that there was no complete series that sought simply to apply the message of Genesis through to Malachi to the concerns of believers today.

The authors of these volumes are not scholars of the original languages and rely on others for guidance on the best modern views of word meanings and similar matters. However, all the authors share the conviction that the Bible in its entirety is the Word of God. They believe it to be reliable, accurate, and intended "for our learning" (Rom 15.4). This view has been explained further by Mr Stevely in a short series of articles that appeared in "The Believer's Magazine", also published by John Ritchie Ltd., in 1999.

The two Testaments fit together so that principles and illustrations from the Old are brought to bear on issues that arise on nearly every page of the New. Knowledge of the Old is therefore an indispensable aid to the proper understanding of the New. In particular the Lord Jesus can be seen in prophecy and picture again and again. He, Himself, as described in the Gospels, is an exemplar of this approach to the Old Testament through His constant reference to people and incidents whose histories are recorded for us, and to those prophetic statements that applied to Him.

Given this understanding of the nature and purpose of the Scriptures, the main lessons of the books are considered and applied to our circumstances today by authors experienced in preaching and teaching the Word of God.

Since no attempt is being made to produce an academic series the technical apparatus has been kept to a minimum. Where authors have judged it of value attention is drawn to linguistic and other issues. Transliteration, where appropriate, is accompanied by reference to the numerical system devised by Strong to allow the reader without knowledge of the original languages to gain access to the various lexical aids which have adopted this system. For clarity, numerical references to New Testament words only are given in italics, following the practice used in Strong's Concordance.

The system of transliteration generally used is that adopted by the *Theological Wordbook of the Old Testament* (TWOT), edited by Harris, Archer and Waltke, and published by Moody Press, Chicago, 1980. However, there are occasions when account has been taken of the commonly recognised English spelling of some Hebrew words.

References to Scripture without attribution are taken from the Authorised (King James) Version. Where other translations are quoted the source is indicated.

Biblical measurements are usually given in cubits. For ease of calculation the general assumption has been adopted that 1 cubit = 18 inches/46cms.

Since the commentaries do not necessarily follow a verse-by-verse approach, and to save space and cost, in general the text of Scripture is not included. It is assumed that all readers have available a copy of the Bible.

The complete Old Testament is expected to be covered in around fifteen to eighteen volumes. These will not appear in the order in which they are found in the Scriptures but simply in order of completion by the authors commissioned for the series.

W. S. STEVELY
D. E. WEST

CONTRIBUTOR

JOHN M. RIDDLE

John Riddle was born into a Christian family in North London, saved as a boy of 13, and received into fellowship in New Barnet, Hertfordshire at the age of 15. Throughout his business life, he was employed by Shipping Companies, latterly as a pension fund manager. On early retirement in 1989, he undertook part-time consultative work for some years. He travels widely, principally in the British Isles, conducting Bible Readings and ministering the Word of God, and contributes to assembly periodicals.

ABBREVIATIONS

AV	Authorised Version of the Bible also known as the King James Version).
JND	New Translation by J. N. Darby.
LXX	The Septuagint: the ancient translation of the Old Testament into Greek. Often quoted in the New Testament.
NASB	The New American Standard Bible (also referred to as The New American Standard Version).
NEB	New English Bible.
Newberry	The AV as edited by Thomas Newberry (also known as "The Englishman's Bible").
NIV	New International Version.
RV	Revised Version, 1885 (published in England; a revision of the AV).
RSV	Revised Standard Version (a revision of the American Standard Version).
Vulgate	A Latin translation of the Bible by Jerome and others in the 4th Century AD.
YLT	Young's Literal Translation of the Bible.

JEREMIAH

J. M. Riddle

CONTENTS

BIBLIOGRAPHY

Baxter, J. Sidlow. *Explore the Book, Vol.3: Job to Lamentations*. Marshall, Morgan & Scott, Ltd., 1952.
A good introduction to, and analysis of, Jeremiah and Lamentations.

Birmingham, G. A. *God's Iron: A Life of the Prophet Jeremiah*. Geoffrey Bles, 1956.
As the title suggests, the author deals with the history of the prophet and its practical lessons.

Broadbent, E. H. *The Book of the Prophet Jeremiah*. Pickering & Inglis. *Not of particular value.*

Davidson, R. *The Daily Study Bible, Jeremiah: Vol. 1*. The Saint Andrew Press, Edinburgh and The Westminster Press, Philadelphia, 1983.
While this commentary helpfully explains the text, with good application, the way in which the writer questions in several ways the sole authorship of Jeremiah casts a shadow over the entire volume.

Ellicott, C. J. (Ed). *A Bible Commentary for English Readers, Vol.5: Jeremiah to Malachi*. Cassell & Co., Ltd.
A particularly helpful general commentary, with attention to detail on a verse- by-verse basis.

Feinberg, C. L. *Jeremiah. A Commentary*. Zondervan Publishing House, 1982.
No student of Jeremiah can afford to be without this detailed commentary which is both scholarly and readable. In the words of the publishers, "The author is clear in his exposition, dealing forthrightly with difficult problems and giving insights that reveal his own extensive background in Semitic lore and Biblical studies".

Gesenius, H. W. F. *Hebrew-Chaldee Lexicon to the Old Testament*. Baker Book House, 1979.
While this Lexicon's scholarly approach is particularly helpful to the technically-minded language student, Gesenius nevertheless gives valuable help to the non-specialist in understanding more accurately the meaning of Hebrew words and expressions.

Goddard, B. L. *Meet Jeremiah*. Kregel Publications, 1992.
Devotional meditations on selected passages. A welcome and refreshing volume in the midst of more technical studies.

Habel, N. C. *Concordia Commentary*: *Jeremiah; Lamentations*. Saint Louis, London, 1968.
For all its 416 pages, the commentary, based on the RSV, is minimal, with little attention to detail.

Harrison, R. K. *Tyndale Old Testament Commentaries: Jeremiah and Lamentations*. Inter-Varsity Press, 1973.
A compact yet quite comprehensive commentary, which is more

satisfactory than IVP's subsequent publication. See under D. A. Kidner below.

Ironside, H. A. *Jeremiah; Lamentations*. Loizeaux Brothers, Inc. New Edition, 1928.

By no means exhaustive, but clear and precise. An excellent introduction to the books of Jeremiah and Lamentations.

Jensen, I. L. *Jeremiah and Lamentations*. Moody Press, 1974.

A helpful compact commentary that makes no attempt to be exhaustive. A good introductory volume.

Kelly, W. *Jeremiah, The Tender Hearted Prophet of the Nations*. Bible Truth Publishers. Reprinted 1978.

A brief commentary in which the reader will probably find some help.

Kidner, D. A. *The Bible Speaks Today: The Message of Jeremiah*. Inter-Varsity Press, 1987.

A compact commentary which nicely conveys the atmosphere of the prophecy, although a little vague, perhaps deliberately, when dealing with passages predicting Israel's future.

Laetsch, T. *Jeremiah*. Concordia Publishing House, 1952.

Conservative in dealing with the text of both Jeremiah and Lamentations, with helpful grammatical notes and explanations, but persists in identifying Israel with the church, leading to some bizarre statements and conclusions. However, the commentary does include some good practical application.

Meyer, F. B. *Jeremiah: Priest and Prophet*. Morgan and Scott, 1911.

Selected devotional studies. A heart-warming volume in the best tradition of F. B. Meyer.

Morgan, G. C. *Studies in the Prophecy of Jeremiah*. Oliphants Ltd. Copyright Fleming H. Revell, New York, 1931.

Not a commentary in the accepted sense, but rather, as the title states, a series of studies, evidently sermonic. As to be expected from Campbell Morgan, the studies are marked by eloquence, clarity and relevance.

Newell, D. *The Prophecy of Jeremiah*. An unpublished introduction to Bible Class Studies in Jeremiah at Eastpark Gospel Hall, Glasgow.

Most helpful, and thoroughly recommended.

Orelli, C. von. *The Prophecies of Jeremiah*. T. & T. Clark, 1889.

Particularly helpful in explaining the text of Jeremiah, but less detailed in exposition, with little application.

Pulpit Commentary. *Jeremiah*. Kegan Paul, Trench & Co, 1883.

Following the usual pattern in the series, the volume dealing with Jeremiah provides an exposition of each chapter together with a homily and a digest of comments from various authors. A volume worth keeping, but not a great loss if absent from the believer's library.

Streane, A. W. *The Cambridge Bible for Schools and Colleges: Jeremiah and Lamentations*. Cambridge University Press, 1883.

A highly recommended volume containing a detailed examination and explanation of the text. Always most helpful and illuminating.

Unger, M. F. *Unger's Commentary on the Old Testament, Vol.2: Isaiah to Malachi*. Moody Press, 1981. *A helpful commentary, abounding with Scriptural cross-references which do need to be read.*

INTRODUCTION

It has been rightly said that the similarities between Jeremiah's day and the modern world "could hardly be stronger: today is a time of deep sin, as then; apostasy and hypocrisy abound today, as then; the balance of power among nations totters precariously and alliances change with apparent recklessness from decade to decade; God's heralds are in a lonely minority; and the rumblings of doomsday, like an approaching avalanche, get louder by the minute" (Jensen). In it all, together with the rejection he experienced from the very people he endeavoured to help, Jeremiah found joy and strength in the word of God: "Thy words were found, and I did eat them; and thy word was unto me the joy and rejoicing of mine heart: for I am called by thy name, O Lord God of hosts" (15.16). His confidence was not misplaced. He saw the fulfilment of his own predictions when Jerusalem fell to the besieging Chaldeans. Some of his prophecies have subsequently been fulfilled, including the return of Jewish captives from Babylon after seventy years in exile (29.10), together with the destruction of the Babylonian Empire itself (25.12). Among his unfulfilled prophecies is the restoration of both Israel and Judah under the direct rule of the long-promised son of David (30.9), but only after they have passed through the unprecedented period of Jacob's trouble (30.7), the Great Tribulation, out of which a remnant will be saved. Of the fulfilment of this there can be no doubt since "For ever, O Lord, thy word is settled in heaven" (Ps 119.89).

The book of Jeremiah is therefore replete with practical and prophetical lessons, proving, as ever, that "All scripture is given by inspiration of God, and is profitable for doctrine, for reproof, for correction, for instruction in righteousness: That the man of God may be perfect, throughly furnished unto all good works" (2 Tim 3.16-17).

The Background of the Book

Jeremiah's service, which spanned more than forty years, commenced some eighty years after the ministry of Isaiah, and continued during and after the reign of Judah's five last kings. Leaving aside Josiah, the names of Jehoahaz, Jehoiakim, Jehoiachin and Zedekiah are forever associated with the demise of Judah, and in consequence, Jeremiah has been called "the prophet of Judah's midnight hour" (Sidlow Baxter). Her final four kings were little more than puppet rulers subject to either Egypt or Babylon. It can be said, therefore, that Jeremiah lived and preached amidst political and national uncertainty. Over one hundred years previously, Rab-shakeh had described Egypt as a "bruised reed" (2 Kings 18.21), and nothing had changed during the intervening century. With the arrival of Pharaoh-hophra's army in Judah, the Chaldeans lifted their siege of Jerusalem, only to return when the Egyptian king decided not to fight and went back home, leaving Jerusalem again at the mercy of Nebuchadnezzar (Jer 37.5-10). Hopes were raised, and dashed. The twenty-first century is little different. Political, economic and national uncertainties are the order of the day.

Judah was not a victim of "quirks of fate". Jeremiah lived at a time when David's throne was occupied by wicked kings who could rightly be described as "men of corrupt minds, reprobate concerning the faith" (2 Tim 3.8). The religious leadership was no better. The prophets and priests of the day could also be described in New Testament language: they were "evil men and seducers", waxing "worse and worse, deceiving, and being deceived" (2 Tim 3.13).

It must be said, however, that Jeremiah was equally "the prophet of Judah's new dawn", and not for Judah only, "For, lo, the days come, saith the Lord, that I will bring again the captivity of my people Israel and Judah, saith the Lord: and I will cause them to return to the land that I gave to their fathers, and they shall possess it" (30.3). If the defeat and captivity of Judah were historical, tangible and visible events, then her recovery and restoration cannot be otherwise than literal. To take any other view is to evacuate words of their clear meaning and, even more seriously, to impugn the unconditional promises made by God to the patriarchs.

The final captivity of Judah and destruction of Jerusalem (588 BC according to some authorities, or 586 BC according to others) was far more than a further triumph for the mighty Babylonian Empire. In 605 BC Nebuchadnezzar had defeated Pharaoh-necho at Carchemish, an event which changed the balance of world-power, and following this Babylon incorporated Judah into her territory as a tributary (2 Kings 24.1; 2 Chr 36.6). This marked the commencement of a new era in world history, still in place, described by the Lord Jesus as "the times of the Gentiles" (Lk 21.24), so called because Nebuchadnezzar's reign "began the succession of the four great kingdoms that exercised world dominion" (Feinberg). But Gentile supremacy will end, and Israel, having been brought into the blessings of the "new covenant" (31.31-36), will enjoy the recognition they once forfeited through disobedience: "And all people of the earth shall see that thou art called by the name of the Lord; and they shall be afraid of thee" (Deut 28.10). The promise is clear: "For I am with thee, saith the Lord, to save thee: though I make a full end of all nations whither I have scattered thee, yet will I not make a full end of thee" (30.11).

The Writer of the Book

While we know little of Isaiah personally, this is certainly not the case with Jeremiah. He was of priestly descent (1.1), although there is no indication that he ever functioned as a priest. His home was the Levitical town of Anathoth in Benjamin. It therefore seems reasonable to assume, although proof is lacking, that he was descended from Abiathar, the sole survivor of the priests massacred at Nob (1 Sam 22.20). Abiathar, having ministered during the reign of David, was exiled by Solomon to Anathoth, where he evidently had property (1 Kings 2.26). Unlike Isaiah and Ezekiel, Jeremiah was not allowed to marry (16.2). Moreover, there is no record that he ever attracted disciples, and his closest companion was his faithful secretary and scribe, Baruch the son of Neriah.

While in his day, he was "unquestionably the greatest spiritual personality in Israel" (Feinberg) and spoke "from the mouth of the Lord" (2 Chr 36.12), he was nevertheless a lone voice, leading him to say, "I sat not in the assembly of the mockers, nor rejoiced; I sat alone because of thy hand: for thou hast filled me with indignation" (Jer 15.17). During the course of his ministry, Jeremiah discovered, not only that his home town, Anathoth, and his own family opposed him (11.21-23; 12.6), but that he was regarded as "man of strife and a man of contention to the whole earth!", adding, "I have neither lent on usury, nor men have lent to me on usury; yet every one of them doth curse me" (15.10).

David Newell points out that there are parallels between the life and service of Jeremiah and that of the Apostle Paul: "Both Jeremiah and the great apostle of the Gentiles were called before their birth (Jer 1.5; Gal 1.15); both were commissioned to preach to Israel and the Gentiles (Jer 1.10,18; Acts 9.15); both were assured of conflict with their own people (Jer 15.20; Acts 22.17-22); both were marked by prayerful compassion for their nation despite the maltreatment they received (Jer 14.7-9; Rom 9.1-3; 10.1)".

As Harrison observes, "Jeremiah is unusual among the Hebrew prophets because of the extent to which he revealed his personal feelings". There were occasions when he was deeply disturbed about his personal circumstances, even to the extent of bitter complaint. For example, "Why is my pain perpetual, and my wound incurable, which refuseth to be healed? wilt thou be altogether unto me as a liar, and as waters that fail?" (15.18). While there are certainly occasions on which believers today approach God with "inarticulate prayer" - "groanings which cannot be uttered" (Rom 8.26) - Jeremiah certainly did articulate his turbulent emotions! Having cried, "Sing unto the Lord, praise ye the Lord", he continues, "Cursed be the day wherein I was born: let not the day wherein my mother bare me be blessed" (20.13,14). This was a mood-swing of huge proportions, and the prophet made no attempt to camouflage his inward thoughts with pious platitudes. While believers today would probably refrain from expressing their deep feelings in this way, there might well be occasions when they are tempted to described Jeremiah, like Elijah, as "a man subject to like passions as we are" (James 5.17).

In surveying the life and service of Jeremiah, Sidlow Baxter draws attention to his suffering sympathy, patient perseverance, and utter faithfulness, all of which are well worth emphasising.

His suffering sympathy

Jeremiah was no automaton: there was nothing dispassionate or mechanical about his ministry. It is not without good reason that he is often called "the weeping prophet". These were not "crocodile tears". He loved his people: "Oh that my head were waters, and mine eyes a fountain of tears, that I might weep day and night for the slain of the daughter of my people!…mine eye shall weep sore, and run down with tears, because the Lord's flock is carried away captive…Let mine eyes run down with tears night and day, and let them not cease: for the virgin daughter of my people is broken with a great breach, with a very grievous blow" (9.1; 13.17; 14.17). Centuries later a greater than Jeremiah wept over the same city (Lk 19.41), and some years after that Paul wrote, "I have great heaviness and continual sorrow in my heart. For I could wish that myself were accursed from Christ for my brethren, my kinsmen according to the flesh" (Rom 9.2-3). But, at the same time, Jeremiah was filled with revulsion over the sin of Judah: "Oh…that I might leave my people, and go from them! for they be all adulterers, an assembly of treacherous men" (9.2). There was a tension between his sorrow over their suffering and his horror over their sin.

But it was more than sorrow for his people. In Sidlow Baxter's words, "His sorest inward trial was the tearing of his heart between two rival sympathies - on the one hand a sympathy with God such as few men have entered into, and on the other hand a grieving, yearning, loving sympathy with his fellow-countrymen, which made him suffer with them. In all their afflictions he himself was afflicted. Somehow, in his relation with God, Jeremiah was a prophet, and something more; and similarly in his ardent identification of himself with his people he was a patriot, and something more. He entered both into the life of his people, and into that of Jehovah. He did not merely speak *for* God; he felt *with* Him: and he did not merely speak *to* the people; he felt *with* them".

His patient perseverance

Although, as already noted, Jeremiah's ministry spanned approximately four decades, there is no evidence of any measure of reform as a result of his preaching. As the prophet looked back over long and difficult years, he could not say that in his case, "He that goeth forth and weepeth, bearing precious seed, shall doubtless come again with rejoicing, bringing his sheaves with him" (Ps 126.6), neither could he say from experience, "Cast thy bread upon the waters: for thou shalt find it after many days" (Eccl 11.1). Jeremiah's last recorded message, delivered in Egypt (44.20-30), was addressed to people who persisted in worshipping "the queen of heaven" even after divine judgment had fallen on Judah and Jerusalem. What a dismal end to a lifetime's work for God!

It should be said, however, that this does not mean that Jeremiah was a failure. His contemporary, Ezekiel, was told, "And they, whether they will hear, or whether they will forbear…yet shall know that there hath been a prophet among them" (Ezek 2.5), and it is important to remember that "every man shall receive his own reward according to his own labour" (1 Cor 3.8), not according to the blessing seen on the labour. Nevertheless, to persevere in these circumstances requires immense resolution and, on the threshold of his ministry, doubtless with this in mind, the Lord assured His servant that he was the chosen man for the hour: "Before I formed thee in the belly I knew thee; and before thou camest forth out of the womb I sanctified thee, and I ordained thee a prophet unto the nations" (1.5). Moreover, Jeremiah was assured that the word of God would not fail: "I will hasten my word ('I am watchful over my word', JND) to perform it" (1.12). Further, he was promised divine help: "kings…princes… priests…people…shall fight against thee; but they shall not prevail against thee; for I am with thee, saith the Lord, to deliver thee" (1.18-19). The patient perseverance of Jeremiah was sustained by his God-given conviction that, in Mordecai's words to Esther, he had "come to the kingdom for such a time as this" (Est 4.14), and that God's word, whether in judgment or in blessing, would not be void of result (Is 55.11). At the end of it all, Jeremiah could well have said with Paul, "I have fought a good fight, I have finished my course, I have kept the faith". Like the apostle, he could have added: "no man stood with me…Notwithstanding the Lord stood with me, and strengthened me" (2 Tim 4.7,16-17).

His utter faithfulness

Jeremiah not only persisted in his ministry, he was unswervingly faithful in proclaiming the word of God. During the earlier years of his service he was commanded to "Stand in the gate of the Lord's house, and proclaim there this word, and say, Hear the word of the Lord, all ye of Judah, that enter in at these gates to worship the Lord" (7.2). This involved predicting the unthinkable: "Therefore will I do unto this house, which is called by my name, wherein ye trust, and unto the place which I gave to you and to your fathers, as I have done to Shiloh" (7.14). But Jeremiah never deviated from the terms of his commission: "speak unto them all that I command thee: be not dismayed at their faces, lest I confound thee before them" (1.17).

Jeremiah's greatest enemy was, undoubtedly, Jehoiakim, and at the beginning of his reign the prophet was told, "Stand in the court of the Lord's house, and speak unto all the cities of Judah, which come to worship in the Lord's house, all the words that I command thee to speak unto them; diminish not a word" (26.2). Little did he know at the time that Jehoiakim would become "a Bible-burning monarch who, unlike his father (who had trembled at the word and had thus been spared), deliberately tore the scriptures and oppressed their advocate (36.23)" (Newell). But even the rage of such an implacable enemy did not intimidate Jeremiah, and he "diminished not a word" when commanded to tell the king that he would "have none to sit upon the throne of David: and his dead body shall be cast out by the day to the heat, and in the night to the frost" (36.30).

There was no lack of false prophets in Judah. As ever, error was more popular than truth, and the distinction between the two was clearly made: "The prophet that hath a dream, let him tell a dream; and he that hath my word, let him speak my word faithfully. What is the chaff to the wheat? saith the Lord" (23.28). It should be added that Jeremiah was not always enthusiastic in his faithfulness. Being "subject to like passions as we are", pressure took its toll, and he determined at one point not to "make mention of him, nor speak any more in his name", only to discover that his feelings in this way gave place to a greater compulsion: "But his word was in mine heart as a burning fire shut up in my bones, and I was weary with forbearing, and I could not stay" (20.9). The fire continued to burn within him, and his last recorded words chronologically proclaim his faithfulness: "all the remnant of Judah…shall know whose words shall stand, mine, or theirs. And this shall be a sign unto you, saith the Lord, that I will punish you in this place, that ye may know that my words shall surely stand against you for…I will give Pharaoh-hophra king of Egypt into the hand of his enemies, and into the hand of them that seek his life" (44.28-30).

The Theme of the Book

The prophecy majors on two principal themes: coming retribution; and coming restoration.

Coming retribution

Coming judgment is prominent in the book from its very commencement. Having seen "a rod of an almond tree", signifying God's watchfulness over His word, Jeremiah is immediately confronted with "a seething pot; and the face thereof is toward the north ('from the north', JND)". The meaning of the sign follows: "Out of the north an evil shall break forth upon all the inhabitants of the land. For, lo, I will call all the families of the kingdoms of the north, saith the Lord; and they shall come, and they shall set every one his throne at the entering of the gates of Jerusalem…and against all the cities of Judah" (1.13-15). References to an enemy from "the north" continue (cp. 4.6; 6.1,22; 10.22; 13.20) without precise identification, but not without further detail (5.15-17), and it is not until Jeremiah confronts Pashur the son of Immer that Babylon is specifically mentioned (20.4-6). Thereafter, the coming final invasion of Judah by the Babylonians, and its successful outcome for Nebuchadnezzar, is constantly mentioned until "in the eleventh year of Zedekiah, in the fourth month, the ninth day of the month, the city was broken up. And all the princes of the king of Babylon came in, and sat in the middle gate" (39.2-3). In all this, Nebuchadnezzar was the Lord's servant (43.10) in the same way that that the Assyrian had served Him many years before: "O Assyrian, the rod of mine anger, and the staff in their hand is mine indignation" (Is 10.5).

The reason for the overthrow of Judah and Jerusalem is made abundantly clear. The Lord had not failed to warn His people, but his warnings over centuries had been ignored and rejected. In this connection, the Lord had repeatedly risen "up early" in speaking to His people through His servants, but to no avail (7.13,25; 11.7; 25.3,4; 26.5; 29.19; 32.33; 35.14,15; 44.4). The eleven references to God's deep concern for the welfare of His people in this way, and their response, all stress His deep earnestness and their blatant refusal to listen. The first references to the Lord rising "up early" occur in the prophet's "Temple message": "I spake unto you, rising up early and speaking, but ye heard not…Since the day that your fathers came forth out of the land of Egypt unto this day I have even sent unto you all my servants the prophets, daily rising up early and sending them: Yet they hearkened not unto me" (7.13,25-26); and the last in his final address to the exiles in Egypt: "Howbeit I sent unto you all my servants the prophets, rising early and sending them, saying, Oh, do not this abominable thing that I hate. But they hearkened not" (44.4-5).

Coming restoration

If imminent judgment were the only subject of the book, it would have to be said that Jeremiah was "of all men most miserable" (1 Cor 15.19) and that the appellation, "the weeping prophet" was fully justified. But the prophecy is not unrelieved gloom from its commencement to its conclusion. In fact the book ends with a decided note of hope: "Evil-merodach king of Babylon in the first year of his reign lifted up the head of Jehoachin king of Judah…and set his throne above the throne of the kings that were with him in Babylon" (52.31-32). The elevation of the king of Judah in this way points down the centuries to the ultimate restoration of David's throne.

Following the time of "Jacob's trouble" (30.7), when the nation will pass through "a time of trouble, such as never was since there was a nation even to that same time" (Dan 12.1), the captivity of Israel and Judah will cease, and they will return to possess the land given to their fathers (30.3) and "it shall come to pass in that day, saith the Lord of hosts, that I will break his yoke (the yoke of Gentile domination) from off thy neck, and will burst thy bonds, and strangers shall no more serve themselves of him: But they shall serve the Lord their God, and David their king, whom I will raise up unto them" (30.8-9). While there are earlier references in the prophecy to coming blessing (3.14; 16.14-15; 23.3-8), chapters 30-33 describe the felicity of this coming "golden age" in Israel's history, when the Lord will "make a new covenant with the house of Israel, and with the house of Judah", under which He will "forgive their iniquity, and…remember their sin no more" (31.31,34). Moreover, "In those days shall Judah be saved, and Jerusalem shall dwell safely: and this is the name wherewith she shall be called, The Lord our righteousness" (33.16). The certainty of national restoration and the restoration of David's throne is beautifully confirmed: "Thus saith the Lord; if ye can break my covenant of the day, and my covenant of the night, and that there should not be day and night in their season; Then may also my covenant be broken with David my servant, that he should not have a son to reign upon his throne" (33.20-21).

The Structure of the Book

The book comprises four major sections (chs.2-20; 21-39; 40-45; 46-51) together with an introduction (ch.1) and a conclusion (ch.52). It should be noted that chapters 1-39 describe Jeremiah's ministry before the fall of Jerusalem, whereas chapters 40-45 refer to his ministry to the Jews after the fall of Jerusalem. It should also be observed that chapters 2-20 are "general and undated" whereas chapters 21-39 are "particular and dated" (Sidlow Baxter).

The introduction (ch.1)

The book is introduced with the commissioning of Jeremiah. The prophet was told, as already noted, "Before I formed thee in the belly I knew thee; and before thou camest forth out of the womb I sanctified thee, and I ordained thee a prophet unto the nations" (v.5). He was given a wide brief: "See, I have this day set thee over the nations and over the kingdoms, to root out, and to pull down, and to destroy, and to throw down, to build, and to plant" (v.10).

Undated prophecies (chs.2-20)

There is, in fact, one chronological reference of a very general nature: "in the days of Josiah" (3.6). It has been suggested (Jensen) that these chapters may be subdivided as follows: public sermons (chs.2-10); personal experiences (chs.11-20), although it might be more accurate to say that these chapters comprise public sermons (chs.2-12), and public signs (chs.13-20). While divisions of this nature can sometimes be rather arbitrary and carry inexact titles, it is suggested that the public sermons are four in number (2.1-3.5; 3.6-6.30; 7.1-10.25; 11.1-12.17), and that the public signs include those of the linen girdle (13.1-27), the drought (14.1-15.21), the unmarried prophet (16.1-17.18), and the potter's vessels (18.1-19.13). As a result of his ministry, Jeremiah was consigned to the stocks (20.1-3), and the section ends with the prophet in deep depression (20.14-18). It should be said that there is no sharp division between Jeremiah's public preaching and the signs that followed. The signs were accompanied by preaching.

While only Josiah is mentioned in these chapters, and only once, as noted above, it is usually said that the messages and signs were given during the reigns of both Josiah and Jehoiakim. The reason evidently lies in the fact that Jeremiah's confinement in the stocks (20.2) could hardly have taken place in Josiah's lifetime. The Temple message in this section of the prophecy (7.1-2), is regarded by some commentators as having been reinserted later in the book with reference to the reign of Jehoiakim (26.1-2), leading to the conclusion that chapters 2-20 must therefore be dated with reference to the reign of Jehoiakim as well as to that of Josiah, but another explanation is offered in the commentary.

Dated prophecies (chs.21-39)

The chronological order of the prophecies in this section of the book is not without difficulty. This commentary attempts to elucidate the problem, but draws back from dogmatism. However, the present writer takes strong exception, indeed very strong exception, to such statements as the following: "The book of Jeremiah naturally suggests to us a book written by a man called Jeremiah. Yet anyone who sits down and seriously tries to read through this book from beginning to end must soon begin to doubt this. If this book has been written by a sane man with an orderly mind, he has done his best to confuse us. It is scrappy, built up of many bits and pieces which do not always seem to follow on easily from one another. It is badly ordered" (Robert Davidson).

The "dated prophecies", like other sections of the prophecy, are not "built up of many bits and pieces" and the following suggestions are made on the basis that there is good reason for the arrangement of these particular chapters. They are certainly not "badly ordered".

Chapters 21-24 record Jeremiah's reply to an enquiry by Zedekiah. Very clearly, the inspiring Spirit of God directed Jeremiah to use a message delivered immediately before the fall of Jerusalem, in the days of Zedekiah, as an introduction to the entire section. The message of these particular chapters (chs.21-24) refers not only to Zedekiah himself (22.1), but to Shallum, otherwise known as Jehoahaz (22.11), Jehoiakim (22.18), and Coniah, otherwise known as Jehoiachin (22.24). These were the "pastors that destroy and scatter the sheep of my pasture! saith the Lord" (23.1). Having painted the overall picture in chapters 21-24, the following chapters provide, from previous messages in the reign of Jehoiakim and the earlier part of Zedekiah's reign, a more detailed account of the wickedness of these kings, which led to the destruction of Jerusalem and captivity of Judah. It must be said, however, that against such a dark background, the prophet delivers a marvellous message of hope (chs.30-33).

Chapters 25-26 refer to Jeremiah's earlier preaching during the reign of Jehoiakim whose name is given at the beginning of both chapters.

Chapters 27-29 revert to the reign of Zedekiah for the simple reason that they continue the subject of chapters 25-26, namely that of Babylonian supremacy. The reader should note that the difficulty arising from the mention of both Jehoiakim (27.1) and Zedekiah (27.3) is addressed in the commentary.

Chapters 30-33 have a common theme, and the fact that at least one of the messages was imparted to Jeremiah in "in the tenth year of Zedekiah king of Judah" (32.1), makes it most likely that all four chapters, which have been called "The Book of Consolation" in view of their dark background (chs.25-29), belong to the reign of Zedekiah.

Chapter 34 is clearly dated. With Nebuchadnezzar at the gates of Jerusalem, Jeremiah is told, "Go and speak to Zedekiah king of Judah" (v.2). The reader should note that the chronological place of this chapter in the reign of Zedekiah is discussed in the commentary.

Chapters 35-36 revert to the reign of Jehoiakim, but the reason is not difficult to ascertain. With the king of Babylon poised to conquer Judah and Jerusalem in the reign of Zedekiah, the people are reminded of two things that took place in the reign of Jehoiakim which were contributory factors to the coming disaster. In the first place, the Lord's people had been guilty of rank disobedience (35.12-17), and in the second, the roll containing the word of God had been deliberately and contemptuously destroyed by the king in the presence of his indifferent court officials (36.22-24).

Chapters 37-39 return, after the previous two "explanatory chapters", to the reign of Zedekiah. The section includes the imprisonment of

Jeremiah (37.15), his rescue from the dungeon of Malchiah (38.13), the capture of Zedekiah (39.5), the destruction of Jerusalem (39.8), and the release of Jeremiah (39.14).

Prophecies after the fall of Jerusalem (chs.40-45)

Chapters 40-42 are concerned with prophecies and details of events in Judah and chapters 43-44 with those in Egypt. Chapter 45 is addressed to Baruch, Jeremiah's secretary, who was taken with the prophet into Egypt (43.6). It is evidently included at this point in the book to emphasise that the Lord had fulfilled His promise to preserve Baruch's life (45.5).

Prophecies against Gentile nations (chs.46-51)

These chapters describe the Lord's judgment on Egypt (46.1-26); Philistia, with passing reference to Tyre and Zidon (47.1-7); Moab (48.1-47); Ammon (49.1-6); Edom (49.7-22); Damascus (49.23-27); Kedar and Hazor (49.28-33); Elam (49.34-39); Babylon (50.1-51.64). It should be remembered that God is not a tribal deity. He is "the Judge of all the earth" (Gen 18.25) and "the God of the earth" (Rev 11.4).

The conclusion (ch.52)

This chapter is usually called "a historical supplement", but perhaps its purpose is to demonstrate that the Lord had not forgotten the house of David, even though its surviving representative had been in exile for thirty-seven years. It has already been pointed out that the faint flicker of hope here is the bright flame of absolute certainty in "The Book of Consolation" (chs.30-33).

The Lord Jesus and the Book

In the words of Meyer, "Jeremiah has always a fascination to Christian hearts, because of the close similarity that exists between his life and that of Jesus Christ. Each of them was 'a man of sorrows, and acquainted with grief'; each 'came unto his own, and his own received him not'; each passed through hours of rejection, desolation and forsakenness. And in Jeremiah we may see beaten out in detail, experiences which, in our Lord, are but lightly touched on by the evangelists". This was evidently recognised in some degree by at least some of the contemporaries of the Lord Jesus, for when He "asked his disciples, saying, Whom do men say that I the Son of man am?", they replied, "Some say that thou art John the Baptist: some, Elias; and others, Jeremias, or one of the prophets" (Mt 16.13- 14).

Whether it is the specific prophecies concerning Christ in the Old Testament, or its types and shadows relating to Him, nothing should delight the believer more than to behold "in all the scriptures the things concerning himself" (Lk 24.27).

JEREMIAH 1

Verses 1-3: The Historical Preface

"The words of Jeremiah the son of Hilkiah, of the priests that were in Anathoth, in the land of Benjamin: To whom the word of the Lord came in the days of Josiah the son of Amon king of Judah, in the thirteenth year of his reign. It came also in the days of Jehoiakim the son of Josiah king of Judah, unto the end of the eleventh year of Zedekiah the son of Josiah king of Judah, unto the carrying away of Jerusalem captive in the fifth month." These introductory verses briefly describe the priestly descent of Jeremiah, and the period of his ministry.

His priestly descent (v.1)

Whilst it is an attractive proposition, there is no reason to identify Hilkiah, Jeremiah's father, with the high priest who discovered "the book of the law" in the Temple during the reign of Josiah (2 Kings 22.8). Jeremiah's family belonged to a colony of priests in Anathoth (meaning "answers to prayers"), some three or four miles north-east of Jerusalem. In all probability their ancestors were deposed from official priestly duties in Jerusalem by King Solomon, and banished to Anathoth (1 Kings 2.26). Anathoth was one of the towns assigned to, and inhabited by, priests (Josh 21.18; 1 Chr 6.60). Jeremiah's name means, literally, "Jah is high", or "whom Jah appoints".

The period of his ministry (vv.2-3)

These verses give the historical framework of Jeremiah's ministry. In all probability, the names of Jehoahaz and Jehoiachin are omitted because their reigns were so short-lived. It might be useful, however, to recall first the larger context by giving a summary of events from the death of Solomon in 975 BC. Following his demise, the kingdom was divided between Israel in the north and Judah in the south, as follows.

In the north, *Israel*, comprising ten tribes, with its capital Samaria (Tirzah at first), and its first king, Jeroboam the son of Nebat. His name is often followed by the chilling epithet, "who made Israel to sin" (e.g. 1 Kings 22.52). Israel was ultimately taken into captivity by Assyria in 721 BC. The reasons are clearly set out in 2 Kings 17.

In the south, *Judah*, comprising the tribes of Judah and Benjamin, together with the priests and the Levites (2 Chr 11.12-14), with its capital Jerusalem, and its first king, Rehoboam, the son of Solomon. Whilst Israel was ruled by kings who were wicked without exception, the kings of Judah (and one queen, Athaliah) were a mixed bag. Some began their reign with great promise, but ultimately failed. Others were wicked throughout. One (Manasseh) began abysmally, but repented under divine judgment and ended his days commendably. Then there were kings who reigned well from beginning to end, and the last of these was Josiah (2 Chr 34.2; 35.26-

27). He came to the throne at the tender age of eight in 641 BC, and it was in "the thirteenth year of his reign" that "the word of the Lord" first came to Jeremiah (Jer 1.2; 25.3). The year was 628 BC. His ministry therefore commenced one year after Josiah began to purge Judah and Jerusalem of idolatry and five years before he began to restore the Temple (2 Chr 34.3,8). Josiah was killed in battle at Megiddo in 610 BC, and Jeremiah was amongst the mourners: "And all Judah and Jerusalem mourned for Josiah. And Jeremiah lamented for Josiah" (2 Chr 35.24-25).

After the death of Josiah, three sons and one grandson (though not in that order) sat on the throne of David.

The first was *Jehoahaz*. His short-lived reign of only three months ended when Pharaoh-Necho, king of Egypt removed him, took him off to Egypt, and replaced him with his brother (2 Chr 36.2-4). This was *Jehoiakim*. Jehoiakim and Judah became subject to Babylon (Nebuchadnezzar) in 606 BC. Although the Temple was not destroyed until 588 BC, the nation became part of the Babylonian Empire from 606 BC, and its remaining two rulers were really only vassal kings. Although Nebuchadnezzar "bound him in fetters, to carry him to Babylon" (2 Chr 36.6), it appears that he changed his mind, and left him in Jerusalem (2 Kings 24.1-6). But a number of "the children of Israel, and of the king's seed, and of the princes" were taken to Babylon, including Daniel and his three friends, Hananiah, Mishael and Azariah (Dan 1.3,6).

Jehoiakim ultimately rebelled against Babylon, but died before Nebuchadnezzar could reassert his authority. He was succeeded by his son *Jehoiachin* who reigned for three months and ten days before surrendering to Nebuchadnezzar. He was taken off to Babylon, together with everything and everybody of value (2 Kings 24.10-16), and this wholesale deportation included Ezekiel (Ezek 1.1-2).

Nebuchadnezzar replaced Jehoiachin with his uncle *Zedekiah* who ultimately rebelled, and after a long siege Jerusalem was destroyed, Zedekiah's eyes were put out and he was taken off to Babylon in chains (2 Kings 25.7).

Bible history is far more than a recitation of facts. It is intended to convey important and undated lessons, and for that reason Old Testament history is selective. It is therefore significant that since Jeremiah began his ministry in the reign of Josiah, and lived through the reigns of Jehoahaz, Jehoiakim, Jehoiachin and Zedekiah (and beyond), Daniel and Ezekiel were his contemporaries. According to Daniel 9.2, Daniel read the prophecy of Jeremiah. It is important to notice God's faithfulness to His people. He ensured that His word reached them wherever they went. Daniel was involved in the first deportation in the days of Jehoiakim, Ezekiel with the second deportation in the days of Jehoiachin, and Jeremiah remained in Jerusalem throughout this entire period. God will not "leave himself without a witness", not even in the darkest days at the end-time as Revelation 11 makes clear.

Jeremiah lived through turbulent and uncertain times. The last four occupants of David's throne were wicked in the extreme. Their reigns are described in 2 Chronicles 36, and make miserable reading. The future of Judah was always in jeopardy, and the Babylonian axe finally fell with devastating results. Jeremiah had anything but ideal conditions in which to preach, but he remained unswervingly faithful in proclaiming his unpalatable message. He might well have uttered the words of David, "the reproaches of them that reproached thee are fallen upon me" (Ps 69.9). He certainly exemplifies Paul's injunction to Timothy: "Preach the word; be instant in season, out of season; reprove, rebuke, exhort, with all longsuffering and doctrine" (2 Tim 4.2). There is a striking similarity between conditions in Jeremiah's day and those described by Paul: "For the time will come when they will not endure sound doctrine; but after their own lusts shall they heap to themselves teachers, having itching ears; And they shall turn away their ears from the truth, and shall be turned unto fables" (2 Tim 4.3-4). The false prophets of Jeremiah's day were the forerunners of the false teachers centuries later.

The Call of Jeremiah

Following the introduction in vv.1-3, the remainder of the chapter can be divided into three main paragraphs:

> His Divinely-given Call (vv.4-10)
> His Divinely-given Confidence (vv.11-16)
> His Divinely-given Command (vv.17-19).

Verses 4-10: His Divinely-given Call
The purpose for Jeremiah (vv.4-5)
"Then the word of the Lord came unto me, saying, Before I formed thee in the belly I knew thee; and before thou camest forth out of the womb I sanctified thee, and I ordained thee a prophet unto the nations." The Lord's sovereignty in calling His servant is emphasised by the expressions: "*I knew thee...I sanctified thee...I ordained thee*". The divine "I" occurs seven times in vv.5-8. The following attributes of the Lord should be noticed: His *omniscience* in v.5 - "*I knew thee*"; His *omnipotence* in v.5 - "*I formed thee*"; His *omnipresence* in v.8 - "*I am with thee*". The last of these is repeated in v.19 to stress its importance. Jeremiah began his ministry with the assurance that his life's work had been predetermined by the Lord. It is with a sense of deep wonder that the children of God learn that He has both chosen them "to salvation through sanctification of the Spirit and belief of the truth" (2 Thess 2.13), and appointed their sphere of service for Him. The risen Lord has given "some, apostles; and some, prophets; and some, evangelists; and some, pastors and teachers; For the perfecting of the saints, for the work of the ministry, for the edifying of the body of Christ" (Eph 4.11-12).

Rightly understood, the call of God should promote *humility*. Jeremiah was chosen by the Lord before his birth. He could not claim to have earned divine favour. Like Paul, he was "a chosen vessel" (Acts 9.15). In fact, there is a striking correspondence between the description of Jeremiah's calling, and Paul's calling: "it pleased God, who separated me from my mother's womb, and called me by his grace, To reveal his Son in me, that I might preach him among the heathen" (Gal 1.15-16). The believer's calling leaves no room for self-gratification. The Lord Jesus made this clear to His disciples: "Ye have not chosen me, but I have chosen you, and ordained you, that ye should go and bring forth fruit" (Jn 15.16). Paul was obliged to censure pride at Corinth: "what hast thou that thou didst not receive? now if thou didst receive it, why dost thou glory, as if thou hadst not received it?" (1 Cor 4.7). No servant of God has any reason to boast: "Who then is Paul, and who is Apollos, but ministers by whom ye believed, even as the Lord gave to every man? I have planted, Apollos watered; but God gave the increase. So then neither is he that planteth any thing, neither he that watereth; but God that giveth the increase" (1 Cor 3.5-7).

Rightly understood, the call of God should also promote *assurance*. Jeremiah was to face intense pressure and persecution and is therefore assured that, although he would be beset by difficulty and opposition, he was the Lord's man for the time. The terms of his calling made it clear that, like Esther, he had "come to the kingdom for such a time as this" (Est 4.14). He really was the man "whom Jehovah has appointed". The necessity for this conviction becomes very clear as the book proceeds. His ministry was accompanied by intensifying pressure. His home town was against him (11.21); his family was against him (12.6); he describes himself as a "man of strife and a man of contention to the whole earth!" (15.10); he is consigned to the stocks by Pashur (20.2); his book is destroyed by Jehoiakim (36.23); he is committed to prison (37.21); he is lowered into the dungeon in the court of the prison (38.6). No wonder he cried, "Wherefore came I forth out of the womb to see labour and sorrow, that my days should be consumed with shame?" (20.18).

The plea by Jeremiah (v.6)

"Then said I, Ah! Lord God! behold, I cannot speak: for I am a child." Jeremiah pleaded his youth and inexperience. Whilst it is true that the Hebrew word can mean "child", it also means "young man", as in Genesis 14.24 (where the plural form is used). It is used of Absalom in 2 Samuel 18.5. In fact the same Hebrew word (NAAR – 5288) is used of Josiah at age sixteen: "For in the eighth year of his reign, while he was yet *young*..." (2 Chr 34.3). It is also used of Joshua at an older age (Ex 33.11). It is generally believed that Jeremiah was between twenty and twenty-five when he was called by God. Very clearly, Jeremiah realised that "public speaking was essential to the prophetic office" (Feinberg), and argued his inability to preach. Moses made a similar objection, and received a similar answer (Ex 4.10-12)!

The provision for Jeremiah (vv.7-10)

God answered Jeremiah's objections in the reverse order. Verses 7-8 answer his second objection, "I am a child". Verses 9-10 answer his first objection, "I cannot speak".

"I am a child"

This plea arose from his consciousness of inexperience as a prophet and weakness against colossal opposition. The Lord therefore tenderly assures Jeremiah that divine power and guidance would more than compensate for his inexperience. The "I" of Jeremiah gives place to the "I" of Jehovah! "Say not, *I* am a child: for thou shalt go to all that *I* shall send thee, and whatsoever *I* command thee thou shalt speak. Be not afraid of their faces: for *I* am with thee to deliver thee, saith the Lord" (vv.7-8). It should also be noted that the man who said, "I am a child", is made acutely aware of his responsibility. God exercises the sole right to direct the movements of His servants. The servant has no freedom of choice: *thou shalt go* to all that *I shall send* thee". God alone has the authority to direct the message of His servants. The servant has no freedom of choice here either: "whatsoever *I command* thee *thou shalt speak*". It is God's prerogative to direct the movement and message of His servants. It is the servant's responsibility to act on His command, and to impart His word faithfully.

But the Lord also assured Jeremiah of divine help and strength in contending with opposition. He is promised the Lord's presence – "I am with thee", and the Lord's preservation – "to deliver thee". In New Testament language, "all that will live godly in Christ Jesus shall suffer persecution" (2 Tim 3.12), but they are not left to face "the afflictions of the gospel" (2 Tim 1.8) alone. Kenneth Wuest explains: "It is the power of God which enables Timothy to endure suffering for the sake of the gospel".

"I cannot speak"

Jeremiah now learns that God will equip him for service. "Then the Lord put forth his hand, and touched my mouth. And the Lord said unto me, Behold, I have put my words in thy mouth" (v.9). This should be compared with Isaiah 6.5-7. But the Lord gave him far more than ability to speak. He gave him His word: "I have put my words in thy mouth". He was to be the Lord's mouthpiece and this was recognised by the writer of 2 Chronicles 36.12: "And he (Zedekiah) did that which was evil in the sight of the Lord his God, and humbled not himself before Jeremiah the prophet, speaking from the mouth of the Lord".

Jeremiah was therefore a forerunner of the Lord Jesus, of whom God said to Moses, "I will raise them up a Prophet from among their brethren, like unto thee, and will put my words in his mouth; and he shall speak unto them all that I shall command him" (Deut 18.18). The prophets frequently introduced their preaching with the words, "Thus saith the

Lord", and Jeremiah began his ministry in this way (2.2). God both calls and equips His servants. This was the experience of Gideon (Judg 6.12-16) and of Ezekiel: "And he said unto me, Son of man, stand upon thy feet, and I will speak unto thee. And the spirit entered into me when he spake unto me, and set me upon my feet, that I heard him that spake unto me. And he said unto me, Son of man, I send thee to the children of Israel" (Ezek 2.1-3). Centuries later, the Lord Jesus said, "All power is given unto me in heaven and in earth. Go ye therefore, and teach all nations...and, lo, I am with you alway, even unto the end of the world" (Mt 28.18-20); "But ye shall receive power, after that the Holy Ghost is come upon you: and ye shall be witnesses unto me" (Acts 1.8). The call of God is still accompanied by divinely-given power and ability.

The man who said, "I cannot speak", is given an awesome task: "See, I have this day set thee over the nations and over the kingdoms, to root out, and to pull down, and to destroy, and to throw down, to build, and to plant"(v.10; cp. 18.7; 45.4). Through Jeremiah, God would pronounce the doom and destiny of nations. Chapters 46-51 deal particularly with the foreign nations, and are introduced by the words: "The word of the Lord which came to Jeremiah the prophet against the Gentiles" (46.1). His ministry would be both *destructive* - "to root out, and to pull down, and to destroy, and to throw down", and *constructive* - "to build, and to plant". Ministry in this present day is equally two-fold. Gospel preaching is both negative and positive. Having declared that "all the world" is "guilty before God", and that "by the deeds of the law there shall no flesh be justified in his sight: for by the law is the knowledge of sin", Paul continues, "But now the righteousness of God without the law is manifested...Even the righteousness of God which is by faith of Jesus Christ unto all and upon all them that believe" (Rom 3.19-22). Bible teaching must also be two-fold, but it must be said that demolition and construction are quite different things! Goddard has a very telling piece in this connection: "There is something wrong with a Christian who criticises and condemns, but who fails to live and speak the good news of salvation and forgiveness. There is something wrong with the church that has no positive message and program, but is free in its attack upon various sects and individuals. The wrong lies in the fact that it has undertaken *only part* of the task of the prophet, and *only part*, whichever part it may be, is utterly wrong in the sight of God".

Verses 11-16: His Divinely-given Confidence
The Lord now assures Jeremiah that he will never have cause to be ashamed of his message. Absolute certainty attached to his prophetic utterances, and this assurance is conveyed in two connected signs introduced by the words, "What seest thou?". In the first place, Jeremiah is asked to look at "a rod of an almond tree" (v.11); in the second, he is asked to observe "a seething pot" (v.13). The call of Isaiah was associated with the Temple vision in which he "saw also the Lord sitting upon a throne,

high and lifted up, and his train filled the temple" (Is 6.1). The call of Ezekiel was associated with the vision of God's chariot throne, and "upon the likeness of the throne was the likeness as the appearance of a man above upon it" (Ezek 1.26). But the call of Jeremiah is accompanied by two signs based upon ordinary country life. The order in which the two signs are given to Jeremiah is significant.

The sign of the almond tree (vv. 11-12)

"Moreover the word of the Lord came unto me, saying, Jeremiah, what seest thou? And I said, I see a rod of an almond tree. Then said the Lord unto me, Thou hast well seen: for I will hasten my word to perform it." The almond tree blossoms in January when other trees remain dormant. It is the forerunner of spring, when "the winter is past, the rain is over and gone; The flowers appear on the earth; the time of the singing of birds is come, and the voice of the turtle is heard in our land" (Song 2.11-12). Feinberg observes: "It is the harbinger of spring, as though it watches over the beginning of the season". The significance of the sign lies in a play on Hebrew words which is not evident in our English versions. J. N. Darby points us in the right direction with the rendering: "And the word of Jehovah came to me, saying, Jeremiah, what seest thou? And I said, I see a rod of an almond-tree (SHAQED - 8247). And Jehovah said unto me, Thou hast well seen; for I am *watchful* (SHAQAD - 8245) over my word to perform it". Darby points out that "almond-tree" derives from a word meaning watchful or vigilant, so that "the rod of an almond tree" was a sign that God was "watching over" His word to fulfil it. This has not changed; like Abraham, we can have every confidence in the Word of God. The patriarch was "fully persuaded that, what he had promised, he was able also to perform" (Rom 4.21). The Lord Jesus declared that "Heaven and earth shall pass away, but my words shall not pass away" (Mt 24.35). God's people can rest in the assurance that He has said, "my word...shall not return unto me void, but it shall accomplish that which I please, and it shall prosper in the thing whereto I sent it" (Is 55.11). As Laetsch observes, "No preacher should ever forget that he is the messenger of Him Who watches over His word; Who will suffer no promise to fall to the ground, Who will with equal wakefulness watch over the fulfilment of His threats".

The sign of the seething pot (vv. 13-16)

The Lord had something particularly in mind when assuring Jeremiah that He was "watching over" His word. "And the word of the Lord came unto me the second time, saying, What seest thou? And I said, I see a seething pot; and the face thereof is toward (from) the north" (v.13). Once again, God uses "something utterly common-place, a cauldron suspended over a fire on a cottage hearth" (Birmingham). The "boiling pot" was "tilting away from the north", that is, facing toward the south, where its contents would be poured out (Feinberg). It was "an ominous sign that God's stringent judgments against His wayward people would soon pour out from the north" (Habel). The verses following confirm that the "seething pot" signifies coming calamity and disaster: "Then the Lord said unto me, Out of the north an evil shall break forth upon all the inhabitants of the land. For, lo, I will call all the families of the kingdoms of the north, saith the Lord; and they shall come, and they shall set every one his throne at the entering of the gates of Jerusalem, and against all the walls thereof round about, and against all the cities of Judah" (vv.14-15). The reasons for divine judgment follow: "And I will utter my judgments against them touching all their wickedness, who have forsaken me, and have burned incense unto other gods, and worshipped the works of their own hands" (v.16). It must never be forgotten that the rise and fall of nations cannot be attributed to quirks of fate or fortunes of war. God is in control. He is the God of history.

When the Lord predicts that the coming "evil" would issue "out of the north" (cp. 4.6; 6.1,22; 10.22), He refers to Babylon. Although Babylon is located east of Judah, the impassable Arabian desert meant that the invasion would come from the north. Jeremiah records the fulfilment of this prophecy in ch.39, where "all the princes of the king of Babylon came in, and sat in the middle gate" (v.3). The fulfilment of this prophecy seemed totally unlikely at the time. Egypt was a powerful ally, and God was obliged to censure Judah for reliance on her southern neighbour. "And now what hast thou to do in the way of Egypt, to drink the waters of Sihor?…thou also shalt be ashamed of Egypt, as thou wast ashamed of Assyria" (2.18,36). A threat from the north was not realistic. But God was "watching over" His word to fulfil it. The significance of the two signs now becomes apparent. Jeremiah's prediction of an invasion from the north would be greeted with derision and rejection, but God would assuredly fulfil His word. It was totally reliable, and could not fail. Peter writes in similar vein; he assures us that "the day of the Lord *will* come" (2 Pet 3.10), although "there shall come in the last days scoffers, walking after their own lusts, And saying, Where is the promise of his coming?" (2 Pet 3.3-4). However unlikely the fulfilment of God's word may seem, His servants can have every confidence that He "will bring it to pass".

Verses 17-19: His Divinely-given Command

The Lord had commissioned and equipped His servant. The time had now come for Jeremiah to commence his ministry, and he was given every encouragement for the difficult task ahead. Two important things should be noticed in the closing paragraph of this chapter.

Jeremiah is to be faithful to God (v.17)

"Thou therefore gird up thy loins, and arise, and speak unto them all that I command thee: be not dismayed at their faces, lest I confound thee before them."

He was to be *unencumbered* in his service: "gird up thy loins". The long voluminous garments of the Easterner were a positive hindrance when it came to work and activity, and to ensure maximum freedom of movement they would be tucked into his belt. Peter exhorts, "Wherefore gird up the loins of your mind" (1 Pet 1.13). W. E. Vine explains that "The figure is taken from the circumstances of the Israelites as they ate the passover in readiness for their journey (Ex 12.11); the Christian is to have his mental powers alert in expectation of Christ's Coming" (*Expository Dictionary of Bible Words*).

He was to be *unwearied* in his service: "arise". The service of God demands action. God did not intend Jeremiah, or His servants now, to have an "armchair" ministry. When Deborah and Barak celebrated victory over the Canaanites, they referred to the inactivity of Reuben. "For the divisions of Reuben there were great thoughts of heart" (Judg 5.15), and there it remained! There was plenty of debate (JND margin), but no contribution to the war effort. God's people today must ensure that they are not the spiritual successors of "the divisions of Reuben".

He was to be *uncompromising* in his service: "speak unto them *all* that I command thee". He was reminded of this at the beginning of Jehoiakim's reign: "Thus saith the Lord; Stand in the court of the Lord's house, and speak unto all the cities of Judah, which come to worship in the Lord's house, all the words that I command thee to speak unto them; *diminish not a word*", (26.2). God's servants still have a responsibility to "declare...all the counsel of God" (Acts 20.27).

He was to be *undaunted* in his service: "be not dismayed at their faces, lest I confound thee before them". Failure to bear witness would bring shame to Jeremiah. Paul reminded Timothy that he was not to be "ashamed of the testimony of our Lord". He had the moral right to say this, since he, himself, was "not ashamed" (2 Tim 1.8,12).

God would be faithful to Jeremiah (vv.18-19)

"For, behold, I have made thee this day a defenced city, and an iron pillar, and brasen walls against the whole land, against the kings of Judah, against the princes thereof, against the priests thereof, and against the people of the land. And they shall fight against thee, but they shall not prevail against thee; for I am with thee, saith the Lord, to deliver thee." The promise occurs again in 15.20. The repetition of the earlier promise, "I am with thee to deliver thee, saith the Lord" (1.8), must have reassured Jeremiah. As Habel observes, "Such an omen was enough to scare a seasoned prophet, to say nothing of a hesitant young priest". Opposition would come from all quarters. Civil leaders, religious leaders, and common people would all oppose and harry him, but Jeremiah is assured of God's strength. "I have made thee this day a defenced city, and an iron pillar, and brasen walls against the whole land". Ezekiel was given a similar promise: "Behold, I have made thy face strong against their faces, and thy forehead strong against their foreheads. As an adamant harder than flint have I made thy forehead: fear them not, neither be dismayed at their looks, though they be a rebellious house" (Ezek 3.8-9). Orelli points out that the figures in v.18 "set off the unyielding, unconquerable firmness peculiar to Jeremiah as the divinely sent and equipped prophet, in strong contrast with the gentleness and tenderness of his disposition. As man he melts in tears and pines away in sympathy; as the bearer of God's word, he is firm and hard like pillar and wall, on which the storm of a nation's wrath breaks in vain". But Jeremiah is assured of God's presence, "they shall not prevail against thee; for I am *with thee,* saith the Lord", and God's preservation, "I am with thee, saith the Lord, to *deliver thee*". God's people today enjoy the peace of mind that this brings: "He hath said, I will never leave thee, nor forsake thee. So that we may boldly say, The Lord is my helper, and I will not fear what man shall do unto me" (Heb 13.5-6). Whilst His people are certainly not exempt from suffering, or even death, in the service of God, they are assured of divine deliverance from the spiritual damage intended by Satan by this means. It was with this in mind that Paul wrote, "And the Lord shall deliver me from every evil work, and will preserve me unto his heavenly kingdom: to whom be glory for ever and ever. Amen" (2 Tim 4.18).

JEREMIAH 2.1-3.5

After his call and commission in chapter 1, the ministry of Jeremiah now commences with God's case against His people. It is important to notice that this is based on His claim upon them. He calls them, "My people", four times in chapter 2, but on each occasion they had acted as if this were not the case: "*my people* have changed their glory for that which doth not profit" (v.11); "*my people* have committed two evils" (v.13); "wherefore say *my people*, We are lords; we will come no more unto thee" (v.31); "*my people* have forgotten me days without number" (v.32). Sinful though they were, they remained in covenant relationship with God. They were His people, causing Him to say, "Turn, O backsliding children, saith the Lord; for I am married unto you" (3.14). It was God's covenant love for His people that constrained Him to cry, "How shall I give thee up, Ephraim? how shall I deliver thee, Israel? how shall I make thee as Admah? how shall I set thee as Zeboim? mine heart is turned within me, my repentings are kindled together" (Hos 11.8). In anticipating the ultimate deliverance and blessing of Israel, Paul observes, "As concerning the gospel, they are enemies for your sakes: but as touching the election, they are beloved for the fathers' sakes. For the gifts and calling of God are without repentance" (Rom 11.28-29).

But the expression, "My people", must be understood in terms of the mutual love between bride and bridegroom. The Lord's case against His people is based on the fact that whilst He had been faithful to them, they had been unfaithful to Him. The section therefore commences with reference to their original love for Him (v.2), continues with reference to the withdrawal of their love for Him in favour of many lovers (v.20), with forgetfulness of their pledge to Him (v.32), and concludes with an appeal for the resumption of the marriage relationship (3.1). It is deeply significant that the ministry of Jeremiah should begin in this way, and it must never be forgotten that if love for God and for Christ declines, the believer becomes vulnerable to every evil. The deterioration described by Malachi begins just here: "I have loved you, saith the Lord. Yet ye say, Wherein hast thou loved us?" (Mal 1.2).

The section falls into four major paragraphs:

> The Response of Love to God (vv.1-3)
> The Refusal of Love to God (vv.4-8)
> The Replacement of Love for God (vv.9-37)
> The Restoration of Love for God (3.1-5).

Verses 1-3: The Response of Love to God

God recalls the promise of their fidelity, and the proof of their fidelity. "I remember thee, the kindness of thy youth, the love of thine espousals, when thou wentest after me in the wilderness, in a land that was not sown" (v.2). The Hebrew word rendered "kindness (CHESED – 2617) is often translated as "lovingkindness" as well as "kindness"'. Laetsch puts it beautifully: it "denotes tender, kind, merciful, condescending love on the part of God towards man; on the part of man to man, that loving-kindness clinging to its object with tender affection and mercy in complete self-forgetfulness, as the loving bride clings to her beloved bridegroom". These verses recall Israel's early devotion to God, and refer to the period immediately following deliverance from Egypt until the arrival at Sinai. This was the betrothal period, and it was followed by acceptance of the covenant at Sinai. Their love for God was displayed "in the wilderness, in a land that was not sown". These are telling words: "Thou wentest after *me* in the wilderness". After all, the "waste howling wilderness" (Deut 32.10) provided no incentive. It had nothing to offer. The people were drawn to God Himself. Spiritual life is at a very low ebb indeed if devotion to God is dependent on material blessings. Another prophet cried, "Although the fig tree shall not blossom, neither shall fruit be in the vines; the labour of the olive shall fail, and the fields shall yield no meat; the flock shall be cut off from the fold, and there shall be no herd in the stalls: Yet I will rejoice in the Lord, I will joy in the God of my salvation" (Hab 3.17-18). Sadly, the people of whom God said, "thou wentest *after me* in the wilderness", ultimately said themselves, "I have loved strangers, and *after them* will I go" (v.25).

Israel's early devotion to God recalls the solemn charge brought against the church at Ephesus by the Lord Jesus. There was so much to commend, but the assembly had become an empty shell: "Nevertheless I have somewhat against thee, because thou hast left thy first love". The matter was so serious, that the Lord Jesus continued: "Remember therefore from whence thou art fallen, and repent, and do the first works; or else I will come unto thee quickly, and will remove thy candlestick out of his place, except thou repent" (Rev 2.4-5). An assembly that has lost its love for Christ has lost its reason to exist.

Israel's devotion made them a holy people: "Israel was holiness unto the Lord, and the firstfruits of his increase" (v.3). It is important to remember that holiness is not cold and clinical. It is marked by a love for God which excludes any rival claim, and this is confirmed by the words, "the firstfruits of his increase". James reminds us that believers too are "a kind of firstfruits of his creatures" (1.18). The firstfruits were all for God, and since "the Lord's portion is his people" (Deut 32.9), no one else could eat them with impunity: "all that devour him shall offend ('are guilty', JND); evil shall come upon them, saith the Lord". This is stressed in vv.6-7 which recall divinely-given deliverance from Egypt, divinely-given guidance through the wilderness, and divinely-given rest in Canaan. Sadly, it should be noticed that God who said, "Israel was holiness unto the Lord", was also obliged to say, "thine iniquity is marked before me" (v.22).

Verses 4-8: The Refusal of Love for God

This section can be summarised as follows: injustice (v.5), ingratitude (vv.6-7), ignorance (v.8), and idolatry (v.8). Past devotion had given place to present departure: "What iniquity ('injustice', JND) have your fathers found in me that they are gone far from me, and have walked after vanity, and are become vain?" (v.5). The expression, "walked after vanity", refers to idolatry (cp. 8.19; 10.15, etc). It is a most appropriate description in view of the fact that idols have no existence of their own: "we know that an idol is nothing in the world, and that there is none other God but one" (1 Cor 8.4). It is striking to note that Israel's backsliding implied that there was some fault on God's part. The prophecy of Micah reads similarly: "O my people, what have I done unto thee? and wherein have I wearied thee? testify against me" (Micah 6.3). Backsliding implies doubt and distrust; it is an affront to God's proven love and faithfulness. In this case, as has already been noticed, He had delivered them from Egypt, guided them through the wilderness, and settled them in "a plentiful country" (v.7). God had not been "a wilderness unto Israel" (v.31), but He was obliged to say, "Ye defiled my land, and made mine heritage an abomination" (v.7). The believer has every reason to rejoice that his inheritance is beyond the defiling and corrupting influences of this world (1 Pet 1.4). It could be said of Israel, as it was said of the Galatians, "Ye did run well; who did hinder you that ye should not obey the truth?" (Gal 5.7). Reference is made to "priests", "pastors" and "prophets" (v.8).

The priests

These were the men who represented the people, but they had failed. "The priests said not, Where is the Lord?" (v.8). They did not seek Him. The priesthood is censured again later: "A wonderful and horrible thing is committed in the land; The prophets prophesy falsely, and the priests bear rule by their means (i.e. their own authority); and my people love to have it so" (5.30-31). Whilst it is usual to think of the priests in terms of ministry Godward, it was His original purpose that men in priestly communion with Him should also teach His people: "For the priest's lips should keep knowledge, and they should seek the law at his mouth: for he is the messenger of the Lord of hosts" (Mal 2.7). The expression "a teaching priest" occurs in 2 Chronicles 15.3. The failure of the priesthood resulted in the emergence of the prophet. Both aspects of priesthood are expressed in the words, "The priests said not, Where is the Lord? and they that handle the law knew me not". This is deeply disturbing. Men handling the law without knowing the law-giver! "It needs knowledge of God and fellowship with Him to be able constantly to draw from the law-book and rightly to apply the real Torah, instruction in the divine will" (Orelli). It is still sadly possible to know the Word of God, but not to know God Himself. Every preacher should be solemnly warned. Teachers and preachers must not become "blind leaders of the blind". Instruction for God's people can only be effective when it flows from priestly communion with God. Every gospel preacher, and every Bible teacher, should function as a priest by praying for their hearers as well as for their ministry. Paul describes himself as "the minister of Jesus Christ to the Gentiles, ministering the gospel of God, that the offering up of the Gentiles might be acceptable, being sanctified by the Holy Ghost" (Rom 15.16). The words "minister" *(leitourgos)* and "ministering" *(leitourgeo)* refer to his "evangelical ministry, fulfilling it as a serving priest" (W. E. Vine, *Expository Dictionary of Bible Words*).

The pastors

These were the men who should have cared for the people, but they had failed: "the pastors (RA'A – 7462) also transgressed against me". Further references to their failure occur in 10.21; 12.10; 23.1-2, and they are severly censured by Ezekiel: "Woe be to the shepherds (RA'A) of Israel that do feed themselves! should not the shepherds feed the flocks?" (Ezek 34.2). Ultimately, Israel will enjoy the ministry of "pastors according to mine heart, which shall feed you with knowledge and understanding" (Jer 3.15). God loves shepherd-work. It is invested with the highest possible character in Scripture. We have only to think of the shepherd-character of Jehovah Himself (Is 40.11), and of the Lord Jesus (Jn 10.11; Heb 13.20; 1 Pet 5.4). Every assembly elder should therefore remember the importance of His work for God. It is beautifully summed up in the words, "take care of the church of God" (1 Tim 3.5), where the expression "take care" is best illustrated by the tender ministrations of the good Samaritan (Lk 10.35).

The prophets

These were the men through whom God continued to speak to His people, but they too had failed: "the prophets prophesied by Baal, and walked after things that do not profit" (v.8).The expression "walked after things that do not profit", like the expression "walked after vanity" (v.5), refers to idolatry (v.11). The question is asked, "What profiteth the graven image that the maker thereof hath graven it?" (Hab 2.18). The true prophet "stood in the counsel of the Lord, and hath perceived and heard his word" (Jer 23.18). Paul has similar advice for the New Testament prophet, and for every Bible teacher as well: "If any man think himself to be a prophet, or spiritual, let him acknowledge that the things that I write unto you are the commandments of the Lord" (1 Cor 14.37).

Verses 9-37: The Replacement of Love for God

"Wherefore I will yet plead with you, saith the Lord, and with your children's children will I plead" (v.9). Feinberg explains this as follows: "Having shown clearly the nation's deep ingratitude, Jeremiah now presents the Lord's expostulation with His people under the figure of a court case". The word "plead", meaning "bring charges", is a legal term. God takes the role of a plaintiff introducing his case in court.

The reason for the charge (vv.10-13)
They had turned from reality to falsehood (vv.10-12)
This is emphasised by the word "changed" (v.11). "Hath a nation changed their gods, which are yet no gods? but *my people* have changed their glory for that which doth not profit." The expression "no gods", an ironical description of idols, occurs in Galatians 4.8, "Howbeit then, when ye knew not God, ye did service unto them which by nature are no gods". Idolatry had been substituted for the worship of Jehovah, in particular the gods of Egypt and Assyria (v.18). "Chittim" (v.10) refers to Cyprus and, more generally, to the western islands and coasts, and "Kedar" (v.10) to the Arabs of the desert. If God's people were to look west to Chittim and east to Kedar, they would find that pagan nations stayed loyal to their worthless deities. But by contrast, "my people have changed their glory for that which doth not profit". The English proverb says that "Fair exchange is no robbery", but this was the most unequal exchange imaginable. The expression, "their glory", refers to the Lord Himself: "They made a calf in Horeb, and worshipped the molten image. Thus they changed their glory into the similitude of an ox that eateth grass" (Ps 106.19-20). He is called "The God of glory" (Acts 7.2). Paul refers to the privileges of Israel: "Who are Israelites; to whom pertaineth the adoption, and the glory" (Rom 9.4). The very heavens themselves are horrified witnesses of Israel's surrender of glory for shame. Centuries later, those same heavens witnessed the reverse. Paul writes of the Thessalonians, "ye turned to God from idols to serve the living and true God" (1 Thess 1.9).

They had turned from satisfaction to disappointment (v.13)
This is emphasised by the word, "forsaken": "For my people have committed two evils; they have forsaken me the fountain of living waters, and hewed them out cisterns, broken cisterns, that can hold no water". A similar passage occurs in Jeremiah 17.13. There is all the difference between a perennial spring and a cistern. The first is God-given: the second is man-made. God himself is called "the fountain of life" (Ps 36.9). The "broken cisterns" are explained in vv.17-19. This section of the chapter emphasises that to turn from God is "evil". It is "evil" itself, then and now, and brings "bitter" results (v.19). "The eternal Fountainhead of life is God, the Lord, who makes His Son the Fountainhead of everlasting life for all sinners. What a wicked thing to leave this Fountain and to imagine that man can produce something better!" (Laetsch).

The results of their crime (vv.14-19)
Israel had become a slave: "Is Israel a servant? is he a homeborn slave?

why is he spoiled? (become a prey)" (v.14). Israel was certainly not "a servant" or a "homeborn slave". Israel was God's son: "When Israel was a child, then I loved him, and called my *son* out of Egypt" (Hos 11.1). Or, to use the language of Jeremiah 2.2-3, Israel was betrothed to Jehovah, and was "holiness unto the Lord". The third question is therefore most pertinent: "why is he spoiled?" Before answering the question, those who spoiled them are identified.

The responsible powers (vv.15-16)

"The young lions roared upon him, and yelled, and they made his land waste: his cities are burned without inhabitant. Also the children of Noph and Tahapanes have broken ('fed on', JND) the crown of thy head." The "young lions" (v.15) are evidently the Assyrians, and the verse therefore refers to their conquest and deportation of the northern kingdom, the ten tribes, in 721 BC, and to their invasion of Judah. Reference should be made to 2 Kings 17 for their conquest of Israel in the north, and Isaiah 10 for their invasion of Judah in the south. The "children of Noph and Tahapanes" are the Egyptians. Noph refers to Memphis, the capital of Lower Egypt, and Tahapanes was located on the north-east border of Egypt. Further references to these two cities occur in chs.43 and 44. The reference to Egypt is not quite so easily explained as the reference to Assyria. Some commentators suggest that this refers to the expedition of Pharaoh-necho against the Assyrians and its sequel (2 Kings 23.29-35; 2 Chr 36.3-4), but this seems untenable if Jeremiah's ministry at this point took place in Josiah's reign. An alternative suggestion can be based on Isaiah 30 and 31, where God warned against alliance with Egypt.

The reason for bondage (vv.17-19)

God sets out three "ways" in these verses. There was His "way": "Hast thou not procured this unto thyself, in that thou hast forsaken the Lord thy God, when he led thee by the *way*?" (v.17). But they had forgotten the lessons of God's "way", and sought "the *way* of Egypt" (v.18) and "the *way* of Assyria" (v.18). Here are the "broken cisterns" of v.13. They are "the waters of Sihor", referring to the Nile, and "the waters of the river", referring to the Euphrates. "Sihor" means the "Black River" and is so named from the incidence of black soil in the water after the annual flooding. Alliances with Egypt and Assyria had brought ruin. Hosea makes the same point: "Ephraim, he hath mixed himself among the people ('peoples', JND); Ephraim is a cake not turned" (Hos 7.8); "Ephraim also is a silly dove without heart: they call to Egypt, they go to Assyria" (Hos 7.11); "They shall not dwell in the Lord's land; but Ephraim shall return to Egypt, and they shall eat unclean things in Assyria" (Hos 9.3).

There are solemn lessons here. Israel courted the favour of Egypt and Assyria, and became subject to them. If believers court the favour of the world, they must not be surprised if the world makes a takeover bid for them. Then, in the case of Egypt, Israel was in bondage to the very power from which she had been originally delivered. Sadly, it happens all too frequently amongst God's children. The conclusion is given in v.19: "Thine own wickedness shall correct (chastise) thee, and thy backslidings shall reprove thee: know therefore and see that it is an evil thing and bitter, that thou hast forsaken the Lord thy God, and that my fear is not in thee, saith the Lord God of hosts". This is substantially repeated in 4.18. "Sin and apostasy are hard schoolmasters, stern judges, knowing no pity, and showing no mercy" (Laetsch). In the New Testament, the warning is, "Be not deceived; God is not mocked: for whatsoever a man soweth, that shall he also reap" (Gal 6.7).

The review of their condition (vv.20-37)

This section of the chapter amplifies the statement in v.19, "know, therefore, and see that it is an evil thing and bitter, that thou hast forsaken the Lord thy God". These verses deal with the following:

Their obsession with idols (vv.20-28)

It brought *degeneration* (vv.20-22). The words, "For of old time I have broken thy yoke, and burst thy bands; and thou saidst, I will not transgress; when upon every high hill and under every green tree thou wanderest, playing the harlot" (v.20) could be understood with reference to the deliverance from Egypt. However, JND renders the verse: "For of old thou hast broken thy yoke, and burst thy bands; and thou saidst, I will not serve. For upon every high hill, and under every green tree, thou bowest down, playing the harlot". Idolatry is described as immorality, but whilst this could be pictorial language, idolatry and immorality are closely connected. At the time when Jeremiah wrote, they were connected in a literal sense, just as they were at the foot of Mount Sinai (1 Cor 10.7-8). James refers to spiritual immorality as follows: "Adulteresses, know ye not that friendship with the world is enmity with God?" (James 4.4, JND). God had planted Judah as a "noble vine" (v.21) which alludes to "a high-quality red grape" called a "Sorek vine" (Feinberg). They were "wholly a right seed", referring to Israel's early history, but they had become "the degenerate plant of a strange vine" to the Lord. Their sin was so deep-dyed that it resembled stains that neither "nitre" (a mineral alkali) nor potash (AV "soap": a vegetable alkali) could remove (v.22).

It brought *domination* (vv.23-25). Idolatry completely dominated them to the extent that they could not be turned back. They could deny the charges as much as thy liked ("How canst thou say, I am not polluted, I have not gone after Baalim?, v.23), but the fact remained that they were totally governed by idolatrous pursuits. In this they resembled "a swift dromedary" ('young camel', RV margin), and the "wild ass" (v.24), both seeking mates. Feinberg amplifies this: "Shamelessly, like a young she-camel that has not foaled runs around to seek satisfaction, impelled by uncontrolled instinct, so Judah went to extremes of idolatry, chasing ever-new objects of worship. Modesty and self-control have gone. As a wild donkey in heat sniffs at the wind to find a male (v.24), so the people sought idols; the idols did not need to woo them. Jeremiah pleads with them not to run their feet bare nor their throats dry in their lust for strange gods (v.25). But they reply that they are determined to do so in spite of God's warnings". Judah exhibited outright refusal to terminate idol-worship.

It brought *disillusion* (vv.26-28). The utter senselessness of worshipping "the creature more than the Creator" (Rom 1.25) is especially evident when trouble breaks: "they have turned their back unto me, and not their face: but in the time of their trouble they will say, Arise, and save us. But where are thy gods ('the tree stump and the stone pillar, symbols of the Canaanite fertility cult', Habel) that thou hast made thee? let them arise, if they can save thee in the time of thy trouble" (vv.27-28). This is an on-going warning. God must never be used as a talisman. Nehemiah certainly prayed when confronted by a crisis (Neh 2.4), but he was accustomed to spending time at length in prayer (Neh 1.6). God's people cannot count on His help in an emergency when they habitually live without reference to Him.

Their objection against God (vv.29-35)

"Wherefore will ye yet plead with me? ye all have transgressed against me, saith the Lord" (v.29). Believe it or not, Judah now launches her own lawsuit. The word "plead" reappears in the chapter (cp. v.9), but now Judah is the plaintiff! However, the charge was baseless. Judah herself was at fault: "ye all have transgressed against me, saith the Lord". The case is rejected on the following grounds. *First*, they had refused His correction: "In vain have I smitten your children; they received no correction" (v.30). *Second*, they had slain His servants, that is, the very men sent to chastise them with a view to restoration: "your own sword hath devoured your prophets, like a destroying lion" (v.30). *Third*, they had rejected His authority: "wherefore say my people, We are lords ('We have dominion', JND); we will come no more unto thee?" (v.31). *Fourth,* they had forgotten His love: "Can a maid forget her ornaments, or a bride her attire? yet my people have forgotten me days without number" (v.32). Painfully, God remembers: but not His people. They were intent on every illicit liaison. "Why trimmest thou thy way to seek love? therefore hast thou also taught the wicked ones thy ways" (v.33). The RSV renders this as follows: "How well you direct your course to seek lovers! So that even to wicked women you have taught your ways". Harrison comments: "So skilled are they that they can now instruct experienced prostitutes in the techniques of their nefarious trade". *Fifth*, they had transgressed his law: "Also in thy skirts is found the blood of the souls of the poor innocents: I have not found it by secret search, but upon all these" (v.34). JND renders this as follows: "Yea, in thy skirts is found the blood of the souls of the innocent poor, whom thou didst not encounter breaking in, but it is found upon all these". This alludes to Exodus 22.2: "If a thief be found breaking up, and be smitten that he die, there shall no blood be shed for him". But this was not the case here. "The blood had been shed illegally, for the victims had not been caught in the act of breaking in" (Harrison). Manasseh was guilty of the same crime; he "filled Jerusalem with innocent blood" (2 Kings 24.4). Innocent people were involved in the wicked behaviour of others.

In spite of all this, Judah pleaded her innocence: "Yet thou sayest, Because I am innocent, surely his anger shall turn from me" (v.35), but that very attitude only sufficed to heighten divine anger: "Behold, I will plead with thee, because thou sayest, I have not sinned" (v.35). Like the lawyer in Luke 10.29, we can all be adept at self-justification. The Pharisees were no better (Lk 16.14-15).

Their occupation with Egypt (vv.36-37)
Judah had failed to learn from past mistakes. When Ahaz was troubled by Edomite incursions and Philistine invasion, he sent "unto the kings of Assyria to help him". Tilgath-pilneser responded, but it proved disastrous. The Assyrian king "came unto him, and distressed him, but strengthened him not. For Ahaz took away a portion out of the house of the Lord, and out of the house of the king, and of the princes, and gave it unto the king of Assyria: but he helped him not" (2 Chr 28.16,20-21). Confidence in Egypt would produce the same result as confidence in Assyria. "Why gaddest (goest) thou about so much to change thy way? thou also shalt be ashamed of Egypt, as thou wast ashamed of Assyria" (v.36). Egypt would fail to help them, and the details are given in 37.5-8. God graphically describes their coming misery, and makes it clear that this could not be explained by the fortunes of war: "Yea, thou shalt go forth from him, and thine hands upon thine head: for the Lord hath rejected thy confidences ('those thou confidest in', JND), and thou shalt not prosper in them" (v.37). The lesson is repeated: "friendship with the world is enmity with God" (James 4.4, JND). Prosperity lies in happy obedience to the Word of God.

CHAPTER 3

Verses 1-5: The Restoration of Love for God
These verses are a fitting conclusion to the section which began with reference to Israel's devotion to God: "I remember thee, the kindness of thy youth, the love of thine espousals" (2.2). The following should be noted.

The call (v.1)
The paragraph begins with a tender appeal: "They say, If a man put away his wife, and she go from him, and become another man's, shall he return unto her again? shall not that land be greatly polluted? but thou hast played the harlot with many lovers; yet return again to me, saith the Lord". Commentators and scholars vary in their understanding of this verse.

Some understand the words "yet return again to me" as an interrogative: "And shalt thou return unto me?", or "Would you now return unto me (in spite of all that you have done)?". The law forbad a man to take his former wife again in such circumstances, but they expected God to do this! Habel espouses this view, and explains that "By this reproach, Jeremiah insists that Israel's repentance was only superficial". He understands the reference to Judah's return as an allusion to Josiah's reforms which really had little effect on the people. Others also take the same words in an interrogative sense, and explain that the reference to Deuteronomy 24.1-4 makes it clear that God could not allow them to return anyway without transgressing His own law. But Feinberg, together with Laetsch, is surely right in saying that "it is hard so see, however, how the Lord would be declaring a reconciliation impossible when, throughout the remainder of the chapter, He is pleading for that very thing, urging Judah to repent". (He refers to vv.7,12-14,22 here.) Feinberg continues persuasively: "We must never forget that God, as He wills, exercises grace beyond the law. Ruth was a Moabitess and was excluded from Israel (cp. Deut 23.3); how then does she become the ancestress of David and the Lord Jesus? God operated by grace beyond the law. So God was ready to forgive Judah in spite of all her past failures. Legal claims to the contrary, God calls Judah to the solution to her predicament - namely, repentance". Jensen describes it as "the sun of God's grace outshining the searchlight of God's law".

The charge (v.2)

God endeavours to impress upon them the deep need for repentance: "Lift up thine eyes unto the high places, and see where thou hast not been lien with. In the ways hast thou sat for them, as the Arabian in the wilderness; and thou hast polluted the land with thy whoredoms and with thy wickedness". The "Arabian in the wilderness" is evidently a reference to the marauding Bedouin. Israel was as eager to commit idolatry as the desert tribes were for plunder.

The consequences (v.3)

"Therefore the showers have been withholden, and there hath been no latter rain; and thou hadst a whore's forehead, thou refusedst to be ashamed." This should be compared with Amos 4.7-8. The absence of rain and dew was evidence of divine displeasure. Elijah referred to Deuteronomy 28.23-24 in proclaiming, "As the Lord God of Israel liveth, before whom I stand, there shall not be dew nor rain these years, but according to my word" (1 Kings 17.1). This will be repeated at the end-time when God's "two witnesses" will have "power to shut heaven, that it rain not in the days of their prophecy" (Rev 11.6).

On a practical note, it should be remembered that just as the withholding of dew and rain was evidence of divine displeasure, so the absence of divine blessing in the lives of God's people is a sure sign that something is terribly wrong. If the Bible has become arid, prayer has become a lifeless form, and there are conditions of drought in the soul, then God's appeal to Judah is His appeal to His people today: "Return again to me, saith the Lord".

The claim (vv.4-5)

The Lord Jesus cited Isaiah 29.13 in saying, "This people draweth nigh unto me with their mouth, and honoureth me with their lips; but their heart is far from me" (Mt 15.8). This is evidently the meaning here: "Wilt thou not from this time cry unto me, My father, thou art the guide of my youth? Will he reserve his anger for ever? will he keep it to the end?". To which the Lord replies, "Behold, thou hast spoken and done evil things as thou couldest ('and thou art so determined', JND)". The words "this time" strongly suggest the period of Josiah's reforms. But the profession that God would now be their guide was superficial. They came with the right language, "My father", but that was all. They traded on God's mercy, without exhibiting true repentance. On the contrary, they pursued their wicked intentions with vigour and determination. The words, "thou art the guide of my youth", refer back to 2.2: "I remember thee, the kindness of thy youth…" when they were "brought…up out of the land of Egypt", "led…through the wilderness", and "brought…into a plentiful country" (2.6-7). But former blessings cannot be repeated without former devotion and faithfulness. Israel's appeal was unsupported by reality: they were determined to do evil. So often God's people are right in *lip*, but far from right in *life*. The Lord Jesus said, "If ye love me, *keep my commandments*" (Jn 14.15).

JEREMIAH 3

The second message of Jeremiah is introduced with the words, "The Lord said also unto me in the days of Josiah the king" (3.6), and continues to the end of ch.6. In this section of the prophecy the Lord censures the hypocrisy of Judah, and reaffirms the pending invasion from the north previously predicted (1.13-16). The "seething pot" (1.13) had begun to tip towards the south: "I will bring evil from the north, and a great destruction" (4.6); "for evil appeareth out of the north, and great destruction" (6.1); "Behold, a people cometh from the north country" (6.22). The enemy is called "the destroyer of the Gentiles" (4.7) and comes "from a far country" (4.16). He is described as "a mighty nation...an ancient nation, a nation whose language thou knowest not, neither understandest what they say" (5.15). Although not named, the description points to the Babylonians.

In the first message (2.1-3.5), the Lord charged His people with *change* (cp. 2.10-13,21). Now he charges them with *cloaking* their sin. This is implied at the very beginning of the second message, and later stated, "And yet for all this her treacherous sister Judah hath not turned unto me with her whole heart, but *feignedly,* saith the Lord" (v.10). This is a sad commentary on Josiah's excellent reforms. The sincerity and godliness of Josiah are unquestioned, but the nation was superficial in its profession, and this is confirmed by the speed with which Judah returned to her idolatry after his death.

The burden of the opening part of the second message is the hypocrisy of Judah. She failed to learn from the history of Israel in the north, but even worse, while Israel made no secret of her apostasy, Judah covered *her* apostasy with empty profession. The Lord makes it clear that He would rather deal with people who were overtly sinful, than people who endeavoured to cover their sins with a religious veneer. Bearing this in mind, the passage may be summarised as follows:

> The Example of Backsliding Israel (vv.6-11)
> The Appeal to Backsliding Israel (vv.12-18)
> The Confession of Backsliding Israel (vv.19-25).

Jeremiah is instructed to appeal to "backsliding Israel" in the hearing of Judah, and then to appeal to "the men of Judah and Jerusalem" (4.3). It therefore appears that the appeal to Israel, the northern kingdom, includes the first two verses of ch.4, after which Judah is addressed directly.

Verses 6-11: The Example of Backsliding Israel
The northern kingdom is called "backsliding Israel" three times in this passage (vv.6,8,11). In each case, together with vv.12,22, the word "backsliding" means "turning away", or "defection" (Gesenius), and is so translated in Proverbs 1.32. The southern kingdom is called "her

treacherous sister Judah" and "treacherous Judah" (vv.7,8,10,11). The RSV dubs the two sisters "Faithless" and "False". Ezekiel deals with them at length, and calls Samaria (Israel) and Jerusalem (Judah) "Aholah" and "Aholibah" respectively, thus: "And Aholah played the harlot when she was mine; and she doted on her lovers, on the Assyrians her neighbours…And when her sister Aholibah saw this, she was more corrupt in her inordinate love than she, and in her whoredoms more than her sister in her whoredoms" (23.5,11).

This section illustrates at least three solemn lessons: that it is important

(i) To learn from the experience of other people. Judah had not learned from the history of Israel, so "I have cut off the nations: their towers are desolate; I made their streets waste…I said, Surely thou wilt fear me, thou wilt receive instruction; so that their dwelling should not be cut off" (Zeph 3.6-7);

(ii) To remember that censure attaches, not only to those who *set* a bad example, but to those who *follow* it: thus, "I marvel that ye are so soon removed from him that called you into the grace of Christ unto another gospel" (Gal 1.6);

(iii) To bear in mind that sin progresses in strength. It has been said in connection with Isaiah 5.18 ("Woe unto them that draw iniquity with cords of vanity, and sin as it were with a cart rope"), "an evil inclination is at the first like a fine hair-string, but the finishing like a cart rope" (quoted by A. R. Fausset). With these things in mind, attention is drawn to the following.

Judah's interest in idolatry (vv.6-7)

"Hast thou seen that which backsliding Israel hath done? she is gone up upon every high mountain and under every green tree, and there hath played the harlot. And I said after she had done all these things, Turn thou unto me. But she returned not. And her treacherous sister Judah *saw it*." Israel (the northern kingdom) persisted in idolatry ("played the harlot") in spite of God's warnings, and Judah watched her sister-nation's determination. This was no fleeting glance. Judah did not see and abhor the example of Israel. She looked with interest and desired to emulate her, even though the Lord had warned Israel of her folly. The temptations and allurements of the world persistently cry for the attention of the Lord's people today, and it is impossible to avoid seeing and hearing things which are evil. But they must beware of the second look or the second thought. Eve "saw that the tree was good for food" (Gen 3.6); Achan "saw among the spoils a goodly Babylonish garment, and two hundred shekels of silver, and a wedge of gold of fifty shekels weight" (Josh 7.21); David "saw a woman washing herself" (2 Sam 11.2). "The lust of the eyes" leads to worse things. God's people must not develop an interest, or even curiosity, in what is wrong.

Judah's participation in idolatry (v.8)

"And I saw, when for all the causes whereby backsliding Israel committed adultery I had put her away, and given her a bill of divorce (referring to Israel's captivity and deportation by the Assyrians in 722 BC); yet her treacherous sister Judah feared not, but *went and played the harlot also.*" Judah had watched, now she "went and played the harlot also". She practised idolatry even after judgment had fallen on Israel because of her harlotry. There was no "fear of the Lord", and therefore no hatred of evil (Prov 8.13).

This should be compared with the effect on others of the death of Ananias and Sapphira: "And great fear came upon all the church, and upon as many as heard these things" (Acts 5.11). But the men of Judah were impervious to the message of divine judgment on Israel. The Apostle Paul was obliged to warn the assembly at Corinth against disorderly conduct by referring to the way in which God had already intervened: "But let a man examine himself...For he that eateth and drinketh unworthily, eateth and drinketh damnation to himself...For this cause many are weak and sickly among you, and many sleep" (1 Cor 11.28-30). God's dealings with His people in both Old and New Testaments should be a warning to His people today. Failure to learn from the mistakes and sins of others, not to mention their own mistakes and sins, means that they are likely to repeat them.

Judah's superficial withdrawal from idolatry (vv.9-11)

"And it came to pass through the lightness of her whoredom, that she defiled the land, and committed adultery with stones and with stocks. And yet for all this *her treacherous sister Judah* hath not turned unto me with her whole heart, but feignedly (hypocritically), saith the Lord" (vv.9-10). While opinion is divided, the pattern of the previous verses suggests that the Lord is describing Israel in v.9. Feinberg renders this as follows: "Because Israel's immorality mattered so little to her, she defiled the land and committed adultery with stone and wood. In spite of all this, her unfaithful sister Judah did not return unto me with all her heart, but only in pretence, saith the Lord".

The graphic language, "she...committed adultery with stones and with stocks" (v.9), is matched by that of James: "Ye adulteresses, know ye not that the friendship of the world is enmity with God? Whosoever therefore would be a friend of the world maketh himself an enemy of God" (James 4.4, RV). John contributes to the subject in saying, "Love not the world, neither the things that are in the world. If any man love the world, the love of the Father is not in him" (1 Jn 2.15). Judah's deep-seated idolatry is emphasised by the failure of Josiah's reforms to touch the heart of the nation. Judah was ostensibly repentant, but the Lord was obliged to say, "...her treacherous sister Judah hath not turned unto me with her whole heart, but feignedly, saith the Lord". As Feinberg observes, "Such falsity could not hoodwink God. Apostasy Israel and Treachery Judah were spiritual sisters, and the latter was worse than the former". This is a clear warning for the Lord's people today. The Lord Jesus said, "Ye hypocrites, well did Esaias prophesy of you, saying, This people draweth nigh unto me with their mouth, and honoureth me with their lips; but their heart is far from me" (Mt 15.7-8). In the words of Laetsch, "Their sacrifices were deliberate deception; their weepings, crocodile tears; their hymns, lip service; their avowals of faithfulness, perfidious dissembling". It is all too easy to pay lip-service to the Word of God. There is terrible danger in apparently doing and saying the right thing, but without conviction and reality.

Judah's hypocrisy brings the solemn conclusion: "The backsliding Israel hath justified herself more than *treacherous Judah*" (v.11). The word "justified" here "is used in the sense of causing oneself to appear as righteous (cp. Ezek 16. 51-52)" (Laetsch). By her pretence, Judah had sunk even lower than Israel. God cannot deal with hypocrisy. It is obnoxious to Him: "He that covereth his sins shall not prosper: but whoso confesseth and forsaketh them shall have mercy" (Prov 28.13). Israel had displayed herself in her true colours; she was at least consistent, whilst Judah had endeavoured to mask her real character. The Lord Jesus censured the religious leaders for the same sin: "Woe unto you, scribes and Pharisees, hypocrites! for ye make clean the outside of the cup and of the platter, but within they are full of extortion and excess...Woe unto you, scribes and Pharisees, hypocrites! for ye are like unto whited sepulchres, which indeed appear beautiful outward, but are within full of dead men's bones, and of all uncleanness. Even so ye also outwardly appear righteous unto men, but within ye are full of hypocrisy and iniquity" (Mt 23.25,27-28).

Verses 12-18: The Appeal to Backsliding Israel

Whilst it might have been expected that the Lord would have announced the dissolution of His covenant with His people, He now "unfolds one of the most marvellous manifestations of divine grace found in the Old Testament" (Laetsch): "Go and proclaim these words toward the north, and say, Return, thou backsliding Israel, saith the Lord; and I will not cause mine anger to fall upon you: for I am merciful, saith the Lord, and I will not keep anger for ever" (v.12). It is important to notice that the appeal is addressed to "backsliding Israel" who, unlike Judah, had made no attempt to cloak her true moral and spiritual decline. Judah continued under the cloak of spiritual deceit. In spite of evidence to the contrary, she had protested her innocence (2.34-35). Judah was therefore outside the divine appeal. It is also important to remember that the appeal to Israel was made in the hearing of Judah. Attention is drawn to the repetition of the word, "Return" (3.12,22; 4.1). It has been suggested that "the technique used in the following oracles seems designed to stimulate Judah's return by arousing her jealousy (cp. Romans 10.19; 11.11)" (Habel).

The conclusion cannot be avoided that this was a *bona fide* appeal at the time, and that following repentance, the Lord would have taken them "one of a city, and two of a family" (v.14), from wherever the Assyrians had scattered them (2 Kings 17.6), and brought them "to Zion" (v.14). At the same time, the passage clearly anticipates the day when the nation will be regathered and reunited. In this connection the following should be noticed.

The announcement of mercy (v.12)

"I am merciful, saith the Lord, and I will not keep anger for ever." It was no delight to Him that Israel had sinned so grievously, and that He had been obliged to "put her away" and give her "a bill of divorce" (v.8). The prophet Micah foresaw national restoration, including return from Assyria (Mic 7.12), and exclaimed, "Who is a God like unto thee, that pardoneth iniquity, and passeth by the transgression of the remnant of his heritage? He retaineth not his anger for ever, because he delighteth in mercy" (Micah 7.18). God is not a hard tyrant who delights in the distress of His people.

The acknowledgement of sin (v.13)

"Only acknowledge thine iniquity, that thou hast transgressed against the Lord thy God, and hast scattered thy ways to the strangers under every green tree, and ye have not obeyed my voice, saith the Lord. Turn, O backsliding children…". This should be compared with 1 John 1.9: "If we confess our sins, he is faithful and just to forgive us our sins, and to cleanse us from all unrighteousness". It should be remembered that there can be no reconciliation or restoration apart from repentance. This is not generally appreciated today. From time to time, news is given of nations forgiving nations, and individuals forgiving individuals, for past crimes, but in the Word of God, forgiveness is based upon repentance.

The assurance of restoration (v.14)

The divine promise is clear, "*I will* take you…*I will* bring you…". Such promises rest upon Israel's confession ("Only acknowledge thine iniquity", v.13) and Israel's covenant relationship with God: "I am married unto you". This is remarkable in view of the fact that God had "put her away, and given her a bill of divorce" (v.8). The fact remained that there was an abiding covenant relationship, and Hosea ch.2 should be read in this connection. The precise language of the promise should be noted: "I will take you one of a city, and two of a family, and I will bring you to Zion". Reference is made here to the remnant and the place. God would bring them, not to Samaria, but to Zion.

The plenitude of divine blessing on restoration is next described (vv.15-18).

The pastoral care (v.15)

"And I will give you pastors (shepherds) according to mine heart, which shall feed you with knowledge and understanding." Through Hosea, God was obliged to say, "There is no truth, nor mercy, nor knowledge of God in the land...My people are destroyed for lack of knowledge" (Hos 4.1,6). In the past, God's people had suffered from abysmal shepherding (Ezekiel ch.34), but in the future they would enjoy the ministry of "pastors according to *mine* heart". In that day the "ruler in Israel" (Mic 5.2) will "stand and feed in the strength of the Lord, in the majesty of the name of the Lord his God" (Mic 5.4). God loves a shepherd, and still provides "pastors according to mine heart", cp. Acts 20.28.

The prosperity in the land (v.16a)

"And it shall come to pass, when ye be multiplied and increased in the land, in those days, saith the Lord." The expression, "in those days", is significant. It has prophetic implications. There can be no doubt about the literality of the promise. This is later confirmed: "I will multiply them, and they shall not be few; I will also glorify them, and they shall not be small" (30.19). The increase in population will result in shortage of land, and "place shall not be found for them" (Zech 10.10).

The presence of the Lord (vv.16b-17)

"They shall say no more, The ark of the covenant of the Lord: neither shall it come to mind: neither shall they remember it; neither shall they visit it; neither shall that be done any more." In this coming age, the absence of the ark of the covenant will not be regretted because the true Ark will be there! God in Christ will rule in person, with Jerusalem, rather than the ark, as His throne. Similarly, the Lord's Supper will be no longer necessary when the Lord Jesus returns for His people today.

> Then in worship purer, sweeter,
> Thee Thy people shall adore,
> Tasting of enjoyment greater
> Far than thought conceived before –
> Full enjoyment,
> Full, unmixed, and evermore.
>   (Thomas Kelly)

This leads to:

The place of gathering (v.17)

"At that time they shall call Jerusalem the throne of the Lord; and all the nations shall be gathered unto it, to the name of the Lord, to Jerusalem." It will be the centre of universal gathering. Idolatry will be eliminated: "neither shall they walk any more after the imagination of their evil heart". The fearful situation described in Romans 1.21 will no longer obtain.

The peaceful relationships (v.18)

"In those days the house of Judah shall walk with the house of Israel, and they shall come together out of the land of the north to the land that I have given for an inheritance unto your fathers." The prophets expand this elsewhere, and examples are found in Isaiah 11.11-13 and Ezekiel 37.15-22.

Verses 19-25: The Confession of Backsliding Israel

The previous verses are prophetic in character, and this is emphasised by the expressions, "And it shall come to pass...At that time...In those days" (vv.16,17,18). The ultimate restoration of Israel having been described, vv.19-20 record a divine interjection which Feinberg translates as follows: "I myself said, How gladly would I treat you like sons and give you a desirable land, the most beautiful inheritance of any nation. I thought you would call me 'Father' and not turn away from following me, But like a woman unfaithful to her husband, so you have been unfaithful to me, O house of Israel, declares the Lord". The charge of treachery against Judah (vv.7,8,10,11) is now applied to the house of Israel. The AV rendering, "How shall I put thee among the children, and give thee a pleasant land, a goodly heritage of the hosts of the nations ('the most lovely inheritance of the hosts of the nations', JND margin)?" (v.19) makes difficult reading. Feinberg's rendering above is helpful here, and Laetsch suggests that "it is preferable to render this clause, 'an inheritance of glory of glories', (the) superlative glory of the nations, the greatest glory known to the nations". As already noted, it is evidently better to construe these verses, not as a question, but as an exclamation. The realisation of God's desire for His people still lies in the future, and their present state was marked by unfaithfulness and apostasy, but not for ever.

The verses that follow (vv.21-25) describe national confession and repentance. This involves:

Sorrow for sin (v.21)

Israel's realisation of her "treachery" (v.20) produces deep sorrow: "A voice was heard upon the high places, weeping and supplications of the children of Israel: for they have perverted their way, and they have forgotten the Lord their God". It must not be forgotten that there is such a thing as "godly sorrow". It "worketh repentance to salvation not to be repented of" (2 Cor 7.10).

Confession of sin (vv.22-25)

In response to the appeal, "Return, ye backsliding children, and I will heal your backslidings", Israel replies, "Behold, we come unto thee; for thou art the Lord our God" (v.22). In the past, Israel had looked to the hills and mountains (with all their idolatrous associations) for salvation, but now they say, "truly in the Lord our God is the salvation of Israel" (v.23). Idolatry had brought nothing but shame: "For shame hath devoured the labour of our fathers from our youth; their flocks and their herds, their sons and their daughters. We lie down in our shame, and our confusion covereth us: for we have sinned against the Lord our God, we and our fathers, from our youth even unto this day, and have not obeyed the voice of the Lord our God" (vv.24-25). The three expressions are noteworthy: "*we* come unto thee...We lie down in our shame...*we* have sinned".

They had cried, "My father, thou art the guide of my youth" (v.4), recalling the Lord's words of them, "I remember thee, the kindness of thy youth" (2.2). Now they cry, "shame hath devoured the labour of our fathers from our youth" (v.24) and "we have sinned against the Lord our God, we and our fathers, from our youth" (v.25). The shameful thing (v.24) is Baal, the god of shame: "according to the number of the streets of Jerusalem have ye set up altars to that shameful thing, even altars to burn incense unto Baal" (11.13). In expanding the word "shame", Laetsch makes the incisive observation that "people usually spend far more money in serving their idols, in the maintenance of false religions, in service of the triple deity of this world (1 Jn 2.16), than God's children would think of sacrificing for their Saviour and His church...Idolatry is an expensive business, and its net results are an accusing conscience, a heavy burden of guilt, death and damnation".

In response to the charge, "they have forgotten the Lord their God" (v.21), Israel will say: "thou art the Lord our God" (v.22), "in the Lord our God is...salvation" (v.23), "we have sinned against the Lord our God" (v.25), "we...have not obeyed the voice of the Lord our God" (v.25). But confession of sin is not enough. Repentance is required, and the opening verses (vv.1-2) of the next chapter draw attention to this, after which the message to Israel is applied to Judah (vv.3-4).

JEREMIAH 4

The opening verses (vv.1-2) of this chapter conclude the appeal to Israel. This commenced with the words, "Go, and proclaim these words toward the north, and say, Return, thou backsliding Israel, saith the Lord" (3.12). The balance of the chapter (vv.3-31) is addressed to Judah.

In connection with the conclusion of God's appeal to Israel, it should be noted that sorrow for sin (3.21) and confession of sin (3.22-25) must be accompanied by turning from sin. Repentance is required: "If thou wilt return, O Israel, saith the Lord, return unto me: and if thou wilt put away thine abominations out of my sight, then shalt thou not remove" (v.1). The expression, "Then shalt thou not remove", refers, not to captivity, but to stability. This is clear from the translation, "If thou wilt return, O Israel, saith Jehovah, return unto me; and if thou wilt put away thine abominations out of my sight, then thou shalt not be a wanderer" (JND). That is, "not roam, rove, run to and fro to other gods, but remain true to God" (Laetsch), or "no longer go astray" (Feinberg). Repentance involves the removal of all that is displeasing to God. The words "thine abominations", or "detestable things", refer to their idols.

But the removal of idolatry must be accompanied by heartfelt devotion to the Lord: "And thou shalt swear, The Lord liveth, in truth, in judgment, and in righteousness". The Lord Jesus illustrated the danger of external profession without inward reality: "When the unclean spirit is gone out of a man, he walketh through dry places, seeking rest; and finding none, he saith, I will return unto my house whence I came out. And when he cometh, he findeth it swept and garnished. Then goeth he, and taketh to him seven other spirits more wicked than himself; and they enter in and dwell there: and the last state of the man is worse than the first" (Lk 11.24-26). J. C. Ryle calls these verses in Luke "a solemn warning to us never to be satisfied with religious reformation without heart conversion". Whereas Judah "hath not turned unto me with her whole heart, but feignedly" (3.10), the Lord looked for allegiance, not only by word of mouth, but in righteous living. It is striking to notice the result: "and the nations shall bless themselves in him, and in him shall they glory" (v.2), fulfilling the earlier prediction, "At that time they shall call Jerusalem the throne of the Lord; and all the nations shall be gathered unto it, to the name of the Lord, to Jerusalem: neither shall they walk any more after the imagination of their evil heart" (3.17). These passages recall New Testament teaching that "if the fall of them be the riches of the world, and the diminishing of them the riches of the Gentiles; how much more their fulness?...For if the casting away of them be the reconciling of the world, what shall the receiving of them be, but life from the dead?" (Rom 11.12,15). They also call to mind the teaching of the Lord Jesus: "Ye are the light of the world. A city that is set on a hill cannot be hid...Let your light so shine before men, that they may see your good works, and glorify your Father which is in heaven" (Mt 5.14,16).

The message of these verses is applied to Judah in vv.3-4. They have seen what had happened to Israel (3.6-11), and the grounds on which Israel will be restored (3.12-4.2). In addressing Judah, the Lord says, "For thus saith the Lord to the men of Judah and Jerusalem, Break up your fallow ground, and sow not among thorns. Circumcise yourselves to the Lord, and take away the foreskins of your heart, ye men of Judah and the inhabitants of Jerusalem: lest my fury come forth like fire, and burn that none can quench it, because of the evil of your doings". This divine judgment is outlined in vv.5-31 where Jeremiah graphically describes the invasion of Judah. With this in mind, vv.3-31 may be divided as follows:

> The Prevention of the invasion (vv.3-4)
> The Proclamation of the Invasion (vv.5-6)
> The Progress of the Invasion (vv.7-31).

Verses 3-4: The Prevention of the Invasion
The reality demanded of Israel (v.2) is now demanded of Judah. It is a final appeal. Divine judgment was imminent. The necessity for thorough-going repentance should be noted. This is emphasised by the occurrence in the passage of the word "heart" (vv.4,14,18). Three things are urged:

"Break up your fallow ground" (v.3a)
This should be compared with, "Sow to yourselves in righteousness, reap in mercy; break up your fallow ground" (Hos 10.12). The very expression implies deep repentance. Thus far they had only "scratched the surface". There was a hard crust of resistance to the word of God. In the words of Kidner, "The expression 'fallow ground' was extraordinarily well suited to describe a people doubly impervious to the good seed of the word of God, both by the tangled growth of worldly notions and preoccupations which had taken hold of them, and by the hard crust beneath it all, of wills and attitudes never broken into penitence". As Feinberg points out, "No farmer will sow seed on unploughed ground. So the plough of repentance and obedience was needed to remove the outer layer of weeds and thorns that had resulted from idolatry".

"Sow not among thorns" (v.3b)
It would be pointless to sow the seeds of repentance in unsuitable soil, for the simple reason that the weeds and thorns grow more quickly than the grain, and will speedily choke it. The lesson is driven home by the Lord Jesus: "And some fell among thorns; and the thorns sprung up, and choked them…He also that received seed among the thorns is he that heareth the word; and the care of this world, and the deceitfulness of riches, choke the word, and he becometh unfruitful" (Mt 13.7,22). This constitutes a warning to God's people today that however frequently they read God's Word, and listen to teaching from it, nothing lasting will be

accomplished in their lives unless they "receive with meekness the engrafted (implanted) word" (James 1.21).

"Circumcise yourselves to the Lord" (v.4)

Circumcision is first mentioned in Genesis 17, where God promised a son to Abraham and Sarah. The New Testament comments on this as follows: "And being not weak in faith, he considered not his own body now dead, when he was about an hundred years old, neither yet the deadness of Sarah's womb: He staggered not at the promise of God through unbelief; but was strong in faith, giving glory to God; And being fully persuaded that, what he had promised, he was able also to perform" (Rom 4.19-21). According to Romans 4.11, circumcision was the outward sign of Abraham's faith in Genesis 15.6. The removal of the flesh by circumcision was an apt symbol that Abraham had no confidence in himself, but every confidence in God. It was, literally, cutting off something natural, and that is precisely what faith does. It took place on the "eighth day" (cp. Phil 3.5), which suggests the commencement of something new. Circumcision therefore distinguished God's people from the world, hence the division between the "circumcised" and the "uncircumcised".

The Jews carefully practised circumcision, but in many cases, it was a mere outward form. Hence the command, "Circumcise therefore the foreskin of your heart, and be no more stiffnecked" (Deut 10.16). Stephen described the Jewish leaders as "uncircumcised in heart and ears" (Acts 7.51) and Paul wrote, "For he is not a Jew, which is one outwardly; neither is that circumcision, which is outward in the flesh: But he is a Jew, which is one inwardly; and circumcision is that of the heart" (Rom 2.28-29). Jeremiah was to say, "Behold, their ear is uncircumcised, and they cannot hearken: behold the word of the Lord is unto them a reproach; they have no delight in it" (6.10); "Egypt, and Judah, and Edom, and the children of Ammon, and Moab, and all that are in the utmost corners, that dwell in the wilderness: for all these nations are uncircumcised, and all the house of Israel are uncircumcised *in the heart*" (9.26).

Believers today enjoy the *spiritual* significance of circumcision: "For we are the circumcision, which worship God in the spirit ('who worship by the Spirit of God', JND), and rejoice in Christ Jesus, and have no confidence in the flesh" (Phil 3.3). It is called "the circumcision made without hands, in putting off the body of the sins of the flesh by the circumcision of Christ" (Col 2.11).

The command, "take away the foreskins of your heart, ye men of Judah and inhabitants of Jerusalem", demanded an instant response. Divine judgment was pending: "…lest my fury come forth like fire, and burn that none can quench it". God still demands true faith and devotion from His people. Believers today are to "draw near with a true heart in full assurance of faith, having our hearts sprinkled from an evil conscience, and our bodies washed with pure water" (Heb 10.22). This leads to:

Verses 5-6: The Proclamation of the Invasion

This supposes the rejection of the appeal to "the men of Judah and Jerusalem" (vv.3-4). The situation is not without precedent in the Old Testament. Moses told Israel, "I know that after my death ye will utterly corrupt yourselves, and turn aside from the way which I have commanded you; and evil will befall you in the latter days" (Deut 31.29). As Feinberg points out, "The remainder of the chapter is occupied with vivid portrayals of the invasion of the land, the siege of Jerusalem, the devastation of the land, and the decimation of the population. So certain is the judgment that Jeremiah sees the imminent invasion as already present".

"Declare ye in Judah, and publish in Jerusalem; and say, Blow ye the trumpet in the land: cry, gather together, and say, Assemble yourselves, and let us go into the defenced cities. Set up the standard toward Zion: retire, stay not; for I will bring evil from the north, and a great destruction." Jeremiah describes the alarm: "Blow ye the trumpet in the land" (cp. 6.1; Amos 3.6), and the flight of the people to the fortified cities: "Assemble yourselves, and let us go into the defenced cities". Attention is drawn to the words, "*I* will bring". This emphasises that the coming invasion was no quirk of fate, and had nothing to do with the fortunes of war. Comparable passages are everywhere in the Old Testament, and an example occurs in the introduction to the book of Daniel, "And *the Lord* gave Jehoiakim king of Judah into his (Nebuchadnezzar's) hand, with part of the vessels of the house of God" (Dan 1.2). It is noteworthy that Ezekiel "looked, and, behold, a whirlwind came out of the north" (Ezek 1.4) from which emerged the "chariot-throne of Jehovah" occupied by "the likeness as the appearance of a man" (Ezek 1.26). God's throne is both static (Rev 4.2) and mobile! The Ezekiel passage points to the fact that the coming invasion from the north described by Jeremiah was subject to the throne of God. He controls the rise, fall and movements of the nations. The words, "evil from the north, and a great destruction" (v.6) recall the words, "I see a seething pot; and the face thereof is toward (from the face of) the north…Out of the north an evil shall break forth upon all the inhabitants of the land" (1.13-14). Jeremiah makes numerous references to the northern invader. Examples are found in 6.22; 10.22; 13.20.

Verses 7-31: The Progress of the Invasion

These verses describe

> The departure of the invader (vv.7-10)
> The despatch of the invader (vv.11-13)
> The deployment of the army (vv.14-18)
> The desolation of the land (vv.19-29)
> The disenchantment of her allies (vv.30-31).

The departure of the invader (vv.7-10)

"The lion is come up from his thicket, and the destroyer of the Gentiles (cp. Jer 25.9) is on his way; he is gone forth from his place" (v.7). Laetsch describes him as "a killer lion". According to Feinberg, "Lions in enamel have been removed from the Processional Way of Babylon". However, we are not dependent on archeology: the Scriptures describe the kingdom of Babylon as a lion: "And four great beasts came up from the sea, diverse from one another. The first was like a lion" (Dan 7.3-4). Towards the end of the prophecy, Jeremiah refers to Babylon again in this way: "Israel is a scattered sheep; the lions have driven him away...and last this Nebuchadrezzar king of Babylon hath broken his bones" (Jer 50.17). Attention is drawn to the following:

The object of the invasion (v.7)

This was "to make thy land desolate; and thy cities shall be laid waste, without an inhabitant". The land would be destroyed and depopulated. Nebuchadnezzar "carried away all Jerusalem, and all the princes, and all the mighty men of valour, even ten thousand captives" (2 Kings 24.14), and Jeremiah 52.28-30 refers to a total of 4,600 "carried away captive".

The effect on the people generally (v.8)

In general terms, the people are told to lament, for there was no way in which judgment could be averted or escaped: "For this gird you with sackcloth, lament and howl: for the fierce anger of the Lord is not turned back from us". The nation faced nothing but doom.

The effect on the leadership particularly (v.9)

The civil and religious leaders are specified here: "And it shall come to pass at that day, saith the Lord, that the heart of the king shall perish, and the heart of the princes; and the priests shall be astonished, and the prophets shall wonder". This is not surprising. These classes are censured by one of Jeremiah's contemporaries: "Her princes within her are roaring lions; her judges are evening wolves...Her prophets are light and treacherous persons: her princes have polluted the sanctuary" (Zeph 3.3-4). The leadership was particularly culpable, and it is worth remembering that "unto whomsoever much is given, of him shall be much required" (Lk 12.48).

The reaction of Jeremiah (v.10)

"Then said I, Ah, Lord God! surely thou hast greatly deceived this people and Jerusalem, saying, Ye shall have peace; whereas the sword reacheth unto the soul." Later, Jeremiah was to cry, "O Lord, thou hast deceived *me*, and I was deceived" (20.7).

It has been pointed out that "at no time had Jeremiah prophesied that Jerusalem would have peace. His message was always the opposite...Actually it was the false prophets who constantly deceived the people with false promises of peace and prosperity regardless of their ways"

(Feinberg). This is confirmed in later passages: "The prophets prophesy falsely, and the priests bear rule by their means, and my people love to have it so" (5.31); "They have healed also the hurt of the daughter of my people slightly, saying, Peace, peace; when there is no peace" (6.14).

The statement, "surely thou hast greatly deceived this people and Jerusalem", is explained by the New Testament (the best commentary on the Bible is always the Bible itself). Paul refers to "him, whose coming is after the working of Satan with all power and signs and lying wonders, And with all deceivableness of unrighteousness in them that perish; because they received not the love of the truth, that they might be saved. And for this cause *God shall send them strong delusion, that they should believe a lie*: That they might all be damned who believed not the truth, but had pleasure in unrighteousness" (2 Thess 2.9-12). Similarly here, God's people had refused to obey the truth, and had reaped the consequences. God deliberately allowed the false prophets to preach their lies.

The despatch of the invader (vv.11-13)

The speed and ferocity of divine judgment is described in two ways. In the first place, the Babylonian armies would be like a dry scorching wind, the Sirocco or Khamsin, which blows in from the desert bringing fierce heat and dust. "A dry wind of the high places in the wilderness toward the daughter of my people, not to fan, nor to cleanse, Even a full wind from those places shall come unto me", or "A wind more vehement than that (necessary for winnowing) shall come from me" (vv.11-12, JND). This describes wind which is far more powerful than the wind necessary for winnowing: it would have the effect of dispersing the entire nation. This will happen at God's command: "now also will I give sentence against them" (v.12). Secondly, the advance of the northern armies is described as "clouds, and his chariots shall be as a whirlwind: his horses are swifter than eagles" (v.13). The reference to "eagles" identifies the invader yet again as Babylon. Attention is drawn in this connection to Habakkuk 1.6,8: "For, lo, I raise up the Chaldeans, that bitter and hasty nation…their horsemen shall come from far; they shall fly as the eagle that hasteth to eat". This should be compared with Ezekiel's parable of the great eagle (Ezek 17.1-24).

The deployment of the army (vv.14-18)

This is preceded by a further appeal: "O Jerusalem, wash thine heart from wickedness, that thou mayest be saved. How long shall thy vain (i.e. idolatrous) thoughts lodge within thee" (v.14). The enemy is coming progressively nearer. Even at this late hour, there was opportunity for repentance. Hence the appeal. The progress of the invader is described.

Entering the land (v.15a)

"For a voice declareth from Dan." Dan was the northern boundary of the land. Another reference to the northern border is made in Jeremiah's

"Temple Discourse" (7.1-10.25), "The snorting of his horses was heard from Dan" (8.16).

Entering Judah (v.15b)

"And publisheth affliction from mount Ephraim." Mount Ephraim was the northern border of Judah, not far from Jerusalem, some ten miles away.

Encircling Jerusalem (vv.16-17)

"Make ye mention to the nations; behold, publish against Jerusalem, that watchers (i.e. the besiegers) come from a far country, and give out their voice against the cities of Judah. As keepers of a field, are they against her round about." Feinberg comments here as follows: "As watchmen guard their fields from predatory animals, so Jerusalem will be surrounded to cut off any who would escape". The reason for the presence of the encircling army, "because she hath been rebellious against me, saith the Lord" (v.17), emphasises that succeeding generations had become "as their fathers, a stubborn and rebellious generation; a generation that set not their heart aright, and whose spirit was not stedfast with God" (Ps 78.8).

This is followed by an explanation: "Thy way and thy doings have procured these things unto thee (cp. 2.17); this is thy wickedness, because it is bitter, because it reacheth unto thine heart" (v.18). It is bitter to bear because the people now realise that they have brought it upon themselves. This illustrates, yet again, that "whatsoever a man soweth, that shall he also reap" (Gal 6.7).

The desolation of the land (vv.19-29)

This section of the chapter commences with deep distress, and this has been variously understood. While these words could have reference to the Lord Himself, or to the nation at large, it does seem more likely that Jeremiah is expressing here his personal grief. His deep emotion over the impending destruction affects him physically. At the same time, he most certainly expressed the Lord's deep feelings for His people. Attention is drawn to the following.

The distress of the prophet (vv.19-22)

"My bowels, my bowels! I am pained at my very heart; my heart maketh a noise in me; I cannot hold my peace, because thou hast heard, O my soul, the sound of the trumpet, the alarm of war. Destruction upon destruction is cried; for the whole land is spoiled: suddenly are my tents spoiled, and my curtains in a moment. How long shall I see the standard, and hear the sound of the trumpet? For my people is foolish, they have not known me; they are sottish (stupid) children, and they have none understanding: they are wise to do evil, but to do good they have no knowledge."

Jeremiah was not alone in his distress over the low straits of God's people. Confronted with news of the same city, Nehemiah "sat down, and wept, and mourned certain days, and fasted, and prayed before the God heaven" (Neh 1.4). The Lord Jesus wept over Jerusalem as He, like Jeremiah, contemplated its coming destruction: "And when he was come near, he beheld the city, and wept over it, Saying, If thou hadst known, even thou, at least in this thy day, the things which belong unto thy peace!" (Lk 19.41). Paul foresaw "grievous wolves…not sparing the flock", and had "ceased not to warn every one night and day with tears" (Acts 20.29,31). Preachers, and others, often expostulate and condemn but, alas, seldom weep over God's people. Paul wrote 1 Corinthians "out of much affliction and anguish of heart" (2 Cor 2.4). The parchment was stained with his tears.

The destruction of the land (vv.23-26)
Jeremiah exclaims, "I beheld…and lo…" (vv.23,24,25,26). While the language is applicable to the end-time, there can be no doubt that Jeremiah anticipates and describes here the results of the Babylonian invasion. "I beheld the earth, and, lo, it was without form, and void (as in Genesis 1.2); and the heavens, and they had no light. I beheld the mountains, and, lo, they trembled, and all the hills moved lightly. I beheld, and, lo, there was no man, and all the birds of the heavens were fled. I beheld, and, lo, the fruitful place was a wilderness, and all the cities thereof were broken down at the presence of the Lord, and by his fierce anger". It seemed to Jeremiah that the land once "flowing with milk and honey", had returned to the conditions that existed before "the Spirit of God moved upon the face of the waters" (Gen 1.2). As Feinberg observes, "It was as though the work of creation had been cancelled out. Sin is catastrophic in its consequences".

The deliverance of the remnant (v.27)
"For thus hath the Lord said, The whole land shall be desolate (summarising vv.23-26); yet will I not make a full end". The same statement, "I will not make a full end", also occurs in 5.10 and 18. Fuller references are found in 30.11 ("though I make a full end of all nations whither I have scattered thee, yet will I not make a full end of thee: but I will correct thee in measure"), and 46.28. Faced with Babylonian invasion, and yet assured that God was in complete control of the situation, Habakkuk exclaimed, "Art thou not from everlasting, O Lord my God, mine Holy One? we shall not die. O Lord, thou hast ordained them for judgment; and, O mighty God, thou hast established them for correction" (Hab 1.12).

The determination of the Lord (vv.28-29)
"For this shall the earth mourn, and the heavens above be black: because I have spoken it, I have purposed it, and will not repent, neither will I turn back from it. The whole city shall flee for the noise of the horsemen and

bowmen; they shall go into thickets, and climb up upon the rocks: every city shall be forsaken, and not a man dwell therein." Although the Lord had determined that He would not make "a full end" of His people, this did not mean that they would be spared the horrors of the coming invasion. Divine judgment was irrevocable. Some one hundred years before, He had announced irreversible judgment upon Judah and Jerusalem: "I will stretch over Jerusalem the line of Samaria, and the plummet of the house of Ahab: and I will wipe Jerusalem as a man wipeth a dish, wiping it, and turning it upside down" (2 Kings 21.13). The only place of refuge was the surrounding hills, with their thickets and rocks, just as it will be the only place of refuge at the end time (Mt 24.15-16).

The disenchantment of her allies (vv.30-31)

"And when thou art spoiled, what wilt thou do? Though thou clothest thyself with crimson, though thou deckest thee with ornaments of gold, though thou rentest thy face with painting, in vain shalt thou make thyself fair; thy lovers will despise thee, they will seek thy life" (v.30). From the description, it is clear that Jerusalem was still playing the harlot. Although she had gone to considerable lengths to gain favour with her lovers, all her efforts were in vain. The expression "rentest thy face with painting" refers to the practice of using a black mineral powder (antimony or stibium) which women applied to their upper and lower eyelids to "rend" (widen or increase) the apparent size of the eyes (cp. Ezekiel 23.40). Instead of "clinging to her true spouse" (Harrison), she had "played the harlot with many lovers" (Jer 3.1) and continued to do so until the very end. But the foreign nations (her "lovers") would simply despise her. Courting their favour brings apparent benefit in prosperous times, but ruin in poverty.

"Jeremiah depicts her final agonies under the figure of a miscarriage of a first child with the mother in her final gasps for breath" (Feinberg). "For I have heard a voice as of a woman in travail, and the anguish as of her that bringeth forth her first child" (v.31), referring not to the birth of a remnant (Is 66.7-8; Mic 5.3), but having "become tainted with a mortal disease" through her behaviour in courting lovers, and, "using the figure of a fatal miscarriage, the prophet depicts the nation moribund and gasping spasmodically with arms outstretched, 'Help, the murderers have killed me'. Like the wanton she has been, Judah is now paying the price for her iniquity" (Harrison).

JEREMIAH 5

Chapter 4 has described, prophetically, the invasion of Judah and the consequent desolation of the land. In order to emphasise the righteousness of this divine judgment and to prove that it was fully justified, Jeremiah is now commanded to "seek in the broad places thereof, if ye can find a man, if there be any that executeth judgment, that seeketh the truth; and I will pardon it" (v.1). Alas, there was no such man, whether in the "broad places" (v.1) or amongst "the great men" (v.5), and the Lord had therefore no alternative but to say, "Shall I not visit for these things? saith the Lord: and shall not my soul be avenged on such a nation as this?" (vv.9,29). The instruction, "seek…if ye can find a man", recalls Abraham's question, "Wilt thou also destroy the righteous with the wicked?" (Gen 18.23). Abraham was well aware that there was not a sufficiently large number of "the righteous" in Sodom to justify Lot's salvation on that ground alone, and pleaded to the extent that the Lord said, "I will not destroy it for ten's sake" (Gen 18.32).

The present chapter may be divided as follows:

A Fruitless Search (vv.1-6)
A Fearful Condition (vv.7-13)
A Ferocious Invasion (vv.14-19)
A Foolish People (vv.20-25)
A False Prosperity (vv.26-31).

Verses 1-6: A Fruitless Search
This stresses the isolation of Jeremiah. As Feinberg points out, "Obviously, some godly people like Josiah, Baruch, Zephaniah and Jeremiah himself were living in Jerusalem. But the words certainly applied to the mass of the populace. In short, corruption was so widespread that exceptions were not significant". Jeremiah made enquiries amongst two classes.

Amongst common men (vv.1-4)
"Run ye to and fro through the streets of Jerusalem, and see now, and know, and seek in the broad places thereof, if ye can find a man, if there be any that executeth judgment, that seeketh the truth" (v.1). Lip-service would not do. Jeremiah was to look for a man who was actively engaged in implementing judgment and pursuing truth. People were using the right words, but it was pretence: "And though they say, the Lord liveth; surely they swear falsely" (v.2). It was a "spurious profession of piety. They used the most binding and the right form of oath, but their conduct showed it to be perjury" (Feinberg). The necessity for reality amongst God's people has already been stressed: "If thou wilt return, O Israel, saith the Lord,

return unto me...And thou shalt swear, The Lord liveth, in truth, in judgment, and in righteousness" (4.1-2). The Lord Jesus condemned the lip-service and insincerity of His day: "This people draweth nigh unto me with their mouth, and honoureth me with their lips; but their heart is far from me" (Mt 15.8). The Lord's people are to "draw near with a true heart" (Heb 10.22).

The Lord saw through their pretence: "O Lord, are not thine eyes upon the truth?" (v.3). It is salutary for the Lord's people to remember that "Neither is there any creature that is not manifest in his sight: but all things are naked and opened unto the eyes of him with whom we have to do" (Heb 4.13). In this case, the Lord was well aware that His severe chastisements had made no difference to their lives, causing Jeremiah to say, "Thou hast stricken them, but they have not grieved; thou hast consumed them, but they have refused to receive correction: they have made their faces harder than a rock; they have refused to return" (v.3). He concludes, perhaps thinking of "extenuating circumstances" (Feinberg), "Surely these are poor; they are foolish: for they know not the way of the Lord, nor the judgment of their God" (v.4). The prophet therefore looks elsewhere.

Amongst great men (vv.5-6)

The "great men", reasons Jeremiah, "have known the way of the Lord, and the judgment of their God" (v.5). Their responsibility was therefore heightened, for "unto whomsoever much is given, of him shall be much required" (Lk 12.48). But there was no difference between them and the common man: "these have altogether broken the yoke, and burst the bonds". Their higher station in life did not mean great piety. They had cast off all restraint. "Their idea of freedom was lawlessness, licence to do as they pleased, freedom from every restraint imposed by man or the Lord" (Laetsch). Judgment was therefore inevitable: "Wherefore a lion (marked by strength) out of the forest shall slay them, and a wolf (marked by rapacity) of the evenings shall spoil them, a leopard (marked by swiftness) shall watch over their cities: every one that goeth out thence shall be torn to pieces: because their transgressions are many, and their backslidings are increased" (v.6). While some commentators suggest that this refers to literal beasts, and others feel that there is an allusion here to various predatory nations, it seems more probable that the coming Babylonian invasion is in view. Strength, rapacity, and swiftness were certainly Babylonish characteristics.

Six hundred years later, there *was* a Man in Jerusalem after God's heart. He *did* know "the way of the Lord". It was said of Him, "Behold my servant, whom I uphold; mine elect, in whom my soul delighteth...A bruised reed shall he not break, and the smoking flax shall he not quench: he shall bring forth judgment unto truth" (Is 42.1,3). The nation's leaders had "altogether broken the yoke, and burst the bonds", but He said, "Lo, I come: in the volume of the book it is written of me, I delight to do thy will, O my God: yea, thy law is within my heart" (Ps 40.7-8).

Verses 7-13: A Fearful Condition
They resorted to idolatry and immorality (vv.7-11)

"How shall I pardon thee for this? thy children have forsaken me, and sworn by them that are no gods" (v.7). Their transgression is expressed in two ways: they had forsaken the Lord, and they had espoused idolatry. Both have already been emphasised in the ministry of Jeremiah. As to the former, "they have forsaken me the fountain of living waters" (2.13); "Hast not thou procured this unto thyself, in that thou hast forsaken the Lord thy God?" (2.17); "know therefore and see that it is an evil thing and bitter, that thou hast forsaken the Lord thy God" (2.19). As to the latter, "Hath a nation changed their gods, which are yet no gods? but my people have changed their glory for that which doth not profit" (2.11).

Idolatry is frequently associated with immorality. Feinberg calls apostasy and adultery "a horrendous pair". The two are associated in 1 Corinthians 10.7-8: "Neither be ye idolaters, as were some of them; as it is written, The people sat down to eat and drink, and rose up to play. Neither let us commit fornication, as some of them committed". It should be noted that idolatry and fornication are linked by the words, "the people sat down to eat and drink, and rose up to play". This is the case here: "when I had fed them to the full, they then committed adultery, and assembled themselves by troops in the harlots' houses" (v.7). What a way to respond to God's provision for them! According to JND, this should read, "they troop to the harlots' house", suggesting that Jeremiah refers here to the idol temple. But this is evidently not the case since the passage continues, "They were as fed horses in the morning: every one neighed after his neighbour's wife" (v.8). Laetsch is clearly of this opinion: "They roam about like well-fed stallions, each one lusting for his neighbour's wife, only one example of their atrocious wickedness". As Feinberg rightly observes, "Idolatry, now as then, always opens the door to immorality".

The Lord is therefore completely justified in pronouncing judgment upon the nation: "Shall I not visit for these things? saith the Lord: and shall not my soul be avenged on such a nation as this?" (v.9). The command that follows is evidently addressed to the invader: "Go ye up upon her walls, and destroy; but make not a full end (cp. 4.27; 5.18): take away her battlements; for they are not the Lord's. For the house of Israel and the house of Judah have dealt very treacherously against me, saith the Lord" (vv.10-11). The word "battlements" has been otherwise rendered by translators. According to JND (in a marginal note), "Some, referring to the figure of a vine, read 'tendrils' or 'shoots'". The RV concurs, with the rendering, "take away her branches: for they are not the Lord's", and commentators seem unanimous in supporting this view. Orelli understands that "the idea is that of a vine (not a vineyard) running on a wall. But the city walls suggest the figure; they are represented as a protecting wall, on which the living vine (the population) hangs". Feinberg is worth quoting in full on this point: "The immediate context that speaks of stripping away the braches is a full pruning, not a complete desolation. Only the branches are involved, not the root or stock. Moreover, the broad context and the other prophets reveal that God always intended a remnant of His people to survive". The passage should be compared with Isaiah 18.5.

They ridiculed the prophets (vv.12-13)

They denied the Lord by denying the word of the Lord: "They have belied ('denied', JND) the Lord" by saying, "It is not he ('He is not', JND), neither shall evil come upon us; neither shall we see sword nor famine" (v.12). They denied the very thought of divine intervention and coming judgment: "They have lied about the Lord; they said, He will do nothing!" (Feinberg). This is strikingly familiar! Peter writes, "There shall come in the last days scoffers, walking after their own lusts, And saying, Where is the promise of his coming? for since the fathers fell asleep, all things continue as they were from the beginning of the creation" (2 Pet 3.3-4). The relevance of the double sign to Jeremiah on the occasion of his commissioning becomes clear. Referring to "a rod of an almond tree", the Lord told the prophet, "I am watchful over my word to perform it" (1.11-12, JND) even though the advent of a northern invader, described as "a seething-pot, and its face is from the north" (1.13, JND) looked most unlikely at the time.

The words, "And the prophets shall become wind, and the word is not in them: thus shall it be done unto them" (v.13), reveal the contempt with which the Lord's prophets were regarded. Scholars point out the play on the Hebrew word RUACH (7307) here. The prophets claimed that they had the Spirit (RUACH) of the Lord (an example occurs in Micah 3.8), but the people claimed that they were only "wind" (RUACH). Laetsch goes as far as to say the people regarded the prophets as "windbags", and gives the amplified translation, "Thus, as they threaten us, it shall be done unto them". The word of God through the prophets was completely rejected, and the consequences follow.

Verses 14-19: A Ferocious Invasion

"Wherefore thus saith the Lord God of hosts, Because ye speak this word (the word in vv.12-13), behold, I will make my words in thy mouth fire, and this people wood, and it shall devour them" (v.14). The people had dismissed the message of the prophets as just "wind" (v.13), but they would discover that the preaching of Jeremiah had the force of a consuming fire. "The complete identity between the prophet's words and God's word to Judah" (Harrison) should be observed, together with the identity between the words of Jeremiah and their fulfillment. The ability of the Lord to fulfil His word is conveyed by the title "the Lord God of hosts". He is the Commander of all the armies of heaven and earth, of whom Nebuchadnezzar said, "He doeth according to his will in the army of heaven, and among the inhabitants of earth: and none can stay his hand, or say unto him, What doest thou?" (Dan 4.35). It is perilous to trifle with the Word of God.

There follows a second description of the Babylonian invasion. The first is described in the previous chapter. The following should be noted.

The devouring of Judah (vv.14-17)

The devouring fire (v.14) is now identified. "Lo, I will bring a nation upon you from far, O house of Israel, saith the Lord: it is a mighty nation, it is an ancient nation, a nation whose language thou knowest not, neither understandest what they say. Their quiver is as an open sepulchre, they are all mighty men" (vv.15-16). Feinberg suggests that the address to the entire nation ("O house of Israel", as opposed to Judah), has reference to the fact that "at this time Josiah exercised some rule over the remnant of Israel in the north (2 Kings 23)". Although not named, the description of the invader points clearly to the Babylonians. Moses had predicted this very invasion: "The Lord shall bring a nation against thee from far, from the end of the earth, as swift as the eagle flieth; a nation whose tongue thou shalt not understand; A nation of fierce countenance, which shall not regard the person of the old, not shew favour to the young" (Deut 28.49-50). Laetsch describes the invader as a nation "whose manpower is as unlimited as its natural resources are inexhaustible". As "an ancient nation", its history stretched back to Nimrod (Gen 10.10). Their language would be "unintelligible to the Jews, they will not be able to understand their demands and for that very reason be treated by a merciless enemy as disobedient, rebellious people, maltreated, tortured, killed" (Laetsch). They would be "invincible because their quivers would be filled with death-dealing arrows, always bringing more destruction. Every arrow could be depended on to slay someone" (Feinberg).

The result of the invasion follows: "And they shall eat up thine harvest, and thy bread, which thy sons and thy daughters should eat: they shall eat up thy flocks and thine herds: they shall eat up thy vines and thy fig trees: they shall impoverish thy fenced cities, wherein thou trustedst, with the sword" (v.17). Moses had predicted this exactly: "And he shall eat the fruit of thy cattle, and the fruit of thy land, until thou be destroyed: which also shall not leave thee either corn, wine, or oil, or the increase of thy kine, or flocks of thy sheep, until he have destroyed thee. And he shall besiege thee in all thy gates, until thy high and fenced walls come down, wherein thou trustedst" (Deut 28.51-52). Some eight hundred and fifty years separate the two passages, but the course of the centuries serves to emphasise the complete harmony of God's Word. How tragic to read, "thy fenced cities, wherein thou trustedst" (v.17). Israel said something similar about the ark: "when it cometh among us, it may save us" (1 Sam 4.3). God's people have infinitely greater security than man-made walls: "Sanctify the Lord of hosts himself; and let him be your fear, and let him be your dread. And he shall be for a sanctuary" (Is 8.13-14).

The deliverance of a remnant (v.18)

"Nevertheless in those days, saith the Lord, I will not make a full end with you." This was fulfilled in the preservation of the remnant which went into exile following the Babylonian invasion, and the repatriation seventy years later following the edict of Cyrus (Ezra 1.1-4). The nation, and the world population in general, will be decimated in the future to the extent that "except those days should be shortened, there should no flesh be saved: but for the elect's sake those days shall be shortened...And he (the Son of man) shall send his angels with a great sound of a trumpet, and they shall gather together his elect from the four winds, from one end of heaven to the other" (Mt 24.22,31). Very clearly, God has not, and will not, "make a full end" of His people.

The deportation of Judah (v.19)

"And it shall come to pass, when ye shall say, Wherefore doeth the Lord our God all these things unto us? then thou shalt answer them, Like as ye have forsaken me, and served strange gods in your land; so shall ye serve strangers in a land that is not yours." Habel calls this "a new element in the preaching of Jeremiah: punishment by exile", and adds, "When the day of wrath comes, however, the punishment will fit the crime. For serving pagan gods, Judah must serve pagan peoples!".

Verses 20-25: A Foolish People

In these verses, the Lord rebukes the nation for its stupidity and stubbornness. They were worshipping lifeless idols (vv.20-21) rather than fearing the living God (vv.22-25).

Their lifeless idols (vv.20-21)

"Declare this in the house of Jacob, and publish it in Judah, saying, Hear now this, O foolish people, and without understanding; which have eyes, and see not; which have ears, and hear not." Jeremiah's description of the people is akin to the Psalmist's description of the idols they worshipped: "They have mouths, but they speak not: eyes have they, but they see not: they have ears, but they hear not: noses have they, but they smell not" (Ps 115.5-6) The Psalmist concludes, "They that make them are like unto them; so is every one that trusteth in them" (v.8).

The living God (vv.22-25)

They worshipped lifeless idols, but there was no fear of God who withholds (vv.22-23) and imparts (vv.24-25). In the first case, the question is asked, "Fear ye not me?" (v.22), and in the second the statement is made, "Neither say they in their heart, Let us now fear the Lord our God" (v.24).

The "fear of the Lord" is an attitude of mind and heart which recoils from the very thought of grieving Him. It can be defined as an abhorrence of anything and everything that will bring Him grief and displeasure. It flows, not from dread *of* God (as in Isaiah 2.19), but from love *for* God. Love for God and the fear of God are not mutually exclusive: they are mutually complementary. Hebrews 12.28-29 puts it as follows: "Wherefore we receiving a kingdom which cannot be moved, let us have grace, whereby we may serve God acceptably with reverence and *godly fear*: For our God is a consuming fire". The "fear of the Lord" is not a cringing or craven fear, but an attitude of devotion. It has been defined as being akin to "the attitude of a devoted son to his much loved and honoured father, lest anything should mar the perfect harmony that subsisted between them" (Montague Goodman). The idea is conveyed in Psalm 119.38, "Stablish thy word unto thy servant, who is devoted to *thy fear*". Two things are emphasised.

Creation respects boundaries (vv.22-23)
"Fear ye not me? saith the Lord: will ye not tremble at my presence, which have placed the sand for the bound of the sea by a perpetual decree, that it cannot pass it: and though the waves thereof toss themselves, yet can they not prevail; though they roar, yet can they not pass over it?" (v.22). Sadly, God's people had no such respect for boundaries: "But this people hath a revolting and a rebellious heart; they are revolted and gone" (v.23). They had overstepped God-given boundaries, quite unlike the sea which stays within its God-given limits. God's people today are subject to restrictions. It should be remembered that "ye have been called unto liberty; only use not liberty for an occasion to the flesh" (Gal 5.13). More specifically, "For this is the will of God, even your sanctification, that ye should abstain from fornication…That no man go beyond and defraud his brother in any matter ('the matter', JND): because that the Lord is the avenger of all such" (1 Thess 4.3,6).

Creation withholds blessings (vv.24-25)
"Neither say they in their heart, Let us now fear the Lord our God, that giveth rain, both the former and the latter, in his season: he reserveth unto us the appointed weeks of the harvest" (v.24). But God's people had forfeited this: "Your iniquities (cp. Is 59.2) have turned away these things, and your sins have withholden good things from you" (v.25). Jeremiah had already drawn their attention to this: "Therefore the showers have been witholden, and there hath been no latter rain" (3.3). This should be compared with Amos 4.6,7,9: "And I also have given you cleanness of teeth in all your cities, and want of bread in your places: yet have ye not returned unto me, saith the Lord. And also I have withholden the rain from you, when there were yet three months to the harvest…yet ye have not returned unto me, saith the Lord". It should be remembered that "no good thing will he withhold from them that walk uprightly" (Ps 84.11).

Verses 26-31: A False Prosperity

These verses draw attention to two particular aspects of the "iniquities" which had robbed the Lord's people of His blessings. The following should be noted.

Wealth built on wickedness (vv.26-29)

There was social evil. It was a case of the rich oppressing the poor. In New Testament language, it was a case of the "members of the body" not having "the same care one for another" (1 Cor 12.25). There was widespread social injustice.

What they did

"For among my people are found wicked men: they lay wait, as he that setteth snares; they set a trap, they catch men. As a cage is full of birds, so are their houses full of deceit: therefore they are become great, and waxen rich" (vv.26-27). "Jeremiah use a fowling metaphor…Like a poacher coming home with a wicker-work cage containing the day's catch, so these iniquitous men steadily amass illegal gains" (Harrison). Others suggest that the basket was used to trap birds. This involved placing tame birds in a cage, thus luring wild birds into captivity. These hunters were successful in catching men, either in the sense that they deceived others into joining their wicked schemes, making themselves wealthy in the process, or trapping men by their schemes, and prospering handsomely from their downfall. It is therefore refreshingly different to hear the Lord Jesus say to Peter, in the very best sense, "Fear not; from henceforth thou shalt catch men" (Lk 5.10).

What they did not do

"They are waxen fat, they shine: yea they overpass the deeds of the wicked: they *judge not* the cause, the cause of the fatherless, yet they prosper; and the right of the needy do they *not judge*" (v.28). In all their ill-gotten prosperity, "they could not have troubled themselves less over whether the cause of the orphan was maintained" (Feinberg). God is "the helper of the fatherless" (Ps 10.14), and "Pure religion and undefiled before God and the Father is this, To visit the fatherless and widows in their affliction, and to keep himself unspotted from the world" (James 1.27).

In view of this the Lord says for the second time (cp. v.9), "Shall I not visit for these things? saith the Lord: shall not my soul be avenged on such a nation as this?" (v.29).

Warmth built on wrong (vv.30-31)

There was religious evil: "A wonderful ('appalling', JND) and horrible thing is committed in the land; The prophets prophesy falsely, and the priests bear rule by their means; and my people love to have it so: and what we will ye do in the end thereof?". According to Laetsch, the word rendered "horrible" (8186) derives from a stem denoting filthiness, dirt, rottenness, and occurs only in Hosea 6.10; Jeremiah 18.13; 23.14; and its co-derivative at 29.17. While the whole situation was reprehensible, it is particularly horrifying to read, "my people love to have it so". At first glance it scarcely seems possible that God's people should actually take delight in the way in which the prophets and priests functioned, but it is not difficult to ascertain the reason. Their consciences were undisturbed. They were not reproved by prophet or priest, the very men entrusted with the spiritual welfare of the nation. Worse still, the people acquiesced with all that their leaders, or "misleaders" (Feinberg) did. Their leadership in this was welcomed by the masses.

The prophets
They "prophesy falsely" (v.31) saying, for example, "Peace, peace, when there is no peace" (6.14; 8.11). The prophets failed to tell the truth. The servant of God is to "Preach the word; be instant in season, out of season; reprove, rebuke, exhort with all longsuffering and doctrine" (2 Tim 4.2).

The priests
They "bear rule by their means" (v.31) that is, by their own authority. They did not implement the word of God, but their own will. Centuries before, Hophni and Phinehas, the sons of Eli, put their own interests above the word of God (1 Sam 2.12-17), with fearful results.

The people
They "love to have it so" (v.31).The very people who despised and ridiculed the prophets of the Lord (v.13) loved the prophets who told them what they wanted to hear. Paul paints the same picture: "For the time will come when they will not endure the sound doctrine; but, having itching ears, will heap to themselves teachers after their own lusts; and will turn away their ears from the truth, and turn aside unto fables" (2 Tim 4.3-4, RV). Failure to accept the truth will facilitate the reception of lies. Thus will be the case at the end-time (2 Thess 2.9-11).

The solemn words, "and what will ye do in the end thereof?" (v.31), introduce the following chapter in which "the end thereof" is described yet again. As Habel rightly observes, "There is always something appalling and sad about the situation when this happens, for it means the beginning of 'the end'. When the end comes, Judah will stand helpless before the overwhelming condemnation it deserves".

JEREMIAH 6

Once again, Jeremiah announces impending doom. God's people had failed to take account of His inevitable judgment on their total disregard for His word. "Shall I not visit for these things? saith the Lord: shall not my soul be avenged on such a nation as this?" (5.29). Evil in the nation went uncondemned. The men who should have given spiritual guidance had utterly failed: "A wonderful and horrible thing is committed in the land; The prophets prophesy falsely, and the priests bear rule by their means" (by their own authority), and this was completely acceptable to the people in general whose consciences were untroubled by their deceitful leaders: "and my people love to have it so" (5.30-31). The solemn question is then asked, "...and what will ye do in the end thereof?" (5.31). The "end thereof" is described in the current chapter which may be divided as follows:

> The Undelayed Attack (vv.1-9)
> The Uncircumcised Ear (vv.10-17)
> The Unmerciful Enemy (vv.18-26)
> The Unproductive Refining (vv.27-30).

Verses 1-9: The Undelayed Attack

This passage depicts the determination and resolution of the northern invader. The exact identification of "the...evil out of the north" (cp. 1.14-15; 3.12,18; 4.6) is not given in the early chapters of the prophecy. The Babylonians are first mentioned in the book by name in 20.4, and the Chaldeans in 21.4. It should be said that "BABYLON THE GREAT" (Rev 17.5) is currently expanding its power and influence, and is gradually, but successfully, acquiring fresh territory. In some cases, it is recovering former possessions. The spiritual degeneration of professing Christians makes them easy prey. These verses describe three stages in the assault on Jerusalem:

> The advance of Jerusalem (vv.1-5)
> The siege of Jerusalem (vv.6-8)
> The fall of Jerusalem (v.9).

The advance on Jerusalem (vv.1-5)

In view of the coming siege and fall of the Jerusalem, the only hope for personal safety was to flee the city: "O ye children of Benjamin, gather yourselves to flee out of the midst of Jerusalem" (v.1). The people could never plead that they had not been warned of pending disaster and it is still the business of God's servants to counsel men and women to "flee from the wrath to come" (Lk 3.7). Geographically, Jerusalem belonged to the territory of Benjamin. Feinberg points out that it "was settled by Judeans and Benjamites (cp. 1 Chr 9.3), separated by the Valley of Hinnom. Moreover, Jeremiah was a Benjamite and had strong ties with his own tribesmen". The warning that the enemy was advancing was to be given by trumpet and fire-signal, or beacon (v.1). Tekoa, the home of the prophet Amos (Amos 1.1), was some twelve miles south of Jerusalem. It was the last town of Judah and located on the edge of the desert. The people would evidently "be safer in his hilly area…than in the fortified capital" (Harrison). Beth-haccerem (meaning "house of the vineyard") is believed by some to be three miles north-east of Tekoa, in which case the fire signal would be used to show the way rather than to warn of coming danger.

Zion is described as "a comely and delicate woman" (v.2). According to Laetsch the words "I have likened" mean, "I will destroy", and this is supported by Darby with the rendering, "The comely and delicate one do I cut off, the daughter of Zion". Laetsch continues, "The Lord loved his bride, showered her with bridal gifts (Deut 32.9-14); but Israel repaid her Spouse with basest ingratitude (cp. Deut 32.15), and now the Lord prepares to fulfil His threat (Deut 32.19-25)". The invader is likened to "shepherds with their flocks" who "shall come unto her; they shall pitch their tents against her round about; they shall feed every one in his place" (v.3). The land would be denuded in the same way that sheep graze pasture until nothing but bare soil remains. They would both lay siege to the city and devastate the land to the point of exhaustion.

Scholars point out that the word "Prepare" (6942), or "hallow" (v.4, JND margin), means to sanctify or consecrate, and can refer to the offering of sacrifices prior to battle. The utter determination of the enemy is described: "arise, and let us go up at noon. Woe unto us! for the day goeth away, for the shadows of the evening are stretched out. Arise, and let us go by night, and let us destroy her palaces" (vv.4-5). Laetsch captures the atmosphere in graphic language: "We hear their eager shouts as they urge each other to the greatest possible hurry and exertion. Let us go up at noon! Usually the scorching midday hours were given to relaxation and rest. Not here! Noontime passes, the afternoon hours pass by, and still they have not reached their goal. And still they go on. The lengthening evening shadows announce the coming of the night. Instead of cooling their ardour, they incite them only to greater exertion. Let us go by night!".

The siege of Jerusalem (vv.6-8)

Whilst the Babylonians might have thought that they were in command of the situation, they were in fact under divine control. The Lord was using them as His agent of judgment: "For thus hath the Lord of hosts said, Hew ye down trees, and cast a mount against Jerusalem: this is the city to be visited; she is wholly oppression in the midst of her" (v.6). The northern invaders were commanded to lay siege to Jerusalem by God Himself! The disreputable conduct of God's people had turned His hand against them. In the "Temple Discourse" that follows (chs.7-10) it is emphasised that the coming destruction of the Temple at Jerusalem and the removal of the nation would be divinely initiated: "Therefore will I do unto this house, which is called by my name, wherein ye trust, and unto the place which I gave to you and to your fathers, as I have done to Shiloh. And I will cast you out of my sight, as I have cast out all your brethren, even the whole seed of Ephraim" (7.14-15). A similar situation is threatened in the New Testament where the church at Ephesus, urged by the Lord Jesus to "repent, and do the first works", would suffer divine judgment if its "first love" for Him was not renewed: "I will come unto thee quickly, and will remove thy candlestick out of his place, except thou repent" (Rev 2.4,5).

Having described the preparations for the siege by felling trees to make "battering rams and catapults and other engines of war" (Laetsch), and constructing siege-mounds, the reasons for the siege are given. "She is wholly oppression in the midst of her" (v.6); there was no care for the underprivileged and no just resolution of their cause. Moreover, her iniquity was perpetual: "As a fountain casteth out her waters, so she casteth out her wickedness: violence and spoil is heard in her". The Lord's perfect knowledge is emphasised by the words, "before me continually is grief and wounds" (v.7). As Harrison observes, "The current social evils have led to profound moral decay, represented by *sickness and wounds* (RSV)". But even though the enemy was "at the doors of Jerusalem", the Lord exhibits His longsuffering in appealing to them: "Be thou instructed, O Jerusalem, lest my soul depart from thee; lest I make thee desolate, a land not inhabited" (v.8). Judgment is His "strange work...his strange act" (Is 28.21). The Lord's people do well to take heed to the words of Oded to Asa: "The Lord is with you, while ye be with him; and if ye seek him, he will be found of you; but if ye forsake him, he will forsake you" (2 Chr 15.2).

The fall of Jerusalem (v.9)

It is "as if convinced that even this last appeal (v.8) will be futile, He now foretells the complete destruction of the land" (Laetsch). "Thus saith the Lord of hosts, They shall throughly glean the remnant of Israel as a vine: turn back thy hand as a grapegatherer into the baskets", or "pass your hand over the braches again, like one gathering grapes" (Feinberg). It does seem that Judah is called here "the remnant of Israel", and that possibly the deportation of the northern tribes is regarded as the main grape harvest. The repeated movement of the gleaners until every grape has been harvested strongly suggests repeated invasion and deportation. Sin must be thoroughly punished. A different figure is used in Zephaniah 1.12, "I will search Jerusalem with candles".

Verses 10-17: The Uncircumcised Ear

Having said, "Thus saith the Lord of hosts" (v.9), Jeremiah asks, "To whom shall I speak, and give warning, that they may hear?" (v.10). He had already looked for "a man...that executeth judgment, that seeketh the truth" in "the broad places" of Jerusalem, and spoken to "the great men" of the city (5.1,5), but all to no avail. A century before, the Lord had said, "Wherefore, when I came, was there no man? when I called, was there none to answer?" (Is 50.2). There had been no improvement in a hundred years.

Their condition described (v.10)

"Behold, their ear is uncircumcised, and they cannot hearken: behold, the word of the Lord is unto them a reproach; they have no delight in it". Laetsch points out that "For the first time the prophet voices his discouragement, complains of the difficulty and hopelessness of the task". In an earlier passage, the Lord had said, "Circumcise yourselves to the Lord, and take away the foreskins of your heart, ye men of Judah and inhabitants of Jerusalem: lest my fury come forth like fire, and burn that none can quench it, because of the evil of your doings" (4.4). The significance of circumcision has already been discussed in connection with that passage. The metaphor is used in the Old Testament of lips and of the heart, but this is its only application to the ears. In the New Testament, Stephen charged the people, particularly the leadership, with being "stiffnecked and uncircumcised in heart and ears, ye do always resist the Holy Ghost: as your fathers did, so do ye" (Acts 7.51). In both cases, they resolutely refused to listen to God.

The words, "they cannot hearken", indicate that they had reached that stage because their ears had been made "heavy" by divine judgment (Is 6.10). There was no "hearing of faith" (Gal 3.2,5); this calls to mind the words of the Lord Jesus, "Take heed therefore how ye hear" (Lk 8.18), and the repeated "He that hath an ear, let him hear what the Spirit saith unto the churches" (Rev chs.2-3). The Lord's people do well to search their hearts in this connection. It has to be said that "their ear is uncircumcised" if the Word of God is not accepted and obeyed, and if it brings them no joy and delight. To reject God's Word must inevitably close their ears to His voice. Jeremiah exhibited the very opposite in saying, "Thy words were found, and I did eat them; and thy word was unto me the joy and rejoicing of mine heart" (15.16). He was certainly a man of whom it could be said, "But his delight is in the law of the Lord; and in his law doth he meditate day and night" (Ps 1.2).

Their condemnation announced (vv.11-13)

"Therefore I am full of the fury of the Lord; I am weary with holding in: I will pour it out upon the children abroad ('And I am full of the fury of Jehovah, I am weary with holding in. Pour it out upon the children in the street', JND), and upon the assembly of young men together: for even the husband with the wife shall be taken, the aged with him that is full of days" (v.11). When, at a later point in his ministry, the prophet had determined to remain silent, the power of God's word overcame his reticence: "But his word was in mine heart as a burning fire shut up in my bones, and I was weary with forbearing, and I could not stay" (20.9). Harrison notes that "The stern message of destruction is aimed at the five stages of life mentioned here: the children in carefree play (cp. Zech 8.5); the adolescents in their clubs or groups (cp. 15.17); the married adults; the more senior citizens; and finally those advanced in age". The very fabric of society would be destroyed: "And their houses shall be turned unto others, with their fields and wives together: for I will stretch out my hand upon the inhabitants of the land, saith the Lord" (v.12). Harrison continues: "The Judeans will be deprived of all the material things which they have cherished. Property will be transferred violently to new owners, and all the old relationships of life will be changed when Jerusalem collapses before the enemy onslaught".

The reason follows: "For from the least of them even unto the greatest of them every one is given to covetousness" (v.13). Because of their covetousness and greed, they would lose everything. They would pay the price "for trust in materialism rather than in the living God: the wages of sin have indeed become death (Rom 6.23)" (Harrison). The leadership is singled out: "and from the prophet even unto the priest every one dealeth falsely" (v.13), of which Laetsch says, "And this dangerous state is due largely to the flattering, soft-soaping, self-seeking priests and prophets". This should be compared with 5.30-31. The content of vv.12-15 is recapitulated in 8.10-12.

Their crimes specified (vv.14-17)
There was no truth (v.14)
"They have healed also the hurt of the daughter of my people slightly ('lightly', JND), saying, Peace, peace; when there is no peace". It was nothing less than gross deception. Ezekiel goes further and calls it seduction: "they have seduced my people, saying, Peace; and there was no peace" (Ezek 13.10). The gravity of the situation was totally ignored. Feinberg gives the rendering, "they dress the wound of my people as though it was not serious". The word rendered "hurt" (7667) means breach, referring to the breach between the Lord and Judah. The priests and the prophets were certainly "physicians of no value" (Job 13.4).

There was no shame (v.15)
"Were they ashamed when they had committed abomination? nay, they were not at all ashamed, nether could they blush." Ezra did not belong to this category: "O my God, I am ashamed and blush to lift up my face to thee, my God: for our iniquities are increased over our head" (Ezra 9.6). They were "insensible to reproach, so hardened and shameless" (Orelli). Their total insensitivity to sin would be met by unsparing judgment: "therefore they (the priests and prophets) shall fall among them that fall: at the time that I visit them they shall be cast down, saith the Lord".

There was no obedience (vv.16-17)

They would not walk in the ways of God. The appeal, "Stand ye in the ways, and see", or "stand at the crossroads" (Feinberg), was met with the stubborn reply, "We will not walk therein" (v.16). Here are people who have lost their way but, having come to the crossroads, have to make a decision. It would be good to "ask for the old paths" which could be summarised in the words of the Lord Jesus as "the weightier matters of the law, judgment, mercy, and faith" (Mt 23.23). They are described as "the old paths, where is the good way, and walk therein, and ye shall find rest for your souls". While there is "no peace, saith the Lord, unto the wicked" (Is 48.22; cp. Is 57.21), the "old paths" bring rest. The "effect of righteousness" is "quietness and assurance for ever" (Is 32.17). The invitation of the Lord Jesus remains: "Come unto me, all ye that labour and are heavy laden, and I will give you rest" (Mt 11.28). They would not listen to the warnings of God: "Also I set watchmen over you, saying, Hearken to the sound of the trumpet. But they said, We will not hearken" (v.17). "Since they did not know and take the right way of themselves, God set watchers over them, who were to deter them from the evil way by the warning cry of the trumpet; even to those loud sounds they were deaf" (Orelli).

Verses 18-26: The Unmerciful Enemy

In these verses, the Lord calls upon the Gentile nations to witness the righteousness of his judgment: "Therefore hear, ye nations, and know, O congregation, what is among them" (v.18). Laetsch suggests that the purpose was to make the nations "apply to themselves the lesson He is about to teach in the punishment of His people". It has been pointed out that the word "congregation" (5712) usually refers in the Old Testament to Israel, and its use here in connection with Gentiles indicates that He no longer regards the people of Judah as His congregation. The following should be noted.

Unalterable law (v.19)

"Hear, O earth: behold, I will bring evil upon this people, even the fruit of their thoughts, because they have not hearkened unto my words, nor to my law, but rejected it." The whole earth would witness the consequences of rejecting the Lord's "words" and the Lord's "law". The voice of God through Moses ("my law") and the voice of God through the prophets ("my words") had been rejected, with fearful consequences. It was the law of sowing and reaping, clearly conveyed in New Testament language: "Be not deceived; God is not mocked: for whatsoever a man soweth, that shall he also reap" (Gal 6.7).

Unacceptable religion (vv.20-21)

"To what purpose cometh there to me incense from Sheba, and the sweet cane from a far country? your burnt-offerings are not acceptable, nor your sacrifices sweet unto me" (v.20). The incense came from Sheba, in south-western Arabia (modern Yemen), and the sweet cane or calamus was probably imported from India. These are costly commodities, but valueless as far as the Lord was concerned.

The rejection of God's word cannot be compensated by religious ceremony. "When sin is not forsaken, sacrifices are useless...offerings are worthless when the heart is not right in making them" (Feinberg). The same point is made in Jeremiah 7.21-23. Solomon wrote, "The sacrifice of the wicked is abomination: how much more, when he bringeth it with a wicked mind" (Prov 21.27). The New Testament is not lacking on the subject: "But let a man examine himself, and so let him eat of that bread, and drink of that cup. For he that eateth and drinketh unworthily, eateth and drinketh damnation to himself, not discerning the Lord's body" (1 Cor 11.28-29). The "stumblingblocks" (v.21) are best understood to be the Babylonians who will bring about Judah's destruction. Empty religion would not save them.

Unsparing cruelty (vv.22-23)

Judah is told once again (cp. 1.14,15; 4.6) that the invader who will bring about her destruction will come from the north: "Behold, a people cometh from the north country, and a great nation shall be raised from the sides of the earth" (v.22). According to Feinberg the expression "sides of the earth" means "from the remote parts of the then-known earth". The invader had one object before him, and that was the total destruction of Judah. To this end "They shall lay hold on bow and spear; they are cruel, and have no mercy; their voice roareth like the sea; and they ride upon horses, set in array as men for war against thee, O daughter of Zion" (v.23). The nation responsible for the destruction of Babylon is described in similar terms (50.41-42).

Unrelieved panic (vv.24-26)

These verses describe the panic and despair of the people as they hear of the approaching enemy. "We have heard the fame thereof: our hands wax feeble: anguish hath taken hold of us, and pain, as of a woman in travail. Go not forth into the field, nor walk by the way; for the sword of the enemy and fear is on ever side" (vv.24-25). Anguish akin to that of a woman in travail grips them. Harrison describes the coming conflict "as unequal as that between a fully-equipped soldier and a defenceless woman demoralised by shock". The pain of childbirth (v.24) is followed is followed by the death of an only son: "O daughter of my people, gird thee with sackcloth, and wallow thyself in ashes: make thee mourning, as for an only son, most bitter lamentation: for the spoiler shall suddenly come upon us" (v.26). All this brought no pleasure to the prophet; he calls Judah, "O daughter of my people". But although he still loves them as a father loves his daughter, they will have to "shed the bitter, anguished tears of hopeless despair" (Laetsch).

Verses 27-30: The Unproductive Refining

The final verses of this chapter emphasise that the coming judgment is completely justified. Just as there was no one, low or high, in Judah's society, "that executeth judgment, that seeketh the truth" (5.1), so there was no valuable residue after the nation had been assayed. Attention is drawn to the assayer (v.27) and to the assaying (vv.28-30).

The assayer (v.27)

This is evidently Jeremiah himself. "I have set thee for a tower and a fortress among my people, that thou mayest know and try their way", or "I have set thee among my people as an assayer, a fortress, that thou mayest know and try their way" (JND). Commentators vary in their understanding of "tower" (AV) and, having considered the various views and explored the grammatical difficulties, Laetsch concludes that the AV rendering "is not impossible and would also fit well into the context". In this case, Jeremiah is assured of his personal safety in acting as "an assayer and tester of the moral worth of Judah" (Feinberg). This accords with the promise made to him at the outset of his preaching: "I have made thee this day a defenced city, and an iron pillar, and brasen walls against the whole land…And they shall fight against thee; but they shall not prevail against thee; for I am with thee, saith the Lord, to deliver thee" (1.18-19). Feinberg thinks otherwise and states, referring to the first noun, that "all ancient translations (except the Targum) and modern commentators agree on 'trier', 'prover', rather than 'tower'". He also suggests that the second noun may be better translated "assayer" (NASB, RSV) or "tester of metals". The word "try" (974) is certainly used in connection with the proving of metals.

The assaying (vv.28-30)

Although the work of the assayer is thorough, nothing of value emerges from the process. "They are all grievous revolters, walking with slanders: they are brass and iron; they are all corrupters" (v.28). Laetsch points out that they were unfaithful to God ("grievous revolters") and unfaithful to man ("walking with slanders"). He calls them "backsliders and backstabbers". The assayer does not spare himself in attempting to obtain a desirable result. "The bellows are burned ('the bellows puff', JND margin), the lead is consumed of the fire; the founder melteth in vain: for the wicked are not plucked away" (v.29). Feinberg explains this as follows: "In antiquity, lead was put with silver in a crucible; when heated, the lead, acting as a flux, oxidized and carried off the alloy. But here, the ore is so impure that the alloys are not removed". The material makes success impossible. There is no silver in the ore, and therefore no righteous from which the wicked could be separated! "With the failure of the refining process, all that is left is slag or dross instead of the purified nation" (Harrison). Harrison continues: "With "subtle wordplay on *refuse* (AV 'reprobate') and *rejected*, both terms coming from the same root, Jeremiah sums up his message to Judeans. Because they are *Refuse silver* (RSV), God has 'refused' to turn their punishment away. The ore is far too adulterated to be worth further effort at refining".

There will be a different result when the Lord returns to establish His millennial Kingdom: "he shall sit as a refiner and purifier of silver: and he shall purify the sons of Levi, and purge them as gold and silver, that they may offer unto the Lord an offering in righteousness" (Mal 3.3). Solomon said, "The fining pot is for silver, and the furnace for gold: but the Lord trieth the hearts" (Prov 17.3), and Peter uses the figure of refining in connection with the Lord's people today: "That the trial of your faith, being much more precious than of gold that perisheth, though it be tried with fire, might be found unto praise and honour and glory at the appearing of Jesus Christ" (1 Pet 1.7).

JEREMIAH 7

The third message (or series of messages) of Jeremiah, occupying chs.7-10, has been called "The Temple Discourse" (Jensen) and this title is supported by the introductory words: "The word that came to Jeremiah from the Lord, saying, Stand in the gate of the Lord's house, and proclaim there this word" (vv.1-2). It should be noted that a similar passage occurs in 26.1-7, and that some commentators have little doubt that both chapters refer to the same occasion. Feinberg states that the "affinities between chapters 7 and 26 are too many and too minute for them not to relate to the same address". It has been pointed out, however, that the prophets frequently spoke in the gates and courts of the Temple, and that there is no reason why Shiloh should not have been repeatedly mentioned as an example of divine judgment on those whose correct religious practices and phraseology were not accompanied by godliness of life and conduct. Laetsch observes that "In ch.7 there is not the slightest suggestion of opposition" and that this "would fit well into the time of Josiah's reform". This is not the case in ch.26 where opposition immediately follows Jeremiah's preaching: "Now it came to pass, when Jeremiah had made an end of speaking all that the Lord had commanded him to speak unto all the people, that the priests and the prophets and the people took him, saying, Thou shalt surely die" (26.8).

The references to the Temple, "this house (or the house), which is called by my name", (vv.10,11,14,30) point to the overall lesson of the chapter. In the words of Feinberg, "The temple-gate address is an eloquent attack on the people's confidence in the temple as insuring Jerusalem's inviolability from all enemies". The teaching of the chapter may be summarised as follows:

> The Need for Reality (vv.1-7)
> The Condemnation of Hypocrisy (vv.8-11)
> The Warning from History (vv.12-16)
> The Practice of Idolatry (vv.17-20)
> The Rejection of Ceremony (vv.21-28)
> The Resulting Misery (vv.29-34).

Verses 1-7: The Need for Reality

Jeremiah's position at the gate of the Temple (said to be the gate that connected the outer and inner courts) ensured a large audience. It is possible that the address was given on the occasion of one of three annual pilgrimages to Jerusalem (cp. Deut 16.16). In keeping with the overall subject, the chapter commences, "Stand in the gate of the Lord's house, and proclaim there this word, and say, Hear the word of the Lord, all ye of Judah, that enter into these gates to worship the Lord" (v.2). The connected references to the house of the Lord, the word of the Lord, and the worship of the Lord should be carefully noted. Those who desire to worship the Lord in the house of the Lord must be subject to the word of the Lord. It is important to remember that there is a standard of conduct appropriate to the house of God. This is always the case in Scripture. When Jacob was told, "Arise, go up to Bethel, and dwell there", he "said unto his household, and to all that were with him, Put away the strange gods that are among you, and be clean, and change your garments" (Gen 35.1-2). Having dealt with various aspects of local church practice, Paul wrote: "But if I tarry long, that thou mayest know how thou oughtest to behave thyself in the house of God, which is the church of the living God, the pillar and the ground of the truth" (1 Tim 3.15). The "house which is called by my name" in the Old Testament has its counterpart today in the local assembly.

Jeremiah made it abundantly clear that lip service would not do: "Thus saith the Lord of hosts, the God of Israel, Amend your ways and your doings, and I will cause you to dwell in this place. Trust ye not in lying words, saying, The temple of the Lord, The temple of the Lord, The temple of the Lord, are these ('these buildings', JND margin)" (vv.3-4). The Lord describes the assurances of the false prophets as "lying words". Occupation and enjoyment of the land depended, not on external ceremonies and pious words, but on obedience to His word. "The people were using these words like a magical incantation. The words were true, but what the people inferred from them was entirely erroneous. The Temple had become a kind of fetish and object of faith" (Feinberg). These verses emphasise that words and sayings have no value apart from "ways and…doings". To adorn or cover evil "ways and…doings" with pious words and sayings is a case of "Having a form of godliness, but denying the power thereof" (2 Tim 3.5). The lesson is emphasised and amplified in vv.5 & 7. "For if ye throughly ('thoroughly', JND) amend your ways and your doings…Then will I cause you to dwell in this place, in the land that I gave to your fathers, for ever and ever". The Lord's people were to "thoroughly amend" their "ways and…doings" in four respects.

i) "If ye throughly execute judgment between a man and his neighbour" (v.5). The law specified procedure in the case of crimes and disputes (cp. Ex 21.12–22.15; Deut 17.8-13), but as in the days of Habakkuk, "the law is slacked, and judgment doth never go forth: for the wicked doth compass about the righteous; therefore wrong judgment proceedeth" (Hab 1.4). The Lord's people today must "throughly execute judgment" in settling offences: "Moreover if thy brother shall trespass against thee, go and tell him his fault between thee and him alone: if he shall hear thee, thou hast gained thy brother" (Mt 18.15); "If ye then have judgments of things pertaining to this life, set them to judge who are least esteemed in the church…But brother goeth to law with brother, and that before the unbelievers" (1 Cor 6.4,6).

ii) "If ye oppress not the stranger, the fatherless, and the widow" (v.6). The law required the protection of these vulnerable people: "Thou shalt not pervert the judgment of the stranger, nor of the fatherless; nor take a widow's raiment to pledge" (Deut 24.17). There is no lessening of this standard in the New Testament. In general terms, the Lord's people should be marked by mutual care: "there should be no schism in the body; but...the members should have the same care one for another" (1 Cor 12.25). In specific terms, it should be remembered that "Pure religion and undefiled before God and the Father is this, To visit the fatherless and widows in their affliction, and to keep himself ('oneself', JND) unspotted from the world" (James 1.27).

iii) "If ye...shed not innocent blood in this place" (v.6). Feinberg calls this "judicial murders" and examples occur in 19.4 and 26.23. The Lord's people can be guilty of character assassination: "But if ye bite and devour one another, take heed that ye be not consumed one of another" (Gal 5.15). "Innocent blood" can still be shed amongst the people of God.

iv) "Neither walk after other gods to your hurt" (v.6). "The cause of this widespread lack of love and loyalty toward their fellow men was their failure to remain faithful to their Covenant God, their 'walking after other gods' (v.6b), to their 'hurt', their own harm, for idolatry leads deeper and deeper into sin and its dire consequences" (Laetsch). No wonder that John writes, "Little children, keep yourselves from idols" (1 Jn 5.21).

Verses 8-11: The Condemnation of Hypocrisy

Having appealed to Judah to "throughly amend" their "ways and...doings", Jeremiah now addresses the fearful wickedness of the people. "Lying words" (cp. v.4) covered blatant evil. "Behold ye trust in lying words, that cannot profit. Will ye steal, murder, and commit adultery, and swear falsely, and burn incense unto Baal, and walk after other gods whom ye know not; And come and stand before me in this house, which is called by my name, and say, We are delivered to do all these abominations?" (vv.8-10). The expression, "that cannot profit", occurs with variations in 2.8,11; 12.13; 16.19; 23.32.

Their confidence that the Temple would ensure their preservation from harm gave them the impression that they could violate the law with impunity. No wonder then that this is followed by divine expostulation. This is brought out by the translation, "We are delivered, - in order to do all these abominations!" (JND). Alternatively, "Will you come...and stand before me in this house, which bears my Name, and say, We are safe - safe to do all these detestable things?" (Feinberg). It is almost unbelievable that in the midst of their gross wickedness the people actually imagined that they would be delivered from impending destruction by their religious practices.

There are practical issues and searching lessons here for God's people today. They *have* been delivered "from the wrath to come" (1 Thess 1.10), but salvation, whatever its aspect, is to have moral effect in their lives. This is expressed as follows: "For the grace of God that bringeth salvation hath appeared to all men, Teaching us that, denying ungodliness and worldly lusts, we should live soberly, righteously, and godly, in this present world; Looking for that blessed hope, and the glorious appearing of the great God and our Saviour Jesus Christ; Who gave himself for us, that he might redeem us from all iniquity, and purify unto himself a peculiar people, zealous of good works" (Tit 2.11-14). God's people are not to "henceforth live unto themselves, but unto him which died for them, and rose again" (2 Cor 5.15).

Since "the eyes of the Lord run to and fro throughout the whole earth" (2 Chr 16.9) He was thoroughly aware of the hypocrisy of His people: "Behold, even I have seen it, saith the Lord" (v.11). This should never be forgotten. To each of the seven churches (Revelation chs.2-3) the Lord says, "I know thy works", and the Lord's people do well to constantly remember that "all things are naked and opened unto the eyes of him with whom we have to do" (Heb 4.13). The words, "Is this house, which is called by my name, become a den of robbers in your eyes?" (v.11) are cited by the Lord Jesus in Matthew 21.13 and in the parallel passages in Mark and Luke. Feinberg explains the expression "den of robbers" as follows: "Ultimately the people were treating the Temple, the house of God, as robbers do their dens. It was a temporary refuge till they sallied forth on another foray. Limestone caves in Palestine were used as robbers' dens; so Jeremiah's metaphor was clear to his hearers".

Verses 12-16: The Warning from History

The expression, "this house, which is called by my name" (vv.10,11) recalls another place: "But go ye now unto my place which was in Shiloh, where I set my name at the first, and see what I did to it for the wickedness of my people Israel" (v.12). Until the time of Samuel, Shiloh was the location of the Tabernacle (cp. Joshua 18.1; 1 Samuel 1.3). But as a result of the sinfulness of His people, particularly the priests, "he forsook the tabernacle of Shiloh, the tent which he placed among men" (Ps 78.60). Shiloh had been destroyed by the Philistines, and lay in territory under the control of Assyria. Now, "this house" would be similarly destroyed: "And now, because ye have done all these works, saith the Lord, and I spake unto you, rising up early and speaking, but ye heard not; and I called you, but ye answered not; Therefore will I do unto this house, which is called by my name, wherein ye trust, and unto the place which I gave to you and to your fathers, as I have done to Shiloh. And I will cast you out of my sight, as I have cast out all your brethren, even the whole seed of Ephraim" (vv.13-15). There are solemn lessons here for God's people today.

i) The Lord does not keep places in existence on sentimental grounds. He does not bless them "for old time's sake". The very idea that Jerusalem with its Temple would be destroyed and its people deported, was an unthinkable prospect to those who trusted in "lying words". But its illustrious history and sacred associations in the past would avail nothing. A New Testament parallel can be found in the history of the church at

Ephesus. It was planted by none other than the Apostle Paul (Acts 19.9-10); its elders had a personal interview with Paul at Miletus (Acts 20.17ff); Timothy ministered there (1 Tim 1.3). What an illustrious history! But with all this, the Lord Jesus said to the same church, "I have somewhat against thee, because thou hast left thy first love. Remember therefore from whence thou art fallen, and repent, and do the first works; or else I will come unto thee quickly, and will remove thy candlestick out of his place, except thou repent" (Rev 2.4-5). It must never be forgotten that current blessing depends on current spirituality. An assembly may have been well-founded and enjoyed past prosperity, but that is no guarantee of ongoing progress and preservation. While changes in working patterns, such as migration from rural areas to cities, account for reduced numbers and closures in some cases, many companies of God's people have foundered on the rocks of wrong teaching, not to mention internal dissension.

ii) The Lord had not failed to warn His people. "I spake unto you, rising up early and speaking, but ye heard not; and I called you, but ye answered not". The Lord had done this "daily" (v.25). The eleven similar references in the book of Jeremiah (7.13,25; 11.7; 25.3-4; 26.5; 29.19; 32.33; 35.14-15; 44.4) convey divine earnestness. The Lord is deeply concerned about the welfare of His people.

iii) The Lord can be displaced in the very place bearing His name. The Lord refers to "this house, which is called by my name, wherein ye trust". A similar situation occurred in the days of Samuel: "Let us fetch the ark of the covenant of the Lord out of Shiloh unto us, that, when it cometh among us, it may save us out of the hand of our enemies" (1 Sam 4.3). Israel treated the ark like a lucky mascot: "when *it* cometh among us, *it* may save us". The presence of the ark at Eben-ezer was purely cosmetic. It is a serious mistake to glory in the assembly, however orthodox it might seem. Paul quotes from Jeremiah 9.24, in saying, "He that glorieth, let him glory in the Lord" (1 Cor 1.31).

The section concludes with chilling words: "Therefore pray not thou for this people, neither lift up cry nor prayer for them, neither make intercession to me: for I will not hear thee" (v.16). Similar instructions are given to Jeremiah in 11.14; 14.11. These references should be compared with 1 John 5.16-17. There is a point at which judgment is inevitable. This was so in the case of Judah - cp. 2 Chronicles 34.25: "Because they have forsaken me, and have burned incense unto other gods, that they might provoke me to anger with all the works of their hands; therefore my wrath shall be poured out upon this place, and shall not be quenched". This passage serves to introduce the next section of the chapter.

Verses 17-20: The Practice of Idolatry

"Seest thou not what they do in the cities of Judah and in the streets of Jerusalem? The children gather wood, and the fathers kindle the fire, and the women knead their dough, to make cakes to the queen of heaven, and to pour out drink-offerings unto other gods, that they may provoke me to anger?" (vv.17-18). The term "queen of heaven" is also found in 44.17-19, and it appears that this goddess was worshipped mainly by women. According to Laetsch, "The Queen of Heaven is evidently to be identified with Astarte (Ashtarte), or Ashtoreth, a Semitic goddess, the Ishtar of the Balylonian-Assyrian cult". She was known by the name Ashtoreth to the Phoenicians and Zidonians, by the name Ishtar to the Babylonians, by the name Aphrodite to the Greeks, and by the name Venus to the Romans. Laetsch continues, "The cult of the Queen of Heaven, or the Mother Goddess, was an ancient custom extending through the Orient in various forms under various names, but of the same nature". Feinberg states, "The fact is that Ishtar was known by the Babylonian title *sharrat shame* (Queen of Heaven), goddess of the planet Venus". In some countries she was regarded as the lunar deity and, according to Feinberg, the "cakes" have been described as "round and flat, resembling the moon".

A female "deity" was therefore the object of Israel's veneration in that day of apostasy and decline. This has particular significance today. In 1950, Pope Pius XII proclaimed the Dogma of the Assumption, raising Mary to divine status and making it necessary for the faithful to believe that, after death, Mary rose bodily to heaven. In 1954, the encyclical announcing the Marian Year went further and proclaimed that the assumption had been followed by a coronation: Mary had been crowned and enthroned as "Queen of Heaven". The twentieth century AD, in which these proclamations were made, was evidently not far removed from the seventh century BC. The worship of a woman is no new concept: the doctrines of the apostate church are rooted in ancient heathendom. Notice, too, that the all-embracing religious system at the end-time is portrayed as a woman in Revelation ch.17 who proudly boasts, "I sit a queen" (Rev 18.7).

Judgment upon Judah was therefore inevitable: "Do they provoke me to anger? saith the Lord: do they not provoke themselves to the confusion of their own faces? Therefore thus saith the Lord God; Behold, mine anger and my fury shall be poured out upon this place, upon man, and upon beast, and upon the trees of the field, and upon the fruit of the ground; and it shall burn, and shall not be quenched" (vv.19-20). The answer to the question, "Do they provoke me to anger?", is evidently "No!". Idolatry was a deliberate declaration of rebellion against God, but they were quite wrong in thinking that they could "disturb God's peace of mind, make Him feel unhappy, miserable, wretched, by willful transgressions of His commandment" (Laetsch). When "The kings of the earth set themselves, and the rulers take counsel together, against the Lord, and against his anointed...He that sitteth in the heavens shall laugh: the Lord shall have them in derision" (Ps 2.2,4). But their rebellion, in both passages, will "seriously vex them, be to them what they hoped it would be to Jehovah, a source of vexation, misery, anguish" (Laetsch). The result for them would be devastating (v.20).

Chapter 7

Verses 21-28: The Rejection of Ceremony

"Thus saith the Lord of hosts, the God of Israel; Put your burnt-offerings unto your sacrifices, and eat flesh" (v.21). According to Leviticus ch.1 the burnt-offering was wholly for the Lord, but He wanted nothing now. The people could eat their sacrifices themselves. They were mere flesh. This should be compared with, "To what purpose is the multitude of your sacrifices unto me? saith the Lord: I am full of the burnt-offerings of rams, and the fat of fed beasts; and I delight not in the blood of bullocks, or of lambs, or of he goats" (Is 1.11). Nothing had changed by the end of the Old Testament: "Oh that there were one among you who would shut the doors, that you might not kindle a fire upon my altar in vain!" (Mal 1.10, RSV). Solomon said that "To do justice and judgment is more acceptable to the Lord than sacrifice" (Prov 21.3).

The rejection of their sacrifices, however orthodox, arose from the fact that they were made by people who had little, if any, desire to obey God's word, and who had conveniently forgotten that He had commanded obedience before commanding sacrifices: "For I spake not unto your fathers, nor commanded them in the day that I brought them out of the land of Egypt, concerning burnt-offerings or sacrifices: But this thing commanded I them, saying, Obey my voice, and I will be your God, and ye shall be my people: and walk ye in all the ways that I have commanded you, that it may be well unto you" (vv.22-23). Before ever the Levitical sacrifices were introduced, obedience was required: "If thou wilt diligently hearken to the voice of the Lord thy God, and wilt do that which is right in his sight, and wilt give ear to his commandments, and keep all his statutes, I will put none of these diseases upon thee" (Ex 15.26); "Now therefore, if ye will obey my voice indeed, and keep my covenant, then ye shall be a peculiar treasure unto me above all people" (Ex 19.5). Apart from this, the worship of God's people was meaningless. Samuel made this clear to Saul: "Hath the Lord as great delight in burnt-offerings and sacrifices, as in obeying the voice of the Lord? Behold, to obey is better than sacrifice, and to hearken than the fat of rams" (1 Sam 15.22-23). The same lesson occurs later in the Old Testament: "Wherewith shall I come before the Lord, and bow myself before the high God? shall I come before him with burnt-offerings, with calves of a year old?...He hath shewed thee, O man, what is good; and what doth the Lord require of thee, but to do justly, and to love mercy, and to walk humbly with thy God?" (Mic 6.6,8). These are the "old paths" in which the Lord's people were to walk (cp. Jer 6.16).

It should be carefully noted that this passage does not invalidate the whole sacrificial system. Jeremiah is not "repudiating the value of sacrifice as such, but is denouncing the wicked and apostate who have made the rituals an end in themselves" (Harrison).

All this was met by downright disobedience: "But they hearkened not, nor inclined their ear, but walked in the counsels and in the imagination of their evil heart, and went backward, and not forward" (v.24). The Lord had not remained silent: "Since the days that your fathers came forth out of the land of Egypt unto this day I have even sent unto you all my servants the prophets, daily rising up early and sending them" (v.25). This was no exaggeration. It would be instructive to construct a complete table of the prophets sent by God with effect from the exodus from Egypt. It would begin with Moses (Deut 18.15; 34.10) and Aaron (Ex 7.1) and include a great number of men (and some women), some named and some unnamed. The "writing prophets" alone cover approximately five centuries (401-900 BC), and the ninth century (801-900 BC) brings us to the era of Elijah and Elisha. (Elijah did write at least one letter, cp. 2 Chr 21.12.) The tenth century included the unnamed prophet who cried against Jeroboam's altar (1 Kings 13.1,18), and the "old prophet in Bethel" (1 Kings 13.11). David was a prophet (Acts 2.30). These examples prove that God did send "unto you all my servants the prophets, *daily* rising up early and sending them". While the oft-quoted words in Acts 14.17 do not refer to the prophets, we can *apply* them in that way, and say that God "left not himself without witness" so far as the prophetic testimony was concerned. This should be an encouragement to the Lord's people today. He will continue to maintain testimony to "all the counsel of God" (Acts 20.27), and even when Jerusalem becomes the darkest moral blot on earth He will give power to His "two witnesses...these two prophets" (Rev 11.3,10).

But the nation had not hearkened to the voice of God in the prophets (v.26). Indeed, they had both gone "backward, and not forward" (v.24) and done "worse than their fathers" (v.26). Jeremiah was therefore warned that they would not listen to him either: "Therefore thou shalt speak all these words unto them; but they will not hearken to thee: thou shalt also call unto them; but they will not answer thee" (v.27), obliging him to say, "This is a nation that obeyeth not the voice of the Lord their God, nor receiveth correction: truth is perished, and is cut off from their mouth" (v.28).

Verses 29-34: The Resulting Misery

While the command, "Cut off thine hair, O Jerusalem, and cast it away" (v.29) could be understood with reference to mourning in a general sense (cp. Job 1.20; Micah 1.16), the use of the word "hair" (NEZER - 5145) suggests that the passage refers to the vow of the Nazarite (Num 6.1-21) where it is translated "consecration" (vv.7,9) and "separation" (v.19). When the Nazarite contracted ceremonial defilement, he was to shave his head as a sign that his consecration to the Lord had been abrogated (v.19). Judah, like the Nazarite, had become unclean: she was no longer consecrated to the Lord, with disastrous results: "take up a lamentation on high places; for the Lord hath rejected and forsaken the generation of his wrath" (v.29).

Two reasons are given: first, "they have set their abominations in the house which is called by my name, to pollute it" (v.30), and second, "they have built the high places of Tophet, which is in the valley of the son of

Hinnom, to burn their sons and their daughters in the fire; which I commanded them not, neither came it into my heart" (v.31). The people had not only brazenly set up idols ("abominations") in the Temple, they had burned their children in Tophet, which was near the eastern end of the southern part of the Valley of Hinnom. This was to appease the fire God, Molech, and the children were not merely made to pass through an ordeal by fire: they were burnt to death. Indeed, "Since the whole city had become a Topheth by its idol worship (cp.19.12; 32.35), Jerusalem also shall meet the fate of Topheth (cp. 19.3-15)" (Laetsch). As Feinberg points out, "This heartless worship was clearly proscribed by the law of Moses (Lev 18.21; 20.2-5)". Feinberg continues, "Since they so flagrantly disobeyed God, therefore where the children were slaughtered, they themselves would be slaughtered. The slaughter of the coming doom of the city will be so great that Tophet will have to be used for burial, thus changing the name of the place to The Valley of the Slaughter (the definite article being used)". So great would be the loss of life, that there would be none to drive away the birds and beasts of prey from the bodies (v.33). The misery of the land will be so complete that all joy, even the joy of marriage will disappear: "Then will I cause to cease from the cities of Judah, and from the streets of Jerusalem, the voice of mirth, and the voice of gladness, the voice of the bridegroom, and the voice of the bride: for the land shall be desolate" (v.34). The removal of joy in this way is repeated in 16.9; 25.10, but it will be restored in the millennial reign of Christ (cp. 33.10-11).

JEREMIAH 8

The opening verses of this chapter (vv.1-3) are so closely connected with the closing verses of chapter 7 (vv.32-34) that commentators often expound the two passages together. Having said that following the coming slaughter in Jerusalem "the carcases of this people shall be meat for the fowls of the heaven, and for the beasts of the earth; and none shall fray them away" (7.33), Jeremiah now declares that such appalling bloodshed will not be enough for the invader: even the remains of the long buried inhabitants of Jerusalem would be disinterred (8.1).

Far from being "a quirk of fate" or part of "the fortunes of war", this was nothing less than divine judgment, and the reasons are given as the chapter proceeds. With this in mind, the passage may be divided as follows.

> Insulting the Dead (vv.1-3)
> Intractable Disobedience (vv.4-7)
> Incorrect Assumptions (vv.8-13)
> Inevitable Judgment (vv.14-17)
> Inconsolable Sorrow (vv.18-22).

Verses 1-3: Insulting the Dead

These verses describe the desecration of the dead (vv.1-2), and the suffering of the living (v.3).

The desecration of the dead (vv.1-2)

"At that time, saith the Lord, they shall bring out the bones of the kings of Judah, and the bones of his princes, and the bones of the priests, and bones of the prophets, and the bones of the inhabitants of Jerusalem, out of their graves" (v.1). The purpose of the invader opening the graves in this way has been variously explained. It has been suggested that since the dead, particularly the ruling classes, were often buried with their valuables, this was a case of grave-robbing. Feinberg observes that "excavations in Egypt and Babylon show that this was common". It seems more likely, however, that the invader was bent on the complete humiliation of Jerusalem. His final insult to the community was the desecration of its dead. The nation would be completely dishonoured, the dead with the living. Moab was guilty of such an insult: "For three transgressions of Moab, and for four, I will not turn away the punishment thereof; because he burned the bones of the king of Edom into lime" (Amos 2.1). In the case of Jerusalem "the bones of kings and princes, of priests and prophets, will be treated no better than the bones of the people they ruled" (Laetsch).

But whatever the human motive for such barbarity, it is abundantly clear that this was nothing less than a complete exposure of the utter folly of idol-worship: "And they shall spread them before the sun, and the moon, and all the host of heaven, whom they have loved, and whom they have served, and after whom they have walked, and whom they have sought (consulted), and whom they have worshipped: they shall not be gathered, nor be buried; they shall be for dung upon the face of the earth" (v.2). Horticulturists today make good use of bone meal, but it is to be hoped that this fertilizer is made from animal rather than human bones. The inhabitants of Jerusalem were totally committed to idolatry, but to no avail whatsoever: "The language of the verse is derisive. The astral deities, whom the people of Judah loved so fanatically, looked down on their former devotees with cold concern!" (Unger). Josiah had "put down the idolatrous priests…them also that burned incense unto Baal, to the sun, and to the moon, and to the planets, and to all the host of heaven" (2 Kings 23.5), but his reforms were short-lived. After his death, idolatry reared its ugly head in the reign of his son, Jehoiakim (cp. 2 Chr 36.8).

Solomon declared that "It is better to go to the house of mourning, than to go to the house of feasting: for that is the end of all men; and the living will lay it to his heart" (Eccl 7.2). The chilling record of the lives of these people, and their end, should promote serious and sober thought on the part of God's people: they should "lay it to heart". Solomon also said that "The memory of the just is blessed: but the name of the wicked shall rot" (Prov 10.7). The Apostle Paul could look back over his life and say, "I am now ready to be offered, and the time of my departure is at hand. I have fought a good fight, I have finished my course, I have kept the faith" (2 Tim 4.6-7). The first readers of the Epistle to the Hebrews were told: "Remember your leaders who have spoken to you the word of God; and considering the issue of their conversation, imitate their faith" (Heb 13.7, JND). It would be tragic beyond words to come to the end of life's journey and not to have heeded the exhortation, "Little children, keep yourselves from idols" (1 Jn 5.21).

The suffering of the living (v.3)

"And death shall be chosen rather than life by all the residue of them that remain of this evil family, which remain in all the places whither I have driven them, saith the Lord of hosts." This had been predicted centuries before: "And upon them that are left alive of you I will send a faintness into their hearts in the lands of their enemies…And they that are left of you shall pine away in their iniquity in your enemies' lands" (Lev 26.36,39); "And thy life shall hang in doubt before thee; and thou shalt fear day and night, and shalt have none assurance of thy life: In the morning thou shalt say, Would God it were even! and at even thou shalt say, Would God it were morning!" (Deut 28.66-67). The survivors of the carnage at Jerusalem would prove the inerrancy of the word of God, causing at least some of them to say, "Like as the Lord of hosts thought to do unto us, according to our ways, and according to our doings, so hath he dealt with us" (Zech 1.6). The desire for death will be a worldwide condition at the end-time. Men everywhere, "tormented…as the torment of a scorpion, when he striketh a man", shall "seek death, and shall not find it; and shall desire to die, and death shall flee from them" (Rev 9.5-6). Rebellion against God and disregard for His Word always bring a bitter harvest.

Verses 4-7: Intractable Disobedience

In these verses it should be noted what men do (vv.4-6); and what birds do (v.7). The section is summarised at the end: birds "observe the time of their coming; but my people know not the judgment of the Lord" (v.7).

What men do (vv.4-6)

"Moreover thou shalt say unto them, Thus saith the Lord; Shall they fall, and not arise? shall he turn away, and not return?" (v.4). The conduct of His people was completely contrary to normal behaviour. When people fall, they instinctively get up again; when they turn off the right path, they return as soon as possible. It would be quite as unnatural for a person to make no effort to rise as it would be for a traveller on the wrong path to make no effort to adjust his route. The question is therefore asked, "Why then is this people of Jerusalem slidden back by a perpetual backsliding?", and the answer follows: "they hold fast deceit, they refuse to return" (v.5). Their conduct in this way was deliberate: they manifested no desire to rise or return. "The nation is incorrigible in her apostasy. Judah shows no desire to correct her ways but holds tenaciously to her deceitful idolatry" (Feinberg). Apart from divine intervention, all men would be dominated by evil in this way, but the Lord's people can say with the Apostle Paul, "But God be thanked, that ye were the servants of sin, but ye have obeyed from the heart that form of doctrine which was delivered you. Being then made free from sin, ye became the servants of righteousness" (Rom 6.17-18).

Alas, this was not so with Judah and Jerusalem: "I hearkened and heard, but they spake not aright: no man repented him of his wickedness, saying, What have I done? every one turned to his course, as the horse rusheth into the battle" (v.6). The words, "every one turned to his course, as the horse rusheth into the battle", describe their determination to continue in their rebellion against God, and recall the situation described in the book of Judges where "every man did that which was right in his own eyes" (Judg 21.25).

The Lord "hearkened and heard", but there was no word of repentance. It is so refreshingly different to read that on another occasion, the Lord "hearkened and heard" something entirely different: "Then they that feared the Lord spake often one to another: and the Lord hearkened, and heard it, and a book of remembrance was written before him for them that feared the Lord, and that thought upon his name" (Mal 3.16).

What birds do (v.7)

"Yea, the stork in the heaven knoweth her appointed times; and the turtle and the crane and the swallow observe the time of their coming; but my people know not the judgment of the Lord." Feinberg points out that the birds named (he has "the stork, dove, swift and thrush") are migratory "and follow the seasons of their migration instinctively", adding that "they know more about God's appointed way for them, than Judah knows about God's appointed way for her!". Approximately 150 years before, the Lord had said, "The ox knoweth his owner, and the ass his master's crib: but Israel doth not know, my people doth not consider" (Is 1.3), but nothing had changed. The Lord's people had sunk below the level of the lower creation.

Verses 8-13: Incorrect Assumptions

These verses draw attention to their empty professions (vv.8-9), and to the resulting loss of possessions (vv.10-13).

Their empty professions (vv.8-9)

"How do ye say, We are wise, and the law of the Lord is with us? Lo, certainly in vain made he it; the pen of the scribes is in vain" (v.8), or "How do ye say, We are wise, and the law of Jehovah is with us? Behold, certainly the lying pen of the scribes hath made it falsehood" (JND). Two most important things must be noticed here.

i) Possession of the Word of God does not in itself guarantee divine favour. The same point is made in the New Testament: "Behold, thou art called a Jew, and restest in the law, and makest thy boast of God, And knowest his will, and approvest the things that are more excellent, being instructed out of the law…Thou that makest thy boast of the law, through breaking the law dishonourest thou God?" (Rom 2.17-18,23).

While it is an immense privilege, and a solemn responsibility to possess God's Word, divine blessing rests upon those who are "doers of the word, and not hearers only" (James 1.22). The Lord Jesus made this abundantly clear: "Therefore whosoever heareth these sayings of mine, and doeth them, I will liken him unto a wise man, which built his house upon a rock" (Mt 7.24). The Apostle Paul prayed that the believers at Colosse "might be filled with the knowledge of his will in all wisdom and spiritual understanding; that ye might walk worthy of Lord unto all pleasing" (Col 1.9-10). True wisdom lies in obeying the Word of God. The Lord Jesus said, "He that hath my commandments, and *keepeth* them, he it is that loveth me" (Jn 14.21).

ii) The teaching of the Word of God can be falsified. The scribes (this is said to be the first mention of them in the Old Testament as a professional class) had interpreted the law "in such a way as to assure the people that they could sin with impunity" (Feinberg). They were the forerunners of the scribes and lawyers of the New Testament of whom the Lord Jesus said, "Thus have ye made the commandment of God of none effect by your tradition" (Mt 15.6). Happily, Ezra was not in this category. He was "a ready scribe in the law of Moses" and "prepared his heart to seek the law of the Lord, and to do it, and to teach in Israel statutes and judgments" (Ezra 7.6,10).

The men who had the temerity to say "We are wise" (v.8) would be "ashamed...dismayed...taken" because "they have rejected the word of the Lord; and what wisdom is in them?" (v.9). The answer to this question is simply that there is no wisdom when God's word is rejected, for "The fear of the Lord is the beginning of knowledge: but fools despise wisdom and instruction" (Prov 1.7).

Their loss of possessions (vv.10-13)

"Therefore will I give their wives unto others, and their fields to them that shall inherit them: for every one from the least even unto the greatest is given to covetousness, from the prophet even to the priest every one dealeth falsely. For they have healed the hurt of the daughter of my people slightly, saying, Peace, peace; when there is no peace. Were they ashamed when they had committed abomination? nay, they were not at all ashamed, neither could they blush: therefore shall they fall among them that fall: in the time of their visitation they shall be cast down, saith the Lord" (vv.10-12). This substantially repeats 6.12-15, and Laetsch points out that "such repetitions are part of Jeremiah's style". The repetition is significant. There had been no repentance since the first message was given, and Jeremiah did not hesitate to repeat the solemn warning.

In a completely different setting, Peter wrote, "I think it meet, as long as I am in this tabernacle, to stir you up by putting you in remembrance" (2 Pet 1.13); "This second epistle, beloved, I now write unto you; in both which I stir up your pure minds by way of remembrance" (2 Pet 3.1). The Bible teacher must remember that there is everything to be gained by going over "old ground". The assumption that all the Lord's people are familiar with what are sometimes called the "foundation truths" of Scripture could lead to an appalling ignorance of them on the part of younger believers and the generations that follow.

Returning to the immediate text, the coming devastation of the land is described: "I will surely consume them, saith the Lord: there shall be no grapes on the vine, nor figs on the fig tree, and the leaf shall fade; and the things that I have given them shall pass away from them" (v.13), or "I will give them up to those that shall pass over them" (JND: cp. 5.24-25). Feinberg points out that "the failure of the vintage and the harvest is a frequent Old Testament metaphor of complete devastation". In the millennial age, "they shall sit every man under his vine and under his fig tree; and none shall make them afraid: for the mouth of the Lord of hosts hath spoken it" (Micah 4.4). The "godly man" "bringeth forth his fruit in his season; his leaf also shall not wither ('fadeth not', JND); and whatsoever he doeth shall prosper" (Ps 1.3).

Verses 14-17: Inevitable Judgment

In these verses, attention is drawn to the flight from the countryside (v.14); the folly of the false prophets (vv.15-16); and the futility of resistance (v.17).

The flight from the countryside (v.14)

Having predicted the coming calamity (v.13), the prophet returns to the progress of the invasion (cp. 4.7) by describing the flight from the rural areas to the fortified cities where, although death seemed inevitable, they might be saved from death at the hands of the enemy: "Why do we sit still? assemble yourselves, and let us enter into the defenced cities, and let us be silent there ('let us perish', JND margin): for the Lord our God hath put us to silence ('made us to perish', JND margin), and given us water of gall to drink, because we have sinned against the Lord" (v.14). By remaining where they were, they would be exposed to the brutality and savagery of the pitiless invader. But they did not expect to survive even in the fortified cities. They were aware that divine judgment was certain. "The water of gall", meaning "poisoned water" has "a penal significance" (Feinberg: cp. 9.15; 23.15). Their remembrance of the Lord, and their confession of sin was too late. They were rather like Esau who "found no place of repentance, though he sought it carefully with tears" (Heb 12.17). There may be a veiled allusion here to Exodus 32.20.

The folly of the false prophets (vv.15-16)

"We looked for peace, but no good came; and for a time of health, and behold trouble!" (v.15). There is clear reference here to the false hopes conveyed by the false prophets who had "healed the hurt of the daughter of my people slightly, saying, Peace, peace; when there is no peace" (v.11). Indeed, the very opposite had happened: "The snorting of his horses was heard from Dan (in the north of the land: cp. 4.6): the whole land trembled at the neighing of his strong ones ('his steeds', JND); for they are come, and have devoured the land, and all that is in it; the city, and those that dwell therein" (v.16). Like the "men of corrupt minds" described in the New Testament, it can be said of the false prophets that "their folly shall be manifest unto all" (2 Tim 3.8-9).

The futility of resistance (v.17)

Nothing can halt the invasion; the enemy is irresistible. Perhaps the reference to snake-charming indicates the futility of negotiation. Either way there is no possibility of escape: "For, behold, I will send serpents, cockatrices ('vipers', JND), among you which will not be charmed, and they shall bite you, saith the Lord". The Psalmist describes the wicked in similar terms: "Their poison is like the poison of a serpent: they are like the deaf adder that stoppeth her ear; Which will not hearken to the voice of charmers, charming never so wisely" (Ps 58.4-5). There may be an allusion here to Numbers 21.4-9.

Verses 18-22: Inconsolable Sorrow

In his sorrow, Jeremiah refers here to the complaint of the exiles (vv.18-19a); the condition of the people (vv.19b-20); and the cure available (vv.21-22).

The complaint of the exiles (vv.18-19a)

The prophet now looks beyond the invasion of the land to the captivity of the people. He is deeply moved at the distress of the captives: "When I would comfort myself against sorrow, my heart is faint in me. Behold the voice of the cry of the daughter of my people because of them that dwell in a far country: Is not the Lord in Zion? is not her king in her?". Far from gloating over the accuracy of his predictions, Jeremiah is thoroughly heartbroken. The question, "Is not the Lord in Zion? is not her king in her?" (v.19) implies that if this were the case, how had disaster overtaken His people? As Feinberg observes, they were "trying to harmonise their theology with their deplorable condition!". Gideon posed a similar question: "Oh my Lord, if the Lord be with us, why then is all this befallen us?" (Judg 6.13). The complaint is answered by a counter question which highlights:

The condition of the people (vv.19b-20)

"Why have they provoked me to anger with their graven images, and with strange (foreign) vanities?" (v.19). Their captivity was the direct result of ongoing defiance of the word and will of the Lord. The repeated warnings of the prophets had not been heeded and in consequence the people had lost every opportunity of repentance given to them, so that they were now entirely without hope: "The harvest is past, the summer is ended, and we are not saved" (v.20). While Laetsch understands this to be the cry of the captives themselves as "the cold, icy winter of abject despondency holds them in its icy grip", the following verses suggest that it is the lament of Jeremiah as he identifies himself with the sore plight of his people.

The gospel preacher will capitalise on this verse by noting the progress of time: "The harvest is past"; the passing of opportunity: "the summer is ended"; and the peril of delay: "and we are not saved".

The cure available (vv.21-22)

As already noted, Jeremiah not only expresses his deep sorrow over the distress of his people, he identifies himself with them: "For the hurt of the daughter of my people am I hurt ('crushed', JND); I am black ('I go mourning', JND); astonishment (or horror) hath taken hold on me" (v.21). His heavy burden was intensified by the fact that healing was available: "Is there no balm in Gilead; is there no physician there? why then is not the health (referring to the growth of sound flesh over a wound) of the daughter of my people recovered?" (v.22). The northern part of Gilead was heavily wooded and noted for its balm which was used medicinally. Elijah came from Gilead (1 Kings 17.1) and his ministry was rather like balm which stings before it soothes. Perhaps the significance of the reference also includes the fact that Gilead lay in close proximity to Judah. Further references to balm are found in Jeremiah 46.11; 51.8. Gilead certainly exported this commodity: "behold, a company of Ishmeelites came from Gilead with their camels bearing spicery and balm and myrrh, going to carry it down to Egypt" (Gen 37.25). Balm was traded in the markets of Tyre (Ezek 27.17).

God's people had received the wrong medication, "they have healed the hurt of the daughter of my people slightly" (v.11), and the correct remedy had been rejected. At this, Jeremiah melts into tears: "Oh that my head were waters, and mine eyes a fountain of tears, that I might weep day and night for the slain of the daughter of my people!" (9.1). According to scholars, this is the concluding verse of ch.8 in the Hebrew text. However, for present purposes the verse will be considered as part of ch.9.

JEREMIAH 9

Jeremiah's horror over the dire condition of his people (8.20-22) brought him to tears. It has already been noted that in the Hebrew text the opening verse of this chapter is the concluding verse of the previous chapter. Jeremiah has been rightly called "The Weeping Prophet".

The chapter may be divided in the following way:

> The Despairing Prophet (vv.1-2)
> The Deceitful Tongue (vv.3-9)
> The Desolate Land (vv.10-16)
> The Distress of Zion (vv.17-22)
> The Delight of the Lord (vv.23-26).

Verses 1-2: The Despairing Prophet

Jeremiah was deeply moved over the suffering of Judah (v.1) but at the same time he was filled with revulsion over the sin of Judah (v.2). The tension between his sorrow over their suffering and his revulsion over their sin should be carefully noted. He was gripped by two strong emotions.

His sorrow over Judah's suffering (v.1)

"Oh that my head were waters, and mine eyes a fountain of tears, that I might weep day and night for the slain of the daughter of *my people!*" (v.1). Their refusal to accept the available cure for their sickness (8.22) has resulted in death. The depth and intensity of Jeremiah's sorrow is conveyed by the prophet's reference to his eyes as "a fountain of tears" where, according to Laetsch, the word "fountain" denotes "a reservoir fed by perennial springs". For all their sins, he cannot forget that they are his people. There is certainly an affinity between Jeremiah and Paul in this regard. When the apostle thought about his "kinsmen according to the flesh" (Rom 9.3) he said, "I have great heaviness and continual sorrow in my heart" (Rom 9.2). If Jeremiah has been called "The Weeping Prophet", then Paul could be described as "The Weeping Apostle" (Acts 20.19,31; 2 Cor 2.4; Phil 3.18). It is one thing to denounce error stridently and thump the pulpit, but quite another to denounce error, and weep with "godly sorrow" (2 Cor 7.10). The Lord's people can be quick to condemn, but not quite so quick to weep.

Centuries later, the Lord Jesus, of whom it was said, "a great prophet is risen up among us" (Lk 7.16), wept over the same city (Lk 19.41). That particular generation had also rejected the available cure for their sickness: "O Jerusalem, Jerusalem, which killest the prophets, and stonest them that are sent unto thee; how often would I have gathered thy children together, as a hen doth gather her brood under her wings, and ye would not!" (Lk 13.34).

His revulsion over Judah's sin (v.2)

"Oh that I had in the wilderness a lodging place of wayfaring men; that I might leave *my people*, and go from them!" (v.2). In both cases, Jeremiah refers to Judah as "my people". His sorrow reveals that he was not hard or unfeeling, and his revulsion discloses that he was not given to compromise and lowered standards. He describes the people as "adulterers" and "treacherous". They were "adulterers" in a spiritual sense: they had "committed adultery with stones and with stocks" (3.9). They were "treacherous" in their observance of "the feasts of the Lord" (Lev 23.2). The word "assembly" (6116) refers to "an assembly...especially an assembly of people for the keeping of festivals" (Gesenius). These were to be "holy convocations" (Lev 23.2), but the idolatry of the Lord's people meant that they celebrated them with hypocrisy and deception. Their "treachery" can be described in the words of the Lord Jesus: "Ye hypocrites, well did Esaias prophesy of you, saying, This people draweth nigh unto me with their mouth, and honoureth me with their lips; but their heart is far from me" (Mt 15.7-8). The Lord's people today must give heed to the lesson.

Verses 3-9: The Deceitful Tongue

These verses continue the reasons for Jeremiah's revulsion over Judah. The use of the tongue is emphasised throughout the section (vv.3,5,8). Attention is drawn to the destructive power of the tongue (vv.3-4); the deliberate misuse of the tongue (vv.5-7); and the deception of the tongue (vv.8-9).

The destructive power of the tongue (vv.3-4)

Jeremiah employs the picture of an archer: "And they bend their tongues like their bow for lies: but they are not valiant for the truth upon the earth ('in the land', JND)" (v.3). Their tongues, like the bow, were offensive weapons! A similar statement is made in v.8: "Their tongue is as an arrow shot out". It is an appalling picture of "completely abandoned moral and social standards. Mutual trust had vanished. The inner cohesiveness of the nation had broken down. Judah was laden with deceit" (Feinberg). The people were intent on "lies" rather than "truth".

The New Testament insists that the Lord's people should be men and women of complete integrity: "Wherefore putting away lying, speak every man truth with his neighbour: for we are members one of another" (Eph 4.25); "Lie not one to another, seeing that ye have put off the old man with his deeds" (Col 3.9). It is to be feared that one way in which the Lord's people can "bend their tongues like their bow for lies" is by indulging in tale-bearing. This practice is specifically prohibited in the Old Testament: "Thou shalt not go up and down as a talebearer among thy people" (Lev 19.16). Solomon made a number of references to the talebearer, including the following: "A froward man soweth strife: and a whisperer separateth chief friends" (Prov 16.28); "Where no wood is, there the fire goeth out: so where there is no talebearer, the strife ceaseth" (Prov 26.20). It should be said that "them which are of the house of Chloe" (1 Cor 1.11) were not in this category. There is a great difference between tale-bearing and bringing a serious matter to the attention of a man who is competent to deal with the situation.

There is another way in which the words, "but they are not valiant for the truth upon the earth", may be applied today. Jude urged his readers to "earnestly contend for the faith which was once delivered unto the saints" (Jude v.3). All too frequently when danger looms for the Lord's people and testimony is threatened, competent teachers and elders stay silent. Paul was not amongst them; speaking of false teachers he exclaimed, "To whom we gave place by subjection, no, not for an hour; that the truth of the gospel might continue with you" (Gal 2.5).

Jeremiah draws attention to the deterioration in the situation: "they proceed from evil to evil (go from one sin to another, Feinberg)" (v.3). The reason follows: "and they know not me, saith the Lord". Paul describes a deteriorating situation in the New Testament: "But evil men and seducers shall wax worse and worse, deceiving, and being deceived" (2 Tim 3.13). Jeremiah also draws attention to the damage caused in society: "Take ye heed every one of his neighbour ('friend', JND), and trust ye not in any brother: for every brother will utterly supplant, and every neighbour ('friend', JND) will walk with slanders" (v.4). The very fabric of society had been destroyed. The unity of the nation was threatened. A similar passage occurs in the prophecy of Micah: "Trust ye not in a friend, put ye not confidence in a guide: keep the doors of thy mouth from her that lieth in thy bosom. For the son dishonoureth the father, the daughter riseth up against her mother, the daughter in law against her mother in law; a man's enemies are the men of his own house" (Micah 7.5-6). According to Harrison, the words "every brother will utterly supplant" are "a pun on the name of Jacob" (Gen 27.36), and in this respect "they were all true offspring of their father Jacob at his worst, before he became Israel" (Laetsch).

The deliberate misuse of the tongue (vv.5-7)

This is another feature of the deceitful tongue. "And they will deceive every one his neighbour, and will not speak the truth: they have taught their tongue to speak lies, and weary themselves to commit iniquity" (v.5). As Feinberg points out, "Lying takes more effort than speaking the truth, but they were willing to endure the drudgery of sin". It was more than a case of speaking lies (v.3), which was bad enough: they had deliberately "taught their tongue to speak lies". Furthermore, it was more than a case of not knowing the Lord (v.3) - that too was bad enough: "Thine habitation is in the midst of deceit; through deceit they refuse to know me, saith the Lord" (v.6). The whole atmosphere of society was permeated by deception: they had deliberately and purposefully excluded the Lord from their lives.

Judgment was inevitable: "Therefore thus saith the Lord of hosts, Behold,

I will melt them, and try them; for how shall I do for the daughter of my people?" (v.7). For the second time in his preaching, Jeremiah refers to the figure of smelting (cp. 6.28-30). He has not abandoned His people but will endeavour to cleanse them from their impurity by "casting them into the furnace of tribulation" (Laetsch). He had no other choice, but at the same time He still yearns over Judah, calling them "the daughter of my people". They were dear to Him as an only daughter.

Judah had "taught their tongue to speak lies", but the Lord Jesus was able to say, "The Lord God hath given me the tongue of the learned" (Is 50.4), meaning "the tongue of the instructed" (JND), or "learned...the same word as that for disciples" (JND margin). As the perfect Servant, He had the "tongue of the learned" because "he wakeneth morning by morning, he wakeneth mine ear to hear as the learned" (Is 50.4). The Lord Jesus listened carefully to the voice of God whom He served, and was able to say, "as my Father hath taught me, I speak these things" (Jn 8.28); "the Father which sent me, he gave me a commandment, what I should say, and what I should speak" (Jn 12.49).

The deception of the tongue (vv.8-9)

This is a third feature of the deceitful tongue. "Their tongue is as an arrow shot out ('a murderous arrow', JND); it speaketh deceit: one speaketh peaceably to his neighbour with his mouth, but in heart he layeth his wait." They shoot suddenly, but so does the Lord: "Hide me from...the workers of iniquity: Who whet their tongue like a sword, and bend their bows to shoot their arrows, even bitter words: That they may shoot in secret at the perfect: suddenly do they shoot at him, and fear not...But God shall shoot at them with an arrow; suddenly shall they be wounded" (Ps 64.2-4,7). Solomon warns against cordiality without reality: "He that hateth dissembleth with his lips, and layeth up deceit within him; When he speaketh fair, believe him not: for there are seven abominations in his heart" (Prov 26.24-25). The Lord Jesus was not deceived by His adversaries when they said, "Master, we know that thou art true, and carest for no man: for thou regardest not the person of men, but teachest the way of God in truth" (Mk 12.14). He knew that they were like the man in the current passage: "A man speaketh peaceably to his neighbour with his mouth, but in his heart he layeth his ambush" (JND).

The inevitability of divine judgment is stressed yet again (cp. v.7). For the third time (cp. 5.9,29) the warning is given: "Shall I not visit them for these things? saith the Lord: shall not my soul be avenged on such a nation as this?" (v.9).

Verses 10-16: The Desolate Land

In this section of the chapter we should notice the land denuded (v.10); the cities deserted (v.11); the reason declared (vv.12-14); and the judgment described (vv.15-16).

The land denuded (v.10)

"For the mountains will I take up a weeping and wailing, and for the habitations ('pastures', JND) of the wilderness a lamentation, because they are burned up, so that none can pass through them; neither can men hear the voice of the cattle." With the exile of the inhabitants of the land, the pastures in the Judean wilderness will be left unattended. There will be "no one to water and care for them" (Feinberg). As the result of human sin "the whole creation groaneth and travaileth in pain together until now" (Rom 8.22). The "groaning creation" includes both bird and beast: "the fowl of the heavens and the beast are fled; they are gone" (cp. 4.25).

The cities deserted (v.11)

"And I will make Jerusalem heaps, and a den of dragons ('jackals', JND); and I will make the cities of Judah desolate, without an inhabitant." Jerusalem is not the only place where jackals would scavenge: Jeremiah refers to Hazor (49.33) and Babylon (51.37) in the same way. Harrison points out that "the scene is reminiscent of Christ lamenting the fate of Jerusalem in a later age (Mt 24.1-28; Mk 13.1-23; Lk 21.5-24), with the spiritual causes of destruction remaining constant".

The reason declared (vv.12-14)

The destruction of the pastures with the attendant disappearance of cattle, bird and beast, together with the reduction of Jerusalem and the Judean cities to ruins, would surely lead wise men in the nation to the reason for these calamities: "Who is the wise man, that may understand this? and who is he to whom the mouth of the Lord hath spoken, that he may declare it, for what the land perisheth ('Why is the land perished?', JND) and is burned up like a wilderness, that none passeth through?" (v.12). The fact that the Lord himself answers these questions indicates the total lack of understanding in the nation. It almost seems as if the people had accepted the situation without any enquiry whatsoever. This is not unknown today. All too often, when spiritual life is at a low ebb, and the Lord's work appears to be so ineffective, it is said that this is "the day of small things" (Zech 4.10) as if to say that nothing more can really be expected. The call to "Remember...from whence thou art fallen, and repent, and do the first works" (Rev 2.5) so often goes unheeded.

Three reasons are given for the disaster that was about to overtake Judah. Divine judgment is never executed without adequate reason and never without advance warning.

i) "Because they have forsaken my law which I *set* before them" (v.13). There was no excuse. The law had been "set before them". It was not therefore difficult to discern or discover! Moses had said as much: "For this commandment which I command thee this day, it is not hidden from thee, neither is it far off...But the word is very nigh unto thee, in thy mouth, and in thy heart, that thou mayest do it" (Deut 30.11,14).

ii) Because they "have not obeyed my voice, neither walked therein" (v.13). It cannot be emphasised too strongly that divine blessing is dependent upon obedience. Spiritual life for the children of God begins with obedience - "ye were the servants of sin, but ye have obeyed from the heart that form of doctrine which was delivered you" (Rom 6.17), and continues with obedience - "As obedient children, not fashioning yourselves according to the former lusts in your ignorance" (1 Pet 1.14).

iii) Because they "have walked after the imagination of their own heart, and after Baalim ('after the Baals', JND), which their fathers taught them" (v.14). This is quite horrifying! The Psalmist said, "I will open my mouth in a parable: I will utter dark sayings of old: Which we have heard and known, and our fathers have told us. We will not hide them from their children, shewing to the generation to come the praises of the Lord, and his strength, and his wonderful works that he hath done" (Ps 78.2-4), and, "One generation shall praise thy works to another, and shall declare thy mighty acts" (Ps 145.4). Continuity of testimony is most important, and this is emphasised in the New Testament as well (cp. 2 Timothy 2.2). But here is continuity in idolatry. Their sinful practices were handed down from one generation to another. Baal means "master, lord, possessor, owner" (Scofield). How tragic that Baal had replaced Jehovah in the lives of God's people. How equally tragic when God's people fail to enthrone the Lord Jesus as "Lord of all" (Acts 10.36). Peter's words, "Not so, Lord" (Acts 10.14), are a contradiction in terms.

The judgment described (vv.15-16)

"Therefore thus saith the Lord of hosts, the God of Israel; Behold, I will feed them, even this people, with wormwood, and give them water of gall to drink. I will scatter them also among the heathen, whom neither they nor their fathers have known: and I will send a sword after them, till I have consumed them." In connection with "wormwood" and "water of gall", Feinberg points out that "the first is a plant with bitter juice, the second a poisonous bitter herb. They represent the bitter suffering in the fall of the kingdom and the Babylonian exile". The wages of sin are always death (Rom 6.23). Jeremiah refers here to the judgments described by Moses (Leviticus 26.33; Deuteronomy 28.64). It should be noted that the words, "till I have consumed them", do not imply the annihilation of the nation, but divine judgment on the ungodly. Jeremiah clearly states that the nation would not be completely eliminated (cp. 4.27; 5.18; 30.11).

Verses 17-22: The Distress of Zion

"Thus saith the Lord of hosts, Consider ye, and call for the mourning women, that they may come; and send for the cunning ('skilful', JND) women, that they may come" (v.17). The death of the nation was at hand! Feinberg explains that "the wailing women (v.17) were professionals employed to arouse relatives and others at funerals to outward display of their grief. They used plaintive cries, baring their breasts, flailing their arms, throwing dust on their heads, and dishevelling their hair". This explanation is borne out here: "And let them make haste, and take up a wailing for us, that our eyes may run down with tears, and our eyelids gush out with waters" (v.18). Jeremiah himself was involved in the lamentations over Josiah's death: "And Jeremiah lamented for Josiah: and all the singing men and the singing women spake of Josiah in their lamentations to this day" (2 Chr 35.25). The custom continued in New Testament times (see Mt 9.23) and still exists among certain peoples today.

The reason for this dirge is given: "For a voice of wailing is heard out of Zion, How are we spoiled! we are greatly confounded, because we have forsaken the land, because our dwellings have cast us out ('for they have cast down our dwellings', JND)" (v.19). National devastation meant that they must leave their land; their houses had been torn down, and the death knell had been tolled over Judah. The death toll would be so great that the professional mourners would need to recruit further women in order to meet demand for their services: "Yet hear the word of the Lord, O ye women, and let your ear receive the word of his mouth, and teach your daughters wailing, and every one her neighbour lamentation. For death is come up into our windows, and is entered into our palaces, to cut off the children from without, and the young men from the streets" (vv.20-21). Orelli points out that "The whole nation is to become a mourner; all women are to assume this character, for they will all have enough to lament, when horrid death penetrates into the ostensibly impregnable city, and reaps its fearful harvest among young and old". There would be no respect to age or sex. Death would enter the homes of rich and poor alike, and children and young people would die in public places.

The saying that death is "the grim reaper" finds support here: "Speak, Thus saith the Lord, Even the carcases of men shall fall as dung upon the open field, and as the handful after the harvestman, and none shall gather them" (v.22). In the words of Unger, "Death was about to take a relentless harvest, and so many mourners had to be trained to meet the need". The grim picture is explained by Feinberg: "The custom was for a reaper to hold in his arm what a few strokes of his sickle had cut. Then he put it down, and behind him another labourer then gathered it into bundles and bound it into a sheaf. So death was to cover the ground with corpses, but the carcases would lie there unburied because of the paucity of survivors and the great number of dead".

Verses 23-26: The Delight of the Lord

In view of the looming crisis described in vv.19-22, there was only one course of action acceptable to the Lord. Since all human wisdom and strength will prove futile in the time of inevitable judgment, His people must both seek Him and recognise the things which bring Him pleasure. In vv.23-24 Jeremiah contrasts the things in which the Lord has no delight (v.23) with the things in which he does delight (v.24).

The things in which the Lord has no delight (v.23)

"Thus saith the Lord, Let not the wise man glory in his wisdom, neither let the mighty man glory in his might, let not the rich man glory in his riches." Wisdom, strength and wealth are three things which are valued and admired in the world; more than that, they are things in which men and women place their confidence. But "these cannot ward off disaster and the Lord's displeasure" (Feinberg). In fact, "the wisdom of this world is foolishness with God" (1 Cor 3.19), "a mighty man is not delivered by much strength" (Ps 33.16), and "Riches profit not in the day of wrath" (Prov 11.4). Solomon wrote: "Labour not to be rich: cease from thine own wisdom. Wilt thou set thine eyes upon that which is not? for riches certainly make themselves wings; they fly away as an eagle toward heaven" (Prov 23.4-5).

The child of God can rejoice, not "in the wisdom of men" and "the wisdom of this world" (1 Cor 2.5,6), but in "the wisdom of God…Which none of the princes of this world knew" (1 Cor 2.7-8). Above all, believers can say, whether Jew or Gentile, "Christ the power of God, and the wisdom of God" (1 Cor 1.24). Moreover, believers can rejoice in the Lord Jesus who is "The mighty God" (Is 9.6). They are therefore to be "strong in the Lord, and in the power of his might" (Eph 6.10). Further, though often having little of this world's goods, they can rejoice in the words of the Apostle Paul: "For ye know the grace of our Lord Jesus Christ, that, though he was rich, yet for your sakes he became poor, that ye through his poverty might be rich" (2 Cor 8.9).

The things in which the Lord does delight (v.24)

"But let him that glorieth glory in this, that he understandeth and knoweth me, that I am the Lord which exercise lovingkindness, judgment, and righteousness, in the earth: for in these things I delight, saith the Lord." True wisdom, strength and riches subsist in the knowledge of God. Laetsch explains the words "understandeth and knoweth" as follows: "The two terms combined express all the powers and faculties of the mind being focused on, and motivated and directed, by the Lord at all times". The word "lovingkindness" (2617) is "commonly used in the Old Testament for covenant love, hence God is emphasising His own moral consistency as against the infidelity of His people" (Harrison).

When the Lord Jesus came, He fulfilled the words of Psalm 40.7-8: "Lo, I come: in the volume of the book it is written of me, I delight to do thy will, O my God: yea, thy law is within my heart". His life was marked by "lovingkindness, judgment, and righteousness". No wonder that "there came such a voice to him from the excellent glory, This is my beloved Son, in whom I am well pleased" (2 Pet 1.17).

What is admired and valued in the world is to have no place in the local assembly. The believers at Corinth, who were glorying in men (1 Cor 3.21), are reminded that they owed everything to the Lord: "For ye see your calling, brethren, how that not many *wise* men after the flesh, not many *mighty*, not many *noble* ('high born', JND) are called: But God hath chosen the *foolish* things of the world to confound the *wise*; and God hath chosen the *weak* things of the world to confound the things which are *mighty*; And base things of the world, and things which are despised, hath God chosen, yea, and things which are not, to bring to nought things that are: That no flesh should glory in his presence. But of him are ye in Christ Jesus, who of God is made unto us wisdom, and righteousness, and sanctification, and redemption: That, according as it is written, He that glorieth, let him glory in the Lord" (1 Cor 1.26-31). Paul makes the same application to himself: "But we will not boast of things without our measure…Not boasting of things without our measure…But he that glorieth, let him glory in the Lord. For not he that commendeth himself is approved, but whom the Lord commendeth" (2 Cor 10.13,15,17-18).

Further things in which the Lord has no delight (vv.25-26)

Without a true desire to understand and know the Lord (v.24), outward circumcision availed nothing. The rite did not mean that Judah was exempted from judgment. The nation lacked the circumcision of heart of which outward circumcision was a symbol, and they were "therefore as little immune against God's wrath as other nations" (Laetsch). Circumcision would not save Judah anymore than the wisdom of the wise, the mighty of the mighty, and the riches of the rich: "Behold, the days come saith the Lord, that I will punish all them which are circumcised with the uncircumcised; Egypt, and Judah, and Edom, and the children of Ammon, and Moab…for all these nations are uncircumcised, and all the house of Israel are uncircumcised in the heart" (vv.25-26).

The words, "and all that are in the utmost corners, that dwell in the wilderness" (v.26), or "and all that have the corners of their beard cut off" (JND) evidently describes the heathen practice of "trimming the hair away from the temples" (Harrison). According to Feinberg, "The Hebrew may be rendered 'corner-clipped' (cp. 25.23 margin; 49.32 margin)". Both Harrison and Feinberg suggest that this may refer to the way in which "certain Arab tribes" honoured Bacchus, the God of wine. The practice was forbidden to Israel (Lev 19.27; Deut 14.1).

JEREMIAH 10

This chapter has been called "the final charge of the Temple discourse" (Jensen). The section commenced with people entering the Temple gates "to worship the Lord" with the repeated words of the false prophets ringing in their ears, "The temple of the Lord, The temple of the Lord, The temple of the Lord, are these ('these buildings', JND margin)" (7.2,4). They ascribed "talismanic power to the temple" (Feinberg), but their idolatry and its associated depravity made it clear that they had abandoned faith in the Lord whom they professed to worship. The utter futility of idolatry is now fully exposed before the people are sent into the exile they so richly deserved. The chapter may be divided into two sections:

> The Folly of Idolatry (vv.1-16)
> The Flight into Exile (vv.17-25).

Verses 1-16: The Folly of Idolatry

Whilst these verses treat idolatry with the contempt it deserves, they are far more than an iconoclastic diatribe. The passage demonstrates beyond the slightest doubt that in Jehovah Israel enjoyed an infinitely better position than the heathen, and to imitate their customs and practices incurred the loss of divinely-given privileges and blessings. Israel's privileged position is summed up in the closing words of the section: "The portion of Jacob is not like them" (v.16).

The passage comprises three sections, each of which contrasts idols and idolatry with the "true God" (v.10), and there is a different emphasis in each section:

(i) Idols have no *power* (vv.1-8): they "move not...speak not...cannot go...cannot do evil, neither also is it in them to do good" (vv.4-5), but the Lord is the "King of nations" (v.7).

(ii) Idols have no *permanence* (vv.9-13). "The gods that have not made the heavens and the earth...shall perish" (v.11), but the Lord is "an everlasting king ('the King of eternity', JND)" (v.10).

(iii) Idols bring no *pleasure* (vv.14-16): "every founder is confounded (put to shame) by the graven image" (v.14), but the Lord is "the portion of Jacob" (v.16).

Idols have no power (vv.1-8)

"Hear ye the word which the Lord speaketh unto you, O house of Israel" (v.1). Having warned his people against faith in religious orthodoxy as seen in their observance of circumcision, the Lord now warns them against paganism as seen in idolatry. The message is addressed to the "house of Israel" in its entirety. As Feinberg points out, "this includes not just the Ten Tribes already in exile for more than a century", for "those who remained in the land still retained the customs of their heathen neighbours before them". The contrast in these verses, and in those that follow, is clear: idols are powerless (vv.1-5); but the Lord is powerful (vv.6-8).

Idols are powerless

"Thus saith the Lord, Learn not the way of the heathen" (v.2). Israel was constantly warned against compromise with her pagan neighbours, and with the original peoples of Canaan. For example, "Take heed to thyself that thou be not snared by following them...and that thou inquire not after their gods, saying, How did these nations serve their gods? even so will I do likewise" (Deut 12.30). The New Testament repeats the warning: "Be ye not unequally yoked together with unbelievers: for what fellowship hath righteousness with unrighteousness? and what communion hath light with darkness? And what concord hath Christ with Belial? or what part hath he that believeth with an infidel? And what agreement hath the temple of God with idols? for ye are the temple of the living God...Wherefore come out from among them, and be ye separate, saith the Lord, and touch not the unclean thing" (2 Cor 6.14-17). Two things are named:

Signs in heaven (v.2). "Be not dismayed at the signs of heaven; for the heathen are dismayed at them." Feinberg explains that "the signs of heaven" refer to "unusual phenomena like eclipses, comets, and meteors, which were supposed to portend extraordinary events". This was a characteristic of Babylonian life: "Let now the astrologers, the stargazers, the monthly prognosticators, stand up, and save thee from these things that shall come upon thee" (Is 47.13). Babylon would not be saved by its "enchantments" and "sorceries" (Is 47.12), let alone by the predictions of those who claimed to read "the signs of heaven". Writing as far back as 1973, Hobart E. Freeman observed that "in the United States alone an estimated five thousand chart the heavens for over ten million Americans, who plan their lives according to the alleged influence of the heavenly bodies on human affairs". It should hardly be necessary to add that the Lord's people today should not have recourse to horoscopes!

Idols on earth (vv.3-5). If God's people were not to be "dismayed at the signs of heaven", then they were not to be "afraid" of idols (v.5). In spite of appearances, idols were totally impotent. In the first place, they were "the work of the hands of the workman" (v.3), and all the craftsmanship and expense involved could not disguise the fact that they were utterly lifeless: "They deck it with silver and with gold; they fasten it with nails and with hammers, that it *move not*" (v.4). As Feinberg sarcastically observes, "The mighty god has to be kept from tottering!". But that was not all: "They are upright as the palm tree ('a palm-column of turned work', JND), but *speak not*" (v.5). While this does appear to be the correct rendering, it is interesting, if not faintly amusing, to notice alternatives: "like a scarecrow in a melon patch" (NIV) and "like scarecrows in a cucumber field" (RSV). No wonder Jeremiah remarks that "the customs of the people are vain" (v.3). Idols in themselves are totally incapable of harming anybody, let alone giving counsel, aid, help or comfort: "they cannot do evil, neither also is it in them to do good" (v.5). The images and icons of Roman Catholicism and the Orthodox Churches are exactly the same.

The New Testament sums it up as follows: "we know that an idol is nothing in the world, and that there is none other God but one" (1 Cor 8.4). But this does not mean that idolatry was harmless. Apart from the commandment, "Thou shalt have no other gods before me" (Ex 20.3), idolatry was the habitat of demon power: "What say I then? that the idol is any thing, or that which is offered in sacrifice to idols is any thing? But I say, that the things which the Gentiles sacrifice, they sacrifice to devils (demons), and not to God: and I would not that ye should have fellowship with devils (demons)" (1 Cor 10.19-20). The subject must not be dismissed as having no relevance today. Having said, "Mortify therefore your members which are upon the earth", Paul concludes the list that follows with "…covetousness, which is *idolatry*" (Col 3.5).

The Lord is powerful (vv.6-8)

The words, "there is none like unto thee", occur twice in these verses: in v.6 the Lord is incomparable in *might*, and in vv.7-8, He is incomparable in *wisdom*.

In might (v.6). "Forasmuch as there is none like unto thee, O Lord; thou art great, and thy name is great in might." The Lord is "great in might" as opposed to the impotence of idols. The divine title "LORD" (Jehovah) is most impressive. Thomas Newberry explains that the title derives from the Hebrew words YEHI, meaning "he will be"; HOVE, meaning "being"; HAHYAH, meaning; "he was". Its meaning is expressed in the New Testament: "Grace be unto you, and peace, from him which is, and which was, and which is to come" (Rev 1.4); "I am Alpha and Omega, the beginning and the ending, saith the Lord, which is, and which was, and which is to come, the Almighty" (Rev 1.8). The meaning of "Jehovah" gives weight to the words which follow: "thou art great, and thy name is great in might". This should be compared with the words of Moses and the children of Israel: "Who is like unto thee, O Lord, among the gods? who is like thee, glorious in holiness, fearful in praises, doing wonders?" (Ex 15.11). David exclaimed, "Wherefore thou art great, O Lord God: for there is none like thee, neither is there any God beside thee, according to all that we have heard with our ears" (2 Sam 7.22).

In wisdom (vv.7-8). "Who would not fear thee, O King of nations? for to thee doth it appertain: forasmuch as among all the wise men of the nations, and in all their kingdoms, there is none like unto thee" (v.7). The Lord is incomparable in wisdom, as opposed to the stupidity of idolatry: "But they are altogether brutish (senseless) and foolish: the stock is a doctrine of vanities". His wisdom is incomparable in world affairs (v.7), in creation (v.12), and in redemption (1 Cor 1.18-25). The "signs of heaven" and idols of earth were *not* to be feared (vv.2,5), but "Who would not fear *thee*, O

King of nations?", and the words that follow, "for to *thee* doth it appertain", make it clear that such fear did not "appertain" elsewhere! The "fear of the Lord" is a vast subject in the Scriptures, and the reader is referred to comments made in connection with 5.22-25.

Attention is drawn to the title, "King of nations" (v.7). Solomon said, "Where the word of a king is, there is power: and who may say unto him, What doest thou?" (Eccl 8.4). How much more the "King of nations"! One of the associates of Chedorlaomer was "Tidal king of nations" (Gen 14.1,9), but he pales into insignificance beside the true "King of nations"! Proud Nebuchadnezzar was humbled "to the intent that the living may know that the most High ruleth in the kingdom of men, and giveth it to whomsoever he will, and setteth up over it the basest of men" (Dan 4.17). It is ironic that Israel worshipped the gods of the very nations over which their God was King! The title is used in the New Testament: "Great and wonderful are thy works, Lord God Almighty; righteous and true are thy ways, O King of nations ('King of saints', AV). Who shall not fear thee, O Lord, and glorify thy name? for thou only art holy; for all nations shall come and do homage before thee; for thy righteousnesses have been made manifest" (Rev 15.3-4, JND). There can be little doubt that the singers here ("them that had gotten the victory over the beast", v.2) are referring to the words of Jeremiah. God's people today can rejoice, as they will in the future, that "The Lord hath prepared his throne in the heavens; and his kingdom ruleth over all" (Ps 103.19). They can say, "Sing praises to God…For God is the King of all the earth: sing ye praises with understanding. God reigneth over the heathen: God sitteth upon the throne of his holiness" (Ps 47.6-8). This leads to:

Idols have no permanence (vv.9-13)

These verses contain a further contrast - idols are manufactured and will perish (vv.9,11), but the Lord is the Creator and everlasting (vv.10,12,13).

Idols are manufactured and will perish (vv.9,11)

"Silver spread into plates is brought from Tarshish, and gold from Uphaz, the work of the workman, and of the hands of the founder: blue and purple is their clothing: they are all the work of cunning men" (v.9). But however well-produced and expensively adorned, the "gods that have not made the heavens and the earth, even they shall perish from the earth, and from under these heavens" (v.11).As Laetsch observes, "Who still fears Marduk and Baal and the thousand and one gods and goddesses of antiquity whose very names are forgotten?". According to Harrison, "Tarshish was the westward limit of the ancient world, perhaps Tartessus in Spain, and supplied silver, iron, tin and lead to Tyre (Ezek 27.12)". Uphaz (cp. Dan 10.5) is unidentified, but may be "a metallurgical term for 'refined gold' (cp. 1 Kings 10.18, PAZAZ)" (Harrison).

The second of the two verses quoted above (v.11) is unique: it is the only verse in Jeremiah in Aramaic, which was "a cognate language to Hebrew" and "the *lingua franca* of the time" (Feinberg). The language is appropriate since it is a message from the one true God to *all* idolaters, whether in Judah or not. "Keil correctly states that it has not the nature of a gloss and that a copyist would not have placed an Aramaic gloss into a Hebrew text accidently or purposely. Moreover, it is found in all the ancient versions" (Laetsch).

The Lord is the Creator and everlasting (vv.10,12,13)

"But the Lord is the true God, he is the living God, and an everlasting king: at his wrath the earth shall tremble, and the nations shall not be able to abide his indignation" (v.10). This is a majestic statement and the following should be noted.

"The Lord is the true God", or "God of truth" (margin). He is the "God of truth" as opposed to idols which are described as "a doctrine of vanities" (v.8) and "falsehood" (v.14). They are *false*: He is *true*. The Hebrew word translated "God" is *Elohim*. Thomas Newberry explains that *Elohim* is the plural form of *Eloah*, and states that "*Eloah*...from *ahlah,* to worship, to adore, presents God as the one supreme object of worship, the Adorable One". It is used in Genesis 1.1: "In the beginning God (*Elohim*) created the heaven and the earth". He reveals Himself on the threshhold of Scripture as the God who is to be worshipped and adored. In their worship "in spirit and in truth" (Jn 4.24), believers fulfill the purpose of creation, let alone the purpose of redemption. While idolaters worship "the work of the workman, and of the hands of the founder...the work of cunning men" (v.9), the Lord is the true object of worship. Alas, men have "changed the glory of the uncorruptible God into an image made like to corruptible man, and to birds, and fourfooted beasts, and creeping things" (Rom 1.23). The AV margin reading, "God of truth", suggests more than "the true God". Just as a system of falsehood centred on idolatry, so truth surrounds all the ways of God.

"He is the living God." Both words are in the plural form. These words are cited in 1 Thessalonians 1.9: "ye turned to God from idols to serve the living and true God". He is "the living God" as opposed to lifeless idols: "there is no breath in them" (v.14). They are *dead*; He is *living*. Elijah could confidently address Ahab because he believed in the living God: "As the Lord God of Israel *liveth*, before whom I stand, there shall not be dew nor rain these years, but according to my word" (1 Kings 17.1). God's people today are "the children of the *living* God" (Rom 9.26); they have "the Spirit of the *living* God" (2 Cor 3.3); they meet together as "the church of the *living* God" (1 Tim 3.15).

He is "an everlasting King", or "the King of eternity" (JND). He is "an everlasting King" as opposed to impermanent idols: "they shall perish" (v.11). They are *transitory* and subject to *destruction*; He is *eternal*: "The

Lord sitteth King for ever" (Ps 29.10). The Lord Jesus is "The everlasting Father ('Father of eternity', JND)" (Is 9.6). The eternal security of every believer is vested in Him!

As the "everlasting king" He will assert His rights: "at his wrath the earth shall tremble, and the nations shall not be able to abide his indignation" (v.10). He will subject all things to Himself, and heaven will ring with the words, "We give thee thanks, O Lord God Almighty, which art, and wast, and art to come; because thou hast taken to thee thy great power, and hast reigned" (Rev 11.17).

The statement, "The gods that have not made the heavens and the earth, even they shall perish from the earth, and from under these heavens" (v.11), is set against the Lord's creatorial power in vv.12-13. The *past tense* is used in v.12: "He hath made the earth by his power, he hath established the world by his wisdom, and hath stretched out the heavens by his discretion ('understanding', JND)". Creation reflects His "power... wisdom...discretion". Idols are conspicuously absent! He preceded His own creation, and must therefore be outside His own creation. He will succeed creation: "And, Thou, Lord, in the beginning hast laid the foundation of the earth; and the heavens are the works of thine hands: They shall perish; but thou remainest; and they all shall wax old as doth a garment; And as a vesture shalt thou fold them up, and they shall be changed: but thou art the same, and thy years shall not fail" (Heb 1.10-12). But there is more. The Lord Jesus is not only "before all things", but "by him all things consist" (Col 1.17), and the Lord's maintenance of creation is described in v.13 where the *present tense* is used: "When he uttereth his voice, there is a multitude of waters in the heavens, and he causeth the vapours to ascend from the ends of the earth; he maketh lightnings with rain, and bringeth forth the wind out of his treasures". What happens when "he uttereth his voice" is described in Psalm 29.

It should be noted that vv.12-16 are repeated, with reference to Babylon, in 51.15-19. The above leads to a conclusion:

Idols bring no pleasure (vv.14-16)
These verses describe the ultimate shame of idol-worshippers, and this is emphasised by a third contrast: idols will disappoint (vv.14-15), but God will satisfy (v.16).

Idols will disappoint (vv.14-15)
"Every man is brutish (cp. v.8) in his knowledge: every founder is confounded ('put to shame', JND) by the graven image: for his molten image is falsehood, and there is no breath in them. They are vanity, and the work of errors: in the time of their visitation they shall perish". In the words of Feinberg, "For a thinking person to engage in idol making and worship is no less than a degrading of his God-given endowments. The prophet's final word on idols is that they are not only worthless but also a

work of mockery, worthy only of being ridiculed. In essence, instead of helping their devotees in time of need, idols will themselves be destroyed".

God will satisfy (v.16)

"The portion of Jacob is not like them: for he is the former of all things; and Israel is the rod of his inheritance: The Lord of hosts is his name." While the "*founder*" of idols will be confounded, God is the "*former*" of everything: "it is he that hath formed all things" (JND).

What a sad commentary on the nation! Their recourse to idolatry had deprived them of the highest possible blessing and enjoyment. They had followed idols to their "hurt" (7.6). The expressions, "The portion of *Jacob*", and, "*Israel* is the rod of his inheritance", should be noted. "Jacob" emphasises that the nation was naturally undeserving of divine blessing, and "Israel" stresses their divinely-given position. The words, "rod of his inheritance" (or 'tribe', JND margin), are explained by the Psalmist: "Remember thy congregation, which thou hast purchased of old; the rod of thine inheritance, which thou hast redeemed" (Ps 74.2). Behind these words lies the practice of marking off a portion of land with a measuring rod. Jacob therefore has a portion in the Lord, and the Lord has a portion in Israel. In connection with the latter, Moses said, "For the Lord's portion is his people; Jacob is the lot of his inheritance" (Deut 32.9).

Believers today can say with Jeremiah, in the most difficult and harrowing circumstances, "The Lord is my portion, saith my soul; therefore will I hope in him" (Lam 3.24). They have been "blessed…with all spiritual blessings in heavenly places in Christ" (Eph 1.3) and have been made "meet to be partakers of the inheritance of the saints in light" (Col 1.12). It is also true that while "Israel is the rod of his inheritance", the Lord has an inheritance in His people today: Paul prayed that the believers at Ephesus "may know what is the hope of his calling, and what the riches of the glory of his inheritance in the saints" (Eph 1.18). The Lord Jesus described His disciples as "the men which thou gavest me out of the world: thine they were, and thou gavest them me" (Jn 17.6).

The section concludes by emphasising the greatness of Israel's God: "The Lord of hosts is his name". It has been suggested that this title finds its origin in the completion of creation: "Thus the heavens and the earth were finished, and all the host of them" (Gen 2.1). Most certainly, "They fought from heaven; the stars in their courses fought against Sisera" (Judg 5.20). The Lord has infinite resources at His command: "he doeth according to his will in the army of heaven, and among the inhabitants of the earth: and none can stay his hand, or say unto him, What doest thou?" (Dan 4.35). Joshua met the "captain of the Lord's host" (Josh 5.15). There can be no doubt that the earthly Joshua and the heavenly Joshua stood face to face on that memorable day! His resources include angelic powers: "And Jacob went on his way, and the angels of God met him. And when Jacob saw them, he said, This is God's host" (Gen 32.1-2).

The passage therefore stresses both the folly and futility of idolatry, not to mention its utter sinfulness. The Lord's people must heed the injunction, "keep yourselves from idols" (1 Jn 5.21) and remember that "this is life eternal, that they might know thee the only true God, and Jesus Christ, whom thou hast sent" (Jn 17.3).

But with all these powerful arguments before them, Israel still refused to worship and serve the "true" and "living" God. With such a God as this, it is nothing less than tragic to find that in the second part of the chapter His people are about to be exiled from their God-given land.

Verses 17-25: The Flight into Exile

This section of the chapter may be divided as follows:

> Leaving for exile (vv.17-18)
> Lamentation over exile (vv.19-22)
> Intercession in connection with the exile (vv.23-25).

Leaving for exile (vv.17-18)

"Gather up thy wares ('baggage', JND) out of the land, O inhabitant of the fortress ('O thou that abidest in the siege', RV). For thus saith the Lord, Behold, I will sling out the inhabitants of the land at this once, and will distress them, that they may find it so." According to Laetsch, the Hebrew word translated "fortress" (4692) means both "fortress" and "siege". Laetsch also explains that the word rendered "wares" (3666), which only occurs here, "may have been chosen because it derived from the same stem as Canaan. The Canaanites were great tradesmen, and commercialism had become the besetting sin of Judah; money dictated their policies". Departure from Jerusalem and Judah was imminent, and it would be a violent departure: "I will sling out the inhabitants of the land". Whereas on past occasions sieges had been lifted, this would not be the case now: they would be evicted "at this once".

Lamentation over exile (vv.19-22)

In these verses, Jeremiah laments the coming catastrophe and expresses the distress of his people. The prophet identifies himself with the exiles. The following should be noted.

The anguish of Jerusalem (vv.19-20)

Habel suggests that having heard Jeremiah plead "with Jerusalem to pack her bags in preparation for the worst", her "response is a cry from the depths of her intolerable affliction": "Woe is me for my hurt! my wound is grievous: but I said, Truly this is a grief, and I must bear it" (v.19). It is difficult to differentiate between the personal feelings of Jeremiah and the feelings of the exiles, but Feinberg is probably right in saying that "The people now recognise and admit that they have merited divine judgment.

They are resigned to God's punishment". Personified Jerusalem laments her dire condition. She speaks "as a tent-dwelling mother, deprived of her children and home" (Feinberg): "My tabernacle is spoiled, and all my cords are broken: my children are gone forth of me, and they are not: there is none to stretch forth my tent any more, and to set up my curtains" (v.20).

The guilt of the pastors (v.21)

The blame is placed on the leadership of the nation: "For the pastors are become brutish (beastlike, senseless), and have not sought the Lord: therefore they shall not prosper, and all their flocks shall be scattered". Jeremiah later asks the question, "Where is the flock that was given thee, thy beautiful flock?" (13.20). Ezekiel 34 describes the failure of Israel's shepherds in detail (vv.1-10), together with the restoration of shepherd care in the millennial age (vv.11-31). The Lord Jesus established the pattern for shepherd care in John 10.1-15, and elders today must heed the exhortation: "Take heed therefore unto yourselves, and to all the flock, over the which ('in the which', RV) the Holy Ghost hath made you overseers, to feed (shepherd) the church of God, which he hath purchased with his own blood" (Acts 20.28). An overseer is both a shepherd and a steward. As a shepherd he is responsible for the flock: as steward he is responsible to the Lord, "For a bishop (overseer) must be blameless, as the steward of God" (Titus 1.7). Israel's shepherds would not "receive a crown of glory that fadeth not away" (1 Pet 5.4), but this will be the reward of every faithful assembly shepherd at the Lord's coming.

The advance of the enemy (v.22)

Rumours of invasion for the north (1.14,15; 3.12,18; 4.6; 6.1,22) are about to become reality: "Behold, the noise of the bruit ('The voice of a rumour', JND) is come, and a great commotion out of the north country, to make the cities of Judah desolate, and a den of dragons ('jackals', JND)". The "great commotion" refers to the preparation for war in Babylonia.

Intercession in connection with the exile (vv.23-25)

Jeremiah pleads extenuating circumstances: "O Lord, I know that the way of man is not in himself: it is not in man that walketh to direct his steps. O Lord, correct me, but with judgment; not in thine anger, lest thou bring me to nothing" (vv.23-24). He refers to "the basic moral weakness of man and his congruent inability to overcome temptation consistently and walk uprightly before God" (Harrison). Although Jerusalem and Judah merited judgment, the prophet requests that God's people will not suffer more than they can endure. He pleads in effect for the continuance of the nation. His prayer was answered - the nation did continue even though it was bereft of the very features of national life: "For the children of Israel shall abide many days without a king, and without a prince, and without a sacrifice, and without an image, and without an ephod, and without teraphim: Afterward shall the children of Israel return, and seek the Lord their God, and David their king; and shall fear the Lord and his goodness in the latter days" (Hos 3.4-5).

Having requested the Lord to spare His people from consuming judgment, Jeremiah turns to the very people whose desire it was to consume them: "Pour out thy fury upon the heathen that know thee not, and upon the families that call not on thy name: for they have eaten up Jacob, and devoured him, and consumed him, and have made his habitation desolate" (v.25). They had "been moved by a spirit of vindictiveness and out of proportion to what God had intended. They wanted to destroy Israel utterly" (Feinberg). In the words of Laetsch, "It is a prayer that God might destroy them before they could accomplish their wicked intention to destroy His people". The Lord heard his prayer, and the prophet later wrote: "For I am with thee, saith the Lord, to save thee: though I make a full end of all nations whither I have scattered thee, yet will I not make a full end of thee: but I will correct thee in measure, and will not leave thee altogether unpunished" (30.11).

JEREMIAH 11

Jensen suggests that, after the introduction (ch.1), the first major section of the prophecy (chs.2-20) comprises "Public Sermons (2.1-10.25)" and "Personal Experiences (11.1-20.18)". This view is well worth consideration. Jeremiah's "Personal Experiences" include opposition from Anathoth (11.18-23) and from his own family (12.5-6), not to mention further opposition in the chapters that follow. They also include the various ways in which he was to act, as well as preach, notably the sign of the linen girdle (13.1-11). Feinberg entitles his analysis of chs.11-20, "Signs to Awaken Repentance".

Broad divisions, however helpful, are seldom exact, and Jeremiah is still engaged in public preaching. From another vantage point, it is therefore generally held that the fourth section of the prophecy is represented by chapters 11 and 12, and this view is supported by the absence of any break between the two chapters, which Scofield calls, "The message on the broken covenant". The current chapter describes the rejection of God's covenant (vv.1-17) and the rejection of God's servant (vv.18-23). In the first case, the nation rejected the message, and in the second, they rejected the messenger. With this in mind the chapter may be divided into three sections:

> Judah Rejects the Lord's Covenant (vv.1-10): the word "covenant" occurs five times in the section (vv.2,3,6,8,10)
> The Lord Rejects Judah's Cry (vv.11-17): the word "cry" occurs four times in the section (vv.11,12,14 where it occurs twice)
> Anathoth Rejects the Lord's Servant (vv.18-23).

Verses 1-10: Judah Rejects the Lord's Covenant

Although this is not specifically stated, it seems most likely that the message of this chapter was delivered in view of the discovery of "the book of the law" in the Temple during the eighteenth year of Josiah's reign (2 Kings 22.8-10). This suggestion, "which is now generally accepted by scholars" (Harrison), is supported by the Lord's commands to Jeremiah: "Hear ye the words of this covenant, and speak unto the men of Judah, and to the inhabitants of Jerusalem" (v.2); "Proclaim all these words in the cities of Judah, and in the streets of Jerusalem, saying, Hear ye the words of this covenant, and do them" (v.6). According to Feinberg, the date of the message "might even have been soon after the discovery of the Book of the Law before the reform became widespread…Many take this section as teaching that, in sponsoring Josiah's reforms, Jeremiah itinerated as he urged the people to follow the ideals of the reformation". Josiah recognised the importance of the covenant: "he read in their ears all the words of the book of the covenant which was found in the house of the Lord. And the king stood by a pillar, and made a covenant before the Lord, to walk after the Lord, and to keep his commandments and his testimonies and his statutes with all their heart and all their soul, to perform the words of this covenant that were written in this book. And all the people stood to the covenant" (2 Kings 23.2-3). A parallel passage is found in 2 Chronicles 34.29-32. Jeremiah later refers to "the book...which was found in the house of the Lord": "Thy words were found, and I did eat them; and thy word was unto me the joy and rejoicing of mine heart" (15.16).

Attention is drawn to the terms of the covenant (vv.1-5); the transgression of the covenant (vv.6-8); and the turning from the covenant (vv.9-10).

The terms of the covenant (vv.1-5)

Judah and Jerusalem are reminded of the terms of the covenant, with a warning: "Cursed be the man that obeyeth not the words of this covenant" (v.3). This repeats the warning given by Moses: "Cursed be he that confirmeth not all the words of this law to do them" (Deut 27.26). The same warning is cited in the New Testament: "Cursed is every one that continueth not in all things which are written in the book of the law to do them" (Gal 3.10). The terms of the covenant had been made clear: "Now therefore, if ye will obey my voice indeed, and keep my covenant, then shall ye be a peculiar treasure unto me above all people: for all the earth is mine: And ye shall be unto me a kingdom of priests, and an holy nation" (Ex 19.5-6). The Lord undertook to perform His covenanted obligations, providing Israel fulfilled their part of the covenant. His promise is reiterated here: "Obey my voice, and do them, according to all which I command you: so shall ye be my people, and I will be your God: That I may perform the oath which I have sworn unto your fathers, to give them a land flowing with milk and honey, as it is this day" (vv.4-5). The people accepted the terms of the covenant (Ex 19.8), and it was inaugurated with blood (Ex 24.3-8; cp. Hebrews 9.18-20).

Failure on Israel's part to keep the covenant did not mean that the Lord had ceased to acknowledge them as His people. The unconditional promises made to the patriarchs will be fulfilled, not on the basis of the old covenant, but on the basis a new covenant. Jeremiah describes the terms of this covenant, and it is noteworthy that the Lord Himself undertakes all of its obligations: "But this shall be the covenant that *I will* make with the house of Israel; After those days, saith the Lord, *I will* put my law in their inward parts, and write it in their hearts; and will be their God, and they shall be my people" (31.33). The old covenant made demands on human nature, which human nature could not meet; it was "weak through the flesh" (Rom 8.3). But the new covenant depends entirely upon God Himself. The terms of the new covenant are the terms of the gospel: "For by grace are ye saved through faith; and that not of yourselves: it is the gift of God: Not of works, lest any man should boast" (Eph 2.8-9). No small wonder then that Paul describes himself and his fellow-labourers as "ministers of the new testament ('covenant', JND)" (2 Cor 3.6).

It should also be said that in the course of his ministry, Jeremiah refers not only to the new covenant with Israel, but to the immutability of the Lord's covenant with David: "Thus saith the Lord; If ye can break my covenant of the day, and my covenant of the night, and that there should not be day and night in their season; Then may also my covenant be broken with David my servant, that he should not have a son to reign upon his throne" (33.20-21). Every day and every night should remind the Lord's people today that the Lord Jesus will sit "upon the throne of David, and upon his kingdom, to order it, and to establish it with judgment and with justice from henceforth even for ever" (Is 9.7). Let every a-millennialist take careful note!

The practical teaching of these verses must be carefully noticed. They clearly set out the consequences of disobedience (v.3), and the consequences of obedience (vv.4-5), and do so with reference to the redemption, obligations, and inheritance of the Lord's people.

Their redemption

"I brought them (the fathers) forth out of the land of Egypt, from the iron furnace" (v.4). Moses referred to the deliverance of Israel in this way (Deut 4.20), and Solomon showed his acquaintance with the Mosaic passage by quoting it in 1 Kings 8.51. This is not surprising: every king was required to make his own copy of the law (Deut 17.18). Believers today have been delivered from cruel bondage: they were once the "servants of sin" (Rom 6.17).

Their obligations

"Obey my voice, and do them ('the words of this covenant', v.3), according to all which I command you: so shall ye be my people, and I will be your God" (v.4). The redeemed people were to be an obedient people. Obedience is obligatory. The words "commanded" and "command" emphasise that obedience is not merely an option. Fellowship with God is dependent on obedience: "so shall ye be my people, and I will be your God". The New Testament emphasises that redeemed people are to be godly in life: the Lord Jesus "gave himself for us, that he might redeem us from all iniquity, and purify unto himself a peculiar people, zealous of good works" (Titus 2.14); "pass the time of your sojourning here in fear: Forasmuch as ye know that ye were not redeemed with corruptible things, as silver and gold...but with the precious blood of Christ" (1 Pet 1.17-19).

Their inheritance

"Obey my voice...That I may perform the oath which I have sworn unto your fathers, to give them a land flowing with milk and honey, as it is this day" (vv.4-5). Obedience will bring blessing. The words, "a land flowing with milk and honey", signify the fertility of the land. Israel's disobedience ultimately cost them their good inheritance, and disobedience on the part of God's people today will deprive them of the joy of their salvation.

Jeremiah's response, "So be it, O Lord" (v.5), or "Amen, Jehovah!" (JND), indicates his total agreement with divine justice. It follows a long sentence beginning with "Thus saith the Lord God of Israel; Cursed be the man that obeyeth not the words of this covenant…". The Lord will be faithful to His own word, even though it means judgment and chastening. The believer today must remember this: "If we suffer, we shall also reign with him: if we deny him, he also will deny us: If we believe not ('if we are unfaithful', JND), yet he abideth faithful: he cannot deny himself" (2 Tim 2.12-13). If the Lord's people are unfaithful (lacking in fidelity) He will be unswervingly faithful to His word in withholding reward. After all, He is "the righteous judge" (2 Tim 4.8).

The transgression of the covenant (vv.6-8)

Like the preceding verses, this section recalls the obligations resting upon the covenant people to obey God. For the second time in this chapter the command is given, "Obey my voice" (v.7), but whereas vv.1-5 warn against disobedience, reference is now made to the practice of disobedience: "Yet they obeyed not, nor inclined their ear, but walked every one in the imagination of their evil heart" (v.8). These verses contain a proclamation (v.6), a protest (v.7), and a promise (v.8).

The proclamation

"Proclaim all these words in the cities of Judah, and in the streets of Jerusalem, saying, *Hear* ye the words of this covenant, and *do* them" (v.6). Familiarity with the covenant was insufficient, and it is equally insufficient today to be merely acquainted with the Word of God. James makes the point: "But be ye *doers* of the word, and not *hearers* only, deceiving your own selves" (James 1.22). Paul makes the same point: "Those things, which ye have both learned, and received, and *heard*, and seen in me, *do*: and the God of peace shall be with you" (Phil 4.9).

The protest

"For I earnestly protested unto your fathers in the day that I brought them up out of the land of Egypt, even unto this day, rising early and protesting, saying, Obey my voice" (v.7). This is the third of eleven occurrences of the words "rising early". In ten instances, it is the Lord who 'rises early' (7.13,25; 11.7; 25.4; 26.5; 29.19; 32.33; 35.14,15; 44.4), and in one case it is Jeremiah himself (25.3). The following should be noted: "rising up early and *speaking*", or "rising early and speaking" (7.13; 25.3; 35.14); "rising up early and *sending*", or "rising early and sending" (7.25; 25.4; 26.5; 29.19; 35.15; 44.4); "rising early and *protesting*" (11.7); "rising up early and *teaching*" (32.33). The reader is referred to more extensive comments made in connection with the words, "*daily* rising up early and sending them" (7.25).

The promise

"Yet they obeyed not, nor inclined their ear, but walked every one in the imagination of their evil heart: *therefore* I will bring upon them all the words of this covenant, which I commanded them to do; but they did them not" (v.8). The lesson is clear: God cannot be disobeyed with impunity. Passively, "they obeyed not, nor inclined their ear". This was because "their ear is uncircumcised, and they cannot hearken" (6.10). There was no "hearing of faith" (Gal 3.2,5). Actively, they "walked every one in the imagination of their evil heart". They resembled their ancestors in the days of the judges, when "every man did that which was right in his own eyes" (Judg 21.25).

The turning from the covenant (vv.9-10)
"And the Lord said unto me, A conspiracy is found among the men of Judah, and among the inhabitants of Jerusalem. They are turned back to the iniquities of their forefathers…the house of Israel and the house of Judah have broken my covenant which I made with their fathers." It is salutary that this charge should be brought against Judah and Jerusalem at this particular time. Following the discovery of the "book" in the Temple, Josiah determined to "perform the words of this covenant that were written in this book. And all the people stood to the covenant" (2 Kings 23.3). But the godly example of Josiah was not wholeheartedly followed by the nation. His reforms only had a superficial effect on national life. The people of Judah and Jerusalem were required to submit personally to the word of God, but this did not happen. The covenant may have been outwardly acknowledged, but it was inwardly resisted. The reforms did not secure lasting change, and this is more than adequately proven by the wholesale apostasy that followed Josiah's death. This should lead the Lord's people today to examine their own spiritual reality and their own spiritual convictions. It is one thing to pay lip service to the "status quo", especially if that is required by the spiritual leadership, but quite another to obey the Word of God genuinely and enthusiastically.

Verses 11-17: God Rejects Judah's Cry
Attention is drawn in these verses to the unheard cries (vv.11-13); the unoffered prayer (v.14); and the unholy conduct (vv.15-17).

The unheard cries (vv.11-13)
There are intensely solemn lessons here: in the first place their cries to the Lord *would* not be heard (v.11), and in the second their cries to idols *could* not be heard (vv.12-13).

Their cry to God would not be heard
"Though they shall cry unto me, I will not hearken unto them" (v.11). He would not hear. It has been rightly said that there is no such thing as unanswered prayer, even if the answer is sometimes, "No". But there is certainly such a thing as unheard prayer: "If I regard iniquity in my heart,

the Lord will not hear me" (Ps 66.18). This was never applicable to the
Lord Jesus and, indeed, it never could be applicable to Him. He "offered
up prayers and supplications with strong crying and tears unto him that
was able to save him from death ('out of death', JND), and was heard in
that he feared ('because of his piety', JND)" (Heb 5.7).

Their cry to idols would not be heard
   "Then shall the cities of Judah and inhabitants of Jerusalem go, and cry
unto the gods unto whom they offer incense: but they shall not save them
at all in the time of their trouble" (vv.12). They could not hear. Jeremiah
has already drawn attention to impotence of idols: "in the time of their
trouble they will say (to stocks and stones), Arise, and save us. But where
are thy gods that thou hast made thee? let them arise, if they can save thee
in the time of thy trouble: for according to the number of thy cities are thy
gods, O Judah" (2.27-28). They were gods "that cannot save" (Is 45.20).
Idolatry had proliferated: it was "according to the number of thy cities",
and "according to the number of the streets of Jerusalem" (v.13). Baal
would certainly prove to be "that shameful thing" ('the Shame', JND; cp.
"shame ('the shameful [idol]', JND margin) hath devoured the labour of
our fathers from our youth" (3.24). Bearing in mind that Baal means lord,
master, possessor, owner, what a "shameful thing" it would be for the Lord's
people to allow anything or anybody to displace Him on the throne of
their hearts and lives.

The unoffered prayer (v.14)
   "Therefore pray not thou for this people, neither lift up a cry or prayer
for them: for I will not hear them in the time that they cry unto me for
their trouble". Similar instructions are given to Jeremiah in 7.16 and 14.11.
When God's word has been deliberately, wilfully, and persistently rejected,
judgment is inevitable.

The unholy conduct (vv.15-17)
   Wide variations in translation meet every commentator here: "What hath
my beloved to do in mine house, seeing she hath wrought lewdness with
many, and the holy flesh is passed from thee? when thou doest evil, then
thou rejoicest" (v.15). According to Feinberg, "the text is obscure…and
many interpreters have despaired of translating it intelligibly". The
difficulties in translation do not, however, obscure the basic meaning of
the verse. The Lord refers here to the religious practices of His people.
They were in the Temple, and they were offering sacrifices. But the whole
procedure was empty and meaningless. "What hath my beloved to do in
my house, seeing that the more part practise their evil devices" (JND);
"What is my beloved doing in my temple as she works out her evil schemes
with many?" (NIV). As Feinberg points out, "All are agreed…that this
parallels 7.10,11,21-23". Comparison should also be made with 6.20. The

remaining part of the verse could mean that the sacrifices ("holy flesh"; cp. Haggai 2.11-12) could not remove the evil of Judah and Jerusalem, and Scofield understands it in this way: "To what purpose the 'holy flesh' of sacrifices? Its efficacy is 'passed from thee' who rejoicest in evil" (The Scofield Reference Bible). An alternative suggestion is made by Harrison: "Ritual sacrifices clearly offered no immunity from calamity". If that were the case, then they could certainly rejoice! But sacrifices would not avert the coming doom. A fellow-prophet reminded Judah that the Lord was not "pleased with thousands of rams, or with ten thousands of rivers of oil". On the contrary, "He hath shewed thee, O man, what is good; and what doth the Lord require of thee, but to do justly, and to love mercy, and to walk humbly with thy God?" (Micah 6.7-8).

This does not suggest for one moment that the Lord is vindictive. Although abhorring their hypocrisy, He calls them "my beloved". He later describes His people as "the dearly beloved of my soul" (12.7). But the nation had proved unfaithful: "she hath wrought lewdness with many" (v.15), and had provoked the Lord "to anger in offering incense unto Baal" (v.17). The Lord's people today must not forget the solemn words, "Ye adulterers and adulteresses, know ye not that the friendship of the world is enmity with God?" (James 4.4).

If Judah and Jerusalem, as the Lord's "beloved", had been persistently unfaithful to Him, there would be no refuge from divine wrath. The past could not save them: "The Lord called thy name, A green olive tree, fair, and of goodly fruit: with the noise of a great tumult he hath kindled fire upon it, and the branches of it are broken" (v.16). Past blessings are no defence against divine displeasure when the Lord's people defect: "But though it was He who had established her, it is He who has to destroy her because, to her hurt, she adores Baal" (Broadbent). Scholars usually suggest that in the picture of coming judgment the destruction of the olive tree is due to lightning. Both Israel in the north and Judah in the south are comprehended here (v.17). Paul alludes to this passage in Romans 11.13-25, and goes further by describing, not only the results which follow when the branches are "broken off", but the results which follow when the branches are "graffed into their own olive tree". When this takes place, "His branches shall spread, and his beauty shall be as the olive tree, and his smell as Lebanon" (Hos 14.6). His people will, again, be beautiful and fruitful.

Verses 18-23: Anathoth Rejects the Lord's Servant

Having rejected the word of God, His people now go further, as so often in the past, by rejecting the servant of the Lord. The "conspiracy" against the Lord in v.9, is followed by a conspiracy against Jeremiah: "I knew not that they had devised devices against me" (v.19). The message and the messenger cannot be disassociated. If the message is rejected, it is inevitable that the messenger will also be rejected. Paul calls this "the offence of the cross" (Gal 5.11). But there is another connection. The Lord had been rejected by His own people, whom He calls "my beloved". Now Jeremiah is rejected by *his* own people. He was able, therefore, like Hosea, to understand God's deep grief over Judah and Jerusalem. It could be called, "the fellowship of his sufferings" (Phil 3.10). The Lord Jesus prepared His disciples for future persecution and animosity: "If the world hate you, ye know that it hated me before it hated you...Remember the word that I said unto you, The servant is not greater than his lord. If they have persecuted me, they will also persecute you; if they have kept my saying, they will keep yours also" (Jn 15.18,20).

This is the first indication of enmity against Jeremiah personally. It began in Anathoth, his home town (1.1; 32.6-12). Centuries later the Lord Jesus "came to Nazareth, where he had been brought up" (Lk 4.16), and his fellow-citizens were ultimately "filled with wrath, And rose up, and thrust him out of the city, and led him unto the brow of the hill whereon their city was built, that they might cast him down headlong" (Lk 4.28-29). For Jeremiah, the next display of animosity came from his own family (12.6). The pressure on him intensifies as the book proceeds, just as it intensified on the Lord Jesus until, ultimately, He was crucified.

According to Gesenius, Anathoth means "answers to prayers". Abiathar was exiled there by Solomon: "Get thee to Anathoth, unto thine own fields; for thou art worthy of death" (1 Kings 2.26). Feinberg suggests that the ill-feeling against Jeremiah at Anathoth could reflect long-standing resentment of Abiathar's rejection which had been fuelled by the prophet's "support for Josiah's reforms, with its abolition of local sanctuaries - something that would have been hard for the priests of Anathoth to swallow". Three things should be noted in this section of the chapter: the conspiracy against Jeremiah (vv.18-19); the confidence of Jeremiah (v.20); and the condemnation of Anathoth (vv.21-23).

The conspiracy against Jeremiah (vv.18-19)

Jeremiah would have remained in ignorance of the plot to kill him had it not been revealed to him by the Lord. "And the Lord hath given me knowledge of it, and I know it: then thou shewedst me their doings" (v.18). The conspirators speak here: "Let us destroy the tree with the fruit thereof, and let us cut him off from the land of the living, that his name may be no more remembered" (v.19). Bearing in mind that Jeremiah was unmarried (16.1-2), and therefore without family, his death would effectively terminate his name in Israel. The "tree" was the man himself, and the "fruit" was his preaching. As Laetsch observes, "Once he is gone, his very memory will be forgotten".

There is a striking similarity between the intended treatment of Jeremiah, and the treatment given to the Lord Jesus. Jeremiah describes himself as "like a lamb or an ox that is brought to the slaughter" (v.19). The Lord Jesus was "brought as a lamb to the slaughter" (Is 53.7). The men of

Anathoth intended to "cut him off from the land of the living, that his name may be no more remembered" (v.19). The Lord Jesus was "taken from prison and from judgment: and who shall declare his generation? for he was cut off out of the land of the living" (Is 53.8).

The confidence of Jeremiah (v.20)

Now Jeremiah speaks. "But, O Lord of hosts, that judgest righteously, that triest the reins and the heart, let me see thy vengeance on them: for unto thee have I revealed my cause." It should be noted that Jeremiah is praying, not for his own, but for the Lord's vengeance on the plotters. They were the Lord's enemies. Jeremiah is probably alluding to Deuteronomy 32.35 here: "To me belongeth vengeance, and recompence", and this is certainly the case in the New Testament: "Dearly beloved, avenge not yourselves, but rather give place unto wrath: for it is written, Vengeance is mine; I will repay, saith the Lord" (Rom 12.19). It should, of course, be noted that the Lord Jesus taught His disciples to "Love your enemies, bless them that curse you, do good to them that hate you, and pray for them which despitefully use you, and persecute you" (Mt 5.44). He was the perfect example of His own ministry (cp. Lk 23.34).

The condemnation of Anathoth (vv.21-23)

Now the Lord speaks. The men of Anathoth had "sown the wind", and they would certainly "reap the whirlwind" (Hos 8.7). They had threatened Jeremiah with death if he persisted in his preaching. They said, "Prophesy not in the name of the Lord, that thou die not by our hand" (v.21). If they could not silence the preaching, then they would silence the preacher. Their successors did exactly the same with Stephen: "they were not able to resist the wisdom and the spirit by which he spake" (Acts 6.10), and took steps to ensure that he did not preach again. It is deeply significant that the very people who said of Jeremiah, "Let us cut him off from the land of the living, that his name be no more remembered" (v.19), would suffer disaster in their own families: "Therefore thus saith the Lord of hosts, Behold, I will punish them: the young men shall die by the sword; their sons and their daughters shall die by famine" (v.22). The words of Paul are applicable: "Be not deceived; God is not mocked: for whatsoever a man soweth, that shall he also reap" (Gal 6.7). Approximately one hundred years before, Isaiah had cried, "O poor Anathoth" (Is 10.30) in connection with an Assyrian invasion. But now, "the year of their visitation" (v.23) would come with the conquest of the land by Nebuchadnezzar.

JEREMIAH 12

Chapters 11 and 12 are linked by Jeremiah's perplexity over God's promised judgment on the men of Anathoth. The latter part of ch.11 (vv.18-23) describes the first eruption of opposition to the Lord's servant. He had been warned of this at the very commencement of his ministry (1.18-19), and the pressure on him intensifies as the book proceeds. In ch.11 he encounters antagonism in his home town, and in ch.12 he encounters antagonism in his family circle.

But this is not the end of the matter for Jeremiah. Whilst he does not doubt that the Lord would deal with the matter, he is at a loss to understand how wicked men can flourish in the first place, and this occupies his mind at the beginning of this chapter. The passage may be divided as follows:

> The Perplexity he Felt (vv.1-4)
> The Patience he Needed (vv.5-13)
> The Purpose of the Lord (vv.14-17).

Verses 1-4: The Perplexity he Felt

These verses reflect the certainty and uncertainty of Jeremiah: "Righteous art thou, O Lord, when I plead with thee: yet let me talk with thee of thy judgments: Wherefore doth the way of the wicked prosper? wherefore are all they happy that deal very treacherously?" (v.1). Jeremiah was certainly not theorising here. He was right in the middle of wickedness and treachery. The irony of it! They were wicked and treacherous, but prospering and at ease ("happy", AV), and apparently free to plot the downfall of God's faithful servant. Jeremiah was certainly not "at ease" in the situation, especially in view of his personal integrity: "But thou, O Lord, knowest me: thou hast seen me, and tried mine heart toward thee" (v.3).

His certainty (v.1a)

"Righteous art thou, O Lord, when I plead with thee." His cry to the Lord "that judgest righteously, that triest the reins and the heart" (11.20), had been answered: the Lord would "bring evil on the men of Anathoth, even the year of their visitation" (11.23). That much was perfectly clear, and stresses that when the Lord's people are faced with uncertainty it is always helpful to rest upon what *is* certain. They can say with Abraham, "Shall not the Judge of all the earth do right?" (Gen 18.25), and be assured that "The eyes of the Lord are upon the righteous, and his ears are open unto their cry. The face of the Lord is against them that do evil, to cut off the remembrance of them from the earth" (Ps 34.15-16). Solomon gave good advice in saying, "Fret not thyself because of evil men, neither be thou envious at the wicked; For there shall be no reward to the evil man; the candle of the wicked shall be put out" (Prov 24.19-20).

Such confidence is a sheet anchor in uncertainty and bewilderment, and enables the Lord's people to trust in Him when they see "the wicked in great power, and spreading himself like a green bay tree" (Ps 37.35). It is equally true in every crisis of life. Job said, "Though he slay me, yet will I trust in him" (Job 13.15), and Habakkuk majestically declared, "Although the fig tree shall not blossom, neither shall fruit be in the vines; the labour of the olive shall fail, and the fields shall yield no meat; the flock shall be cut off from the fold, and there shall be no herd in the stalls: Yet I will rejoice in the Lord, I will joy in the God of my salvation" (Hab 3.17-18).

His uncertainty (vv.1b-4)

While Jeremiah had no doubts about the righteousness of God in dealing with evil, he was not quite so sure about the way in which it would be implemented. He was completely persuaded that the wicked would be judged by God, but why were they allowed to prosper for the time being? Hence his words, "yet let me talk with thee of thy judgments" (v.1). Asaph could not understand "the prosperity of the wicked" until he "went into the sanctuary of God". Then he "understood…their end" (Ps 73.3,17). But although Jeremiah *did* know "their end", he was *still* perplexed over their "prosperity".

Having said this, it should be noted that Jeremiah did not brood over the problem, and become indignant or even bitter. He brought the problem to the Lord. In fact, he made a practice of speaking to Him about his problems and perplexities (15.16-18). Habakkuk, one of Jeremiah's contemporaries, did the same (Hab 1.2-4, 12-17), although he was well aware that there must be a flaw in his reasoning, and fully expected to be corrected: "I will stand upon my watch, and set me upon the tower, and will watch to see what he will say unto me, and what I shall answer when I am reproved" (Hab 2.1). Both prophets would have fully acquiesced with the hymn-writer:

> Have we trials and temptations?
> Is there trouble anywhere?
> We should never be discouraged:
> Take it to the Lord in prayer.
> (J. M. Scriven)

In New Testament language, "Let us therefore come boldly unto the throne of grace, that we may obtain mercy, and find grace to help in time of need" (Heb 4.16).

Jeremiah's uncertainty surrounded two problems: Why should the wicked prosper in view of the way they treated *God*? (v.2), and Why should they prosper in view of the way they treated *him*? (vv.3-4).

Their response to God's goodness (v.2)

The wicked prospered, even though they rejected God, to whom they owed everything: "Thou hast planted them, yea, they have taken root:

they grow, yea, they bring forth fruit: thou art near in their mouth, and far from their reins". They are firmly established ("they have taken root"), they make good progress ("they grow"), and they are successful ("they bring forth fruit"). The Lord Jesus instructed His disciples to love and do good to their enemies, and thus display their spiritual parentage: "That ye may be the children of your Father which is in heaven: for he maketh his sun to rise on the evil and on the good, and sendeth rain on the just and on the unjust" (Mt 5.45). It should be noticed that the success of the wicked was not accompanied by blatant opposition to God. To the contrary, they used His name and created the impression that they were His people. But it was empty profession: "thou art near in their mouth, and far from their reins". They paid lip-service to the Lord. Religious hypocrisy is nauseating to Him. The spiritual children of Jeremiah's contemporaries were censured in the same way by the Lord Jesus: "Ye hypocrites, well did Esaias prophesy of you, saying, This people draweth nigh unto me with their mouth, and honoureth me with their lips; but their heart is far from me" (Mt 15.7-8). Ezekiel describes the same situation, which must have brought him some discouragement, as it would any preacher: "And they come unto thee as the people cometh, and they sit before thee as my people, and they hear thy words, but they will not do them: for with their mouth they shew much love, but their heart goeth after their covetousness" (Ezek 33.31). The Lord's people today do well to heed the warning of this passage, and examine the depth and reality of their profession of devotion to the Lord.

Their response to Jeremiah's ministry (vv.3-4)

The wicked prospered even though they rejected the servant of God. Bearing in mind his personal integrity and faithful ministry, why were they permitted to threaten him? Unlike them, he did not speak hypocritically: "But thou, Jehovah, knowest me; thou hast seen me, and proved my heart toward thee" (v.3, JND). Jeremiah's reference to his heart emphasises his inward reality, as opposed to the hypocrisy of the wicked: the Lord was "far from their reins". Jeremiah's language here is similar to that of David: "Thou hast proved *mine* heart; thou hast visited *me* in the night; thou hast tried *me*, and shalt find nothing" (Ps 17.3). David also said, "O Lord, thou hast searched me, and known me. Thou knowest my downsitting and mine uprising, thou understandest my thoughts afar off...Search me, O God, and know my heart: try me, and know my thoughts: And see if there be any wicked way in me, and lead me in the way everlasting" (Ps 139.1-2, 23-24).

In view of the way in which the wicked had responded to the goodness of the Lord, and to the testimony of His servant, Jeremiah calls on Him to "pull them out like sheep for the slaughter, and prepare them for the day of slaughter" (v.3). He wanted action at once! How could the situation possibly continue without divine intervention? The whole land was suffering as a result of their wickedness: "How long shall the land mourn, and the herbs of every field wither, for the wickedness of them that dwell therein? the beasts are consumed, and the birds; because they said, He shall not see our last end" (v.4). Chapters 14 and 15 describe in detail the effect of "the dearth" (14.1), where the land was experiencing drought, and this is clearly the situation here, with dire results on vegetation, beasts and birds. This is an eloquent reminder that as the result of sin: "the whole creation groaneth and travaileth in pain together until now" (Rom 8.22). But this does not move the wicked. Like the "scoffers" of the New Testament, they firmly believe that "all things continue as they were from the beginning of the creation" (2 Pet 3.4). There will be no divine intervention, in spite of Jeremiah's predictions. As Laetsch observes, "They sneeringly exclaim, He shall not see our end. Who cares for the predictions of a prophet whose prophecies of doom have never been fulfilled?". Or, as Unger understands this: "We shall not be destroyed according to his foreboding predictions".

As Laetsch notes, "Jeremiah has presented his case and awaits the Lord's answer. This answer is not what the prophet had expected".

Verses 5-13: The Patience he Needed

The Lord now answers His perplexed servant. In the first place, Jeremiah would have to be patient. His experiences in Anathoth would prove insignificant when compared with the further trials which awaited him. In particular, his own family had turned against him (vv.5-6). In the second place, the Lord had already intervened in judgment. The Lord's own family had turned against Him and He had been obliged to act accordingly (vv.7-13).

Jeremiah's family was against him (vv.5-6)

Jeremiah received, initially, an unexpected answer. Things were going to get worse! The Lord likens his present problem to the rigours of a race against men. But coming problems are likened to a race against horses! "If thou hast run with the footmen, and they have wearied thee, then how canst thou contend with horses?" (v.5). To enforce the point, God uses a second metaphor: "...if in the land of peace, wherein thou trustedst, they wearied thee ('if in a land of peace thou thinkest thyself in security', JND), then how wilt thou do in the swelling of Jordan?" (v.5). Jeremiah's present problems were like those of a man who thought he lived in a peaceful land, but coming problems would be, comparatively, like "the swelling of Jordan" (v.5). While this appears to refer to the annual inundation of the Jordan valley (cp. Josh 3.15), other passages suggest another kind of danger. Both Edom and Babylon would be overthrown by an enemy who would "come up like a lion from the swelling of Jordan against the habitation of the strong" (49.19), or "unto the habitation of the strong (50.44). The expression is also rendered, "the pride of Jordan" (Zech 11.3). Gesenius has "the glory of Jordan", and explains that the phrase is "used of its green and shady banks, beautifully clothed with willows, tamarisks and cane, where lions used to lie among the reeds". By referring to the "swelling of Jordan", with its lurking danger, the Lord prepares His servant for even greater troubles, and immediately identifies them: "For even thy brethren, and the house of thy father, even they have dealt treacherously with thee; yea, they have called a multitude after thee: believe them not, though they speak fair words unto thee" (v.6). There can be nothing worse than when "a man's foes shall be they of his own household" (Mt 10.36). It should be noted that the Lord Jesus prepared His disciples for coming troubles (Lk 21.12-19). Paul warned the Thessalonians in the same way: "For verily, when we were with you, we told you before that we should suffer tribulation; even as it came to pass, and ye know" (1 Thess 3.4).

Perhaps the reference to "fair words" reminded Jeremiah that Solomon had said, "He that hateth dissembleth with his lips, and layeth up deceit within him; When he speaketh fair, believe him not: for there are seven abominations in his heart" (Prov 26.24-25). The enemies of the Lord Jesus approached Him with "fair words", but they masked treachery (Mk 12.14). It should be noted that even this was not the end of opposition to Jeremiah. First of all, his own *city* was against him (11.21), now it is his own *family* (12.6), and it would not be long before he discovered that his own *nation* was against him (15.10). The Lord Jesus was opposed in His own city (Lk 4.16-29), and there was a time when "neither did his brethren believe in him" (Jn 7.5). Eventually, like Jeremiah. He was rejected by the nation: "He came unto his own, and his own received him not" (Jn 1.11).

The disclosure to Jeremiah that he was opposed by his own family appears only to exacerbate his problem. But the prophet now learns that the treatment that he received from his family reflected the Lord's opposition from *His* family:

The Lord's family was against Him (vv.7-13)

"I have forsaken mine house, I have left mine heritage; I have given the dearly beloved of my soul into the hand of her enemies. Mine heritage is unto me as a lion in the forest; it crieth out against me: therefore have I hated it. Mine heritage is unto me as a speckled bird, the birds round about are against her; come ye, assemble all the beasts of the field, come to devour" (vv.7-9). Broadbent sees the connection with the preceding verses as follows: "'Now turn from your own griefs to Mine. I have had to forsake my temple, leave my peculiar treasure, give the object of my affection unto the power of cruel invaders. My chosen people are so violently opposed to Me that I have had to turn from them altogether". Unger writes in similar vein: "His experience at having to forsake family and friends because of treachery, closely paralleled the Lord's experience of being compelled to turn away from His people for the same reason. Accordingly the Lord's lament is placed here in conjunction with Jeremiah's grief over his alienated home and family".

It is delightful for believers to be able to say, "We have not an high priest which cannot be touched with the feeling of our infirmities" (Heb 4.15), but how often are they touched by His grief? Rightly understood, their experiences enable them to share His feelings. This is illustrated by the experiences of Hosea. When God told him to "love a woman beloved of her friend, yet an adulteress", he became acutely aware of "the love of the Lord toward the children of Israel, who look to other gods, and love flagons of wine" (Hos 3.1). The vicissitudes of Hosea's own marriage taught him how deeply the Lord loved His erring people. In undertaking service for Him, it is so important to share His thoughts and feelings, and in this connection the depth of the Lord's grief over His people should be noted. He refers to them as "mine house" (v.7); "mine heritage" (vv.8,9); "my vineyard" (v.10); "my portion" (v.10).

"Mine house"

"I have forsaken mine house" (v.7). Whilst this could refer to the Temple, it is more likely that it describes the people amongst whom He dwelt. They are addressed as, "O house of Israel" (10.1). The spiritual and moral condition of His people made it impossible for Him to dwell with them any longer. The Lord's people today must ensure that the oft-quoted words, "For where two or three are gathered together in my name, there am I in the midst of them" (Mt 18.20), do not become a façade. The "house of God" in the New Testament demands appropriate conduct and behaviour (1 Tim 3.15).

"Mine heritage"

"I have left mine heritage" (v.7). Moses described the Lord's people in similar language: "the Lord's portion is his people; Jacob is the lot of his inheritance" (Deut 32.9). The Lord loved His inheritance (Deut 7.6-8). They were "beloved for the fathers' sakes" (Rom 11.28). The Lord's people today are his inheritance: Paul prayed that the Ephesian believers might know "what the riches of the glory of his inheritance in the saints" (Eph 1.18).

Sadly, the very people who should have brought Him joy had turned against Him. There was no reciprocal love, and He was obliged, with deep grief, to say, "I have given the dearly beloved of my soul into the hand of her enemies" (v.7). The reasons follow: His heritage had become "as a lion in the forest; it crieth out against me", and "as a speckled bird ('a speckled bird of prey', JND), the birds round about are against her" (vv.8,9). As "a lion in the forest", His people opposed Him as fiercely as "the king of beasts". As Laetsch observes, "Their declaration of independence from God was actually pronouncing their own death warrant". As a "speckled bird", they were vulnerable to other predatory birds. "Speckled birds are unusually coloured birds, which are attacked by other birds, who will not allow a strange bird among them" (Feinberg). But the "speckled bird" may well describe Israel's syncretism. Her indulgence in idolatry, whilst retaining a nominal acknowledgement of Jehovah, had made her unique amongst her neighbours. The "beasts of the field" are the Lord's "evil neighbours" (v.14).

"My vineyard"

"Many pastors have destroyed my vineyard" (v.10). Israel is described as a vineyard in other Old Testament passages including the following: "Now will I sing to my wellbeloved a song of my beloved touching his vineyard" (Is 5.1), and "In that day sing ye unto her, A vineyard of red wine. I the Lord do keep it" (Is 27.2-3). A vineyard serves no purpose whatever if it is unfruitful (Ezek 15.1-8). Israel yielded no fruit for God, and had therefore been progressively destroyed. The "pastors" ('shepherds', JND) have already been identified: "The shepherds with their flocks shall come unto her...they shall feed every one in his place" (6.3). These particular "shepherds" come, ominously, from "the north" (6.1). The words "because no man layeth it to heart" (v.11) mean that no one actually sat down and carefully considered the reasons for such desolation and destruction.

The fact that the Lord's people then had become an unfruitful vineyard is a warning to believers today, and John 15.1-16 should be read in this connection. Every assembly should resemble a vineyard by exhibiting "the fruit of the Spirit" (Gal 5.22).

"My portion"

"They have trodden my portion under foot, they have made my pleasant portion a desolate wilderness" (v.10). The word translated "portion" (2513) refers to "a portion of a field" (Gesenius; cp. Ruth 2.3). A field is a place where labour and energy are expended, and the Lord had worked diligently amongst His people. The same figure is used in the New Testament. "I have planted, Apollos watered; but God gave the increase...Now he that planteth and he that watereth are one: and every man shall receive his own reward according to his own labour. For we are labourers together with God: ye are God's husbandry (field of labour), ye are God's building" (1 Cor 3. 6, 8-9).

God was already implementing judgment. The present tense should be noted: "Spoilers are come upon all heights in the wilderness; for the sword of Jehovah devoureth from one end of the land even to the other end of the land: no flesh hath peace. They have sown wheat, and they reap thorns; they have put themselves to pain, and do not profit. Be ye therefore ashamed of your revenues, because of the fierce anger of Jehovah" (vv.12-13, JND). The "spoilers" were "the sword of the Lord": it was through them that divine judgment was administered. The word "revenues" refers to the produce of the land; it is elsewhere rendered "increase" (Num 18.30), and "fruit" (Josh 5.12). The prosperous wicked, who had caused Jeremiah so much perplexity, were subject to "the fierce anger of the Lord". Feinberg comments as follows: "They gain nothing. They reap the opposite of what they expect. Their crops are a failure (compare 14.3-4). In fact, the harvests are so poor that even the farmers are ashamed of them". This should be compared with: "Ye have sown much, and bring in little; ye eat, but ye have not enough…he that earneth wages earneth wages to put it into a bag with holes" (Hag 1.6).

Verses 14-17: The Purpose of the Lord
But the despoliation of Judah, either by invasion or by famine, was not the end of the story. The chapter now anticipates divine judgment on the very nations which had invaded the land, but also, depending on their obedience, their ultimate blessing. In these verses, Jeremiah begins to fulfill the ministry committed to him: "See, I have this day set thee over the nations and over the kingdoms, to root out, and to pull down, and to destroy, and to throw down, to build and to plant" (1.10). It anticipates his ministry in chs.47-49.

Divine judgment on the nations (v.14)
On Judah's neighbours
Although divine judgment rested upon Judah (v.7), they remained His people. They were "the apple of his eye" (Zech 2.8); the Lord had said to Abram, "I will bless them that bless thee, and curse him that curseth thee" (Gen 12.3), and this is equally true of his descendents. When the Lord Jesus, as "the Son of man", comes "in his glory, and all the holy angels with him", the living nations will be judged in respect of their treatment of His earthly "brethren" (Mt 25.31-46).

The imminent deportation of Judah's neighbours is now described: "Thus saith the Lord against all mine evil neighbours, that touch the inheritance which I have caused my people to inherit; Behold, I will pluck them out of their land, and pluck out the house of Judah from among them". He calls Judah, "my people" four times in these closing verses (vv.14,16), and describes her enemies as "mine evil neighbours". As Laetsch observes, "Judah's land is Jehovah's land (Lev 25.23; 2 Chr 7.20; Jer 2.7; 16.18), and therefore Judah's neighbours are Jehovah's neighbours. What a wealth of practical application comes to our mind as we apply this truth to our own homes and possessions!" The "evil neighbours" are identified: "In his (Jehoiakim) days Nebuchadnezzar king of Babylon came up, and Jehoiakim became his servant three years: then he turned and rebelled against him. And the Lord sent against him bands of the Chaldees, and…of the Syrians, and…of the Moabites, and…of the children of Ammon, and sent them against Judah to destroy it" (2 Kings 24.1-2). It was the policy of the Babylonians to deport subjugated nations to other parts of their empire, and it was by this means that God would "pluck them out of their land".

On Judah herself
"I will pluck them (Judah's neighbours) out of their land, and pluck out

the house of Judah from among them." They too would be deported from their lands. The Psalmist records their lament in Babylonia: "By the rivers of Babylon, there we sat down, yea, we wept, when we remembered Zion. We hanged our harps upon the willows in the midst thereof. For there they that carried us away captive required of us a song; and they that wasted us required of us mirth, saying, Sing us one of the songs of Zion. How shall we sing the Lord's song in a strange land?" (Ps 137.1-4). God would implement the warnings given in Leviticus 18.24-30.

Divine restoration of the nations (vv.15-17)
The nations generally (v.15)

While so far as Judah was concerned, there was a partial fulfilment of this prophecy in the return from exile under Zerubbabel (Ezra 1.1-4) and Ezra (7.1-9), the passage looks on to the end-time. It anticipates the return of deported nations to their homelands, and includes both Jews and Gentiles: "I will return, and have compassion on them, and will bring them again, every man to his heritage, and every man to his land" (v.15). This is a striking passage. Without losing sight of His particular relationship with Israel, it emphasises God's pity and compassion on all men, both Jew and Gentile. Further details are given in chs.47-49: "Yet will I bring again the captivity of Moab in the latter days, saith the Lord" (48.47); "And afterward I will bring again the captivity of the children of Ammon, saith the Lord" (49.6); "But it shall come to pass in the latter days, that I will bring again the captivity of Elam, saith the Lord" (49.39). Even Egypt and Assyria will be divinely blessed in the millennial age (Is 19.23-25). In divine mercy, God's righteous judgment on Jew and Gentile will be followed by their ultimate blessing.

Israel particularly (vv.16-17)

The restored nation, Israel with Judah, will become a role model for the whole world: "And it shall come to pass, if they will diligently learn the ways of my people, to swear by my name, The Lord liveth; as they taught my people to swear by Baal; then shall they be built again in the midst of my people". The Lord will be able to draw attention to "the ways of my people" as an example to the nations. As a regenerate people, the Lord will make them "the head, and not the tail" of the nations (Deut 28.13). Their moral excellence is described when "the Redeemer shall come to Zion" (Is 59.20): "My spirit that is upon thee, and my words which I have put in thy mouth, shall not depart out of thy mouth, nor out of the mouth of thy seed, nor out of the mouth of thy seed's seed, saith the Lord, from henceforth and for ever" (Is 59.21). The opening verses of Isaiah 60 describe the glory of Israel when "the Gentiles shall come to thy light, and kings to the brightness of thy rising" (Is 60.3). The nations will then recognise that Jehovah is "the true God, he is the living God" (Jer 10.10), and exclaim, "The Lord liveth" (12.16). But disobedience on the part of the nations will bring judgment: "But if they will not obey, I will utterly pluck up and destroy that nation, saith the Lord" (v.17). Further details are found in Zechariah 14.16-19. The principle that blessing follows obedience, and judgment follows disobedience, is applicable at all times.

Laetsch sums up the chapter succinctly: "Jeremiah and all children of God, impatient with His mysterious and unfathomable ways, have no reason to quarrel with Him, to judge Him by their feeble sense. God is His own Interpreter, and He will make both His justice and His grace plain in His own time". This was the Lord's message to Habakkuk: "the vision is yet for an appointed time, but at the end it shall speak, and not lie: though it tarry, wait for it; because it will surely come, it will not tarry" (Hab 2.3).

JEREMIAH 13

As already noted, Jensen suggests that chs.11-20 comprise Jeremiah's "Personal Experiences", which include opposition from various sources. In addition Jeremiah was called upon to act as well as preach, and in the current chapter the prophet is told, amongst other things, to engage in what has been called an acted oracle (vv.1-11). This forms the first of four sections into which the chapter may be divided:

> The Parable of the Linen Girdle (vv.1-11)
> The Proverb of the Wine Bottles (vv.12-14)
> The Pride of the Nation (vv.15-19)
> The Punishment of Jerusalem (vv.20-27).

Jeremiah uses four pictures to describe coming judgment: a marred girdle, a full bottle, a captive flock, and an uncovered woman. The passage does not comprise four unrelated paragraphs. The details in the parable of the linen girdle are amplified in the balance of the chapter. For example, the pride that led to the marring of the girdle (vv.9-10) is emphasised in vv.15-18; the direction from which judgment would come (the Euphrates, vv.4,5,6,7) is confirmed in v.20; the way in which the girdle would be marred is described in v.14; the obstinacy to God's will (v.11) is illustrated in v.23.

Verses 1-11: The Parable of the Linen Girdle
The New Testament words, "God, who at sundry times and in divers manners spake in time past unto the fathers by the prophets, Hath in these last days spoken unto us by his Son" (Heb 1.1), bring joy to the Lord's people, and while they rejoice particularly in the final and complete revelation of God in Christ, the "divers manners" in which He spoke in the past make an absorbing study. God spoke through direct preaching, through dreams and visions, and through signs, some of which took the form of acted parables. An example occurs in the ministry of Ezekiel where the prophet symbolically bore the iniquity of the house of Israel by lying on his left side for 390 days, and the iniquity of the house of Judah by lying on his right side for 40 days (Ezek 4.4-6), and a further example occurs here. Consideration must be given to the sign (vv.1-7), and the significance (vv.8-11).

The sign (vv.1-7)
It makes good sense to take the sign quite literally, even though it involved two long return journeys to the banks of the Euphrates: "And the word of the Lord came unto me the second time, saying…go to Euphrates" (vv.3-4); "the Lord said unto me, Arise, go to Euphrates" (v.6). The distance involved has led some to the conclusion that these could not have been literal journeys. It is worth pointing out in this connection that the prophet

was not necessarily commanded to trek east across the desert to the Euphrates, but probably north to Syria, possibly to the Euphrates at Carchemish. Others suggest that the word *perath,* translated "Euphrates" is actually an abbreviation of "Ephratah" (Bethlehem), some six miles south of Jerusalem, but this destroys the whole significance of the parable. The absence of the word "river", which some commentators use to support their argument for a much shorter journey, is not unique to this passage (cp. Gen 2.14; 2 Chron 35.20; Jer 51.63). The parable of the linen girdle prefigured coming events. Like the linen girdle, the nation would be "marred". The Lord would bring an enemy, the Chaldeans, across the Euphrates, and use them to "mar the pride of Judah, and the great pride of Jerusalem" (v.9). The following should be considered.

The original condition of the girdle (v.1a)

Jeremiah was to take a "*linen* girdle". Linen is particularly associated with priesthood. The prophet himself was "of the priests that were in Anathoth in the land of Benjamin" (1.1). When removing the ashes of the burnt-offering, the priest was to "put on his linen garment, and his linen breeches shall he put upon his flesh" (Lev 6.10). On the Day of Atonement, Aaron was to wear "the holy linen coat...the linen breeches...a linen girdle...with the linen mitre" (Lev 16.4). Samuel "ministered before the Lord, being a child, girded with a linen ephod" (1 Sam 2.18). Saul commanded Doeg to "fall upon the priests", and he "slew on that day fourscore and five persons that did wear a linen ephod" (1 Sam 22.18). Bearing in mind that the linen girdle depicts God's people, "the whole house of Israel and the whole house of Judah" (v.11), it can be concluded that the girdle describes His purpose for them: "And ye shall be unto me a kingdom of priests, and an holy nation" (Ex 19.6). Ultimately, Israel will be "named the Priests of the Lord: men shall call you the Ministers of our God" (Is 61.6). Whatever the obstacles, the Lord will accomplish His purpose! This is, of course, the happy position of His people *now*: "Ye also, as lively stones, are built up a spiritual house, an holy priesthood, to offer up spiritual sacrifices, acceptable to God by Jesus Christ...But ye are a chosen generation, a royal priesthood, an holy nation, a peculiar people; that ye should shew forth the praises of him who hath called you out of darkness into his marvellous light" (1 Pet 2.5,9).

The fact that it was a "linen *girdle*" emphasises the character of the priesthood. The girdle was probably not a sash or an outer band over other garments, but the usual undergarment of the day, a short skirt worn about the hips and reaching midway down the thighs. Its nearness to the body illustrates God's desire for intimate fellowship with His people. He did not want them to be at a distance from Him. The linen girdle is therefore descriptive of Israel's purity in fellowship with God. "As a girdle wound close round a man's body is near to him (Ps 18.39; 30.11), so Israel and Judah were near to the Lord" (Broadbent).

Jeremiah was told, "put it upon thy *loins*". In Scripture, the loins are associated with fruitfulness; reference is made to "the fruit of his loins" (Acts 2.30); "the loins of Abraham" (Heb 7.5); "the loins of his father" (Heb 7.10). The loins are also associated with strength: "She girdeth her loins with strength" (Prov 31.17); "make thy loins strong" (Nah 2.1). Fruitfulness and strength flow from fellowship with the Lord.

The deterioration of the girdle (vv.1b-2)

Jeremiah is told, "put it not in water". It was not to be washed, and therefore it became increasingly soiled. This is precisely what God's people had become! They were defiled by idolatry to the extent that "according to the number of thy cities were thy gods, O Judah; and according to the number of the streets of Jerusalem have ye set up altars to that shameful thing, even altars to burn incense unto Baal" (11.13). The "linen girdle" had become filthy. While godly kings of Judah had initiated reforms, these had no long-lasting effects. God's people had rejected the cleansing power of His word, and national life had progressively deteriorated. In accordance with divine instructions, the prophet obtained and wore the girdle, breaking all the laws of hygiene in the process.

The decay of the girdle (vv.3-7)

While we do not know how long it was before "the word of the Lord" came to Jeremiah "the second time" (v.3), it does not require a great deal of imagination to visualise either the state of the girdle or its condition when the prophet made his second journey to the Euphrates (vv.6-7) having hidden it "there in a hole of the rock" sometime before (vv.4-5). Jeremiah was soon to discover the significance of his journeys, namely that as a result of their filthiness Judah would become subject to Babylon, and suffer deportation across the Euphrates. This much is clear. But why was Jeremiah commanded to make two journeys to the Euphrates? On his first visit, the prophet buried the girdle in close proximity to Chaldea, and there it rotted for "many days" (v.6). In exactly the same way, Judah had become entranced with the Chaldeans: "And as soon as she saw them with her eyes, she doted upon them, and sent messengers unto them into Chaldea. And the Babylonians came to her into the bed of love, and they defiled her with their whoredom, and she was polluted with them, and her mind was alienated from them" (Ezek 23.16-17). This brought final ruin to Judah, and when, after "many days", Jeremiah went again to the Euphrates, the girdle was "marred, it was profitable for nothing" (v.7). The very people upon whom Judah "doted" would execute divine judgment on her, and the nation eventually crossed the Euphrates *en route* to exile.

Notice should be taken of Jeremiah's strict obedience to the word of God. In the midst of a people who "would not hear" (v.11), there was at least one man who did hear and obey. God spoke to him on three occasions, and on each occasion he obeyed implicitly: "Thus saith the Lord unto me,

Go and get thee a linen girdle, and put it upon thy loins…*So I got a girdle* according to the word of the Lord, and put it on my loins (vv.1-2); "And the word of the Lord came unto me the second time, saying, Take the girdle…and arise, go to Euphrates, and hide it there in a hole of the rock. *So I went*, and hid it by Euphrates, as the Lord commanded me" (vv.3-4); "the Lord said unto me, Arise, go to Euphrates, and take the girdle from thence…*Then I went* to Euphrates, and digged, and took the girdle from the place where I had hid it" (vv.6-7). Jeremiah illustrates perfectly the instructions to the servants at Cana: "Whatsoever he saith unto you, do it" (Jn 2.5). The believers at Rome "obeyed from the heart that form of doctrine which was delivered" to them (Rom 6.17). Saul was reminded that "to obey is better than sacrifice, and to hearken than the fat of rams" (1 Sam 15.22).

The significance (vv.8-11)

Up to this point, Jeremiah was evidently unaware of the significance of the linen girdle. But obedience precedes understanding, and leads to understanding: "Through faith we understand" (Heb 11.3). The meaning now becomes clear. Reversing the order of events, the Lord first explains the meaning of the marred girdle, and then the meaning of its original condition. Bearing in mind that it represented His people, two points are emphasised.

What they had become (vv.9-10)

Like the girdle, God's people had become "good for nothing" (v.10). He would therefore reject them, and "mar the pride of Judah, and the great pride of Jerusalem" (v.9). Two questions arise.

How would God mar them? As already noted, in associating the girdle with the Euphrates, God predicted their deportation across the river into captivity: "The cities of the south shall be shut up, and none shall open them: Judah shall be carried away captive all of it, it shall be wholly carried away captive" (v.19).

How did they show their pride? Their pride is described as follows: "This evil people, which refuse to hear my words, which walk in the imagination of their heart, and walk after other gods, to serve them, and to worship them, shall even be as this girdle, which is good for nothing" (v.10). Instead of walking "humbly with…God" (Micah 6.8), Judah had substituted their own will for the will of God. "It was pride, as foolish as it was wicked, that caused them to cast away their God as a man casts away the trinkets of his childhood, once cherished so highly, now regarded as outmoded and out of date, and to choose, instead, strange gods, to serve those who could not help them, to worship them who could not even hear their prayers" (Laetsch). The Lord had described the surrounding nations as "mine evil neighbours" (12.14), but now He is obliged to call Judah, "this evil people". If believers today refuse the Word of God, and follow the dictates of their own will, they too will become "good for nothing". If, like the girdle, they have become dirty, they too stand in danger of complete destruction in terms of usefulness to God.

What God intended for them (v.11)
The Lord intended His people to be unto Him "for a people, and for a name, and for a praise, and for a glory". This must not lead any to think that the degeneration of the Lord's people, to the extent that they had become "good for nothing", left His desire for them permanently unfulfilled. His purposes cannot fail, and the Lord himself states that the nation will be "to me a name of joy, a praise and an honour before all the nations of the earth" (33.9). It was with this in view that He said, "For as the girdle cleaveth to the loins of a man, so have I caused to *cleave* unto me the whole house of Israel and the whole house of Judah, saith the Lord". His people should have actively pursued their God-given calling: "Thou shalt fear the Lord thy God; him shalt thou serve, and to him shalt thou *cleave*, and swear by his name" (Deut 10.20); "Ye shall walk after the Lord your God, and fear him, and keep his commandments, and obey his voice, and ye shall serve him, and *cleave* unto him" (Deut 13.4). But they had failed to fulfill their fourfold divinely-given role. They should have been to the Lord:

"For a people." To this end they were a *chosen people*: "For thou art an holy people unto the Lord thy God: the Lord thy God hath chosen thee to be a special people unto himself, above all people that are upon the face of the earth" (Deut 7.6). His choice was rooted in His love for them: "The Lord did not set his love upon you, nor choose you, because ye were more in number than any people; for ye were the fewest of all people: But because the Lord loved you" (Deut 7.7-8). With this in view, they had become a *redeemed people*: "Thou in thy mercy hast led forth the people which thou hast redeemed…The people shall hear, and be afraid…till thy people pass over, O Lord, till the people pass over, which thou hast purchased" (Ex 15.13,14,16). Moreover, it was the Lord's intention that they should be a *peculiar people*: "Now therefore, if ye will obey my voice indeed, and keep my covenant, then ye shall be a peculiar treasure unto me above all people: for all the earth is mine" (Ex 19.5). The word "peculiar" involves the idea of an enclosure (Young's Concordance), emphasising that "the Lord's portion is his people" (Deut 32.9).

Although the Lord was obliged to say, "*my people* have changed their glory for that which doth not profit" (Jer 2.11), and "*my people* have committed two evils" (Jer 2.13), His purpose for them has not been cancelled by their failure: "I will put my law in their inward parts, and write it in their hearts; and will be their God, and they shall be *my people*" (Jer 31.33).

"For a name." The Lord had chosen Israel that through them His name should be honoured and promoted: "In Judah is God known: his name is great in Israel" (Ps 76.1); "For he hath looked down from the height of his

sanctuary; from heaven did the Lord behold the earth…To declare the name of the Lord in Zion, and his praise in Jerusalem; When the people are gathered together, and the kingdoms, to serve the Lord" (Ps 102.19, 21-22); "As a beast goeth down into the valley, the Spirit of the Lord caused him to rest: so didst thou lead thy people, to make thyself a glorious name" (Is 63.14). Tragically, Paul was obliged to say, "For the name of God is blasphemed among the Gentiles through you" (Rom 2.24).

"For a praise." At their redemption, "Then believed they his words; they sang his praise", but "They soon forgat his works; they waited not for his counsel" (Ps 106.12,13). Sadly, it was necessary to say: "This people have I formed for myself; they shall shew forth my praise. But thou hast not called upon me, O Jacob; but thou hast been weary of me, O Israel" (Is 43.21-22). But as it has already been noted, this is not the end of the story: "Violence shall no more be heard in thy land, wasting nor destruction within thy borders; but thou shalt call thy walls Salvation, and thy gates Praise" (Is 60.18).

"For a glory." The word "glory" can be rendered "beauty" or "adornment" (JND margin). It occurs as "beauty" in the following: "Woe to the crown of pride, to the drunkards of Ephraim, whose glorious beauty is a fading flower" (Is 28.1); "And the glorious beauty…shall be a fading flower…In that day shall the Lord of hosts be for a crown of glory, and for a diadem of beauty, unto the residue of his people" (Is.28.4-5).

Sadly, Israel failed to fulfill the purpose for which God had brought them so near to Him: "but they would not hear". They must therefore follow the footsteps of Jeremiah to the Euphrates, in fulfilment of the sign of the marred linen girdle. In the first of his two closing addresses to Israel, Joshua urged Israel to "cleave unto the Lord your God, as ye have done unto this day" (Josh 23.8). The words, "as ye have done unto this day", are a marvellous testimony! He followed with a warning, "Else if ye do in any wise go back, and cleave unto the remnant of these nations…Know for a certainty that the Lord your God will no more drive out any of these nations from before you" (Josh 23.12-13). This is a salutary lesson for believers today. When Barnabas came to Antioch, he "exhorted them all, that with purpose of heart they would cleave unto the Lord ('abide with the Lord', JND)" (Acts 11.23). In the language of the hymn-writer:

> Keep us, Lord, oh, keep us cleaving
> To Thyself, and still believing,
> Till the hour of our receiving
> Promised joys in heaven!
> (Thomas Kelly)

Verses 12-14: The Proverb of the Wine Bottles

These three verses may be divided simply as follows: the saying (v.12), and the significance (vv.13-14).

The saying (v.12)

"Thus saith the Lord God of Israel, Every bottle shall be filled with wine: and they shall say unto thee, Do we not certainly know that every bottle shall be filled with wine?" Feinberg explains that this was "a proverbial saying about jars and wine, which was probably a platitude concerning hope for future prosperity". They fully expected that their wine jars would be filled.

The significance (vv.13-14)

They would not be disappointed. In fact, they would be sated with wine, to the extent that they became helplessly drunk. But it would be the wine of God's wrath: "Then shalt thou say unto them, Thus saith the Lord, Behold, I will fill all the inhabitants of this land, even the kings that sit upon David's throne, and the priests, and the prophets, and all the inhabitants of Jerusalem, with drunkenness" (v.13). The very classes of people whom Jeremiah knew would oppose him (1.18) would be destroyed. Like judgment on Babylon at the end-time, it would be "the cup of the wine of the fierceness of his wrath" (Rev 16.19), and like the judgment on the nations, it would be "the wine cup of this fury at my hand" (Jer 25.15). The effect of God's judgment on the nations is described in terms of drunkenness: "Drink ye, and be drunken, and spue, and fall, and rise no more, because of the sword which I will send among you" (25.27). Drunkenness means helplessness and irrationality, and Judah would be helpless when divine judgment fell.

These verses amplify the statement, "After this manner will I mar the pride of Judah, and the great pride of Jerusalem" (v.9). As Laetsch observes, "The Lord whom they discarded now discards them". He visits them in unsparing judgment: "And I will dash them one against another, even the fathers and the sons together, saith the Lord: I will not pity, nor spare, nor have mercy, but destroy them" (v.14).

Verses 15-19: The Pride of the Nation

These verses address both the nation at large (vv.15-17) and the royal house in particular (vv.18-19). Pride was their undoing in both cases. "Proud of their favoured position before God as His chosen people, they refused to hear His message through the prophets" (Feinberg). The following should be noted: the appeal (vv.15-16); the anguish (v.17); and the announcement (vv.18-19).

The appeal (vv.15-16)

This is self-explanatory. The appeal is made in view of the promise of coming judgment. It calls on the people to repent before it is too late: "Hear ye, and give ear; be not proud: for the Lord hath spoken. Give glory to the Lord your God, *before* he cause darkness, and *before* your feet stumble upon the dark mountains, and, while ye look for light, he turn it

into the shadow of death, and make it gross darkness". In the words of
Laetsch, "Take the Lord as your Guide and Protector lest He withdraw the
sunshine of His grace, and cause you to be enveloped by darkness, so that
your feet will stumble in the ever-increasing dusk of twilight".

The anguish (v.17)

This is also self-explanatory: "But if ye will not hear it, my soul shall
weep in secret places for your pride; and mine eye shall weep sore, and
run down with tears, because the Lord's flock is carried away captive".
This is the second reference to the tears of Jeremiah (cp. 9.1). The prophet
found no joy in the prospect of coming misery for his proud and rebellious
people.

The connection with previous verses is clear. The parable of the linen
girdle ends with the words "but they would not *hear*" (v.11). Having cried,
"*Hear ye*, and give ear" (v.15), the prophet exclaims, "But if ye will not
hear it, my soul shall weep in secret places for your pride". The nation,
depicted in the linen girdle, would be marred: "After this manner will I
mar the pride of Judah, and the great pride of Jerusalem" (v.9). The marring
of the girdle, and the drunkenness of the nation, is now fully explained:
"the Lord's flock is carried away captive". The lesson is clear for the Lord's
people at all times - failure to cleave to the Lord and persistence in self-will
bring exposure to defeat and captivity.

The announcement (vv.18-19)

The announcement is addressed to the royal house: "Say unto to the
king and to the queen, Humble yourselves, sit down: for your principalities
shall come down, even the crown of your glory" (v.18), or "Say unto the
king and to the queen ('the queen-mother'; lit. 'mistress', margin): Humble
yourselves, sit down low; for from your heads shall come down the crown
of your magnificence" (JND). This evidently refers to Jehoiachin, otherwise
known as Coniah (22.24), who had several wives, and to his mother,
Nehushta (2 Kings 24.8,12,15; Jer 22.24-26). Feinberg points out that
"because kings practiced polygamy, their mothers were highly influential
(cp. 1 Kings 2.19; 15.13; 2 Kings 10.13). This was all the more true of
Jehoiachin because he was only eighteen when he began his short reign
of three months". It was of Jehoiachin that the Lord said: "Write ye this
man childless, a man that shall not prosper in his days: for no man of his
seed shall prosper, sitting upon the throne of David, and ruling any more
in Judah" (22.30).

When the time for deportation came, "The cities of the south (referring
to the Negev, the barren area in the south of Judah) shall be shut up, and
none shall open them: Judah shall be carried away captive all of it, it shall
be wholly carried away captive" (v.19). According to Harrison this indicates
that "the cities of the area (the Negev) would be barricaded to prevent
entry by refugees fleeing the fury of the invader".

Verses 20-27: The Punishment of Jerusalem

A case might be made for suggesting that the question, "where is the flock that was given thee, thy beautiful flock?" (v.20), is addressed to Jehoiachin, and that the royal house had failed to exercise proper shepherd care. However the subject of this verse and of the verses that follow is evidently Jerusalem (v.27) and this is supported by the language of the passage. Jerusalem was the place in which the kings resided and from which the nation should have been properly governed. The city "is addressed under the figure of a shepherdess who had abandoned her flock. She is called on to account for the sheep entrusted to her...Jerusalem was responsible for protecting the entire nation" (Feinberg). As a result, the once "beautiful flock" would now be scattered by the northern invader (v.20) "as the stubble that passeth away by the wind of the wilderness" (v.24).

Both Old and New Testaments assign great importance to shepherd work. The Lord "chose David also his servant, and took him from the sheepfolds: From following the ewes great with young he brought him to feed Jacob his people, and Israel his inheritance. So he fed them according to the integrity of his heart; and guided them by the skilfulness of his hands" (Ps 78.70-72). His successors lamentably failed to follow his example, but a shepherd-king of impeccable character and unfailing ministry will tend the flock of Israel after national regathering and restoration: "David my servant shall be king over them; and they all shall have one shepherd: they shall also walk in my judgments, and observe my statues, and do them" (Ezek 37.24). Every assembly elder should bear the in mind the importance of his work. Does it have to be said today: "Where is the flock that was given thee, thy beautiful flock?" It was "the Lord's flock" (v.17) and elders today tend "the flock of God" (1 Pet 5.2).

Attention is drawn to two questions and the answers to them: "What wilt thou say when he shall punish thee?" (v.21), and "Wherefore come these things upon me?" (vv.22-27).

"What wilt thou say when he shall punish thee?" (v.21)

Jerusalem would reap where she had sown, and therefore she could have nothing to say! Her alliances with surrounding nations, particularly with Babylon, would result in her own captivity: "What wilt thou say when he shall visit thee, since *thou thyself* hast trained them to be princes in chief over thee?" (JND). This is best explained by an earlier passage: "And when thou art spoiled, what wilt thou do? Though thou clothest thyself with crimson, though thou deckest thee with ornaments of gold, though thou rentest thy face with painting, in vain shalt thou make thyself fair; thy lovers will despise thee, they will seek thy life" (4.30). Israel, the northern kingdom, had acted similarly: "Ephraim also is like a silly dove without heart: they call to *Egypt*, they go to *Assyria*" (Hos 7.11), with this result: "Ephraim shall return to *Egypt*, and they shall eat unclean things in *Assyria*"

(Hos 9.3). The punishment of the Lord's people is likened to the agony of a mother in childbirth.

"Wherefore come these things upon me?" (vv.22-27)

In answer to the question, which indicates that continuance in sin had so deadened the nation's conscience that she feels that she is suffering unjustly, the Lord replies: "For the greatness of thine iniquity are thy skirts discovered, and thy heels made bare" (v.22). "The shameful way the conquerors will treat the people would be like the shaming of a prostitute" (Feinberg). This was completely justified. Their iniquity had become natural to them: "Can the Ethiopian change his skin, or the leopard his spots? then may ye also do good, that are *accustomed* to do evil" (v.23). As Laetsch points out, "His sin is not merely an acquired habit, which they might give up at any time they chose to do so. They can relinquish their sinful nature as little as the Ethiopian can rid himself of his skin or the leopard erase his spots". Judgment was both inevitable and calculated: "Therefore will I scatter them as the stubble that passeth away by the wind of the wilderness. This is thy lot, the portion of thy measures from me, saith the Lord; because thou hast forgotten me, and trusted in falsehood" (vv.24-25). The word "falsehood" (v.25) is literally "the lie" and refers to Baal. Divine retribution would mean complete and utter disgrace: "Therefore will I discover thy skirts upon thy face, that thy shame may appear" (v.26), which repeats the penalty described in v.22 and is further described by Hosea: "Plead with your mother, plead: for she is not my wife, neither am I her husband: let her therefore put away her whoredoms out of her sight, and her adulteries from between her breasts; Lest I strip her naked, and set her as in the day that she was born...And now will I discover her lewdness in the sight of her lovers, and none shall deliver her out of mine hand" (Hos 2.2-3, 10). The cause is restated: "I have seen thine adulteries, and thy neighings, the lewdness of thy whoredom, and thine abominations on the hills in the fields" (v.27).

The chapter closes on a despairing note: "Woe unto thee, O Jerusalem! wilt thou not be made clean? when shall it once be?". Laetsch renders this: "You will not be clean even after how long a time!", and comments, "She steadfastly prefers her filth to the purity He offers to her, a hardened, incurably wicked harlot".

JEREMIAH 14.1-15.9

"The word of the Lord that came to Jeremiah concerning the dearth ('drought', JND)" (14.1). The absence of chronological references precludes the assignment of a date to this oracle. Chapters 14 and 15 belong together. The message "concerning the dearth" commences in ch.14 and continues in ch.15. The connection between the two chapters is clear. Chapter 14 concludes with three questions: "Are there any among the vanities of the Gentiles that can cause rain? or can the heavens give showers? art not thou he, O Lord our God? therefore we will wait upon thee: for thou hast made all these things" (v.22). Chapter 15 commences with the answer: "Then said the Lord unto me, Though Moses and Samuel stood before me, yet my mind could not be toward this people: cast them out of my sight, and let them go forth" (v.1). In the remaining verses of ch.15 (vv.10-21), Jeremiah expresses his resentment of the lonely path that he was called to tread as a most unpopular prophet.

Taken together, the two chapters may be divided by the expression "called by thy name" (14.9; 15.16).

Jeremiah, speaking on behalf of Judah, appeals to the Lord for help on the basis that they were His people: "thou, O Lord, art in the midst of *us*, and *we* are *called by thy name*; leave *us* not" (14.9). But it was an empty claim; the Lord would not hear them.

Jeremiah, now speaking personally, appeals to the Lord for help on the basis that he was one of His people: "Thy words were found, and *I* did eat them; and thy word was unto *me* the joy and rejoicing of *mine* heart: for *I* am *called by thy name*, O Lord God of hosts" (15.16). It was a valid claim - the Lord heard him. In summary, these chapters describe the nation called by the Lord's name (14.1-15.9); and the man called by the Lord's name (15.10-21).

The first of these two major divisions has two parts.

The message of the drought (14.1-6): droughts were a solemn indication of divine displeasure.

The ministry of Jeremiah (14.7-15.9). His ministry at this juncture took the form of three appeals to the Lord, each of which is followed by a divine answer: 14.7-12; 14.13-18; 14.19-15.9. The first appeal (14.7-9) is based on the Lord's promises: Jeremiah addresses Him as "the hope of Israel" (v.8); the second (14.13) is based on the vulnerability of Judah: they had been deceived by the false prophets; the third (14.19-22) is based on the Lord's apparent change of heart towards them (v.19).

Verses 14.1-6: The Message of the Drought

"Judah mourneth, and the gates thereof languish; they are black unto the ground; and the cry of Jerusalem is gone up" (v.2). Black is the colour of famine: "Our skin was black like an oven because of the terrible famine" (Lam 5.10). The third of four universal conditions described in Revelation

6.1-8 is famine: "And I beheld, and lo a black horse; and he that sat on him had a pair of balances in his hand" (Rev 6.5). "The two main cereals (wheat and barley, v.6) which constitute the staff of life are to be doled out by weight and sold at famine prices" (Walter Scott, *Exposition of the Revelation of Jesus Christ*). In the current passage, there was "no water" (v.3), "no rain" (v.4) and "no grass" (vv.5,6). The passage graphically describes distraught children returning from the dry water pits (v.3), the parched and cracked earth (v.4), the idle ploughmen (v.4), and frantic animals (vv.5-6). In the words of Laetsch, "The scrubby, shaggy wild ass, inured to the hardships of the desert, dies of hunger and thirst. The dry wind it sniffs to detect the slightest trace of moisture which might lead it to water, only sucks up like a greedy vampire what little moisture is left in that walking skeleton". The reference to jackals ('dragons', AV) emphasises "their wide-open, wolf-like jaws" (Laetsch).

The existence of the drought ("dearth", AV: it is a plural word, which may suggest a series of droughts) testified against the wickedness of Judah: "our iniquities testify against us...our backslidings are many; we have sinned against thee" (v.7). It must not be thought that the Lord was unmindful of Judah's distress. As Broadbent observes, "Yet He suffered with both man and beast, as is seen in this His description to Judah of the drought".

Drought was never a chance occurrence in the Old Testament. It was a sign of divine displeasure, and evidence of the disciplinary hand of God: "Take heed to yourselves, that your heart be not deceived, and ye turn aside, and serve other gods, and worship them; And then the Lord's wrath be kindled against you, and he shut up the heaven, that there be no rain, and that the land yield not her fruit; and lest ye perish quickly from off the good land which the Lord giveth you" (Deut 11.16-17; cp. Deut 28.23-24). Elijah was evidently aware of these passages when he said to Ahab, "As the Lord God of Israel liveth, before whom I stand, there shall not be dew nor rain these years, but according to my word" (1 Kings 17.1). This statement should be compared with Revelation 11.6. Both passages refer, significantly, to a period of three and half years (James 5.17; Rev 11.3, where the period is expressed in days). The object of drought in the land was to bring Israel to repentance and this is strikingly illustrated in the preaching of Amos: "And also I have withholden the rain from you, when there were yet three months to the harvest: and I caused it to rain upon one city, and caused it not to rain upon another city (so judgment was discriminatory): one piece was rained upon, and the piece whereupon it rained not withered...yet have ye not returned unto me, saith the Lord" (Amos 4.7-8).

There is an important lesson here for God's people now. If, in Bible times, drought was a clear sign that the Lord's people were subject to divine discipline because of sin, then spiritual drought in the lives of His people today indicates that sin has interrupted communion with God and marred the enjoyment of His blessing. If the Word of God and prayer have lost their attraction, and Bible reading has become a lifeless routine which brings no spiritual joy, then His people are in a state of spiritual famine. God deliberately withholds His blessing on these spiritual activities, in order to highlight their departure from Him and to bring them to repentance. In short, drought in spiritual life is a sure signal that something is wrong. This lesson was impressed on the Lord's people by Haggai: "Ye looked for much, and, lo, it came to little; and when ye brought it home, I did blow upon it. Why? saith the Lord of hosts. Because of mine house that is waste, and ye run every man unto his own house. Therefore the heaven over you is stayed from dew, and the earth is stayed from her fruit" (Hag 1.9-10).

Verses 14 7–15.9: The Ministry of Jeremiah

The miserable condition of Judah touched the heart of Jeremiah, and in the verses which follow, he makes three appeals to the Lord.

The first appeal (14.7-12)
The appeal (vv.7-9)

Whilst it is possible that the appeal is voiced by the stricken nation, it seems more likely that Jeremiah himself is speaking on their behalf, in which case the command, "Pray not for this people for their good" (v.11), indicates that their rebellion was so great that God was not prepared to respond to intercession on their behalf. Even Moses and Samuel would not prevail, if had been possible for them to intercede (15.1). Jeremiah's appeal here, together with his second and third appeals (v.13; vv.19-22), disclose his deep distress over the reduced circumstances of God's people. This is the man who had said, "Oh that my head were waters, and mine eyes a fountain of tears, that I might weep day and night for the slain of the daughter of my people!" (9.1). He was not impervious to the suffering of Judah, even though they were reaping the bitter harvest of their own waywardness. Jeremiah pronounced divine judgment, but did so with tears in his eyes: "But if ye will not hear it, my soul shall weep in secret places for your pride; and mine eye shall weep sore, and run down with tears, because the Lord's flock is carried away captive" (13.17).

Jeremiah's appeal here begins with the confession of sin: "O Lord, though our iniquities testify against us, do thou it for thy name's sake: for our backslidings are many; we have sinned against thee" (v.7). He calls on the Lord to deliver His people for His own name's sake, even though they are totally unworthy and undeserving. His appeal rests upon the Lord's honour: "do thou it for thy name's sake". Jeremiah evidently refers here to the revelation made to Moses: "And the Lord descended in the cloud, and stood with him there, and proclaimed *the name* of the Lord. And the Lord passed by before him, and proclaimed, The Lord, The Lord God, merciful and gracious, longsuffering, and abundant in goodness and truth" (Ex 34.5-6). He appeals to the Lord as "the hope of Israel" (v.8). Jeremiah uses this expression again in 17.13, and Paul uses it in Acts 28.20. At the time of national restoration, the Lord will say, "O Israel, thou hast destroyed thyself;

but in me is thine help" (Hos 13.9). He is both "the hope of Israel, the saviour thereof in time of trouble" (v.8). The word "saviour" is used for the first time to describe the Lord in 2 Samuel 22.3, and occurs eight times in the prophecy of Isaiah (19.20; 43.3,11; 45.15,21; 49.26; 60.16; 63.8). Apart from Him, there could be no hope and no salvation. But He appeared to have lost interest in His people, and acted as "a non-resident traveler" (Laetsch): "O the hope of Israel, the saviour thereof in time of trouble, why shouldest thou be as a stranger in the land, and as a wayfaring man that turneth aside to tarry for a night?" (v.8). He graced them with His presence, and they bore His name, but He was evidently unwilling to act on their behalf. Jeremiah therefore calls upon God to vindicate his own name, and deliver His people: "Why shouldest thou be as a man astonied (taken by surprise), as a mighty man that cannot save? yet thou, O Lord, art in the midst of us, and we are called by thy name; leave us not" (v.9).

While the personal sincerity and reality of Jeremiah cannot be doubted, the people he represented were anything but sincere. Confession of sin did not necessarily mean true repentance. It was one thing to call upon the Lord as "the hope of Israel", but something quite different to really trust and rely upon Him. To say, "We are called by thy name", does not necessarily mean conformity to that name! Samuel's two sons had fine names: Joel, meaning "Jehovah is God", and Abiah, meaning "whose father is Jehovah" (1 Sam 8.2). But Jehovah was not Joel's God, and Jehovah was not Abiah's father. It is one thing to pronounce the name of the Lord Jesus Christ, but another thing entirely to "put…on the Lord Jesus Christ, and make not provision for the flesh, to fulfil the lusts thereof" (Rom 13.14).

The answer (vv.10-12)

The appeal is rejected. "Their own profession of faith will not now avail, their judgment is irrevocable" (Broadbent). Their determined disobedience and inveterate desire to sin placed them beyond divine mercy: "Thus saith the Lord unto this people, Thus have they loved to wander, they have not refrained their feet, therefore the Lord doth not accept them; he will now remember their iniquity, and visit their sins" (v.10). This highlights the solemn lesson that the Lord's people cannot trade on His mercy. Judah had sinned "unto death" (1 Jn 5.16), and Jeremiah is told, for the third time, "Pray not for this people for their good" (v.11; cp. 7.16; 11.14). This would have come as a heavy blow to Samuel in his day: "God forbid that I should sin against the Lord in ceasing to pray for you" (1 Sam 12.23).

Their pious words and pious practices were devoid of reality. Some 150 years before, God had expressed his total disgust at their religious hypocrisy: "And when ye spread forth your hands, I will hide mine eyes from you: yea, when ye make many prayers, I will not hear" (Is 1.15). The intervening years had not witnessed the slightest improvement and now the Lord is obliged to say, "When they fast, I will not hear their cry; and when they offer burnt-offering and an oblation, I will not accept them" (v.12). They had already experienced the rigours of drought; worse would follow: "I will consume them by the sword, and by the famine, and by the pestilence" (v.12). The inevitability of divine judgment in this way is emphasised by the repetition of the words "sword…famine…pestilence" throughout the book (cp. 21.9; 24.10; 27.8,13).

Religious hypocrisy is detestable to God. The centuries between the preaching of Isaiah and Jeremiah, and the coming of the Lord Jesus, saw no improvement, and Matthew 15.7-8 should be read in this connection. The Lord's people today must heed the warning of these passages, not only in connection with their relationship with Him, but in their relationships with each other: "Let love be without dissimulation" (Rom 12.9); "Seeing ye have purified your souls in obeying the truth through the Spirit unto unfeigned love of the brethren, see that ye love one another with a pure heart fervently" (1 Pet 1.22). The Apostle Paul could say, "For we are not as many, which corrupt the word of God: but as of sincerity, but as of God, in the sight of God speak we in Christ" (2 Cor 2.17).

The second appeal (14.13-18)
The appeal (v.13)

Jeremiah now appeals to God for mercy towards Judah on the grounds that they had been misled by the false prophets. They had totally contradicted God's intention to judge His people "by the sword, and by the famine, and by the pestilence" (v.12), and proclaimed peace rather than judgment: "Then said I, Ah, Lord God! behold, the prophets say unto them, Ye shall not see the sword, neither shall ye have famine; but I will give you assured peace in this place".

The answer (vv.14-18)

In His answer, the Lord deals, firstly, with the false prophets themselves (vv.14-15), and then with the people they had deceived (vv.16-18). In both cases, there was no prospect but divine judgment.

The false prophets assured the nation that all would be well, but the predicted "sword" and "famine" (v.12), which they denied (v.13), would consume them (v.15), together with their audiences (vv.16,18). They had lulled the nation into a sense of complacency and false security. This is a familiar charge: "from the prophet even unto the priest every one dealeth falsely. They have healed also the hurt of the daughter of my people slightly, saying, Peace, peace; when there is no peace" (6.13-14; 8.10-11). While Jeremiah does not deny the sinfulness of Judah, he pleads mitigating circumstances; the false prophets had deluded the people. By their very nature, false prophets do not face the truth.

The judgment passed upon the false prophets is all the more merited because they professed to speak from the Lord: "The prophets prophesy lies in my name: I sent them not, neither have I commanded them, neither spake unto them" (v.14); "the prophets that prophesy in my name, and I sent them not, yet they say, Sword and famine shall not be in this land" (v.15). They were given to deception: "they prophesy unto you a false vision and divination, and a thing of nought, and the deceit of their heart" (v.14), and would experience destruction: "By sword and famine shall those prophets be consumed" (v.15). It is characteristic of false prophets, and false teachers, that they preach to suit their audiences, and therefore continue to enjoy great popularity: "For the time will come when they will not endure sound doctrine; but after their own lusts shall they heap to themselves teachers, having itching ears ('but, having itching ears, will heap to themselves teachers after their own lusts', RV); And they shall turn away their ears from the truth, and shall be turned unto fables" (2 Tim 4.3-4).

Through Jeremiah, the Lord then addresses the nation which had listened, with pleasure, to the deceit of the false prophets: "And the people to whom they prophesy shall be cast out in the streets of Jerusalem because of the famine and the sword; and they shall have none to bury them, them, their wives, nor their sons, nor their daughters: for I will pour their wickedness upon them" (v.16). As Feinberg observes: "The people should have known that the Lord punishes sin, and they should not have believed the false prophets. The judgment of the nation is spoken of here because the people were willing to be deceived". The churches of Galatia were in the same position: "I marvel that ye are so soon removed from him that called you into the grace of Christ unto another gospel" (Gal 1.6). While Paul censures the false teachers who had invaded the assemblies in Galatia, he also censures the Galatians themselves for imbibing false teaching. They should have known better.

The section concludes with the preaching of the true prophet (vv.17-18). There is a marked contrast between this section and the previous verses. Jeremiah is told: "Therefore thou shalt say this word unto them" (v.17), but the Lord had said nothing to the false prophets: "I sent them not, neither have I commanded them, neither spake unto them" (v.14). Like Haggai, Jeremiah was the "Lord's messenger in the Lord's message" (Hag 1.13). There were no tears of grief in the eyes of the false prophets, but godly men weep at the prospect of divine judgment. Jeremiah has not been called the "weeping prophet" without reason: "Therefore thou shalt say this word unto them; Let mine eyes run down with tears night and day, and let them not cease: for the virgin daughter of my people is broken with a great breach, with a very grievous blow" (v.17). There would be no refuge from the sword in the countryside, and no refuge from the famine in the city. The prophets and priests who had deceived the people would live to see divine judgment: "If I go forth into the field, then behold the slain with the sword! and if I enter into the city, then behold them that are sick with famine!" (v.18).

Various suggestions have been made in connection with the words, "both the prophet and the priest go about into a land that they know not", but there is considerable weight in the opinion that the AV rendering conveys the meaning of the original text: the surviving prophets and priests would be deported.

The third appeal (14.19-15.9)
The appeal (vv.19-22)
"Hast thou utterly rejected Judah? hath thy soul lothed Zion? why hast thou smitten us, and there is no healing for us? we looked for peace, and there is no good; and for the time of healing, and behold trouble!" (v.19). "Jeremiah cannot believe that God has utterly abandoned Zion" (Broadbent). Judah was the tribe which, with Benjamin, remained loyal to the throne of David, and Zion was the place where God saw fit to place His name. But an excellent past does not secure present blessing (cp. 7.12-15).

The "hope of Israel" (v.8) had apparently failed them. Although the nation had broken the Lord's covenant, Jeremiah pleads with God not to abandon His covenant faithfulness towards them. He refers to the Lord's name: "Do not abhor us, for thy name's sake"; the Lord's glory: "do not disgrace the throne of thy glory"; and the Lord's covenant: "remember, break not thy covenant with us" (v.21). Jeremiah argued that if God continued to abandon them, His name and His throne would be brought into disrepute. Moses used a similar argument: "Now if thou shalt kill all this people as one man, then the nations which have heard the fame of thee will speak, saying, Because the Lord was not able to bring this people into the land which he sware unto them, therefore he hath slain them in the wilderness" (Num 14.15-16). Joshua did the same: "For the Canaanites and all the inhabitants of the land shall hear of it, and shall environ us round, and cut off our name from the earth: and what wilt thou do unto thy great name?" (Josh 7.9).

The appeal ends with clear reference to the drought. "Are there any among the vanities of the Gentiles that can cause rain? or can the heavens give showers? art not thou he, O Lord our God? therefore we will wait upon thee: for thou hast made all these things." The expression "vanities of the Gentiles" refers to Judah's devotion to "the sun, and the moon, and all the host of heaven, whom they have loved, and whom they have served" (8.2). Hence the second question: "Can the heavens give showers?". Only the Lord can do this.

The answer (15.1-9)
Like its predecessors, the third appeal is unavailing. Jeremiah had now interceded three times, and even if it were possible for Moses and Samuel to join him, the position would not alter. Feinberg describes Moses and Samuel as "exemplary intercessors for Israel". In the case of Moses, reference can be made to Exodus 32.11-14, 30-34; Numbers 14.13-20; Deuteronomy 9.18-20, 25-29, and in the case of Samuel to 1 Samuel 7.8-9; 12.19-25. Both are mentioned in the same connection by the Psalmist:

"Moses and Aaron among his priests, and Samuel among them that call upon his name; they called upon the Lord, and he answered them" (Ps 99.6).

The Lord was no longer prepared to change His mind towards Judah: "Though Moses and Samuel stood before me, yet my mind could not be toward this people: cast them out of my sight, and let them go forth" (v.1). The word "mind" (5315) carries the thought of "heart" or "affection". The Lord could tolerate them no longer. This does not signal the end of His covenant relations with Israel. This very prophecy anticipates national restoration. The Lord "will bring again the captivity of Jacob's tents, and have mercy on his dwellingplaces" (30.18). He will then say, "I have loved thee with an everlasting love: therefore with lovingkindness have I drawn thee" (31.3). "As touching the election, they are beloved for the fathers' sakes" (Rom 11.28).

But in the immediate future, some would die by the sword and by famine; others would go into exile: "And it shall come to pass, if they say unto thee, Whither shall we go forth? then thou shalt tell them, Thus saith the Lord; Such as are for death, to death; and such as are for the sword, to the sword; and such as are for the famine, to the famine; and such as are for the captivity, to the captivity" (v.2). Those who died would be denied decent burial: they would be consumed by fowls and beasts: "And I will appoint over them four kinds, saith the Lord: the sword to slay, and the dogs to tear, and the fowls of the heaven, and the beasts of the earth, to devour and destroy" (v.3), and those who suffered exile would be scattered "into all kingdoms of the earth" (v.4). Particular reference is made in this connection to the sins of Manasseh (v.4) who reversed the reforms initiated by his father, Hezekiah, and "did that which was evil in the sight of the Lord, like unto the abominations of the heathen, whom the Lord had cast out before the children of Israel". Amongst other things, "he built again the high places which Hezekiah his father had broken down, and he reared up altars for Baalim, and made groves, and worshipped all the host of heaven, and served them" (2 Chr 33.2-3). In consequence, "the Lord spake by his servants the prophets, saying, Because Manasseh king of Judah hath done these abominations...Therefore thus saith the Lord God of Israel, Behold, I am bringing such evil upon Jerusalem and Judah, that whosoever heareth of it, both his ears shall tingle" (2 Kings 21.10-12). Very clearly, divine judgment was not attributable to his sins alone, but it was during his reign that Israel's wickedness reached its zenith. While he "seduced them to do more evil than did the nations whom the Lord destroyed before the children of Israel" (2 Kings 21.9), Israel had provoked the Lord to anger "since the day their fathers came forth out of Egypt, even unto this day" (2 Kings 21.15).

Then there would be no pity. In the first place, there would no pity from men: "For who shall have pity upon thee, O Jerusalem? or who shall bemoan thee? or who shall go aside to ask how thou doest?" (v.5). In the second place, there would be no pity from the Lord. His people had now gone too far. They had continually flouted His goodness to them, to the extent that He could withhold judgment no longer: "Thou hast forsaken me, saith the Lord, thou art gone away backward: therefore will I stretch out my hand against thee, and destroy thee; I am weary with repenting. And I will fan them with a fan in the gates of the land; I will bereave them of children, I will destroy my people, since they return not from their ways" (vv.6-7). The "fan" was used in winnowing: "As a farmer winnows the wheat to remove the chaff, so the Lord will disperse the people from their cities - the 'city gates' standing for the whole country" (Feinberg). It will not escape notice that the Lord actually moves against His people: "I will appoint" (v.3); "I will cause" (v.4); "I will fan them…I will bereave them of children, I will destroy my people" (v.7)". Judah would not suffer because of "the quirks of fate", or "the fortunes of war"; the Lord would bring judgment upon them.

The bloodshed would be appalling. The words, "Their widows are increased to me above the sand of the seas" (v.8), graphically describes the slaughter when Jerusalem, described as "the mother of the young men", is suddenly and unexpectedly attacked at noonday (v.8). Laetsch points out that "usually armies rested at noon because of the intense heat". The blessings of a large family are shortlived: "She that hath borne seven languisheth: she hath given up the ghost; her sun is gone down while it was yet day" (v.9). Any survivors of the attack would be put to the sword: "and the residue of them will I deliver to the sword before their enemies, saith the Lord" (v.9).

JEREMIAH 15.10-21

Attention has been drawn to the connection between chs.14 and 15 - they describe the nation called by the Lord's name (14.1-15.9) and the man called by the Lord's name (15.10-21).

As could be expected, the message of "the dearth" (14.1) made Jeremiah thoroughly unpopular. The false prophets, claiming that the Lord had sent them, had raised Judah's expectation by assuring them of a secure future: "Ye shall not see the sword, neither shall ye have famine; but I will give you assured peace in this place" (14.13). This was exactly what the nation wanted to hear, and they gladly accepted the message. But the future was quite different: "If I go forth into the field, then behold the slain with the sword! and if I enter into the city, then behold them that are sick with famine!" (14.18). The perpetual wickedness of Judah had exhausted the Lord's mercy and patience. He rejected Jeremiah's appeals (14.7-9,13,19-22), and even the combined intercession of Moses and Samuel could not have secured deliverance from judgment: "Though Moses and Samuel stood before me, yet my mind could not be toward this people: cast them out of my sight, and let them go forth" (15.1).

Like Micaiah before him, of whom Ahab said, "I hate him; for he never prophesied good unto me, but always evil" (2 Chr 18.7), this left Jeremiah isolated and lonely. Everyone was against him: "Woe is me, my mother, that thou hast borne me a man of strife and a man of contention to the whole earth ('land', JND)!" (v.10). This was the direct result of his preaching: "thou shalt say this word unto them" (14.17); "if they say unto thee, Whither shall we go forth? then thou shalt tell them, Thus saith the Lord" (15.2). When Jeremiah was commissioned, the Lord warned him that he would face opposition from all sectors of society, and promised him deliverance (1.18-19). This promise is repeated in the current passage (15.20). He had experienced opposition in his home town (11.21), from his own family (12.6), and now from the whole land (15.10).

The passage may be divided as follows:

> Jeremiah's Position (v.10)
> Jeremiah's Preservation (vv.11-14)
> Jeremiah's Protest (vv.15-21).

Verse 10: Jeremiah's Position

"Woe is me, my mother, that thou hast borne me a man of strife and a man of contention to the whole earth! I have neither lent on usury, nor men have lent to me on usury; yet every one of them doth curse me." The prophet refers to his unpopular ministry, and his unblemished character.

His unpopular ministry

Jeremiah felt keenly the reproach of the message committed to him.

The prophets were not a race of supermen. Elijah was "a man subject to like passions as we are" (James 5.17), and so were his successors. This is encouraging! If the Lord used these men so effectively, then He is able to use His people today in the same way. The raw material is the same! It does mean, of course, that they must be like the prophets who "stood in the counsel of the Lord" and who "perceived and heard his word" (23.18). It also means faithfulness in communicating God's word: "The prophet that hath a dream, let him tell a dream; and he that hath my word, let him speak my word faithfully" (23.28). But faithfulness in God's service does not mean popularity. Centuries later, Paul referred to "the offence of the cross" (Gal 5.11). Tragically, Jeremiah was unpopular amongst *God's people*, and the same sad situation is anticipated in the New Testament (cp. 2 Tim 4.3). Paul was obliged to write: "This thou knowest, that all they which are in Asia be turned away from me" (2 Tim 1.15). Faithful men of God have so often been regarded as men of "strife and...contention" in so-called "Christian circles". The clear teaching of God's word is often dismissed as "fundamentalism", and branded "controversial" or "contentious".

His unblemished character

"I have neither lent on usury, nor men have lent to me on usury; yet every one of them doth curse me." Jeremiah stood apart from the forbidden practices of the day. Usury, money-lending as a profit-making business, was strictly forbidden amongst God's people: "If thou lend money to any of my people that is poor by thee, thou shalt not be to him as an usurer, neither shalt thou lay upon him usury" (Ex 22.25). Other examples are found in Leviticus 25.35-37 and Deuteronomy 23.20. The demands implied by the questions, "Lord, who shall abide in thy tabernacle? who shall dwell in thy holy hill?", can be met only by people of exemplary conduct, including "He that putteth not out his money to usury" (Ps 15.1,5).

Jeremiah's character could not be maligned. He was cursed, purely and simply, because of his preaching. This is most important. Jeremiah had the moral right to preach, and although his message was totally unacceptable, he could not be charged with inconsistency. It was to avoid this very charge that Paul wrote: "Take heed unto thyself, and unto the doctrine" (1 Tim 4.16). For the same reason he said to the Ephesian elders, "Take heed therefore unto yourselves, and to all the flock" (Acts 20.28). The Lord Jesus charged the religious leaders of the day with inconsistency between doctrine and practice: "The scribes and the Pharisees sit in Moses' seat: All therefore whatsoever they bid you observe, that observe and do; but do not ye after their works: for they say, and do not" (Mt 23.2-3). He Himself displayed perfect consistency between practice and doctrine: "The former treatise have I made, O Theophilus, of all that Jesus began both to do and teach" (Acts 1.1). There should be no inconsistency between the talk and walk of God's people.

Verses 11-14: Jeremiah's Preservation

God reassures His distressed and complaining servant: "The Lord said, Verily it shall be well with thy remnant; verily I will cause the enemy to entreat thee well in the time of evil and in the time of affliction" (v.11). According to Feinberg, the rendering, "Verily it shall be well with thy remnant" (AV), "seems to be the least likely translation". The term "thy remnant" (8293) has been understood as a noun (as in the AV) and as a verb. There are numerous variations in translation, and this indicates the difficulty of the original text. Scholars are evidently in some agreement that "the obvious force appears to be verbal rather than nominal" (Feinberg), hence the renderings, "Verily I will set thee free for thy good" (JND); "I will set you free for purposes of good" (NASB). However, the verb may mean "to establish", or "to strengthen", rather than "to set free", or "to release", and in this case the sense of the words, bearing in mind the context, is that, in spite of the opposition, Jeremiah would be established and strengthened to accomplish the good purposes of the Lord.

The promise, "verily I will cause the enemy to intreat thee well ('make supplication unto thee', RV) in the time of evil and in the time of affliction", refers, not to the protection and liberty given to him by Nebuchadnezzar and Nebuzar-adan (39.11-14; 40.1-6), but to the recognition given to him by his opponents, including Zedekiah (21.1-2; 37.3,17; 38.14-16). "God assures him that his enemies, now cursing him, will acknowledge him as God's prophet" (Laetsch). "The foe, who in his time of calamity goes humbly at God's instigation to the prophet whom he hated before, and especially to obtain the prophet's intercession with God, is, of course, not the Chaldean; the hostile Judaeans are meant" (Orelli). Jeremiah lived to prove that "the Lord thy God, he it is that doth go with thee; he will not fail thee, nor forsake thee" (Deut 31.6).

Having assured Jeremiah that he would be preserved when the captivity came, the Lord then assures the nation that they would be powerless to resist the enemy: "Shall iron break the northern iron and the steel?", or "Will iron break? iron from the north? and bronze?" (JND). Unusually hard iron was manufactured in the area of the Black Sea and the northern enemy would be just like that iron. He would sweep into Judah with irresistible force, the land would be plundered, its wealth and treasures carried away, and its inhabitants taken into exile: "Thy substance and thy treasures will I give to the spoil without price, and that for all thy sins, even in all thy borders. And I will make thee to pass with thine enemies into a land which thou knowest not" (vv.13-14). These events could not be classed as "the fortunes of war": they represented divine judgment: "a fire is kindled in mine anger, which shall burn upon you" (v.14).

Verses 15-21: Jeremiah's Protest

Although he had been assured of divine preservation, the prophet remained deeply disturbed and deeply distressed by the antagonism of Judah. He refers to his "persecutors" (v.15), and to his perpetual pain and incurable wound (v.18). Although he had been faithful to the Lord and His word (vv.16-17), there was no vengeance on his enemies and no relief from his suffering. The Lord had seemingly let him down badly: "wilt thou be altogether unto me as a liar, and as waters that fail?" (v.18). In response, the Lord tenderly rebukes and encourages his overwrought servant (vv.19-21). The section can therefore be divided as follows: Jeremiah's recrimination (vv.15-18); and the Lord's reply (vv.19-21).

Jeremiah's recrimination (vv.15-18)

God's people can cry, in times of adversity and difficulty, whatever their character, "O Lord, thou knowest" (v.15). David said, "Thou knowest my downsitting and mine uprising, thou understandest my thought afar off. Thou compassest my path and my lying down, and art acquainted with all my ways" (Ps 139.2-3). In this particular case Jeremiah was persuaded that the Lord was aware of his righteousness, and the total unrighteousness of his enemies. In view of his exemplary character he called for divine vengeance on his enemies: "O Lord, thou knowest: remember me, and visit me, and revenge me of my persecutors; take me not away in thy longsuffering" (v.15). The words, "take me not away in thy longsuffering", mean that he looked for vindication in his lifetime. He wanted to see the judgment of God on his adversaries. Whilst the history and experiences of Jeremiah remind us of the life and experiences of the Lord Jesus, there is a sharp divergence here. The Lord Jesus prayed, "Father, forgive them; for they know not what they do" (Lk 23.34), and this must have been on Peter's heart and mind when he wrote: "Who, when he was reviled, reviled not again; when he suffered, he threatened not; but committed himself to him that judgeth righteously" (1 Pet 2.23). Stephen followed the footsteps of the Lord Jesus when he cried, "Lord, lay not this sin to their charge" (Acts 7.60).

Jeremiah gives three reasons for crying to the Lord for the destruction of his enemies, and deliverance from their persecution. It perplexed him that in view of these reasons the Lord had still not acted on his behalf, and this constrained him to complain bitterly (v.18).

He was reproached for the sake of the Lord (v.15)

"Know that for thy sake I have suffered rebuke." His willingness to stand alone was engendered by His desire for the Lord's glory and the honour of the Lord's name. It was Jeremiah's devotion to the Lord that made him bear the stigma of "a man of strife and a man of contention to the whole earth!" (v.10), just as it was the devotion of the Lord Jesus to His Father that motivated His perfect service. The "Spirit of Christ" (1 Pet 1.11) was surely in David when he wrote, "for thy sake I have borne reproach; shame hath covered my face. I am become a stranger unto my brethren, and an alien unto my mother's children. For the zeal of thine house hath eaten me up; and the reproaches of them that reproached thee are fallen upon me" (Ps 69.7-9). It should be remembered that since it was for our sakes that the Lord Jesus "became poor" (2 Cor 8.9) we should be willing to be "fools for Christ's sake" (1 Cor 4.10), "servants for Jesus' sake" (2 Cor 4.5), and, if necessary, to be "delivered unto death for Jesus' sake" (2 Cor 4.11). The Lord Jesus taught that "whosoever will save his life shall lose it; but whosoever shall lose his life for my sake and the gospel's, the same shall save it" (Mk 8.35).

He rejoiced in the word of the Lord (v.16)
"Thy words were found, and I did eat them; and thy word was ('words were', JND) unto me the joy and rejoicing of my heart: for I am called by thy name, O Lord God of hosts." The expression, "thy words were found", are significant. In was in the eighteenth year of Josiah's reign that "Hilkiah the high priest said unto Shaphan the scribe, I have found the book of the law in the house of the Lord" (2 Kings 22.8). The book is thereafter called "this book that is found" (2 Kings 22.13); "the book of the covenant which was found in the house of the Lord" (2 Kings 23.2); "the book that Hilkiah the priest found in the house of the Lord" (2 Kings 23.24). Jeremiah's language strongly suggests that he refers here to the discovery of "the book" in the Temple, and that he made its teaching part of his very life.

The words "I did eat them" suggest far more than study, which can be an intellectual exercise and no more. By "eating" the words of "the book" Jeremiah lived in the good of their teaching, in exactly the same way that we benefit from the food we consume. The Word of God is intended to maintain spiritual life. More than informing the minds of God's people, it maintains and develops their spiritual lives. Food is initially swallowed, but its nourishment is made good by the process of digestion, and in the same way the Word of God, which His people read and hear, is made good to them by the processes of reflection and meditation. Hence the injunction, "Meditate upon these things; give thyself wholly to them; that thy profiting ('progress', JND) may appear to all" (1 Tim 4.15). Joshua was told that "This book of the law shall not depart out of thy mouth; but thou shalt meditate therein day and night, that thou mayest observe to do according to all that is written therein: for then thou shalt make thy way prosperous, and then thou shalt have good success" (Josh 1.8). Both Ezekiel (Ezek 3.1-3) and John (Rev 10.10-11) were required to assimilate the Word of God, and then preach.

While Jeremiah's preaching was often solemn, causing him grief and tears, he rejoiced in the Word of God: "thy word was unto me the joy and rejoicing of my heart". The Word of God should bring to joy to the hearts of the Lord's people. The godly man finds "his delight...in the law of the Lord; and in his law doth he meditate day and night" (Ps 1.2). As a result of the public reading of the Scriptures by Ezra and his colleagues, the people first wept and then made "great mirth, because they had understood the words that were declared unto them" (Neh 8.9,12). The Psalmist expressed his joy over the Word of God: "Thy testimonies have I taken as an heritage for ever: for they are the rejoicing of my heart...I rejoice at thy word, as one that findeth great spoil" (Ps 119.111,162). Jeremiah evidently had great joy in reading and assimilating the word of God, but even this must have been exceeded by the Lord Jesus who could say prophetically, "I delight to do thy will, O my God: yea, thy law is within my heart" (Ps 40.8).

Jeremiah not only rejoiced in the word of the Lord, he also rejoiced in the name of the Lord: "I am called by thy name, O Lord God of hosts". The name Jeremiah means "Jehovah is high", or "whom Jehovah appoints". James refers to "that worthy name by the which ye are called" (James 2.7), or "the excellent name which has been called upon you" (JND). G. P. Waugh (*What the Bible Teaches : James*) suggests that "The name which is 'worthy' may well be 'Christian', first associated with the Christians at Antioch". It has already been noted that some Bible characters had excellent names, but failed to display their reality. The title, "O Lord God of hosts", signifies His immense resources and infinite power: "he doeth according to his will in the army of heaven, and among the inhabitants of the earth: and none can stay his hand, or say unto him, What doest thou?" (Dan 4.35).

He was restrained by the hand of the Lord (vv.17-18)

"I sat not in the assembly of the mockers, nor rejoiced; I sat alone because of thine hand: for thou hast filled me with indignation" (v.17). The contrast with the previous verse is clear: there the word of God was the "rejoicing" of his heart (v.16), but the constraints of His word meant that Jeremiah was unable to rejoice with others. The word "mockers" (7832) is not used here in its English sense: it means "to make merry...laugh...rejoice" (Laetsch). Jeremiah did not "sit in the circle of profane merrymakers and mockers" (Unger). The Psalmist puts it as follows: "Blessed is the man that walketh not in the counsel of the ungodly, nor standeth in the way of sinners, nor sitteth in the seat of the scornful" (Ps 1.1). The word of God rested heavily upon Jeremiah, and restrained him from fellowship with his contemporaries.

In the first place, this involved separation from evil: "I sat alone because of thy hand". Faithfulness to the Word of God often involves a lonely path and means withdrawal from the pleasures, pursuits and practices of the world: "Be ye not unequally yoked together with unbelievers: for what fellowship hath righteousness with unrighteousness? and what communion hath light with darkness?...Wherefore come out from among them, and be ye separate, saith the Lord" (2 Cor 6.14,17). Peter describes the lonely path of the believer as follows: "they think it strange that ye run not with them to the same excess of riot ('the same sink of corruption', JND), speaking evil of you" (1 Pet 4.4). In the second place, Jeremiah did not adopt a disinterested attitude. He *hated* the sin of Judah; it filled him with indignation.

In all this, Jeremiah felt that the Lord had failed him. His faithfulness had not been vindicated. After opposition from his home town and his own family (11.21; 12.6), and now from entire nation (v.10), even the Lord had apparently abandoned him: "Why is my pain perpetual, and my wound incurable, which refuseth to be healed? wilt thou be altogether unto me as a liar, and as waters that fail?" (v.18), or "wilt thou be altogether unto me as a treacherous spring, as waters that fail" (JND). Jeremiah's imagery is clearly explained by Job; "My brethren have dealt deceitfully as a brook, and as the stream of brooks they pass away; Which are blackish by reason of the ice, and wherein the snow is hid: What time they wax warm, they vanish: when it is hot, they are consumed out of their place" (Job 6.15-17). The Lord had promised to deliver him (1.18-19), but had not done so. He had not fulfilled His promises.

The Lord's reply (vv.19-21)

In His tender mercy, the Lord restores (v.19a), cautions (v.19b), and reassures (vv.20-21) His despairing servant who, like Moses before him, had spoken "unadvisedly with his lips" (Ps 106.33).

Jeremiah's restoration (v.19a)

"If thou return, then will I bring thee again, and thou shalt stand before me: and if thou take forth the precious from the vile, thou shalt be as my mouth." Jeremiah faithfully records the Lord's rebuke. In the first place, he must "return"; his hasty accusation necessitated repentance. The example of Job in this respect should be noted (Job 42.6). In the second place, he must "take forth the precious from the vile", or "if you utter worthy, not worthless words" (Feinberg). Given these conditions, the prophet would again stand before the Lord and be His mouthpiece. It is heartening to notice that Jeremiah did again speak "from the mouth of the Lord" (2 Chr 36.12) and that the captivity in Babylonia eventually ended in fulfillment of "the word of the Lord by the mouth of Jeremiah" (2 Chr 36.21). The Lord's people have every reason to rejoice with David when he said, "He restoreth my soul" (Ps 23.3).

Jeremiah's cautioning (v.19b)

"Let them return unto thee; but return not thou unto them." The man who "sat alone" (v.17) is warned against compromise. If necessary, even though it be fraught with difficulty, he must continue his lonely pathway. At his commissioning, he was told, "be not dismayed at their faces, lest I confound thee before them" (1.17). Ezekiel was also warned against compromise: "Be not thou rebellious like that rebellious house" (Ezek 2.8). Relentless pressure always brings the danger of compromise. It has to be said, sadly, that in some cases very little pressure is necessary to this end.

Jeremiah's reassurance (vv.20-21)

"I will make thee unto this people a fenced brasen wall: and they shall fight against thee, but they shall not prevail against thee: for I am with thee to save thee and to deliver thee, saith the Lord" (v.20). The Lord restates His original promise to Jeremiah (1.18-19). For a brief moment, he had lost sight of the Lord's promise, and without that sure foundation had begun to sink in despair and recrimination. Now, he stands again on the bedrock of God's unchangeable word. The added words provided Jeremiah with even more assurance: "And I will deliver thee out of the hand of the wicked, and I will redeem thee out of the hand of the terrible" (v.21). While Feinberg observes that "This word of encouragement was sufficient for the prophet's need: and though opposition to his message mounted perilously, he never again complained to the Lord as he did in 15.15-18", it has to be said that what has been described as his saddest and bitterest complaint was yet to come (20.7-18).

JEREMIAH 16

While the formula, "The word of the Lord came also unto me" (v.1), introduces a new and distinct message which extends to 17.18, there is a clear connection with the preceding oracle. Having complained bitterly about the lonely path he was called upon to tread (15.17-18), and having been assured of the Lord's presence and preservation on repenting of his hasty accusations (15.19-21), Jeremiah now discovers that his heavy burdens are to be aggravated rather than removed. The Lord promises him no immediate relief in his loneliness. The prophet had been forewarned that his ministry would mean isolation, "speak unto them all that I command thee: be not dismayed at their faces, lest I confound thee before them" (1.17), and now his solitary life is subject to even more limitations. His words, "I sat alone because of thy hand" (15.17) now acquire an additional dimension. It is noteworthy that although Jeremiah was denied the blessings of married life (v.2) he found joy and strength in the Lord whom he describes as "my strength, and my fortress, and my refuge in the day of affliction" (v.19).

The chapter may be divided as follows:

> The Loneliness of Jeremiah (vv.1-9)
> The Dispersion of Israel (vv.10-18)
> The Confession of the Gentiles (vv.19-21).

Verses 1-9: The Loneliness of Jeremiah
Three prohibitions are placed on Jeremiah: he was to forego marriage (vv.1-4), mourning (vv.5-7), and mirth (vv.8-9). "Jeremiah could not have felt the gnawing pain of utter loneliness more intensely than when he heard God speak these words to him" (Jensen). These commands involved considerable sacrifice and self-discipline for Jeremiah. Marriage, mourning, and mirth are perfectly proper, but the Lord's interests took precedence over even legitimate activities. This is a salutary reminder that believers today should not "live unto themselves, but unto him which died for them, and rose again" (2 Cor 5.15). Obedience to the Lord's will continues to involve sacrifice on the part of His people.
As in the case of the sign of the linen girdle (13.1-11), Jeremiah was called upon to proclaim the message by an acted parable. Through these prohibitions and abstentions "Jeremiah's life and activities became a continuous sermon, a visible living word. His whole life had a symbolic dimension. As the alienated prophet he visibly portrayed the complete alienation of God from Judah and the ensuing loneliness of His forsaken people" (Habel).

No marriage (vv.1-4)
"The word of the Lord came also unto me, saying, Thou shalt not take

thee a wife, neither shalt thou have sons or daughters in this place" (vv.1-2). Jeremiah's compliance with the Lord's command not to marry displays complete submission to His will, but at great cost. "The desire to perpetuate the family name led to almost universal marriage in Israel" (Feinberg). In order to convey the word of the Lord, Jeremiah paid a price. This remains the case. Serving the Lord involves a different price for different people. The Lord Jesus referred to those who leave "house, or brethren, or sisters, or father, or mother, or wife, or children, or lands, for my sake, and the gospel's" (Mk 10.29). The words "in this place" (Jerusalem) may imply that the command was limited to Jeremiah's days in the city, and that there was no prohibition to marry after divine judgment had fallen.

Needless to say, the command to Jeremiah should not be understood either as a blanket prohibition on marriage, or as a prohibition on marriage for servants of God. Marriage is God's provision for the orderly arrangement and development of the human race: "Therefore shall a man leave his father and his mother, and shall cleave unto his wife: and they shall be one flesh" (Gen 2.24). It is a provision for this life only (Mk 12.25).

The humanly-imposed injunction, "forbidding to marry" (1 Tim 4.3), suggests that celibacy is superior to marriage: hence the marital status of Romish priests, and the rise of monasticism. It also suggests that marriage is restrictive and inhibiting to the human spirit, but this is nothing less than a denial of the wisdom and goodness of God. People who perpetrate such ideas are divinely censured: "Woe unto them that call evil good, and (even worse) good evil" (Is 5.20). The Word of God teaches that "Marriage is honourable in all, and the bed undefiled: but whoremongers and adulterers God will judge" (Heb 13.4).

The prohibition placed on Jeremiah was a sign, and therefore differs from the position of Paul who did not exercise his liberty to marry. He had "power to lead about a sister, a wife, as well as other apostles" (1 Cor 9.5), but did not do so in the interests of His service for the Lord. In his own words: "He that is unmarried careth for the things that belong to the Lord, how he may please the Lord: But he that is married careth for the things that are of the world, how he may please his wife" (1 Cor 7.32-33). In the case of Jeremiah, the denial of wife and children was a warning of the way in which "the family life of the nation was to be disrupted" (Feinberg). His presence in Jerusalem without the joys and blessings of family life would be a constant reminder to the people that the time was approaching when marriages would no longer be contracted, and the voices of bridegroom and bride would no longer be heard (v.9). The reason follows: "For thus saith the Lord concerning the sons and concerning the daughters that are born in this place, and concerning their mothers that bare them, and concerning their fathers that begat them in this land; They shall die of grievous deaths; they shall not be lamented; neither shall they be buried; but they shall be as dung upon the face of the earth: and they shall be consumed by the sword, and by famine; and their carcases shall be meat for the fowls of heaven, and for the beasts of the earth" (vv.3-4). The words "grievous deaths", or "deadly diseases", suggest "epidemic diseases" (Feinberg). The number of deaths, resulting from war and famine, would be so great that time would not permit mourning or burial. The picture is appalling: "decomposing bodies being eaten by birds and rodents" (Harrison). The same dreadful picture is painted in 15.3.

No mourning (vv.5-7)

Once again, the embargo placed upon Jeremiah was a sign: "For thus saith the Lord, Enter not into the house of mourning, neither go to lament nor bemoan them: for I have taken away my peace from this people, saith the Lord, even lovingkindness and mercies" (v.5). This is quite different from the advice given by Solomon: "A good name is better than precious ointment; and the day of death than the day of one's birth. It is better to go to the house of mourning, than to go to the house of feasting: for that is the end of all men; and the living will lay it to his heart. Sorrow is better than laughter: for by the sadness of the countenance the heart is made better. The heart of the wise is in the house of mourning; but the heart of fools is in the house of mirth" (Eccl 7.1-4). Death should cause serious reflection; it should result in sorrow for sin and sobriety in life. The Lord Jesus went to "the house of mourning" (Lk 8.49-56), and believers are to "weep with them that weep" (Rom 12.15).

According to Feinberg, abstinence from mourning "was abnormal and was cause for criticism". Jeremiah's behaviour in this way would forcibly remind the people that the Lord hath withdrawn his "peace…lovingkindness and mercies" (v.5). The Lord would retract covenant mercy and sympathy from His own people. These verses also emphasise that the death-roll would be so large, and the people would become so accustomed to the situation, that they would lose "the faculty of mourning over the loss" (Laetsch). "Both the great and the small shall die in this land: they shall not be buried, neither shall men lament for them, nor cut themselves, nor make themselves bald for them" (v.6). Reference is made here to the pagan expressions of grief: "cut themselves (as the prophets of Baal: 1 Kings 18.28)…make themselves bald" (as prohibited for Israel: Lev 19.27; Deut 14.1). Shaving the head, or part of the head, was a forbidden pagan custom, but evidently practised by Israel (Ezek 7.18; Amos 8.10; Micah 1.16).

It was the custom to fast at time of death and then, after the burial, for the friends of the mourners to prepare a meal for them. But the dire circumstances described (v.6) meant that even this custom would be abandoned: "Neither shall men tear themselves for them in mourning, to comfort them for the dead; neither shall men given them the cup of consolation to drink for their father or for their mother" (v.7). The words, "Neither shall men tear themselves for them in mourning" are often translated, "break bread for them in mourning" (as in JND). While there is no connection between the bread and wine here and the bread and cup at the Lord's supper (1 Cor 11.23-25), the Lord's people can at least rejoice at the contrast: Israel took bread and wine as they mourned the dead whereas believers take the bread and cup in remembrance of their Lord who said, "I am he that liveth, and was dead; and, behold, I am alive for evermore" (Rev 1.18).

No mirth (vv.8-9)

The third embargo placed upon Jeremiah was also a sign: "Thou shalt not also go into the house of feasting, to sit with them to eat and drink. For thus saith the Lord of hosts, the God of Israel; Behold, I will cause to cease out of this place in your eyes, and in your days, the voice of mirth, and the voice of gladness, the voice of the bridegroom, and the voice of the bride". Similar words are found in 7.34; 25.10; 33.11. The abstinence of Jeremiah in this way was to remind the people of the imminence of divine judgment. It would occur "in your eyes, and in your days" (v.9). As Feinberg observes, Jeremiah "could have little joy at marriage festivities when he remembered the threat hanging over them all".

It could be said that Jeremiah obeyed God's word when others were celebrating, just as Noah "walked with God" (Gen 6.9) when judgment was coming whereas men were "eating and drinking, marrying and giving in marriage...And knew not until the flood came, and took them all away...", to which the Lord Jesus added, "...so shall also the coming of the Son of man be" (Mt 24.38-39). Believers should conduct themselves as "men that wait for their lord" (Lk 12.36). It is sadly possible for even children of God to say, "Soul...take thine ease, eat, drink, and be merry", forgetting that God might say, "This night thy soul shall be required of thee" (Lk 12.19,20).

Verses 10-18: The Dispersion of Israel

The explanation of Jeremiah's "acted parables" would generate questions: "And it shall come to pass, when thou shalt shew this people all these words, and they shall say unto thee, Wherefore hath the Lord pronounced all this great evil against us? or what is our iniquity? or what is our sin that we have committed against the Lord our God? Then shalt thou say unto them..." (vv.10-11). Three things follow: the reason for the dispersion (vv.11-13); the restoration after the dispersion (vv.14-15); and the recompense by the dispersion (vv.16-18).

The reason for the dispersion (vv.11-13)

The questions are quite unbelievable: the people had succumbed to the preaching of the false prophets, who proclaimed, "Peace, peace; when there is no peace" (6.14; 8.11), to the extent that they were completely unaware of their apostasy. A similar passage is found in 5.19. The church at Laodicea was in a similar position: "thou sayest, I am rich, and increased with goods, and have need of nothing; and knowest not that thou art wretched, and miserable, and poor, and blind, and naked" (Rev 3.17). Both passages have a warning voice for believers today; it is sadly possible for the Lord's people to be quite insensitive to their spiritual waywardness. Having urged the believers at Ephesus to "have no fellowship with the unfruitful works of darkness, but rather reprove them", Paul issues a clarion call: "Wherefore he saith, Awake thou that sleepest, and arise from the dead, and Christ shall give thee light. See then that ye walk circumspectly, not as fools, but as wise" (Eph 5.11,14-15).

The answer to the three questions follows. In the first place the Lord had pronounced judgment upon them "Because your fathers have forsaken me, saith the Lord, and have walked after other gods, and have served them, and have worshipped them, and have forsaken me, and have not kept my law" (v.11). Attention is drawn to the expressions "forsaken *me*…have not kept *my law*". The Lord and His word cannot be separated; to forsake one is to forsake the other. A further example occurs in the New Testament: "I marvel that ye are so soon removed from *him that called you* into the grace of Christ unto another gospel" (Gal 1.6). In the second place, and bearing in mind that "The son shall not bear the iniquity of the father" (Ezek 18.20), divine judgment had been pronounced because "ye have done worse than your fathers; for, behold, ye walk every one after the imagination of his evil heart, that they may not hearken unto me" (v.12). They had not learned the lessons from the past, and therefore they were even more culpable. The Lord Jesus made the same point in Matthew 23.29-36.

As a result, the people of Judah and Jerusalem would be deported: "Therefore will I cast you out of this land into a land that ye know not, neither ye nor your fathers; and there shall ye serve other gods day and night; where I will not shew you favour" (v.13). The expression "a land that ye know not" (a similar expression occurs in 14.18 and 15.14) does not mean that they did not know that it existed but rather that they had never lived there. Laetsch observes that "In a land unknown to them and their fathers they would serve idols to their hearts' content, for there He would no longer be gracious to them, but turn them over to their imaginations, the hardness of their own heart". He continues, "Many of the exiled Jews were paganized in Babylon, as were the Jews going down to Egypt against the Lord's will (Jer 44.15-27)". The words, "and there shall ye serve other gods day and night" are "spoken in the bitterness of irony" (Ellicott's Commentary). The commentator there (Plumptre) suggests that since they had "chosen to serve the gods of other nations in (their) own land: therefore, by a righteous retribution, (they) shall serve them in another sense, as being in bondage to their worshippers".

The restoration after the dispersion (vv.14-15)

These verses make clear reference to deliverance from captivity. They imply national deportation, but emphasise restoration. Judgment is never God's last word: "Therefore, behold, the days come, saith the Lord, that it shall no more be said, The Lord liveth, that brought up the children of Israel out of the land of Egypt; But, The Lord liveth, that brought up the children of Israel from the land of the north, and from all the lands whither he had driven them: and I will bring them again into their land that I gave unto their fathers". Feinberg must be right in saying that, rather than an interpolation, as some suggest, the promise occurs at this point "so that the godly among the people might not be overwhelmed with despair". The repatriation of God's people will take place in fulfilment of His faithfulness to the unconditional covenant made with the patriarchs (Gen 12.7; 13.14-17; 26.3; 35.12; Ps 105.8-12). This will be accomplished by divine power (Mt 24.31). The first exodus was amazing: the second exodus will be even more wonderful.

The recompense in the dispersion (vv.16-18)

Returning now to the dispersion, Jeremiah is told: "Behold, I will send for many fishers, saith the Lord, and they shall fish them; and after will I send for many hunters, and they shall hunt them from every mountain, and from every hill, and out of the holes of the rocks" (v.16). The following verses (vv.17-18) make it clear that the "fishers" and the "hunters" are not employed in recovering the nation from captivity. The section describes the judgment of God on His people because of their evil, and prior to the recovery described in vv.14-15. It stresses the thorough nature of coming judgment; this will be inescapable. The "fishers" and "hunters" are the invaders. The Chaldeans, "that bitter and hasty nation, which shall march through the breadth of the land" are described as fishermen: "They take up all of them with the angle, they catch them in their net, and gather them in their drag: therefore they rejoice and are glad. Therefore they sacrifice unto their net, and burn incense unto their drag; because by them their portion is fat, and their meat plenteous. Shall they therefore empty their net, and not spare continually to slay the nations?" (Hab 1.6,15-17). The "prince in Jerusalem" would be one of "fish" in the Chaldeans' net (Ezek 12.10,13). The figure of a fisherman, this time with a fishhook, is also used to describe the Assyrian when deporting the people of Samaria (Amos 4.2). The "fishers" and "hunters" would dislodge the people of Judah and Jerusalem from their hiding places. The same process is described differently by Zephaniah: "And it shall come to pass at that time, that I will search Jerusalem with candles" (Zeph 1.12).

The coming judgment would be inescapable, however much the people attempted to hide on mountains and hills and in "holes of the rocks" (v.16), because the Lord was thoroughly aware of their sinfulness: "For mine eyes are upon all their ways: they are not hid from my face, neither is their iniquity hid from mine eyes" (v.17). The Word of God emphasises His omniscience: "the eyes of the Lord run to and fro throughout the whole

earth" (2 Chr 16.9); "Neither is there any creature that is not manifest in
his sight: but all things are naked and opened unto the eyes of him with
whom we have to do" (Heb 4.13). The fact that the wheels of God's chariot
throne are "full of eyes round about them four" (Ezek 1.18) indicates that
the movements of the throne are governed by His perfect knowledge.

The words, "And first (suggesting that priority must be given to divine
judgment) I will recompense their iniquity and their sin *double*" (v.18) are
most solemn and should be compared with the statement "she hath
received of the Lord's hand double for all her sins" (Is 40.2). The significance
of the word "double" (4932) has been understood in different ways. It has
been suggested that its "exact force…is not to be pressed…it simply points
to an abundance" (Young). According to Feinberg, "the word cannot be
understood outside the context of the Hebrew viewpoint, which used the
term to express ample, full, complete punishment". Commentators refer
to the use of the word on an Alalkah tablet (Alalkah is in the plain of Antioch
in Syria) where it has the sense of "proportionate". It should be said that
the word "double" (8147) means exactly what it says in Exodus 22.4,7,9.
However, since the Lord regarded Israel as "my son, even my firstborn"
(Ex 4.22), and that the "firstborn" received a "double portion" (Deut 21.17),
the use of "double" here might point to the principle that privilege
determines responsibility. If Israel were doubly privileged then, equally, it
was doubly responsible. While the idea of receiving "double" after suffering
points to divine blessing in Isaiah 61.7, the present passage, together with
17.18, refers to the punishment and misery which Judah and Jerusalem
would experience. This was thoroughly deserved: the Lord would
"recompense their iniquity…because they have defiled my land, they have
filled mine inheritance with the carcases of their detestable and abominable
things" (v.18). According to Laetsch, the word "carcases" is singular and is
therefore used in a collective sense. It indicates "not only the lifelessness
of idols, but their unclean, defiling character".

Verses 19-21: The Confession of the Gentiles

The chapter commences with reference to the lonely and isolated
position of Jeremiah (vv.1-9) but it concludes by emphasising that he was
not alone: "O Lord, my strength, and my fortress, and my refuge in the day
of affliction" (v.19). Like Paul, isolated and alone at his "first answer" in
Rome, he could say, in effect, "Notwithstanding the Lord stood with me
and strengthened me" (2 Tim 4.16-17). He could exclaim with David, "The
Lord is my strength and shield; my heart trusted in him, and I am helped"
(Ps 28.7) and with Solomon, "The name of the Lord is a strong tower: the
righteous runneth into it, and is safe" (Prov 18.10). The reason for his joy
is that he had before him "the end of the Lord" (James 5.11). His present
circumstances, necessitated by the dire condition of the nation which was
about to be visited with divine judgment, were illumined not only by the
future restoration of Israel (vv.14-15), but now by the ultimate repentance

and blessing of Gentile nations. Universal blessing lay ahead. This was not the first time that Jeremiah had been made aware of the magnitude of the Lord's mercy: "At that time they shall call Jerusalem the throne of the Lord; and all the nations shall be gathered unto it, to the name of the Lord, to Jerusalem: neither shall they walk any more after the imagination of their evil heart" (3.17). The Gentile nations will recognise two things: the emptiness of idolatry (vv.19-20); and the reality of the Lord (v.21).

The emptiness of idolatry (vv.19-20)

"The Gentiles shall come unto thee from the ends of the earth, and shall say, Surely our fathers have inherited lies, vanity, and things wherein there is no profit" (v.19). The words "things wherein there is no profit" refer to idolatry, and similar expressions occur in 2.8,11. Zephaniah describes the effect of this on idolatry: "The Lord…will famish all the gods of the earth; and men shall worship him, every one from his place, even all the isles of the heathen" (Zeph 2.11). Idols will have no devotees, because all will worship the Lord!

The emptiness of idolatry is stressed by the question, "Shall a man make gods unto himself, and they are no gods?" (v.20). The term "no gods" occurs elsewhere: "whosoever cometh to consecrate himself with a young bullock and seven rams, the same may be a priest of them that are no gods" (2 Chr 13.9); "thy children have forsaken me, and sworn by them that are no gods" (Jer 5.7); "Howbeit then, when ye knew not God, ye did service unto them which by nature are no gods" (Gal 4.8).

The reality of the Lord (v.21)

"Therefore, behold, I will this once cause them to know, I will cause them to know mine hand and my might; and they shall know that my name is The Lord." In that day "The kings of Tarshish and of the isles shall bring presents: the kings of Sheba and Seba shall offer gifts. Yea, all kings shall fall down before him: all nations shall serve him" (Ps 72.10-11); "the earth shall be filled with the knowledge of the glory of the Lord, as the waters cover the sea" (Hab 2.14); "from the rising of the sun even until the going down of the same my name shall be great among the Gentiles" (Mal 1.11).

JEREMIAH 17

The first part of this chapter (vv.1-18) completes the message that commenced in ch.16, and the remaining verses (vv.19-27) are devoted to a new oracle in a new location: "Thus said the Lord unto me; Go and stand in the gate of the children of the people" (v.19).

The way in which Gentile nations will ultimately come to the Lord, confessing their idolatry and receiving divinely-given enlightenment (16.19-21), is contrasted with Judah's preference for evil: "The sin of Judah is written with a pen of iron, and with the point of a diamond" (17.1). A similar passage is found in the prophecy of Malachi: "from the rising of the sun even unto the going down of the same my name shall be great among the Gentiles…But ye have profaned it, in that ye say, The table of the Lord is polluted; and the fruit thereof, even his meat, is contemptible" (Mal 1.11-12). How tragic that the very nation to which the Lord had uniquely revealed Himself should become so adamant in their evil practices! The very people who should have been a role-model to the whole world had lamentably failed. They had persistently disobeyed the very God whose "name shall be continued as long as the sun: and men shall be blessed in him: all nations shall call him blessed" (Ps 72.17).

The chapter may be divided as follows:

> The Sin of Judah (vv.1-13)
> The Service of Jeremiah (vv.14-18)
> The Sanctity of the Sabbath (vv.19-27).

Verses 1-13: The Sin of Judah
The "sin of Judah" (v.1) was exhibited in deep-seated disobedience (vv.1-4); deliberate choice (vv.5-8); deceit of heart (vv.9-11); and departure from the Lord (vv.12-13).

Deep-seated disobedience (vv.1-4)
"The sin of Judah is written with a pen of iron, and with the point of a diamond: it is graven upon the table of their heart, and upon the horns of your altars" (v.1). While the word "written" (3789) does not in itself suggest "engrave" this is evidently the meaning. An iron stylus was used for engraving upon hard surfaces (cp. Job 19.24). According to Gesenius the point of a stylus was made of diamonds, although the word used (8068) does not necessarily indicate this stone. It is rendered "adamant" in Ezekiel 3.9; Zechariah 7.12. Judah's sin was indelible. Idolatry had become an integral part of national life. Attention is drawn to the following:

The description of her sin (vv.1-2)
Judah's sin was *inward*: it was "graven upon the table of their heart"

(v.1). In divine grace and by divine power the inward life of God's people will ultimately undergo an amazing transformation: "I will put my law in their inward parts, and write it in their hearts" (Jer 31.33); "I will give them one heart, and I will put a new spirit within you; and I will take the stony heart out of their flesh, and will give them an heart of flesh" (Ezek 11.19). The Lord's people today are in possession of these new covenant blessings: the believers at Corinth were "manifestly declared to be the epistle of Christ…written not with ink, but with the Spirit of the living God; not in tables of stone, but in fleshy tables of the heart" (2 Cor 3.3).

Judah's sin was *outward*: it was "graven…upon the horns of your altars" (v.1). The state of the heart will always be displayed in practice: "an evil man out of the evil treasure of his heart bringeth forth that which is evil: for of the abundance of the heart his mouth speaketh" (Lk 6.45). The plural "altars" probably points to idolatrous altars rather than, as some suggest, to the brazen altar and altar of incense in the Temple which they had polluted. Details of their practices follow: "their children remember their altars and their groves by the green trees upon the high hills" (v.2). While there are variations, the explanation favoured by Feinberg seems the most acceptable: "the children of Judah will be so steeped in idolatry by their parents that the desire for it will emerge at the slightest provocation". These were altars dedicated to the Baalim, and the groves (poles or wooden columns) were the symbols of the Phoenician goddess Asherah, possibly the same as Astarte. In this connection, the reader is referred to comments made at 7.17-18.

The children were terribly affected by the bad example set before them. There are clear lessons here for the present day. The Old Testament placed a solemn responsibility on one generation to teach the next: "And thou shalt teach them diligently ('impress them', JND) unto thy children" (Deut 6.7). The Psalmist cried, "Now also when I am old and greyheaded, O God, forsake me not; until I have shewed thy strength unto this generation, and thy power to every one that is to come" (Ps 71.18). The New Testament speaks with the same voice: "the things that thou hast heard of me among many witnesses, the same commit thou to faithful men, who shall be able to teach others also" (2 Tim 2.2). This should be compared with Psalm 78.2-7.

The deliverance to her enemies (vv.3-4)

As a result of her iniquities the nation would lose its wealth to her enemies: "O my mountain in the field, I will give thy substance and all thy treasures to the spoil, and thy high places for sin, throughout all thy borders" (v.3). This anticipates the plunder of Jerusalem, perhaps particularly the plunder of the Temple. The city is described in this way because of its "eminent position at the centre of the country" (quoted by Feinberg). It has been pointed out that the word "field" does "not necessarily mean a level field, but the open country in contrast to the city"

(Laetsch). A similar expression occurs later in the book: "Behold, I am against thee, O inhabitant of the valley, and rock of the plain, saith the Lord" (21.13). It is "a poetic phrase…its greatness consisting not in its material elevation above the 'field' or surrounding country, but in being 'my mountain', the mountain of Jehovah" (Ellicott's Commentary).

The words "O my mountain in the field" appear to have the touch of deep pathos about them. The sack of Jerusalem would bring pain to the Lord, as well as loss of inheritance for His people: "And thou, even thyself, shalt discontinue from thine heritage that I gave thee; and I will cause thee to serve thine enemies in the land which thou knowest not: for ye have kindled a fire in mine anger, which shall burn for ever" (v.4). This stresses that Judah herself was responsible for the coming calamity: "And of thyself thou shalt let go thine inheritance which I gave thee" (JND) with the marginal note: "or, 'on thine own account thou shalt leave'". Feinberg quotes the NIV here: "Through your own fault you will lose the inheritance I gave you". The words, "ye have kindled a fire in mine anger, which shall burn for ever", together with 15.14, refer to Deuteronomy 32.22. This does not mean that the Lord's wrath will burn incessantly against Judah nationally, but rather against those that have given themselves to idolatry.

Deliberate choice (vv.5-8)

The heart is involved again: "Thus saith the Lord; Cursed be the man that trusteth in man, and maketh flesh his arm, and whose heart departeth from the Lord" (v.5). The coming judgment described in v.4 was the result of a wrong choice. Judah's trust in man and reliance upon "an arm of flesh" had led them to alliances with Assyria and Egypt. After attempting to buy his way out of trouble, Hezekiah saw the folly of this: "With him (Sennacherib) is an arm of flesh; but with us is the Lord our God to help us, and to fight our battles" (2 Chr 32.8). The hymn puts it clearly:

> Stand up! Stand up for Jesus!
> Stand in His strength alone;
> The arm of flesh will fail you;
> Ye dare not trust your own.
> (G. Duffield)

These verses contrast the results of trusting in man (vv.5-6), and trusting in the Lord (vv.7-8).

Trust in man (vv.5-6)

"He shall be like the heath in the desert, and shall not see when good cometh; but shall inhabit the parched places in the wilderness, in a salt land and not inhabited" (v.6). It has been well said that "where one depends on man, spiritual life cannot thrive; that person is like the dwarf juniper of the desert" (Feinberg). The word rendered "heath" (6199), evidently referring to the tamarisk or dwarf juniper, comes from the same root as "destitute" (Ps 102.17). According to Harrison, the plant has "a particularly stark and naked appearance which has no prospect of improvement, since its stunted roots do not penetrate to the water-levels beneath the surface". The words "shall not see when good cometh" refer to rain that "falls too late on the dead or withered heath" (Ellicott's Commentary). The grim prospects for the "the man that trusteth in man" are spelt out by Laetsch: "All that remains for him is the solitary, parched, salty wilderness of eternal despair and damnation. Cursed indeed!"

Trust in the Lord (vv.7-8)
    "Blessed is the man that trusteth in the Lord, and whose hope the Lord is. For he shall be as a tree planted by the waters, and that spreadeth out her roots by the river, and shall not see (regard or feel) when heat cometh, but her leaf shall be green; and shall not be careful (anxious) in the year of drought, neither shall cease from yielding fruit." This man does not resemble a "heath in the desert" but rather "a tree planted by the waters". He is not conditioned by the "wilderness" of this world, but enjoys the nourishment and life supplied by a perennial stream which finds its source in "the fountain of living waters" (2.13). Whereas the "man that trusteth in man" will "not see when good cometh", this man will not fear when faced with the "heat" of trial and tribulation. These words are almost a paraphrase of Psalm 1.3. In summary, the "man that trusteth in the Lord" enjoys *stability*: "a tree planted"; *fertility*: "roots by the river" (cp. Job 29.19); *continuity*: "her leaf shall be green"; *productivity*: "neither shall cease from yielding fruit".
    Sadly, Judah had chosen "man" and "flesh" with dire results. The child of God today must trust in the Lord, with all the blessings that this brings: growth and fruitfulness are assured. The reason for Judah's dreadful decision follows.

Deceit of heart (vv.9-11)
    For the third time the heart is involved. It should be said that the word "heart" signifies man's inward life. This is evident from the first three occurrences of the word in the Bible: "every imagination of the thoughts of his (man's) heart was only evil continually" (Gen 6.5); "it grieved him (the Lord) at his heart" (Gen 6.6); "the Lord said in his heart, I will not again curse the ground any more for man's sake" (Gen 8.21). These three verses indicate that the word "heart" embraces intellect ("the thoughts of his heart"); emotions (grief is an emotion); volition (or "will"). This gives immense weight to the current verses, and attention is drawn to the following.

The deceitfulness of the heart (v.9)
    "The heart is deceitful above all things, and desperately wicked: who can know it?" The word "deceitful" (6121) means "tortuous" or "crooked";

literally, "following the heel". The name Jacob comes from the same root. The expression "desperately wicked" translates one word (605) meaning "sick" or "beyond cure". It is rendered "incurable" in 15.18; 30.12,15. The heart's greatest deceit is its self-deception, its failure to realise that it is incurable. It is so deceitful that even its owner does not know that it is "desperately wicked". The measure of this can be seen in the oft-repeated expression, "out of the goodness of my heart"! Man's intellect, emotions and will have been invaded by sin and rendered "desperately wicked". The Lord Jesus said, "For out of the heart proceed evil thoughts, murders, adulteries, fornications, thefts, false witness, blasphemies" (Mt 15.19).

The discerner of the heart (vv.10-11)
"I the Lord search the heart, I try the reins, even to give every man according to his ways, and according to the fruit of his doings" (v.10). While men and women do not know their own hearts, hence the rhetorical question, "who can know it?" (v.9), the Lord does know and will ultimately judge in perfect righteousness. His word has the same power: it is "quick, and powerful…piercing even to the dividing asunder of soul and spirit, and of the joints and marrow, and is a discerner of the thoughts and intents of the heart" (Heb 4.12). Samuel was told that "the Lord seeth not as man seeth; for man looketh on the outward appearance, but the Lord looketh on the heart" (1 Sam 16.7). As Laetsch points out, "This Searcher of the heart is also the Judge!". He gives to "every man according to his ways, and according to the fruit of his doings". He judges the inward lives of men and women; He searches the "heart" and tries the "reins". He judges the outward lives of men and women; He is aware of their "ways" and "doings".

The way in which the Lord gives to "every man according to his ways, and according to the fruit of his doings" is now illustrated, and with it "the fatal folly of trusting in anything but the Lord" (Laetsch): "As the partridge sitteth on eggs, and hatcheth them not; so he that getteth riches, and not by right, shall leave them in the midst of his days, and at his end shall be a fool" (v.11), or "As the partridge sitteth on eggs it hath not laid, so is he that getteth riches and not by right" (JND). This verse is not without its difficulties, particularly the fact that partridges do not hatch the eggs of other birds, but it has been pointed out that the word rendered "partridge" (7124) could refer to some variety of sand grouse. Leaving aside the technicality, the meaning is clear: ill-gotten gains are soon lost in the same way as a bird is soon bereft of the brood she has not hatched. It appears that the warning is given here in view of the evil example set by King Jehoiakim (22.13-19). He certainly ended his days on earth as a fool! The New Testament comments as follows: "But they that will be rich fall into temptation and a snare…For the love of money is the root of all evil: which while some coveted after, they have erred from the faith, and pierced themselves through with many sorrows" (1 Tim 6.9-10).

Departure from the Lord (vv.12-13)

The impermanence of unjustly acquired riches (v.11) gives place to the permanent security afforded by the throne of the Lord: "A glorious high throne from the beginning is the place of our sanctuary" (v.12). While most commentators suggest that this refers to Jerusalem (cp. 3.17; 14.21), the language strongly suggests a heavenly Sanctuary: "For he hath looked down from the height of his sanctuary; from heaven did the Lord behold the earth" (Ps 102.19); "Thus saith the Lord, The heaven is my throne, and the earth is my footstool" (Is 66.1). When Judah, under Ahaz, sought help from Assyria, Isaiah counselled otherwise: "Sanctify the Lord of hosts himself; and let him be your fear, and let him be your dread. And he shall be for a sanctuary" (Is 8.13-14). Believers today have "a glorious high throne" as their Sanctuary: it is called "the throne of grace" (Heb 4.16) and "the throne of the Majesty in the heavens" (Heb 8.1).

In view of this, how could the Lord's people forsake Him in favour of unjust gain or, for that matter, in favour of anything? He was their true hope (v.13) as opposed to riches which "certainly make themselves wings; they fly away as an eagle toward heaven" (Prov 23.5). Having said of such a person that "his end shall be a fool" (v.11), Jeremiah adds, "all that forsake thee shall be ashamed, and they that depart from me shall be written in the earth, because they have forsaken the Lord, the fountain of living waters" (v.13). Those who forsake the Lord "are as unenduring as names written in the dust" (Feinberg). Their names would certainly not be "written in heaven" (Lk 10.20). The section therefore concludes by contrasting the impermanence of life outside fellowship with the Lord and the permanence of divine blessing from "the fountain of living waters". The New Testament refers to this verse in warning believers today: "Take heed, brethren, lest there be in any of you an evil heart of unbelief, in departing from the living God" (Heb 3.12).

Verses 14-18: The Service of Jeremiah

The unwelcome ministry of Jeremiah did not leave him unscathed, and he was certainly not unaffected by the unfavourable response of the people. His faithful service had brought him nothing but difficulty, and he now pleads for divine help. This leads to an illuminating insight into his pastoral work. Attention is drawn to his plea for deliverance (v.14); his predictions were questioned (v.15); his pastoral ministry (v.16); and his persecutors' judgment (vv.17-18).

His plea for deliverance (v.14)

"Heal me, O Lord, and I shall be healed; save me, and I shall be saved." It is suggested that the healing and salvation he desires refers to the damage inflicted on him by his opponents. Verbal abuse can be as damaging as physical affliction. The confidence with which he makes his appeal follows: "for thou art my praise". He speaks of the Lord as "He whom I have to praise for past benefits as well as future favours" (Unger). Jeremiah would have found a kindred spirit in David: "Hold not thy peace, O God of my praise" (Ps 109.1).

His predictions were questioned (v.15)

The need for healing and salvation arose from the taunts and sneers of the people: "Behold, they say unto me, Where is the word of the Lord? let it come now ('let it be fulfilled')". Jeremiah had consistently predicted the fall of Jerusalem, but the city was still intact. Their taunting unbelief has its counterpart in "the last days" when "scoffers, walking after their own lusts" will say, "Where is the promise of his coming? for since the fathers fell asleep, all things continue as they were from the beginning of the creation?" (2 Pet 3.3-4). It seems possible that Jeremiah's opponents were citing Moses: "When a prophet speaketh in the name of the Lord, if the thing follow not, nor come to pass, that is the thing which the Lord hath not spoken" (Deut 18.22). The fulfilment of the word of the Lord was something in which Jeremiah had no delight (v.16). The people had no concept of what they were saying! The word of the Lord by Jeremiah was ultimately fulfilled, just as "the day of the Lord will come" (2 Pet 3.10).

His pastoral ministry (v.16)

Jeremiah was a faithful and compassionate shepherd, and the following features of his work should be noted.

He did not leave his work

Other pastors had utterly failed (2.8; 10.21), but Jeremiah did not hasten, or hurry away, from his pastoral responsibilities. "I have not hastened from being a shepherd in following thee" (JND), or "I have not run away from being your shepherd" (NIV, quoted by Feinberg). Only the "hireling…leaveth the sheep, and fleeth" (Jn 10.12). Assembly shepherds are to hold "fast the faithful word" in order "by sound doctrine both to exhort and to convince the gainsayers" (Titus 1.9). Since the word "shepherd" usually refers to a king in the Old Testament, its use here indicates the abysmal leadership of the monarchy.

He took no delight in coming judgment

Jeremiah found no joy in predicting doom: "neither have I desired the woeful day". His enemies had evidently accused him of wanting judgment to overtake the nation. The "woeful day ('fatal day', JND)" was the day on which the city would fall. Coming judgment must never be the occasion of exuberant joy, rather of sorrowful intercession. Jeremiah had stood before the Lord on behalf of the people and had endeavoured to turn away His wrath from them (18.20).

He faithfully communicated God's word

"That which came out of my lips was right before thee." Paul followed in the footsteps of Jeremiah in saying, "For we are not as many, which corrupt the word of God: but as of sincerity, but as of God, in the sight of God speak we in Christ" (2 Cor 2.17); "For our exhortation was not of deceit, nor of uncleanness, nor in guile…For neither at any tine used we flattering words, as ye know, nor a cloke of covetousness; God is witness" (1 Thess 2.3,5).

His persecutors' judgment (vv.17-18)

"Be not a terror unto me: thou art my hope in the day of evil" (v.17). Jeremiah evidently felt that as a result of his loyalty to the Lord and His word, he might be left to face his enemies alone, and cries to Him for protection and deliverance. He therefore asks the Lord to fulfil His initial promise to preserve him (1.17-19). In order to be vindicated before his enemies Jeremiah's predictions must be fulfilled, and the prophet prays accordingly: "Let them be confounded that persecute me, but let not me be confounded: let them be dismayed, but let not me be dismayed: bring upon them the day of evil, and destroy them with double destruction" (v.18). As Feinberg points out, "There is no contradiction between v.18 and v.16 because the people in view are not the same". For the meaning of "double destruction" the reader is referred to comments made at 16.18.

Verses 19-27: The Sanctity of the Sabbath

In pronouncing this new message, Jeremiah was required to "Go and stand in the gate of the children of the people, whereby the kings of Judah come in, and by the which they go out, and in all the gates of Jerusalem" (v.19). The "gate of the children of the people" is not clearly identified. It was apparently one of the Temple gates, but the message was to be proclaimed "in all the gates of Jerusalem", which evidently refers to the city gates. The message of these verses is summed up in the words "hallow ye the sabbath day" (v.22), and "hallow the sabbath day" (vv.24,27).

In the first place the sabbath recognised the Lord as Creator, and therefore refuted idolatry. It was "the sign between the Lord and Israel and a perpetual reminder to them of their separation to God" (Unger) and this is earlier confirmed: "it is a sign between me and you throughout your generations; that ye may know that I am the Lord that doth sanctify you" (Ex 31.13). The sabbath is first mentioned by name in Exodus 16.23: "This is that which the Lord hath said, To morrow is the rest of the holy sabbath unto the Lord". Its association with the manna indicates that it was a day in which the nation was to enjoy the Lord's goodness and provision. It was also a day in which His people were to remember their deliverance from Egypt: "But the seventh day is the sabbath of the Lord thy God: in it thou shalt not do any work…And remember that thou wast a servant in the land of Egypt, and that the Lord thy God brought thee out thence through a mighty hand and by a stretched out arm: therefore the Lord thy God commanded thee to keep the sabbath day" (Deut 5.14-15).

For the Lord's people to pollute the sabbath was therefore to treat their deliverance and redemption lightly. The keeping of the sabbath was to be regarded as the means of honouring God who had so blessed them; it was therefore to be "a delight...holy...honourable" (Is 58.13).

While sabbath-keeping is not a divine requirement in the current dispensation, God's people today must not allow anything in their lives which either reduces, minimises, or even removes their appreciation of the goodness of "God our Saviour" (Titus 2.10). Commerce and pleasure, with their demands on time and energy, can so easily make believers forget His claims upon them. He has every right to their devotion, and they are to live and act in a way that honours Him and brings Him pleasure.

The message of Jeremiah has three component parts: the failure to keep the sabbath (vv.20-23); the blessings through keeping the sabbath (vv.24-26); and the consequences of profaning the sabbath (v.27).

The failure to keep the sabbath (vv.20-23)

Jeremiah was required to remind the people of the Lord's commandment, "Remember the sabbath day, to keep it holy" (Ex 20.8): "Take heed to yourselves, and bear no burden on the sabbath day, nor bring it in by the gates of Jerusalem...but hallow ye the sabbath day, as I commanded your fathers" (vv.21-22). But the commandment had not been kept: "they obeyed not, neither inclined their ear, but made their neck stiff, that they might not hear, nor receive instruction" (v.23). Approximately 160 years later, Nehemiah was confronted by the same situation (Neh 13.15-22).

The blessings through keeping the sabbath (vv.24-26)

Obedience to the word of the Lord would secure three distinct blessings: the continuance of the throne of David - "Then shall there enter into the gates of this city kings and princes sitting upon the throne of David, riding in chariots and on horses, they, and their princes, the men of Judah, and the inhabitants of Jerusalem" (v.25); the permanent settlement of Jerusalem - "and this city shall remain for ever" (v.25); and the resumption and continuance of Temple worship at the heart of national life - "And they shall come from the cities of Judah, and from the places about Jerusalem, and from the land of Benjamin, and from the plain (the Shephelah, the lowlands between the Judean mountains and the Mediterranean Sea), and from the mountains (the central highland ridge), and from the south (the Negev, the desert south of Judah), bringing burnt offerings, and sacrifices, and meat offerings, and incense, and bringing sacrifices of praise (thank-offerings), unto the house of the Lord". The passage must be understood as a *bona fide* appeal to the nation even though divine wrath was imminent. The fact that it was ignored does not mean that the Lord's desires for His people will never be fulfilled. In the millennial Kingdom, the Lord's people will hallow His sabbaths (Ezek 44.24) and "the people of the land shall worship at the door of this gate ('the gate of the inner court that looketh toward the east') before the Lord in the sabbaths and in the new moons" (Ezek 46.1,3).

The consequences of profaning the sabbath (v.27)

The passage concludes with the consequences of disobedience. The city would be destroyed: "But if ye will not hearken unto me to hallow the sabbath day, and not to bear a burden, even entering in at the gates of Jerusalem on the sabbath day; then will I kindle a fire in the gates thereof, and it shall devour the palaces of Jerusalem, and it shall not be quenched". A similar passage, detailing the blessings of obeying the word of God and the consequences of disobedience, is found in 22.1-7.

JEREMIAH 18

The Word of God often uses commonplace objects and experiences to teach important spiritual lessons. Jeremiah was prepared for future service by lessons drawn from "a rod of an almond tree" and "a seething pot" (1.11-14). Now, in the opening verses of this chapter, he is asked to watch a potter at work: "The word which came to Jeremiah from the Lord, saying, Arise, and go down to the potter's house" (vv.1-2). This is probably the most familiar of the figures employed in the book. The lessons from the potter's house are not unconnected with the preceding message in which the Lord had promised to bless His people if they turned from their disobedience and were prepared to "hallow the sabbath day", with the solemn warning of sweeping judgment if they refused (17.19-27), cp. 18.7-10.

This oracle clearly divides into three sections:

> The Lesson of the Potter (vv.1-10): "cannot I do with you as this potter?" (v.6)
> The Appeal to the People (vv.11-17): "return ye now every one from his evil way, and make your ways and your doings good" (v.11)
> The Rejection of the Prophet (vv.18-23): "Come, and let us devise devices against Jeremiah" (v.18).

Verses 1-10: The Lesson of the Potter

This section of the chapter is in two parts: the illustration (vv.1-4) and the interpretation (vv.5-10). To these can be added: the application.

The illustration (vv.1-4)

Jeremiah delivered his previous message "in the gate of the children of the people" (17.19), but the potter's house was evidently outside the city. It is generally thought that he went down to the slopes of the Valley of Hinnom, to the south of Jerusalem, where water and clay were found. The simple obedience of Jeremiah must not be overlooked: "Arise, and go down to the potter's house, and *there* I will cause thee to hear my words. Then I went down to the potter's house" (vv.2-3). Elijah was similarly instructed: "Get thee hence, and turn thee eastward, and hide thyself by the brook Cherith...and I have commanded the ravens to feed thee *there*" (1 Kings 17.3-4); "Arise, get thee to Zarephath...behold, I have commanded a widow woman *there* to sustain thee" (1 Kings 17.9). Servants of God are only taught and fed when they obey the Lord!

The prophet describes the potter at work: "Then I went down to the potter's house, and, behold, he wrought a work on the wheels" (v.3). The "wheels" refer to the upper and lower horizontal stones used in the ancient craft of the potter. The lower "wheel" was operated by the foot, and attached by an axle to the upper "wheel" on which the clay was worked.

Two things happened that day in the course of the potter's work.

"The vessel that he made of clay was marred in the hand of the potter" (v.4a)

This was not through the mismanagement of the potter, as the explanation makes clear (vv.9-10), but because of a defect in the clay itself. The work could be marred by the presence of a foreign body, or a hard lump in the clay.

"He made it again another vessel, as seemed good to the potter to make it" (v.4b).

It is important to notice the ability of the potter to work in this way. He did not cast aside the clay, but re-used it: "he made it again another vessel". As Meyer observes, "It was a memorial of the potter's patience and longsuffering, of his careful use of material, and of his power of repairing loss and making something out of failure and disappointment".

The interpretation (vv.5-10)

It must be said that the potter's work as described above is used as an illustration of the Lord's work in relation to Israel, although the parable is meant principally for Judah (v.11). He can do with Israel what the potter did with the clay: "Then the word of the Lord came to me, saying, O house of Israel, cannot I do with you as this potter? saith the Lord. Behold, as the clay is in the potter's hand, so are ye in mine hand, O house of Israel" (vv.5-6). Israel (the whole nation), likened here to a vessel "marred in the hand of the potter", can be "another vessel" (v.4).

The application emphasises the *power* of the potter, rather than any *arbitrary decision* by the potter. "There is one important difference between men and clay. Clay is a lifeless substance. It is entirely passive in the potter's hands. Men and women are the glory of God's creation, endued with life, and possessing wills of their own. They know the difference between right and wrong, and have the capability to make moral choices. The Potter's hand on them is sovereign, but never shapes them contrary to their own will. Entire responsibility for their actions and for their final end is laid upon them" (Goddard). These verses display what Feinberg calls "a true but mysterious blending of the divine sovereignty and human responsibility".

The passage emphasises the conditional element in the Lord's dealings with nations generally, and therefore widens the application; what can be true for Israel (v.6) can be true for any nation (vv.7-10). Whatever the nation, He "does not exercise His omnipotence arbitrarily or capriciously, but conditions everything ethically" (Feinberg). The will of the divine Potter will be done, but always on the principles of perfect grace (vv.7-8) and perfect righteousness (vv.9-10).

A nation that repents can be saved from destruction in the same way that a potter does not destroy the clay, but reshapes it: "At what instant I shall speak concerning a nation, and concerning a kingdom, to pluck up, and to pull down, and to destroy it; If that nation, against whom I have pronounced, turn from their evil, I will repent of the evil that I thought to do unto them" (vv.7-8).

A nation that will not repent will not be refashioned: "And at what instant I shall speak concerning a nation, and concerning a kingdom, to build and to plant it; If it do evil in my sight, that it obey not my voice, then I will repent of the good, wherewith I said I would benefit them" (vv.9-10).

In both cases, "Repentance can always change the Lord's decree of judgment" (Feinberg). It must be borne in mind that divine repentance is altogether different from human repentance. "God is not a man, that he should lie; neither the son of man, that he should repent" (Num 23.19). However, the Lord does repent! But He does not repent as men and women repent, for the simple reason that He has never done wrong. With the Lord, repentance is not a change of mind and will, but a response consistent with a change of conduct on the part of a nation as in the case of Nineveh: "And God saw their works, that they turned from their evil way; and God repented of the evil, that he had said that he would do unto them; and he did it not" (Jonah 3.10).

Very clearly, in divine grace the Lord is giving Judah and Jerusalem the opportunity to repent: "Thus saith the Lord…return ye now every one from his evil way (v.11), but their failure to do so at that time (v.12) does not mean that His "marred" people (v.4) have been permanently rejected. The clay remains in the Potter's hand and when, at the end-time, national repentance takes place, He will make it "again another vessel" (v.4; cp. Zech 12.10-13.1).

The application

God desires that every one of His people should be a "vessel unto honour, sanctified, and meet for the master's use, and prepared unto every good work" (2 Tim 2.21). With this in view children of God should be as yielding as clay in His gracious hands. The New Testament reveals the purpose of the Master Potter for them: "For whom he did foreknow, he also did predestinate to be conformed to the image of his Son, that he might be the firstborn among many brethren" (Rom 8.29). His work begins with a shapeless piece of clay which, through the skill and strength of the Potter's fingers, becomes a vessel for His praise and glory! Like the potter observed by Jeremiah, there is never any mismanagement on His part, even though, at times, His skill is not readily understood. One thing is sure: He makes no mistakes. Weak men are not in a position to question the wisdom of God. To criticise His ways is akin to the absurdity of the clay pot challenging the potter, or the impropriety of child questioning its birth: "Shall the clay say to him that fashioneth it, What makest thou? or thy work, He hath no hands? Woe unto him that saith unto his father, What begettest thou? or to the woman, What hast thou brought forth?" (Is 45.9-10).

Failure to understand God's ways should never cause His people to question His superior wisdom, but rather to say:

> Have thine own way, Lord!
> Have Thine own way!
> Thou art the Potter; I am the clay.
> Mould me and make me after Thy will,
> While I am waiting, yielded and still.
>
> Have Thine own way, Lord!
> Have Thine own way!
> Hold o'er my being absolute sway!
> Fill with Thy Spirit till all shall see
> Christ only, always, living in me.
>   (A. A. Pollard)

But how often He has to make them again, causing them to cry: "But now, O Lord, thou art our father; we are the clay, and thou our potter; and we all are the work of thy hand. Be not wroth very sore, O Lord, neither remember iniquity for ever: behold, see, we beseech thee, we are all thy people" (Is 64.8-9).

The ability of the divine Potter to make His people again is clear from Scripture. "He made Jacob again, when He met him at the Jabbok ford; finding him a supplanter and a cheat, but after a long wrestle, leaving him a prince with God. He made Simon again, on the resurrection morning, when He found him somewhere near the open grave, the son of a dove - for so his old name Bar-jonas signified - and left him Peter, the man of the rock, the apostle of Pentecost. He made Mark again, between his impulsive leaving of Paul and Barnabas, as though frightened by the first touch of sea-sickness, and the times when Peter spake of him as his son, and Paul from the Mamertime prison described him as being profitable" (Meyer). His grace is so evident, reminding us, in different imagery, that "A bruised reed shall he not break, and the smoking flax shall he not quench" (Is 42.3).

Verses 11-17: The Appeal to the People

It is very clear that these verses bring the message of the potter's house to bear upon the nation. The Lord had said, "If that nation, against whom I have pronounced, turn from their evil, I will repent of the evil that I thought to do unto them" (v.8). Jeremiah is therefore instructed to convey this very message to Judah and Jerusalem (v.11). The Lord had also said that if that nation "do evil in my sight, that it obey not my voice, then I will repent of the good, wherewith I said I would benefit them" (v.10). Since this was the case, Jeremiah is instructed to pronounce divine judgment on them (vv.15-17). This part of the chapter describes the appeal (v.11); the answer (v.12); and the anger (vv.13-17).

The appeal (v.11)

"Now therefore go to, speak to the men of Judah, and to the inhabitants of Jerusalem, saying, Thus saith the Lord; Behold, I frame evil against you, and devise a device against you: return ye now every one from his evil way, and make your ways and your doings good." It was an urgent appeal: "return ye *now* every one from his evil way". Judgment was imminent. A similar urgency pervaded His appeal through Isaiah: "Seek ye the Lord while he may be found, call ye upon him while he is near" (Is 55.6). Significantly, the word "frame" (3335) means, literally, "to form, or fashion, as a potter, clay" (Gesenius). According to Feinberg, "The Hebrew verb is the same as the word for potter, so there is a play on words".

The answer (v.12)

"And they said, There is no hope: but *we will* walk after our own devices, and *we will* every one do the imagination of his evil heart." There is no evidence of "yielding clay" here! This is not the first time that Jeremiah had encountered such obduracy: "There is no hope: no; for I have loved strangers, and after them will I go" (2.25). According to Ellicott's Commentary, the present tense is used here: "But they say…". This was "the ever-recurring answer which they made to the prophet's pleas. It was the answer of defiance rather than of despair".

The anger (vv.13-17)

Such a response to the Lord's appeal cannot pass unheeded. Time had run out for Judah and the solemn implications of their behaviour are spelt out (vv.13-15) before judgment is announced (vv.16-17).

They had marred their testimony for the Lord

"Therefore thus saith the Lord; Ask ye now among the heathen, who hath heard such things: the virgin of Israel hath done a very horrible thing" (v.13). Similar condemnation is found in Jeremiah's earlier ministry: "pass over the isles of Chittim, and see; and send unto Kedar, and consider diligently, and see if there be such a thing. Hath a nation changed their gods, which are yet no gods? but my people have changed their glory for that which doth not profit" (2.10-11). The Lord's people had become worse than the heathen. The expression, "the virgin of Israel", stresses that the nation "should have kept herself untainted by pagan orgiastic rites, just as an unmarried woman keeps herself chaste for her future husband" (Harrison). This emphasises the culpability of the nation.

They had turned from the blessings of the Lord

"Will a man leave the snow of Lebanon which cometh from the rock of the field? or shall the cold flowing waters that come from another place be forsaken?" (v.14), or "Shall the snow of Lebanon cease from the rock of the field? Shall the cool flowing waters coming from afar be dried up?" (JND). According to Feinberg this verse is "unusually obscure" and some commentators go to great lengths in giving the various ways in which it could be understood. Without criticising the painstaking work of scholars, it is worth bearing in mind the aphorism, "Beware of long explanations" (J. Hunter). The simplest explanation often proves to be the best! Ellicott's Commentary is clear: "The strength of Jehovah was like the unfailing snow of Lebanon (the 'white' or snow mountain), like the dashing stream that flows from heights so distant that they belong to a strange country, and which along its whole course was never dried up, and yet men forsook that strength for their own devices". Feinberg is in agreement: "The snow from Lebanon and cold running water are dependable, but Judah had proved herself fickle in the extreme. Her conduct has been wholly unnatural...Nature's reliability puts to shame Judah's instability". Men will not leave a dependable supply of water, but Judah had forsaken God, "the fountain of living waters" (2.13; 17.13).

They had forgotten their relationship with the Lord
"Because my people hath forgotten me, they have burned incense to vanity" (v.15). As previously (2.11,13,32), He calls them "my people", but they had acted as if this were not the case. They were devoted to idols, described here as "vanity", with the result that "they (the false prophets and false priests) have caused them to stumble in their ways from the ancient paths, to walk in paths, in a way not cast up" (v.15). According to Ellicott's Commentary, different words are translated "paths" here. The "ancient paths" (5769,7635) are, literally, "the paths of the age, or of eternity", and "point to the old immemorial faith of the patriarchs". The second reference to "paths" (5410) implies rather "by-ways", as contrasted with the "way cast up" or "raised causeway...on which a man could not well lose his way". Put differently: "The nation had lost its way. The ancient paths were those of blessing through obeying the Lord (cp. 6.16). The contrast is between a rough track in the country and an elevated causeway" (Feinberg). The results follow.

(a) The land would be desolate. The land would be "desolate ('an astonishment', JND), and a perpetual hissing" (v.16). "The Hebrew word rendered 'hissing' (8292) is onomatopoetic, and expresses the inarticulate sound which we utter on seeing anything that makes us shudder, rather than 'hissing' in its modern use as an expression of contempt or disapproval" (Ellicott's Commentary).

(b) The passers by would be amazed. "Every one that passeth thereby shall be astonished, and wag his head" (v.16; cp. 2 Chr 7.21-22). The same passers-by "shall be astonished and hiss because of all the plagues thereof" (19.8). But amazement would not be limited to the passers-by: "The kings of the earth, and all the inhabitants of the world, would not have believed

that the adversary and the enemy should have entered into the gates of Jerusalem" (Lam 4.12). Unlike Judah and Jerusalem, all believers, not only "younger women", must "give none occasion to the adversary to speak reproachfully" (1 Tim 5.14).

   (c) The people would be scattered "I will scatter them as with an east wind (the sirocco, a hot dry wind coming from the eastern deserts) before the enemy; I will shew them the back, and not the face, in the day of their calamity" (v.17). This is exactly what they had done to the Lord: "they have turned their back unto me, and not their face" (2.27). The "face" of the Lord indicates His favour: "The Lord bless thee, and keep thee: The Lord make his face shine upon thee, and be gracious unto thee: The Lord lift up his countenance upon thee, and give thee peace" (Num 6.24-26).

Verses 18-23: The Rejection of the Prophet
   As a result of his faithful preaching, Jeremiah faced a further conspiracy towards him, cp. 11.18-23; 12.6; 15.10-11. The passage records their antagonism towards him (v.18); and his prayer for judgment on them (vv.19-23).

Their antagonism towards him (v.18)
   "Then said they, Come, and let us devise devices against Jeremiah." His enemies deeply resented the way in which he attacked the *status quo* in Judah by disturbing or threatening "the established order of society in which the official priests pronounced the authoritative interpretation of God's law, the wise men gave appropriate counsel for social, moral, and political issues, and the professional prophet gave official oracles to popular requests for valid answers from God" (Habel). All three classes would prove impotent when judgment fell: "Mischief shall come upon mischief, and rumour shall be upon rumour; then shall they seek a vision of the prophet; but the law shall perish from the priest, and counsel from the ancients" (Ezek 7.26). They opposed the Lord's servant in three ways.

They said that they did not need him
   "The law shall not perish from the priest, nor counsel from the wise, nor the word from the prophet." They were perfectly satisfied with their leaders, which is not surprising since they told the people exactly what they wanted to hear! They cried, "Peace, peace; when there is no peace" (6.14; 8.11). Moreover, "The prophets prophesy falsely, and the priests bear rule by their means (their own authority); and my people love to have it so" (5.31). It is no small wonder they did all in their power to silence Jeremiah! "The priests said not, Where is the Lord? and they that handle the law knew me not: the pastors also transgressed against me, and the prophets prophesied by Baal, and walked after things that do not profit" (2.8). Truth was rejected in favour of error.

They attempted to silence him

"Let us smite him with the tongue." Feinberg suggests that they proposed to charge Jeremiah with treason: "His messages against Judah's policies provide ample basis for accusing him of treason". They levelled the same accusation against the Lord Jesus: "We found this fellow perverting the nation, and forbidding to give tribute to Caesar, saying that he himself is Christ a King" (Lk 23.2). Their opposition was more than verbal - they plotted to kill Jeremiah: "Lord, thou knowest all their counsel against me to slay me" (v.23). Later, Pashur, the son of Immer, "smote Jeremiah the prophet, and put him in the stocks that were in the high gate of Benjamin" (20.1-2). This is a salutary reminder that "all that will live godly in Christ Jesus shall suffer persecution" (2 Tim 3.12).

They decided to ignore him

"Let us not give heed to any of his words." They would rather listen to the voice of falsehood, than to the voice of the Lord.

His prayer for judgment on them (vv.19-23)

The people, perhaps the leaders particularly, would not heed him (v.18), but Jeremiah now calls on the Lord to heed him: "Give heed to me, O Lord, and hearken to the voice of them that contend with me" (v.19). In saying, "Shall evil be recompensed for good? For they have digged a pit for my soul", he refers to the "good" that he had showed to Judah: "Remember that I stood before thee to speak good for them, and to turn away thy wrath from them" (v.20). Like Amos before him (Amos 7.1-6), Jeremiah had repeatedly prayed for them (14.7-9, 19-22) only to be rejected by the very people whose welfare he sought.

While his prayer for divine judgment upon his enemies is "admittedly strong" (Feinberg), it was not just a cry for personal vindication but rather for the Lord to avenge the rejection of His word. "The prophet had always been faithful to his people and to his God. Now let God be faithful to His word and fulfil His threats...which His loyal messenger had proclaimed so boldly even against his personal feelings. The prayer of the prophet not to forgive the iniquity of these self-hardened people merely re-echoes the Lord's refusal to forgive (cp. 7.16; 14.10-12; 15.1,6; 16.5)" (Laetsch). While it could be argued that the imprecations in these verses are directed against the apostate nation in its entirety, it seems more likely that he has particularly in mind those that directly accused him ("them that contend with me", v.19). Particular mention is made of "their children...their wives...their children...their men...their young men...Let a cry be heard from their houses, when thou shalt bring a troop suddenly upon them: for they have digged a pit to take me, and hid snares for my feet. Yet, Lord, thou knowest all their counsel against me to slay me: forgive not their iniquity, neither blot out their sin from thy sight, but let them be overthrown before thee; deal thus with them in the time of thine anger" (vv.21-23).

When judgment fell it was Judah's leadership that particularly suffered (cp. 39.6; 52.24-27).

The attitude of children of God today should be markedly different: "Love your enemies, bless them that curse you, do good to them that hate you, and pray for them that despitefully use you, and persecute you" (Mt 5.44). The Lord Jesus was the perfect example of His own teaching: "Who, when he was reviled, reviled not again; when he suffered, he threatened not; but committed himself to him that judgeth righteously" (1 Pet 2.23). On the cross, He prayed, ""Father, forgive them; for they know not what they do" (Lk 23.34).

JEREMIAH 19

In the previous chapter the "house of Israel" is described as "clay…in the potter's hand" (18.6), but the picture now changes and the nation is likened to a broken "potter's vessel, that cannot be made whole again" (19.11). Ellicott's Commentary describes the solemn teaching in this chapter as "the darker side of the imagery of 18.3-4. There the vessel was still on the potter's wheel, capable of being re-shaped. Now we have the vessel which has been baked and hardened. No change is possible. If it is unfit for the uses for which it was designed, there is nothing left but to break it. As such it became now the fit symbol of the obdurate people of Israel". The lesson of the broken bottle is clearly stated at the conclusion of the chapter: "Behold, I will bring upon this city and upon all her towns all the evil that I have pronounced against it, because they have hardened their necks, that they might not hear my words" (v.15). The symbol of the "potter's earthen bottle" (v.1) extends the message of the "marred" vessel (18.4). The Lord's sovereignty and long-suffering are emphasised in "the potter's house" (18.2), whereas the complete and irreversible nature of impending judgment is emphasised in "the valley of the son of Hinnom" (19.2).

Jeremiah's preaching at this time caused considerable disquiet to Pashur who put the prophet "in the stocks that were in the high gate of Benjamin" (20.1-2), an indignity which would hardly have been bestowed upon the prophet in the reign of Josiah. As Laetsch observes, "No temple guard would have dared to imprison Jeremiah as long as this pious king and friend of Jeremiah occupied the throne". There seems therefore little reason to doubt the general opinion that chs.18-20 refer to events which took place in the early years of Jehoiakim's reign.

The chapter falls into two clear sections:

> The Prophecy in Tophet (vv.1-13)
> The Prophecy in the Temple (vv.14-15).

Verses 1-13: The Prophecy in Tophet
This took place before "the ancients of the people, and…the ancients of the priests" (v.1). Jeremiah was told how to prepare (vv.1-2) and what to proclaim (vv.3-13).

The preparation (vv.1-2)
"Thus saith the Lord, Go and get a potter's earthen bottle, and take of the ancients of the people, and of the ancients of the priests; And go forth unto the valley of the son of Hinnom, which is by the entry of the east gate." The prophet is specifically told what to take, whom to take, and where to go.

What he was to take (v.1)

Nearly all commentators remark on the onomatopoetic nature of the Hebrew word (1228) rendered "bottle" ('flagon', JND), "sounding like the gurgling of outpouring water" (Feinberg). Attention has already been drawn to significance of the vessel; it symbolised the final form of Judah's spiritual obduracy. Like the "earthen bottle", the nation had become hardened in their rebellion against the Lord and in their rejection of His word.

Whom he was to take (v.1)

Jeremiah was to take representatives of the civil and ecclesiastical rulers to witness the "acted prophecy" (Ellicott's Commentary) about to take place in "the valley of the son of Hinnom". These were men who occupied positions of honour because of their age or rank. As representatives of the leadership, they were about to witness in symbolic form the terrible result of their failure to guide properly the Lord's people. Perhaps Laetsch is just a little imaginative in saying, "In solemn procession the prophet, carrying the bottle, and the representatives of the priesthood and civic power marched through the streets of Jerusalem, attracting wide attention. Soon multitudes of people gathered and followed the dignitaries, anxious to ascertain the purpose of this strange procession".

Where he was to go (v.2)

Jeremiah and his party were to go to the valley of Hinnom via the "Pottery-gate" (JND). The translation "east gate" (AV) comes from "equating the Hebrew word (2777) with the archaic word for 'sun'…hence, the east gate. Jerome preferred a connection with the word for 'earthenware', which is probably correct" (Feinberg). Bearing in mind that Jeremiah had been previously instructed to "go down to the potter's house" (18.2), and that it is generally thought that he went down to the slopes of the Valley of Hinnom where water and clay were found, it seems likely that the "pottery gate" led not only to the potter's house but to the place where the potter's waste was dumped. It has been suggested that the gate in question is elsewhere known as the "dung gate" (Neh 3.14). Both the dung gate and the fountain gate led into the valley of Hinnom. Because it had been connected with child-sacrifice (cp. Jer 7.31), Josiah "defiled Tophet, which is in the valley of the children of Hinnom" (2 Kings 23.10) and it is generally understood that he did this by making the valley into a garbage dump for Jerusalem. According to Harrison, the valley also became the site for cremating the bodies of criminals. In New Testament times, the rubbish fires there constantly smouldered, and the Lord Jesus alluded to this in solemnly declaring that "it is better for thee to enter into life maimed, than having two hands to go into hell ('gehenna', a Jewish corruption of 'Ge [valley of] Hinnom'), into the fire that shall never be quenched" (Mk 9.43).

The nation would be broken and become just like the fragments of broken pottery found in the valley.

The proclamation (vv.3-13)

Jeremiah is told how he was to impart the message (vv.3-9), and how he was to illustrate the message (vv.10-13).

The message imparted (vv.3-9)

"Hear ye the word of the Lord, O kings of Judah, and inhabitants of Jerusalem; Thus saith the Lord of hosts, the God of Israel; Behold, I will bring evil upon this place, the which whosoever heareth, his ears shall tingle" (v.3). The message is addressed to an absent audience. The plural, "kings of Judah", indicates that the message was not only for the reigning king, but for his successors, all of whom proved to be equally wicked. The expression, "his ears shall tingle", occurs in connection with the destruction of the Sanctuary at Shiloh (1 Sam 3.11) as well as with the destruction of Jerusalem (2 Kings 21.12).

Jeremiah was to speak in this way "Because they have forsaken me, and have estranged this place, and have burned incense in it unto other gods…and have filled this place with the blood of innocents; They have built also the high places of Baal, to burn their sons with fire for burnt-offerings unto Baal, which I commanded not, nor spake it, neither came it into my mind" (vv.4-5). The words "have estranged this place" have the meaning "made this a place of foreign gods" (quoted by Feinberg), or "made God's city and land a heathen land by introducing foreign cults unknown to the fathers" (Laetsch).

This led to the most fearful crimes, both civil and religious. In the first place they had shed the blood of innocent people (not referring to children since they are mentioned next), possibly referring to the murders recorded in 2 Kings 21.16. This might include the deaths of those who opposed idolatry. In the second place, they had engaged in child-sacrifice, following the rites of both Baal and Molech worship (cp. Jer 32.35). The Lord's total abhorrence of these degraded practices is expressed in His words: "which I commanded not, nor spake it, neither came it into my mind" (cp. 7.31). All this was the result of forsaking the Lord (v.4). Failure "to love the Lord thy God with all thine heart, and with all thy soul, and with all thy might" (Deut 6.5) opens the floodgates to fearful evil.

This in turn opens the floodgates of divine wrath. "Therefore, behold, the days come, saith the Lord, that this place shall no more be called Tophet (meaning 'fire' or 'the place of fire'), nor The valley of the son of Hinnom, but The valley of slaughter" (v.6). Feinberg suggests "that because the valley had water, an invading force would besiege it first; and its defenders would suffer casualties in seeking to defend it". If this were the case, then the very people who had slain their children in the valley would be slain in the same place. Alternatively, the description "The valley of slaughter" could mean that the bodies of Jerusalem's inhabitants would be buried in the very valley that had been defiled by their idolatry.

The certainty of divine judgment in this way is emphasised: "And *I will* make void the counsel of Judah and Jerusalem in this place; and *I will* cause them to fall by the sword before their enemies…and their carcases *will I* give to be meat for the fowls of the heaven, and for the beasts of the earth. And *I will* make this city desolate, and a hissing (8322, referring to scorn)…And *I will* cause them to eat the flesh of their sons and the flesh of their daughters" (vv.7-9).

Scholars point out that the expression, "I will make void" (v.7), referring to the frustration of any plans they had for their deliverance, represent a play on words. The underlying Hebrew verb (1238) is onomatopoetic and represents the gurgling sound of water flowing from the mouth of a jar. It contains the root of the word rendered "bottle" (v.1) and seems to have been chosen with this in mind. According to Ellicott's Commentary, "The primary meaning is 'to pour out, to spill', and so to 'waste', or 'bring to nought'". In fact, some have suggested that the words of Jeremiah here were accompanied by the emptying of the earthen bottle in the sight of the witnesses. The fearful results of siege are described. Famine would lead to cannibalism. This had happened in Samaria (2 Kings 6.28-29); now it would happen in Jerusalem. The nation had been warned by Moses that this would be the case (Deut 28.53-57), and Jeremiah later recorded the fulfillment of his own prophecy: "Behold, O Lord, and consider to whom thou hast done this. Shall the women eat their fruit, and children of a span long?" (Lam 2.20); "The hands of the pitiful women have sodden their own children: they were their meat in the destruction of the daughter of my people" (Lam 4.10).

The message illustrated (vv.10-13)

"Then shalt thou break the bottle in the sight of the men that go with thee" (v.10). As they observed his "acted parable", the representatives of the civil and religious leadership were faced with the results of their abuse of power. Approximately one hundred years before, Isaiah had likened divine judgment on Judah to "the breaking of the potters' vessel" (Is 30.14) and as the time drew near for that prophecy's fulfilment, its solemnity is brought home in this dramatic way.

The sign (v.10) is followed by its significance: "Thus saith the Lord of hosts; Even so will I break this people and this city, as one breaketh a potter's vessel, that cannot be made whole again: and they shall bury them in Tophet, till there be no place to bury" (v.11). The punishment would fit the crime. The very place where Judah had worshipped false gods in such a vile manner would become "the local dump for human corpses" (Habel). Tophet was the place where Jerusalem expressed its abominable idol worship to the full. More than this, Jerusalem itself would become as Tophet: "Thus will I do unto this place, saith the Lord, and to the inhabitants thereof, and even make this city as Tophet: And the houses of Jerusalem, and the houses of the kings of Judah, shall be defiled as the place of Tophet" (vv.12-13). The very houses in Jerusalem whose flat roofs had been used for idol worship would be defiled by corpses. It does seem that the women were particularly responsible for burning "incense unto all the host of heaven" and pouring out "drink-offerings unto other gods" (v.13; cp. 7.18; 44.15-19).

Verses 14-15: The Prophecy in the Temple

This took place before "all the people" (v.14). Having delivered his prophecy in "the valley of the son of Hinnom" (v.2), Jeremiah returns to the Temple precincts to recapitulate the divine sentence upon Jerusalem: "Then came Jeremiah from Tophet, whither the Lord had sent him to prophesy; and he stood in the court of the Lord's house; and said to all the people, Thus saith the Lord of hosts, the God of Israel; Behold, I will bring upon this city and upon all her towns all the evil that I have pronounced against it, because they have hardened their necks, that they might not hear my words".

Commentators have remarked on the fact that these two verses (with 20.1-6) are in the third person and it is usually suggested that this section may have been the work of Baruch, Jeremiah's scribe (cp. 36.4 *et al*). The reference here to "this city and…all her towns" (v.15) is to Jerusalem and the cities of Judah (cp. 34.2).

Centuries later, Stephen charged their successors with the same sin: "Ye stiffnecked and uncircumcised in heart and ears, ye do always resist the Holy Ghost: as your fathers did, so do ye", and continued by saying, "Which of the prophets have not your fathers persecuted?" (Acts 7.51,52). Jeremiah was no exception to this, as the following chapter makes clear.

JEREMIAH 20

The preaching of Jeremiah "in the court of the Lord's house" (19.14) did not go unnoticed and unheard by the Temple authorities. It resulted in the first recorded instance of violence against the prophet. Some commentators suggest that he was beaten with "forty stripes" (Deut 25.3) which in Paul's day was reduced to "forty stripes save one" (2 Cor 11.24) for fear of exceeding the legal limit. Jeremiah was certainly amongst the men that James had in mind in saying, "Take, my brethren, the prophets, who have spoken in the name of the Lord, for an example of suffering affliction, and of patience" (James 5.10). The New Testament makes it clear that the Lord's people today can expect opposition, for "all that will live godly in Christ Jesus shall suffer persecution" (2 Tim 3.12).

Having delivered his message of pending judgment, Jeremiah was apprehended and punished by "Pashur the son of Immer the priest, who was also chief governor in the house of the Lord" (v.1). The prophet's preaching, with its theme of coming "violence and spoil" (v.8), was totally unacceptable. This is not surprising, for Pashur had evidently been prophesying himself but his message was totally different from the burden of Jeremiah. He had "prophesied lies" (v.6). No doubt he was one of the prophets who cried "Peace, peace; when there is no peace" (6.14; 8.11).

The chapter may be divided in the following way:

> The Confinement of Jeremiah (vv.1-6): "Then Pashur smote Jeremiah the prophet, and put him in the stocks" (v.2)
> The Complaint of Jeremiah (vv.7-10): he describes himself as being "deceived" by the Lord, and "in derision daily, every one mocketh me" (v.7)
> The Confidence of Jeremiah (vv.11-13): "But the Lord is with me as a mighty terrible one…he hath delivered the soul of the poor from the hand of evildoers" (vv.11,13)
> The Cursing of Jeremiah (vv.14-18):"Cursed be the day wherein I was born…Cursed be the man who brought tidings to my father, saying, A man child is born unto thee; making him very glad" (vv.14-15).

Verses 1-6: The Confinement of Jeremiah

These verses record the antagonism of Pashur (vv.1-2); and the answer of Jeremiah (vv.3-6).

The antagonism of Pashur (vv.1-2)

"Now Pashur the son of Immer the priest, who was also chief governor in the house of the Lord, heard that Jeremiah prophesied these things. Then Pashur smote Jeremiah the prophet, and put him in the stocks that

were in the high gate of Benjamin, which was by the house of the Lord."
This is the first occurrence in the book of the words "Jeremiah the prophet"
and Feinberg suggests that "the prophet" stands in apposition to
"Jeremiah", as if to indicate the sacrilege of Pashur's act. According to
Harrison, *"Pashur ben Immer* was the chief officer of the temple at the
close of the monarchy". He "was apparently the immediate subordinate of
the high priest and maintained order in the area of the temple". The
"stocks", where the prophet was confined, were evidently intended not
only for restraint, but also for torture. The Hebrew word (4115) implies
"causing distortion". "The stocks…held the feet, hand, and neck, so that
the body was almost doubled up…Jeremiah was put in the stocks at the
Upper Benjamin Gate, the northern gate of the upper temple court. It was
one of the most conspicuous places in the city" (Feinberg). It is said to be
the gate built by Jotham (cp. 2 Kings 15.35).

It is noteworthy that Jeremiah was punished, not because he had
transgressed the law, but for preaching the word of God. It should also be
noted that he suffered at the hands of the religious authorities. This has
its counterpart in the days of the New Testament, and in the succeeding
centuries. The greatest opposition to the gospel has always come from
institutionalised religion. In the case of the Jews, Paul observes that they
"both killed the Lord Jesus, and their own prophets, and have persecuted
us; and they please not God, and are contrary to all men: Forbidding us to
speak to the Gentiles that they might be saved" (1 Thess 2.15-16). The
dreadful persecutions initiated by papal Rome illustrate religious
hostility to the gospel over many centuries. This is a salutary reminder
that suffering and persecution are the norm in Christian experience
(cp. Philippians 1.29-30).

In the New Testament, Paul and Silas followed in the footsteps of
Jeremiah. They were beaten with "many stripes" and "cast…into prison"
with their feet "fast in the stocks" (Acts 16.23-24). How Jeremiah fared at
midnight it is impossible to say, but God "who giveth songs in the night" (Job
35.10) enabled Paul and Silas, with their bleeding backs, cramped feet, and in
unrelieved darkness, to pray and sing at that very hour (Acts 16.25).

The answer of Jeremiah (vv.3-6)
If Pashur thought that a night in the stocks would silence this
troublesome preacher, he was in for a shock!

Jeremiah was not silenced by opposition
The prophet was not intimidated by his overnight confinement in the
stocks. His release the following morning was accompanied by a
restatement of coming judgment on Judah, with particular reference to
Pashur himself: "And it came to pass on the morrow, that Pashur brought
forth Jeremiah out of the stocks. Then said Jeremiah unto him, the Lord
hath not called thy name Pashur (said to mean 'ease' or 'tranquility'), but

Magor-missabib (meaning 'terror on every side')" (v.3). Feinberg points out that the root of this compound name is found in four other places in the book (6.25; 20.10; 46.5; 49.29) as well as in Lamentations 2.22. The renderings vary, including "fear is on every side" (6.25), and "fear was round about" (46.5). The way in which Jeremiah used the expression evidently registered with his hearers to the extent that they made it a nickname for him: "For I heard the defaming of many, fear on every side" (v.10).

Like Jeremiah, Paul and Silas were not silenced by their time in the stocks. Having answered the jailor's initial question, "Sirs, what must I do to be saved?", the preachers "spake unto him the word of the Lord, and to all that were in his house" (Acts 16.30-32). Later, Paul wrote, "But even after that we had suffered before, and were shamefully entreated, as ye know, at Philippi, we were bold in our God to speak unto you the gospel of God with much contention" (1 Thess 2.2).

Jeremiah did not alter his message because of persecution

He clearly restated his preaching in "the valley of the son of Hinnom" (19.2) and in the Temple precincts (19.14) with added details: "For thus saith the Lord, Behold I will make thee a terror to thyself, and to all thy friends: and they shall fall by the sword of their enemies, and thine eyes shall behold it: and I will give all Judah into the hand of the king of Babylon, and he shall carry them captive into Babylon, and shall slay them with the sword. Moreover I will deliver all the strength of this city, and all the labours thereof, and all the precious things thereof, and all the treasures of the kings of Judah will I give into the hand of their enemies, which shall spoil them, and take them, and carry them to Babylon" (vv.4-5). These are the first direct references to Babylon in the book; previous references have been to "the north" of which examples occur in 1.14,15; 4.6; 6.1,22; 10.22; 13.20. A century before, Isaiah had told Hezekiah, who had entertained the representatives of "Merodach-baladan, the son of Baladan, king of Babylon" (Is 39.1), that "all that is in thine house, and that which thy fathers have laid up in store unto this day, shall be carried to Babylon: nothing shall be left, saith the Lord" (Is 39.6). The time had now come for this prophecy to be fulfilled; the Lord always honours His word.

Having reminded Timothy that "evil men and seducers shall wax worse and worse, deceiving, and being deceived", Paul urges him to "continue...in the things which thou hast learned and hast been assured of" (2 Tim 3.13-14). Jeremiah did not bend under pressure and Timothy was not to do so either.

Jeremiah did not spare Pashur

Jeremiah described in detail the Lord's judgment upon him: "And thou, Pashur, and all that dwell in thine house shall go into captivity: and thou shalt come to Babylon, and there thou shalt die, and shalt be buried there, thou, and all thy friends, to whom thou hast prophesied lies" (v.6). Pashur, having presumed to be a prophet, would live to see the fulfilment of Jeremiah's prophecy, and the emptiness of his own lying words. It seems quite possible that he was among the prophets described earlier: "Then said I, Ah, Lord God! behold, the prophets say unto them, Ye shall not see the sword, neither shall ye have famine; but I will give you assured peace in this place. Then the Lord said unto me, The prophets prophesy lies in my name" (14.13-14).

The fact that in Zedekiah's reign Pashur's office was held by Zephaniah (29.25-26), strongly suggests that after Jehoiakim's death, Pashur was carried into captivity with Jeconiah (24.1). Further details of this particular captivity, including reference to the removal of the Temple and royal treasures, are given in 2 Kings 24.11-16 where Jeconiah's name is given as Jehoiachin.

Verses 7-10: The Complaint of Jeremiah

After this clear and boldly-pronounced message from Jeremiah, it may seem at first glance somewhat surprising to discover that the Lord's servant was far from "cool, calm and collected". While dealing with Pashur, he had remained like "a defenced city, and an iron pillar, and brasen walls" (1.18) but when alone, "a reaction sets in...he breaks down completely" (Laetsch). "Set free, Jeremiah went to his home, and there poured forth that marvellous combination of heroic faith and wailing grief, which is recorded for us that we may know the weakness of his nature, and learn how earthen was the vessel in which God had placed his heavenly treasure" (Meyer). He felt deeply the reproach and indignity which attached to his ministry. Jeremiah was not insensitive to the constant opposition he faced: "I am in derision daily" (v.7); "a derision, daily" (v.8). This led him to complain to the Lord. He describes himself as deceived (v.7a); derided (vv.7b-8); despairing (v.9); and defamed (v.10).

He felt deceived (v.7a)

"O Lord, thou hast deceived me ('enticed me', JND), and I was deceived ('enticed', JND): thou art stronger than I, and hast prevailed." The same word (6601) is rendered "enticed" in v.10. This is the last of Jeremiah's so-called "confessions" and is an amazing revelation of his inner feelings. This, his saddest and bitterest complaint, is not expressed publicly, but to God alone. According to Feinberg, the intensive form of the verb "deceived" (6601) "means 'to seduce' as a virgin is seduced (Ex 22.16; 1 Kings 22.20-22)". He continues, "To be sure, Jeremiah is not accusing God of misrepresentation; but what he calls seduction is the divine compulsion upon his spirit. He is claiming that the Lord over-persuaded him to be a prophet. He pleads that, though the Lord overcame his resistance to His call (1.4-10), and he believed the Lord's promises, he has now been abandoned to shame".

Nevertheless Jeremiah had been told that he would be subject to relentless pressure. The prophet had been warned that "the kings of Judah…the princes…the priests…and the people of the land" would all oppose him (1.18-19), but he evidently felt that he had been persuaded to embark on the Lord's service without realising the magnitude and viciousness of the opposition. In the words of Feinberg, he "clearly speaks like a man overtaxed and overwrought", to which the commentator adds, "Who of us can feel justified in censuring him for what he said here?".

He was derided (vv. 7b-8)

Jeremiah explains why he felt so hurt in this way: "I am in derision daily, every one mocketh me. For since I spake, I cried out, I cried violence and spoil; because the word of the Lord was made a reproach unto me, and a derision, daily", or "For as oft as I speak, I cry out; I proclaim violence and spoil; for the word of Jehovah is become unto me a reproach and a derision all the day" (JND). The Lord's servant was derided because his hearers saw no apparent evidence that his gloomy message, which he describes as "violence and spoil", would be fulfilled. The New Testament paints a similar picture: "there shall come in the last days scoffers…saying, Where is the promise of his coming? For since the fathers fell asleep, all things continue as they were from the beginning of the creation" (2 Pet 3.3-4). It would be quite wrong to charge Jeremiah with unbelief. He had been assured that the Lord would fulfil His word: "I will hasten my word to perform it…I will call all the families of the kingdoms of the north…and they shall come" (1.12,15). It was the mockery he had to endure because of the apparent delay in the fulfilment of God's word which grieved him so deeply. Believers today are assured that although men and women scoff at the very idea of divine intervention, God has already intervened in human affairs, and will do so again: "the day of the Lord will come" (2 Pet 3.5-6,10).

He was in despair (v.9)

The intense daily pressure on the prophet persuaded him to terminate his service: "Then I said, I will not make mention of him, nor speak any more in his name". The burden had become so heavy that Jeremiah finally decided that he would no longer serve as a prophet. It was all just too much for him! But his feelings in this way gave place to a greater compulsion: "But his word was in mine heart as a burning fire shut up in my bones, and I was weary with forbearing, and I could not stay", or "I am weary of holding it in; indeed, I cannot" (NIV). As Meyer observes, "The difficulty, therefore, with him was, not in speaking, but in keeping silent - not in acting, but in refraining". For Jeremiah, the word of God was overpowering. "He found out the impossibility of denying his call. He learned that it was irreversible, and that God's word was irrepressible" (Feinberg). The tension in the heart of the prophet is clear; on the one hand he faced the prospect of "continually reaping the hateful ridicule and scornful rejection of his message", and on the other "his sense of duty, his prophetic obligation, his willingness to obey the Lord, and above all the Lord's Word that burnt in his heart as a fire" (Laetsch).

It is noteworthy that others in the Scriptures bear witness to the inward compulsion of God's word, including David: "My heart was hot within me, while I was musing the fire burned: then spake I with my tongue" (Ps 39.3); Amos: "The lion hath roared, who will not fear? the Lord God hath spoken, who can but prophesy?" (Amos 3.8); Peter and John: "For we cannot but speak the things which we have seen and heard" (Acts 4.20); Paul: "For though I preach the gospel, I have nothing to glory of: for necessity is laid upon me; yea, woe is unto me, if I preach not the gospel!" (1 Cor 9.16). It was at Corinth that Paul was "pressed in the spirit ('constrained by the word', RV), and testified to the Jews that Jesus was Christ" (Acts 18.5). Perhaps Elihu speaks for them all, and for Jeremiah, in saying: "I am full of matter, the spirit within me constraineth me. Behold, my belly is as wine which hath no vent; it is ready to burst like new bottles" (Job 32.18-19). The Lord's people today must remember that the proclamation of His Word must never be regarded as a hobby or a pastime, but the earnest expression of a burdened heart.

He was defamed (v.10)

Jeremiah now enlarges on the reason that he was so determined to resign his prophetic ministry: "For I heard the defaming ('whispering', RSV) of many, fear on every side. Report, say they, and we will report it. All my familiars watched for my halting, saying, Peradventure he will be enticed, and we shall prevail against him, and we shall take our revenge on him". This expands the "reproach" and "derision" mentioned earlier (v.8). Attention is drawn to the following.

They whispered about him

According to Gesenius the word "defaming" (1681) means "slander" or "calumny". Feinberg suggests that the "defaming is that of people whispering in twos or threes apart". Ezekiel had a similar experience: "Also, thou son of man, the children of thy people still are talking against thee by the walls and in the doors of their houses" (Ezek 33.30). It does not need too much imagination to visualise the picture! In the case of Jeremiah they mimicked him with the phrase "fear (or 'terror') on every side". They called him "Mr Terror All Around" or "Mr Magor-missabib" (Feinberg).

They watched him

"Report, and we will report it. All my familiars are watching for my stumbling" (JND). Even those who "greet him with the familiar greeting of friendship" (Laetsch) plot to report him for treason, hoping for some unguarded words which could justify a charge against him (cp. 26.11). The enemies of the Lord Jesus did exactly the same: "Then went the

Pharisees, and took counsel how they might entangle him in his talk" (Mt 22.15); "And they watched him, and sent forth spies, which should feign themselves just men, that they might take hold of his words, that so they might deliver him unto the power and authority of the governor" (Lk 20.20). David had to say "Yea, mine own familiar friend, in whom I trusted, which did eat of my bread, hath lifted up his heel against me" (Ps 41.9), but it is noticeable that the Lord Jesus omitted the words, "in whom I trusted", when quoting this verse in John 13.18.

The Lord's people are under constant observation and must give those who oppose the gospel no just cause for criticism and condemnation. All believers, not only bondservants, are to conduct their lives so that "the name of God and his doctrine be not blasphemed" (1 Tim 6.1) and all believers, not only "younger women", must "give none occasion to the adversary to speak reproachfully" (1 Tim 5.14).

Verses 11-13: The Confidence of Jeremiah

Jeremiah moves rapidly from complaint to confidence (vv.10-11), just as he moves equally rapidly from confidence to cursing immediately afterwards (vv.13-14). For a brief moment a "note of hope and joy pervades the gloom of the section as a whole" (Harrison). Three things should be noted in connection with these verses.

The presence of the Lord (v.11)

"But the Lord is with me as a mighty terrible one ('a mighty warrior', NIV)". Jeremiah rested on the repeated promise made to him at the commencement of his ministry: "I am with thee to deliver thee, saith the Lord" (1.8); "I am with thee, saith the Lord, to deliver thee" (1.19). He was therefore assured that his adversaries would be totally defeated: "therefore my persecutors shall stumble, and they shall not prevail: they shall be greatly ashamed; for they shall not prosper: their everlasting confusion shall never be forgotten". The Lord's people today can rest in His ultimate triumph over the greatest enemy: "And the God of peace shall bruise Satan under your feet shortly" (Rom 16.20). In the words of the hymn,

> Jehovah is our strength,
> And He shall be our song;
> We shall o'ercome at length,
> Although our foes be strong:
> In vain doth Satan now oppose,
> For God is stronger than His foes.
> (Samuel Barnard)

The prayer to the Lord (v.12)

"But, O Lord of hosts, that triest the righteous, and seest the reins and the heart, let me see thy vengeance on them: for unto thee have I opened my cause." Jeremiah, who had prayed like this before (11.20), confidently commits his cause to the Lord. He prays with the consciousness that he has the moral right to ask for judgment upon his enemies. David prayed on similar grounds: "Thou hast proved mine heart; thou hast visited me in the night; thou hast tried me, and shalt find nothing" (Ps 17.3). Believers today are to act differently: "Bless them which persecute you: bless, and curse not…if thine enemy hunger, feed him; if he thirst, give him drink" (Rom 12.14,20).

The praise to the Lord (v.13)

Having committed his cause to the Lord, he voices his grateful trust in Him in anticipation of his ultimate vindication: "Sing unto the Lord, praise ye the Lord: for he hath delivered the soul of the poor from the hand of evildoers". This section therefore begins with Jeremiah's assurance of the Lord's presence, and ends with his assurance of deliverance from all who opposed him.

Verses 14-18: The Cursing of Jeremiah

The chapter, and this section of the prophecy, concludes with a mood-swing of gigantic proportions! "Sing unto the Lord, praise ye the Lord" (v.13) suddenly turns to "Cursed be the day wherein I was born: let not the day wherein my mother bare me be blessed. Cursed be the man who brought tidings to my father, saying, A man child is born unto thee; making him very glad" (vv.14-15). The quick transition from triumph to gloom and despair has been variously explained, including the suggestion that vv.14-18 have been transposed. But, as Feinberg observes, "The transition and contrast are psychologically understandable in view of the constant pressures on Jeremiah. Feeling an utter failure after being in the stocks, he wished he had never been born". The experience of Elijah is comparable. Having been party to the great victory over the false prophets at Mount Carmel (1 Kings 18.17-40) and then having to run for his life from the wrath of Jezebel, the prophet is found sitting under a juniper tree in the wilderness with the request, "It is enough; now, O Lord, take away my life; for I am not better than my fathers" (1 Kings 19.4). There is considerable merit in the comments of Laetsch: "Any Christian that knows Satan's tactics in tempting God's children, knows from his own experience that Satan will not always cease the fight after he has once been beaten back, but that the inveterate foe may return immediately with still greater ferocity in order to attack the Christian rejoicing in his victory and less ready or altogether unprepared for such a second attack".

It is noteworthy that in his bitterness, Jeremiah does not curse his parents: to do so carried the severest penalty under Mosaic law (Ex 21.17). The way in which he curses the man who brought news of his birth is, of course, strictly rhetorical: "Cursed be the man who brought tidings to my father, saying, A man child is born unto thee; making him very glad. And let that man be as the cities which the Lord overthrew, and repented not: and let him hear the cry in the morning, and the shouting at noontide" (vv.15-16). Feinberg explains that "the outcry in the morning represents a call for help when under attack", whereas "the shout of alarm or trumpet blast is an alarm of war (cp. 4.19)". Jeremiah's reference to his mother's womb (v.17) is equally rhetorical. The prophet wishes that "his mother's womb had been at once his birthplace and his grave" (Feinberg): he complains bitterly "Because he slew me not from the womb; or that my mother might have been my grave, and her womb to be always great with me" (v.17). Comparable language is found in Job 3.3-16.

Jeremiah's concluding words reveal "the inmost recesses of his mind" (Streane): "Wherefore came I forth out of the womb to see labour and sorrow, that my days should be consumed with shame?" (v.18). Under the extreme pressure of the time, he had evidently forgotten the divinely-ordained purpose for his life: "Before I formed thee in the belly I knew thee; and before thou camest forth out of the womb I sanctified thee, and I ordained thee a prophet unto the nations" (1.5). Like Elijah before him, Jeremiah was deeply troubled by the apparent failure of his mission. Feinberg suggests that Jeremiah's "shame" was his inability to avert the coming catastrophe.

The chapter therefore concludes with an unanswered question. There was no apparent answer from the Lord, unlike the previous occasion on which he had complained (15.17-21). But this was not the end of his ministry. The very next chapter, describing events which took place some ten to fifteen years later, commences: "The word which came unto Jeremiah from the Lord, when king Zedekiah sent unto him Pashur the son of Melchiah, and Zephaniah the son of Maaseiah the priest" (21.1). As Laetsch observes, "The God of infinite loving-kindness and unlimited patience overlooked this outburst of Jeremiah's flesh, and did not deal with him after his sins nor reward him according to his iniquity. He applies to His prophet His own promise: 'I will forgive their iniquity and I will remember their sin no more' (Jer 31.34)".

JEREMIAH 21

Chapter 21 marks the commencement of a new division in the book. Chapters 1-20 evidently relate in part to the earlier years of Jeremiah's ministry: in the first place to the reign of Josiah (cp. 3.6: "The Lord said also unto me in the days of Josiah the king"), and in the second to the reign of Jehoiakim. Some of things which happened to Jeremiah in chapters 11-20 could hardly have taken place if Josiah had been on the throne. It has already been said that chapters 2-10 are devoted to public sermons and chapters 11-20 to personal experiences, where there is certainly more autobiographical material and more narrative.

Streane can be quoted at length here: "This commences a new division of the whole book. The substance of the roll of Chapter 36 had been given in the preceding chapters, while fragments of the same are doubtless included in this portion. We here pass at once from the time of Jehoiakim to that of Zedekiah the last king of Judah, and the occasion on which the city was attacked by the Chaldeans (v.4)...Zedekiah under these circumstances follows the example set by Hezekiah towards Isaiah the great prophet of *his* time (2 Kings 19.2) and sends Pashur and Zephaniah to Jeremiah to ask for a declaration of the future. The prophet replies in this and the three following chapters to the effect that the successive crimes of kings, prophets and priests, of which he speaks in detail, have secured for Judah the unenviable fate now visibly at hand, while there appear however from time to time gleams of brighter things".

It does therefore seem that chapters 21-24 are a unit, locked together by references to Zedekiah, but embracing all four kings who succeeded Josiah, namely Shallum (22.11), Jehoiakim (22.18), Coniah (22.24), and Zedekiah (21.1-7; 24.8). Shallum is otherwise known as Jehoahaz, and Coniah as Jeconiah or Jehoiachin. Chapters 21 and 22 describe the sins of these successive kings who are described as "pastors" (22.22) and, having emphasised their total failure in this role, the following chapter, which continues this section of the prophecy, describes "shepherds" who will not fail (23.4) and whose ministry will be exercised under the reign of "a King" who "shall reign and prosper, and shall execute judgment and justice in the earth ('land', JND)" (23.5). The failure of the national "pastors" leads to the sharp censure of the prophets and priests, principally the former (23.9-40), and chapter 24 "shews under the similitude of baskets of figs the rottenness to which the State under Zedekiah had been reduced" (Streane). Thus kings, prophets and priests had all failed, but the section points forward to the coming of the Messiah, the Lord Jesus Christ, who, as Prophet, Priest and King, can never fail!

Zedekiah (597-586 BC) is mentioned first in this section of the book and therefore out of chronological order. He was young, weak, and dominated by the princes. In the latter part of his reign (to which this chapter refers) he rebelled against Nebuchadnezzar, who responded by laying siege to the city of Jerusalem (2 Kings 25.12). It has to be asked why the record of his request to Jeremiah should be included at this point in the book. After all, the event in question took place some time after other events mentioned in the chapters that follow. The reason is not easily ascertained, but perhaps its inclusion at this point is to give the key to what follows in the book. In Jeremiah 21, the end was near. The Babylonians were besieging Jerusalem (v.4), and the Lord was on the side of the invaders! He was actually fighting against Jerusalem! Why was this so? The reason lay in the infamous conduct of all four kings whose reigns are reviewed in chapters 21 and 22.

It should be noted that the Babylonian siege was temporarily lifted. Details are given in 37.3-10. Jeremiah's help is sought in petitioning the Lord that the respite might become permanent, but to no avail. Zephaniah was again one of the messengers sent by Zedekiah on this occasion (37.3)

The present chapter may be divided as follows:

> The Alarm of Zedekiah (vv.1-2)
> The Answer from Jeremiah (vv.3-7)
> The Alternatives for the People (vv.8-10)
> The Avoidance of Judgment (vv.11-14).

Verses 1-2: The Alarm of Zedekiah
"The word which came unto Jeremiah from the Lord, when king Zedekiah sent unto him Pashur the son of Melchiah, and Zephaniah the son of Maaseiah the priest" (v.1). The deputation was evidently sent before Jeremiah was imprisoned (37.15-16). Attention is drawn to the following: the delegation (v.1); the danger (v.2a); and the deliverance (v.2b).

The delegation (v.1)
Quite clearly, "Pashur the son of Melchiah", who is mentioned later in the book as "Pashur the son of Malchiah (38.1) should not be confused with "Pashur the the son of Immer" (20.1). Zephaniah is "mentioned again in 29.25; 37.3; 52.24. In the last place he is spoken of as the 'second priest', meaning, next to the high-priest in rank. He was one of those slain by Nebuchadnezzar at Riblah. Both he (as we may gather from that fact) and Pashur (38.1,4) belonged to the party who were for refusing to recognise and submit to Nebuchadnezzar's overwhelming power, and were thus politically hostile to Jeremiah" (Streane).

Pashur and Zephaniah make a significant pair. Pashur was one of the princes (38.4) and Zephaniah was a priest (52.24). The secular world and the religious world were brought together in the delegation. The political and religious worlds combined to oppose the Lord Jesus in His ministry (Mt 22.15-16) and were similarly involved in His death (Acts 4.27).

On a practical note, it is heartening to see that sinful, weak and vacillating

Zedekiah at least knew to whom he could go for reliable information and help. Such was the spiritual stature of Jeremiah. Ought not the Lord's people today be recognised as men and women in touch with God?

The danger (v.2a)

"Inquire, I pray thee, of the Lord for us; for Nebuchadrezzar king of Babylon maketh war against us." The "war" had progressed to the point of besieging Jerusalem (v.4), albeit in its early stages. "When the text indicates that the Babylonians were besieging them, the meaning is 'closing in on you', 'blockading you', or 'pressing you hard' (so Bright) because the actual siege had not yet begun" (Feinberg). There were still defenders outside the city (v.4).

The first direct reference to the king of Babylon is in 20.4: "I will give all Judah into the hand of the king of Babylon, and he shall carry them captive into Babylon". Previous references have been to "the north". The exact identification of "the…evil out of the north" (cp.1.14,15; 3.12,18; 4.6; 6.1,22; 10.22; 13.20; 16.15) is not given in the early chapters of the prophecy.

It should be noted that the king of Babylon's name is spelt "Nebuchadrezzar" as opposed to the usual "Nebuchadnezzar". According to Orelli, "The form Nebuchadrezzar, supplied by the Hebrew text here…corresponds better to the Assyrio-Babylonian form of the name than the Jewish-Aramaean Nebuchadnezzar". "Nebuchadrezzar" transliterates the Babylonian spelling. The name has been variously interpreted by scholars: examples are "Nebo protects against misfortune"; "Nebo protects the crown"; "Nebo protects landmarks".

The deliverance (v.2b)

"Inquire, I pray thee, of the Lord for us…if so be that the Lord will deal with us according to all his wondrous works, that he (Nebuchadrezzar) may go up from us."

As Laetsch points out, "This plea, however, was not the humble petition of penitent sinners, confessing their wickedness and imploring God's grace. Not a word is said of repentance, of desire for forgiveness. Jeremiah is asked to procure an oracle. They hope that God will deal with them according to all His wondrous works, manifested so often in the history of Israel". The message "repent, and do the first works" (Rev 2.5) did not occur to Zedekiah. Neither does it occur to God's people so often today.

Zedekiah may well have been thinking of divine deliverance in the days of Jehoshaphat (2 Chr 20.1-30), but it must be noted that this king "feared, and set himself to seek the Lord, and proclaimed a fast throughout all Judah" (2 Chr 20.3). In later years Judah was delivered from the Assyrians (2 Kings 18.13-19.37), but Hezekiah "did that which was right in the sight of the Lord" (2 Kings 18.3), and when the Assyrian threat emerged, he "rent his clothes, and covered himself with sackcloth, and went into the house of the Lord" (2 Kings 19.1). Zedekiah wanted Jeremiah's prayers, and fully expected deliverance from God, though he uttered no syllable of repentance or desire to do God's will.

The lessons here are clear: God does not "just intervene". There must be moral and spiritual conditions pleasing to Him.

Verses 3-7: The Answer from Jeremiah

"Then said Jeremiah unto them, Thus shall ye say to Zedekiah" (v.3). In effect, the Lord would not deal with them "according to all his wondrous works". To the contrary, He would fight against them (vv.4-7). It has been said that "the army of Nebuchadnezzar was the visible extension of God's arm" (Habel). A similar passage is found in the book of Isaiah: "O Assyrian, the rod of mine anger, and the staff in their hand is mine indignation" (Is 10.5). The certainty of the Lord God of Israel's warfare against Judah and Jerusalem is emphasised.

a) "*I will* turn back the weapons of war that in are in your hands" (v.4). "Those who are engaged outside the walls in trying to baffle the Chaldeans as they take up their positions for the siege, are to be driven back by the foe into the city" (Streane).

This is the first reference in the book to the Chaldeans by name. "The Chaldeans were originally a semi-nomadic tribe occupying the district between northern Arabia and the Persian Gulf. The tenth-century BC Assyrians gave the name *Kaldu* to the territory earlier known as the 'Sea-Land', and in the following century several Chaldean chiefs were included among the vassals of Adadnirari (c. 805-782 BC). Subsequently the designation of 'Chaldea' was used to include Babylonian as a whole (cp. Ezek 23.23; Dan 3.8)" (Harrison).

b) "*I will* assemble them into the midst of this city" (v.4). That is, the outside defenders of the city would be driven back into the city. "And I myself will fight against you with an outstretched hand and with a strong arm, even in anger, and in fury, and in great wrath" (v.5). The expressions "outstretched hand" and "strong arm" could well be taken from the book of Deuteronomy, where similar expressions occur several times. Examples are found there in 4.34; 5.15; 26.8. The fact that the Lord fought against His people at this time is also expressed in the Lamentations of Jeremiah: "The Lord was as an enemy: he hath swallowed up Israel" (Lam 2.5). The Lord's opposition to His own people is not confined to the Old Testament: speaking to the angel of the church in Pergamos the Lord Jesus said, "But I have a few things against thee, because thou hast there them that hold the doctrine of Balaam, who taught Balac to cast a stumblingblock before the children of Israel, to eat things sacrificed unto idols, and to commit fornication. So hast thou also them that hold the doctrine of the Nicolaitans, which thing I hate. Repent; or else I will come unto thee quickly, and will fight against them with the sword of my mouth" (Rev 2.14-16).

c) "And *I will* smite the inhabitants of this city, both man and beast: they shall die of a great pestilence" (v.6). There would be an onset of plague. As Feinberg observes, "During a siege, an epidemic is always a threat. A fearful plague would weaken the people".

d) "*I will* deliver Zedekiah...from the pestilence, from the sword, and from the famine, into the hand of Nebuchadrezzar king of Babylon...and he shall smite them with the edge of the sword; he shall not spare them, neither have pity, nor have mercy" (v.7). The final declaration spells out the ruthless and merciless end for Jerusalem's defenders together with the doom of Zedekiah. The Lord would deliver him into the invader's hands, and although he was not slain, he "died in exile as a blinded deposed monarch (Jer 34.4; 2 Kings 25.6-7; Ezek 12.13)" (Feinberg). Alas, "the captain of the host of the Lord" is no longer for Judah and against her adversaries (Josh 5.13-14). While he is still the Lord of wondrous works, He will now do a work (which whosoever heareth, his ears shall tingle' (Jer 19.3)" (Laetsch).

Verses 8-10: The Alternatives for the People

"And unto this people thou shalt say, Thus saith the Lord; Behold, I set before you the way of life, and the way of death" (v.8). It has been suggested that this is not part of Jeremiah's message to the king's deputation but rather a separate message from the Lord. If this is the case, it is not evident from the passage. The figure of a choice between two ways comes from Deuteronomy 30.19: "I call heaven and earth to record this day against you, that I have set before you life and death, blessing and cursing: therefore choose life, that both thou and thy seed may live". Harrison observes that in Matthew 7.13-14 "Christ spoke of 'two ways', and the difficulty which many people experienced in finding the one leading to eternal life".

As Feinberg points out, "Though Jeremiah was actually counselling desertion, which was ordinarily treason, as a prophet of God he spoke with an authority higher than even that of a king": "He that abideth in this city shall die by the sword, and by the famine, and by the pestilence: but he that goeth out, and falleth to the Chaldeans that besiege you, he shall live, and his life shall be unto him for a prey" (v.9). This must have been extraordinarily difficult for the Lord's servant, surrounded as he was with men and women engaged in "a life-and-death struggle with a powerful invader" (Feinberg). It is no small wonder that Jeremiah's counsel made him unpopular to the extent that he was regarded as unpatriotic and traitorous (26.8-9; 38.1-4). The declaration of God's will runs counter to public opinion and often results in His servants treading a lonely path.

The words "his life shall be unto him for a prey" mean he will "escape with his life" (Feinberg). Those who surrendered would lose all but their lives. It was a stark choice. There were no other options. The city would not survive: "For I have set my face against this city for evil (cp. 44.11; Amos 9.4), and not for good, saith the Lord: it shall be given into the hand of the king of Babylon, and he shall burn it with fire" (v.10). The Babylonians, tired of repeated rebellions, would destroy the city.

Verses 11-14: The Avoidance of Judgment

Having addressed the people (vv.8-10), Jeremiah now turns to the royal family: "And touching the house of the king of Judah, say, Hear ye the word of the Lord; O house of David, thus saith the Lord" (vv.11-12). These verses introduce the following chapter which commences, "Thus saith the Lord; Go down to the house of the king of Judah, and speak there this word, And say, Hear the word of the Lord, O king of Judah, that sittest upon the throne of David" (22.1-2). It should be noted that the reference to the "gates", which at first glance might suggest that there was liberty to enter and re-enter Jerusalem and that therefore that the Babylonians were not besieging the city, are in fact "the gates of his house" (22.4). It should also be carefully noted that Zedekiah is not mentioned by name, although he was the reigning monarch at the time. This is because the emphasis is placed in these verses (21.11-22.30) on the dire condition of the "house of David" which will only be recovered when the Lord raises "unto David a righteous Branch, and a King shall reign and prosper" (23.5). In fact, ch.22 concludes with the extinguishing of the royal line. But ch.23 introduces a new King!

With this in mind, the passage urges the royal house to "Execute judgment in the morning, and deliver him that is spoiled out of the hand of the oppressor, lest my fury go out like fire, and burn that none can quench it, because of the evil of your doings" (vv.11-12). This is expanded in the following chapter: "Thus saith the Lord; Execute ye judgment and righteousness, and deliver the spoiled out of the hand of the oppressor: and do no wrong, do no violence to the stranger, the fatherless, nor the widow, neither shed innocent blood in this place" (22.3). This had long been one of the burdens of the prophets, and Jeremiah himself had already called for these reforms to be implemented (cp. 7.5-7). His message here is evidently a last-ditch appeal to Zedekiah. Two matters needed immediate attention.

Justice must be executed (v.12)

"Execute judgment in the morning, and deliver him that is spoiled out of the hand of the oppressor." The words "execute judgment in the morning" refer "to pre-exilic kings dispensing justice before the day's heat became too great' (cp. 2 Sam 4.5)" (Harrison). He adds, "Along with the false prophets and immoral cultic priests, the monarchy must take its share of responsibility for the moral and social degradation of the people because the king's highest duty was the administration of justice (2 Sam 15.4)". For deliverance from destruction, there must be "a change of their policy of tolerating and thus encouraging oppression and social injustice" (Laetsch). Failure to act would incur sweeping judgment.

Pride must cease (vv.13-14)

"Behold, I am against thee, O inhabitant of the valley, and rock of the plain, saith the Lord; which say, Who shall come down against us? or who shall enter into our habitations?" (v.13). Laetsch calls this "A cessation of their insane pride in privileges and favours promised by the Lord to His people and the royal dynasty (1 Kings 9.4-5) but long ago forfeited by their wickedness; and a cessation of their paradoxical trust in the saving power of the Lord, whom they had turned against themselves by their unbelief and disobedience, which called down upon themselves His consuming wrath". The lesson here is clear: in New Testament language, "let him that thinketh he standeth take heed lest fall" (1 Cor 10.12).

The expression, "O inhabitant of the valley, and rock of the plain", referring as it evidently does to Jerusalem, has been the occasion of lengthy comment. Streane is succinct here: "Jerusalem is called both 'valley' and 'rock'…because, although it is lower than the surrounding mountains, yet the hills on which it is built rise high above the plain". A comparable expression is found in 17.3.

Failure to turn from their foolish pride would, again, incur divine judgment: "But I will punish you according to the fruit of your doings, saith the Lord: and I will kindle a fire in the forest thereof, and it shall devour all things round about it" (v.14). While some take the reference to "forests" literally, arguing that forests covered a larger area than in later times, it seems more probable that Jeremiah is referring to the royal palace, called "the house of the forest of Lebanon", with its "cedar pillars, with cedar beams" (1 Kings 7.2).

JEREMIAH 22

This chapter continues Jeremiah's reply to Zedekiah's request for the prophet's help in securing divine deliverance from the besieging Babylonian army: "Inquire, I pray thee, of the Lord for us; for Nebuchadrezzar king of Babylon maketh war against us; if so be that the Lord will deal with us according to all his wondrous works, that he may go up from us" (21.2).

Attention has been drawn to the chronology of this oracle, which covers chapters 21-24. Zedekiah was the last of the four kings of Judah who succeeded Josiah, but he is mentioned first, and this is particularly apparent in the current chapter where reference is made to his predecessors, Shallum alias Jehoahaz, Jehoiakim, and Coniah alias Jeconiah or Jehoichin (vv.11,18,24). Zedekiah had been told that the Lord was fighting against Judah (21.4-5) and that this was attributable, not only to his own iniquities, but to the iniquities of the three kings who reigned before him. The message to Zedekiah evidently reviews the history of these kings and apparently reproduces the very words of the warnings issued to them. But Zedekiah had not learned anything from God's dealings with his predecessors, and God's people today do well to ask themselves how much they have learned from His dealings with them and with others.

It has also been noted that, having referred to Zedekiah by name and pronounced judgement of him as an individual (21.7), Jeremiah then addresses the royal house: "And touching the house of the king of Judah, say, Hear ye the word of the Lord; O house of David" (21.11-12). This paragraph (21.11-14) forms the introduction to chapter 22 which begins, "Go down to the house of the king of Judah, and speak there this word, And say, Hear the word of the Lord, O king of Judah, that sittest upon the throne of David (vv.1-2), and ends, "no man of his seed shall prosper, sitting upon the throne of David, and ruling any more in Judah" (v.30). Put differently, the chapter begins with a king sitting upon the throne, and ends with an empty throne or, perhaps more accurately, no throne at all. But this is not the end, for chapter 23 describes the restoration of David's throne when "a King shall reign and prosper, and shall execute judgment and justice in the earth" (23.5).

The chapter may be divided as follows:

> The Destruction of Jerusalem (vv.1-9)
> The Deportation of Shallum (vv.10-12)
> The Dishonour of Jehoiakim (vv.13-23)
> The Discontinuance of the throne after Coniah (vv.24-30).

Verses 1-9: The Destruction of Jerusalem
These verses, which are evidently addressed to the ruling king at the time, that is, to Zedekiah, fall into two sections introduced by the words:

"Hear the word of the Lord" (vv.2-4), and "But if ye will not hear these words" (vv.5-9). In the words of Campbell Morgan, Jeremiah "charged the king to remember that the way of repentance is the way to restoration, and that the way of disobedience is the way of destruction".

Obedience will bring continuance (vv.2-4)

"Hear the word of the Lord...Execute ye judgment and righteousness, and deliver the spoiled out of the hand of the oppressor: and do no wrong, do no violence to the stranger, the fatherless, nor the widow, neither shed innocent blood in this place. For if ye do this thing indeed, then shall there enter in by the gates of this house kings sitting upon the throne of David, riding in chariots and on horses, he, and his servants, and his people." A similar promise is made earlier in the book (17.24-25) but with reference to "the gates of this city" rather than to "the gates of this house".

These verses expand the earlier message: "Execute judgment in the morning, and deliver him that is spoiled out of the hand of the oppressor" (21.12). In both cases the message is addressed to the leadership. The royal house was to ensure that the law was implemented, and that no advantage was taken of the disadvantaged and vulnerable members of society. David had said, "He that ruleth over men must be just, ruling in the fear of God" (2 Sam 23.3). The Lord intended His people to be a caring society, just as He intends the local assembly to resemble the human body where "the members should have the same care one for another" (1 Cor 12.25).

The message and its lessons are clear. But when did Jeremiah "Go down to the house of the king of Judah, and speak there this word"? It was clearly at a time when the king, his servants and his people could "enter in by these gates". Could such a statement be made with the Babylonians outside the walls, even if the siege proper had not actually begun (21.4)? The answer is evidently that the gates in question were not the city gates, but the palace gates: "the gates of this house" (v.4).

Disobedience will bring destruction (vv.5-9)

The desolation

"But if ye will not hear these words, I swear by myself, saith the Lord, that *this house* shall become a desolation" (v.5). According to Ellicott's Commentary, "The formula, 'I swear by myself', is an exceptionally rare one, but meets us in Genesis 22.16. In Deuteronomy 32.40 the same thought is embodied the language of the loftiest poetry. The principle in both cases is that on which the writer of the Epistle to the Hebrews dwells in 6.13. Men swear by the greater, but God can swear by nothing greater than Himself". While the expression "this house" is often used in relation to the Temple, in the present context it evidently refers to the royal palace: "then shall there enter in by the gates of this house...this house shall become a desolation" (vv.4-5). While the words "this house shall become a desolation" could refer to the dynasty, the word "desolation" makes it more likely that they refer to a literal building. But at the same time, the destruction of the building does point to the destruction of the dynasty. The continuance of the royal house depended on strong moral leadership and due attention to the needs of the disadvantaged classes in society. There are important lessons here for assembly leaders. Paul urges the elders at Thessalonica to "warn them that are unruly, comfort the feebleminded, support the weak" (1 Thess 5.14).

The destroyers
"For thus saith the Lord unto the king's house of Judah; Thou art Gilead unto me, and the head of Lebanon: yet surely I will make thee a wilderness, and cities which are not inhabited. And I will prepare destroyers against thee, every one with his weapons: and they shall cut down thy choice cedars, and cast them into the fire" (vv.6-7). Ellicott's Commentary points out that "'the oaks of Bashan' in the Gilead district (Is 2.13; Zech 11.2) were as famous as the cedars of Lebanon, and were both alike the fit symbol of the glory of sovereignty (Is 37.24; Ezek 17.3)". While some commentators refer to the "choice cedars" as metaphoric language "for the princes of the royal house of Judah, and the chief counsellors and generals" (Ellicott's Commentary), it does seem that the reference is to the buildings in Jerusalem. David's house was "an house of cedar" (2 Sam 7.2). The cedars of Lebanon were largely used in the construction of Solomon's palace (1 Kings 7.2-5).

The discernment
"And many nations shall pass by this city, and they shall say every man to his neighbour, Wherefore hath the Lord done thus unto this great city? Then they shall answer, Because they have forsaken the covenant of the Lord their God, and worshipped other gods, and served them" (vv.8-9). This should be compared with the words of Moses: "Even all nations shall say, Wherefore hath the Lord done thus unto this land? what meaneth the heat of this great anger? Then men shall say, Because they have forsaken the covenant of the Lord God of their fathers" (Deut 29.24-25). Believers today are reminded that they should "give none occasion to the adversary to speak reproachfully" (1 Tim 5.14).

Verses 10-12: The Deportation of Shallum
According to 1 Chronicles 3.15, Shallum (otherwise known as Jehoahaz) was the fourth son of Josiah, although Streane suggests that "there is some ground (he does not give his authority for saying this) for believing that the Johanan of that verse is the Shallum here". It is known, however, that Jehoahaz was two years younger than his brother Jehoiakim who succeeded him (2 Chr 36.2-5).

After Josiah's death at the battle at Megiddo in 609 BC, "all Judah and Jerusalem mourned for Josiah. And Jeremiah lamented for Josiah: and all the singing men and the singing women spake of Josiah in their lamentations to this day, and made them an ordinance in Israel: and, behold, they are written in the lamentations" (2 Chr 35.24-25; cp. 2 Kings 23.29-30; Zech 12.11). But Jeremiah now tells the people at large, "Weep ye not for the dead, neither bemoan him: but weep sore for him that goeth away: for he shall return no more, nor see his native country" (v.10). "It had become customary among God's people to sing dirges for departed rulers. But now they were to reserve their weeping for Josiah's son, Shallum-Jehoahaz, who was to be forever exiled from the land. The fate of King Josiah was better than that of his son who was exiled to Egypt and died there (2 Kings 23.34)" (Feinberg). Josiah had been "taken away from the evil to come" (Is 57.1).

The permanence of Jehoahaz's exile is emphasised three times: "he shall return no more, nor see his native country" (v.10); he "went forth out of this place; He shall not return thither any more" (v.11); "he shall die in the place whither they have led him captive, and shall see this land no more" (v.12). Jehoahaz means "the Lord will help", but there would be no help for him. It is not known for how long Shallum survived in Egypt. "There is no trace of him being alive when the prophet is dragged by his countrymen to Egypt (43.6-7)" (Ellicott's Commentary). Ezekiel 19.1-4 also refers to the deportation of Shallum.

It has been suggested that Shallum's removal to Egypt was the consequence of his father's encounter with Pharaoh-nechoh (otherwise known as Necho) but it is noticeable that during his short reign (2 Chr 36.1-4) he had sufficient time to reverse his father's godly policies: "he did that was evil in the sight of the Lord, according to all that his fathers had done" (2 Kings 23.32). This is rather staggering: in such a short space of time (three months) he undid his father's reforms. How quickly evil policies can follow on the heels of godly example and legislation!

Verses 13-23: The Dishonour of Jehoiakim

In the words of Laetsch, "In a few lines Jeremiah here presents the picture of a wicked, selfish, vainglorious, cruel, covetous ruler; a man lacking every virtue sought in a king, yet immensely proud of his achievements". Jeremiah paints a grim portrait of this monarch, and the following should be noted.

The exposure of his injustice (vv.13-14)

"Woe unto him that buildeth his house by unrighteousness, and his chambers by wrong; that useth his neighbour's service without wages, and giveth him not for his work; That saith, I will build me a wide house and large chambers, and cutteth him out windows; and it is ceiled with cedar, and painted with vermilion." In the words of Feinberg, "The building mania, common amongst Oriental monarchs had seized him". According to 2 Kings 23.35, he was in straitened circumstances financially. Ellicott's Commentary (written late Nineteenth Century) states that "like the modern rulers of Constantinople, Jehoiakim went on building palaces when his kingdom was on the verge of ruin, and his subjects were groaning under their burdens".

Forced labour without wages was in direct violation of the law of Moses (Lev 19.13; Deut 24.14-15). It is said that the verb "cutteth him out windows" is "the same as that used in 4.30 for dilating the eyes by the use of antimony and implies accordingly the construction of windows of unusual width". It is also said that vermilion is "Probably the red pigment still conspicuous in the buildings of Egypt…The king was probably impelled by a vainglorious desire to imitate the magnificence of the Egyptian king (Pharaoh-Necho) who had placed him on the throne" (Ellicott's Commentary). Jehoiakim had built for himself a sumptuous palace.

The contrast with his father (vv.15-17)

"Shalt thou reign, because thou closest thyself in cedar? did not thy father eat and drink, and do judgment and justice, and then it was well with him? He judged the cause of the poor and needy; then it was well with him: was not this to know me? saith the Lord" (vv.15-16). According to Streane, the words "closest thyself in cedar" mean "viest in cedar (palaces)" or "viest with the cedar" and that "the context sufficiently suggests his ancestor Solomon with his cedar-palaces as the person whom he sought to rival". Whilst Jehoiakim thought that a splendid palace was the mark of a true king, Josiah, whilst enjoying the normal comforts of life ("did not thy father eat and drink?"), thought otherwise: he involved himself in "judgment and justice" and "judged the cause of the poor and needy". Most significant words follow: "Was not this to know me? saith the Lord". What a telling expression! The New Testament says the same: "And hereby we do know that we know him, if we keep his commandments" (1 Jn 2.3). Paul refers to those "supposing that gain is godliness" (1 Tim 6.5). True greatness lies, not in the possession of material things, but in the exercise of spiritual values and in obeying the Word of the Lord. "In choosing what was righteous he shewed himself acquainted with the character of Him whose pleasure he was doing" (Streane).

The contrast is stark: "But thine eyes and thine heart are not but for thy covetousness ('gain'), and for to shed innocent blood, and for oppression, and for violence, to do it" (v.17). Josiah excelled in judgment and justice, but Jehoiakim excelled in self-indulgence and iniquity. An example of his shedding innocent blood is given in the extradition of Urijah from Egypt, and his subsequent murder (26.20-23).

His dishonourable death (vv.18-19)

There would be no mourning for Jehoiakim. "Therefore thus saith the Lord concerning Jehoiakim the son of Josiah king of Judah; they shall not lament for him, saying, Ah, my brother! or, Ah sister! they shall not lament for him, saying, Ah lord! or, Ah his glory! He shall be buried with the burial of an ass, drawn and cast forth beyond the gates of Jerusalem." No lamentation would be expressed by his kith and kin. Family members would not be heard to exclaim as they normally did, "Ah, my brother! or, Ah sister!" (the latter would not be applicable in Jehoiakim's case) and his subjects would also be silent. None would say, "Ah lord! or, Ah his glory!". There would be no wailing over the death of their "lord" and the departure of his "glory". All this stands in striking contrast with the widespread and continued lamentation for Josiah (2 Chr 35.24-25). Jehoiakim would not be accorded the normal courtesies, and, even more shocking, he would be buried with "the burial of an ass". In other words, no burial at all: "his dead body shall be cast out in the day to the heat, and in the night to the frost" (36.30).

There is no discrepancy between this and the record of his death in 2 Kings 24.6: "So Jehoiakim slept with his fathers". As Feinberg points out, "Resting, sleeping, or being gathered with the fathers is not tantamount to burial with the fathers". Streane concurs: "The same is said of Ahab, although dying in battle ('so Ahab slept with his fathers', 1 Kings 22.40)".

The man who had lived for himself and wallowed in self-indulgence and iniquity would suffer a most ignominious end. Like one of his predecessors, Jehoram, "he departed without being desired" (2 Chr 21.20). How unlike Stephen: "And devout men carried Stephen to his burial, and made great lamentation over him" (Acts 8.2). The Lord's people do well to remember that "The memory of the just is blessed: but the name of the wicked shall rot" (Prov 10.7), and it is for this reason that Solomon also said, "A good name is better than precious ointment; and the day of death than the day of one's birth" (Eccl 7.1).

The condemnation of Jehoiakim is accompanied by a statement of coming judgment on the entire nation. It has been said that here Jeremiah mourns "the disastrous results brought on the land by the foolish international policy of Jehoiakim" (Feinberg). He rebelled against the king of Babylon, with dire results for Judah (2 Kings 24.1-2).

The consequences of his reign (vv.20-23)

"Go up to Lebanon, and cry; and lift up thy voice in Bashan, and cry from the passages ('cry from the heights of Abarim', JND): for all thy lovers are destroyed" (v.20). According to Feinberg, this comprehends the entire land: "The regions mentioned - Lebanon, Bashan, and Abarim represent the land in its entirety, from north to north-east to south-east. The invaders would overrun the whole land. Abarim refers to the regions beyond the Jordan, that is, the mountains of Moab (including Mount Nebo), east of the Dead Sea (cp. Num 27.12; Deut 32.49)". Streane substantially agrees with this: "The people, under the figure of a woman...is called upon the ascend the heights which the Chaldean hosts would successfully pass in their advance southwards upon Jerusalem, *viz.* Lebanon in the north, the hills of Bashan (Ps 68.15-16) in the north-east and Abarim in the south-east". The "lovers" are most probably Egypt and other nations upon whom Jehoiakim relied for aid against the Babylonians (cp. Jer 4.30; Ezek 23.5-9).

The judgment of the Lord upon His people was the result of longstanding rebellion against Him and the rejection of His word: "I spake unto thee in thy prosperity; but thou saidst, I will not hear. This hath been thy manner from thy youth, that thou obeyedst not my voice" (v.21). What an awful testimony! Therefore "The wind shall eat up all thy pastors, and thy lovers shall go into captivity: surely then shalt thou be ashamed and confounded for all thy wickedness" (v.22). The winds of adversity and invasion will carry off both the national leaders and their allies.

The words, "O inhabitant of Lebanon, that makest thy nest in the cedars, how gracious shalt thou be ('how wilt thou sigh', JND margin; or 'how wilt thou groan', RV margin) when pangs come upon thee, the pain as of a woman in travail!" (v.23), evidently refer, not to the region of Lebanon, but to "the king and his nobles in their cedar palaces. Jerusalem considered herself secure, like the eagles nesting in the cedars of Lebanon (cp. 21.13)" (Feinberg). Other commentators agree: "The king in his cedar palace is as one who has made Lebanon his home" (Ellicott's Commentary); "Lebanon here is Jerusalem with its royal palace and the mansions of the rich built of cedarwood from Lebanon" (Laetsch).

Verses 24-30: The Discontinuance of the throne after Coniah

Coniah (vv.24,28; 37.1) is the abbreviated form of Jeconiah and the alternative form of Jehoiachin, which was probably the regal title assumed on his accession. Jeconiah means "the Lord will establish", but because of his wickedness, he was disestablished. He is described in four ways:

A rejected signet (v.24)

"As I live, saith the Lord, though Coniah the son of Jehoiakim king of Judah were the signet upon my right hand, yet would I pluck thee thence." The unfaithfulness of Jehoiachin (Coniah) must be contrasted with the faithfulness of his grandson, Zerubbabel: "In that day, saith the Lord of hosts, will I take thee, O Zerubbabel, my servant, the son of Shealtiel, saith the Lord, and I will make thee as a signet: for I have chosen thee, saith the Lord of hosts" (Hag 2.23). The pronouncement on Coniah is reversed in the case of Zerubbabel. "The signet ring, engraved with the king's seal, was used to endorse all official documents (cp. Esther 8.10). It was so precious that, to guard against theft, it was usually worn on the king's person" (J. G. Baldwin). The words, "I will make thee as a signet", therefore, emphasise the security of Zerubbabel, the closeness of his relationship with God, and the importance of his future role, but this did not apply in the case of Coniah. Every believer today ought to be deeply concerned that his or her conduct and behaviour does not disqualify them from the honour of serving the Lord.

An exiled king (vv.25-27)

"I will give thee into the hand of them that seek thy life, and into the hand of them whose face thou fearest, even into the hand of Nebuchadrezzar king of Babylon, and into the hand of the Chaldeans. And I will cast thee out, and thy mother that bare thee, into another country, where ye were not born; and there shall ye die. But to the land whereunto they desire to return, thither shall they not return." He was exiled with his mother (Nehushta) in 597 BC (cp. 2 Kings 24.8-16; 25.27-30; Jer 29.1-2; Ezek 19.5-9) after reigning for three months and ten days, and was imprisoned for thirty-seven years in Babylon. According to 2 Kings 25.27-30 and Jeremiah 52.31-34, his punishment was mitigated, and Evil-merodach "spake kindly unto him, and set his throne above the throne of the kings that were with him in Babylon" (52.32). Amongst the captives taken to Babylon at this time was Ezekiel (Ezek 1.1-3). Hananiah, a false prophet, predicted that Jeconiah would be restored to the throne "within two full years" (28.1-4), but the word of God cannot be broken and Hananiah paid with his life for his lies (28.15-17).

A broken vessel (v.28)

"Is this man Coniah a despised broken idol? is he a vessel wherein is no pleasure? wherefore are they cast out, he and his seed, and are cast into a land which they know not?" The word rendered "idol" is not the customary one, but refers to "the potter rejecting and breaking what his own hands had made" (Ellicott's Commentary).

An heirless king (vv.29-30)

Before the Lord makes a final pronouncement on Jehoiachin, Jeremiah calls three times on the "land" (JND margin) to "hear the word of the Lord" (v.29). The repetition implies the strongest emphasis, solemnity, and intensity: "O earth, earth, earth, hear the word of the Lord". The Lord continues: "Thus saith the Lord, Write ye this man childless, a man that shall not prosper in his days: for no man of his seed shall prosper, sitting upon the throne of David, and ruling any more in Judah". In fact Jehoiachin, who is described as "Jeconiah, the captive" (RV), had seven sons (cp. 1 Chr 3.17-18) but as pointed out by Orelli the "verse does not say that he is to be absolutely childless, but only that he is to be legally counted so, no son or descendant succeeding to him". His grandson, Zerubbabel, became governor of Judah (Hag 1.1), but neither he nor any of his descendants ever ruled as king. As Feinberg observes, "Jehoiachin's uncle, Zedekiah, reigned after him, but died before him (Jer 52.10-11). Jehoiachin was therefore the last of the Judaean kings. In him the royal line became extinct. So ch.23 goes on to speak of the new king to be raised up by the Lord (23.5-6)".

Having said this, it will be noted that Jehoiachin is found in the genealogy of the Lord Jesus as given by Matthew: "And Josias begat Jechonias and his brethren, about the time they were carried away to Babylon: And after they were brought to Babylon, Jechonias begat Salathiel (Shealtiel); and Salathiel begat Zorobabel (Zerubbabel)" (Mt 1.11-12). This, however, is no contradiction of Jeremiah's prophecy that "no man of his seed shall prosper, sitting upon the throne of David, and ruling any more in Judah". As Ironside observes, "In him (Coniah) the line of Solomon's succession ends. Royalty passes over to the line of David's son, Nathan. This explains why we have the two genealogies of our Lord in the New Testament. Matthew gives Joseph's line through this very Coniah. But if Christ came through him, He would not be able to sit upon the throne. In Luke we evidently have the line of Mary the daughter of Heli, Joseph's father-in-law, through Nathan, thus preserving the blood-line of David while avoiding the curse of Coniah". Matthew's record of David's lineage indicates only that Joseph, descended from Shealtiel, was the *legal* father of the Lord Jesus, in the sense that he was Mary's husband. Matthew's Gospel very carefully emphasises that Joseph was not the father of the Lord Jesus by omitting the word "begat" in the case of Joseph, and saying, "and Jacob begat Joseph the husband of Mary, of whom was born Jesus, who is called Christ" (Mt 1.16). Joseph was clearly told by the angel that the child conceived in Mary was "of the Holy Spirit" (Mt 1.20). It can therefore be concluded that no man of Jehoiachin's seed sat upon the throne of David. Messiah was not of Coniah's line.

JEREMIAH 23

This chapter continues the "word which came unto Jeremiah from the Lord" in answer to Zedekiah's desire for the prophet's help in obtaining divine deliverance from the besieging Babylonians (21.1-2). Having pronounced the Lord's response to Zedekiah, and drawn his attention to the divine judgment which fell upon his predecessors, Shallum (otherwise known as Jehoahaz), Jehoiakim, and Coniah (otherwise known as Jeconiah or Jehoiachin), Jeremiah cries, "Woe be unto the pastors that destroy and scatter the sheep of my pasture! saith the Lord" (v.1). During the reign of Jehoiakim the Lord had said "The wind shall eat up all thy pastors" (22.22), and the opening verses (vv.1-2) of the current chapter evidently refer to the same men.

The word rendered "pastors" (7462) is often translated "shepherds" and an example occurs later in this passage: "And I will set up shepherds over them" (v.4). While it has been suggested that the words "pastors" or "shepherds" describe the leadership generally, including kings, prophets and priests, the present context suggests that Jeremiah is censuring the kings of Judah. An earlier passage (2.8) certainly distinguishes the "pastors" from the priests and the prophets. Ezekiel was commanded to "prophesy against the shepherds of Israel" who had totally disregarded the welfare of the sheep (Ezek 34.1-10). These verses evidently refer to the pre-exilic kings of Judah who were altogether unlike David whom the Lord "brought...to feed Jacob his people, and Israel his inheritance", and who "fed them according to the integrity of his heart; and guided them by the skilfulness of his hands" (Ps 78.71-72).

Bearing in mind the connection between chapters 21, 22 and 23, it should be noted that while it was said of Coniah, the penultimate king of Judah, that "no man of his seed shall prosper, sitting upon the throne of David, and ruling any more in Judah" (22.30), this cannot possibly mean that the Lord had annulled His covenant with David (2 Sam 7.4-17). Chapter 23 clearly states that the Lord will "raise unto David a righteous Branch, and a King shall reign and prosper...In his days Judah shall be saved, and Israel shall dwell safely" (vv.5-6). It should also be noted that the name Zedekiah, borne by the final king of Judah, means "the Lord is my righteousness". This monarch was anything but righteous. He is called the "profane wicked prince of Israel" (Ezek 21.25), but the throne of David will be occupied by another King, and "his name...shall be called, THE LORD OUR RIGHTEOUSNESS" (v.6).

The chapter may be divided into two major sections:

The Exercise of Pastoral Care (vv.1-8)
The Exposure of False Prophets (vv.9-40).

Having described the heads of state, past and future (vv.1-8), Jeremiah then describes the leaders of religious life in the nation (vv.9-40).

Verses 1-8: The Exercise of Pastoral Care

These verses describe the scattering of the flock (vv.1-2); the regathering of the flock (vv.3-4); and the reign of the Shepherd-King (vv.5-8).

The scattering of the flock (vv.1-2)

"Woe be unto the pastors that destroy and scatter the sheep of my pasture! saith the Lord. Therefore thus saith the Lord God of Israel against the pastors that feed my people." As already noted, the subject is dealt with more extensively in Ezekiel 34.1-10. The way in which these "pastors" totally misused their position to the complete detriment of the flock is paralleled in the New Testament: "For I know this, that after my departing shall grievous wolves enter in among you, not sparing the flock. Also of your own selves shall men arise, speaking perverse things, to draw away disciples after them" (Acts 20.29-30). The Lord describes His people as "the sheep of *my* pasture" (v.1); "*my* people" (v.2); "*my* flock" (v.2). Elders today tend "the flock of God" (1 Pet 5.2). There is a twofold aspect to their work: in relation to the assembly they act as shepherds (Acts 20.28, where the word "feed" means to act as a shepherd) and in relation to God they act as stewards (Titus 1.7). Every elder, as a steward, should bear in mind the question: "Where is the flock that was given thee, thy beautiful flock?" (13.20).

It should be noticed that the culpability of the "pastors" is emphasised. It was bad enough that the Lord had to say, "My sheep wandered through all the mountains...yea, my flock was scattered upon all the face of the earth, and none did search or seek after them (Ezek 34.6), but this was even worse: "Ye have scattered my flock, and driven them away" (v.2). Feinberg points out the double sense of the Hebrew word PAQAD (6485), meaning either "to care for" or "to chastise", in the words "ye...have not *visited* them: behold I will *visit* upon you the evil of your doings, saith the Lord". The shepherds had not bestowed care on the flock; so God would bestow punishment on them. It is worth pointing out in this connection that in the New Testament the words rendered "bishop" (overseer) and "visitation" are almost identical, which strongly suggests, apart from other considerations, that every assembly overseer should engage in visitation.

The regathering of the flock (vv.3-4)

If the scattering of Israel was literal, then their regathering must also be literal. "And I will gather the remnant of my flock out of all countries whither I have driven them" (v.3). Ezekiel uses similar language: "As a shepherd seeketh out his flock in the day that he is among his sheep that are scattered; so will I seek out my sheep...And I will bring them out from the people, and gather them from the countries, and will bring them to their own land" (Ezek 34.12-13). Attention is drawn to the following.

The regathering will be divinely accomplished

"And *I* will gather the remnant of my flock out of all countries whither *I* have driven them" (v.3). This regathering is emphasised by Isaiah: "And it shall come to pass in that day, that the Lord shall set his hand again the second time to recover the remnant of his people…And he shall set up an ensign for the nations, and shall assemble the outcasts of Israel, and gather together the dispersed of Judah from the four corners of the earth" (Is 11.11-12). While it is said to the "pastors", "Ye have scattered my flock, and driven them away" (v.2), their actions "in driving the people away is now attributed to the Lord because He ultimately carried out the penalty brought on the people by their own sins and by the sins of their leaders" (Feinberg). "The remnant of my flock" are the "elect" at the end-time of whom the Lord Jesus, referring to the coming "great tribulation", said, "And except those days should be shortened, there should no flesh be saved: but for the elect's sake those days shall be shortened" (Mt 24.22). The "remnant" are the "all Israel" (Rom 11.26). No apostate Jew will be saved.

The regathering will involve the entire world

"And I will gather the remnant of my flock out of *all countries*" (v.3). While some commentators consider that this was fulfilled in the return from Babylonian exile, the reference to "all countries" points to the end-time and to the regathering described the Lord Jesus: "And then shall appear the sign of the Son of man in heaven…And he shall send his angels with a great sound of a trumpet, and they shall gather together his elect from the four winds, from one end of heaven to the other" (Mt 24.30-31). This is not at variance with such passages as Isaiah 49.18-23. The exiles will be gathered by divine power, but Gentiles will be the vehicles through whom it will be accomplished.

The regathering will be to their former land

"I…will bring them again to their folds" where "they shall be fruitful and increase" (v.3). The sheep will be returned to their own pasture. Ezekiel expresses it as follows: "I will multiply upon you man and beast; and they shall increase and bring fruit: and I will settle you after your old estates, and will do better unto you than at your beginnings" (Ezek 36.11). In fact, the land will be too small for them. This is implied by Zechariah: "I will bring them into the land of Gilead (presently part of the country of Jordan) and Lebanon; and place shall not be found for them" (Zech 10.10).

The regathering will be accompanied by permanent care

"And I will set up shepherds over them which shall feed them: and they shall fear no more, nor be dismayed, neither shall they be lacking, saith the Lord" (v.4). This should be compared with, "And I will give you pastors according to mine heart, which shall feed you with knowledge and understanding" (3.15). The faithless shepherds of the past (v.2) will be replaced by faithful shepherds. At this time the Lord's people will enjoy the care of "seven shepherds, and eight principal (princely) men" (Micah 5.5). The words "*seven* shepherds" could refer to the completeness of shepherd care, and "*eight* principal men" could refer to a totally new character of rule, bearing in mind that the number eight indicates the commencement of something new.

The reign of the Shepherd-King (vv.5-8)
Having denounced the faithless shepherds and predicted the coming of faithful shepherds, Jeremiah now completes the picture of the future blessing of the Lord's people by describing the Shepherd-King who will "feed his flock like a shepherd: he shall gather the lambs with his arm, and carry them in his bosom, and shall gently lead those that are with young" (Is 40.11). It has been pointed out that the formula "the days come" has Messianic implications. He is described in three ways.

"A righteous Branch"
"Behold, the days come, saith the Lord, that I will raise unto David a righteous Branch" (v.5). While some of the kings of Judah were praiseworthy, no other scion of the house of David could be described in this way. All would have to say with David, "Behold, I was shapen in iniquity; and in sin did my mother conceive me" (Ps 51.5). Only the Lord Jesus can be called "a righteous Branch". His was not an acquired righteousness. He was born as "that holy thing" (Lk 1.35).

This is one of five similar references to the Lord Jesus Christ in the Old Testament: Is 4.2; Jer 33.15; Zech 3.8; 6.12. The word "Branch" (6780) means "shoot" or "sprout" and it is significant that the Lord Jesus is not described here as a stately tree, but as a shoot from the roots. This indicates the simple but important fact that the Lord will bring new life to the nation of Israel when, humanly speaking, all seems lost. It should be noted that a different word (5342) is used in Isaiah 11.1, although the words, "there shall come forth a rod ('shoot', RV) out of the stem ('stock', RV) of Jesse", also indicate new life for the nation.

It is not difficult to relate these five references to the four Gospels. The promise here, "I will raise unto David a righteous Branch" points to Matthew's Gospel: it is the Gospel of the "Branch....unto David" (Jer 33.15). Mark is the Gospel of "my servant the BRANCH" (Zech 3.8). Luke is the Gospel of "the man whose name is The BRANCH" (Zech 6.12). John is the Gospel of "the branch of the Lord" (Is 4.2). The context of each reference is most instructive, and merits careful examination.

A reigning King
"A King shall reign and prosper, and shall execute judgment and justice in the earth ('land', JND)" (v.5). Zedekiah, the last king of Judah was really only a puppet-king. He was appointed by Nebuchadnezzar (2 Chr 36.10) and paid the terrible penalty of rebelling against him. The Lord Jesus will

reign as a true King. Unlike the wicked kings of Judah, particularly Josiah's successors, whose sinfulness meant that they presided over unrelieved disaster, He will bring unparalleled prosperity. "He shall come down like rain upon the mown grass: as showers that water the earth. In his days shall the righteous flourish; and abundance of peace so long as the moon endureth" (Ps 72.6-7). He will "reign in righteousness" (Is 32.1), and "righteousness shall be the girdle of his loins, and faithfulness the girdle of his reins" (Is 11.5). Moreover, He will rule over a reunited kingdom that will enjoy peace and security: "In his days Judah shall be saved, and Israel shall dwell safely" (Jer 23.6).

The righteousness of His people
"And this is his name whereby he shall be called, THE LORD OUR RIGHTEOUSNESS" (v.6). While, in a similar context, Jerusalem is called "The Lord our righteousness" (33.16) it would be quite unwarranted in the present context for Jeremiah "to be speaking of a Davidic descendant and then without warning or preparation to turn to a name for Jerusalem" (Feinberg). Laetsch points out that Jeremiah "does not mean merely to repeat what he had said a moment before, that the King is to be personally righteous in all His actions. He adds a new thought. As a king or ruler He is to make, create, establish a new norm, a new righteousness, because of which He shall be called 'Our Righteousness', sinful man's righteousness". Laetsch continues, thinking in terms of believers today: "By His vicarious, substitutionary fulfilment of all the demands of the mandatory and punitive justice of God He became 'Our Righteousness'". According to Harrison, "The designation *the Lord is our righteousness* means 'the one who secures our vindication'".

In view of the above, both the manner in which the Lord's people will be regathered and the character of their Shepherd-King, their future restoration will exceed anything in the past. It will surpass the deliverance from Egypt: "Therefore, behold, the days come, saith the Lord, that they shall no more say, The Lord liveth, which brought up the children of Israel out of the land of Egypt; But, The Lord liveth, which brought up and which led the seed of the house of Israel out of the north country, and from all countries whither I had driven them; and they shall dwell in their own land" (vv.7-8).

Verses 9-40: The Exposure of the False Prophets
Having denounced the "pastors" (vv.1-2), Jeremiah turns to the prophets. The section of the chapter commences with his deep distress over the state of the prophetic office. "Mine heart within me is broken because of the prophets; all my bones shake; I am like a drunken man, and like a man whom wine hath overcome, because of the Lord, and because of the words of his holiness" (v.9). The prophet was deeply shocked. When "he contrasted their evil ways and words with the holy words of God, it was

more than he could contemplate without deep agony of soul" (Feinberg). Jeremiah does not show vindictiveness towards his opponents; he is utterly heart-broken at the situation. It could be said that Jeremiah shows by his anguish that he has the heart of a true pastor (cp. 17.16).

This section of the chapter denounces the prophets in four ways: they disregarded God's word (vv.10-15); they were devoid of God's word (vv.16-22); they displaced God's word (vv.23-32); and they debased God's word (vv.33-40).

They disregarded God's word (vv.10-15)

These men had no moral right to prophesy. Their behaviour disqualified them from office. They were depraved. This is clear from the words, "they commit adultery, and walk in lies: they strengthen also the hands of evildoers" (v.14). The following should be noted.

The result of their evil ways

Their influence on the nation was totally evil: the people followed their evil ways. In consequence, gross immorality abounded: "the land is full of adulterers"; the Lord had withdrawn His blessings: "for because of swearing (using the Lord's name in vain, Ex 20.7) the land mourneth; the pleasant places of the wilderness are dried up"; the only strength in the nation was the power to do wrong: "their course is evil, and their force is not right" (v.10). The reason for the abysmal state of the nation follows: "*For* both prophet and priest are profane" (v.11). It is for good reason that Timothy was told: "Take heed unto *thyself*, and unto the doctrine; continue in them: for in doing this thou shalt both save thyself, and them that hear thee" (1 Tim 4.16).

The extent of their evil ways

"For both prophet and priest are profane; yea, in my house have I found their wickedness, saith the Lord" (v.11). The prophets and the priests were "partners in crime". The religious leaders, whether prophets or priests, were totally corrupt. The word "profane" (2610) means impious or godless (Gesenius). Their wickedness was not confined to their personal and secular lives. Inevitably, it permeated the house of God. Ezekiel draws a horrifying picture of the corruption which had invaded the Temple at Jerusalem (Ezek 8.5-18), and the Lord Jesus said, "It is written, My house is the house of prayer: but ye have made it a den of thieves" (Lk 19.46). The Lord's people today should never forget that sin in their lives will affect the local assembly.

The judgment on their evil ways

Sin is a hard taskmaster. "Wherefore their way shall be unto them as slippery ways in the darkness: they shall be driven on, and fall therein: for I will bring evil upon them, even the year of their visitation, saith the Lord" (v.12). "Their way, the way they chose, will be a slippery, dangerous one, on which they will have to walk in the darkness of sin and unbelief. No light from God will illumine their path. Unmercifully they will be driven on by Satan to their ruin" (Laetsch).

The hypocrisy of their evil ways

Jeremiah examines the evil behaviour of the false prophets in Samaria and in Jerusalem. The former were devoted to Baal and made no attempt to cover their idolatry: "And I have seen folly in the prophets of Samaria; they prophesied in Baal, and caused my people Israel to err" (v.13). The latter blatantly practised evil, and by their example hardened the nation against repentance, yet at the same time they professed to be the Lord's spokesmen: "I have seen also in the prophets of Jerusalem an horrible thing: they commit adultery, and walk in lies: they strengthen also the hands of evildoers, that none doth return from his wickedness" (v.14). The prophets in Samaria were at least honest: they "prophesied in Baal". But the prophets in Jerusalem had the effrontery to say "the Lord hath said" (v.17), and practised immorality and idolatry at the same time. Their influence on Jerusalem was catastrophic: it had become a second Sodom and Gomorrah (v.14). Isaiah had said the same (Is 1.9-10), and at the end-time Jerusalem is described as "the great city, which spiritually is called Sodom and Egypt, where also our Lord was crucified" (Rev 11.8). It has to be said that the fearful increase in sodomy today has been aided and abetted by men who profess to be ministers of religion.

The spread of their evil ways

"Therefore thus saith the Lord of hosts concerning the prophets; Behold, I will feed them with wormwood, and make them drink the water of gall: for from the prophets of Jerusalem is profaneness gone forth into all the land" (v.15). Because they had "poisoned the nation's spiritual springs, the Lord would inflict drastic judgment on them" (Feinberg).

They were devoid of God's word (vv.16-22)

This section begins with a warning: "Thus saith the Lord of hosts, Hearken not unto the words of the prophets that prophesy unto you" (v.16). The reason for the warning is very clearly stated throughout the section: "they speak a vision of their own heart, and not out of the mouth of the Lord" (v.16); "For who (that is, 'whom of them') hath stood in the counsel of the Lord, and hath perceived and heard his word?" (v.18); "I have not sent these prophets, yet they ran: I have not spoken to them, yet they prophesied" (v.21).

These prophets were like the people described by Jude: "clouds they are without water" (Jude v.12), which evidently alludes to Proverbs 25.14: "Whoso boasteth himself of a false gift is like clouds and wind without rain". There were certainly not like Haggai who rightly describes himself as "the Lord's messenger in the Lord's message" (Hag 1.13).

Their pronouncements proved that they were without God's word (vv.16-18)

The outstanding feature of false prophecy is its presentation of false hope. False prophets never counselled repentance in view of coming judgment. The true prophet "roused the conscience, caused pain and anger by his reproofs; the other soothed and quieted men with a false assurance (6.14; 14.13)" (Ellicott's Commentary). The false prophets told the people what they wanted to hear rather than what the Lord wanted them to hear. This gave the people false assurance: "Thus saith the Lord of hosts, Hearken not unto the words of the prophets that prophesy unto you: *they make you vain* ('they lead you to vanity', JND)" (v.16). The "vanity" to which Jeremiah refers is then explained: "They say still unto them that despise me, The Lord hath said, Ye shall have peace; and they say unto every one that walketh after the imagination of his own heart, No evil shall come upon you" (v.17). This immediately identifies them as prophets which "speak a vision of their own heart, and not out of the mouth of the Lord" (v.16). Jeremiah did not belong to this category of prophet: he spoke from "the mouth of the Lord" (2 Chr 36.12).

The people addressed by the false prophets are described as "them that despise me" and "every one that walketh after the imagination of his own heart" (v.17). The prophets who spoke "a vision of their own heart" appealed to people who walked after the imagination of their heart. Speaker and hearer were certainly on the same wavelength!

The fact that their message lacked divine authority simply proved that they had not heard the voice of the Lord. They said, "The Lord hath said" (v.17) but none of them "stood in the counsel of the Lord": "For who hath stood in the counsel (or 'council', 5475) of the Lord, and hath perceived and heard his word? who hath marked his word, and heard it?" (v.18). These prophets had not stood in "the council of Jehovah" (JND), that is, they were not amongst those with whom He shared His mind and will, and of whom Amos said, "Surely the Lord God will do nothing, but he revealeth his secret unto his servants the prophets" (Amos 3.7). "Could any of the false prophets say that they had been called as into the privy council of Jehovah?" (Ellicott's Commentary).

The New Testament places great responsibility on those who preach and teach the Word of God: "If any man speak, let him speak as the oracles of God" (1 Pet 4.11). This statement places great responsibility on the man who speaks publicly. When he speaks, God's voice should be heard. The preacher or teacher has good cause to remember that "to this man will I look, even to him that…trembleth at my word" (Is 66.2). When a man stands up in the assembly to teach, his ministry must come from the Sanctuary. When a brother preaches the gospel, the message must be written on his heart by the Spirit of God. The standard for the Bible Class leader or the Sunday School teacher cannot be less.

Coming judgment would prove that they were without God's word (vv. 19-20)

The false hopes engendered by the false prophets would evaporate when divine judgment fell on the nation: "Behold, a whirlwind of the Lord is gone forth in fury, even a grievous whirlwind: it shall fall grievously upon the head of the wicked. The anger of the Lord shall not return, until he have executed, and till he have performed the thoughts of his heart: in the latter days ye shall consider it perfectly ('clearly', JND)". There is a vast difference between the "vision of their own heart (the heart of the false prophet)" (v.16) and the "thoughts of his heart (the heart of the Lord)" (v.20).

Lack of effect proved that they were without God's word (vv.21-22)

"I have not sent these prophets, yet they ran: I have not spoken to them, yet they prophesied" (v.21). The false prophets "ran" with "unbecoming eagerness to assume the prophetic office without the Lord's sanction. How unlike God's prophets! (Ex 3.11; 4.1 ff; Is 6.1-8; Jer 1.1-15; Amos 7.14-15)" (Laetsch). The false prophets had no influence whatsoever on the state and course of the nation: "But if they had stood in my counsel ('council', JND), and had caused my people to hear my words, then they should have turned them from their evil way, and from the evil of their doings". In the words of Feinberg, "If they had been in the intimate circle where God divulges His plans to His faithful followers…the result would have been the repentance of the nation and their restoration to godliness. The proof of the true prophet was his desire to win others to the way of godliness in which he himself was walking. The results of his ministry were indicators of the genuineness of his call and message".

But was Jeremiah's own work successful in this sense? Must not the prophet speak "whether they will hear, or whether they will forbear?" (Ezek 2.5). The question is answered as follows in Ellicott's Commentary: "true teaching seldom fails altogether of its work", and "where it seems to fail it satisfies the other test, and at least stirs and rouses men from lethargy, even if it stirs them to antagonism. It is never satisfied with speaking smooth things and acquiescing in the evil that surrounds it". One thing is very clear: men without God's word can do nothing: they cannot avert divine judgment. They may tell people what they want to hear (v.17) but it will make no moral impact upon them (v.22).

They displaced God's word (vv.23-32)

They displaced God's word with their dreams. Jeremiah bluntly describes the "vision of their own heart" (v.16) as "the deceit of their own heart" (v.26) saying that the false prophets prophesied "lies in my name, saying,

I have dreamed, I have dreamed" (v.25). The words "dreamed", "dreams" or "dream" occur six times in these verses. So much for their visions - they were just dreams! Jeremiah is not denying that there were times when divine revelation was given by dreams, but the false prophets claimed authority for their own alleged dreams. Attention is drawn to the following.

The Lord's awareness of their false dreams (vv.23-25)
The false prophets evidently thought that their pronouncements went unnoticed and unheard by the Lord. The words of Eliphaz to Job could well be addressed to them: "And thou sayest, How doth God know? can he judge through the dark cloud? Thick clouds are a covering to him, that he seeth not; and he walketh in the circuit of heaven" (Job 22.13-14). But the Lord is omnipotent and omniscient: "Am I a God at hand, saith the Lord, and not a God afar off? Can any hide himself in secret places that I shall not see him? saith the Lord. Do not I fill heaven and earth? saith the Lord. I have heard what the prophets said, that prophesy lies in my name, saying, I have dreamed, I have dreamed". These three questions emphasise that the Lord is not "a localised deity whom it is easy to avoid" (Feinberg).

The evil purpose of their false dreams (vv.26-27)
"How long shall this be in the heart of the prophets that prophesy lies? yea, they are prophets of the deceit of their own heart; Which think to cause my people to forget my name by their dreams which they tell every man to his neighbour, as their fathers have forgotten my name for Baal". The object of false prophecy has always been the same: to lead people away from the true God. This will reach universal proportions at the end-time with the advent of "that Wicked...whose coming is after the working of Satan with all power and signs and lying wonders, And with all deceivableness of unrighteousness in them that perish; because they received not the love of the truth, that they might be saved" (2 Thess 2.8-10).

The superiority of God's word over false dreams (vv.28-29)
"The prophet that hath a dream, let him tell a dream; and he that hath my word, let him speak my word faithfully. What is the chaff to the wheat? saith the Lord" (v.28). If a prophet had a dream, he was to relate it as a dream and nothing more so that all who listened were under no misunderstanding. The true prophet was to "diminish not a word" of the message committed to him (26.2). He was to "declare...all the counsel of God" (Acts 20.27). The dreams of the false prophets were to the word of God as chaff to the wheat. The pronouncements of the false prophets had no value, but those of the Lord's true servants were food and strength to all who received them. But this was not all. God's word is likened, not only to wheat, but to a fire and to a hammer: "Is not my word like as a fire? saith the Lord; and like a hammer that breaketh the rock in pieces?" (v.29). The false prophets preached a message of hope and reassurance which had no

foundation in repentance and righteousness, and was therefore useless and powerless. But the Word of God in the mouths of His true servants is penetrating, purifying and consumes evil. Jeremiah himself knew its power in this way (5.14; 20.9). Moreover, the Word of God is powerful in its ability to crush the most resistant barriers, and there is nothing so obstinate as the human heart (17.9). As Feinberg observes, "His message does not lull men in their sins: it crushes the heart to bring it to repentance. The true word convicts and converts, it neither amuses nor entertains".

Bearing in mind that the New Testament indicates further ways in which teaching can be assessed, these verses nevertheless provide a means by which all pronouncements, including alleged dreams, can be tested. They also provide a means by which the true word of God can be identified. It could be said here, "if they speak not according to this word, it is because there is no light in them" (Is 8.20).

Divine judgment on the perpetrators of false dreams (vv.30-32)
Three reasons for divine judgment are given, and in each case the Lord's opposition to the false prophets is clearly stated.

In the first case, "*I am against* the prophets, saith the Lord, that steal my words every one from his neighbour" (v.30). This suggests that these lying prophets were misappropriating and using the prophecies of God's true servants to their own ends. The word "neighbour" must mean a fellow-prophet, and in his case, "one who had really received a revelation at first-hand from Jehovah" (The Pulpit Commentary). "The false prophets, not trusting to their dreams alone, listen greedily to the discourses of men like Jeremiah, not with a view to spiritual profit, but to make their own utterances more effective" (The Pulpit Commentary). It has to be said that the most dangerous opponents of the gospel today are men who can camouflage their doctrines with acceptable language and phraseology.

In the second case, "*I am against* the prophets, saith the Lord, that use their tongues, and say, He saith" (v.31). By claiming that they have the word of God they endeavour to give their pronouncements the ring of authenticity. The bulwark against these claims is to emulate the Jews at Berea of whom it is said, "they...searched the scriptures daily, whether those things were so" (Acts 17.11). The Lord's people today need "good Berean blood flowing through their veins!" (Jeffrey Harrison).

In the third case, "*I am against* them that prophesy false dreams, saith the Lord, and do tell them, and cause my people to err by their lies, and by their lightness; yet I sent them not, nor commanded them: therefore they shall not profit this people at all, saith the Lord" (v.32). It does appear that one objective of the false prophets was to raise national morale. But this was far from being in the best interests of the Lord's people. The "false dreams", the "lies" and the "lightness" was nothing but empty talk. The true welfare of Jerusalem and Judah lay in repentance and morality. The expression "their lightness" calls for attention. According to Ellicott's Commentary, "The Hebrew word is the same in meaning as the 'unstable as water' of Genesis 49.4, the 'light persons' of Judges 9.4 and Zephaniah 3.4, and points primarily to the gushing or spurting forth of water. Here it points to what we may call the 'babbling' of the false prophets".

They debased God's word (vv.33-40)

Of these verses, Campbell Morgan writes: "The last charge was the most serious of all. They were profane in another sense of the word. They were profane in that they claimed to speak with divine authority. They said, 'This is the utterance of God'…This was the last sin of these prophets, the debasing of spiritual formulae, the using of the language of orthodoxy, but in false way, the claiming to speak in the name of Jehovah, while they were seeking no message from God". The following should be noted.

The way in which they were debasing God's word (vv.33-34)

The word "burden" (4853) occurs eight times in this section: vv.33 (twice), 34, 36 (twice), 38 (thrice). According to Feinberg, it is important to realise that there is a play on this word which "had a primary meaning from which was derived an important secondary meaning. In the first instance the word comes from a verb meaning 'to lift' or 'to lift up' with the noun (the thing lifted up) denoting a 'burden' in the physical sense, but by usage the word came to mean that which was placed as a burden on the heart of a prophet, having already been such on the heart of God". It seems likely that the question put to Jeremiah, "What is the burden of the Lord?" (v.33), was asked sarcastically "in a manner similar to the American idiom, 'What's new?'" (Habel). The AV rendering of Jeremiah's reply makes good sense as it stands: "What burden? I will even forsake you, saith the Lord" (v.33). The "burden" was nothing else but exile and shame. However, nearly all commentators point out that without any change of consonants in the Hebrew text but only by another division of them, the question, "What burden?", can be translated, as in the Septuagint, "You are the burden!". The idea is evidently extended in the words, "I will even cast you off, saith Jehovah" (JND), that is, the Lord would shortly unburden Himself of them in judgment.

The question asked, it is suggested, flippantly, "What is the burden of the Lord" (v.33), leads to the stringent condemnation of the way in which such solemn language was being debased: "And as for the prophet, and the priest, and the people, that shall say, The burden of the Lord (meaning, 'This is the burden of the Lord'), I will even punish that man and his house" (v.34).

The prohibition on debasing God's word (vv.35-37)

"Thus shall ye say every one to his neighbour, and every one to his brother, What hath the Lord answered? and, What hath the Lord spoken?"

(v.35). This is repeated in v.37. Rather than continuing their affectation of using solemn words that had become hollow and meaningless, which was nothing less than hypocrisy which showed itself in cant, Jeremiah "calls men back to the simpler terms, which were less open to abuse" (Ellicott's Commentary). "And the burden of the Lord shall ye mention no more: for every man's word shall be his burden; for ye have perverted the words of the living God, of the Lord of hosts our God" (v.36). It has been pointed out that if they "continued to apply it (the word 'burden') to the words of their own heart, they would find it a 'burden' (the prophet plays once more on the etymology of the word) too heavy to be borne. This would be the righteous punishment of the reckless levity with which they had treated the sacred Name" (Ellicott's Commentary). Feinberg makes the pertinent observation that "though the term "oracle" ('burden', AV) was used by canonical prophets (e.g. Is 13.1; Nahum 1.1; Hab 1.1; Zech 9.1; Mal 1.1) Jeremiah never used it of his own prophecies because it had become the hallmark of the lying prophets".

The consequences of debasing God's word (vv.38-40)

"But since ye say (or, 'if ye say'), The burden of the Lord; therefore thus saith the Lord; Because ye say this word, The burden of the Lord, and I have sent unto you, saying, Ye shall not say, The burden of the Lord; Therefore, behold, I, even I, will utterly forget you, and I will forsake you, and the city that I gave you and your fathers, and cast you out of my presence: And I will bring an everlasting reproach upon you, and a perpetual shame, which shall not be forgotten." According to Ellicott's Commentary "many modern commentators" adopt the Septuagint which by "a very sight alteration of a single letter of the Hebrew verb" connects it with the root of the word translated "burden", giving the rendering, "I will take you up as a burden, and cast you off". While this may seem to have some contextual support, care should be exercised over "very slight alterations" of this nature. Feinberg is perhaps to be preferred here: "The horrifying prospect of being utterly forgotten of God loomed before the lying prophets".

JEREMIAH 24

This chapter relates the vision of the two baskets of figs and represents the final part of the Lord's answer to Zedekiah's request for the help of Jeremiah in securing the lifting of the Babylonian siege of Jerusalem (21.1-2). This section of the prophecy (chs.21-24) commences and ends with Zedekiah's name (21.1; 24.8) which is therefore used as an *inclusio*. The section begins with his anticipated deliverance into the hand of Nebuchadnezzar, when all who remain in Jerusalem would "die by the sword, and by the famine, and by the pestilence" (21.9), and ends in the same way: he would be amongst the "evil figs" (24.8) in the vision, who were to be "removed into all the kingdoms of the earth for their hurt" and upon whom the Lord would send "the sword, the famine and the pestilence, among them, till they be consumed from off the land" (24.9-10). The final king of Judah would pass off the scene, not only as a "profane wicked prince of Israel" (Ezek 21.25), but as an "evil fig".

The use of figs in describing the Lord's people here was far from random choice. Both the vine and the fig tree depict the nation of Israel (cp. Micah 4.4) and the Lord Jesus clearly had Israel in mind when cursing the barren fig tree (Mt 21.18-19) and in relating the parable of the barren fig tree (Lk 13.6-9). Matthew 24.32 and John 1.48 should also be considered in this connection.

The chapter divides clearly into two sections:

The Illustration (vv.1-3)
The Interpretation (vv.4-10).

Verses 1-3: The Illustration
"The Lord shewed me, and, behold, two baskets of figs were set before the temple of the Lord, after that Nebuchadrezzar king of Babylon had carried away captive Jeconiah son of Jehoiakim king of Judah, and the princes of Judah, with the carpenters and smiths, from Jerusalem, and had brought them to Babylon" (v.1). Jeremiah sent a letter to these very people (29.1-29), encouraging them to settle down in Babylon until "seventy years be accomplished" (29.10).

The historical background to these verses is found in 2 Kings 24.10-16. It has been suggested that the deportation of Jeconiah (alias Coniah or Jehoiachin) and the princes of Judah was in effect the removal of potential troublemakers, and that the deportation of the "carpenters ('craftsmen', JND) and smiths" (a figure of 3,023 is given in Jeremiah 52.28) was "partly a matter of policy, making the city more helpless by removing those who might have forged weapons or strengthened its defences, partly, doubtless, of ostentation, that they might help in the construction of buildings with which Nebuchadnezzar was increasing the splendour of his city" (Ellicott's Commentary).

While this may have been Nebuchadnezzar's purpose, the Lord had other objectives in mind, and these become clear in the subsequent verses. The fact that Jeremiah was party to the Lord's will in this way is confirmed by the fact that the verb "shewed" (7200) is frequently used in the Old Testament to indicate the divine origin of a vision (cp. Ex 25.9; Amos 7.1,4,7; Zech 1.20; 3.1), and therefore emphasises that, unlike the false prophets who "speak a vision of their own heart, and not out of the mouth of the Lord" (23.16), Jeremiah "stood in the counsel of the Lord, and hath perceived and heard his word" (23.18).

The two baskets of figs are now described: "One basket had very good figs, even like the figs that are first ripe: and the other basket had very naughty figs, which could not be eaten, they were so bad". The fig harvest is in August. Sometimes, however, the figs ripen early, in June, and these are regarded as a delicacy. It should be said that the word rendered "naughty" (7451) is usually translated "evil". According to Ellicott's Commentary, "The 'naughty' (i.e. worthless) fruits were those that had been left behind on the tree, bruised and decayed. The word was not confined in the 16th century to the language of the nursery, and was applied freely to things as well as persons".

Some commentators suggest that the words, "two baskets of figs were set before the temple of the Lord", imply that they had been literally brought to the Lord as an offering (cp. Deut 26.2), but this overlooks the fact that Jeremiah saw the baskets in a vision and that their position before the Lord in the vision indicates that He was both thoroughly aware and in complete control of His people's future. The pleasure that "first ripe" figs gives to the eater should remind the Lord's people today that it should be said of them that "the Lord taketh pleasure in his people" (Ps 149.4). The purpose of the question "What seest thou, Jeremiah?" (v.3) was evidently to concentrate Jeremiah's mind on the vision and its explanation.

Verses 4-10: The Interpretation

There seems no reason to doubt the general view that the purpose of the vision was to disabuse the Jews remaining in Jerusalem of the idea that they were in a superior position to their brethren in captivity. After all, Nebuchadnezzar had spared the city and given them another king, albeit a mere puppet, and all this pointed to the fact that "they were now God's specially chosen remnant and that only those in exile were under God's direct condemnation (cp. Ezek 11.15; 33.24). The message of Jeremiah affirms that the reverse is true" (Habel). The two baskets of figs, "the good figs, very good" (v.3) and "the evil, very evil" (v.3), represented, respectively, the people of Judah in captivity (vv.4-7) and the people remaining in Jerusalem (vv.8-10). Had they been asked to which basket they belonged, the Jews in Jerusalem would have doubtless replied that they were the "very good figs" and that their brethren had been carried off because they were "very naughty figs" (v.2). But this was not the case.

It must be said that the two classes do not necessarily mean that those who were deported by Nebuchadnezzar were morally better than those that remained in Jerusalem. Rather that, in His sovereign grace, the Lord would deal with the deportees as with "very good figs", leaving those remaining in Jerusalem as very "naughty" figs which could not be eaten, they were so bad (v.3). The chapter clearly teaches that the Lord's hand lay behind the apparent tragedy of the captivity which terminated Jehoiachin's reign; the exiles were removed by His determining will so that He could purge the land of its evil before restoring a godly people at a later date.

The good figs (vv.4-7)

As already noted, the basket of "very good figs" represents the exiles: "Thus saith the Lord, the God of Israel: Like these good figs, so will I acknowledge them that are carried away captive of Judah, whom I have sent out of this place into the land of the Chaldeans for their good" (v.5). Feinberg rightly points out that "The word 'good' refers not the character of the exiles, but to their circumstances. They were not taken to Babylon for their piety and godliness. But the Lord promised that He would look with favour on them (v.6). His feeling of concern for them was manifested in their exemption from the horrors of the Fall of Jerusalem in 586 BC and their being cured of idolatry". Their captivity was designed by the Lord for their ultimate blessing. The following should be noted.

The Lord would "acknowledge them" (v.5)

"Like these good figs, so will I regard for good them that are carried away captive of Judah, whom I have sent out of this place into the land of the Chaldeans" (JND). The words "for their good" (AV) refer to His acknowledgement of them rather than to their actual exile. This is confirmed in the following verse: "I will set mine eyes upon them for good" (v.6). The Lord would look with favour upon the exiles. In fact they were to "seek the peace of the city" to which they had been taken, and "pray unto the Lord for it: for in the peace thereof shall ye have peace" (29.7). Divine favour in this way was not based on compromise with their sinful ways. The Babylonian exile had a salutary effect on the Lord's people there: "Their very contact with the monstrous idolatry of Babylon made them more conscious than they had ever been before of the greatness of their own faith. The process which, at the end of the seventy years of exile, made them once more and forever a purely monotheistic people, had already begun" (Ellicott's Commentary).

The Lord would restore them (v.6a)

"For I will set mine eyes upon them for good, and I will bring them again to this land." There was certainly a partial fulfillment of this promise in the return to the land following the decree of Cyrus (2 Chr 36.22-23;

Ezra 1.1-3). The Lord had set His "eyes upon them for good" in preparation for their repatriation. They had gone to Babylon as slaves and prisoners; they returned with gifts of "silver, and with gold, and with goods, and with beasts, beside the freewill offering for the house of God that is in Jerusalem" (Ezra 1.4). But it is clear from what follows that this does not represent the complete fulfilment of the promise:

The Lord would establish them (v.6b)

"I will build them, and not pull them down; and I will plant them, and not pluck them up." Ironside writes with clarity: "He would watch over them in grace, and eventually restore them (the remnant) to their land, to be once more planted, never to be plucked up again. This last phrase negatives effectively the unworthy theory that would consider the promise fulfilled in the days of Ezra and Nehemiah. Have they not 'been plucked again'? Surely. But when Jehovah's set time has come, they shall be established in their land never to be rooted out of it again". The matter is put beyond all doubt in the following:

The Lord would regenerate them (v.7)

"And I will give them an heart to know me, that I am the Lord: and they shall be my people, and I will be their God: for they shall return unto me with their whole heart." At this point some commentators fall strangely silent, but the Old Testament prophets have a great deal to say on the subject, including Jeremiah himself: "Behold, the days come, saith the Lord, that I will make a new covenant with the house of Israel, and with the house of Judah…this shall be the covenant that I will make with the house of Israel; After those days, saith the Lord, I will put my law in their inward parts, and write it in their hearts; and will be their God, and they shall be my people…they shall all know me, from the least of them unto the greatest of them, saith the Lord" (31.31-34). Ezekiel contributes to the subject as follows: "I will take you from among the heathen, and gather you out of all countries, and will bring you into your own land…A new heart also will I give you, and a new spirit will I put within you: and I will take away the stony heart out of your flesh, and I will give you an heart of flesh" (Ezek 36.24-26). It is worth pointing out that the desire to turn to the Lord "with their whole heart" was not evidence of their own spiritual initiative, but the result of His initiative. He will bring about a change of heart in His people.

The evil figs (vv.8-10)

The basket of "evil figs, which cannot be eaten, they are so evil", represents "Zedekiah the king of Judah, and his princes, and the residue of Jerusalem, that remain in this land, and them that dwell in the land of Egypt" (v.8). A similar passage is found in ch.29: "Because ye have said, The Lord hath raised us up prophets in Babylon; Know that thus saith the

Lord of the king that sitteth upon the throne of David, and of all the people that dwelleth in this city, and of your brethren that are not gone forth with you into captivity; Thus saith the Lord of hosts; Behold I will send upon them the sword, the famine, and the pestilence, and will make them like *vile figs, that cannot be eaten, they are so evil*" (29.15-17).

Divine judgment would encompass Jews both remaining in Jerusalem and dwelling in Egypt. So far as the latter are concerned, it is generally said that they were either people who had been taken into captivity with Jehoahaz by Pharaoh-nechoh (cp. 2 Kings 23.34), or Jews who had fled during the subsequent reigns of Judaean kings in order to escape from the clutches of Nebuchadnezzar. Egypt was opposed to the Babylonian power. While Feinberg suggests that to "understand them as those involved in the events of chapters 43 and 44 is to leap too far ahead in the narrative of the book", the judgment described in these chapters could well include Jews living in Egypt before the arrival of Johanan the son of Kareah and his party (43.4-7).

The predicted judgment looks beyond the immediate success of Nebuchadnezzar both in Judah and in Egypt (cp. 43.8-13), to world-wide dispersion: "And I will deliver them to be removed into all the kingdoms of the earth for their hurt, to be a reproach and a proverb, a taunt and a curse, in all places whither I shall drive them" (v.9). Moses had said that failure to obey the Lord would have exactly this result: "The Lord shall cause thee to be smitten before thine enemies: thou shalt go out one way against them, and flee seven ways before them: and shalt be removed into all the kingdoms of the earth...And thou shalt become an astonishment, a proverb, and a byword, among all nations whither the Lord shall lead thee" (Deut 28.25,37). They would be utterly consumed: "And I will send the sword, the famine, and the pestilence, among them, till they be consumed from off the land that I gave unto them and to their fathers" (v.10). Commentators point out that this prophecy was fulfilled in part in the fall of Jerusalem to the Babylonians but more so in the siege of Jerusalem by the Roman Emperor Titus in AD 70.

JEREMIAH 25

Attention is drawn to the vexed question of the chronological order of Jeremiah's prophecies in chapters 21-44. The message in chapter 25 was given in "the fourth year of Jehoiakim" whereas the previous message (chs.21-24) belongs to the later reign of Zedekiah. While J. Heading rightly points out that there should be no "casual thought that the historical order throughout the book appears rather haphazard", it is far from easy to identify "the historical order". The reader is referred to suggestions already made in connection with chapters 21-24. So far as chapters 25-44 are concerned, Heading suggests that their order reflects the two alternatives presented to Jerusalem in her closing days, namely "the way of life, and the way of death" (21.8) and that chapters 25-34 represent the first alternative (for those that leave Jerusalem, the promise of restoration through the New Covenant) whilst chapters 35-44 represent the second (for those remaining in the city, their judgment and their final worse state in Egypt). An alternative explanation will be given when considering the relevant verses in chapters 34, 35, and 37.

There can be no doubt that this chapter is particularly significant, and its precise dating serves to emphasise it importance. "The word that came to Jeremiah concerning all the people of Judah in the fourth year of Jehoiakim the son of Josiah king of Judah, that was the first year of Nebuchadrezzar king of Babylon" (v.1). It was in this year (605 BC, perhaps 606 BC) that the balance of world power changed when Nebuchadrezzar defeated "Pharaoh-necho king of Egypt...by the river Euphrates in Carchemish" (46.2). Reference is made to the same battle in 2 Chronicles 35.20. According to F. A. Tatford, the Egyptians had held Carmechish for at least three years prior to the date of the battle, "but Nabopolassar, king of Babylon, was simply biding his time, and in due course, he gathered a great army together and placed it under the leadership of his son Nebuchadnezzar". Having inflicted a crushing and decisive defeat upon the army of Pharaoh-necho (46.1-12), Nebuchadrezzar, having heard of his father's death, returned, evidently via Jerusalem, to Babylon where the throne awaited him, and with it the mastery of Western Asia, otherwise known as the Near East. With him began the long era of present world history described by the Lord Jesus as "the times of the Gentiles" (Lk 21.24), so called because Nebuchadrezzar's reign "began the succession of the four great kingdoms that exercised world dominion" (Feinberg).

It should also be said that that "the fourth year of Jehoiakim" marked the lowest point in that monarch's eleven year reign. It was then that he consigned the roll containing Jeremiah's prophecy to the fire in his winter-house (36.1,21-23).

Scholars have pointed out that there is no discrepancy between the words "the fourth year of Jehoiakim" (v.1) and "the third year of the reign of Jehoiakim king of Judah" (Dan 1.1). According to F. F. Bruce, "Jeremiah reckoned regnal years in the Palestinian fashion, Daniel in the Babylonian fashion. In the Palestinian fashion, a king's first year began on the date of his accession and lasted till the next New Year's Day, when his second year began. In the Babylonian fashion, a king's first year did not begin until the first New Year's Day of his reign; the period between his accession and the following New Year's Day was called 'the beginning of his reign'".

Leaving aside now these interesting and absorbing technicalities, sight must not be lost of the outstanding importance of the chapter. It describes the beginning, character and end of "the times of the Gentiles". These began when Babylon incorporated Judah into her territory as a tributary (2 Kings 24.1; 2 Chr 36.6), not with Jerusalem's destruction which ultimately followed (Jer 25.9-11), and will end with fearful world-wide conflagration when it will be said that the Lord "hath forsaken his covert, as the lion: for their land (the lands of the nations) is desolate because of the fierceness of the oppressor, and because of his fierce anger" (v.38).

With these things in mind, the chapter may be divided as follows:

> The Warnings of Judgment on Judah (vv.1-7)
> The Instrument of Judgment upon Judah (vv.8-14)
> The Extension of Judgment to the Nations (vv.15-29)
> The Severity of Judgment on the Nations (vv.30-38).

The chapter therefore commences with judgment on Judah, and ends with judgment on the nations.

Verses 1-7: The Warnings of Judgment on Judah

Having noted the occasion of the prophecy (vv.1-2), attention is drawn to the extent of the warnings (vv.3-4); the content of the warnings (vv.5-6); and the response to the warnings (v.7).

The extent of the warnings (vv.3-4)

Jeremiah commenced to preach in "the thirteenth year of Josiah the son of Amon king of Judah" (v.3), and with unflagging zeal he had faithfully continued to proclaim the word of the Lord for twenty-three years. He had received the "the word of the Lord", and earnestly conveyed it to His people: "I have spoken unto you, rising early and speaking". There was nothing nonchalant or casual about his ministry. He spoke out of deep conviction and even when opposition threatened to close his mouth he could not resist the inward power of God's word: "his word was in mine heart as a burning fire shut up in my bones, and I was weary with forbearing, and I could not stay" (20.9).

The earnestness of Jeremiah reflected the earnestness of the Lord himself: "And the Lord hath sent unto you all his servants the prophets, rising early and sending them" (v.4). While some commentators suggest that Jeremiah alludes here to contemporary prophets, as Urijah (26.20), Zephaniah and Habakkuk, it seems more likely that he is referring to the centuries-long testimony of the prophets. This is certainly the case in the second and third of the ten occasions (7.13,25; 11.7; 25.4; 26.5; 29.19; 32.33; 35.14,15; 44.4) on which the expression "rising early" or "rising up early" is used by the Lord Himself, or in this case, of the Lord Himself. Alas, Jeremiah followed in the footsteps of his predecessors: the Lord's people had not hearkened to him (v.3) as they had not hearkened to "all his servants the prophets" (v.4).

The content of the warnings (vv.5-6)

Over the centuries, let alone in Jeremiah's time, the Lord's servants had said, "Turn ye again now every one from his evil way, and from the evil of your doings, and dwell in the land that the Lord hath given unto you and to your fathers for ever and ever: And go not after other gods to serve them, and to worship them, and provoke me not to anger with the works of your hands; and I will do you no hurt". Occupancy and enjoyment of the land rested on separation from evil and whole-hearted devotion to the Lord in the same way that believers today can only enjoy their present inheritance in Christ as they are "obedient children" and "holy in all manner of conversation" (1 Pet 1.14,15). In view of the immensity of their blessings in knowing "him that is true" and in being "in him that is true, even in his Son Jesus Christ", it is not surprising that John should say, "Little children, keep yourselves from idols" (1 Jn 5.20,21).

The response to the warnings (v.7)

"Yet ye have not hearkened unto me, saith the Lord; that ye might provoke me to anger with the works of your own hands to your own hurt." Disobedience is nothing less than self-inflicted damage. To reject the message of the Lord's servants is to ignore the voice of the Lord, and it could be said of them, as it was said of their ancestors, "they have not rejected thee (Samuel), but they have rejected me, that I should not reign over them" (1 Sam 8.7).

Verses 8-14: The Instrument of Judgment upon Judah

Harrison points out that since "the disobedient nation would not listen to God's prophetic servants, so now they must pay heed to a different kind of servant (cp. 27.6; 43.10)". This is confirmed by the text: "Therefore thus saith the Lord of hosts; Because ye have not heard my words, Behold, I will send and take all the families of the north, saith the Lord, and Nebuchadrezzar the king of Babylon, my servant, and will bring him against this land" (vv.8-9).

This section of the chapter can be divided as follows: the descent on the land by Babylon (vv.8-9a); the devastation of the land by Babylon (vv.9b-11a); the duration of servitude to Babylon (v.11b); and the defeat and desolation of Babylon (vv.12-14).

The descent on the land by Babylon (vv.8-9a)

As has been noted, Judah was by now tributary to Babylon, and "the times of the Gentiles" had already begun, but after three years Jehoiakim rebelled against Nebuchadnezzar with the result that "the Lord sent against him bands of the Chaldees, and bands of the Syrians, and bands of the Moabites, and bands of the children of Ammon, and sent them against Judah to destroy it, according to the word of the Lord, which he spake by his servants the prophets" (2 Kings 24.2). At least part of "the word of the Lord, which he spake by his servants the prophets" is found in the current passage. The "families of the north" are identified in part in 2 Kings 24.1-2. The Lord's servant for the purpose of judgment upon Judah and Jerusalem was Nebuchadnezzar. As Feinberg observes, "The characterisation of Nebuchadnezzar as the Lord's servant shows the magnitude of the work committed to him. It was not so much that God's pleasure was on him but that as the Lord's instrument he was to execute the divine plan for Judah and the nations. He was unconsciously doing God's will by devoting whole populations to destruction…whether Judah or the surrounding nations". Very clearly, the enthronement of Nebuchadnezzar as king of Babylon in the "fourth year of Jehoiakim" was no quirk of fate. God was preparing His servant. There is evidently far more to history than secular historians have ever realised! It is not without good reason, as Nebuchadnezzar himself discovered, that "the most High ruleth in the kingdom of men, and giveth it to whomsoever he will" (Dan 4.25).

Jeremiah was able to proclaim the beginning of the fulfilment of his own prophecy of some twenty-three years previously: "Then the Lord said unto me, Out of the north an evil shall break forth upon all the inhabitants of the land. For, lo, I will call the families of the kingdoms of the north, saith the Lord; and they shall come, and they shall set every one his throne at the entering of the gates of Jerusalem, and against the walls thereof round about, and against all the cities of Judah" (1.14-15). The prophet lived to see the ultimate fulfilment of this prophecy.

The devastation of the land by Babylon (vv.9b-11a)

While reference is made in passing to the surrounding nations, "and against all these nations round about" (v.9) the section principally concerns Judah: "I will…bring them against this land…And this whole land shall be a desolation, and an astonishment" (vv.9,11). The reference to "these nations round about" is amplified in vv.15-28 and the current reference emphasises that, in judging His own people, the Lord is not unmindful of the surrounding nations "who had seduced them into their idolatrous practices" (Ironside). Judah would be reduced to "an astonishment ('horror', NIV), and an hissing ('mockery', Gesenius), and perpetual desolations" (v.9).

For the third time in the prophecy (cp. 7.34; 16.9) the utter desolation of Judah and Jerusalem is graphically described in terms of its effect on family and domestic life: "Moreover I will take from them the voice of mirth, and the voice of gladness, the voice of the bridegroom, and the voice of the bride, the sound of millstones, and the light of the candle" (v.10). But this would not be permanent, and when national restoration takes place "Again there shall be heard in this place…The voice of joy, and the voice of gladness, the voice of the bridegroom, and the voice of the bride, the voice of them that shall say, Praise the Lord of hosts" (33.10-11). These passages should be compared with Revelation 18.21-23.

The duration of servitude to Babylon (v.11b)

"And these nations shall serve the king of Babylon seventy years." Taken in isolation, it could be concluded that this is a bare statement of fact - simply that Judah and her neighbours, without any further differentiation between them, would be subject to Babylon for seventy years at which point Babylon herself would succumb to her enemies (vv.12-14). While there is no direct reference here to Judah's deportation and exile, this is confirmed later in the prophecy: "For thus saith the Lord, That after seventy years be accomplished at Babylon I will visit you, and perform my good word toward you, in causing you to return to this place" (29.10).

It must be said that while "the most High…set the bounds of the people according to the number of the children of Israel" (Deut 32.8) He also directed the course of history with reference to Israel. The coming seventy-year servitude to Babylon was far more than a mere statement of fact. Its duration had been carefully calculated. "And them that had escaped from the sword carried he (Nebuchadnezzar) away to Babylon; where they were servants to him and his sons until the reign of the kingdom of Persia: To fulfil the word of the Lord by the mouth of Jeremiah, *until the land had enjoyed her sabbaths: for as long as she lay desolate she kept sabbath, to fulfil threescore and ten years*" (2 Chr 36.20-21). This refers to Leviticus 25.3-4: "Six years thou shalt sow thy field, and six years thou shalt prune thy vineyard, and gather in the fruit thereof; But in the seventh year shall be a sabbath of rest unto the land, a sabbath for the Lord: thou shalt neither sow thy field, nor prune thy vineyard". God ensured that His people would not be hungry during "the sabbath of the land" (Lev 25.20-21). Every seventh year reminded them that He was able to preserve and bless His people as tenants in His property. But although this was ignored (Lev 26.33-43: particularly vv.34-35), the Lord secured every one of those sabbaths! Each of the seventy years in captivity represented a "seventh year", which means that Israel had not "kept sabbath" for 490 years. On the assumption that Judah's captivity commenced in 606 BC, the 490 year period stretches back to 1096 BC, the year in which Saul was anointed, and the monarchy commenced.

The Lord's people must not fail to grasp the lesson. The Lord is well aware of their disobedience. It had become the norm to dispense with Leviticus 25.3-4, and, if it ever crossed their minds at all, some Israelites might have concluded that since the Lord had not intervened it obviously no longer mattered. The seventy years' captivity proved that it did matter: the Lord had not forgotten His word, and had not overlooked the disobedience of His people. God's people cannot play fast and loose with His word, and escape unscathed.

While some commentators suggest that the seventy-year period is nothing more than a round number representing a normal life span (Ps 90.10), Daniel evidently thought in precise terms: "I Daniel understood by books (he had been reading Jeremiah) the number of the years, whereof the word of the Lord came to Jeremiah the prophet, that he would accomplish seventy years in the desolations of Jerusalem" (Dan 9.2). The seventy years ended with the decree of Cyrus authorising the Jewish exiles to return to Jerusalem to rebuild the Temple. Cyrus was prompted by the Lord to make this decree: "the Lord stirred up the spirit of Cyrus king of Persia" and did so that the His word "by the mouth of Jeremiah might be accomplished" (2 Chr 36.22; Ezra 1.1). The decree of Cyrus was made in 536 BC and the seventy years therefore commenced in 606 BC, that is, "in the fourth year of Jehoiakim". While the date might have been 605 BC, it remains that the foregoing seems preferable to other views.

Very clearly, God fulfilled His promises. This is not surprising: after all, He "cannot lie" (Titus 1.2), and He "is not a man, that he should lie; neither the son of man, that he should repent: hath he said, and shall he not do it? or hath he spoken, and shall he not make it good?" (Num 23.19). Abraham was "fully persuaded that, what he had promised, he was able also to perform" (Rom 4.21), and the Lord's people today should be equally persuaded that "The Lord is not slack concerning his promise, as some men count slackness" (2 Pet 3.9).

The defeat and desolation of Babylon (vv.12-14)

The seventy years represent a given time for a given purpose, and this is now expressed in the prediction of Babylon's downfall: "And it shall come to pass, when seventy years are *accomplished*, that I will punish the king of Babylon, and that nation, saith the Lord, for their iniquity, and the land of the Chaldeans, and will make it perpetual desolations" (v.12). It should be stressed that Babylon was not to be punished for carrying out God's will, but for her own sins. As Feinberg points out, "It is clear that God used Babylon, not because of her merit, but because of Israel's sin". Habakkuk was so concerned that the instrument used to chasten his people was even more wicked than the people themselves that he exclaimed, "Thou art of purer eyes than to behold evil, and canst not look on iniquity:

wherefore lookest thou upon them that deal treacherously, and holdest thy tongue when the wicked devoureth the man that is more righteous than he?" (Hab 1.13). He soon learned that the Chaldeans, who crushed weaker nations in order to secure financial gain, would reap where they had sown: "Shall they not rise up suddenly that shall bite thee, and awake that shall vex thee, and thou shalt be for booties unto them? Because thou hast *spoiled* many nations, all the remnant of the people shall *spoil* thee; because of men's blood, and for the violence of the land, of the city, and of all that dwell therein" (Hab 2.7-8).

In accordance with "all that is written in this book, which Jeremiah hath prophesied against all the nations", the Lord would "bring upon that land (Chaldea) all my words which I have pronounced against it" (v.13). Some commentators opine that this is an interpolation and that the words "all that is written in this book" are "manifestly the addition of a scribe" (Ellicott's Commentary), but leaving aside the Septuagint text "which need not necessarily be superior in nature" (Harrison), the passage makes good sense as it stands in the AV when it is remembered that Jeremiah is conveying to the people of Judah the message he had received from the Lord (vv.1-2). Harrison suggests that "this book" is "the original prophecy, which was destroyed by Jehoiakim (36.22-23)", in which case "All that is written in the book" could well refer to the immediate passage (vv.12,14).

The "many nations" and great kings" (v.14) refer to the Medes and Persians with their many allies or tributary kings under Cyrus the Great. Babylon would receive retribution in kind: "I will recompense them according to their deeds, and according to the works of their own hands". The words "serve themselves" ("reduce them to servitude, even them", JND margin) indicate that her conquerors "would impose forced labour on the once-invincible Babylonians" (Feinberg).

Verses 15-29: The Extension of Judgment to the Nations

Since the section ends with predicted judgment upon Babylon (Sheshach, v.26), the introductory words, *"For* thus saith the Lord God of Israel unto me" (v.15), indicate that what follows could be regarded as an amplification of vv.8-14 which embraces Judah, the surrounding nations, and Babylon. Attention is drawn to the cup of judgment (vv.15-17); the course of judgment (vv.18-26); and the certainty of judgment (vv.27-29).

The cup of judgment (vv.15-17)

"Take the wine cup of this fury at my hand, and cause all the nations, to whom I send thee, to drink it. And they shall drink, and be moved, and be mad, because of the sword that I will send among them. Then took I the cup at the Lord's hand, and made all the nations to drink, unto whom the Lord had sent me." While the figure of a cup is used in Scripture to denote God's blessing (examples are found in Ps 16.5; 23.5) it is a common figure in signifying the wrath of God (examples of this are found in Is 51.17,22;

Jer 49.12; 51.7). As Feinberg observes, "With the mention of the sword (v.16), fact replaces the figure. The horrors of war will drive the nations mad". It is hardly necessary to say that Jeremiah did not travel to the various kingdoms, neither did he give the cup to their ambassadors who were in Jerusalem, as some have suggested. Rather that through Jeremiah's "prophetic word forces will be set in motion to bring disaster to all the nations involved" (Habel). Making "all the nations to drink" is symbolic language for declaring the Lord's judgment on them. In this the prophet began to fulfil his God-given ministry in connection with the Gentile nations: "See, I have this day set thee over the nations and over the kingdoms, to root out, and to pull down, and to destroy, and to throw down, to build, and to plant" (1.10).

The course of judgment (vv.18-26)

It could be said of these verses, although it is not wholly appropriate, that if "judgment must begin at the house of God...what shall the end be of them that obey not the gospel of God?" (1 Pet 4.17). The course of judgment is clear.

Judgment on Jerusalem and Judah (v.18)

"Jerusalem, and the cities of Judah, and the kings thereof (Jehoiakim, Jehoiachin, Zedekiah), and the princes thereof, to make them a desolation, an astonishment, an hissing and a curse; as it is this day." The instrument of judgment was Babylon.

Judgment on the nations (vv.19-26a)

The instrument of judgment was Babylon: "Babylon hath been a golden cup in the Lord's hand, that made all the earth drunken: the nations have drunken of her wine; therefore the nations are mad" (51.7). All the nations mentioned in chs.46-51 are included here with the exception of Damascus. Kedar and Hazor (49.28-33) were evidently tribes located in the Arabian desert (25.24).

The roster of the nations runs from south to north. The southernmost nation is Egypt. "Pharaoh (Pharaoh-necho) king of Egypt, and his servants, and his princes, and all his people" (v.19) are probably mentioned first in view of their role in the alliance against the Babylonians. The "mingled people" (v.20) are thought to have been "people who were living in Egypt without having acquired citizenship, colonists, or traders, or hired soldiers" (Laetsch). Egypt would be conquered by Nebuchadrezzar (46.13,25-26). According to Lamentations 4.21, Uz (cp. Job 1.1) appears to have been in the region of Edom, possibly extending to the eastern boundary of Egypt, since it is mentioned here between Egypt and Philistia (v.20). Gath is not mentioned in connection with the Philistine pentapolis (v.20), possibly because it has lost its importance. The expression, "the remnant of Ashdod" refers to the destruction of the city after a siege of twenty-nine years.

The roster next mentions Edom, Moab and Ammon (v.21), all lying east of Jordan, before referring to Phoenician territory north of Philistia. Tyre and Zidon (v.22) were the main Phoenician cities. The "isles which are beyond the sea" (v.22) are probably Phoenician colonies on the Mediterranean coasts (including Cyprus). It is said that these colonies were located as far west as Tartessus in Spain. The prophet next turns from the west to east to include "Dedan, and Tema, and Buz, and all that are in the utmost corners ('all that have the corners of their beard cut off', JND), And all the kings of Arabia, and all the kings of the mingled people that dwell in the desert" (vv.23-24). Dedan was a grandson of Abraham by Keturah (Gen 25.3). He was evidently sent, with others, to "the east country" (Gen 25.6). Tema was a son of Ishmael (Gen 25.15). Buz was descended from Nahor, Abraham's brother (Gen 22.21). Zimri (v.25) cannot be identified with certainty. Feinberg suggests that there may be a connection with Zimran, a son of Abraham by Keturah (Gen 25.2). As already noted, reference is later made to territory in this region (49.28-33). Nebuchadrezzar would "spoil the men of the east" (49.28).

The roster ends in the north: "And all the kings of Elam, and all the kings of the Medes (v.25). Elam and Media lay to the east of the river Tigris. Elam was north-east of the Persian Gulf, about two hundred miles east of Babylon and, according to Feinberg, "is here representative of all Persia". Media was north and west of Persia. Under Cyrus, the two kingdoms were merged to become the Medo-Persian world power, which was finally destroyed by Alexander the Great. The "kings of the north, far and near, one with another" (v.26b) probably refers to territory extending north to the Caspian Sea, and the words "all the kingdoms of the world, which are upon the face of the earth" (v.26b) are evidently a summary of the whole roster. Daniel told Nebuchadnezzar that "thy greatness is grown, and reacheth unto heaven, and thy dominion to the end of the earth" (Dan 4.22).

Judgment on Babylon (v.26b)

"And the king of Sheshach† shall drink after them." The name occurs twice in Jeremiah, and is not mentioned elsewhere in the Old Testament. The second reference leaves no doubt that it refers to Babylon: "How is Sheshach taken! and how is the praise of the whole earth surprised! how is Babylon become an astonishment among the nations!" (51.41). "Babylon, the current agent of wrath against God's people (v.9) will not escape her turn" (Habel). The destruction of Babylon is described in detail in chs.50-51.

The certainty of judgment (vv.27-29)

No nation can escape the judgment described by Jeremiah; resistance would be futile: "Thus saith the Lord of hosts, the God of Israel; Drink ye, and be drunken, and spue, and fall, and rise no more, because of the sword which I will send among you. And it shall be, if they refuse to take the cup at thine hand to drink, then shalt thou say unto them, Thus saith the Lord of hosts; Ye shall certainly drink" (vv.27-28). For the second time, the figure gives place to the fact (cp. v.16). Refusal "to take the cup at thine hand" is metaphoric language for dismissing the thought of coming judgment. The New Testament describes this as the attitude of "scoffers, walking after their own lusts, And saying, Where is the promise of his coming?" (2 Pet 3.3-4). It is undoubtedly significant that emphasis is placed on the identity of the Judge. He is no powerless pagan deity, but "the Lord of hosts, the God of Israel".

The certainty of judgment on the nations, including Babylon, is proven by the fact that the Lord is already beginning to "bring evil" on Jerusalem. If "the city which is called by my name" is subject to divine judgment, shall the heathen nations go unpunished? The answer follows: "Ye shall not be unpunished: for I will call for a sword upon all the inhabitants of the earth, saith the Lord of hosts" (v.29). Jensen asks the relevant questions: "What of ungodly nations today, in this age of deification of science and man? Are such nations impregnable?" He answers: "The prophet's words of millennia ago concerning the finality of God's judgments are as pertinent today as then: 'And thou shalt say unto them (the nations), Thus saith the Jehovah of hosts, the God of Israel: Drink ye, and be drunken, and spew, and fall, and rise no more'".

Verses 30-38: The Severity of Judgment on the Nations

The chapter concludes with a restatement of divine wrath in vv.27-29 in what Feinberg describes as "vivid poetry". With the exception of v.33, where Jeremiah uses plain prose to describe the incalculable numbers of unburied dead, the entire section is poetic. "In martial metre, and with graphic delineation, the day of the Lord's controversy with the nations and their shepherds, or kings, is set forth in the closing verses" (Ironside). The metaphor of "the wine cup" (v.15) gives place to the metaphor of the roaring lion (vv.30,38). While, in context, the carnage results from the irresistible conquests of Nebuchadrezzar, the language employed strongly suggests that "future events are casting their shadow before them" and that the passage looks on to divine judgment upon the world at the end-time.

The following should be noticed: the universality of divine wrath (vv.30-32); the ferocity of divine wrath (v.33); and the despair of the shepherds (vv.34-38).

The universality of divine wrath (vv.30-32)

Once again, the prophet begins with Judah and Jerusalem before describing the Lord's sweeping judgment on the whole earth. "The Lord shall roar from on high, and utter his voice from his holy habitation; he shall mightily roar upon his habitation ('fold', RV, or 'pasture', RV margin)" (v.30). Divine judgment follows upon the nations: "he shall give a shout, as they that tread the grapes, against all the inhabitants of the earth" (v.30).

The vintage was evidently attended by shouting (Is 16.10), but here the "shout" (1959) is invested with its other meaning and refers to the shout of soldiers going into battle (cp. Jer 51.14). "It becomes the shout of the Lord treading down the nations" (Feinberg). The universality of divine judgment is emphasised: "A noise shall come even to the ends of the earth; for the Lord hath a controversy with the nations, he will plead with all flesh; he will give them that are wicked to the sword, saith the Lord...Behold, evil shall go forth from nation to nation, and a great whirlwind (evidently referring in the first place to Nebuchadrezzar) shall be raised up from the coasts of the earth" (vv.31-32).

The ferocity of divine wrath (v.33)

The description of the carnage is frightening as it stands: "And the slain of the Lord shall be at that day from one end of the earth even unto the other end of the earth: they shall not be lamented, neither gathered, nor buried; they shall be dung upon the ground". The whirlwind of God's wrath will spread from nation to nation "until the whole earth from one end to the other is a vast necropolis in which the unburied and unlamented corpses lie like dung upon the ground" (Laetsch).

At the end-time, of which the foregoing must be surely a picture, "the Lord will come with fire, and with his chariots like a whirlwind, to render his anger with fury, and his rebuke with flames of fire. For by fire and by his sword will the Lord plead with all flesh: and the slain of the Lord shall be many" (Is 66.15-16). Referring to this time, the Lord Jesus said, "And except those days should be shortened, there should no flesh be saved: but for the elect's sake those days shall be shortened" (Mt 24.22). "The supper of the great God" will provide food for "all the fowls that fly in the midst of heaven" (Rev 19.17). The "great supper" is described in Revelation 19.18,21. The mountains of Israel will see similar carnage (Ezek 39.1-15).

The despair of the shepherds (vv.34-38)

The word "shepherds" and the words "principal of the flock" (leaders of the flock or chief among the sheep) occur three times in these verses (vv.34,35,36). In context, these are not Israel's shepherds and leaders, but the leaders of the nations. Contrary to what often happens to day, when national leaders flee to safe havens when danger threatens, there would be no escape here: "the days of your slaughter and of your dispersions are accomplished; and ye shall fall like a pleasant vessel ('be shattered like fine pottery', NIV). And the shepherds shall have no way to flee, nor the principal of the flock to escape" (vv.34-35). Laetsch describes the "voice of the cry of the shepherds" and the "howling of the principal of the flock" as follows: "Their proud boastings and imperious commands are suddenly changed to shrieks of despair and howls of mortification, for the Lord has destroyed their pastures from which they grew rich, and devastated the fields to which they owed their welfare and prosperity". Streane simply says, 'These pastures so lately abounding in flocks are now silent; in other words the country is denuded of its inhabitants".

While Feinberg suggests that the words, "He hath forsaken his covert, as the lion: for their land is desolate because of the fierceness of the oppressor, and because of his fierce anger" (v.38), mean "As a lion abandons a den that has been destroyed, so the Lord will abandon His own land after He has devastated it with the sword of the oppressive invader", it does seem that Ellicott's Commentary is more to the point: "He is as the lion leaving its hiding-place in the forest, and going forth to do its work of vengeance". It is a case of "The lion hath roared, who will not fear?" (Amos 3.8).

Notes

26 According to Ellicott's Commentary, "Sheshach" is "the earliest known example of the use of a cypher-writing to disguise the meaning of what was written from all but the initiated. The cipher in this instance, known by the significant name of ATBASH (i.e. A taking the place of T, and T of A, B of SH, and SH of B, and so on), consisted in the use of the Hebrew alphabet in an inverted order, thus giving SHeSHaCH as an equivalent of BaBeL". It is not clear why this device is used, particularly as Babylon has already been mentioned by name. Feinberg suggests that Jeremiah might have resorted to the code name while Nebuchadnezzar was at the gates of Jerusalem, but the matter has not been satisfactorily resolved.

JEREMIAH 26

Events in this chapter took place "In the beginning of the reign of Jehoiakim the son of Josiah king of Judah" (v.1). F. F. Bruce points out that while in the "technical Babylonian sense", the period between a monarch's "accession and the following New Year's Day was called 'the beginning of his reign'", the expression "the beginning of the reign" (26.1; 27.1; 28.1) had a different connotation so far as the kings of Judah were concerned. In their case "it simply denotes the earlier part of a king's reign, as is clear from Jeremiah 28.1, where it is actually Zedekiah's fourth year that is referred to".

The similarity between the opening verses of the chapter (vv.1-6) and 7.1-15 has led most commentators to the conclusion that both passages refer to the same occasion, and that the current passage gives a only a brief summary of the Temple address in chapter 7 because the particular purpose is now to emphasise the result of Jeremiah's preaching, something omitted previously. As already noted, Feinberg states that "the affinities between chapters 7 and 26 are too many and too minute for them not to relate to the same address". However, this is not the universal view, and Laetsch strongly suggests that the similarity between the two passages does not necessarily point to the same occasion. He argues, for example, that the absence of even the slightest hint of opposition in chapter 7 is in keeping with the great reforms carried out by Josiah, and that the warning there concurs with the Lord's announcement of "His readiness at that time to fulfil all the threats contained in the rediscovered Book of the Law (2 Kings 22.16-20)". He adds, in pointing out that Jeremiah and others frequently spoke in the gates and courts of the Temple, "Why should not Shiloh have been repeatedly mentioned as a warning example of the folly of relying on external possession of God's house?". The reader must carefully consider both views; the second should not be lightly dismissed.

The chapter may be divided in the following way:

> The Preaching in the Temple (vv.1-6)
> The Preservation of Jeremiah (vv.7-19)
> The Persecution of Urijah (vv.20-24).

Verses 1-6: The Preaching in the Temple

In these verses attention is drawn to the command to Jeremiah (vv.1-2); the object of his message (v.3); and the warning of coming judgment (vv.4-6).

The command to Jeremiah (vv.1-2)

"In the beginning of the reign of Jehoiakim…came this word from the Lord, saying, Thus saith the Lord; Stand in the court of the Lord's house, and speak unto all the cities of Judah, which come to worship in the Lord's house, all the words that I command thee to speak unto them; diminish not a word." Jeremiah stood "in the court of the Lord's house", where he had delivered at least one previous message of pending judgment (19.14), in order to speak to the people who had evidently assembled on one of the feast days. His original commission included the words, "thou shalt go to all that I shall send thee, and whatsoever I command thee thou shalt speak" (1.7) and the current chapter makes it clear that he continued to obey his instructions faithfully (vv.8,12,15). It should be noted that the prophet was to convey the message to his hearers in the very words in which it was delivered to him: "speak…all the words that I command thee to speak unto them; diminish not a word" (v.2). Moses gave similar instructions to the people of Israel (Deut 4.2; 12.32). Jeremiah was not merely to give an outline or the gist of the message committed to him. "Not one word was to be kept back" (Meyer). This stresses that he was not to trim his message to suit his hearers and "play to the gallery". The servant of God is to "Preach the word; be instant in season, out of season" (2 Tim 4.2). He should not be swayed by fear of the consequences of his preaching.

The object of his message (v.3)

The object of the message was to secure the repentance of the people in order to avert coming disaster: "If so be they will hearken, and turn every man from his evil way, that I may repent me of the evil, which I purpose to do unto them because of the evil of their doings". As noted in connection with 18.8-10, divine repentance is altogether different from human repentance. The Lord does not repent as men and women repent, for the simple reason that He has never done wrong. With Him, repentance is not a change of mind and will, but a response consistent with a change of conduct on the part of men and women. The Lord was prepared to do for His people here what He had done for the Ninevites: "they turned from their evil way; and God repented of the evil, that he had said that he would do unto them; and he did it not" (Jonah 3.10). "The true repentance of the people of Judah at any time before the hour of doom would have been met by God's willingness to relent from His former threatened punishment" (Feinberg).

The warning of coming judgment (vv.4-6)

If "on the one side, by his lips, God entreated His people to repent, and turn from their evil ways; on the other, He bade them know that their obduracy would compel Him to make their great national shrine as complete a desolation as the site of Shiloh, which for five hundred years had been in ruins" (Meyer). "If ye will not hearken to me…To hearken to the words of my servants the prophets, whom I sent unto you…Then will I make this house like Shiloh, and will make this city a curse to all the nations of the earth" (vv.4-6).

Shiloh was not far from Jerusalem, and its ruins were a standing reminder that sacred associations in the past were no guarantee of ongoing favour when those conditions changed. The reader is referred to comments made in connection with Shiloh in 7.12-14. The destruction of Shiloh was bad enough, but Jerusalem would be made "a curse to all the nations of the earth" (v.6), or "an object of cursing among all the nations of the earth" (NIV). This is explained in earlier oracles (24.9; 25.18).

Verses 7-19: The Preservation of Jeremiah

The people listened with what Feinberg describes as "hushed respect" until Jeremiah had finished speaking (v.7), and then mayhem broke out. Jeremiah's life was in immediate danger (vv.8,11). The accusation against Jeremiah (vv.8-9); the advocacy of the princes (vv.10-16); and the advice of the elders (vv.17-19) should be noted.

The accusation against Jeremiah (vv.8-9)

To the "blurred spiritual perspective" (Unger) of his audience, Jeremiah's preaching was nothing short of traitorous, making him a false prophet deserving death. They called for the sentence demanded by the Mosaic law: "the prophet, which shall presume to speak a word in my name, which I have not commanded him to speak...even that prophet shall die" (Deut 18.20). Since the Lord had said of Zion, "This is my rest for ever: here will I dwell; for I have desired it" (Ps 132.14), it was utterly reprehensible to say that "this city shall be desolate without an inhabitant" (v.9). Such preaching was particularly intolerable to the false prophets in the audience (they are described as "pseudoprophets" in the Septuagint) who had proclaimed, "The Lord hath said, Ye shall have peace; and they say unto every one that walketh after the imagination of his own heart, No evil shall come upon you" (23.17).

These verses illustrate that error is more popular, and more acceptable, than truth. The faithfulness of Jeremiah was met by the fury of the people. He had discharged his responsibility and "made an end of speaking all that the Lord had commanded him to speak unto all the people" (v.8), only to be met by outright antagonism: "all the people were gathered against Jeremiah in the house of the Lord" (v.9). Stephen faced a similar accusation by false witnesses before the Jewish council: "This man ceaseth not to speak blasphemous words against this holy place, and the law: For we have heard him say, that this Jesus of Nazareth shall destroy this place, and shall change the customs which Moses delivered us" (Acts 6.13-14). Something similar befell Paul when, on the presumption that he had defiled the holy place, he was dragged out of the Temple and would have been killed were it not for intervention by Roman soldiers (Acts 21.27-36). There is little doubt that Jeremiah would also have been put to death by the hostile crowd in the Temple had it not been for the intervention of the princes (v.10).

In commenting on these verses, Meyer makes the following observation: "Such is always the reception given on the part of man to the words of

God. We may gravely question how far our words are God's, when people accept them quietly and as a matter of course. The Word of God to those that hug their sin can only be as a fire, a hammer, and a sharp two-edged sword...That which men approve and applaud may lack the King's seal, and be the substitution on the part of the messenger of tidings which he deems more palatable, and therefore more likely to secure for himself a larger welcome". Paul speaks of "the offence of the cross" (Gal 5.11).

The advocacy of the princes (vv.10-16)
"When the princes of Judah heard these things, then they came up from the king's house unto the house of the Lord, and sat down in the entry of the new gate of the Lord's house" (v.10). It is thought that the "new gate" led to the inner, or priests' court (36.10), and that it was built by Jotham (2 Kings 15.35). The following should be noted.

The charge against Jeremiah (v.11)
"This man is worthy to die; for he hath prophesied against this city, as ye have heard with your ears." As far as the priests and prophets were concerned, it was an open and closed case. They acted as prosecution and pronounced the verdict. It seems possible that in referring only to Jeremiah's words against the city, his accusers were giving a political slant to the charge against him.

The courage of Jeremiah (vv.12-15)
Laetsch describes Jeremiah's defence as "a masterpiece of brevity and convincing argumentation. He does not retract or even apologise for a single word". "The Lord sent me to prophesy against this house and against this city all the words that ye have heard" (v.12). Feinberg is surely right in saying that "Nowhere in the book does he appear in a better light than here". He never moves from his conviction that, like Haggai, he was the "Lord's messenger in the Lord's message" (Hag 1.13). He followed in the steps of Amos who said, "the Lord took me...and the Lord said unto me, Go, prophesy unto my people Israel" (Amos 7.15). Jeremiah made no attempt to amend or deny the content of his preaching, but rather emphasised its origin and authority. In view of the fact that the Lord had sent him, their contention was really with the Lord Himself. In the New Testament, Gamaliel made the same point (Acts 5.38-39).

Moreover, he honed the keen edge of his message by repeating his call for repentance (cp. v.3). Even the threat of death would not divert him from his message: "Therefore now amend your ways and your doings, and obey the voice of the Lord your God; and the Lord will repent him of the evil that he hath pronounced against you" (v.13). It is noteworthy that Jeremiah did not plead for his life. He recognised the power of his enemies, but warned them of the consequences of carrying out their threat to kill him (vv.14-15). To reject and kill Jeremiah (v.15) would be a crime of the greatest magnitude. Centuries later, the same city killed God's perfect Servant and their own cry was later fulfilled: "His blood be on us, and on our children" (Mt 27.25).

The clearance for Jeremiah (v.16)

It is significant that not only the princes (the civil officials) but also the people recognised the God-given authority of Jeremiah: "Then said the princes and all the people unto the priests and to the prophets; This man is not worthy to die: for he hath spoken to us in the name of the Lord our God". There was more spiritual intelligence in the laymen at Jerusalem than there was in the professional religionists. "The judges and people were freer of prejudice than the religious leaders" (Feinberg). Centuries later, another civic official, also free from the prejudice of the religious leaders, declared of the Lord Jesus, "I find no fault in this man" (Lk 23.4).

The advice of the elders (vv.17-19)

"Then rose up certain of the elders of the land, and spake to all the assembly of the people" (v.17). According to Streane, "It has been conjectured that as the princes represented the king in judgment, so the elders represented the people". In this case, they "added their assent to the previously expressed decision". Unger suggests that their "age and dignity gave weight" to their pronouncements and particularly in "citing precedents of past history". They drew attention to the response of King Hezekiah, some one hundred years previously, to the preaching of Micah (vv.18-19). They quoted Micah almost word for word. He had said that in view of the misdeeds of the "heads", the "priests", and "the prophets...Therefore shall Zion for your sake be plowed as a field, and Jerusalem shall become heaps, and the mountain of the house as the high places of the forest" (Micah 3.11-12). Laetsch notes that "these elders were able to quote verbatim the text that has come down to us" and adds, "A remarkable testimony to the general accuracy of the copies current among the people and handed down through the centuries!". It should be said that elders today ought to be able to quote the Scriptures. The elders in Jeremiah's day made the point that Micah's message was effective. Hezekiah and his people heeded the Lord's words through Micah, turned to the Lord instead of threatening Micah's life, and thereby averted the calamity at that time. "Did Hezekiah king of Judah and all Judah put him at all to death? did he not fear the Lord, and besought the Lord, and the Lord repented him of the evil which he had pronounced against them?" (v.19). Although it is not explicitly stated, Jeremiah was evidently acquitted by the princes who recognised the extent of the guilt that would be incurred by mistreating the Lord's servant. In the words of the elders, "Thus might we procure great evil against our souls" (v.19).

Verses 20-24: The Persecution of Urijah

Unger suggests that the story of Urijah's arrest and execution is introduced at this point "to show the grave peril Jeremiah faced and how easily his career could have been terminated, except for the Lord's faithfulness. It also shows the malignant animosity of the king and his ministers to the true prophets of the Lord". The absence of Jehoiakim's name in the earlier part of the chapter could mean that the threat to Jeremiah's life took place in the earliest part of the king's reign before he gained influence over the civil leaders. The fate of Urijah could have been shared by Jeremiah had Jehoiakim been at the height of his power and influence, although it must be remembered that the Lord had said that "they (the kings, princes, priests and people) shall fight against thee; but they shall not prevail against thee; for I am with thee, saith the Lord, to deliver thee" (1.19).

Jeremiah was not a lone voice: "And there was also a man that prophesied in the name of the Lord, Urijah the son of Shemaiah of Kirjath-jearim, who prophesied against this city and against this land according to all the words of Jeremiah" (v.20). Whilst nothing else is known of Urijah, his "record is on high" (Job 16.19) and the fact that he is mentioned here emphasises that the Lord overlooks none of His servants, however obscure they may seem by human standards. It should be carefully noted that while both men faithfully proclaimed the word of God, their respective situations turned out quite differently – Urijah was martyred and Jeremiah was preserved. A comparable case occurs in the New Testament: James was "killed...with the sword" but Peter was delivered from prison and from death (Acts 12.1-17). These situations cannot be readily explained, and there is no alternative but to bow before the inscrutable, but perfect, sovereignty of God.

Whilst it could be said that if Urijah had stood his ground like Jeremiah, the outcome might well have been different, there is no hint of criticism over his flight to Egypt from the wrath of Jehoiakim and his associates (v.21). Jehoiakim had been appointed by Pharaoh-necho (2 Chr 36.4) and the extradition of Urijah would have not posed a problem. According to Harrison, "International treaties often contained extradition clauses, and this was doubtless part of the vassalage terms imposed by Egypt". Elnathan and his party were therefore despatched to Egypt to apprehend Urijah who was duly brought back to Jerusalem and slain by Jehoiakim (vv.22-23). It is not without significance that the very man who had the body of Urijah "cast...into the graves of the common people" (v.23) was given "the burial of an ass" (22.19).

Even though Jeremiah had been acquitted, his life was still in danger, but his cause was espoused by "Ahikam the son of Shaphan" (v.24). He was an official under Josiah (2 Kings 22.12,14) and father of Gedaliah, the governor of Judah under Nebuchadnezzar after the fall of Jerusalem (Jer 39.14). As already noted, in accordance with His promise, the Lord was present to deliver His servant (1.19).

JEREMIAH 27

The references in chapters 25-29 to Nebuchadnezzar and the seventy-year exile in Babylon indicate the distinct theme of this section of the prophecy. As already noted, it is not without significance that reference is made at the beginning of the section to "the first year of Nebuchadrezzar king of Babylon" (25.1). This anticipates his divinely-given role in subjugating both Judah and her neighbours: "Behold, I will send and take all the families of the north, saith the Lord, and Nebuchadrezzar the king of Babylon, my servant, and will bring them against this land…and against all these nations round about" (25.9). Jeremiah then predicts the fall of Babylon itself. Having said that "these nations shall serve the king of Babylon seventy years" (25.11), he continues: "And it shall come to pass, when seventy years are accomplished, that I will punish the king of Babylon, and that nation, saith the Lord, for their iniquity…For many nations and great kings shall serve themselves of them also" (25.12,14). In the meantime, the king of Babylon, called "the king of Sheshach", would be responsible for administering "the wine cup" of the Lord's fury against the nations (25.15-26a), before drinking from that same cup himself (v.26b).

This clear and unambiguous prediction of Babylonian supremacy is accompanied in the prophecy by an appeal for repentance on the part of Judah (26.3). Judgment could be averted, but failure to hearken to the appeal would bring something quite unthinkable to the crowds in Jerusalem: "I will make this house like Shiloh, and will make this city a curse to all the nations of the earth" (26.6).

While the following three chapters (chs.27-29) are set, not in the reign of Jehoiakim as chapters 25 and 26, but in the reign of Zedekiah, they continue the subject of Babylonian supremacy by warning Judah and her neighbours, who by this time were under Nebuchadnezzar's control, not to rebel against their Babylonian overlord (27.1-13). The Lord had given "all these lands into the hand of Nebuchadnezzar the king of Babylon…And all nations shall serve him…until the very time of his land come" (27.6-7). The neighbouring kings and the king of Judah were not therefore to listen to their false prophets who said, "Ye shall not serve the king of Babylon". In both cases it is said, "For they prophesy a lie unto you" (27.10,16). Several false prophets in Judah are then named: Hananiah (28.1), who was present in Jerusalem, together with Ahab (29.21), Zedekiah (29.21), and Shemaiah (29.24) who were evidently in Babylon. Hananiah, presuming to speak in the name of "the Lord of hosts, the God of Israel", predicted that within two years "the vessels of the Lord's house" and Jeconiah (Jehoiachin) would be repatriated from Babylon because the Lord would "break the yoke of the king of Babylon" (28.2-4). Hananiah died under divine judgment two months later (28.17).

In order to counteract the influence of the false prophets amongst the exiles in Babylon, Jeremiah wrote to the Jews there advising them that

they would remain in captivity for seventy years, after which they would
be repatriated (29.10). Babylon was not about to leave the stage of history.
Jeremiah was quite right in saying, "This captivity is long" (29.28). Moreover,
the false prophets Ahab and Zedekiah would be slain by Nebuchadrezzar
(29.21) and Shelamiah would be punished "because he hath taught
rebellion against the Lord" (29.32).

It can therefore be concluded that chapters 25-29 comprise a unit within
the book which is bound together by references to the seventy-year
captivity.

Chapter 27 describes the dangers of rebellion against the king of Babylon,
and comprises three warnings:

> The Warning to Judah's Neighbouring Kings (vv.1-11)
> The Warning to the King of Judah (vv.12-15)
> The Warning to Judah's Priests and People (vv.16-22).

Verses 1-11: The Warning to Judah's Neighbouring Kings
The opening verse of the chapter poses a difficulty as it stands in the AV:
"In the beginning of the reign of Jehoiakim the son of Josiah king of Judah
came this word unto Jeremiah from the Lord" (v.1). Further references in
the chapter name Zedekiah as the reigning monarch (vv.3,12) and the
following chapter begins, "And it came to pass the same year, in the
beginning of the reign of Zedekiah king of Judah" (28.1). In the absence of
any other viable explanation, it does seem that "Jehoiakim" is a scribal
error for Zedekiah. While most manuscripts read "Jehoiakim", Feinberg
notes that "three Hebrew manuscripts, the Syriac, and the Arabic versions
read 'Zedekiah'". It must be said that great caution should be exercised
when reading commentators, almost invariably liberal commentators, who
habitually speak about "scribal errors", "corrupt texts", and "interpolations".
When a commentator cannot understand a passage as it stands, it is nothing
less than sheer dishonesty to rearrange the text to make it suit his
understanding. However, this is not the case here, and it might be worth
adding that the commentators cited in this exposition of Jeremiah are most
conservative when it comes to the text, although this does not mean that
all of them are uniformly conservative when it comes to interpreting the
text.

Attention is drawn to the sign (vv.2-3), and to the significance (vv.4-11).
It should be noted that whereas previously the figure of a "wine cup" was
used in connection with Babylonian conquests (25.15), the figure of "bonds
and yokes" is used here (v.2). The two figures indicate different aspects of
Babylonian suzerainty.

The sign (vv.2-3)
"Thus saith the Lord to me; Make thee bonds and yokes, and put

them upon thy neck, And send them to the king of Edom, and to the king of Moab, and to the king of the Ammonites, and to the king of Tyrus, and to the king of Zidon, by the hand of the messengers which come to Jerusalem unto Zedekiah king of Judah." The yoke was made of wooden bars held together by leather thongs ("bonds and yokes", v.2) and there is no reason to doubt that Jeremiah did exactly what he was told. He was certainly wearing a yoke when challenged by Hananiah (28.10). A yoke was the symbol of submission and servitude (vv.8,11) and is used similarly in the New Testament (Acts 15.10; Gal 5.1). The Lord Jesus used the same figure but with a different emphasis: "Take my yoke upon you, and learn of me; for I am meek and lowly in heart: and ye shall find rest unto your souls. For my yoke is easy, and my burden is light" (Mt 11.29-30).

While Feinberg suggests otherwise, the passage does say "send them" to the kings in question. The kings named were all near-neighbours of Judah: Edom lay to the south, Moab and Ammon to the east, and Tyre (Tyrus) and Zidon (Sidon) to the north. It is commonly held that the "messengers" from these kingdoms were their ambassadors who had come to Jerusalem to discuss plans for breaking their country's subservience to Nebuchadnezzar. The symbol of a yoke was therefore highly appropriate. As Habel observes, "Jeremiah disrupted this top-level conference by employing some rather undiplomatic and sensational tactics".

The significance (vv.4-11)

The returning envoys were given an explanatory message which emphasises, yet again, that "the most High ruleth in the kingdom of men, and giveth it to whomsoever he will" (Dan 4.32). The courage of Jeremiah against his opponents in Jerusalem has already been noted (26.12-15), but now he boldly condemns the strategy of Judah's neighbours. Attention is drawn to the following.

The supremacy of the Lord

"Thus saith the Lord of hosts, the God of Israel…I have made the earth, the man and the beast that are upon the ground, by my great power and by my outstretched arm, and have given it unto whom it seemed meet unto me. And now have I given all these lands into the hand of Nebuchadnezzar the king of Babylon, my servant; and the beasts of the field have I given him also to serve him" (vv.4-6). The God of creation ("I have made") is the God of history ("I have…given"). He is "the Lord of hosts" (v.4) who "doeth according to his will in the army of heaven, and among the inhabitants of the earth: and none can stay his hand, or say unto him, What doest thou?" (Dan 4.35). But at the same time He is "the God of Israel" (v.4). Israel's God is no tribal deity: He is "the everlasting God, the Lord, the Creator of the ends of the earth" (Is 40.28). As the sovereign Creator of the universe He has the right to give earthly dominion to whomsoever He pleases. The New Testament underlines the lesson in saying that "there is no power but of God: the powers that be are ordained of God" (Rom 13.1). They are charged with responsibility for the maintenance of orderly government and, as stewards of the authority committed to them by God, they are ultimately responsible to Him. Nebuchadnezzar is therefore described as "my servant" with the stewardship of a vast dominion extending over all countries, with all their resources down to "the beasts of the field" (v.6). Nebuchadnezzar was told by Daniel that this was the case (Dan 2.37-38). Ellicott's Commentary suggests that the reference to "the beasts of the field" might be "connected with the resistance of the nations to the levies made by the Babylonian officers upon their horses and cattle, or their claim to use the land they had subdued".

The service of Nebuchadnezzar

"All nations shall serve him, and his son, and his son's son (cp. 2 Chr 36.20), until the very time of his land come: and then many nations and great kings shall serve themselves of him" (v.7). The predicted seventy-year dominion by Babylon (25.11-12; 29.10) would see three monarchs of the same family occupying the throne: Nebuchadnezzar himself, his son Evil-merodach (2 Kings 25.27; Jer 52.31), and his grandson Belshazzar (Dan 5.1,30). According to Tatford, Belshazzar was the son of Nabonidus who was not himself a descendant of Nebuchadnezzar but who had married a daughter of Nebuchadnezzar. Nabonidus, who occupied the throne of Babylon, associated his son Belshazzar with him in government. "Daniel describes Belshazzar as the king, but that is quite reasonable if he was actually governing as his father's viceroy" (F. A. Tatford). In accordance with the prophecy here, when the appointed time came for the termination of Babylonian supremacy the forces of Persia, Media and their allies prevailed. "Many nations and great kings" (25.14; 27.7) certainly did "serve themselves of him". The confederacy of nations is described more fully in Jeremiah 51.11,27,28.

The subservience of the nations

While the Babylonian kingdom was not a permanent institution, it was nevertheless the divinely-appointed agent of divine government at the time, and was therefore to be obeyed. Disobedience would be punished: "And it shall come to pass, that the nation and kingdom which will not serve the same Nebuchadnezzar the king of Babylon, and that will not put their neck under the yoke of the king of Babylon, that nation will I punish, saith the Lord, with the sword, and with the famine, and with the pestilence, until I have consumed them by his hand" (v.8). As already noted, these nations were subject to Babylon at the time, and the arrival home of their ambassadors bearing, presumably, the yokes given them by Jeremiah, was a graphic reminder of the folly of attempting to break free from Babylonian dominion. Rebellion would bring disaster because in the final analysis it was rebellion against the Lord. As Laetsch points out, "Behind the rulers of the world and their schemes, behind wars and famines and epidemics, due to natural causes, stands Jehovah".

Like Judah, the surrounding nations had their false prophets, and to heed their pronouncements would prove ruinous: "Therefore hearken ye not to your prophets, nor to your diviners (involving the casting of lots), nor to your dreamers, nor to your enchanters (who practised secret arts), nor to your sorcerers (who muttered and whispered spells), which speak unto you, saying, Ye shall not serve the king of Babylon: For they prophesy a lie unto you, to remove you from your land; and that I should drive you out, and ye should perish" (vv.9-10). Ellicott's Commentary observes that "the five nations of the confederacy were sustained in their rebellion against Nebuchadnezzar by a unanimity of prediction by men of all these classes, like that which lured Ahab to his destruction (1 Kings 22.22). Every oracle was tuned, as it were, in favour of the policy of resistance". The only prudent policy in the circumstances was to submit to Nebuchadnezzar. The nations that did this would remain in peaceful possession of their own lands (v.11).

Verses 12-15: The Warning to the King of Judah

The warning to the kings of Edom, Moab, Ammon, Tyrus and Zidon (v.3) is repeated to the king of Judah: "I spake also to Zedekiah king of Judah according to all these words, saying, Bring your necks under the yoke of the king of Babylon, and serve him and his people, and live. Why will ye die, thou and thy people, by the sword, by the famine, and by the pestilence, as the Lord hath spoken against the nation that will not serve the king of Babylon?" (vv.12-13). The prospect of exile was no idle threat. Zedekiah lived just long enough to prove that the Lord meant exactly what He said. He did choose to rebel against Nebuchadnezzar (2 Kings 24.20) and the nation was largely carried away into captivity, leaving "the poor of the land to be vinedressers and husbandmen" (2 Kings 25.12). It is perilous to ignore God's warnings.

The warning to the five kings against heeding the lies of their false prophets is also repeated to Zedekiah: "Therefore hearken not unto the words of the prophets that speak unto you, saying, Ye shall not serve the king of Babylon: for they prophesy a lie unto you. For I have not sent them, saith the Lord, yet they prophesy a lie in my name; that I might drive you out, and that ye might perish, ye, and the prophets that prophesy unto you" (vv.14-15). The outstanding feature of false prophecy was its message of hope. False prophets, even though claiming to speak in the Lord's name, could easily be identified from their policy of telling people exactly what they wanted to hear. Zedekiah the son of Chenaanah, some three hundred years previously, was a case in point: "Thus saith the Lord, With these (horns of iron) shalt thou (Ahab) push the Syrians, until thou have consumed them" (1 Kings 22.11). On the other hand his contemporary, Micaiah the son of Imlah, "a prophet of the Lord", was so strikingly different that Ahab exclaimed, "I hate him; for he doth not prophesy good concerning me, but evil" (1 Kings 22.7-8).

The activity of the false prophets served the purpose of God in bringing judgment upon unrepentant men and women, in this case, an unrepentant king: "they prophesy a lie in my name; that I might drive you out, and that ye might perish" (v.15). It is illuminating that when the court in heaven, with "the Lord sitting on his throne, and all the host of heaven standing by him", was discussing the death of Ahab, one of its members said, "I will go forth, and I will be a lying spirit in the mouth of all his (Ahab's) prophets" (1 Kings 22.19,22). It was "an evil spirit from the Lord" that troubled King Saul (1 Sam 16.14).

Verses 16-22: The Warning to Judah's Priests and People

"Also I spake to the priests and to all this people, saying, Thus saith the Lord; Hearken not to the words of your prophets that prophesy unto you, saying, Behold, the vessels of the Lord's house shall now shortly be brought again from Babylon: for they prophesy a lie unto you" (v.16). The false prophets had gone further than counselling rebellion against the king of Babylon: they promised an early return of the Temple vessels and evidently made this "a powerful incentive for Judah to revolt against the Babylonians" (Feinberg). Later, one of the false prophets, Hananiah, went still further and predicted not only the return of the Temple vessels within two years, but also the return of Jeconiah (Jehoiachin), Zedekiah's predecessor (28.3-4).

Once again, Jeremiah counsels submission to the king of Babylon as the only way to preserve both the nation and the city (v.17) and then continues, with evident sarcasm, by suggesting that the prophets concerned prove their reality by praying that the vessels remaining in Jerusalem should not also be carried away to Babylon: "But if they be prophets, and if the word of the Lord be with them, let them now make intercession to the Lord of hosts, that the vessels which are left in the house of the Lord, and in the house of the king of Judah, and at Jerusalem, go not to Babylon" (v.18).

Jeremiah was well aware that the false prophets were "prophets of the deceit of their own heart" (23.26) and that the Temple vessels already in Babylon would not be speedily returned. The false prophets had no interest whatsoever in "understanding what the will of the Lord is" (Eph 5.17). Jeremiah also knew that the vessels remaining in Jerusalem would also be taken by the invaders. "The secret of the Lord is with them that fear him" (Ps 25.14) and he was able to say in truth that "thus saith the Lord of hosts concerning the pillars, and concerning the sea, and concerning the bases, and concerning the residue of the vessels that remain in this city...Yea, thus saith Lord of hosts, the God of Israel, concerning the vessels that remain in the house of the Lord, and in the house of the king of Judah and

Jerusalem; They shall be carried to Babylon" (vv.19,21-22). The vessels already in Babylon had been transported from Jerusalem when Zedekiah's predecessor Jeconiah (Jehoiachin) had been carried away captive by Nebuchadnezzar (v.20), and details are given in 2 Kings 24.11-16. In accordance with Jeremiah's prophecy (v.22), the remaining vessels did follow suit, and a detailed record is given in 2 Kings 25.13-17. In the current passage particular mention is made of "the pillars" (called Jachin and Boaz, 1 Kings 7.21), "the sea" (the laver, 1 Kings 7.23), and "the bases" (the wheeled stands for the ten further lavers, 1 Kings 7.38-39), together with a general reference to "the residue of the vessels" (v.19).

The false prophets had been responsible for spreading lies (vv.14,16) but the fulfilment of Jeremiah's prophecy demonstrated that he had truly spoken "in the name of the Lord" (Deut 18.22). But this was not the end of the matter. Jeremiah also prophesied that the Temple vessels would remain in Babylon "until the day that I visit them, saith the Lord; then will I bring them up, and restore them to this place" (v.22). As in every case, the "scripture cannot be broken" (Jn 10.35) and in 536 BC, that "the word of the Lord by the mouth of Jeremiah might be fulfilled" (Ezra 1.1), Cyrus both authorised the rebuilding of the Temple in Jerusalem (Ezra 1.2-3) and restored the Temple vessels. He "brought forth the vessels of the house of the Lord, which Nebuchadnezzar had brought forth out of Jerusalem...and numbered them unto Sheshbazzar, the prince of Judah...All these did Sheshbazzar bring up with them of the captivity that were brought up from Babylon unto Jerusalem" (Ezra 1.7,8,11).

All this emphasises that God's people can have every confidence in His Word. The frequently-repeated expression, "And it shall come to pass", is permeated with confidence. No wonder that Paul describes the Scriptures as "the faithful word" (Titus 1.9).

JEREMIAH 28

In chapter 27 Jeremiah warned neighbouring kings as well as the king of Judah against listening to the pronouncements of their false prophets. In both cases, they prophesied lies (27.10,14-15) and to heed their falsehood would bring the well-known results of war: sword, famine and plague (27.8,13). The false prophets in Judah propagated their lies in the Lord's name: "I have not sent them, saith the Lord, yet they prophesy a lie in my name" (27.15).

Chapter 28 describes a confrontation between Jeremiah and one of these false prophets, Hananiah, who, true to form, claims to speak in the name of the Lord: "Thus speaketh the Lord of hosts, the God of Israel" (v.2); "I will bring again to this place Jeconiah…saith the Lord" (v.4); "Thus saith the Lord; Even so will I break the yoke of Nebuchadnezzar king of Babylon" (v.11). Very clearly, chapter 28 continues the narrative of chapter 27. The incident took place in "the same year" (v.1) and Jeremiah was still wearing the yoke (28.10) which he had donned in obedience to divine instructions (27.2). Feinberg explains that there is no contradiction between the expression "the beginning of the reign of Zedekiah" and the fact that this is said to be "in the fourth year" (v.1). "According to Jewish usage, the date was indeed the beginning of his rule, for the Jews divided periods of time into halves: beginning and end…It means simply 'in the first half of his reign'".

The chapter, which is quite self-explanatory, may be divided as follows:

The Promise of Restoration (vv.1-4)
The Proof of Inspiration (vv.5-9)
The Personal Assault (vv.10-11)
The Punishment for Insubordination (vv.12-14)
The Price of Rebellion (vv.15-17).

Verses 1-4: The Promise of Restoration
"Hananiah the son of Azur the prophet, which was of Gibeon, spake unto me in the house of the Lord, in the presence of the priests and of all the people" (v.1). It has been conjectured that since he came from Gibeon, a few miles north-west of Jerusalem, Hananiah may have been a priest. Gibeon was one of the thirteen cities allocated to "the children of Aaron the priest" (Josh 21.13,17,19). Jeremiah was of priestly descent and came from Anathoth (1.1), another of the thirteen priestly cities (Josh 21.18). While it might be speculative to describe the incident in this chapter as a priestly confrontation, it was most certainly a confrontation between two prophets (cp. v.5).

Hananiah flatly contradicted Jeremiah, claiming divine inspiration for his pronouncement: "Thus speaketh the Lord of hosts, the God of Israel, saying, I have broken the yoke of the king of Babylon" (v.2). Not for Hananiah the doleful message, "Bring your necks under the yoke of the king of Babylon, and serve him and his people, and live" (27.12). The people needed some *esprit de corps* and he had just the message for them. Speaking with unbridled confidence, Hananiah therefore continued: "Within two full years will I bring again into this place all the vessels of the Lord's house, that Nebuchadnezzar king of Babylon took away from this place, and carried them to Babylon: And I will bring again to this place Jeconiah the son of Jehoiakim king of Judah, with all the captives of Judah, that went into Babylon, saith the Lord: for I will break the yoke of the king of Babylon" (vv.3-4). It has been suggested that the predicted return of Jeconiah in this way reflected the view in Judah that he, rather than Zedekiah, was the rightful king. A total of 3,023 captives were taken to Babylon with Jeconiah (52.28).

God's word cannot be denied or altered without serious consequences. This is equally emphasised in the New Testament: "But though we, or an angel from heaven, preach any other gospel unto you than that which we have preached unto you, let him be accursed. As we said before, so say I now again, If any man preach any other gospel unto you than that ye have received, let him be accursed" (Gal 1.8-9). The Word of God, however outdated and outmoded it might appear to those who reject it, stands inviolate. Those who "resist the truth" will "proceed no further: for their folly shall be manifest unto all men" (2 Tim 3.8-9). This was certainly true of Hananiah: he died within two months, and even though Jeconiah (Jehoiachin) was released from prison after thirty-seven years' incarceration in Babylon, he never returned to Judah (52.31-34). Jeremiah's own prophecy concerning this king (22.24-27) was completely fulfilled. There was no doubting the "folly" of Hananiah!

Error is always more popular than truth, and Laetsch may not be far wrong in saying, "We can imagine the enthusiasm bordering on fanaticism that swept through the vast audience, the thunderous applause, the joyous shouts that echoed through the spacious court at this oracle so positively and so publicly proclaimed as the very word of the Lord of Hosts". Feinberg's imagination is a little different: "One can well imagine the confusion created in the minds of the populace by the spectacle of the false prophet's denying the central elements in the message of the prophet of God".

One thing is clear, it does not take too much imagination to visualise Jeremiah standing in the Temple precincts, with the yoke about his neck, listening carefully to Hananiah! How will the Lord's servant react to this peddler of lies?

Verses 5-9: The Proof of Inspiration

Jeremiah's reply does not match expectations. Having already said, "Thus saith the Lord; Hearken not to the words of your prophets that prophesy unto you, saying, Behold, the vessels of the Lord's house shall now shortly be brought again from Babylon: for they prophesy a lie unto you" (27.16), Jeremiah might have been expected to have launched into a sweeping condemnation of Hananiah. But he is remarkably restrained: "Then the prophet Jeremiah said unto the prophet Hananiah in the presence of the priests, and in the presence of all the people that stood in the house of the Lord, Even the prophet Jeremiah said, Amen: the Lord do so: the Lord perform thy words which thou hast prophesied" (vv.5-6). Some commentators are quite convinced that Jeremiah spoke wholeheartedly and that it was his earnest desire that Hananiah's prophecy should prove correct: the speedy end of the Babylonian exile would have been welcomed by the servant of the Lord. However, he knew that this would not be the case which gives strength to the alternative view that Jeremiah spoke ironically. This view is espoused by Harrison: "Jeremiah's reply to this is an ironic *Yes indeed! Would that God might do so*', probably conveying his sense of doubt by his tone of voice". Bearing in mind that Jeremiah knew that the vessels remaining in the Temple were to be carried to Babylon (27.21-22), and that Jeconiah (Coniah) would die in captivity (22.26), this seems a more likely explanation.

It is noteworthy that, as Jeremiah continues his reply to Hananiah he does not say, "Thus saith the Lord", as he does later (v.13). Rather like Paul who wrote, "I have no commandment of the Lord: yet I give my judgment, as one that hath obtained mercy of the Lord to be faithful" (1 Cor 7.25), Jeremiah gave Hananiah the benefit of his spiritual understanding and observation: "Nevertheless hear thou now this word that I speak in thine ears, and in the ears of all the people; The prophets that have been before me and before thee of old prophesied both against many countries, and against great kingdoms, of war, and of evil, and of pestilence. The prophet which prophesieth of peace, when the word of the prophet shall come to pass, then shall the prophet be known, that the Lord hath truly sent him" (vv.7-9). Jeremiah therefore made two points to Hananiah.

i) That his message of joy and hope ran contrary to the messages of all true prophets of the past. Their messages were laden with doom: "war...evil...pestilence" (v.8). They solemnly predicted divine judgment against sin and wickedness. It is noticeable that whereas Jeremiah had called the nation to repentance, of which an example occurs in 26.3, Hananiah had nothing at all to say on the subject. He predicted prosperity unconditionally without the need for repentance. His preaching therefore lacked credibility; it had no historical precedent.

ii) That in the final analysis, the fulfilment of a prophecy was the best proof of its truthfulness (v.9). As Feinberg observes, "This was the time-honoured criterion of true prophecy". In fact it would be quite in order to substitute the word "biblical" for "time-honoured" (cp. Deut 18.20-22).

Verses 10-11: The Personal Assault
The audience in the Temple must have waited with bated breath for

Hananiah's reply. But as in the case of Stephen when his accusers "were not able to resist the wisdom and the spirit by which he spake" (Acts 6.10), the false prophet was quite unable to answer Jeremiah's quiet and convincing argument. He therefore resorted to violence, although this was not necessarily an outburst of bad temper. It is quite possible that since Jeremiah had used yokes to illustrate his message, Hananiah decided to turn his "visual aid" to good account. Dramatically, he "took the yoke from off the prophet Jeremiah's neck, and brake it", adding, "Thus saith the Lord; Even so will I break the yoke of Nebuchadnezzar king of Babylon from the neck of all nations within the space of two full years".

Once again, Jeremiah's response did not match expectations. Instead of a downright denial of Hananiah's message, "the prophet Jeremiah went his way" (v.11). Jeremiah had not lost the argument: he did not leave the Temple having been humiliated by his opponent. Although he was more than capable of answering Hananiah, he did not have the word of the Lord for the occasion and therefore remained silent. Like Solomon he recognised that there is "a time to keep silence, and a time to speak" (Eccl 3.7). The Lord Jesus was complete master of every situation through which He passed, yet when "Pilate asked him again, saying, Answerest thou nothing? behold how many things they witness against thee…Jesus yet answered nothing; so that Pilate marvelled" (Mk 15.4-5). The silence of both Jeremiah and the Lord Jesus, when both might have responded to their opponents, illustrates New Testament teaching that "the servant of the Lord must not strive" (2 Tim 2.24).

While this was far from Hananiah's mind, the Lord will "break the yoke" of Gentile domination at the end-time: "For it shall come to pass in that day, saith the Lord of hosts, that I will break his yoke from off thy neck, and will burst thy bonds, and strangers shall no more serve themselves of him" (30.8).

Verses 12-14: The Punishment for Insubordination

Jeremiah might have said, "He is near that justifieth me" (Is 50.8), for shortly after Hananiah's assault "the word of the Lord came unto Jeremiah…saying, Go and tell Hananiah, saying, Thus saith the Lord; Thou hast broken the yokes of wood; but thou shalt make for them yokes of iron" (vv.12-13). Streane explains this clearly: "Hananiah's act only served, by exciting the Jews to resistance, to render the servitude which they should undergo more harsh. Had Zedekiah not resisted further he and the remainder of the people might have been spared the horrors of a siege and their subsequent exile". This is supported by reference to Zedekiah's stubborn refusal to surrender in the face of Jeremiah's warning in 38.17-21. It should be noted, however, that this was the prospect, not only for Judah, but for the five nations whose envoys had come to Jerusalem (27.3): "I have put a yoke of iron upon the neck of all these nations, that they may serve Nebuchadnezzar king of Babylon; and they shall serve him" (28.14).

A further reference is made here to the inclusion of "the beasts of the field" under Nebuchadnezzar's control (v.14), and the reader is referred to comments made in connection with 27.6. Habel's suggestion that Jeremiah reappeared wearing a yoke of iron seems rather unlikely.

Verses 15-17: The Price of Rebellion

Prophesying falsely in the Lord's name carried the death penalty (Deut 18.20). Jeremiah had been tried on that very charge in the reign of Jehoiakim (26.8-9,11). The Lord now pronounces the sentence through His servant, and effects the punishment. "Hear now, Hananiah; The Lord hath not sent thee; but thou makest this people to trust in a lie. Therefore thus saith the Lord; Behold, I will cast thee from off the face of the earth: this year thou shalt die, because thou hast taught rebellion against the Lord. So Hananiah the prophet died the same year in the seventh month." Habel must be right in saying that "Jeremiah, no doubt, had no more taste for this kind of preaching than he did for continually preaching doom for Israel. But when God spoke, Jeremiah was compelled to act". The death of Hananiah should be compared with the death of Pelatiah (Ezek 11.1-13). It was lies that brought about the death of Ananias and Sapphira (Acts 5.1-11).

JEREMIAH 29

It has already been noted that chapters 25-29 deal principally with the period of Judah's captivity in Babylon. The dominion of Babylon over nations in the Near East was to last for seventy years (25.11), after which the Lord would "punish the king of Babylon, and that nation...for their iniquity, and the land of the Chaldeans, and will make it perpetual desolations" (25.12). Attention has been drawn to the fact that the period of seventy years was calculated with reference to Israel's failure to keep, every seven years, "a sabbath of rest unto the land, a sabbath for the Lord" (Lev 25.4). In consequence the Lord's people were "carried...away to Babylon" by Nebuchadnezzar "where they were servants to him and his sons until the reign of the kingdom of Persia: To fulfil the word of the Lord by the mouth of Jeremiah, until the land had enjoyed her sabbaths: for as long as she lay desolate she kept sabbath, to fulfil threescore and ten years" (2 Chr 36.20-21).

However, it must also be remembered that the seventy years in Babylon were intended to be a testing and purifying period in the history of the Lord's people. As Goddard points out, "This was not their end as a people, but as a nation they had sunk to a state of ignominious sin and disregard for God's law. Something had to be done, or complete degradation would soon result. The corrective measure would have to be a severe one". He continues by noting that there are "two possible responses to chastisement: *resignation* on the one hand, *rebellion* on the other. Open defiance of God's disciplinary measures makes for bitterness of soul and extreme unhappiness. Quiet submission to God's will brings peace and blessing". Both are emphasised in the current chapter.

While Nebuchadnezzar was described by the Lord as "my servant" (25.9; 27.6) and had been given divine authority to accomplish his conquests, false prophets amongst Judah's neighbours (27.9-10) and in Judah herself (27.14-15) thought otherwise, and counselled rebellion against the king of Babylon (27.9,14). Amongst the false prophets in Jerusalem was Hananiah (28.1) who went so far as to say that not only would the Temple vessels which had been carried to Babylon be returned to Jerusalem "Within two full years", but with them "Jeconiah (Jehoiachin) the son of Jehoiakim king of Judah, with all the captives of Judah, that went into Babylon" (28.3-4). Having, in this way, made "this people to trust in a lie", Hananiah "died the same year in the seventh month" (28.15,17).

But the false prophets amongst the Lord's people were not confined to Judah and Jerusalem; they were amongst the Lord's people in Babylon as well. Three of them are named in chapter 29: "Ahab the son of Kolaiah...Zedekiah the son of Maaseiah...Shemaiah the Nehelamite" (vv.21,24). Like Hananiah in Jerusalem, the false prophets in Babylon practised deceit (v.8), falsehood (v.9), and lies (vv.21,31). Whether in Jerusalem or Babylon, their message was the same: the captivity would be of short-lived duration, and having made it clear to the Lord's people in

Jerusalem that the false prophets were lying, Jeremiah now makes the same point in writing to the exiles in Babylon. The captivity would last for seventy years (v.10). Very clearly, chapters 28-29 are closely linked; both relate to the early years of Jeconiah's captivity (28.3-4; 29.2). The people had not yet settled down in Babylon (29.5-6).

The chapter records an exchange of correspondence. Jeremiah wrote from Jerusalem to the captives in Babylon (vv.1-23) to which Shemaiah responded by writing from Babylon to the people remaining in Jerusalem (vv.24-29), referring in his communication to Jeremiah's letter (v.28). Jeremiah then replied to Shemaiah's letter, pronouncing judgment upon him (vv.30-32). The chapter may therefore be divided with reference to these three letters.

Verses 1-23: Jeremiah's First Letter

"Now these are the words of the letter that Jeremiah the prophet sent from Jerusalem" (v.1). Attention is drawn to the following:

> The letter to Babylon (vv.1-3)
> The people in Babylon (vv.4-7)
> The period in Babylon (vv.8-14)
> The prophets in Babylon (vv.15-23).

The letter to Babylon (vv.1-3)

These verses contain some general details about the letter, and the following should be noted:

The recipients of the letter

The letter was written to "the residue of the elders which were carried away captives, and to the priests, and to the prophets, and to all the people whom Nebuchadnezzar had carried away captive from Jerusalem to Babylon" (v.1). Commentators speculate on the meaning of the words "the residue of the elders", and it seems likely that they refer to the men in this category who survived the journey to Babylon. The variety of people mentioned ("elders…priests…prophets…all the people") may suggest that that there was "some form of community organisation like that in Judah" (Feinberg) but the absence of further information makes it impossible to speak with certainty. The letter is addressed to the entire community in Babylon.

The date of the letter

The letter was written, it is suggested, shortly after the deportation of "Jeconiah the king, and the queen, and the eunuchs, the princes of Judah and Jerusalem, and the carpenters, and the smiths" (v.2). These were the "very good figs" which had been "sent…into the land of the Chaldeans for their good" (24.2,5). Jeremiah's advice to build houses and plant gardens (v.5) implies that they had not been very long in Babylon.

The carriage of the letter
The letter was carried to Babylon "by the hand of Elasah the son of Shaphan, and Gemariah the son of Hilkiah, (whom Zedekiah king of Judah sent unto Babylon to Nebuchadnezzar king of Babylon)" (v.3). Elasah was probably the son of Shaphan, the secretary of state under Josiah, and brother of Ahikam (2 Kings 22.8-14; Jer 26.24). Gemariah was probably the son of Hilkiah, the high priest in the reign of Josiah (2 Kings 22.8-14). Both men were evidently loyal to Jeremiah and Laetsch observes that "the families of Hilkiah and Shaphan are living evidence that even among a corrupt priesthood and a venal government the Lord has believing, faithful servants, shining lights among a perverse generation".

No further details are given in connection with the embassy sent by Zedekiah but it seems likely, bearing in mind the earlier presence in Jerusalem of ambassadors from Judah's near-neighbours (27.3), that Elasah and Gemariah had been sent to Babylon to exonerate Zedekiah of any complicity in a possible plot to rebel against Nebuchadnezzar. It should also be said that the correspondence in this chapter indicates that there was some measure of communication between Judah and the exiles.

The people in Babylon (vv.4-7)
Contrary to the prediction of Hananiah (28.2) the exiles were going to be in Babylon for a long time. They were in Babylon because it was the Lord's will for them to be there. Their exile was no quirk of fate; the Lord had caused them "to be carried away from Jerusalem unto Babylon" (v.4). Rather than expecting an early return to their homeland, with the resulting discontent when that did not take place, they were to adopt a normal life-style: "Build ye houses, and dwell in them; and plant gardens, and eat the fruit of them; Take ye wives, and beget sons and daughters…that ye may be increased there, and not diminished" (vv.5-6). It hardly needs to be said that the marriages were intended to be between members of God's people, not with foreigners. They were even to pray for their captors: "seek the peace of the city whither I have caused you to be carried away captives, and pray unto the Lord for it" (v.7). This was something quite "unique in ancient literature" (Feinberg). This is not to say that the Jewish captives were encouraged to forget their homeland. When their captors said, "Sing us one of the songs of Zion", they replied, "How shall we sing the Lord's song in a strange land?" and continued, "If I forget thee, O Jerusalem, let my right hand forget her cunning. If I do not remember thee, let my tongue cleave to the roof of my mouth; if I prefer not Jerusalem above my chief joy" (Ps 137.3-6).

Feinberg makes the very pertinent observation that over "the centuries of their world-wide dispersion, the Jews have tried to follow this pattern. They have identified themselves with the country of their residence, while at the same time looking toward eventual restoration to their native land".

The Lord's people today are to lead normal lives even though they too are in alien territory. Like the Jews in Babylon, who were told to pray for Babylon "for in the peace thereof shall ye have peace" (v.7), believers today are to pray "For kings, and for all that are in authority; that we may lead a quiet and peaceable life in all godliness and honesty. For this is good and acceptable in the sight of God our Saviour" (1 Tim 2.2-3). The Lord Jesus expected His disciples to "pray for them which despitefully use you, and persecute you" (Mt 5.44). Like the Jews in Babylon, believers today are not permanently in the world, and in the meantime they "use this world, as not abusing (over-using) it" (1 Cor 7.31), setting their "affection on things above, not on things on the earth" (Col 3.2).

The period in Babylon (vv.8-14)

These verses contrast the deceit of the false prophets (vv.8-9) with the declaration of the Lord (vv.10-14).

The deceit of the false prophets (vv.8-9)

Little explanation is necessary: they practised outright deception. While it is not specifically stated, the context clearly indicates that they lied particularly about the length of the captivity in Babylon. Through Jeremiah, the Lord had already commanded His people to settle down in Babylon (vv.4-7) and was about to tell them that they could expect to be there for seventy years (v.10). The false prophets, like their counterparts in Jerusalem (27.16; 28.1-4), preached otherwise: "Let not your prophets and your diviners, that be in the midst of you, deceive you, neither hearken to your dreams which ye cause to be dreamed. For they prophesy falsely unto you in my name: I have not sent them, saith the Lord" (vv.8-9). "Rosy predictions were the stock in trade of the falsifiers" (Feinberg). The reference to "your dreams which ye cause to be dreamed" perplexes commentators. Ellicott's Commentary calls it "an altogether exceptional phrase", and according to Streane, "the form of the verb in the original is peculiar". The suggestion that the dreams were supplied on demand is particularly appealing. In the words of Ellicott's Commentary, this "indicates that the supply was created by a demand for visions of this nature".

The declaration of the Lord (vv.10-14)

The false hopes engendered by lying prophets now give place to the certainty of divine promise. The Lord's people in Babylon were not to think that that emptiness and deceit of the "prophets" and "diviners" left them without any hope at all for the future. The Lord did not intend to leave his people in Babylon: "For thus saith the Lord, That after seventy years be accomplished at Babylon I will visit you, and perform my good word toward you, in causing you to return to this place" (v.10). The Lord had already declared His "good word": "They (the remaining Temple vessels) shall be carried to Babylon, and there shall they be until the day that I visit them, saith the Lord; then will I bring them up, and restore them to this place" (27.22). By divine design, the end of Judah's exile would coincide with the demise of the Babylonian Empire (25.11-12). The Lord has a marvellous way of harmonising His purposes.

The false prophets made glowing predictions about the future without demanding those conditions in the hearts and lives of the Lord's people which enabled Him to act in blessing towards them. This is not the case here. In His infinite grace the Lord desired their utmost blessing and would accomplish this when His people turned to Him with whole-hearted reality: "For I know the thoughts that I think toward you, saith the Lord, thoughts of peace, and not of evil, to give you an expected end ('to give you in your latter end a hope', JND). Then shall ye call upon me, and ye shall go and pray unto me, and I will hearken unto you. And ye shall seek me, and find me, when ye shall search for me with all your heart" (vv.11-13). It should be said that this passage in its entirety is permeated with divine initiative. Not only do the promises of future blessing emphasise His gracious initiative, but it is "the goodness of God" that leads "to repentance" (Rom 2.4).

Daniel readily understood this. Having read the current passage and realised that the time for its fulfilment was imminent, he prayed with humility: "I set my face unto the Lord God, to seek by prayer and supplications, with fasting, and sackcloth, and ashes" (Dan 9.3). Daniel's understanding of Bible prophecy did not mean that he sat back and let it all happen! He prayed about it. As W. H. Burnett observes, "Daniel was no fatalist: he believed in the effectiveness of prayer". He knew the will of God from Jeremiah's prophecy, and prayed accordingly. His prayer (Daniel 9.3-19) could certainly be described as the prayer of a man who, in the language of the current chapter, sought the Lord with all his heart (v.13).

It is difficult to escape the conclusion that the prophecy looks far beyond the return from Babylon as described in the book of Ezra. Ultimately God's people experienced world-wide dispersion and this remains the case today. It is still true that the Lord has "thoughts of peace, and not of evil" towards His people and that He has not abandoned His stated purpose for them: "I will turn away your captivity, and I will gather you from all the nations, and from all the places whither I have driven you, saith the Lord; and I will bring you again into the place whence I caused you to be carried away captive" (v.14). In New Testament language, "As concerning the gospel, they are enemies for your sakes: but as touching the election, they are beloved for the fathers' sakes. For the gifts and calling of God are without repentance" (Rom 11.28-29). Such are the "thoughts of peace" that the Lord has for His people!

The prophets in Babylon (vv.15-23)

These verses indicate that when Jeremiah wrote the people were far from seeking the Lord with all their heart (v.13). On the contrary, they still hearkened to the voice of the false prophets saying, "The Lord hath raised us up prophets in Babylon" (v.15), doubtless referring to the "prophets" and "diviners" already mentioned (vv.8-9). Jeremiah now exposes the fallacy of their message (vv.16-19), and pronounces judgment on the men (vv.20-23).

The fallacy of their message (vv.16-19)

The false prophets had dangled the prospect of an early return from Babylon before the eyes of the exiles, but Jeremiah makes it clear that the very people that the exiles hoped to rejoin in Jerusalem would be subject to sweeping judgment. There would be no one left for the exiles to rejoin: "Know that thus saith the Lord of the king that sitteth upon the throne of David, and of all the people that dwelleth in this city, and of your brethren that are not gone forth with you into captivity; Thus saith the Lord of hosts; Behold, I will send upon them the sword, the famine, and the pestilence, and will make them like vile figs, that cannot be eaten, they are so evil. And I will persecute them with the sword, with the famine, and with the pestilence, and will deliver them to be removed to all the kingdoms of the earth, to be a curse, and an astonishment, and an hissing, and a reproach, among all the nations whither I have driven them" (vv.16-18). The words "curse...astonishment...hissing...reproach" are, sadly, commonly used in connection with disgrace that would befall the Lord's people: other examples occur in 19.8; 24.9; 25.18. The people remaining in Jerusalem, soon "to be removed to all the kingdoms of the earth", are described as "vile figs". They had been previously described in similar terms: "very naughty ('evil') figs...evil figs, which cannot be eaten, they are so evil" (24.2,8).

The reason for coming judgment on Zedekiah and his people is expressed in now familiar terms: "Because they have not hearkened to my words, saith the Lord, which I sent unto them by my servants the prophets, rising up early and sending them; but ye would not hear, saith the Lord" (v.19). The change of pronoun (from "they" to "you") emphasises that that the exiles already in Babylon, who would be spared the horrors of siege and death at Jerusalem, were nevertheless not exonerated from guilt; they too had rejected the Lord's word through His servants the prophets.

The judgment of the men (vv.20-23)

Jeremiah was evidently well informed about the affairs of the Lord's people in Babylon, to the extent that he knew both the names and reputation of at least two of the false prophets there. There were evidently others, including Shemaiah (v.24). Nothing further is known of the two men in question, Ahab and Zedekiah (v.21), other than their deceit and gross immorality. The exiles had said, "The Lord hath raised us up prophets in Babylon" (v.15), but now the very same people were to see what the Lord actually thought of the men He was supposed to have given them: "Hear ye therefore the word of the Lord, all ye of the captivity, whom I have sent from Jerusalem to Babylon (this statement exposed the lies of the false prophets): thus saith the Lord of hosts, the God of Israel, of Ahab the son of Kolaiah, and of Zedekiah the son of Maaseiah...Behold, I will deliver them into the hand of Nebuchadrezzar king of Babylon; and he shall slay them before your eyes; And of them shall be taken up a curse by all the captivity of Judah which are in Babylon, saying, The Lord make thee like Zedekiah and like Ahab, whom the king of Babylon roasted in the fire" (vv.20-22). Nebuchadnezzar had quite a shock when he endeavoured to roast Shadrach, Meshach and Abednego in the fire. The "burning fiery furnace" had "no power" upon them, "nor was an hair of their head singed, neither were their coats changed, nor the smell of fire had passed on them" (Dan 3.23,27). But then, unlike Zedekiah and Ahab, Daniel's three companions (Dan 2.17) were not false prophets! The official charge against Zedekiah and Ahab is not specified, but it seems more than likely that their false predictions of a quick return to Jerusalem were regarded as treasonable by the Babylonian authorities. There was no such thing as freedom of speech in Babylon!

The divine charge against the two false prophets is clearly stated: they "prophesy a lie unto you in my name" (v.21); "they have committed villany ('infamy', JND) in Israel, and have committed adultery with their neighbours' wives, and have spoken lying words in my name, which I have not commanded them" (v.23). It has been said that "truth is moral" and to pursue and practise truth, particularly divine truth, brings moral safeguards. These men did the exact opposite: they dabbled in lies, made all the more serious because they peddled their lies in the Lord's name, and practised immorality. A further example of the relationship between lies and immorality occurs in the New Testament: "Who changed the truth of God into a lie (Paul's definition of idolatry), and worshipped and served the creature more than the Creator, who is blessed for ever. Amen. For this cause God gave them up unto vile affections" (Rom 1.25-26).

Wicked men may say, "How doth God know? and is there knowledge in the most High?" (Ps 73.11), but "all things are naked and opened unto the eyes of him with whom we have to do" (Heb 4.13), and this is made very clear here: "even I know, and am a witness, saith the Lord" (v.23). The Lord's people ought always to live in the consciousness that "Thou God seest me" (Gen 16.13).

Verses 24-29: Shemaiah's Letter

Like Zedekiah and Ahab, nothing further is known of Shemaiah the Nehelamite other than information given in these verses. It is not known whether "Nehelamite" refers to his family or to his birthplace. Shemaiah was obviously incensed that Jeremiah should have written to the exiles in Babylon "saying, This captivity is long: build ye houses, and dwell in them; and plant gardens, and eat the fruit of them" (v.28). After all, this was in complete opposition to the pronouncements of the false prophets, amongst whom Shemaiah was evidently numbered. He had therefore written, evidently more than once, to "all the people...at Jerusalem" and in particular to Zephaniah and his fellow-priests in Jerusalem accusing them of dereliction of duty: "Jehovah hath made thee priest in the stead of Jehoiada the priest, that there should be officers in the house of Jehovah, over every madman and self-made prophet, that thou shouldest put him in the stocks and in the shackles. And now, why hast thou not reproved Jeremiah of Anathoth, who maketh himself a prophet to you?" (vv.26-27, JND). Unger points out that Shemaiah "referred contemptuously to Jeremiah, not only as one not called by the Lord to be a prophet, but scornfully as 'Jeremiah of Anathoth', just as the Lord Jesus was called 'Jesus of Nazareth'". Some commentators suggest that Jehoiada, who was Pashur's successor (20.1), had been deposed in favour of Zephaniah because he did not espouse "the stringent policy of the party of revolt" (Ellicott's Commentary), but this seems a little speculative. Others hold that the reference is to "Jehoiada, the energetic high priest, who, according to 2 Kings 11.18, established an overseership in the Temple, after reducing things to order there, and who was thus in a sense the first overseer in God's house, and served as an example of intrepid activity to later generations" (Orelli).

Shemaiah's opinion of Jeremiah was most uncomplimentary; he was nothing but a "madman" and a "self-made prophet" (v.26, JND). This is not the only time in the Old Testament that the Lord's servants were thought to be mad; something similar was said in the days of Hosea, "the prophet is a fool, the spiritual man is mad" (Hos 9.7). Jeremiah's place was "in the stocks and in the shackles". According to Feinberg, the "shackles", or "neck-irons", were "an iron collar that held the head immoveable while the prisoner was in the stocks". Jeremiah was no stranger to the stocks (20.2). It is somewhat ironical that Shemaiah should call Jeremiah a "self-made prophet" when he was himself amongst those who "prophesy falsely" and of whom the Lord said, "I have not sent them" (v.9).

Shemaiah's letter did not get him very far. Zephaniah took no action: all he did was to "read the letter in the ears of Jeremiah the prophet" (v.29). Jeremiah's reply follows.

Verses 30-32: Jeremiah's Second Letter

Like Jeremiah's first letter, this is addressed, not to Shemaiah personally, but to "all them of the captivity" (v.31). Both letters indicate that divine judgment on the false prophets, whether Ahab and Zedekiah in the first case or Shemaiah in the second, was to be a salutary lesson to all God's people in Babylon. Like Hananiah (28.15-17), the divine indictment against Shemaiah is that "he caused you to trust in a lie" (v.31), and "taught rebellion against the Lord" (v.32). In consequence, "I will punish, Shemaiah the Nehelamite, and his seed: he shall not have a man to dwell among this people; neither shall he behold the good that I will do for my people, saith the Lord" (v.32). Shemaiah would have no descendants and "forfeited the privilege of participating in the restoration to the homeland" (Feinberg).

The last word must go to Jensen: "Thus Jeremiah's unpopular message withstood his opponents' destructive plots because it was *God's* message. And God's message, being truth, must inevitably slay falsehood". Perhaps Jensen deliberately forgot to add, "And slay the perpetrators of falsehood as well"!

JEREMIAH 30

Thus far the general tone of Jeremiah's prophecies has been threatening and gloomy. This is not to say that the gloom has been completely unrelieved (cp. 3.14; 16.14-15; 23.3-8), but "any gleams of brightness that have from time to time appeared have borne but a very small proportion of the long stretches of melancholy foreboding and stern declaration of coming punishment which have formed the gist of his prophecies" (Streane). The next section of the prophecy, comprising chapters 30-33, brings a complete change in this respect. The whole character of the section is one of glorious hope, resting on the steadfastness of the Lord's purpose (30.24), which is expressed in the strongest possible terms (31.35-37), and the steadfastness of His love (31.3). It is not without good reason that several commentators call these chapters, "The Book of Consolation".

It cannot be without significance that these four chapters follow a section in the prophecy (chs.25-29) which deals principally with the period of Judah's captivity in Babylon. Against this dark background, Jeremiah now describes national repatriation and restoration, not from Babylon after seventy years, but from world-wide dispersion after many hundreds of years. This is intimated by the words, "the days come, saith the Lord" (v.3), a formula referring to the end-time (cp. 16.14; 23.5; 31.27,31). This section of the book therefore looks forward to what was at that time the distant future of the nation, rather than to events following the dissolution of the Babylonian Empire. It should also be noted that whereas previous chapters have anticipated the return of Judah from Babylonian captivity (27.22; 29.10-14), chapters 30-31 concern both Israel and Judah (30.3-4).

Chapter 30 commences with the words, "The word that came to Jeremiah from the Lord (v.1), and chapter 31 very clearly continues the same message: "At the same time, saith the Lord, will I be the God of all the families of Israel, and they shall be my people" (v.1). It has to be said that in neither case is there a clear reference to the immediate historical background. However, if chapters 32 and 33 belong to the same time, as seems likely, and is generally assumed to be the case since the unity of theme is most evident, then the background to the entire section is the imprisonment of Jeremiah "in the tenth year of Zedekiah king of Judah, which was the eighteenth year of Nebuchadrezzar" (32.1). Chapter 33 clearly belongs to the same time: "the word of the Lord came unto Jeremiah the second time, while he was yet shut up in the court of the prison" (v.1). While it cannot be said with certainty, it does seems that the word of the Lord in these chapters was imparted to Jeremiah "in the tenth year of Zedekiah, when the final blow was about to fall" (Feinberg). Jerusalem was "broken up" in "the eleventh year of Zedekiah" (39.2). As Feinberg therefore observes, "The remarkable feature of chapters 30-33 is that, though written during a time of deep distress for Jerusalem, they foretell a glorious future for the nation". Streane makes a similar observation: "The prophet was in prison, famine and pestilence held possession of the city, and the prospects of the nation were such as to create despair in every mind. It was at such a time as this, when humanly speaking, the people most needed the comfort of hope...that it was announced through Jeremiah that the people of God should not perish".

Chapter 30, which cannot be divided from chapter 31, may be analysed in the following way:

> The Subject of the Prophecy (vv.1-3)
> The Intensity of National Travail (vv.4-7)
> The Assurance of National Salvation (vv.8-11)
> The Restoration of National Health (vv.12-17)
> The Resumption of National Life (vv.18-22)
> The Strength of the Promise (vv.23-24).

Verses 1-3: The Subject of the Prophecy

This section in the prophecy is introduced with familiar language which clearly intimates the commencement of a new message: "The word that came to Jeremiah from the Lord" (v.1). However, the words which follow are not so familiar: "Thus speaketh the Lord God of Israel, saying, Write thee all the words that I have spoken unto thee in a book" (v.2). On the assumption that the Lord spoke to Jeremiah in this way towards the end of the reign of Zedekiah, the Lord's command here cannot refer to the books written some years earlier in the fourth year of Jehoiakim (36.1,2,27,28,32). It therefore appears that the "book" here was to contain only the particular prophecies which follow. The reason for committing them to writing, rather than preaching their message in the usual way, can be explained by Jeremiah's probable imprisonment at the time (32.2; 33.1). It should also be borne in mind that a large proportion of the population was already in Babylon and it was important that they should be able to read the messages of hope and consolation.

The subject of these chapters is clearly stated: "I will bring again the captivity of my people Israel and Judah, saith the Lord: and I will cause them to return to the land that I gave to their fathers, and they shall possess it" (v.3). There is no uncertainty about the strength of these promises: the Lord Himself says, "I will".

Verses 4-7: The Intensity of National Travail

The regathering of the nation, involving Israel and Judah (v.4), will be coincident with national rebirth and, following the pattern of natural childbirth, the rebirth of the nation will be preceded by national travail: "We have heard a voice of trembling, of fear, and not of peace. Ask ye now, and see whether a man doth travail with child? wherefore do I see every man with his hands on his loins, as a woman in travail, and all faces are turned into paleness?" (vv.5-6).

It is not without significance that this period of coming travail is called "the time of Jacob's trouble" (v.7). The expression is best understood in the context of Jacob's own life, which is itself a prophetic history of the nation. In literal terms, "the time of Jacob's trouble" was at Peniel (Gen 32.30) where, having finally succumbed to the power of the man who "wrestled…with him until the breaking of the day" (Gen 32.24), he exclaimed, "I have seen God face to face, and my life is preserved", and "as he passed over Penuel the sun rose upon him" (Gen 32.30,31). Having passed through the future "time of Jacob's trouble", "an afflicted and poor people…shall trust in the name of the Lord", and "The remnant of Israel shall not do iniquity" (Zeph 3.12-13). What is more, just as "the sun rose" on Jacob that day, so "shall the Sun of righteousness arise with healing in his wings" (Mal 4.2) for Israel's blessing.

The awful terror that will strike the nation at this time is likened to a mother in childbirth, a figure of extreme distress (cp.4.31; 6.24; 13.21; 22.23; 49.24; 50.43). Isaiah describes this as follows: "Who hath heard such a thing? who hath seen such things? Shall the earth be made to bring forth in one day? or shall a nation be born at once? for as soon as Zion travailed, she brought forth her children" (Is 66.8).

Daniel refers to the same "travail": "And at that time shall Michael stand up, the great prince which standeth for the children of thy people: and there shall be a time of trouble, such as never was since there was a nation even to that same time" (Dan 12.1). The Lord Jesus cited these words: "For then (that is, 'When ye therefore shall see the abomination of desolation, spoken of by Daniel the prophet, stand in the holy place', Mt 24.15) shall be great tribulation, such as was not since the beginning of the world to this time, no, nor ever shall be" (Mt 24.21). There is good reason for believing that the intervention of Michael here is synonymous with the expulsion of Satan from heaven: "And there was war in heaven: Michael and his angels fought against the dragon; and the dragon fought and his angels, And prevailed not; neither was their place found any more in heaven. And the great dragon was cast out, that old serpent, called the Devil, and Satan, which deceiveth the whole world: he was cast out into the earth, and his angels were cast out with him…And the dragon was wroth with the woman, and went to make war with the remnant of her seed, which keep the commandments of God, and have the testimony of Jesus Christ" (Rev 12.7-9,17). As F. A. Tatford observes, "All the descriptions given in the Scriptures of this dread time show that it will be a period of unprecedented horrors, during which the Jews will suffer torment and hardships unspeakable, as God pours out upon them His unmitigated wrath for their wrongdoing". He will use Satan's malign power to bring His people to repentance. It has been said that, when the Lord resumes direct dealings with the nation, He will fully answer their cry, "His blood be on us, and on our children" (Mt 27.25), and that in the "great tribulation" He will deal with Israel on its own admission of responsibility.

In His "Olivet Discourse" the Lord Jesus added, "And except those days should be shortened, there should no flesh be saved: but for the elect's sake those days shall be shortened" (Mt 24.22). According to Revelation 12.6, this will be a period of 1,260 "days", so that when the Lord said "for the elect's sake those days shall be shortened", he meant "shortened" *to* 1,260 days, not "shortened" to *less than* 1,260 days. The period is also described as "a time, and times, and half a time" (Rev 12.14; cp. Dan 12.7) and "forty and two months" (Rev 13.5). The "great tribulation" (Mt 24.21; Rev 7.14), or "Jacob's trouble" (Jer 30.7) will follow Israel's acceptance of the "beast", and their worship of his image under the direction and command of the "false prophet" (Rev 13.11-18).

Despite all the unparalleled horrors of Israel's coming suffering, the nation will be preserved in the deliverance of God's "elect" (Mt 24.22). In Jeremiah's words: "Alas! for that day is great, so that there is none like it: it is even the time of Jacob's trouble; but he shall be saved out of it" (v.7); "though I make a full end of all nations whither I have scattered thee, yet will I not make a full end of thee: but I will correct thee in measure, and will not leave thee altogether unpunished" (v.11). In Daniel's words: "and at that time thy people shall be delivered, every one that shall be found written in the book" (Dan 12.1), and it is to them that Paul refers in saying, "And so all Israel shall be saved" (Rom 11.26).

It should be carefully noted that the passage refers to the "the time of Jacob's trouble" (v.7) which effectively silences the argument that these verses describe the deliverance from Babylon following the conquest of the city by Cyrus. Had this been the case then the suffering would have been described as "the time of Babylon's trouble". As Feinberg rightly observes, "It is not readily clear why such a situation would be so horrendous for God's people. Actually, Cyrus would be considered their liberator from those who took them captive". At the same time, it should be said that since this period is called "the time of Jacob's trouble" no attempt should be made to include the church. Ironside, recognising that "the time of Jacob's trouble" has universal implications, clearly states the position: "To the church the promise is 'Because thou hast kept the word of my patience, I also will keep thee *from* the hour of temptation, which shall come upon all the world, to try them that dwell upon the earth' (Rev 3.10). The saints of this dispensation shall be kept *from* the hour of travail. Those of the next period will be saved *out of it*: they will pass through it, but find deliverance at last when the Lord returns in glory".

Verses 8-11: The Assurance of National Salvation

The theme of these verses is expressed in the words, "I will save thee" (v.10); "I am with thee…to save thee" (v.11). They expand the statement "that day is great…but he shall be saved out of it" (v.7), making it clear that the "time of Jacob's trouble" will mark an end of the nation's subservience to the Gentile powers, and the commencement of a new era in its history:

"For it shall come to pass in that day, saith the Lord of hosts, that I will break his yoke from off thy neck, and will burst thy bonds, and strangers shall no more serve themselves of him: But they shall serve the Lord their God, and David their king, whom I will raise up unto them" (vv.8-9). The "yoke" (v.8) evidently refers to foreign oppression. Most certainly in the past it refers to "the yoke of the king of Babylon" (27.8), but the current passage clearly refers to the future. Ironside is quite specific here: "The yoke referred to is that of the last great Gentile power, the ten-horned beast of Revelation 13", which he defines as "the Roman empire revived in is last and awful form", a definition that does not appeal to all students of prophecy!

The last four kings of Judah convey a picture of unrelieved moral and spiritual gloom. At the time of Jerusalem's final conquest by Babylon, the throne was occupied by Zedekiah, of whom the Lord testified as follows: "And thou, profane wicked prince of Israel, whose day is come, when iniquity shall have an end, Thus saith the Lord God; Remove the diadem, and take off the crown...I will overturn, overturn, overturn it: and it shall be no more, until he come whose right it is; and I will give it him" (Ezek 21.25-27). The promises made to David will never be cancelled, even though many of his successors were most unworthy to sit on his throne. God had "sworn with an oath to him, that of the fruit of his loins, according to the flesh, he would raise up Christ to sit on his throne" (Acts 2.30). The current passage, one of many, confirms this: "they shall serve the Lord their God, and David their king, whom I will raise up unto them" (v.9). The fulfilment of this delightful prophecy will take place in the millennial age when the Lord Jesus will sit "upon the throne of David, and upon his kingdom, to order it, and to establish it with judgment and with justice from henceforth even for ever. The zeal of the Lord of hosts will perform this" (Is 9.7). The angelic message to Mary reaffirms this ancient promise: "He shall be great, and shall be called the Son of the Highest: and the Lord God shall give unto him the throne of his father David" (Lk 1.32). If unrighteousness had stamped the closing years of the monarchy in Old Testament days, then the restoration of the monarchy will be the complete reverse: "Behold, a king shall reign in righteousness, and princes shall rule in judgment" (Is 32.1).

The references to David in the prophetic Scriptures (Jer 30.9; Ezek 34.22-24; 37.24; Hos 3.5) have been understood either with reference to the Lord Jesus Himself as "the so-called second David...the messianic regent, a scion of the house of David" (Feinberg) or a "new representative of the house who is to restore the kingdom" (Ellicott's Commentary). However, it is difficult to escape the conclusion, particularly from the passage in Ezekiel 34, that it will be David himself, raised from the dead, who will act as vice-regent over Israel in the millennial Kingdom. Having said that the words, "David their king" is taken "to refer antitypically to the Messiah, the Son of David", Unger continues: "But since David as well as other Old

Testament saints are to be resurrected to participate in the Messianic-Davidic Kingdom (Mt 8.11), it is not impossible that the literal, glorified David may be meant".

The end of servitude to the nations and the commencement of a glorious new era in which Israel will serve the Lord is presented as a glorious hope to the whole nation: "Therefore fear thou not, O my servant *Jacob*, saith the Lord; neither be dismayed, O *Israel*: for, lo, I will save thee from afar, and thy seed from the land of their captivity; and *Jacob* shall return, and be in rest, and be quiet, and none shall make him afraid" (v.10). The use of the two national names, Jacob and Israel, has been beautifully explained by J. G. Bellett in saying that Jacob expresses the depths to which the grace of God will go to reach a man, and Israel expresses the heights to which the grace of God will take that same man.

Other nations would cease to exist, or their power would be annulled, but not so the Lord's people: "For I am with thee, saith the Lord, to save thee: though I make a full end of all nations whither I have scattered thee, yet will I not make a full end of thee: but I will correct thee in measure, and not leave thee altogether unpunished" (v.11). The Lord will not overlook the sins of His people. "They can no more sin with impunity than any other persons or nation" (Feinberg). This is now amplified.

Verses 12-17: The Restoration of National Health

The punishment of Israel (v.11) was well-deserved: "For thus saith the Lord, Thy bruise is incurable, and thy wound is grievous" (v.12). Jeremiah's reference to Israel's health in this way echoes Isaiah's earlier description of the nation: "the whole head is sick, and the whole heart faint. From the sole of the foot even unto the head there is no soundness in it; but wounds, and bruises, and putrifying sores: they have not been closed, neither bound up, neither mollified with ointment" (Is 1.5-6). The intervening 150 years had seen no improvement in national health. If anything, the situation had worsened. If the nation's "wounds" and "bruises" figuratively described the devastation inflicted by foreign invasion in Isaiah's day (Is 1.7), how much more at the time of Jeremiah's prophecy when the Babylonians were at the gates of Jerusalem. The utter hopelessness of the situation is described in three ways.

Israel has no advocate: "There is none to plead thy cause" (v.13a). The word rendered "plead" (1777) is used of King Josiah: "He judged the cause of the poor and needy" (22.16). As a defendant in a lawsuit, Israel's sins are so flagrant that she has no one to defend her.

Israel has no medication: "to bind up thy wound; thou hast no healing medicines" (v.13b, JND). This continues the symbolism of v.12. Some suggest that the word "medicines" refers to a plaister, literally something that is placed on a wound.

Israel has no friends: "All thy lovers have forgotten thee; they seek thee not" (v.14). Edom, Moab, Ammon, Tyre, and Sidon had all courted the favour of Judah (27.3), but all had left her to face the consequences of her sins alone, and it is made clear that this was the reason for her distress: "I have wounded thee with the wound of an enemy, with the chastisement of a cruel one, for the multitude of thine iniquity; because thy sins were increased" (v.14). While this could mean that the Lord had used "an enemy" and a "cruel one" to afflict His people, it appears more likely that these terms describe the Lord Himself. So great was Israel's sin that the Lord had become their enemy. This is emphasised in the Lamentations of Jeremiah: "He hath bent his bow like an enemy: he stood with his right hand as an adversary, and slew all that were pleasant to the eye in the tabernacle of the daughter of Zion" (Lam 2.4). Not only had Israel's "lovers" turned from her, the Lord Himself had turned against her. In all this, Israel had no right to complain of her punishment; it was amply deserved: "Why criest thou for thine affliction? thy sorrow is incurable for the multitude of thine iniquity: because thy sins were increased, I have done these things unto thee" (v.15).

The unrelieved darkness of these verses now yields to hope for the future. In the first place, Israel is promised relief from her oppressors (v.16), and in the second, restoration of health (v.17).

Relief from her oppressors

"Therefore all they that devour thee shall be devoured; and all thine adversaries, every one of them, shall go into captivity; and they that spoil thee shall be a spoil, and all that prey upon thee will I give for a prey" (v.16). Commentators call this *lex talionis*, the principle of measure for measure. The Lord had said to Abram, "I will bless them that bless thee, and curse him that curseth thee (Gen 12.3). The arrogance of the nations that the Lord uses to chasten His people will be suitably rewarded, and an example is found in the downfall of the Assyrian Empire. Having described the Assyrian as "the rod of mine anger", the Lord continues: "Wherefore it shall come to pass, that when the Lord hath performed his whole work upon mount Zion and on Jerusalem, I will punish the fruit of the stout heart of the king of Assyria, and the glory of his high looks" (Is 10.5,12). It must be remembered that nations will be judged, not because they have carried out the will of God, but because of their own sin.

Restoration of health

"For I will restore health unto thee, and I will heal thee of thy wounds, saith the Lord; because they called thee an Outcast, saying, This is Zion, whom no man seeketh after" (v.17). According to Feinberg, "the figure is that of a woman put away by her husband (cp. Is 62.4)". He then asks the question, "Why did the Lord consider the treatment of His nation so great an offence?", with the answer, "Because the words and actions of the enemies revealed their disregard of God and His expressed purpose for

His people. Ultimately, calling them an outcast impugned God's faithfulness to His elect people". The restoration of health is next described in greater detail.

Verses 18-22: The Resumption of National Life

Called "an Outcast...Zion, whom no man seeketh after" (v.17), their captivity will be terminated: "I will bring again the captivity of Jacob's tents, and have mercy on his dwellingplaces" (v.18). National life will flourish again. The following should be noted.

The regathering of the nation (v.18a)

"Thus saith the Lord; Behold, I will bring again the captivity of Jacob's tents, and have mercy on his dwellingplaces." This is later expanded, "Behold, I will bring them from the north country, and gather them from the coasts of the earth, and with them the blind and the lame, the woman with child and her that travaileth with child together: a great company shall return thither...Hear the word of the Lord, O ye nations, and declare it in the isles afar off, and say, He that scattered Israel will gather him, and keep him, as a shepherd doth his flock. For the Lord hath redeemed Jacob, and ransomed him from the hand of him that was stronger than he" (31.8,10-11).

That nation had often been warned through Moses that one consequence of disobedience would be scattering amongst the nations and dispossession of their land (cp. Lev 26.33; Deut 4.26-27; 28.63-68). These predictions have already been largely fulfilled and will be completely realised in the coming time of "Jacob's trouble" (v.7). The unspeakable suffering of Jewish people in the Holocaust is described in some measure by Moses: "And among these nations shalt thou find no ease, neither shall the sole of thy foot have rest...And thy life shall hang in doubt before thee; and thou shalt fear day and night, and shalt have none assurance of thy life" (Deut 28.65-66).

The repatriation of God's people to the land following the establishment of the State of Israel in 1948, whilst undoubtedly setting the stage for future events, must not be regarded as the anticipated regathering of Bible prophecy. The current success of Israel must be attributed largely to the inherent genius of the nation; the future regathering will be solely by divine power: "And it shall come to pass in that day, that the Lord shall set his hand again the second time to recover the remnant of his people...And he shall set up an ensign for the nations, and shall assemble the outcasts of Israel, and gather together the dispersed of Judah from the four corners of the earth" (Is 11.11-12). Further passages describing this great event are found in Isaiah 43.5-6, and 49.22-23. The Lord Jesus described this regathering as follows: "And he shall send his angels with a great sound of a trumpet (cp. Is 27.13), and they shall gather his elect from the four winds, from one end of heaven to the other" (Mt 24.31).

The rebuilding of the city (v.18b)

"The city shall be builded upon her own heap ('mound', JND margin), and the palace shall remain after the manner thereof." The word translated "heap" (8510) is the well-known term TEL referring to the mound comprising the ruins of an ancient city. While some understand the word "palace" with reference to the Temple, it indicates rather "that the city will be settled by a king" (Feinberg).

At the time of "Jacob's trouble", the Lord "will gather all nations against Jerusalem to battle; and the city shall be taken" (Zech 14.2). Jerusalem is yet to fall again in battle, but only to be rebuilt for a thousand years of undisturbed peace and security. The glory of the city, with its Temple and environs, is described in Ezekiel 40-48. Isaiah cried, "For Zion's sake will I not hold my peace, and for Jerusalem's sake I will not rest, until the righteousness thereof go forth as brightness, and the salvation thereof as a lamp that burneth" (Is 62.1). In the millennial Kingdom, the city will be the centre of universal government (Ps 2.6; Is 2.2); the centre of divine education (Is 2.3); the centre of universal worship (Zech 14.16). This will be the city over which the Lord Jesus once wept, "Saying, If thou hadst known, even thou, at least in this thy day, the things that belong unto thy peace!" (Lk 19.42).

The rejoicing of the people (v.19a)

"And out of them shall proceed thanksgiving and the voice of them that make merry." At the advent of the Messiah, when they "shall look upon me whom they have pierced, and they shall mourn for him", there "shall be a great mourning in Jerusalem…And the land shall mourn" (Zech 12.10-12). However, the prophetic Scriptures abound with references to the joy of the Lord's people at this time, including the following examples: "For the Lord hath chosen Zion; he hath desired it for his habitation…her saints shall shout aloud for joy" (Ps 132.13,16); "And in that day thou shalt say, O Lord, I will praise thee: though thou wast angry with me, thine anger is turned away, and thou comfortedst me. Behold, God is my salvation; I will trust, and not be afraid: for the Lord JEHOVAH is my strength and my song; he also is become my salvation. Therefore with joy shall ye draw water out of the wells of salvation" (Is 12.1-3); "And the ransomed of the Lord shall return, and come to Zion with songs and everlasting joy upon their heads: they shall obtain joy and gladness, and sorrow and sighing shall flee away (Is 35.10). It will indeed be the "acceptable year of the Lord" then for Israel, and the Messiah will give unto them "beauty for ashes, the oil of joy for mourning, the garment of praise for the spirit of heaviness" (Is 61.2-3). Other similar passages are found in Isaiah 65.19; 66.10.

The resurgence of growth (vv.19b-20)

"And I will multiply them, and they shall not be few; I will also glorify them, and they shall not be small" (v.19). At this time, the Lord will "sow the house of Israel and the house of Judah with the seed of man, and with the seed of beast" (31.27). According to the prophecy of Zechariah, some territorial enlargement will be necessary: "I will bring them into the land of Gilead (presently part of Jordan) and Lebanon; and place shall not be found for them" (Zech 10.10). Space will be at a premium!

The Lord's people will enjoy security in that day: "Their children shall be as aforetime, and their congregation shall be established before me, and I will punish all that oppress them" (v.20). Zechariah paints a beautiful picture of security in the millennial age: "There shall yet old men and old women dwell in the streets of Jerusalem, and every man with his staff in his hand for very age. And the streets of the city shall be full of boys and girls playing in the streets thereof" (Zech 8.4-5). There will be no mugging in the streets then, and no child abduction.

The reinstitution of home rule (v.21)

"And their nobles ('prince', JND) shall be of themselves, and their governor (4910) shall proceed from the midst of them; and I will cause him to draw near, and he shall approach unto me: for who is this that engaged his heart to approach unto me? saith the Lord". With the fall of the city and the imposition of Gentile authority this must have been a great consolation to all who read Jeremiah's "book" (v.2). At His civil trial in Jerusalem, the Lord Jesus was brought before "Pontius Pilate, the governor" (Mt 27.2), and He predicted that the city would "be trodden down of the Gentiles, until the times of the Gentiles be fulfilled" (Lk 21.24). But the coming ruler will not be a foreigner: "And their prince shall be of themselves" (JND), fulfilling the ancient prophecy: "But thou, Bethlehem Ephratah, though thou be little among the thousands of Judah, yet out of thee shall he come forth unto me that is to be ruler (4910) in Israel" (Mic 5.2).

It does appear that the titles "prince" (JND) and "governor" refer to the same person, and bearing in mind he will have the privilege of approaching God without a mediator, implying priestly ministry, it can be concluded that the passage refers to none other than "the man whose name is The BRANCH" who "shall grow up out of his place, and he shall build the temple of the Lord...and he shall bear the glory, and shall sit and rule upon his throne; and he shall be a priest upon his throne" (Zech 6.12-13). As Streane, and others, point out, "None but the priests were permitted to enter the Lord's presence, and the Holy of Holies was open but once a year to the high priest himself. To all others this was a profanity to be punished with death. For Messiah as being God the Son the approach to the Father was open".

The relationship with the Lord (v.22)

"And ye shall be my people, and I will be your God" (v.22). This is amplified in the following chapter: "they shall be my people" (31.1); "I...will be their God, and they shall be my people" (31.33). Whilst it remains that

God has not "cast away his people which he foreknew" (Rom 11.2), for His purposes for Israel are immutable, it remains that at this point in time He does not acknowledge them as His people. They are at present "Loammi: for ye are not my people, and I will not be your God" (Hos 1.9). But "Loammi" is not for ever, for time is yet to be when "it shall come to pass, that in the place where it was said unto them, Ye are not my people, there it shall be said unto them, Ye are the sons of the living God" (Hos 1.10).

Verses 23-24: The Strength of the Promise
  The concluding verses of the chapter virtually repeat 23.19-20: "Behold, the whirlwind of the Lord goeth forth with fury, a continuing whirlwind: it shall fall with pain upon the head of the wicked. The fierce anger of the Lord shall not return, until he have done it, and until he have performed the intents of his heart: in the latter days ye shall consider it".

  Having described the blessings which the Lord intends for the nation, none should labour under the delusion that the wicked amongst His people would escape divine judgment. But even this had in view the achievement of "the intents of his heart". In the millennial age, with judgment ended, the godly will fully understand the purpose of the dark days through which they have passed.

  At "the time of the end...the wise shall understand" (Dan 12.9-10). Nothing, not even human wickedness, can thwart the promises of God.

JEREMIAH 31

It has already been noted that chapter 31 clearly continues the message commencing in chapter 30. Both chapters describe Israel's glory and prosperity in the coming millennial age, and chapter 31 emphasises the regathering and reuniting of the nation. "At the same time, saith the Lord, will I be the God of all the families of Israel, and they shall be my people" (v.1). According to Feinberg, this verse concludes chapter 30 in the Masoretic text. The words "the God of all the families of Israel" indicate the scope of the chapter and comprehend both Israel and Judah. Contrary to the view of some historians, there are no "lost tribes" so far as the Lord is concerned. In the New Testament, James writes to "the twelve tribes which are scattered abroad" (James 1.1) and the true "Jehovah's Witnesses" at the end-time are drawn from the entire nation (Rev 7.4). It should be noted in this connection that Dan and Ephraim are excluded from missionary service amongst the Gentiles, not because they are "missing", but because of their past idolatrous associations. They are, of course, included in the millennial division of the land (Ezek 48.1,6).

Bearing in mind the dominant theme of the chapter, the passage may be divided as follows:

> The Return of Ephraim (vv.1-22)
> The Restoration of Judah (vv.23-26)
> The Regeneration of Israel and Judah (vv.27-40).

Verses 1-22: The Return of Ephraim

The territory of Ephraim included the city of Samaria, the capital of the Ten Tribes, and Ephraim therefore stands for Israel, the northern of the two kingdoms into which the nation was divided after the death of King Solomon. This is confirmed in the book of Ezekiel: "Behold, I will take the stick of Joseph, which is in the hand of Ephraim, and the tribes of Israel his fellows, and will put them with him, even with the stick of Judah, and make them one stick, and they shall be one in mine hand" (Ezek 37.19). The future blessings of Ephraim are emphasised throughout this section of the chapter: "the watchmen upon the mount Ephraim shall cry, Arise ye, and let us go up to Zion unto the Lord our God" (v.6); "I am a father to Israel, and Ephraim is my firstborn" (v.9); "I have surely heard Ephraim bemoaning himself" (v.18); "Is Ephraim my dear son? is he a pleasant child? for since I spake against him, I do earnestly remember him still" (v.20). Samaria is specifically mentioned: "Thou shalt yet plant vines upon the mountains of Samaria" (v.5).

It must be said that the return of Ephraim is described in the context of national regathering, when Jehovah will be "the God of all the families of Israel" (v.1). The northern tribes will not only "come again to their own border" (v.17), and "turn again to these thy cities" (v.21), but they will heed the cry, "Arise ye, and let us go up to Zion unto the Lord our God" (v.6) and "they shall come and sing in the height of Zion" (v.12). The northern tribes, once alienated from Judah and Jerusalem, will return physically to the land, and spiritually to Zion. One of the sad results of the secession of Israel under Jeroboam the son of Nebat was the inauguration of a rival priesthood (1 Kings 12.31), but only one priesthood will function in the millennial Kingdom when the Lord will "satiate the soul of the priests with fatness" (v.14).

These delightful verses contain two major subjects: the love of Jehovah (vv.1-14); and the lamentation of Rachel (vv.15-22).

The love of Jehovah (vv.1-14)

The words "they shall be my people" (v.1) intimate the Lord's determination to bless them. His purposed blessing upon them is rooted in His love, and the past experience of His love is the pledge of His love in the future. While the statement, "The people which were left of the sword found grace in the wilderness; even Israel, when I went to cause him to rest" (v.2), could refer, as most interpreters feel, to the experiences of God's people in exile, it seems preferable to understand this as a distinct allusion to the wilderness journey from Egypt to Canaan. "The grace then shewn God has now determined to repeat" (Streane). The Lord determines to continue the mercy and grace He showed His people in their desert wanderings. This follows: "The Lord hath appeared of old unto me ('from afar unto me', JND), saying, Yea, I have loved thee with an everlasting love: therefore with lovingkindness have I drawn thee". According to the competent authorities, the words "unto me" are a literal translation, but commentators put these words into the mouths of the exiles, "The Lord appeared to us" (Feinberg), with the explanation that "The thought is that of a deliverer who hears the cry of his people in the distance, and then draws near to help them. Jehovah enthroned in Zion, or in the heaven of heavens, hears the cry of the exiles" (Ellicott's Commentary). In this sense, He intervenes "from afar" (JND). A comparable passage is found in connection with the deliverance from Egypt: "I have surely seen the affliction of my people which are in Egypt...And I am come down to deliver them out of the hand of the Egyptians" (Ex 3.7-8).

Moses was deeply conscious of the Lord's "everlasting love" for His people: "The Lord did not set his love upon you, nor choose you, because ye were more in number than any people; for ye were the fewest of all people (cp. Ps 105.11-15): But because the Lord loved you, and because he would keep the oath which he had sworn unto your fathers, hath the Lord brought you out with a mighty hand, and redeemed you out of the house of bondmen, from the hand of Pharaoh king of Egypt" (Deut 7.7-8). As C. H. Mackintosh observes: "It is the settled purpose of God that 'no flesh should glory in his presence' (1 Cor 1.29). All human pretension must be set aside. He will hide pride from man...They were in no wise better than the nations around them; and therefore, if called to account for their high elevation and moral greatness, they had simply to trace it all up to the free love of God, and His faithfulness to His oath" (*Notes on the Pentateuch*). The great statement in the New Testament, "For whom he did foreknow, he also did predestinate…them he also called…them he also justified…them he also glorified", causes Paul to exclaim, "Who shall separate us from the love of Christ?", and that nothing "shall be able to separate us from the love of God, which is in Christ Jesus our Lord" (Rom 8.29-30,35,39).

The Lord's "everlasting love" for His people will secure their utmost blessing, and this is described in vv.4-14 where the following should be noted:

His love secures joy for them (vv.4-7)

"Again I will build thee, and thou shalt be built, O virgin of Israel: thou shalt again be adorned with thy tabrets (or 'timbrels', instruments played like a tambourine), and shalt go forth in the dances of them that make merry" (v.4). As Feinberg observes, "Addressing Israel as a virgin, unsullied before God, Jeremiah implies that the Lord sees her just as appealing as in the time of her departure from Egypt (cp. Jer 2.1-3; Hos 2.14-23). Grace blots out all the failures of the past". The reference to planting "vines upon the mountains of Samaria" (v.5) is a further allusion to national joy (cp. Judg 9.13; Ps 104.15), but since the fruit of newly-planted trees could not be eaten for three years, and even eating in the fourth year was subject to restriction (Lev 19.23-25), the consumption of fruit here implies the ongoing settlement of the land.

Furthermore, there will be joy in worship: "For there shall be a day, that the watchmen upon the mount Ephraim shall cry, Arise ye, and let us go up to Zion unto the Lord our God. For thus saith the Lord; Sing with gladness for Jacob, and shout among the chief of the nations: publish ye, praise ye, and say, O Lord, save thy people, the remnant of Israel" (vv.6-7). This marks the end of the disruption brought about by Jeroboam who saw the danger of losing his kingdom if his people went up "to do sacrifice in the house of the Lord at Jerusalem", and therefore "made two calves of gold, and said unto them, It is too much for you to go up to Jerusalem: behold thy gods, O Israel, which brought thee up out of the land of Egypt" (1 Kings 12.27-28). Israel will then be "the head of the nations" (v.7, JND). In that day, God's people will indeed be "high above all nations which he hath made, in praise, and in name, and in honour" (Deut 26.19). The Lord will make them "the head and not the tail; and…above only, and…not…beneath" (Deut 28.13).

To say, for example, that "to go to Zion in Old Testament prophecy is to join the Christian Church" and that "the blind and the lame" (v.8) describe those who "could never by their own reason or strength believe in Jesus Christ or come to Him and His church" (Laetsch) requires no rebuttal. To treat the Scriptures in this way is bizarre.

His love secures care for them (vv.8-10)

"Behold, I will bring them from the north country, and gather them from the coasts of the earth, and with them the blind and the lame, the woman with child and her that travaileth with child together: a great company shall return thither" (v.8). The Lord will care for His people wherever they are found, not only in "the north country", the principal place of exile, but "from the coasts of the earth", and in whatever condition they are found. None will be excluded. The section bears all the marks of shepherd care. The "Shepherd of Israel" (Ps 80.1) will bring His flock "to walk by the rivers of waters in a straight way (a level path), wherein they shall not stumble" (v.9). They will come weeping with tears of repentance and with prayer (v.9), all of which will be overshadowed by the joy of returning to the land and to the Lord. The nations of the world, even the furthest of them, will recognise that "He that scattered Israel will gather him, and keep him, as a shepherd doth his flock" (v.10). As Feinberg rightly observes, there are "affinities in style and thought with the latter parts of Isaiah". It is Isaiah who said, "He shall feed his flock like a shepherd: he shall gather the lambs with his arm, and carry them in his bosom, and shall gently lead those that are with young" (Is 40.11), and "he that hath mercy on them shall lead them, even by the springs of water shall he guide them. And I will make all my mountains a way, and my highways shall be exalted. Behold, these shall come from far: and, lo, these from the north and from the west; and these from the land of Sinim" (Is 49.10-12).

The shepherd care in these verses is permeated by a father's love. The Lord who had said, "Yea, I have loved thee with an everlasting love" (v.3) now says, "I am a father to Israel, and Ephraim is my firstborn" (v.9). Feinberg makes an important distinction in saying that "Sonship in the Old Testament includes the concept of paternal love and care on a national scale, rather than the New Testament concept of personal membership in the family of God by the Spirit". The expression "firstborn" was used of the nation in its entirety by Moses when addressing Pharaoh: "Thus saith the Lord, Israel is my son, even my firstborn" (Ex 4.22). But here it is transferred to Ephraim, marking him out "as the object of the special favour of Jehovah, the birthright of Reuben having been transferred to the sons of Joseph (1 Chr 5.1)" (Ellicott's Commentary). It does seem that the words "special favour" explain the reference here to Ephraim as "my firstborn". The Ten Tribes, of which Ephraim was the most conspicuous member and who stood as their leader, who were without one good king throughout their history, and totally idolatrous, were the first tribes to enter captivity. They will therefore be the object of "special favour" in the national restoration..

His love secures deliverance for them (v.11)

"For the Lord hath redeemed Jacob, and ransomed him from the hand of him that was stronger than he." As Ironside observes, the Lord "has never given up His purpose of redemption. As a nation they were sheltered by blood from judgment and redeemed by power from Pharaoh's thraldom, when He brought them out of Egypt. He has contemplated them ever since from that standpoint. His grace cannot admit of failure to bring them into fulness of blessing at last, however much their ways necessitated chastisement in the interim". The two verbs "redeemed" (6299) and "ransomed" (1350) express the acts of setting free and intervention as the kinsman-redeemer (the *goel*) respectively.

His love secures provision for them (vv.12-14)
Every need will be supplied: "they shall come and sing in the height of Zion, and shall flow together to the goodness of the Lord, for wheat, and for wine, and for oil, and for the young of the flock and of the herd" (v.12). The exact sense of the words "they…shall flow together to the goodness of the Lord" is not easily understood, but perhaps the best explanation, bearing in mind the use of the word "flow" (5102) in Isaiah 2.2; Jeremiah 51.44; Micah 4.1, is that they describe "the returned tribes assembling in joyful worship on the holy mountain, that they may receive the blessings of a fruitful land" (Streane). The "goodness of the Lord" will be seen in the provision of wheat, wine, oil, and young cattle and sheep. According to Ellicott's Commentary, the picture of a "watered garden" (cp. Is 58.11) is "always among the brightest which an Eastern mind can draw…of the continuous joy and freshness of their life".

It is rather lovely to notice that the consequent joy of the nation is not at the expense of provision for the priests. In the midst of their prosperity, the Lord's people will not forget their responsibilities towards the men who represent them before the Lord. Their joy will be expressed as follows: "Then shall the virgin rejoice in the dance, and the young men and old together; for I will turn their mourning into gladness, and will comfort them, and make them rejoice after their sorrow" (v.13, JND). "The dances of joy, as in the days of Miriam (Ex 15.20), Jephthah (Judg 11.34), and David (1 Sam 18.6) will take the place of lamentation" (Ellicott's Commentary), and, with such abundant provision from the Lord, the tithes will exceed the utmost expectations of the priests: "And I will satiate the soul of the priests with fatness, and my people shall be satisfied with my goodness, saith the Lord" (v.14). In summary, old and young, priest and people, will rejoice together.

The lamentation of Rachel (vv.15-22)
Through Joseph, Rachel was the ancestress of the northern tribes of Ephraim and Manasseh, together with Benjamin in whose territory Ramah was located. Ramah was on the frontier between Israel and Judah. Jeremiah pictures Rachel (Rahel), as a poetical figure, weeping disconsolately over the loss of her children. The connection with the previous verses is clear: having described the coming blessing of Ephraim, the prophet now recalls

the sorrow of the exile which took place in 722-721 BC and gives assurance that the restoration of the northern tribes would bring an end to Rachel's tears. Attention is drawn to Rachel's sorrow (vv.15-17); and to Rachel's son (vv.18-22).

Rachel's sorrow (vv.15-17)
"Thus saith the Lord; A voice was heard in Ramah, lamentation, and bitter weeping; Rahel weeping for her children refused to be comforted for her children, because they were not" (v.15). As Feinberg points out, "She who had so longed for children (cp. Gen 30.1) is cruelly bereaved of them, but God purposes to restore them". The fact that Jeremiah was released at Ramah, to which he had been taken in chains preparatory to deportation (40.1), has led some to suggest that the passage refers to the Judean exile in 586 BC but the context demands the deportation of the northern kingdom. It should be noted that the cry is not said to have been raised in Ramah, but that it was "heard in Ramah", indicating that the sound of sorrow over the exile was sufficiently strong to reach Ramah, the most elevated border-town of the two kingdoms.

The quotation of this prophecy in the New Testament has engaged the minds of commentators at length. Having recorded "Herod's slaughter of the innocents" (Scofield), Matthew continues by saying, "Then was fulfilled that which was spoken by Jeremy the prophet, saying, In Rama was there a voice heard, lamentation, and weeping, and great mourning, Rachel weeping for her children, and would not be comforted, because they are not" (Mt 2.17-18). Feinberg points out that "Matthew's method of quoting an Old Testament reference does not automatically imply a direct fulfilment" and continues, "For proof see the immediate context in Matthew 2.15, where Hosea 11.1 in its original context unmistakably speaks of the nation of Israel, but by analogy and higher fulfilment refers to Christ. Similarly, that which related to Israel in original revelation (v.15) is by analogy used in speaking of Herod's atrocities. In both cases God will overrule the nation's sorrow for her ultimate joy". While the events recorded in Matthew 2.16 were a sad fulfilment of the passage (v.15), the two following verses make it evident that a second and more complete fulfilment is envisaged: "Thus saith the Lord; Refrain thy voice from weeping, and thine eyes from tears: for thy work shall be rewarded, saith the Lord; and they shall come again from the land of the enemy. And there is hope in thine end, saith the Lord, that thy children shall come again to their own border" (vv.16-17). It has been suggested that the "work" to be "rewarded" includes "bearing, rearing, sorrowing over, and praying for her children" (quoted by Feinberg).

Rachel's son (vv.18-22)
The restoration of Ephraim, personifying the Ten Tribes, will take place in conjunction with his repentance. Divine blessing is dependent on appropriate conditions in the hearts and lives of the Lord's people. Ephraim

looks back over his history and expresses sorrow for his sins: "I have surely heard Ephraim bemoaning himself thus; Thou hast chastised me, and I was chastised, as a bullock unaccustomed to the yoke: turn thou me, and I shall be turned; for thou art the Lord my God. Surely after that I was turned, I repented; and after that I was instructed, I smote upon my thigh [evidently an expression of extreme grief]: I was ashamed, yea, even confounded, because I did bear the reproach of my youth" (vv.18-19). Hosea had declared that "Israel slideth back as a backsliding heifer" (Hos 4.16), or "Israel is refractory as an untractable heifer" (JND), and "this is here taken up as their own confession, but they turn to the One so long refused and sinned against" (Ironside). In it all, "the Spirit of God had done His effective work so that Ephraim recognised the shame his earlier sinful life brought on him" (Feinberg).

As in the case of the father of the "prodigal son" (Lk 15.20-24), the Lord's fatherly concern for prodigal Ephraim is beautifully expressed: "Is Ephraim my dear son? is he a pleasant child? for since I spake against him, I do earnestly remember him still: therefore my bowels are troubled for him (an expression of deep yearning); I will surely have mercy upon him, saith the Lord" (v.20). Although obliged to denounce the sins of His people, the Lord nonetheless recalls his early relationship with them (cp. 2.2-3). In spite of his sin, divine love for Ephraim will not be denied, and he is urged "to take the highway leading back from the lands of the nations to their ancestral home in Palestine" (Ironside): "Set thee up waymarks, make thee high heaps: set thine heart toward the highway, even the way which thou wentest: turn again, O virgin of Israel, turn again to these thy cities" (v.21). It was evidently the custom of caravans to mark their routes in various ways and Ephraim is here instructed to trace and mark the route by which they went into exile in order to be able to retrace their steps. There was to be no delay: "How long wilt thou go about ('wander about', JND), O thou backsliding daughter?" (v.22). The words, "turn again, O virgin of Israel, turn again to these thy cities", prompts Ironside to exclaim, "How boundless the grace that owns as a virgin the people that had been so horribly polluted!"

This section of the chapter ends with what is probably the most disputed and enigmatic statement in the entire book: "the Lord hath created a new thing in the earth, A woman shall compass a man" (v.22). Needless to say commentators have made diverse suggestions, but no interpretation has been accepted by a majority of scholars. Perhaps the most ancient explanation comes from the so-called "church fathers" who saw in this verse a prophecy of the incarnation, saying that the "woman" is the Virgin Mary and the "man" is the Lord Jesus Christ. On grammatical and linguistic grounds, let alone on the ground of the context, this view is invalid and is now rejected by the majority of interpreters.

Bearing in mind the context, the repatriation and restoration of God's people, it would seem that any viable explanation of the word "woman" must involve Israel (Ephraim). The expression "O virgin of Israel" occurs in vv.4 and 21, but that is not necessarily a good supporting argument since it has to be said that the word "woman" cannot be made to mean a virgin and is the general word for woman in contradistinction to man (Feinberg). On the assumption, however, that the "woman" is Israel it has to be determined in what way she will "compass ('encompass', JND) a man". Kelly writes with evident confidence in saying, "The meaning is that a woman who is regarded as the weakest of the human race should overcome even the strongest man. The term here for "man" (GEBER - 1397) implies a man of might. He is expressly not an ordinary man but a hero, a man of might; and, contrary to the course of nature, the weak woman overthrows the powerful man. Such is the idea of the phrase. The true force of 'compass' (5437) is not only to oppose or resist but even to defeat all man's strength…The woman is the symbol of the nation in their weakness, and the compassing a man is their victory over all human resources brought to bear against them". Ironside is in agreement with this view in suggesting that the "man" stands here as "the symbol of power in the hands of the Gentile" and that "Israel, weak as a woman, shall compass, or overcome, the power of the nations", adding that "This would harmonise with the context" although admitting that "This verse is confessedly difficult and the meaning obscure". Feinberg calls them "puzzling words" and adds, "On the whole, it seems best to take them as a proverbial saying about something amazing and hard to believe. The meaning is beyond present solution". Nevertheless, the spirit of enquiry must not be stifled, and Kelly's explanation should be carefully considered, something each commentator would doubtless say about his preferred view!

Verses 23-26: The Restoration of Judah

Having described Ephraim's return, Jeremiah addresses Judah with similar assurance and with similar promises. The restoration of the southern kingdom will be accompanied by the renewal of old greetings: "As yet they shall use this speech in the land of Judah and in the cities thereof, when I shall bring again their captivity; The Lord bless thee, O habitation of justice, and mountain of holiness" (v.23). The words "as yet" ('again', JND) mean "as was the case in former times" (Streane). While Jerusalem is yet to be the darkest place on earth (cp. Rev 11), it will ultimately be the most sacred place on earth: the "habitation of justice, and mountain of holiness". The Lord will say, "Yet have I set my king upon my holy hill of Zion" (Ps 2.6). He describes it as "my holy mountain" (Is 11.9; 66.20). Having established the spiritual strength of Judah (v.23), the Lord will bless His people in temporal things: "And there shall dwell in Judah itself, and in all the cities thereof together, husbandmen, and they that go forth with flocks" (v.24). All this stands in sharp contrast with the situation at the time when "the fruitful place was a wilderness, and all the cities thereof were broken down at the presence of the Lord, and by his fierce anger" and "every city shall be forsaken, and not a man dwell therein" (4.26,29).

Having heard the Lord say with reference to Ephraim, "I will satiate the soul of the priests with fatness, and my people shall be satisfied with my goodness" (v.14) and now, with reference to Judah, "I have satiated the weary soul, and I have replenished every sorrowful soul" (v.25), it is not surprising that Jeremiah's sleep was sweet: "Upon this I awaked, and beheld; and my sleep was sweet unto me" (v.26). He would not have said that if, instead of enjoying divine revelation, he had listened to some commentators, one of whom, sadly, goes as far as to say that the "promise of a physical return to Canaan ended with the abrogation of the Old Covenant and is no longer part of God's covenant with His people in the latter days" (Laetsch). Had this been the case, Jeremiah would have been "of all men most miserable".

Verses 27-40: The Regeneration of Israel and Judah

Having described the coming blessings of Ephraim and Judah separately, the passage now describes the bestowal of further blessings upon the northern and southern tribes conjointly: reference is made here to "the house of Israel" and "the house of Judah" together (vv.27,31). Both Israel and Judah are then comprehended in the expression "the seed of Israel" (vv.36,37). The reunion of the nation is described in an earlier passage: "In those days the house of Judah shall walk with the house of Israel, and they shall come together out of the land of the north to the land that I have given for an inheritance unto your fathers" (3.18).

These momentous verses may be divided with reference to the words, "Behold, the days come, saith the Lord" (vv.27,31,38): the care for the nation (vv.27-30); the covenant with the nation (vv.31-37); and the continuance of the city (vv.38-40).

The care for the nation (vv.27-30)

Years of invasions and deportations had denuded the land of man and beast, but not for ever. "Behold, the days come, saith the Lord, that I will sow the house of Israel and the house of Judah with the seed of man, and with the seed of beast" (v.27). It has already been noted that the words, "Behold the days come, saith the Lord", are a formula referring to the end-time. This is certainly not Jeremiah's last word on the subject: "Again there shall be heard in this place, which ye say shall be desolate without man and without beast…The voice of joy, and the voice of gladness, the voice of the bridegroom, and the voice of the bride, the voice of them that shall say, Praise the Lord of hosts" (33.10-11).

The prophets speak eloquently on this subject. "But ye, O mountains of Israel, ye shall shoot forth your branches, and yield your fruit to my people of Israel; for they are at hand to come. For, behold, I am for you, and I will turn unto you, and ye shall be tilled and sown: And I will multiply men upon you, all the house of Israel, even all of it…And I will multiply upon you man and beast; and they shall increase and bring fruit: and I will settle you after your old estates, and will do better unto you than at your beginnings" (Ezek 36.8-11). The Lord will act on behalf of His people in every respect. Thus, "The wilderness and the solitary place shall be glad for them (that is, for "the ransomed of the Lord"); and the desert shall rejoice, and blossom as the rose. It shall blossom abundantly, and rejoice even with joy and singing: the glory of Lebanon shall be given unto it, the excellency of Carmel and Sharon, they shall see the glory of the Lord, and the excellency of our God" (Is 35.1-2). The fertility of the land is described by the prophet Amos: "Behold, the days come, saith the Lord, that the plowman shall overtake the reaper, and the treader of grapes him that soweth seed; and the mountains shall drop sweet wine, and all the hills shall melt" (Amos 9.13).

According to Ellicott's Commentary, some twenty-three years had passed since Jeremiah's call to service, but he had evidently never forgotten the two aspects of the ministry committed to him: "See, I have this day set thee over the nations and over the kingdoms, to root out, and to pull down, and to destroy, and to throw down, to build and to plant" (1.10). In fact the words "watched over" and "watch over" (v.28) recall the "very symbolism of the 'almond' with the play upon its meaning as the 'wakeful' or 'watching' tree (1.11-12)" (Ellicott's Commentary). Having enjoyed the sweetest of sleep (v.26) it must have been equally sweet for the awakened prophet to turn from describing the Lord's judicial hand upon His people, "as I have watched over them, to pluck up, and to break down, and to throw down, and to destroy, and to afflict", to describing national reconstruction, "so will I watch over them, to build, and to plant, saith the Lord" (v.28).

An example of "plucking up" follows. In this case, it is the removal of a false idea, and its replacement by the truth. At the time of writing, the current generation of Israelites, believing themselves to be innocent, were evidently complaining and claiming, mistakenly, that they were reaping the misdeeds of their forefathers, and that this was totally unjust. They said, in their own proverbial language, "The fathers have eaten a sour grape, and the children's teeth are set on edge" (v.29). The exiles in Babylonia were saying the same thing: "What mean ye, that ye use this proverb concerning the land of Israel, saying, The fathers have eaten sour grapes, and the children's teeth are set on edge?" (Ezek 18.2). The principal difference between the two passages is that Jeremiah anticipates what would happen ("In those days they shall say no more…") whereas Ezekiel insists that such talk should stop forthwith. The claim is difficult to understand in view of the principle clearly enunciated by Moses, "The fathers shall not be put to death for the children, neither shall the children be put to death for the fathers: every man shall be put to death for his own sin" (Deut 24.16), and it has been suggested that this misunderstanding arose from a wrong interpretation of Exodus 20.5-6. No such misunderstanding will exist in the millennial Kingdom. It will be readily recognised then that "every one shall die for his own iniquity: every man that eateth the sour grape, his teeth shall be set on edge" (v.30). In Ezekiel's words, "the soul that sinneth, it shall die" (Ezek 18.4,20).

The covenant with the nation (vv.31-37)

As Meyer points out, "The dread commands of Moses, the elaborate forms of Temple-ritual, the pleadings of Deuteronomy, enforced as they had been by the words of contemporary prophets, had all failed to withhold the people from backsliding. What hope was there that the distant future would not repeat the bitter story of the past? But God, who commanded the light to shine out of darkness, shined into His servant's heart, and unveiled the glory of the new covenant, which was to be sealed by the Blood of the Cross – 'the new testament in my blood', as Jesus called it. A covenant which would no longer depend on man's obedience to 'Thou shalt', and 'Thou shalt not'; but would glisten with the ... repeated, I WILL of God".

These verses lie at the heart of the book of Jeremiah, and "many expositors maintain that the concept of the new covenant is Jeremiah's greatest contribution to biblical truth" (Feinberg). Attention is drawn to four aspects of this all-important subject.

The parties to the covenant

"Behold, the days come, saith the Lord, that I will make a new covenant with the house of Israel, and with the house of Judah" (v.31). The time of the covenant is firmly established by the words, "Behold, the days come, saith the Lord", clearly pointing to the end-time. The new covenant will be made "with the house of Israel, and with the house of Judah", that is, with the whole nation. While the blessings of the new covenant are enjoyed by believers today, to the extent that Paul described himself and his colleagues as "able ministers of the new testament ('covenant', JND)" (2 Cor 3.6), the covenant is never said to be made with the church. In the Epistle to the Hebrews, as in the current passage, it is distinctly said that it is to be made with "the house of Israel and the house of Judah" (Heb 8.8). It would be singularly inappropriate to say that the new covenant is made with the church since no former covenant existed so far as the church is concerned. It must nevertheless be emphasised that the blessings of regenerate Israel in the millennial Kingdom, so far as the new covenant is concerned, are possessed by believers today, and that the basis on which Israel will be so wonderfully blessed by God *then* is exactly the same basis on which the Lord's people *now* enjoy divine blessing. In instituting the Lord's Supper, the Lord Jesus said, "This cup is the new testament in my blood, which is shed for you" (Lk 22.20). The current enjoyment of new covenant blessings is emphasised in the second of the two references in the Epistle to the

Hebrews to Jeremiah 31, where direct reference to the nation of Israel is omitted: "For by one offering he hath perfected for ever them that are sanctified. Whereof the Holy Ghost also is a witness to us: for after that he said before, This is the covenant that I will make with them after those days, saith the Lord, I will put my laws into their hearts, and in their minds will I write them; And their sins and iniquities will I remember no more" (Heb 10.14-17). As J. M. Flanigan observes, "Such blessedness could never have been attained under the old covenant. It is ours now, as a present possession, and the Holy Spirit bears witness of it to us" (*What the Bible Teaches: Hebrews*).

The superiority of the covenant
    "Not according to the covenant that I made with their fathers in the day that I took them by the hand to bring them out of the land of Egypt; which my covenant they brake, although I was an husband unto them, saith the Lord" (v.32). The old covenant, the law, placed an obligation on God's people; its blessings were dependent on their obedience: "if ye will obey my voice indeed, and keep my covenant, then ye shall be a peculiar treasure unto me above all people" (Ex 19.5). The law in itself was "holy, and just, and good" (Rom 7.12), but it made demands on imperfect men and women: "For if that first covenant had been faultless, then should no place have been sought for the second. For finding fault with *them*, he saith, Behold, the days come, saith the Lord, when I will make a new covenant with the house of Israel and with the house of Judah" (Heb 8.7-8). It is not without significance that the law is described as "the ministration of death, written and engraven in *stones*" (2 Cor 3.7). The law, like stone, is inflexible; unlike other materials, it cannot be bent and any attempt to do so will result in breakage. In fact, Israel broke the first commandment before Moses descended from Sinai (Ex 32.1). The blame for breaking the covenant rested wholly on Israel and Judah. The Lord had been to them as a faithful husband to his wife, and expected obedience and fidelity to the covenant. The new covenant rests on an entirely different basis, and this follows.

The provisions of the covenant
    "But this shall be the covenant that I will make with the house of Israel" (v.33). In divine grace the Lord will make it possible for the exclusion of failure on the part of the nation by undertaking all the obligations of the covenant Himself. The old covenant was bilateral in nature: the new covenant will be unilateral: "I will put my law in their inward parts, and write it in their hearts; and will be their God, and they shall be my people. And they shall teach no more every man his neighbour, and every man his brother, saying, Know the Lord: for they shall all know me, from the least of them unto the greatest of them, saith the Lord: for I will forgive their iniquity, and I will remember their sin no more" (vv.33-34). The new covenant will involve a change in will, heart, and conscience. Unlike the

law, the old covenant, it will be an internal covenant rather than an external covenant. As already noted, the old covenant was "written and engraven in stones", but the new covenant will be written in the hearts of God's people. Meyer puts it as follows: "That the law of God should not be without as a precept, but within, as though inwrought into the very structure of heart and will; that religion should consist primarily in what God was to His child, rather than in what the child said and did towards Him; that neither priest nor Levite should be needed any more, since each soul would possess the right of direct intercourse with its Lord; that sin should be completely forgiven, as if it had never been – this was the vision which shone in on the prophet's heart, and is realised in Christ for all who belong to Him by faith. This blessed covenant shall yet gather Israel within its provisions".

The New Testament emphasises the basis on which all this is so gloriously possible: "For I will be *merciful* to their unrighteousness, and their sins and their iniquities will I remember no more" (Heb 8.12). Like its use in Luke 18.13, the word "merciful" means far more than the expression of mercy: it denotes the ground on which mercy can be extended. The word mercy *(hileos)* means propitious and recalls the day of atonement when the blood of the sin offering was placed on and before the mercy seat in the Tabernacle (Lev 16.14-15). The ground therefore on which God can bless men and women under the new covenant is the finished work of Christ (cp. Heb 9.15). The effectiveness of the new covenant is emphasised: "their sins and their iniquities will I remember no more" (Heb 8.12). This is far more than "forgiving and forgetting". God says in effect: "I will never reopen the case". The matter will never be raised again! The question is settled – for ever! This was not so under the old covenant: "in those sacrifices there is a remembrance again made of sins every year" (Heb 10.3). But now "their sins and their iniquities *will I remember no more*" (Heb 10.17). This covenant will therefore never be superseded; it is an "everlasting covenant" (32.40).

The permanence of the covenant

As Feinberg observes in connection with vv.35-37, "The permanence of the nation is illustrated from the fixed arrangements in nature". This is expressed in magnificent and quite self-explanatory language: "Thus saith the Lord, which giveth the sun for a light by day, and the ordinances of the moon and of the stars for a light by night, which divideth the sea when the waves thereof roar; The Lord of hosts is his name: If those ordinances depart from before me, saith the Lord, then the seed of Israel also shall cease from being a nation before me for ever. Thus saith the Lord; if heaven above can be measured, and the foundations of the earth searched out beneath, I will also cast off all the seed of Israel for all that they have done, saith the Lord". The continuity of the nation, which seemed impossible at the time of writing, is assured. A similar passage is found in 33.19-26.

The continuance of the city (vv.38-40)

The future of Jerusalem is assured along with the future of the nation. These verses describe some of its future features. The very city besieged by the Chaldeans at the time of writing and shortly to be destroyed by them, would be rebuilt, not as a showpiece and not as an advertisement for the genius and enterprise of the nation, but for the glory of the Lord. It will be built "to the Lord" (v.38) and "be holy unto the Lord" (v.40). A literal nation "must have an actual geographical location in which to reside...a renewed covenant demands a renewed Jerusalem" (Feinberg).

The details given make it clear that Jeremiah is describing a literal city. It has been suggested that the details relate to the four sides of the city, although this cannot be said with certainty. The "tower of Hananeel" (v.38) formed the north-east corner of the city (Neh 3.1; 12.39; Zech 14.10), and it is thought that the "gate of the corner" (v.38) refers to the city's north-west corner (2 Kings 14.13; 2 Chr 26.9). The locations of Gareb and Goath (v.39) are unknown. According to Feinberg, it has been conjectured that Gareb was on the western side of Jerusalem and Goath toward the Valley of Hinnom on the south. The "whole valley of the dead bodies, and of the ashes" (v.40) is generally understood to be the Valley of Hinnom (cp. 7.31), and again, according to Feinberg, it is suggested that the "fields" (v.40) are quarries. The "horse gate" is evidently at the south-east corner of the Temple courts (Neh 3.28; 2 Kings 11.16). Since a permanent nation calls for a permanent capital, this description must look forward to the end-time when "it shall not be plucked up, nor thrown down any more for ever" (v.40). These words cannot apply to any period in the past. "In our Lord's time the filthy stench of the valley of Hinnom still polluted the atmosphere. It was in no sense holy unto Jehovah. To the future alone can we look for a fulfilment that shall accord with, and transcend, the promise. 'The zeal of the Lord of hosts will perform this'" (Ironside).

JEREMIAH 32

It is not uncommon for servants of God to say that they have been "tested on their own ministry". Having urged their hearers to be faithful to the Word of God, circumstances in their own lives require them, sometimes at great cost, to adhere to the very teaching they have imparted to others. Jeremiah is in a very similar position in this chapter. Having described the future restoration of the nation in chapters 30 and 31, the reality of his faith in the Lord's promises is now put to the test. To use modern language, he is asked to make what appeared to be a most unwise investment in a piece of real estate when the property in question was probably in enemy hands and the whole country, including Jerusalem, would shortly be under Chaldean control. Nevertheless, Jeremiah was to proceed with the transaction, being assured by the Lord that, contrary to appearances, "Houses and fields and vineyards shall be possessed again in this land" (v.15). In doing this Jeremiah displayed his faith in the Lord's ability to restore the nation as He had promised, and encouraged others to believe similarly, despite their desperate situation at the time. This is not to say that he never harboured the slightest doubt about the future (vv.24-25), but the Lord graciously reassured him that he was right in saying, "there is nothing too hard for thee" (v.17).

The chapter may be divided as follows:

> The Prediction of Captivity (vv.1-5)
> The Purchase of the Field (vv.6-15)
> The Prayer of the Prophet (vv.16-25)
> The Prospect for the Nation (vv.26-44).

Verses 1-5: The Prediction of Captivity

"The word that came to Jeremiah from the Lord in the tenth year of Zedekiah king of Judah, which was the eighteenth year of Nebuchadrezzar. For then the king of Babylon's army besieged Jerusalem: and Jeremiah the prophet was shut up in the court of the prison, which was in the king of Judah's house" (vv.1-2). The king of Babylon had laid siege to Jerusalem in the ninth year of Zedekiah's reign and the city finally fell in the eleventh year of his reign (39.1-2; 52.4-5). However, the siege was not continuous; it was temporarily lifted at the approach of the Egyptian army, at which time Jeremiah attempted to leave Jerusalem, having warned Zedekiah that the withdrawal of the Chaldeans made no difference to the outcome of the war (37.5-12). His attempt to leave the city was construed as an act of treachery, and he was arrested and imprisoned, firstly "in the house of Jonathan the scribe" and latterly in "the court of the prison" (37.13-21), which is where Jeremiah was confined at the commencement of the current chapter (v.2).

Jeremiah had been imprisoned by Zedekiah because he had foretold
the king's fate. When interviewed by the king after his imprisonment in
the house of Jonathan, he had said, "thou shalt be delivered into the hand
of the king of Babylon" (37.17), but this was evidently a précis of his reply
to the king, and fuller details are given here by angry Zedekiah himself:
"Wherefore dost thou prophesy, and say, Thus saith the Lord, Behold I will
give this city into the hand of the king of Babylon, and he shall take it; And
Zedekiah king of Judah shall not escape out of the hand of the Chaldeans,
but shall surely be delivered into the hand of the king of Babylon, and
shall speak with him mouth to mouth, and his eyes shall behold his eyes;
And he shall lead Zedekiah to Babylon, and there shall he be until I visit
him, saith the Lord: though ye fight with the Chaldeans, ye shall not
prosper?" (vv.3-5). Zedekiah did look into the eyes of Nebuchadrezzar, but
that was almost the last thing he saw before his eyes were put out and he
was taken in chains to Babylon (52.11). Since he died in Babylon, the words
"until I visit him" evidently refer to his death.

The fall of Jerusalem and the captivity of Zedekiah are predicted here in
plain, unequivocal terms to emphasise the dark background to the promise
that "fields shall be bought in this land, whereof ye say, It is desolate without
man or beast; it is given into the hand of the Chaldeans. Men shall buy
fields for money…for I will cause their captivity to return, saith the Lord"
(vv.43-44). With the Chaldeans at the gates, it all looked completely
impossible. But, like a master jeweller, the Lord often displays his brightest
gems against the darkest background, and while the opening section of
the chapter makes miserable reading, this was not the end of the story.
Although all the evidence pointed to the elimination of the nation, Jeremiah
was given the opportunity to demonstrate his faith in the promises of
God. So far as he was concerned, the future of God's people was assured
and he was prepared to declare this publicly by purchasing property for
future possession.

Verses 6-15: The Purchase of the Field

These verses describe the transaction itself and the following should be
noted: the parties to the transaction (vv.6-8); the details of the transaction
(vv.9-12); and the significance of the transaction (vv.13-15).

The parties to the transaction (vv.6-8)

Jeremiah himself now takes up the story: "The word of the Lord came
unto me, saying, Behold, Hanameel the son of Shallum thine uncle shall
come unto thee, saying, Buy thee my field that is in Anathoth: for the right
of redemption is thine to buy it" (vv.6-7). Hanameel's personal
circumstances are not revealed but it has been suggested he was either
childless or found himself in dire financial straits, necessitating the sale of
the field. In such circumstances, provision had been made for keeping
property in the family (Lev 25.23-28) and the present passage provides an

opportunity to see "the duty of redemption and the right of preemption" (Feinberg) in action. The same law applied to the "parcel of land" belonging to Elimelech (Ruth 4.3).

With the arrival of Hanameel in "the court of the prison", the part of the palace area set aside for prisoners, Jeremiah "knew that this was the word of the Lord" (v.8) and this gave him confidence to proceed with the transaction, even though the whole enterprise looked foolish. His willingness to buy the field in Anathoth yields some timeless lessons.

Testimony to others must not be weakened by inconsistency

It has already been noted that having spoken so eloquently of Israel's future restoration and blessing, Jeremiah now had the opportunity to provide a tangible demonstration of his faith in the Word of God. Failure to exhibit confidence in the promises of God by declining to purchase the land would inevitably undermine his preaching. The Lord Jesus told His disciples to be "like unto men that wait for their lord" (Lk 12.36), and the believers at Thessalonica were known for their "patience of hope in our Lord Jesus Christ" and that they waited for God's "Son from heaven" (1 Thess 1.3,10). The lives of believers today should conform to their expectation of the Lord's return.

Changing circumstances must not weaken confidence in God's Word

With the Chaldeans tightening their grip on Jerusalem, Jeremiah might have succumbed to despair. What price now the promises of God? How could the word of God possibly be fulfilled? The inevitable fall of the city must mean that the nation would be extinguished and that all hope of restoration would be gone for ever. Surely the recently-imparted prophecy of Israel's coming glory no longer applied. But it did! The Lord does not renege on His promises. His word is inviolable and unchangeable. The Word of God is "For ever...settled in heaven" (Ps 119.89) and "the gifts and calling of God are without repentance" (Rom 11.29).

Personal feelings must not weaken obedience to God's Word

The property was located "in Anathoth, which is in the country of Benjamin". This was Jeremiah's home town and it was there that he first experienced opposition (11.21) but, more to the point, his own family there opposed him (12.6). It has been said that it is quite possible to know what is right, but to refuse to do it simply because of personal dislike for the individual making the request in the first place. Jeremiah was not influenced in this way. He did not allow incidents in the past to sway his judgment and he certainly did not bear a grudge against his own family.

The details of the transaction (vv.9-12)

"And I bought the field of Hanameel my uncle's son, that was in Anathoth, and weighed him the money, even seventeen shekels of silver" (v.9). According to Harrison, "Before coinage was introduced in the sixth century BC money normally consisted of weighed amounts of gold or silver (cp. Gen 23.16)". He adds, "The actual value of a shekel at this time is uncertain". As Feinberg observes, "We do not know the source of Jeremiah's income, nor can we speculate about the adequacy or inadequacy of the price, or about the size of the field. These details are not important".

The legal precision of the transaction is impressive: "And I subscribed the evidence, and sealed it, and took witnesses, and weighed him the money in the balances. So I took the evidence of the purchase, both that which was sealed according to the law and custom, and that which was open: And I gave the evidence of the purchase unto Baruch the son of Neriah, the son of Maaseiah, in the sight of Hanameel mine uncle's son, and in the presence of the witnesses that subscribed the book of the purchase, before all the Jews that sat in the court of the prison" (vv.10-12). The signing, sealing and witnessing of deeds has continued to the present day, and will be familiar to many readers, although it has to be said that the sealing here is rather different from modern legal practice where a seal is added to a signature. Jeremiah signed and sealed the deed ("I subscribed the evidence, and sealed it"), and paid the purchase price in the presence of witnesses (v.10). Two copies of the deed of purchase ("the evidence of the purchase") were made (v.11). The first copy was sealed in the sense of being sealed up or closed securely, and the other left open. Should it be suspected that the "open" copy of the deed had been tampered with, the closed or "sealed" copy could be consulted. Both copies were then delivered to Baruch in the presence of witnesses (v.12) who then deposited them in an "earthen vessel" (v.14). This is the first reference to Baruch in the book. According to Feinberg, "Deeds were probably executed on papyrus" and "stored in clay jars to ensure their permanence...Usually the jars were sealed with pitch". The title deeds generally went to the buyer, but in this case more was involved. For reasons already given, it was important for the sale to be made as public as possible. After all, this particular transaction conveyed an important message!

The opportunity should be taken to say that if strict legal procedures were in force in Jeremiah's time, and if measures were taken to ensure complete transparency in business and financial matters, then no less a standard should mark the affairs of the Lord's people today. In the New Testament, Paul made careful arrangements to ensure complete confidence in those who conveyed the gift from the assemblies in Macedonia and Achaia to the needy saints in Jerusalem (Rom 15.26). These arrangements are detailed in 2 Corinthians 8.16-24 and include the words, "Providing for honest things, not only in the sight of the Lord, but also in the sight of men" (v.21).

The significance of the transaction (vv.13-15)

These verses are quite self-explanatory: "And I charged Baruch before them, saying, Thus saith the Lord of hosts, the God of Israel; Take these evidences, this evidence of the purchase, both which is sealed, and this evidence which is open; and put them in an earthen vessel, that they may continue many days. For thus saith the Lord of hosts, the God of Israel; Houses and fields and vineyards shall be possessed again in this land". While there was a partial fulfilment of this promise after Judah's return from captivity in 536 BC and at other times thereafter, the ultimate fulfillment awaits the establishment of the millennial Kingdom.

Ironside speaks for several commentators in saying that "No thoughtful Bible student can fail to see in this striking incident the key to the understanding of the vision of the seven-sealed book in the Revelation (Rev 5.1). The latter is unquestionably the title-deed to this world. It remains sealed till the rightful Heir steps forth to claim it. He, the worthy One, has first to purge His heritage by judgment, before entering into possession of it. The opening of the seals is the declaration that He about to enter into His vested rights".

While Harrison observes that "The entire transaction demonstrates the tremendous faith which Jeremiah had in the divine promises of national renewal", the verses that follow show that he had some misgivings.

Verses 16-25: The Prayer of the Prophet

According to James, "Elias was a man subject to like passions as we are, and he prayed" (James 5.17), and the same might be said of Jeremiah. Harrison rightly remarks that "Jeremiah's humanity is apparent here. Like many another person since, he began to have second thoughts about the wisdom of his action once he had purchased the property. In some distress he prayed to God and was reassured concerning the future". The prophets were certainly not supermen, and the Word of God faithfully records the troughs as well as the peaks in their spiritual experience. With so much else, the elation and despondency, sometimes doubt, of the Lord's servants, is "written for our learning, that we through patience and comfort of the scriptures might have hope" (Rom 15.4). The Lord used imperfect men to great effect in Old Testament times, and His people today can be assured that this is still the case.

Jeremiah's difficulty lay in reconciling the imminent fall of Jerusalem and national dissolution, with the purchase of property for future occupation. What he had just done seemed irreconcilable with the Chaldean siege ramps surrounding the city walls (vv.24-25). It was not a case of rank unbelief, but of inability to understand. Jeremiah therefore prays for illumination. Habakkuk was in the same position and also sought divine help (Hab 1.1-2.1). Both men stood firmly on what they did know about the Lord, and then asked for help in matters which eluded their understanding. Jeremiah's prayer has two distinct parts: his assurance (vv.17-23); and his uncertainty (vv.24-25).

His assurance (vv.17-23)

In these verses, Jeremiah dwells upon the way in which the Lord had dealt with Israel over her long history.

He was assured of the Lord's omnipotence (v.17)

"Ah Lord God! behold, thou hast made the heaven and the earth by thy great power and stretched out arm, and there is nothing too hard for thee." The word "hard" (6381) has the meaning of "wonderful", implying that the future transactions envisaged "require a miraculous, wonderful operation of God" (Feinberg). Prayer must always recognise the omnipotence of God. The Lord Himself later reminds Jeremiah that the answer to his problem lay in his own words: "Behold, I am the Lord, the God of all flesh: is there any thing too hard for me?" (v.27).

He was assured of the Lord's grace and government (v.18a)

"Thou shewest lovingkindness unto thousands, and recompensest the iniquity of the fathers into the bosom of their children after them." Jeremiah refers here to Exodus 20.5-6; 34.7. Recompensing "the iniquity of the fathers into the bosom of their children after them" does not contradict the statement that "every one shall die for his own iniquity" (Jer 31.30). It indicates, rather, that "the sins of the fathers impact on families, perhaps through hereditary features, although this is not specifically stated, or in future dealings which the Lord will have with the family" (J. Grant; *What the Bible Teaches: Exodus*). In the present context, this appears particularly relevant. Since the current generation in Judah's society had both ignored the implications of the "iniquity of the fathers" and committed the same sins themselves, they were doubly responsible for the impending calamity.

He was assured of the Lord's omniscience (vv.18b-19)

"The Great, the Mighty God, the Lord of hosts, is his name, Great in counsel, and mighty in work: for thine eyes are open upon all the ways of the sons of men: to give every one according to his ways, and according to the fruit of his doings." The description of the Lord in this way emphasises His complete ability to accomplish His purposes and that He acts at all times in perfect righteousness. In the words of Hanani, "the eyes of the Lord run to and fro throughout the whole earth" (2 Chr 16.9), and in those of Solomon, "The eyes of the Lord are in every place, beholding the evil and the good" (Prov 15.3).

He was assured of the Lord's ability to intervene on behalf of His people (vv.20-21)

He had "set signs and wonders in the land of Egypt, even unto this day, and in Israel, and among other men (literally, 'among men'); and hast made thee a name, as at this day; And hast brought forth thy people Israel out of the land of Egypt with signs, and with wonders, and with a strong hand, and with a stretched out arm, and with great terror". The impact of the exodus on the ancient world was immense. Rahab remarked on this: "I know that the Lord hath given you the land, and that your terror is fallen upon us...For we have heard how the Lord dried up the water of the Red sea for you, when ye came out of Egypt" (Josh 2.9-10). In fact, the awe and wonder engendered by the deliverance of the Lord's people from Egypt will only be exceeded by the sense of wonder at their deliverance at the end-time: when "it shall no more be said, The Lord liveth, that brought up the children of Israel out of the land of Egypt; But, The Lord liveth, that brought up the children of Israel from the land of the north, and from all the lands whither he had driven them" (Jer 16.14-15).

He was assured of the Lord's ability to fulfil His promises (v.22)
"And hast given them this land, which thou didst swear to their fathers to give them, a land flowing with milk and honey." Towards the end of his life, Joshua reminded the people that "not one thing hath failed of all the good things which the Lord your God spake concerning you; all are come to pass unto you, and not one thing hath failed thereof" (Josh 23.14).

He was assured that the Lord was completely justified in dealing with their sin (v.23)
"And they came in, and possessed it; but they obeyed not thy voice, neither walked in thy law; they have done nothing of all that thou commandest them to do: therefore thou hast caused all this evil to come upon them."

In summary, Jeremiah fully understood that the nation had rejected "the Great, the Mighty God" (v.18) by disobeying His word, and that the pending disaster was therefore fully merited. The Lord must judge His people's sin. How, therefore, could this be reconciled with the bright promises enshrined in the recently completed transaction?

His uncertainty (vv.24-25)
Jeremiah presents his problem in the clearest terms. In fulfilment of the word of God, the city was about to fall to the Chaldeans. The earthworks ("the mounts" or siege ramps) used in capturing a city were already in place, and the city was ravaged by the sword, famine and plague (v.24). The outcome of the siege was not in doubt and it seemed incongruous to Jeremiah that the Lord should command him to purchase land when "the end of organised life in Judah was at hand" (Harrison). In the prophet's own words, "and what thou hast spoken is come to pass; and, behold, thou seest it. And thou hast said unto me, O Lord God, Buy thee the field for money, and take witnesses; for the city is given into the hand of the Chaldeans" (vv.24-25).

The Lord was not slow in answering his perplexed servant.

Verses 26-44: The Prospect for the Nation

The Lord fully answered the three main points in Jeremiah's prayer (vv.16-25): confession of faith in the Lord's omnipotence (v.17); recognition that having been signally blessed by the Lord, the nation fully deserved divine judgment (vv.18-24); admission of his lack of understanding (v.25). Each of these is answered in turn.

The Lord confirms His omnipotence (v.27)

"Behold, I am the Lord, the God of all flesh: is there anything too hard for me?" As Feinberg observes, "It was as if the Lord were asking Jeremiah if he believed his own words in v.17". However impossible a bright national future might seem, it was not beyond the Lord's power to accomplish. Ironside strikes an encouraging note in saying, "Precious it is to have to do with One to whom nothing is impossible. What comfort for his imprisoned servant to know that it was the Almighty upon whom he leaned!"

The Lord confirms the guilt of His people (vv.28-35)

In fact, He goes further than Jeremiah had done by describing in detail the devastation of Jerusalem and dilating on the reasons for its destruction.

The coming devastation (vv.28-29)

"Behold, I will give this city into the hand of the Chaldeans…And the Chaldeans, that fight against this city, shall come and set fire on this city, and burn it with the houses, upon whose roofs they have offered incense unto Baal, and poured out drink offerings unto other gods, to provoke me to anger." The Chaldeans would execute the very judgment on idolatrous Jerusalem demanded by the Mosaic Law: "Thou shalt surely smite the inhabitants of that (idolatrous) city with the edge of the sword…and shalt burn with fire the city, and all the spoil thereof every whit" (Deut 13.15-16). Idolatry had been practised openly and blatantly (v.29), and now "The incense-smoke of their false worship had, as its end, the smoke of burning roof and timbers" (Ellicott's Commentary).

The reasons for coming destruction (vv.30-35)

In his prayer, Jeremiah had stressed the faithfulness and goodness of the Lord towards His people (vv.18-22), but the Lord now draws attention to their ongoing rebellion from the beginning of their national existence: "the children of Israel and the children of Judah have only done evil before me from their youth" (v.30). Jerusalem itself had a terrible record stretching back to and including Jebusite days (1 Chr 11.4-6): "For this city hath been to me as a provocation of mine anger and of my fury from the day that they built it even unto this day; that I should remove it from before my face" (v.31). Every section of society was guilty: "their kings, their princes, their priests, and their prophets, and the men of Judah, and the inhabitants of Jerusalem" had all provoked the Lord to anger (v.32). The people persistently rejected the word of the Lord: "they have turned unto me the back (cp. 2.27), and not the face: though I taught them, rising up early and teaching them, yet they have not hearkened to receive instruction" (v.33). National impiety reached its height when the people set up their idols in the Temple of God (v.34). As Feinberg observes, "Their obscene symbols had been removed during Josiah's reforms, but they were reintroduced in the days of apostasy after Josiah's reign (cp. Jer 7.30; 2 Kings 23.4; Ezek 8.3-11)". Gross idolatry was accompanied by child sacrifice: "And they built the high places of Baal, which are in the valley of the son of Hinnom, to cause their sons and their daughters to pass through the fire unto Molech" (v.35). This appalling subject is mentioned in 7.31 and 19.5, and the reader is referred to comments made there. The Lord's total abhorrence of these degraded practices is expressed again in His words: "I commanded them not, neither came it into my mind, that they should do this abomination, to cause Judah to sin" (v.35).

The Lord confirms His intention to bless His people (vv.36-44)

Any uncertainty in Jeremiah's mind is thus banished. The Lord now proves that His servant was quite correct in stating that nothing was too hard for Him (v.17). The impending destruction of Jerusalem would indeed take place, but this did not signal the end of the nation. The passage leaps forward in anticipating, not the return from Babylonian exile, but the return from worldwide dispersion. "And now therefore thus saith the Lord, the God of Israel, concerning this city, whereof ye say, It shall be delivered into the hand of the king of Babylon by the sword, and by the famine, and by the pestilence; Behold, I will gather them out of all countries, whither I have driven them in mine anger, and in my fury, and in great wrath; and I will bring them again unto this place, and I will cause them to dwell safely: And they shall be my people, and I will be their God: And I will give them one heart, and one way, that they may fear me for ever, for the good of them, and of their children after them: And I will make an everlasting covenant with them, that I will not turn away from them, to do them good; but I will put my fear in their hearts, that they shall not depart from me. Yea, I will rejoice over them to do them good, and I will plant them in this land assuredly with my whole heart and with my whole soul" (vv.36-41). Nowhere else in the Old Testament is the phrase "with my whole heart and with my whole soul" used of the Lord.

The passage effectively restates the terms of the New Covenant (31.31-37). "The unity between God and the nation will never again be disrupted, since the returned exiles will be renewed in will and spirit" (Harrison). Attention is drawn to the use of the "prophetic perfect" in the words, "I will gather them out of all countries, whither I have driven them" (v.37); the exile had still not taken place. Feinberg is right in saying that "the promise of restoration is just as certain as the predictions of punishment": "For thus saith the Lord; Like as I have brought all this great evil upon this people, so will I bring upon them all the good that I have promised them" (v.42).

When this is in place, "fields shall be bought in this land, whereof ye say, It is desolate without man or beast; it is given into the hand of the Chaldeans. Men shall buy fields for money, and subscribe evidences, and seal them, and take witnesses...for I will cause their captivity to return, saith the Lord" (vv.43-44). "Following Jeremiah's example, land will again be bought and sold...and again the procedures adopted presuppose a stable economy, flourishing under God's provision" (Harrison). The coming prosperity of the nation is described in ch.33, and the current chapter concludes by mentioning various places in the land (v.44) to emphasise that the entire country will enjoy the Lord's blessing in this way. Feinberg suggests that Benjamin is mentioned first because of the property of Jeremiah at Anathoth.

Having seen something of the blessings attendant on the future restoration of the nation earlier, Jeremiah awoke out of sleep a happy man (31.26). Now, having seen the solution to his problem (32.43-44), it is not beyond reason to suggest he was also a happy man when he went to sleep that night!

JEREMIAH 33

This chapter completes a section of the book, comprising chapters 30-33 which, as already noted, has been called by several commentators "The Book of Consolation". This title has been assigned to these chapters in view of the dark background painted by chapters 25-29 which deal principally with the period of Judah's captivity in Babylon. With the Babylonians outside Jerusalem (32.24), captivity was imminent. But this was not the end for Judah and Jerusalem. Chapters 30-33 describe the regathering and restoration of the Lord's people, and portray a bright picture of their future. As Feinberg observes, "The Lord gives Judah light in her darkest hours".

Since "the word of the Lord came unto Jeremiah the second time, while he was yet shut up in the court of the prison" (33.1), it seems likely that this new message was also imparted to Jeremiah "in the tenth year of Zedekiah king of Judah, which was the eighteenth year of Nebuchadrezzar" (32.1). Quite possibly, as previously suggested, chapters 30 and 31 also belong to this particular time. The four chapters are certainly bound together by a common theme.

After the introduction (vv.1-3), in which the limitations of Jeremiah (v.1) give place to the Lord's limitless ability to fulfil His word (vv.2-3), the chapter briefly refers to the approaching cessation of Judah's national life (vv.4-5), before extensively describing her future restoration and permanence (vv.6-26). With this in mind, the chapter may be divided as follows:

> The Guarantor of National Life (vv.2-3)
> The Cessation of National Life (vv.4-5)
> The Restoration of National Life (vv.6-14)
> The Righteousness of National Life (vv.15-16)
> The Continuity of National Life (vv.17-18)
> The Assurance of National Life (vv.19-26).

It can be reasonably assumed that if Jeremiah's sleep was "sweet" when the word of God was revealed to him earlier (31.26), then life for him became even sweeter after the Lord had given him yet another picture of Israel's future blessing, especially as he was in prison at the time. No doubt he would have agreed entirely with the sentiments of Paul: "I suffer trouble, as an evil doer, even unto bonds; but the word of God is not bound" (2 Tim 2.9).

Verses 2-3: The Guarantor of National Life

At the very beginning of the message, emphasis is placed on the Lord's ability to fulfil His promises. He had previously said, "Behold, I am the Lord, the God of all flesh: is there anything too hard for me?" (32.27). This is now reinforced: "Thus saith the Lord the maker thereof, the Lord that formed it, to establish it; the Lord is his name" (v.2). In view of the weighty promises to be given to the nation through Jeremiah, "the Lord underscores their veracity by affixing His eternal name to them. He Himself is surety for the programme He is unfolding" (Feinberg). While the expressions, "the maker *thereof...* that formed *it,* to establish *it*", are said by some to refer to creation (following the Septuagint), and by others to Jerusalem or David's throne, it seems more likely that they refer to the Lord's purpose to bless His people. This is supported by the close connection with the previous chapter which concludes with reference to the return from captivity: "Men shall buy fields for money, and subscribe evidences, and seal them...for I will cause their captivity to return, saith the Lord" (32.44).

As Harrison observes, "While God is always ready to answer the cry of the human heart, man must first request assistance". The Lord Jesus said, "Ask, and it shall be given you" (Mt 7.7). Bearing in mind Jeremiah's circumstances, which were enough to break the spirit of any man, it seems wholly appropriate that the Lord should say to him, "Call unto me, and I will answer thee, and shew thee great and mighty things, which thou knowest not" (v.3). With Jerusalem and the cities of Judah soon to be, if not already, "desolate without man and without beast" (vv.10,12), the Lord intended to lift the sagging spirit of His servant by revealing "great and mighty things" to him. These were "matters so far beyond human insight that they require divine revelation" (Feinberg). The future blessings eagerly anticipated by believers today are equally "far beyond human insight": "Eye hath not seen, nor ear heard, neither have entered into the heart of man, the things which God hath prepared for them that love him. But God hath revealed them unto us by his Spirit" (1 Cor 2.9-10).

Verses 4-5: The Cessation of National Life

The king and his people were fighting a lost cause; resistance would prove totally ineffective (cp.32.5). "For thus saith the Lord, the God of Israel, concerning the houses of this city, and concerning the houses of the kings of Judah, which are thrown down by the mounts, and by the sword ('because of the mounds and because of the sword', JND); They shall come to fight with the Chaldeans, but it is to fill them with the dead bodies of men" (vv.4-5). It is generally understood that the houses and royal palaces had been demolished, not by the enemy, but by the defenders "against the mounts and against the sword...in order to make room for defensive works against these attacks" (Streane). According to Ellicott's Commentary "the prophet sees, as it were, a *sortie* of the besieged ("they shall come to fight with the Chaldeans"), but it is doomed to failure". The verse is not easily understood, but Orelli is probably right in saying that the result of the foray against the Chaldeans was only to "fill them (the Chaldeans, or their swords) with corpses". Alternatively, it could be the siege mounds that are filled "with the dead bodies of men". The imminent defeat and death which stared the inhabitants of Jerusalem in the face were not due "to the fortunes of war", but to the anger of the Lord against their sin and wickedness. The onslaught of the Chaldeans expressed His wrath: "whom I have slain in mine anger and in my fury, and for all whose wickedness I have hid my face from this city" (v.5).

Verses 6-14: The Restoration of National Life

Against this sombre background, Jeremiah is given a vision of the promised "great and mighty things" (v.3) which the Lord would accomplish on behalf of His people. The change in atmosphere and outlook is dramatic: "Behold, I will bring it health and cure, and I will cure them, and will reveal unto them the abundance of peace and truth" (v.6). According to Feinberg, the word "health" (724) is literally "new flesh", something conspicuously absent in Jeremiah's lifetime: "Is there no balm in Gilead; is there no physician there? why then is not the health (724) of the daughter of my people recovered?" (8.22). But both city ("it") and people ("them") will be healed. "Peace and truth" will be applied, like a bandage (Ellicott's Commentary) to the wounds of the nation. The Lord will fulfil His promise, "I will restore health (724) unto thee, and I will heal thee of thy wounds" (30.17). The verses that follow describe this coming period, and the following features should be noted.

The unity of the kingdom (v.7)

"I will cause the captivity of Judah and the captivity of Israel to return, and will build them, as at the first." It has been pointed out that the restoration of Judah and Israel must refer to the end-time since the captivity of the Lord's people did not end after the seventy-year period in Babylon. Without denying the achievements of Zerubbabel, Ezra and Nehemiah, it remains that Judah was still under the heel of the Persian Empire. In the latter days, Judah and Israel will be restored as one kingdom, as they were before the division of the kingdom in the days of Rehoboam. At the end-time, the Lord "will be the God of all the families of Israel, and they shall be my people" (31.1). The unity and progress of the Lord's people at the end-time will be evidence of His blessing upon them, as it is evidence of His presence amongst His people today. When this is the case, the Lord's people will "follow after the things which make for peace, and things wherewith one may edify another" (Rom 14.19), and endeavour "to keep the unity of the Spirit in the bond of peace" (Eph 4.3).

The purity of the kingdom (v.8)

"I will cleanse them from all their iniquity, whereby they have sinned against me; and I will pardon all their iniquities, whereby they have sinned, and whereby they have transgressed against me." The allusion here to the new covenant is unmistakable: "I will forgive their iniquity, and I will remember their sin no more" (31.34); "In those days, and in that time, saith the Lord, the iniquity of Israel shall be sought for, and there shall be none; and the sins of Judah, and they shall not be found: for I will pardon them whom I reserve ('whom I leave remaining', JND)" (50.20). Very clearly, this comprehends both forensic and moral righteousness. Believers today have been forgiven "for Christ's sake" (Eph 4.32) and their "state" must correspond with their "standing". They are expected to heed the injunction, "keep thyself pure" (1 Tim 5.22), and to recognise the sanctity of the local assembly (1 Cor 3.17). It has been said that "if we lose purity, we lose everything".

The testimony of the kingdom (v.9)

"And it (Jerusalem) shall be to me a name of joy, a praise and an honour before all the nations of the earth, which shall hear all the good that I do unto them: and they shall fear and tremble for all the goodness and for all the prosperity that I procure unto it." According to Gesenius, the word "honour" (8597) is used in the sense of "ornament". Orelli puts it rather nicely in saying that the city will be "a living monument of His saving power and grace...The nations tremble, because this blessing of Zion convinces them of the utter superiority of Jehovah to their gods (cp. Deuteronomy 2.25)". The Lord will be honoured in the eyes of the nations as they witness the singular goodness of the Lord towards His people, just as "one that believeth not, or one unlearned" will observe godly order in the local assembly and "report that God is in you of a truth" (1 Cor 14.24,25).

The felicity of the kingdom (vv.10-11)

"Thus saith the Lord; Again there shall be heard in this place, which ye say shall be desolate without man and without beast, even in the cities of Judah, and in the streets of Jerusalem, that are desolate, without man, and without inhabitant, and without beast, The voice of joy, and the voice of gladness." After the coming desolation, much of which had already taken place, Judah and Jerusalem would ring with the joy of the Lord's people. Two aspects of this are specified.

Marital joy

"The voice of the bridegroom, and the voice of the bride" (v.11). This is the last of four similar references in the book (cp. 7.34; 16.9; 25.10). According to Feinberg, these words are "the closing part of the benediction in the Jewish marriage ceremony today". A member of the UK judiciary is reported as saying (in 2008) that "the breakdown of marriage and family life constitutes a greater threat to this country than global warming". For believers today, the "joy" and "gladness" of bridegroom and bride are maintained as husbands "dwell with them (their wives) according to knowledge, giving honour unto the wife, as unto the weaker vessel, and as being heirs together of the grace of life" (1 Pet 3.7). It should be said that the joy and strength of a believer's married life contributes immeasurably to the strength of the assembly.

Spiritual joy

"The voice of them that shall say, Praise the Lord of hosts: for the

Lord is good; for his mercy endureth for ever: and of them that shall bring the sacrifice of praise into the house of the Lord" (v.11). Joy and gladness will mark both the relationships of the Lord's people and their worship in His Temple. Streane points out that the clauses "Praise the Lord of hosts: for the Lord is good; for his mercy endureth for ever" were evidently "liturgical forms used in the Temple services". He adds, "this we gather from such passages as 2 Chronicles 5.13; 7.3,6; Ezra 3.11; Psalm 106.1". This confirms the earlier statement in the book that "they shall come…bringing sacrifices of praise, unto the house of the Lord" (17.26). The Temple will be rebuilt and its ministry restored. Divine certainty invests this: "For I will cause to return the captivity of the land, as at the first, saith the Lord" (v.11). Ellicott's Commentary puts it rather well: "The Courts of the Temple, now hushed in silence, should once again re-echo with the Hallelujahs of the Priests and Levites". Believers today offer "the sacrifice of praise" (Heb 13.15).

The tranquility of the kingdom (vv.12-14)

"Thus saith the Lord of hosts; Again in this place, which is desolate without man and without beast, and in all the cities thereof, shall be an habitation of shepherds causing their flocks to lie down" (v.12). The word "habitation" (5116) is elsewhere translated "sheepcote" (2 Sam 7.8; 1 Chr 17.7) or "fold" (Is 65.10; Ezek 34.14). The whole land will not only witness properly documented property transactions (32.44), it will also be given to the peaceful work of shepherd care: "In the cities of the mountains, in the cities of the vale, and in the cities of the south, and in the land of Benjamin, and in the places about Jerusalem, and in the cities of Judah, shall the flocks pass again under the hands of him that telleth (counteth) them, saith the Lord" (v.13). In short, nothing will interrupt the peaceful pursuit of animal husbandry. The land will not be subject to enemy invasion then, neither will there be conflict between Palestinians and Israelis. Since "He that scattered Israel will gather him, and keep him, as a shepherd doth his flock" (31.10), something greater than literal shepherding may be implied here. In the words of Harrison, "God's people will then feel the loving touch of the Master's hand".

It is noticeable that shepherd-work figures largely in the Scriptures. It is clothed with the highest possible associations. "The Lord God…shall feed his flock like a shepherd" (Is 40.10-11). Men who act as shepherds in local assemblies undertake work which is particularly precious to the Lord.

The statement, "Behold, the days come, saith the Lord, that I will perform that good thing which I have promised unto the house of Israel and to the house of Judah" (v.14) is pivotal. It both confirms what has already been said (vv.7-13) and gives assurance to what is to follow (vv.15-18). Abraham was "fully persuaded that, what he (God) had promised, he was able also to perform" (Rom 4.21). Sadly, many professing believers today do not appear to believe the clear promises of God here.

Verses 15-16: The Righteousness of National Life

"In those days, and at that time, will I cause the Branch of righteousness to grow up unto David; and he shall execute judgment and righteousness in the land. In those days shall Judah be saved, and Jerusalem shall dwell safely: and this is the name wherewith she shall be called, The Lord our righteousness." It should be noted that while these verses largely repeat the language of 23.5-6, they do so with a remarkable difference. "There the title 'the Lord our righteousness' is given to the future King…Here it is given to the city, and, so given, can only mean that the name will be, as it were, the motto and watchword of her being. She will be a city marked by a righteousness which will be the gift of Jehovah; He will inscribe that name on her banners, and grave it on her portals" (Ellicott's Commentary). Attention is drawn to a threefold righteousness.

The righteousness of the King

"In those days, and at that time, will I cause the Branch of righteousness to grow up unto David" (v.15). The reader is referred in this regard to comments made in connection with 23.5.

The righteousness of His rule

"He shall execute judgment and righteousness in the land" (v.15). The reader is referred again to comments made in connection with 23.5.

The righteousness of His people

"And this is the name wherewith she (Jerusalem) shall be called, The Lord our righteousness" (v.16). When the city was unrighteous there was no security; at the time of writing, the Babylonians were at the gates. But "In those days shall Judah be saved, and Jerusalem shall dwell safely". Righteousness and security are linked - so are unrighteousness and insecurity! Whereas in the parallel passage reference is made to Judah and Israel (23.6), Judah and Jerusalem are the subjects of the promise here, and this reflects the immediate circumstances of the prophecy. The "cities of Judah, and…the streets of Jerusalem" were "desolate" (v.10).

Verses 14-26 are not found in the Septuagint Version and some commentators therefore regard them with suspicion, one even suggesting that the translation "she shall be called" (v.16) is both ignorant and impious, and attempting, in desperation, to alter the text to make it agree with his alternative! Other scholars "are equally convinced that the passage is in the right place" and that it is "perfectly compatible with the revelation made in chapter 23 and with chapters 30-33…Most scholars agree that the name 'The Lord our righteousness' refers to Jerusalem. She can have the same name as the Messiah because she reflects that righteousness the Messiah bestows upon her (so Keil & Delitzsch)" (Feinberg).

Verses 17-18: The Continuity of National Life

The pivotal statement, "I will perform that good thing which I have promised unto the house of Israel and to the house of Judah" (v.14), is now applied to the royal and priestly succession. Two things are clearly stated here.

Continuity of rule

"For thus saith the Lord; David shall never want a man to sit upon the throne of the house of Israel" (v.17). In the words of Ellicott's Commentary, this statement is "hardly more than a repetition of promises like those of 2 Samuel 7.16; 1 Kings 2.4; Psalm 89.29,36, but it is here repeated under very different circumstances. Then it had been given when the line of David was in all the freshness of its strength. Now it is uttered when that line seemed on the very point of dying out. The hope of the prophet is, however, inextinguishable. He is certain that the true King will always be of the house of David". The passage does not claim an uninterrupted succession of Davidic rulers, but rather that David's dynasty will never cease. The Lord Jesus is "the root and the offspring of David" (Rev 22.16) and of Him it was said, "He shall be great, and shall be called the Son of the Highest: and the Lord God shall give unto him the throne of his father David…and of his kingdom there shall be no end" (Lk 1.32-33).

Continuity of worship

"Neither shall the priests the Levites want a man before me to offer burnt offerings, and to kindle meat offerings, and to do sacrifice continually" (v.18). As Feinberg observes, "Simply stated, the passage assures that just as the Davidic covenant (2 Sam 7) is guaranteed by God's promise, so is the Levitical priesthood". It was said of Phinehas, Aaron's grandson, "Behold, I give unto him my covenant of peace: And he shall have it, and his seed after him, even the covenant of an everlasting priesthood" (Num 25.12-13). As with the Davidic rulers, so with the Levitical priests; the passage does not claim their uninterrupted succession, but that Israel's priesthood will always be in their hands. This is confirmed by Isaiah 66.21-23; Ezekiel 43.19; 44.10,15. The entire passage deals with literal Jews and therefore to read the New Testament priesthood into this verse is a classic example of the maxim that "A text taken out of its context becomes a pretext for anything". It should also be said that the new covenant promise, "they shall all know me, from the least of them unto the greatest of them, saith the Lord" (31.34), does not mean that the priesthood would become redundant. In the millennial reign the Levitical priests will offer sacrifices on behalf of the Lord's believing and regenerate people.

Verses 19-26: The Assurance of National Life

What has been stated in 31.35-37 as the assurance of the new covenant is now used to guarantee the continuance of the monarchy and the priesthood. The covenants with David and with the Levites are placed on the same level of permanence as the ordered succession of day and night. As Feinberg observes, "The greater the promises, the stronger the assurances that they will be fulfilled": "Thus saith the Lord; If ye can break my covenant of the day, and my covenant of the night, and that there should not be day and night in their season; Then may also my covenant be broken with David my servant, that he should not have a son to reign upon his throne; and with the Levites the priests, my ministers" (vv.20-21). But there is more: an added promise is given of great increase in the descendents of David and the Levites. What was originally said of the entire nation (Gen 22.17) is now applied specifically to them: "As the host of heaven cannot be numbered, neither the sand of the sea measured: so will I multiply the seed of David my servant, and the Levites that minister unto me" (v.22).

This is reinforced in view of opinion amongst the Lord's people at the time: "Considerest thou not what this people have spoken, saying, The two families (referring to Israel and Judah) which the Lord hath chosen, he hath even cast them off? thus they have despised my people, that they should be no more a nation before them" (v.24). While some commentators regard this as the taunt of heathen nations, the words "this people" are never used of any besides Israel, and Ellicott's Commentary rightly asserts that the Lord's word through Jeremiah was given in response to national despair. The monarchy, represented by Zedekiah was about to fall, together with the Levitical priesthood. What price now the Lord's promises? The answer follows: "Thus saith the Lord; If my covenant be not with day and night, and if I have not appointed the ordinances of heaven and earth; Then will I cast away the seed of Jacob, and David my servant, so that I will not take any of his seed to be rulers over the seed of Abraham, Isaac, and Jacob" (vv.25-26). As Feinberg observes, "The threefold mention of the patriarchs points to the whole chain of promises repeatedly given them. Nature will utterly collapse before God will go back on the slightest promise to His people". The coming disaster for the Lord's people did not signal their end: "I will cause their captivity to return, and have mercy on them" (v.26), and then His promises will be fulfilled. They have not been fulfilled in the church as suggested by some commentators. Laetsch entitles vv.14-26 "The glory of the New Testament Church", and it is hoped that the reader will find this totally unacceptable.

In the New Testament, the Apostle Paul asks the question, "Hath God cast away his people?" (Rom 11.1). It is tempting to think that he may have had in mind Jeremiah 33 where people were saying, "The two families which the Lord hath chosen, he hath even cast them off?" (v.24). This may not be the case, but the answer in vv.25-26 could well be placed alongside Paul's own words (Rom 11.1), leading him to the conclusion, "God hath not cast away his people which he foreknew" (Rom 11.2).

JEREMIAH 34

Commentators generally point out that this chapter marks the resumption of biographical material in the book. The previous four chapters, which anticipate national restoration, end with the assurance of deliverance from all captivity, and the future permanence of the monarchy and of the priesthood (33.19-26). Now, "in glaring contrast to the future stands the present reality. Jerusalem is engaged in a death struggle with mighty Babylon, and the end is fast approaching. Already all the fortified cities have been taken, only Jerusalem, Lachish and Azekah remain unoccupied by the enemy" (Laetsch).

The precise place of the chapter in the chronology of events is not specifically given, but it is clear that although in its early stages, the final assault on Jerusalem had commenced: "The word which came unto Jeremiah from the Lord, when Nebuchadnezzar king of Babylon…fought against Jerusalem, and against all the cities thereof" (v.1); "Then Jeremiah the prophet spake all these words unto Zedekiah king of Judah in Jerusalem, When the king of Babylon's army fought against Jerusalem, and against all the cities of Judah that were left" (vv.6-7). By human reckoning, the invasion of Judah had been provoked by Zedekiah's rebellion against Babylon in 589 BC (2 Kings 24.20; 2 Chr 36.13), but it is equally true that the armies of Nebuchadnezzar were the instruments of divine judgment (cp. 2 Chr 36.14-16). Nebuchadnezzar's army was formidable: "all his army, and all the kingdoms of the earth of his dominion, and all the people" (v.1). This is amplified in 2 Kings 24.2.

However, attention has already been drawn to the fact that the Babylonian siege was not continuous and that it was lifted temporarily at the approach of the Egyptian army, at which time Jeremiah made it clear to Zedekiah that the withdrawal of the Chaldeans would make no difference to the outcome of the war (37.5-10). The concluding verses of the current chapter refer to the withdrawal of the Babylonian army, and to its return: "And Zedekiah king of Judah and his princes will I give…into the hand of the king of Babylon's army, which are *gone up from you*. Behold, I will command, saith the Lord, and cause them to *return* to this city; and they shall fight against it, and take it, and burn it with fire: and I will make the cities of Judah a desolation without an inhabitant" (vv.21-22). According to 37.11-21, the prophet was not imprisoned until after the Chaldean armies had made their temporary withdrawal from Jerusalem, and he was therefore able to respond to the divine command, "*Go* and speak to Zedekiah king of Judah" (v.2). The current chapter therefore predates Jeremiah's imprisonment, whereas chapters 32-33 and, in all probability chapters 30-31, belong to the time when the prophet was "shut up in the court of the prison, which was in the king of Judah's house" (32.2).

The reason for the inclusion of this chapter at this point in the book, out of chronological order, is not easily ascertained. It has been suggested, however, that it forms an addendum to chapters 30-33 in that it amplifies 32.3-5. Ellicott's Commentary is in agreement with this suggestion: "The prophecy that follows is probably a fuller statement of that in chapter 32.3-4, and delivered shortly before it, being referred to there as the cause of his imprisonment".

After the introduction (v.1), there are two major sections in the chapter:

> The Result of the Siege (vv.2-7)
> The Renewal of Servitude (vv.8-22).

The chapter commences with the Babylonians in the process of attacking Jerusalem (vv.1-7) and ends with their temporary withdrawal (vv.21-22).

Verses 2-7: The Result of the Siege

This section of the chapter may be subdivided as follows: the result for the city (v.2); and the result for the king (vv.3-7).

The result for the city (v.2)

"Thus saith the Lord, the God of Israel; Go and speak to Zedekiah king of Judah, and tell him, Thus saith the Lord; Behold, I will give this city into the hand of the king of Babylon, and he shall burn it with fire." "The Israelites who had burned cities with fire as part of the divine curse on the conquered land would now see their own holy city burned to the ground" (Habel).

It is tempting to think that at this point in time the Chaldeans had lifted the siege, and that the purpose of this message was to assure Zedekiah that contrary to appearances, the destruction of Jerusalem was nevertheless inevitable. However, this cannot be the case since the invaders were still actually fighting "against Jerusalem, and against all the cities thereof" (v.1). These verses are therefore a general statement that the city would be destroyed. In view of Jerusalem's destruction by fire, Jeremiah later urged Zedekiah to surrender to the Babylonians: "If thou wilt assuredly go forth unto the king of Babylon's princes, then thy soul shall live, and this city shall not be burned with fire" (38.17), but to no avail. In the process of time, this was completely fulfilled (see 2 Chr 36.19; Neh 1.3).

The result for the king (vv.3-7)

While Zedekiah would "cause this city to be burned with fire" (38.23), the king himself would survive the destruction of the city and the slaughter of its inhabitants (2 Chr 36.17-19). In this connection the following should be noted.

The deportation of the king (v.3)

"And thou shalt not escape out of his hand, but shalt surely be taken, and delivered into his hand; and thine eyes shall behold the eyes of the king of Babylon, and he shall speak with thee mouth to mouth, and thou shalt go to Babylon" (cp. 32.4-5). As already noted, Zedekiah did look into the eyes of Nebuchadnezzar, but that was almost the last thing he saw before his eyes were put out and he was taken in chains to Babylon (52.11). Ezekiel also predicts the deportation of Zedekiah: "My net also will I spread upon him, and he shall be taken in my snare: and I will bring him to Babylon to the land of the Chaldeans; yet shall he not see it, though he shall die there" (Ezek 12.13). As Feinberg observes, "The mention of a face-to-face confrontation with Nebuchadnezzar shows something of the fear he inspired. Zedekiah could not escape the consequences of his treason in breaking his covenant with Nebuchadnezzar".

The death of the king (vv.4-5)

Unlike Jehoiakim (cp. 22.18-19) who died unlamented, Zedekiah would die and be mourned in the traditional way: "Yet hear the word of the Lord, O Zedekiah king of Judah; Thus saith the Lord of thee, Thou shalt not die by the sword: But thou shalt die in peace: and with the burnings of thy fathers, the former kings which were before thee, so shall they burn odours for thee; and they will lament thee, saying, Ah Lord! for I have pronounced the word, saith the Lord" (vv.4-5). The expression "the burnings of thy fathers" (the 'royal funeral rites', Unger) does not refer to cremation, which was not practised by the Hebrews, but to the custom of burning spices at royal funerals (cp. 2 Chr 16.14; 21.19). Contrary to the opinion of some scholars, there is no reason to believe that this prophecy was not fulfilled, even though Zedekiah died in exile. Neither is there any hint that such honours were only conditional on his obedience to the word of God and that his failure in this respect meant their withdrawal.

Since Zedekiah was as wicked as his predecessors (2 Chr 36.11-14), it therefore has to be asked why this "profane wicked prince of Israel" (Ezek 21.25) was not summarily executed by Nebuchadnezzar, and therefore consigned to death in unrelieved disgrace. Contrary to expectations, some mercy is extended to him by the Lord. Possibly, the reason lies in vv.8-9. For whatever reason, Zedekiah had "made a covenant with all the people which were at Jerusalem, to proclaim liberty unto them". For a brief period, Zedekiah had at least obeyed part of God's word: "And ye were now turned, and had done right in my sight, in proclaiming liberty every man to his neighbour" (v.15). Although the course of divine judgment on Jerusalem could not be averted, there was some recognition for the man who, though far from acceptable with the Lord, was nonetheless willing to obey part of His word. There were certainly occasions when Zedekiah, knowing what was right, failed to act out of fear of his princes, and it is noteworthy that whilst it was Zedekiah who proclaimed liberty for the bondservants (v.8), it was the princes and people who re-imposed servitude upon them (v.11). This did not exonerate Zedekiah. It was his responsibility to implement the law of the land.

The declaration to the king (vv.6-7)

While, according to Solomon, "The fear of man bringeth a snare" (Prov 29.25), Jeremiah faithfully communicated his unpalatable message to Zedekiah: "Then Jeremiah the prophet spake all these words unto Zedekiah king of Judah in Jerusalem, When the king of Babylon's army fought against Jerusalem, and against all the cities of Judah that were left, against Lachish, and against Azekah: for these defenced cities remained of the cities of Judah". Lachish and Azekah lay approximately thirty-five and fifteen miles respectively south-west of Jerusalem. According to Feinberg, "Since their fall was necessary to the capture of Jerusalem, they marked the southern limit of Nebuchadnezzar's invasion". Streane thinks differently: "Both these were in the low country of Judah near the borders of Egypt. Nebuchadnezzar would not venture to advance on his career of conquest into Egypt, leaving such important fortresses untaken".

Verses 8-22: The Renewal of Servitude

This section of the chapter commences with the words, "This is the word that came unto Jeremiah from the Lord, after that the king Zedekiah had made a covenant with all the people which were at Jerusalem, to proclaim liberty unto them; That every man should let his manservant, and every man is maidservant...go free" (vv.8-9). The wording could suggest a completely new oracle, but there does appear to be a connection with vv.1-7. In the first place, as suggested above, the proclamation of liberty for the bondservants could possibly have been the reason for the extending of some mercy to Zedekiah, and in the second place (not necessarily in opposition to the first suggestion) the proclamation could have been an attempt by the king, amongst other things, to mollify the Lord's wrath.

Attention is drawn to servitude removed (vv.8-10); and servitude re-imposed (vv.11-22).

Servitude removed (vv.8-10)

The proclamation required liberty for all bondservants: "That every man should let his manservant, and every man his maidservant, being an Hebrew or an Hebrewess, go free; That none should serve himself of them, to wit, of a Jew his brother" (v.9). The law concerning bondservice (cp. Ex 21.1-11; Lev 25.39-55; Deut 15.12-18) had evidently fallen into disuse. The covenant, which was solemnly ratified in the Temple (vv.18-20), went further than the letter of the law in that it provided for the liberation of all bondservants, irrespective of their length of service. According to the law, a Hebrew bondservant, having served for six years, was to be released in the seventh year (Ex 21.2; Deut 15.12) and a Hebrew hired servant was to be set free "in the year of jubilee" (Lev 25.40,54). According to Campbell Morgan, the first category related to house-servants, whereas the second related to those who laboured in the fields.

Commentators are generally suspicious of Zedekiah's motives. Unger opines that Zedekiah's proclamation was "certainly as a matter of expediency, and not as a show of deep piety". According to Feinberg, "Expositors differ about the reasons for the covenant (vv.8,18). It may have been made because under the continuing threat of invasion, the poor – unable to freely work outside the city – were faced with starvation or slavery. Now that the invasion appeared imminent, the liberation of slaves would mean a lessening of the burden on the owners. Perhaps the covenant was an attempt at reform, and was made in the hope that it would lead to the Lord's blessing. More probably the covenant was made with the thought that the liberated slaves would join in defending the city".

Initial response to the proclamation was positive: "Now when all the princes, and all the people, which had entered into the covenant, heard that every one should let his manservant, and every one his maidservant, go free, that none should serve themselves of them any more, then they obeyed, and let them go" (v.10). But the newly-imparted liberty did not last long.

Servitude re-imposed (vv.11-22)

Liberation from bond-service was short-lived: "But afterward they turned, and caused the servants and the handmaids, whom they had let go free, to return, and brought them into subjection for servants and for handmaids" (v.11). The change of mind on the part of the princes and people (v.10) is not categorically explained, but it is generally held by commentators to be the result of the cessation of hostilities by the Chaldeans, and their withdrawal from Jerusalem. The Chaldeans were no longer outside the walls of Jerusalem (v.21), although they would return to complete their task (v.22), and it can be justifiably inferred that, since the danger seemed to have passed, the princes and people quickly reversed their agreement to Zedekiah's proclamation and re-imposed servitude on their hapless bondservants. The remaining verses of the chapter express the Lord's commendation of the release of the bondservants (vv.12-15) and His condemnation of their re-enslavement (vv.16-22).

Commendation (vv.12-15)

These verses are self-explanatory: "Thus saith the Lord, the God of Israel; I made a covenant with your fathers in the day that I brought them forth out of the land of Egypt, out of the house of bondmen, saying, At the end of seven years let ye go every man his brother an Hebrew, which hath been sold unto thee ('who hath sold himself unto thee', JND); and when he hath served thee six years, thou shalt let him go free from thee" (vv.13-14). It is not without significance that reference is made to the deliverance from "the land of Egypt...the house of bondmen". Above all people, Israel should have had compassion on slaves!

As already noted, the "covenant" in question is found in Exodus 21.1-11 and Deuteronomy 15.12-18. It was not a separate covenant, but part of the covenant which Israel accepted at Sinai: "Now therefore, if ye will obey my voice indeed, and keep my covenant, then shall ye be a peculiar treasure unto me", to which the people responded by saying, "All that the Lord hath spoken we will do" (Ex 19.5,8). But this aspect of the covenant, like every other clause, had not been carried out, making it necessary for the Lord to say, "but your fathers hearkened not unto me, neither inclined their ear" (v.14). This was nothing less than a complete disregard for the welfare of bondservants, and attracted divine condemnation. The nation had become devoid of care for the under-privileged classes, something that the Lord's people today, under different conditions, must not repeat: for "whoso hath this world's good, and seeth his brother have need, and shutteth up his bowels of compassion from him, how dwelleth the love of God in him?" (1 Jn 3.17). In contrast to earlier generations (v.14), and for possible reasons already discussed, the decision had been made to release the manservants and maidservants: "And ye were now turned, and had done right in my sight, in proclaiming liberty every man to his neighbour; and ye had made a covenant before me in the house which is called by my name" (v.15). As Feinberg points out, "Their covenant was not only a civil and economic act, but a religious one as well". The covenant was made in the Temple, and it was this that made their subsequent actions so serious.

Condemnation (vv.16-22)

"But ye turned and polluted ('profaned', JND) my name, and caused every man his servant, and every man his handmaid, whom ye had set at liberty at their pleasure, to return, and brought them into subjection, to be unto you for servants and for handmaids" (v.16). Campbell Morgan points out that the Lord's name stands here for His care for bondservants as expressed in His provision for their liberty at the end of six years. The princes and people had "polluted" or "profaned" (2490) His name by their disobedience. In re-imposing bondage upon their servants they had cast dishonour on the Lord's name. This is a salutary warning for God's people today: His name is dishonoured when His Word is disobeyed.

With what Feinberg calls a "pungent play" on the Hebrew word rendered "liberty" (1865), the Lord ironically declares that the people responsible would be granted freedom. They would be freed from His protecting hand: "Ye have not hearkened unto me, in proclaiming liberty, every one to his brother, and every man to his neighbour: behold, I proclaim a liberty for you, saith the Lord, to the sword, to the pestilence, and to the famine; and I will make you to be removed into all the kingdoms of the earth" (v.17).

The severity of coming judgment is attributed to the enormity of their guilt in transgressing the covenant they had made in the Lord's presence: in the Lord's words, they had "transgressed my covenant" and had "not performed the words of the covenant which they had made before me" (v.18). It is a most solemn thing to invoke the Lord's name when making agreements and promises. The way in which the covenant was made is described as follows: "the covenant which they had made before me, when they cut the calf in twain, and passed between the parts thereof, The princes of Judah, and the princes of Jerusalem, the eunuchs, and the priests, and all the people of the land, which passed between the parts of the calf" (vv.18-19). In the words of Ellicott's Commentary, "The passage is interesting, as showing the survival of one of the oldest rites of Patriarchal times (Gen 15.8-21). So, when Jehovah made a covenant with Abraham, the victims that had been slain were cut up and arranged opposite each other, and when the 'burning lamp' passed between the pieces it was the token the Jehovah had completed the covenant, even as men complete it". This evidently formed the pattern for important and binding contracts in later years. The parties entering into the agreement would walk between the pieces of the animals rehearsing the terms of the covenant by which they were binding themselves. Having done that they would then invoke the penalty for breach of the contract, namely, that whoever broke the covenant would be treated in the same way as the animals had been, that is, put to death. This is borne out by the current passage: "And I will give the men that have transgressed my covenant...I will even give them into the hand of their enemies, and into the hand of them that seek their life: and their dead bodies shall be for meat unto the fowls of the heaven, and to the beasts of the earth" (vv.18,20). It must be said that there was no failure, and that there could be no failure, in executing the covenant made with Abraham.

As already noted, the chapter concludes as it begins: Zedekiah and the people are assured that there would be no escape for them, and no protection for the city, when the Babylonians resumed their attack on Jerusalem. The Babylonians did return and destroy the city (39.1-8). "The scripture cannot be broken" (Jn 10.35).

JEREMIAH 35

This chapter, together with chapter 36, forms what Streane calls "a remarkable break in the narrative of chapters 32-44". The events in these two chapters certainly precede chapters 32-34 chronologically and in all probability chapters 30-31 as well. The reader will recall that in view of their unity of theme, chapters 30-33 are generally assumed to belong to the same period and have been called, for good reason, "The Book of Consolation". If, like chapter 36, the current chapter belongs to "the fourth year of Jehoiakim" (36.1), then it predates chapters 32-34 by an estimated seventeen years. It is quite possible, however, that it belongs towards the end of Jehoiakim's reign when, having rebelled against the king of Babylon, "the Lord sent against him bands of the Chaldees, and bands of the Syrians, and bands of the Moabites, and bands of the children of Ammon, and sent them against Judah to destroy it" (2 Kings 24.2). It may well have been this invasion that forced the Rechabites to seek safety in Jerusalem (Jer 35.11).

The reason for the inclusion of these two chapters at this point in the book is not easily explained. Campbell Morgan suggests that "It may be that they are inserted here because Jeremiah made use of them in messages delivered in those last days of the reign of Zedekiah, prior to the fall of the city". If Jeremiah did not actually use them in this way, it may well be that they occur here to emphasise the reasons for the coming sack of Jerusalem and captivity of the people. In the first place, the Lord's people had been guilty of rank disobedience (35.12-17), and in the second, the roll containing the word of God had been deliberately and contemptuously destroyed by the king in the presence of his indifferent court officials (36.22-24). Jensen makes the point that "The account in chapter 35 serves to expose the glaring sin of disobedience described in the previous chapter" and adds, "The chapter is placed here apparently because of its illustration of obedience, the antithesis of the disobedience exemplified in chapter 34".

The chapter may be divided as follows:

> The Identity of the Rechabites (vv.1-2a)
> The Test of the Rechabites (vv.2b-5)
> The Obedience of the Rechabites (vv.6-11)
> The Lesson from the Rechabites (vv.12-17)
> The Reward of the Rechabites (vv.18-19).

Verses 1-2a: The Identity of the Rechabites

"The word which came unto Jeremiah from the Lord in the days of Jehoiakim the son of Josiah king of Judah, saying, Go unto the house of the Rechabites, and speak unto them." In the words of The Pulpit Commentary, "It is refreshing to meet these quiet, simple people after wearying ourselves with the sickening sights of the vice and hypocrisy of the court and city life in Jerusalem".

The Rechabites were the descendants of Rechab the father of Jehonadab (2 Kings 10.15). They were a wandering tribe of Kenite descent (cp. 1 Chr 2.55) who had joined the Israelites on the exodus from Egypt and had settled in the south of Judah (Judg 1.16; 4.17; 5.24; 1 Sam 15.6; 27.10). Jehonadab accompanied Jehu (841-814 BC) in his slaughter of "all that remained unto Ahab in Samaria" and in his elimination of "Baal out of Israel" (2 Kings 10.17,23,28). The association between the two men began with Jehu's question: "Is thine heart right, as my heart is with thy heart?", or "Is your heart true to my heart as mine is to yours" (RSV) to which Jehonadab replied, "It is" (2 Kings 10.15).

It is not specifically stated that it was the religious and moral life of the nation at the time that made Jehonadab (or Jonadab, as he is called in Jeremiah 35) command his family to follow a nomadic life (vv.6-7), but it would be difficult to disagree with the view of Meyer: "He was dismayed at the abounding corruption and iniquity of the time, and especially of the northern kingdom, then under the fatal spell of Jezebel's and Ahab's influence…In his endeavour to save his people from such a fate, this noble man, who afterwards became Jehu's confederate in extirpating idolatry, bound his people under a solemn pledge to drink no wine for ever; neither to build houses, nor sow seed, nor plant vineyards, but to dwell in tents". Solomon observed that "A prudent man foreseeth the evil, and hideth himself: but the simple pass on, and are punished" (Prov 22.3). Jonadab was well aware of the evils of his day, and was determined that his descendents should not become ensnared by the corruption in society. He saw danger, and made provision accordingly. In the New Testament, Paul did the same: "But evil men and seducers shall wax worse and worse, deceiving, and being deceived. But continue thou in the things which thou hast learned and hast been assured of, knowing of whom thou hast learned them" (2 Tim 3.13-14).

Verses 2b-5: The Test of the Rechabites

Having been told by Jonadab, "Ye shall drink no wine, neither ye, nor your sons for ever: Neither shall ye build house, nor sow seed, nor plant vineyard, nor have any: but all your days ye shall dwell in tents; that ye may live many days in the land where ye be strangers" (vv.6-7), the obedience of the Rechabites was put to the test. Jeremiah was instructed to "bring them into the house of the Lord, into one of the chambers, and give them wine to drink" (v.2). It could be argued that the Rechabites had every reason to relax their strong self-discipline.

They were taken "into the house of the Lord"

"Then I took Jaazaniah the son of Jeremiah, the son of Habaziniah, and his brethren, and all his sons, and the whole house of the Rechabites; And

I brought them into the house of the Lord" (vv.3-4). It should be pointed out that the Rechabites were brought into the house of the Lord in order to publicise the important message that was to follow (vv.12-17). In his inimitable way, Meyer makes it clear that the "tribe" (as he calls them) must have "excited much curiosity by reason of its strange and antique manners". When Jeremiah shepherded them into the Temple, all eyes must have been fixed on them.

The Rechabites could not have been in a better environment. What was more, there was wine there; in fact, wine in abundance: "pots full of wine" (v.5). Surely the commandment of their father, Jonadab, did not apply in a place like this! The very fact that they were in "the house of the Lord", with all its sacred associations, must override Jonadab's original commandment and make it right for them to drink the proffered wine.

They were taken into the chamber of "a man of God"
"And I brought them…into the chamber of the sons of Hanan, the son of Igdaliah, a man of God, which was by the chamber of the princes, which was above the chamber of Maaseiah the son of Shallum, the keeper of the door" (v.4). As "a man of God", Hanan (the words "son of Igdaliah" appear to be a parenthesis) followed in the footsteps of Moses (Deut 33.1; Josh 14.6); Shemaiah, in Rehoboam's reign (1 Kings 12.22); Elijah (1 Kings 17.18); and Elisha (2 Kings 4.7). (Moses, Shemaiah and Elisha are all called "the man of God"). "Accordingly, he was a man so reverenced that no one could call in question what was transacted under his supervision" (Unger). If the location was not a sufficiently strong reason to take wine, then surely the association with "a man of God" must clinch the argument. Jonadab's commandment could not possibly override the moral authority of such a man.

They were commanded by a prophet
No less a prophet than Jeremiah! "And I set before the sons of the house of the Rechabites pots full of wine, and cups, and I said unto them, Drink ye wine" (v.5). (It should be noted at Jeremiah did not say, "Thus saith the Lord, Drink ye wine"). The man who addressed them was a prophet of many years standing and of proven faithfulness to the Lord. This surely, was the ultimate argument. There was not a man in the entire realm who spoke with greater authority than Jeremiah. Jonadab's commandment must be superseded. There could be no contest between Jonadab and Jeremiah! It would be called today "an open and closed case".

These compelling arguments were all brought to the same touchstone: "our father commanded us" (v.6). For the Rechabites, the only court of appeal was the word of Jonadab. The believer today must make the Word of God the test of all matters of doctrine and practice. An assembly with a name for spiritual excellence, and preachers with a reputation for sound ministry, should not be the criteria by which believers today test belief and behaviour. Rather, "To the law and to the testimony: if they speak not according to this word, it is because there is no light in them" (Is 8.20). The Jews at Berea "searched the scriptures daily, whether those things were so" (Acts 17.11).

Verses 6-11: The Obedience of the Rechabites

The sacred location and the presence of godly men did not diminish the resolve of the Rechabites. They had obeyed the commands of Jonadab for some three hundred years, and had no intention of changing their minds: "We will drink no wine: for Jonadab the son of Rechab our father commanded us, saying, Ye shall drink no wine, neither ye, nor your sons for ever…Thus have we obeyed the voice of Jonadab the son of Rechab our father in all that he hath charged us, to drink no wine all our days, we, our wives, our sons, nor our daughters" (vv.6,8). More than that, the restrictions placed upon them by Jonadab dictated their entire life-style (v.7). The Rechabites had complied with these instructions in every respect (vv.8-10), but with the invasion of Judah by Nebuchadnezzar they were forced to seek refuge in Jerusalem (v.11). But while this change in their circumstances meant that they could no longer live in tents in the open country, it did not mean that they were compelled to drink wine.

The reply of the Rechabites, "Jonadab the son of Rechab our father commanded us…Thus have we obeyed the voice of Jonadab the son of Rechab our father" (vv.6,8), is clear and distinct. The Lord's people today are to be "obedient children" (1 Pet 1.14). Samuel reminded Saul that "to obey is better than sacrifice, and to hearken than the fat of rams" (1 Sam 15.22), and Paul gave thanks that the believers at Rome had "obeyed from the heart that form of doctrine which was delivered you" (Rom 6.17).

It should be carefully noted that the purpose of offering wine to the Rechabites was not to tempt them deliberately. "It was done in order to give them the opportunity to refuse, and thus prepare the way for the message…that men are more loyal to the commandments of men than they are to the commandments of God" (Campbell Morgan). It must be said that if the Rechabites would not deviate from the commandments of their ancestor, then the Lord's people today should not deviate from "the faith which was once delivered unto the saints" (Jude v.3). Having succumbed to false teaching, the churches in Galatia were strongly admonished by the Apostle Paul: "I marvel that ye are so soon removed from him that called you into the grace of Christ unto another gospel…But though we, or an angel from heaven, preach any other gospel unto you than that which we have preached unto you, let him be accursed. As we said before, so say I now again, If any man preach any other gospel unto you than that ye have received, let him be accursed" (Gal 1.6,8-9).

While the purpose of the passage is not to commend or censure the actual commands of Jonadab, it is certainly worth drawing attention to the salient features of his instructions.

Abstinence from wine

"Ye shall drink no wine, neither ye, nor your sons for ever" (v.6). Meyer calls this, "Abstinence from the spirit of the age", and points out that wine was "closely associated with the luxury, corruption, and abominable revelries of the time (Is 28.1-8)". He continues by saying, "Their abstinence was not only a protest against the evils which were honeycombing their age, but a sure safeguard against participation in them". It has been said that "the best way to keep out of harm, is to keep out of harm's way".

The determination of the Rechabites is noteworthy: "We will drink no wine" (v.6). They were of the same spirit as Daniel who "purposed in his heart that he would not defile himself with the portion of the king's meat, nor with the wine which he drank" (Dan 1.8). Commentators point out the resemblance in this respect with the life-style of the Nazarites (Num 6.1-4), although it must be said that the Nazarite vow was taken for entirely different reasons.

Pursuit of a nomadic life

In their avoidance of a settled life (v.7) they resembled the patriarchs, who "confessed that they were strangers and pilgrims on the earth" (Heb 11.13), and therefore held the world with a very light touch. In the New Testament, Peter addresses his readers as "strangers and pilgrims" (1 Pet 2.11). Meyer addresses what he calls "ties that hold us to the earth" and continues, "We may discover what they are by considering what we cling to; what we find it hard to let go, even into the hands of Christ; what we are always striving to augment; what we pride ourselves in. It may be name, fame, notoriety, pride of fashion, rank, money. But whatever it is, if it hinders us from living on the highest level, if it is a weight that impedes our speed heavenward, it should be laid deliberately on God's altar, that He may do with it as He will, and that we may be able, without let or hindrance, to be wholly for God".

Verses 12-17: The Lesson from the Rechabites

The purpose of the episode is now made clear. This has already been noted: the Rechabites had been obedient to the command of Jonadab, but Judah and Jerusalem had failed to obey the Lord: "Then came the word of the Lord unto Jeremiah, saying, Thus saith the Lord of hosts, the God of Israel; Go and tell the men of Judah and the inhabitants of Jerusalem, Will ye not receive instruction to hearken to my words? saith the Lord" (vv.12-13). Some telling contrasts follow.

Authority is contrasted

The Rechabites obeyed an earthly leader, but Judah had disobeyed the Lord. "The words of Jonadab the son of Rechab, that he commanded his sons not to drink wine, are performed; for unto this day they drink none, but obey their father's commandment: notwithstanding I have spoken unto you, rising early and speaking; but ye hearkened not unto me" (v.14). The Rechabites had fulfilled the commandment of Jonadab, "a fallible leader" (Feinberg), but "the Lord of hosts, the God of Israel" (v.13) had been disregarded by His people. Through Isaiah, the Lord uses an even greater contrast to make the same point: "Hear, O heavens, and give ear, O earth: for the Lord hath spoken…The ox knoweth his owner, and the ass his master's crib: but Israel doth not know, my people doth not consider" (Is 1.2-3).

Frequency is contrasted

The Rechabites had been given commandments once, but God's people had received His word repeatedly. "I have sent also unto you all my servants the prophets, rising up early and sending them, saying, Return ye now every man from his evil way, and amend your doings, and go not after other gods to serve them, and ye shall dwell in the land which I have given unto you and to your fathers: but ye have not inclined your ear, nor hearkened unto me" (v.15). The Lord had spoken earnestly and untiringly to His people, but to no avail.

Response is contrasted

The Rechabites had obeyed the commands of Jonadab for about three hundred years, but the Lord's people had constantly disobeyed: "the sons of Jonadab the son of Rechab have performed the commandment of their father, which he commanded them; but this people (not 'my people') hath not hearkened unto me" (v.16).

Disobedience comes with a price. "Therefore thus saith the Lord God of hosts, the God of Israel; Behold, I will bring upon Judah and upon all the inhabitants of Jerusalem all the evil that I have pronounced against them: because I have spoken unto them, but they have not heard; and I have called unto them, but they have not answered" (v.17). There would be no escape from God's determined judgment upon them. Judah and Jerusalem had been immensely privileged. The Lord had constantly spoken to them. But privilege determines responsibility, and therefore they would be subject to sweeping judgment.

Verses 18-19: The Reward of the Rechabites

If Judah would reap judgment for her disobedience (v.17), then the Rechabites would reap blessing for their obedience. "And Jeremiah said unto the house of the Rechabites, Thus saith the Lord of hosts, the God of Israel; Because ye have obeyed the commandment of Jonadab your father, and kept all his precepts, and done according unto all that he hath commanded you: Therefore thus saith the Lord of hosts, the God of Israel; Jonadab the son of Rechab shall not want a man to stand before me for ever". While the words "stand before me", with their priestly associations (Deut 18.7; 1 Kings 8.11) have led some scholars to the conclusion that the promise points to the incorporation, in some way, of the Rechabites into the tribe of Levi, it has to be said that the expression, or its equivalent, is used in a wider sense in the Old Testament (cp. Gen 19.27; 1 Kings 17.1; Jer 15.1). In general the words point to the privilege of service, and the promise to the Rechabites may therefore be regarded in that way.

Ironside has a nice piece here: "The family of this devoted man has long since been lost to history, both sacred and profane…doubtless, in the Millennium, when all the prophecies regarding Israel and Judah are fulfilled, the house of Rechab will once more appear upon the scene, a testimony to the faithfulness of Him who is 'not a man, that he should lie; neither the son of man, that he should repent: hath he said, and shall he not do it? or hath he spoken, and shall he not make it good?' (Num 23.19). In that day the Rechabites shall drink of the pure joys that flow through the scene of Immanuel's presence; nor will it appear as a hardship that they were denied the fruit of the vine while the curse rested upon the earth for man's sake".

JEREMIAH 36

Attention has already been drawn to the fact that chapters 35 and 36, which record incidents that took place during the reign of Jehoiakim, are preceded and succeeded by chapters dealing with events that took place in the reign of Zedekiah. It has been suggested that the interruption in the chronological order of the book at this point could be accounted for, either by Jeremiah's use of these incidents in messages delivered during the reign of Zedekiah, prior to the fall of Jerusalem, or if he did not use them in this way, to emphasise the reasons for the coming sack of Jerusalem and captivity of the people. In the first place, unlike the Rechabites who had obeyed "their father's commandment", the Lord's people had completely disregarded His word (35.14), and in the second, the written word of God had been both rejected and destroyed by the king (36.22-24).

The current chapter may be divided as follows:

> Writing God's Word (vv.1-4)
> Reading God's Word (vv.5-21)
> Burning God's Word (vv.22-26)
> Re-writing God's Word (vv.27-32).

Verses 1-4: Writing God's Word
The date of this oracle is significant: "And it came to pass in the fourth year of Jehoiakim the son of Josiah king of Judah, that this word came unto Jeremiah from the Lord" (v.1). The "fourth year of Jehoiakim" was the "first year of Nebuchadrezzar king of Babyon" (25.1), and the reader is referred to comments made in introducing chapter 25. Bearing in mind the enormity of Jehoiakim's guilt in cutting the roll containing the word of God "with the penknife" and casting it "into the fire that was on the hearth, until all the roll was consumed in the fire that was on the hearth" (v.23), it can be said that the "the times of the Gentiles" (Lk 21.24) began with the final rejection of God's word by His people. It is interesting to notice, in an entirely different connection, that having listened to Paul as he "expounded and testified the kingdom of God, persuading them concerning Jesus, both out of the law of Moses, and out of the prophets, from morning till evening", the Jews at Rome "departed, after that Paul had spoken one word, Well spake the Holy Ghost by Esaias the prophet unto out fathers, Saying, Go unto this people, and say, Hearing ye shall hear, and shall not understand; and seeing ye shall see, and not perceive….Be it known therefore unto you, that the salvation of God is sent unto the Gentiles, and that they will hear it" (Acts 28.23-28). In both cases, the Jews rejected the word of God, whereupon God turned, in two different ways, to the Gentiles. The rejection of God's word always incurs solemn consequences.

Attention is drawn to the purpose for which the book was written (vv.2-3); and the process by which the book was written (v.4).

The purpose for which the book was written (vv.2-3)

"Take thee a roll of a book, and write therein all the words that I have spoken unto thee against Israel, and against Judah, and against all the nations, from the day I spake unto thee, from the days of Josiah, even unto this day" (v.2). Streane points out that the word "roll" (4039) refers to parchment, as opposed to "a tablet of wood or metal, with a thin coating of wax" upon which Isaiah was commanded to write: "Take thee a great roll (1549)" (Is 8.1). Streane continues: "Several skins were stitched together and attached to a roller of wood at one or both ends. The writing was arranged in columns parallel to the rollers, so that as the parchment was gradually unrolled from one end to the other, the successive columns could be read. Our word *volume* (that which is *rolled up*) points by its derivation to this older form of book". It should be added that the "roll" could have been made from papyrus. While reference is made later to "three or four leaves" (v.23), which suggests a parchment or papyrus book rather than a roll, it should be remembered that the word "leaves" (1817) literally means "doors", and refers to the columns of a book, so called from their resemblance to a door (Gesenius).

Since this was evidently the first time that Jeremiah's messages, given over a period of some twenty years, had been written down, "a prodigious feat of memory would have been required" (Feinberg). Commentators refer to "transcribing parts of records" and to the "aid of notes" made by Jeremiah, but there can be no doubt that the Holy Spirit, of whom the Lord Jesus said, "he shall teach you all things, and bring all things to your remembrance, whatsoever I have said unto you" (Jn 14.26), undertook a similar ministry here. According to the New Testament, "the prophecy came not in old time by the will of man: but holy men of God spake as they were moved by the Holy Ghost" (2 Pet 1.21). Baruch "wrote from the mouth of Jeremiah (v.4), but Jeremiah spoke "from the mouth of the Lord" (2 Chr 36.12).

The purpose of this exercise is clearly stated: "It may be that the house of Judah will hear all the evil which I purpose to do unto them; that they may return every man from his evil way; that I may forgive their iniquity and their sin" (v.3). By restating his preaching in this way it was to be hoped that the written messages would be more effective than the public preaching. As Feinberg rightly observes, "The purpose of all Jeremiah's prophecies was to spur the nation to repentance", and it could be said here that "The Lord is not slack concerning his promise, as some men count slackness; but is longsuffering…not willing that any should perish, but that all should come to repentance" (2 Pet 3.9).

The process by which the book was written (v.4)

Baruch, previously mentioned in connection with the property transaction (32.12-16), acted as scribe, and "wrote from the mouth of Jeremiah all the words of the Lord, which he had spoken unto him, upon a roll of a book". In the New Testament, the Apostle Paul also dictated to a scribe (Rom 16.22; 2 Thess 3.17). As the prophet spoke, Baruch painstakingly penned the word of the Lord letter by letter. This was no "general impression" or interpretation that Jeremiah had "deduced" from what the Lord had spoken. These were "the words of the Lord, which he had spoken unto him". When asked by the princes, "Tell us now, How didst thou write all these words at his mouth?", Baruch replied, "He pronounced all these words unto me with his mouth, and I wrote them with ink in the book" (vv.17-18). It is important to remember that inspiration extends to the very words of Scripture, but it extends even further than that for the Lord Jesus said, "For verily I say unto you, Till heaven and earth pass, one jot or one tittle shall in no wise pass from the law, till all be fulfilled" (Mt 5.18). The "jot" is the smallest letter of the Hebrew alphabet (*yod*), and the "tittle" is the little projection which distinguishes some Hebrew letters. So inspiration extends to the very letters which make up the words of the Bible! No wonder Ezra was a "scribe of the *words* of the commandments of the Lord" (Ezra 7.11)!

The passage does not reveal how long it took Jeremiah and Baruch to complete their enormous task, but some idea of the period may be gained from the fact that the word of the Lord came to Jeremiah in the fourth year of Jehoiakim's reign (v.1), according to Streane, probably early in that year, and that the book was first read publicly in the ninth month of his fifth year.

Verses 5-21: Reading God's Word

Since Jeremiah and Baruch were in a position to hide themselves (v.19), the prophet was not imprisoned at the time (his imprisonment took place during the reign of Zedekiah), but his movements were evidently restricted. Feinberg suggests that the authorities had probably forbidden him to speak in the Temple because of his unpopular Temple address (cp. 26.1-24), but it is quite possible that he was aware of the danger to his life arising from his recent preaching. "And Jeremiah commanded Baruch, saying, I am shut up; I cannot go into the house of the Lord: Therefore go thou, and read in the roll, which thou hast written from my mouth, the words of the Lord in the ears of the people in the Lord's house upon the fasting day: and also thou shalt read them in the ears of all Judah that come out of their cities" (vv.5-6). The public reading of Scripture is most important. The following is worthy of careful consideration: "Let us read the Scriptures in public with such reverence, conviction, and clarity, that the listeners may understand that this is the Word of God! The keen young preacher may be tempted to hurry through his Scripture reading, eager to get on with his comments about the portion read, as if they were really more important than the Word of God. This is patently a misjudgment of the power of

God's Word alone to speak to human hearts" (Gordon S. Bissett, *Precious Seed*, August, 2005).

The Word of God was read on three occasions: on "the fasting day" (vv.6-10); to "the princes" (vv.11-19); and to "the king" (vv.20-21).

Its reading on "the fasting day" (vv.6-10)

Baruch was told by Jeremiah to read "the words of the Lord in the ears of the people in the Lord's house upon the fasting day…And Baruch the son of Neriah did according to all that Jeremiah the prophet commanded him, reading in the book the words of the Lord in the Lord's house" (vv.6,8) and "this concise statement that Baruch discharged the commands laid on him, is followed by the detailed account of the same in the subsequent verses" (Streane). As already noted (v.3), the word of God was to be read publicly in the hope that it would secure the people's repentance: "It may be they will present their supplication before the Lord, and will return every one from his evil way: for great is the anger and the fury that the Lord hath pronounced against this people" (v.7).

The purpose of the fast is not disclosed. Since it was held "in the fifth year of Jehoiakim…in the ninth month" (v.9), it was certainly not the divinely-commanded fast connected with the day of atonement (Lev 16.29; 23.27), which took place in the "seventh month". It could have been called to commemorate the capture of Jerusalem by the Chaldeans one year previously, which was in "the third year of the reign of Jehoiakim king of Judah" (Dan 1.1) by Babylonian reckoning, but his fourth year by Judaean reckoning. The "ninth month" approximates to December, which accounts for the fire burning in the king's winter-house (v.22). The "fasting day" provided the opportunity for the maximum number of people to hear the word of the Lord: the "words of the Lord" were to be read "in the ears of all Judah that come out of their cities" (v.6), and this is precisely what happened (v.8). The details follow: "Then read Baruch in the book the words of Jeremiah in the house of the Lord, in the chamber of Gemariah the son of Shaphan the scribe, in the higher court, at the entry of the new gate of the Lord's house, in the ears of all the people" (v.10). Gemariah was the son of Shaphan, Josiah's secretary of state (2 Kings 22.3,8,12). He was among Jeremiah's small circle of supporters (cp. v.25). His brother, Ahikam, had previously saved Jeremiah's life (26.24). "Evidently Baruch stationed himself at the door to Gemariah's room so that what he read could be heard by the assembled people" (Feinberg).

It is worth noting that the word of God was brought to the attention of men and women where they were gathered. In this case, it was the Temple precincts, but in Paul's day it was, amongst other places, "in the market" (Acts 17.17). According to F. F. Bruce, the "Agora (the market)" was "the centre of Athenian life and activity". Paul took every opportunity to preach the gospel. On Saturdays he was indoors ("in the synagogue"), and during the rest of the week he was in the open air! He did not ask people to "come to church". He took the gospel message to people on their own ground. The Lord Jesus said, "*Go* ye therefore (not, 'sit and wait for people to come'), and teach all nations" (Mt 28.19).

Its reading to "the princes" (vv.11-19)

Amongst those listening to the reading of the word of God was "Michaiah the son of Gemariah, the son of Shaphan", who "went down into the king's house, into the scribe's chamber: and, lo, all the princes sat there...Then Michaiah declared unto them all the words that he had heard, when Baruch read the book in the ears of the people" (vv.11-13). While the word "princes" (8269) can carry the idea of royal descent, here it has a wider significance. According to Gesenius, it includes leaders, nobles and courtiers, and in this case it indicates court officials. "Michaiah doubtless felt that what Baruch had read affected the public interest (v.11); so he told the officials about it (vv.12-13)" (Feinberg). Of these, Jehudi was sent to Baruch with the message, "Take in thine hand the roll wherein thou hast read in the ears of the people, and come" (v.14). It has been suggested that because his great-grandfather was Cushi, Jehudi was a naturalised Jew of Ethiopian descent. Cush and Ethiopia translate the same word (3568). However, it has been pointed out that the prophet Zephaniah was "the son of Cushi" who was "the son of Gedaliah, the son of Amariah, the son of Hizkiah (Hezekiah)" (Zeph 1.1), so that there appears to be no need to assume Jehudi's naturalisation. It is said that Jehudi must have been of some importance in his day, otherwise his ancestry would not have been traced to the third generation.

Having courteously requested Baruch to sit and read from the roll, indicating that they were favourably disposed towards him and Jeremiah, and listened with evident attention, the princes were "afraid both one and other, and said unto Baruch, We will surely tell the king of all these words" (vv.15-16). There can be little doubt that the court officials believed the word of God that he had read to them, otherwise they would not have looked at one another in fear. Moreover, since "the scroll contained such bold announcements at a time of crisis and struggle for the nation's existence" (Feinberg), they felt that the king should hear the message. "They had no hostile purpose in communicating what they had heard to the king, but the matter had come to their official knowledge, and they had no alternative but to report it" (Ellicott's Commentary). The princes anticipated that Jehoiakim would react in two ways.

i) He would wish to know how the scroll had come to be written (vv.17-18). The princes "desired to know how far the words might be Baruch's own, that they might be able to state to the king the amount of responsibility for them which rested upon each" (Streane). With this in mind, Baruch was asked for an explanation: "Tell us now, How didst thou write all these words at his mouth?" (v.17), to which he replied, "He pronounced all these words unto me with his mouth, and I wrote them with ink in the book" (v.18). The word "pronounced" (7121) is usually translated "call" and indicates that Jeremiah "spoke loudly and distinctly while dictating, the only time this term is used in this sense of dictation" (Laetsch). The fact that Baruch specifically states that Jeremiah "pronounced *all* these words unto me with his mouth", indicates that he had added nothing. All Baruch did was to write the words of Jeremiah, with no additions of his own, on the scroll. The ink would have been made by "mixing soot or lampblack with a liquid" (Feinberg).

ii) He would demand the life of Baruch and Jeremiah (v.19). Not only was Jehoiakim no lover of truth, but the princes doubtless remembered that he had been responsible for the death of Urijah who had prophesied against Jerusalem and Judah "according to all the words of Jeremiah", and had been extradited from Egypt so that he could be executed (26.20-23). The princes' concern for the safety of the Lord's servants was therefore a wise precaution: "Go, hide thee, thou and Jeremiah; and let no man know where ye be" (v.19). As events proved, they were not mistaken (cp. v.26).

Its reading to "the king" (vv.20-21)

Having deposited the roll in "the chamber of Elishama the scribe" for safekeeping, the princes "told all the words in the ears of the king" (v.20). It is not unlikely that they surmised how Jehoiakim would respond to the solemn messages of the scroll, and attempted to keep it out of his reach, but to no avail: "the king sent Jehudi to fetch the roll: and he took it out of Elishama the scribe's chamber. And Jehudi read it in the ears of the king, and in the ears of all the princes which stood beside the king" (v.21). His reaction was openly hostile.

Verses 22-26: Burning God's Word

The scene is the palace "winterhouse", which was evidently a special apartment in a sheltered part of the building, probably its southern wing. "As glass windows were unknown, a charcoal fire, placed after the Eastern fashion in a brazier, or earthen pot, in the middle of the room, was a necessity. So we find a fire in the court of the high priest's palace in the raw early morning of a Passover in March or April (Jn 18.18)" (Ellicott's Commentary). According to Streane, "hearths are unknown in the East", hence the rendering, "Now the king was sitting in the winter-house in the ninth month, and with the fire-pan burning before him" (v.22, JND).

Having heard Jehudi read "three or four leaves" (or "columns", as explained in connection with v.2), the king cut the roll with a penknife and consigned it piece by piece to the fire burning in the winterhouse. He "cast it into the fire that was on the hearth ('in the pan', JND), until all the roll was consumed in the fire that was on the hearth ('in the pan', JND)" (v.23). Jehoiakim thus became responsible for "the first recorded instance of the unhallowed mutilation and rejection of the written Word of God - now so common" (Ironside). The "penknife" (8593) was "a writer's penknife, with which he sharpened his reed" (Gesenius). The destruction of God's written word in this way was undertaken without any grief on the part of the king and his courtiers: "Yet they were not afraid, nor rent their garments, neither the king, nor any of his servants that heard all these words" (v.24). Three men, Elnathan, Delaiah and Gemariah, "made intercession to the king that he would not burn the roll: but he would not hear them" (v.25). It is at least heartening to observe that Elnathan (cp. v.12) had changed his stance (cp. 26.22).

Feinberg calls Jehoiakim's action in this way, "an appalling act of blasphemy and contempt for God's revelation in His written word". When wicked Ahab heard the solemn message of Elijah, "he rent his clothes, and put sackcloth upon his flesh, and fasted, and lay in sackcloth, and went softly" (1 Kings 21.27). Jehoiakim's father, Josiah, "rent his clothes" on hearing "the words of the book of the law" (2 Kings 22.11), but Jehoiakim rent the book itself. Streane quotes from the Speaker's Commentary in saying, "And thus passed away 'his last chance, his last offer of mercy: and as he threw the torn fragments of the roll on the fire he threw there in symbol his royal house, his doomed city, the Temple, and all the people of the land'". Jehoiakim compounded his grievous sin by ordering the arrest of Baruch and Jeremiah, but "the Lord hid them" (v.26), presumably through the good offices of friends. The promise made to Jeremiah years previously held good: "I have made thee this day a defenced city, and an iron pillar, and brasen walls against the whole land, against the kings of Judah, against the princes thereof...And they shall fight against thee; but they shall not prevail against thee; for I am with thee, saith the Lord, to deliver thee" (1.18-19).

While this was the first time a portion of the Scriptures was deliberately destroyed, it was certainly not the last. "The Bible bonfires of infidels and even church authorities have lighted the centuries of the Christian era...Voltaire thought to destroy it from the face of the earth and in so doing bring to an end the sect of Christians, and England's skies once burned red from incendiary piles fed by the leaves of God's Book. In this way, people despised God's offer of mercy, rebelled at the accusation of sin, and committed sacrilege against the volume in which is found the way of forgiveness and life everlasting" (Goddard). But the Lord who protected his messengers (v.26), was equally capable of preserving His message.

Verses 27-32: Re-writing God's Word

Another roll is commissioned by the Lord: "Then the word of the Lord came to Jeremiah, after that the king had burned the roll, and the words which Baruch wrote at the mouth of Jeremiah, saying, Take thee again another roll, and write in it all the former words that were in the first roll, which Jehoiakim the king of Judah hath burned" (vv.27-28). God's word was not to be lost, but rewritten.

The hostility of Jehoiakim towards the word of God and the servants of

God was evidently kindled by the references to the return of the king of Babylon. Nebuchadnezzar had already invaded Judah, and Jehoiakim had submitted to him for three years, but "then he turned and rebelled against him" (2 Kings 24.1). His rebellion brought Nebuchadnezzar to Judah for the second time, and the word of God through Jeremiah had made it plain that Judah and Jerusalem would not survive: "And thou shalt say to Jehoiakim king of Judah, Thus saith the Lord; Thou hast burned this roll, saying, Why hast thou written therein, saying, The king of Babylon shall certainly come and destroy this land, and shall cause to cease from thence man and beast?" (v.29). This was finally fulfilled in the reign of Zedekiah, but in the meantime not only would Jehoiakim's rebellion fail, but he would suffer the ignominy of having no son to succeed him on the throne of Judah, and the disgrace of death without burial: "He shall have none to sit upon the throne of David: and his dead body shall be cast out in the day to the heat, and in the night to the frost" (v.30). This double disgrace had already been predicted (22.18-19,30). The king died before the arrival of Nebuchadnezzar, and "it has been conjectured that Jehoiakim died either in a palace uprising or in an uprising of the people (v.31; cp. 22.18-19)" (Feinberg). The man who had endeavoured to dispose of God's word was disposed of himself. While his son Jehoiachin did succeed him, his reign lasted for only three months and ten days (2 Chr 36.9). Feinberg points out that this does not contradict the prediction that Jehoiakim would have no son to succeed him on the throne of Judah since Jehoiachin's reign was "not a valid one but only a token one because he was immediately besieged by Nebuchadnezzar, surrendered in three months, and then went into exile, where he died after many years". No other descendant of Jehoiakim ever ascended the throne: Zedekiah was Jehoiakim's brother.

The destruction of the roll did not in any sense annul its contents: "And I will punish him and his seed and his servants for their iniquity; and I will bring upon them, and upon the inhabitants of Jerusalem, and upon the men of Judah, all the evil that I have pronounced against them; but they hearkened not" (v.31). But more than that, in accordance with the Lord's word (v.27), the written word was replaced with additions: "Then took Jeremiah another roll, and gave it to Baruch the scribe, the son of Neriah; who wrote therein from the mouth of Jeremiah all the words of the book which Jehoiakim king of Judah had burned in the fire: and there were added besides unto them many like words" (v.32). The laborious work of Jeremiah and Baruch began again, and was duly completed. The Lord who communicates His word in the first place will also ensure its preservation. While Feinberg states that "it is certain that our present text of the book of Jeremiah is longer than the original portion that had brief abstracts of Jeremiah's earlier prophecies" and that "the additions doubtless included the doom of the godless king", it must be said that the original roll was contain "all the words" which the Lord had spoken against Israel, Judah, and all the nations (v.2), and that Baruch duly "wrote from the mouth of

Jeremiah all the words of the Lord, which he had spoken unto him, upon a roll of a book" (v.4).

"The Bible may be burned; the witnesses of God's Word may be killed or exiled; in spite of the opposition and enmity of puny mortals, the Word of God liveth and abideth for ever!" (Laetsch).

JEREMIAH 37

Chapters 37-44 are in chronological order and form a continuous narrative. They describe events in the reign of Zedekiah, culminating with the fall of Jerusalem (39.2), together with subsequent events which brought the Jews remaining in Judah (40.5-6) and Jews who returned to Judah from neighbouring countries (40.11-12) into Egypt (43.5-7). The contingent included Jeremiah and Baruch (43.6).

While the current chapter commences with reference to the accession of Zedekiah (v.1), a great deal has already been said about his reign, and it might be helpful at this juncture to briefly review relevant chapters in the book.

Having referred to Zedekiah in the introduction to the book (1.3), Jeremiah next mentions him in 21.1,3,7 and 24.8. The reader will recall that in introducing chapter 21 it was pointed out that chapters 21-24 are a unit, locked together by references to Zedekiah (21.1; 24.8), but embracing all four kings who succeeded Josiah. It was also suggested that details of Zedekiah's request to Jeremiah (21.1-2), together with the infamous conduct of all four kings, are included at that point in the book as an explanation of the disastrous events which were to overtake Judah and Jerusalem. Chapters 21-24 can therefore be regarded as a general introduction to the section of the book dealing with the capture of Jerusalem and the subsequent exile.

Chapters 25-26 deal with events in during the reign of Jehoiakim, but chapters 27-29 revert to the reign of Zedekiah (27.3,12; 28.1; 29.3), evidently in the interests of continuing the theme of Babylonian supremacy which locks together chapters 25-29. (The reader is referred to comments made in connection with 27.1, which mentions the name of Jehoiakim). While chapters 32-34 clearly state the Jeremiah received the word of the Lord during the reign of Zedekiah (32.1; 33.1, "the second time, while he was yet shut up in the court of the prison" 34.4), the fact that these chapters extend the theme of chapters 30 and 31 suggest that they too belong to the same reign. While chapters 35 and 36 revert to the reign of Jehoiakim, it has been pointed out that either Jeremiah used these incidents in messages delivered during the reign of Zedekiah, prior to the fall of Jerusalem, or, if he did not use them in this way, they occur at this point in the book to emphasise the reasons for the coming sack of Jerusalem and captivity of the people.

It is admitted that the chronology of chapters 21-36 is not easily understood, but the above explanation is offered for consideration. The "impious assumption that the various parts of this book have been thrown together haphazardly by some later editor" (Ironside) must be steadfastly rejected. However, chapters 37-44 do not pose the chronological problems of earlier chapters.

Chapter 37 falls into two major sections:

> The Consultation with Jeremiah (vv.1-10)
> The Confinement of Jeremiah (vv.11-21).

The chapter commences with Jeremiah at liberty, and concludes with Jeremiah in prison, but it has to be said that "the word of God is not bound" (2 Tim 2.9). Whilst the prophet was at liberty, he proclaimed the word of the Lord: "Then came the word of the Lord unto the prophet Jeremiah" (v.6), and when he was in prison he did exactly the same: when asked by the king, "Is there any word from the Lord?", he replied, "There is: for, said he, thou shalt be delivered into the hand of the king of Babylon" (v.17).

It should noted that having heard of the approach of the Egyptian army, the Chaldeans lifted the siege of Jerusalem (v.5), which prompted Zedekiah to send Jehucal and Zephaniah to Jeremiah (v.3) in an attempt to ascertain the course of future events, only to be told by the prophet that there would be no escape from the king of Babylon (vv.7-8).

Verses 1-10: The Consultation with Jeremiah

The following should be noted in connection with these verses: the reign of Zedekiah (vv.1-2); the request for prayer (vv.3-4); the relief by the Egyptians (v.5); and the return of the Chaldeans (vv.6-10).

The reign of Zedekiah (vv.1-2)

"And king Zedekiah the son of Josiah reigned instead of Coniah the son of Jehoiakim, whom Nebuchadrezzar king of Babylon made king in the land of Judah" (v.1). The accession of Zedekiah in the place of "Coniah (otherwise known as Jehoiachin) the son of Jehoiakim" fulfilled the prophecy that "Jehoiakim king of Judah…shall have none to sit upon the throne of David" (36.30). Coniah was deported to Babylon after three months on the throne (2 Kings 24.8). Zedekiah, who succeeded him, was Jehoiakim's brother and thus Coniah's uncle. He was appointed by Nebuchadnezzar who "made him swear by God" (2 Chr 36.13), meaning that he solemnly pledged his loyalty to the Chaldean king. Further details are given by Ezekiel: "Behold, the king of Babylon is come to Jerusalem, and hath taken the king thereof (Coniah), and the princes thereof, and led them with him to Babylon; And hath taken of the king's seed, and made a covenant with him (Zedekiah), and hath taken an oath of him: he hath also taken the mighty of the land: That the kingdom might be base, that it might not lift itself up, but that by keeping of his covenant it might stand. But he rebelled against him in sending his ambassadors into Egypt, that they might give him horses and much people" (Ezek 17.12-15). It was Zedekiah's rebellion against Nebuchadnezzar (2 Chr 36.13), in favour of this alliance with Egypt, that brought about the final siege of Jerusalem.

Leaving aside his broken pledge to Nebuchadnezzar, Zedekiah's reign was one of unmitigated disaster: "But neither he, nor his servants, nor the people of the land, did hearken unto the words of the Lord, which he spake by the prophet Jeremiah" (v.2). Zedekiah consulted Jeremiah on at least four occasions (21.1-2; 37.3,17; 38.14), but failed to "hearken unto the words of the Lord". The NIV renders this: "Neither he nor his attendants nor the people of the land *paid any attention* to the words the Lord had spoken through Jeremiah the prophet". This is not the only commentary on his reign: "And he did that which was evil in the sight of the Lord his God, and humbled not himself before Jeremiah the prophet speaking from the mouth of the Lord...Moreover all the chief of the priests, and the people, transgressed very much after all the abominations of the heathen; and polluted the house of the Lord which he had hallowed in Jerusalem" (2 Chr 36.12,14). Zedekiah was not as aggressively wicked as Jehoiakim, his brother, had been, but he was "a weak, vacillating character, hesitating to do what he knew to be right, stubbornly proceeding on his self-chosen paths of compromising" (Laetsch).

The request for prayer (vv.3-4)

"And Zedekiah the king sent Jehucal the son of Shelemiah and Zephaniah the son of Maaseiah the priest to the prophet Jeremiah, saying, Pray now unto the Lord our God for us" (v.3). This was prior to Jeremiah's imprisonment (v.4). It has already been noted that the approach of the Egyptian forces had brought about the withdrawal of the Babylonian army (v.5), and there can be no doubt that Zedekiah, with all his weakness and vacillation, had at least some regard for the Lord's servant. It is noticeable, however, that there is no evidence or expression of repentance. The expression, "the Lord *our* God", was nothing short of hypocrisy in view of the description of his reign and the nation's rejection of the Word of God through Jeremiah (v.2). Jehucal, or Jucal, was no friend of Jeremiah: he was one of the "princes" who demanded the death penalty for God's servant (38.1,4). Bearing in mind that Jeremiah had been forbidden to pray for the nation (7.16; 11.14; 14.11), he responds to the request by announcing the failure of Pharaoh's expedition, and the capture and burning of Jerusalem (vv.6-10).

The relief by the Egyptians (v.5)

"Then Pharaoh's army was come forth out of Egypt: and when the Chaldeans that besieged Jerusalem heard tidings of them, they departed from Jerusalem." As already noted, this explains the reason for the deputation from Zedekiah: his request, "Pray now unto the Lord our God for us" (v.3), was tantamount to asking the Lord "to make the temporary withdrawal of the Babylonians permanent" (Feinberg). It has already been noted that the Egyptian army was advancing on Jerusalem following Zedekiah's appeal for help (Ezek 17.15).

Zedekiah had also sought the help of Jeremiah at the onset of the Chaldean invasion: "Inquire, I pray thee, of the Lord for us; for Nebuchadrezzar king of Babylon maketh war against us; if so be that the Lord will deal with us according to all his wondrous works, that he may go up from us" (21.2). The withdrawal of the Chaldeans in the current chapter, to which reference has already been made in the book (34.21), must have seemed initially to be nothing less than a divine answer to Zedekiah's request. He was soon disabused of that idea (vv.6-10; cp. 34.22)

According to Feinberg, the Pharaoh whose "army was come forth out of Egypt" was Pharaoh-hophra, "the fourth ruler of the Twenty-Sixth Dynasty, ruling from 589-570 BC". He evidently decided to avoid an encounter with the Babylonian forces so that Zedekiah's appeal to him for help availed him nothing. As Jeremiah predicted, Pharaoh-Hophra's army went back to Egypt, whereupon the Chaldeans returned (vv.7-8). Pharaoh-Hophra was later completely defeated by Nebuchadrezzar (44.30; 46.25-26), apparently having already suffered a partial defeat (Ezek 30.21).

The return of the Chaldeans (vv.6-10)

Although circumstances and appearances pointed to the contrary, Jeremiah stood by the word of God. He had already told Zedekiah that the king of Babylon would burn Jerusalem (34.2), and this is now confirmed: "Then came the word of the Lord unto the prophet Jeremiah, saying, Thus saith the Lord, the God of Israel; Thus shall ye say to the king of Judah, that sent you unto me to inquire of me; Behold, Pharaoh's army, which is come forth to help you, shall return to Egypt into their own land. And the Chaldeans shall come again, and fight against this city, and take it, and burn it with fire" (vv.6-8). The king might have been deceived by the lifting of the siege, but not Jeremiah: "Thus saith the Lord; Deceive not yourselves, saying, The Chaldeans shall surely depart from us: for they shall not depart. For though ye had smitten the whole army of the Chaldeans that fight against you, and there remained but wounded men among them, yet should they rise up every man in his tent, and burn this city with fire" (vv.9-10). Feinberg points out that the "hyperbole underscores the hopeless condition of Jerusalem before the Babylonians", and notes that the word "wounded" (1856) is "literally 'thrust through', 'pierced', 'transfixed', thus mortally wounded men". Very clearly, there was no escape for Jerusalem.

Verses 11-21: The Confinement of Jeremiah

This section of the chapter deals with Jeremiah's imprisonment after he was charged with treason by Irijah (v.13), and attention is drawn to the following: his attempt to leave Jerusalem (vv.11-12); his arrest by Irijah (vv.13-16); his answer to Zedekiah (v.17); and his appeal for release (vv.18-21).

His attempt to leave Jerusalem (vv.11-12)

The withdrawal of the Chaldean army gave Jeremiah opportunity to leave the city for his native Benjamin: "And it came to pass, that when the army of the Chaldeans was broken up from Jerusalem for fear of Pharaoh's army, Then Jeremiah went forth out of Jerusalem to go into the land of Benjamin, to separate himself thence in the midst of the people". In the prophet's own words, he was certainly not defecting to the Chaldeans (v.14), and while it could be argued that he was either making his escape before Jerusalem fell (cp. 6.1), or going to inspect his newly-acquired piece of real estate in Anathoth, he was in fact settling his affairs in Benjamin while the opportunity to do so existed. Since his property acquisition in Anathoth (32.7-12) did not take place until he was "shut up in the court of the prison" (32.2), this could not possibly have been in his mind in any case.

The words, "to separate himself thence in the midst of the people" (v.12), or "to have his portion there among the people" (JND), indicate that Jeremiah wished to settle his property affairs in Anathoth. According to Feinberg, the verb translated "to separate" (2505) means "to divide", as of property. Gesenius has, "to receive thence his portion or inheritance", although an additional note suggests that this is not altogether certain. Nevertheless, the majority of English translations favour the suggested explanation and according to Feinberg, "The Vulgate, Targum, and Syriac so understand it as well".

His arrest by Irijah (vv.13-16)

Jeremiah's attempt to leave the city via "the gate of Benjamin" on the north side of the city (cp. 38.7; Zech 14.10), was thwarted by Irijah the son of Shelemiah, "a captain of the ward", or "a Lord of the watch" (Streane), who apprehended him with the charge, "Thou fallest away to the Chaldeans" (v.13). Despite the prophet's denial, "It is false; I fall not away to the Chaldeans" (v.14), he was arraigned before the angry princes who "smote him, and put him in prison in the house of Jonathan the scribe: for they had made that the prison" (vv.14-15). These were not the princes who were favourably disposed to Jeremiah during the reign of Jehoiakim (26.16; 36.12-20) since they were probably in exile by this time (Ezek 17.12). Laetsch suggests that the charge was "as false as it was foolish. If Jeremiah had intended to desert to the Babylonians, he could not have chosen a more inopportune time. The Babylonians were gone!" However, in the eyes of the "princes" the "incident provided a 'legal' excuse to get rid of a prophet whose preaching had weakened the defence of the city (cp. 38.4)" (Habel).

It might be helpful to note the various phases of Jeremiah's confinement. During the reign of Jehoiakim, he was "shut up", saying "I cannot go into the house of the Lord" (36.5). He was not imprisoned at the time (this took place during the reign of Zedekiah), but his movements were evidently restricted. Following his attempt to leave Jerusalem in the current chapter, during the reign of Zedekiah, he was apprehended and committed to prison "in the house of Jonathan the scribe" (v.15). Laetsch rightly observes that "Unbelief, constantly demanding toleration and charity, is unbelievably intolerant and cruel against opposition".

Jeremiah's imprisonment involved his incarceration in a subterranean room adjoining the "the dungeon", meaning, literally, "house of the pit" or "'cistern" (v.16, JND margin). The underground cells are called "cabins" (2588) meaning "vaulted cells". Gesenius quotes another authority who "understands the word to mean *curved posts* or *crooked bars*, in which the captive sat in a distorted position". Harrison is probably right in saying that Jeremiah was placed in "solitary confinement" in "insanitary" conditions. Following his plea to Zedekiah in the king's house (vv.17-18), Jeremiah was not returned to "the dungeon" but allowed remain in the court of the prison (v.21). It was there that he received instructions from the Lord in connection with the purchase of property in Anathoth (32.2,8) and shown "great and mighty things" concerning the future of the nation (33.1-3). While Jeremiah was "in the court of the prison", his enemies secured the permission of Zedekiah to "cast him into the dungeon of Malchiah" from whence he was rescued by Ebed-Melech (38.4-6, 7-13). Having been extricated from the dungeon, Jeremiah remained "in the court of the prison until the day that Jerusalem was taken: and he was there when Jerusalem was taken" (38.28).

Returning to the current chapter, it is recorded that Jeremiah having "entered into the dungeon, and into the cabins" and "remained there many days" (v.16), "Zedekiah the king sent, and took him out" (v.17).

His answer to Zedekiah (v.17)

Having released Jeremiah from his subterranean confinement, Zedekiah "asked him secretly in his house, and said, Is there any word from the Lord?". As Feinberg observes, "the nature of this meeting shows Jeremiah's unpopularity as well as Zedekiah's weakness in confronting his officials face to face. By this time he realised that Jeremiah was a true prophet of God. Evidently he was hoping that Jeremiah would give him a more encouraging word about the Babylonian menace". Jeremiah certainly did have a "word from the Lord". It was short and sharp: "thou shalt be delivered into the hand of the king of Babylon". Jeremiah was unswervingly faithful in declaring the word of the Lord, and Feinberg draws attention to "the contrast between the frightened king in his palace and the resolute prophet in his prison". Jeremiah was no "fair-weather" prophet. While we know him to have had a very tender heart, he did not flinch from pronouncing divine judgment. Zedekiah was faced by a man who was nothing less than an "iron pillar, and brasen walls" (1.18).

His appeal for release (vv.18-21)

Though it is not specifically stated, it seems certain that by this time the Chaldeans had resumed the siege of Jerusalem.

Jeremiah now focuses on the injustice of his imprisonment. He had been incarcerated for telling the truth, whereas, ironically, the false prophets who had been guilty of gross deception, remained at liberty! "Moreover Jeremiah said unto king Zedekiah, What have I offended against thee, or against thy servants, or against this people, that ye have put me in prison? Where are now your prophets which prophesied unto you, saying, The king of Babylon shall not come against you, nor against this land?" (vv.18-19). The servant of God had been falsely accused of attempting to desert the nation (v.13), but the men who had actually betrayed the nation with their lies were the real traitors. "Unbelief is unreasonable in its hate of the prophets of truth! And just as foolish in following their own prophets of peace and prosperity" (Laetsch).

Servants of God are not devoid of human feelings, and the prophet's unjust confinement in his subterranean cell took its toll: "Therefore hear now, I pray thee, O my lord the king: let my supplication, I pray thee, be accepted before thee; that thou cause me not to return to the house of Jonathan the scribe, lest I die there" (v.20). The deep pathos in Jeremiah's voice here is clearly discernible. He does not explode with rage and remonstrate with Zedekiah, but appeals to him on what today would be called "humanitarian grounds". A similar note of deep feeling can be discerned in the voice of Paul in prison at Rome: "The cloke that I left at Troas with Carpus, when thou comest, bring with thee, and the books, but especially the parchments" (2 Tim 4.13). It has been said that "The prophets, like the apostles, were not self-appointed martyrs. They made use of the means at hand to save their life, their safety and convenience" (Laetsch). Jeremiah's petition "shows the cruelty with which the prophet had been treated. Half-starved, and thrust into a foul and foetid dungeon, he felt that to return to it would be death" (Ellicott's Commentary).

Unlike his officials, who would gladly have left Jeremiah to perish in his cell, Zedekiah, who should have authorised the prophet's liberty on the ground of his complete innocence, at least made some provision for him: "Then Zedekiah the king commanded that they should commit Jeremiah into the court of the prison, and that they should give him daily a piece of bread out of the bakers' street, until all the bread in the city were spent" (v.21). Out of fear of his officials Zedekiah failed to free Jeremiah, and his deferment to them became increasingly obvious as the siege continued (38.5). Feinberg observes that "This verse is the only place in Scripture where the name of a street in Jerusalem appears", adding that "It was the Near Eastern custom to name streets after those who worked in them". The "street of the bakers" (NIV) was probably connected with "the tower of the furnaces (or 'ovens', Gesenius)" (Neh 3.11; 12.38). As the siege drew to a close, the predicted famine became a reality.

JEREMIAH 38

This chapter could be entitled, "The story of two men in the mire". The first man was Jeremiah who "sunk in the mire" (v.6) literally, and the second was Zedekiah who was in danger of sinking "in the mire" (v.22) metaphorically. In the first case, help was available, and "they drew up Jeremiah with cords" (v.13); in the second, no help would be available, for the women of his own household would say, "Thy friends...are turned away back" (v.22).

It has already been noted that Jeremiah's ministry was accompanied by intensifying pressure upon him. This began with opposition from his home town (11.21), and from his own family (12.6). He then described himself as a "man of strife and a man of contention to the whole earth!...every one of them doth curse me" (15.10). Later, he experienced physical ill-treatment at the hands of Pashur, who consigned him to the stocks (20.2). His meticulously-written book was destroyed, column by column, by Jehoiakim (36.23), and in the reign of Zedekiah he was committed to a foetid subterranean cell by the princes (37.15-16). Now, in the current chapter, he reaches his lowest ebb in being lowered into the muddy cistern of Malchiah, which was located in the court of the prison (v.6), and there can be no doubt that his enemies hoped that he would die there. It has to be said that even this did not mark the end of the opposition to Jeremiah. The people who were allowed to remain in the land after the fall of Jerusalem, rejected his counsel against fleeing to Egypt (43.1-7), and continued to oppose him in Egypt (44.15-19). His experiences in this way illustrate the New Testament statement that "all that will live godly in Christ Jesus shall suffer persecution" (2 Tim 3.12).

This chapter may be divided as follows:

> The Anger of the Princes (vv.1-6)
> The Aid of Ebed-melech (vv.7-13)
> The Alternatives before Zedekiah (vv.14-23)
> The Advice to Jeremiah (vv.24-28).

Verses 1-6: The Anger of the Princes
These verses draw attention to the warnings of Jeremiah (vv.1-3); the demand of the princes (v.4); the weakness of the king (v.5); and the danger to Jeremiah (v.6).

The warnings of Jeremiah (vv.1-3)
Though in the court of the prison (37.21), which Harrison calls "the palace stockade", Jeremiah was by no means silent, and his preaching enraged Shephatiah, Gedaliah, Jucal and Pashur (v.1) who charged him with undermining the will of the people to resist the besieging Chaldeans

(v.4). The princes listened with dismay to his preaching: "Thus saith the Lord, He that remaineth in this city shall die by the sword, by the famine, and by the pestilence: but he that goeth forth to the Chaldeans shall live; for he shall have his life for a prey, and shall live…This city shall surely be given into the hand of the king of Babylon's army, which shall take it" (vv.2-3).

It is noteworthy that Jeremiah did not change his message under pressure. At the outset of the Babylonian invasion, he had told Zedekiah that the Lord would deliver "such as are left in this city from the pestilence, from the sword, and from the famine, into the hand of Nebuchadrezzar king of Babylon…and he shall smite them with the edge of the sword" (21.7). At the same time, he had cried: "Behold, I set before you the way of life, and the way of death. He that abideth in this city shall die by the sword, and by the famine, and by the pestilence: but he that goeth out, and falleth to the Chaldeans that besiege you, he shall live, and his life shall be unto him for a prey" (21.8-9). Zedekiah would not therefore have been surprised when the princes related to him Jeremiah's preaching in the court of the prison. Even "Pashur the son of Malchiah" (v.1) had heard it before (21.1, where the latter is called Melchiah)!

It should be carefully noted that the passage does not say, as previously, "The word which came unto Jeremiah from the Lord" (21.1), but "Thus saith the Lord" (vv.2,3). Jeremiah did not need a new message from the Lord for the occasion: he needed only to restate what he already knew, and it must be said that there are often circumstances in the lives of believers today, and in the lives of assemblies, in which it is not necessary to ask for divine guidance since the Word of God is perfectly explicit in its teaching. On such occasions, it is necessary to pray, not so much for guidance, but for help in implementing what is clearly taught in the Scriptures.

The demand of the princes (v.4)

In the judgment of the princes, Jeremiah's advice was disastrous for morale, and Zedekiah was informed: "We beseech thee, let this man be put to death: for thus he weakeneth the hands of the men of war that remain in this city, and the hands of all the people, in speaking such words unto them: for this man seeketh not the welfare of this people, but the hurt". Evidently the end was fast approaching: the words, "the men of war that remain", strongly suggest that many, if not most, of the soldiers had either been killed or had deserted. There had certainly been a defection to the Chaldeans (cp. v.19). It is ironical that the princes should say, "this man seeketh not the welfare of this people, but the hurt". As Laetsch points out, "They sought to silence the only true friend the people had", and Ironside is surely right in saying that "Like Paul, the more abundantly he loved them, the less he was loved in return. It is one of the hardest trials a devoted servant has to bear when his good is evil spoken of, and his very affection mistaken for malice, because it makes it impossible for him to hold his peace and to permit the people to sleep on in their sins without lifting a warning voice".

The request of the princes illustrates the New Testament statement that "the natural man receiveth not the things of the Spirit of God: for they are foolishness unto him: neither can he know them, because they are spiritually discerned" (1 Cor 2.14). Quite obviously, it never occurred to the princes that the moral and spiritual state of the nation called for divine judgment, and that Jeremiah must therefore be right in proclaiming the imminent fall of Jerusalem. As "princes of this world" they employed "the wisdom of this world" (1 Cor 2.6,8) in evaluating Jeremiah's preaching. To the spiritually-untutored ear the princes might seem justified in accusing Jeremiah of treasonable behaviour, but they were devoid of spiritual judgment. Jeremiah was amongst those of whom it can be said, "The secret of the Lord is with them that fear him" (Ps 25.14).

The weakness of the king (v.5)

Zedekiah, ever a weakling, succumbed to the demands of his ministers, reneging on his undertaking to provide for Jeremiah (37.21): "Behold, he is in your hand: for the king is not he that can do any thing against you". He was too weak to resist his officials. As Feinberg observes, "His capitulation to them was a clear giveaway of his lack of moral fibre. While he did not actually sign Jeremiah's death warrant, neither did he do anything to prevent it". Ellicott's Commentary points out that "The whole history reminds us of Pilate's conduct in circumstances more or less analogous".

It might be opportune to say that an assembly overseer must hold "fast the faithful word as he hath been taught, that he may be able by sound doctrine both to exhort and to convince the gainsayers" (Titus 1.9). Zedekiah had certainly been taught "the faithful word", but utterly failed to stand by it in refuting the demands of his court officials.

The danger to Jeremiah (v.6)

Jeremiah is consigned to "the dungeon of Malchiah, the son of Hammelech". A worse place can hardly be imagined: "And in the dungeon there was no water, but mire: so Jeremiah sunk in the mire". The word translated "dungeon" (953) refers here to a pit or cistern. According to Feinberg, "In ancient and modern Jerusalem, there are many cisterns to catch the winter rainwater for the dry summer. The depth of this cistern can be judged by the fact that ropes were used to lower Jeremiah into it. By this punishment his enemies tried to salve their consciences from the burden of having actually slain him. Restrained by the Lord, they stopped just short of executing His prophet". Harrison observes that "Most houses in Jerusalem had private cisterns (cp. 2 Kings 18.31) for storing water collected from rainfall or from a spring. They were usually pear-shaped with a small opening at the top, which could be covered over if necessary to prevent accidents or contamination of the water…The cistern in question was apparently not in use, but nevertheless contained a residue of tacky mud in which the prophet was compelled to stand or sit". The prospect for Jeremiah was grim: "A lingering death by starvation in a dreadful dungeon seemed to hang over him" (Orelli).

Verses 7-13: The Aid of Ebed-melech

The plight of Jeremiah came to the attention of "Ebed-melech the Ethiopian, one of the eunuchs which was in the king's house" (v.7). In ancient courts, eunuchs were employed as keepers of the royal harem. Moreover, being a eunuch he was excluded from "the congregation of the Lord" (Deut 23.1), although according to Orelli no difficulty would have arisen "in the case of a slave come from abroad", to which he adds, "In a court so thoroughly worldly, where a great harem existed (v.22), heathenism would be imitated in this respect also".

There was evidently no one amongst God's people who was willing to come to Jeremiah's aid, and it was a foreigner who was sufficiently concerned to act on his behalf. Habel calls Ebed-melech "the 'good Samaritan' of the Old Testament". His intervention on Jeremiah's behalf was engendered by his trust in the Lord (39.18), something conspicuously absent in the inhabitants of Jerusalem. But "like the young man in Acts 23.16 used for Paul's deliverance, here also God had prepared this His servant for Jeremiah's deliverance" (Ironside). Some commentators suggest that since Ebed-melech means "the king's servant", he could actually be anonymous, but "the absence of the article in the Hebrew makes it probable that it had come to be used as a proper name" (Ellicott's Commentary).

Attention is drawn to the alarm of Ebed-melech (vv.7-9); the command of Zedekiah (v.10); and the deliverance of Jeremiah (vv.11-13).

The alarm of Ebed-melech (vv.7-9)

Having "heard that they had put Jeremiah in the dungeon", Ebed-melech hastened to the king to plead Jeremiah's cause: "My lord the king, these men have done evil in all that they have done to Jeremiah the prophet, whom they have cast into the dungeon; and he is like to die for hunger in the place where he is: for there is no more bread in the city" (v.9). Unlike the princes, Ebed-melech recognised the divinely-given authority of God's servant, whom he calls "Jeremiah the prophet". It is ironic that Zedekiah was "sitting in the gate of Benjamin at the time" (v.7). Orelli suggests that the "the gate of Benjamin" was "an important post of observation", but kings also sat in the city gates to dispense judgment (cp. 2 Sam 19.8), something that was completely lacking in the case of Jeremiah. It does seem probable that Zedekiah was not actually aware of the prophet's predicament at the time, and quite possible, in any case, that he was too cowardly to raise the subject with his officials.

The command of Zedekiah (v.10)

"Then the king commanded Ebed-melech the Ethiopian, saying, Take from hence thirty men with thee, and take up Jeremiah the prophet out of the dungeon, before he die." It is generally thought that while thirty men would not have been required to lift Jeremiah from the cistern, they formed a guard of sufficient size to discourage any intervention by the court officials. It is noticeable that, like Ebed-melech, Zedekiah refers to him as "Jeremiah the prophet". Ironside describes the king as "a typical changeling, whose mind is controlled by the last man who gains his ear…The king makes no confession of sin in thus having treated Jehovah's messenger; nor is there a word of apology to the prophet for the indignities so unrighteously heaped upon him after his pledged word as to provision for his comfort".

The deliverance of Jeremiah (vv.11-13)

While "they drew up Jeremiah with cords, and took him up out of the dungeon" (v.13), careful provision was made for the prophet's well-being during the rescue operation. There was nothing "rough and ready" about the procedure. Referring to the "old cast clouts and old rotten rags" which came, above all places, from "the house of the king under the treasury" (vv.11-12), Orelli observes, "He carefully gets this old stuff, because it will form a soft covering for the cords, that the latter may not cut". Feinberg calls this "a fine touch of compassion". Meyer makes a helpful application here: "It was an act of womanly tenderness, which makes it as fragrant as the breaking of the box over the person of the Lord. It is not enough to serve and help those who need assistance; we should do it with the sweetness and gentleness of Christ".

According to Harrison, the words "under the treasury" might be rendered "the wardrobe storeroom", but this does appear to involve an amendment to the text. Ellicott's Commentary calls it the "lumber-room" of the palace. Having done their best to ensure that Jeremiah would be as comfortable as possible, they hauled him of the pit and left him "in the court of the prison" (v.13).

Verses 14-23: The Alternatives before Zedekiah

Yet again, Zedekiah sought the counsel of Jeremiah, removing him from the court of the prison to the Temple for the purpose of a private interview: "Then Zedekiah the king sent, and took Jeremiah the prophet unto him into the third entry that is in the house of the Lord" (v.14). "The third entrance, unmentioned elsewhere, was perhaps the 'royal entry' (cp. 2 Kings 16.18). If so, it would be sufficiently private for a consultation between king and prophet" (Harrison). In his inimitable language, Meyer describes the scene: "Once more and for the last time those two men stood face to face - king and prophet - weakness and strength - representatives, one of the fading glories of David's race, and the other of the imperishable splendour of truth and righteousness".

The following should be noted: the pledge of the king (vv.14-16); the choices before the king (vv.17-18); the apprehension of the king (vv.19-20); and the mockery of the king (vv.21-23).

The pledge of the king (vv.14-16)

Having been so badly treated by permission of the king, even if Zedekiah were unaware at the time of the way in which Jeremiah had suffered, the prophet was apprehensive. Having been told by Zedekiah, "I will ask thee a thing; hide nothing from me" (v.14), the prophet replied, "If I declare it unto thee, wilt thou not surely put me to death? and if I give thee counsel, wilt thou not hearken unto me?" (v.15). Jeremiah evidently knew that the king's question would be a repetition of his previous enquiry, "Is there any word from the Lord?" (37.17), in the hope that there would now be a different answer. Since the prophet knew that he had nothing but renewed bad news for the king, he feared for his life. He also knew that the king would not listen to his advice: "if I give thee counsel, thou wilt not hearken unto me" (JND). Streane points out that this is not an interrogative clause. Jeremiah was under no illusion about the response to his message.

It has to be said that, vacillating as he was, Zedekiah stood by his pledge on this occasion: "As the Lord liveth, that made us this soul ('who has given us breath', NIV), I will not put thee to death, neither will I give thee into the hand of these men that seek thy life" (v.16). Zedekiah was well aware of the intentions of his officials. The force of Zedekiah's oath to Jeremiah can be understood by his reference to the imparting of life by the Lord: "God takes life just as He gives it, and hence He may be expected to take Zedekiah's life if he proves false to his oath" (Harrison).

The choices before the king (vv.17-18)

With the king's assurance of safety, Jeremiah proceeds: "Thus saith the Lord, the God of hosts, the God of Israel; If thou wilt assuredly go forth unto the king of Babylon's princes, then thy soul shall live, and this city shall not be burned with fire; and thou shalt live, and thine house: But if thou wilt not go forth...then shall this city be given into the hand of the Chaldeans, and they shall burn it with fire, and thou shalt not escape out of their hand". No reference is made here to Nebuchadnezzar himself: he was not present at the siege and was located at Riblah (39.5).

Nothing had changed; as already noted, Jeremiah had described these very alternatives at the onset of the siege (21.8-10) and did so again. The choice was crystal clear: surrender and live (v.17) or resist and suffer (v.18).

The apprehension of the king (vv.19-20)

Zedekiah's fear of surrendering lay in the possibility that the Jews who had already defected to the Chaldeans (39.9; 52.15) would be given mastery over him: "I am afraid of the Jews that are fallen to the Chaldeans, lest they deliver me into their hand, and they mock me" (v.19). He was afraid that the Babylonians would turn him over to the Jewish defectors. The word translated "mock" (5953) refers, not just to verbal insult, but to ill-treatment and torture. Feinberg points out that the same word is used in used "in the incident of the extreme abuse of the Levite's concubine by the men of Gibeah (Judg 19.25)". Zedekiah feared men, whether his own court officials ("the princes") or the defectors, rather than the Lord. He lived to prove that "The fear of man bringeth a snare" and thus failed to prove that "whoso putteth his trust in the Lord shall be safe" (Prov 29.25).

Jeremiah's solemn assurance of Zedekiah's personal safety if he opted to "go forth unto the king of Babylon's princes" (v.17) is accompanied by a strong plea: "Obey, I beseech thee, the voice of the Lord, which I speak unto thee: so it shall be well unto thee, and thy soul shall live" (v.20). Jeremiah found no pleasure in the coming catastrophe. Like the Lord whom he served, he had "no pleasure in the death of the wicked; but that the wicked turn from his way and live" (Ezek 33.11).

The mockery of the king (vv.21-23)

The Lord had already indicated that Zedekiah and those associated with him were like "evil figs, which cannot be eaten, they are so evil", and that they would be "removed into all the kingdoms of the earth for their hurt, to be a reproach and a proverb, a taunt and a curse, in all places whither I shall drive them" (24.8-9). Something even worse is indicated here for Zedekiah: "But if thou refuse to go forth, this is the word that the Lord hath shewed me: And, behold, all the women that are left in the king of Judah's house shall be brought forth to the king of Babylon's princes, and those women shall say, Thy friends have set thee on, and have prevailed against thee ('misled you and overcame you', NIV): thy feet are sunk in the mire, and they are turned away back" (vv.21-22).

Zedekiah was afraid of being mocked if he did surrender (v.19): he would, in fact, be mocked if he did not surrender. The women of the royal house, perhaps to gain favour with their new masters, would point out that Zedekiah's "friends" had "impelled him to a suicidal opposition" (Feinberg). "If Zedekiah feared the mockery of deserters, how much more galling that of his own harem!" (Feinberg). The word translated "friends" is earlier rendered "familiars" (20.10) and evidently refers not to the Egyptians nor to the adjoining nations, but to Zedekiah's own "princes" who were set on resistance. In his fear of them, and refusal to heed the voice of Jeremiah, Zedekiah would bring about his personal ruin together with the ruin of his family and the destruction of Jerusalem: "So shall they bring out all thy wives and thy children to the Chaldeans: and thou shalt not escape out of their hand, but shalt be taken by the hand of the king of Babylon: and thou shalt cause this city to be burned with fire" (v.23). Commentators draw attention to the similarity between the latter part of v.23 and Obadiah v.7.

It has already been pointed out that this chapter could be entitled "The story of two men in the mire". The Lord had delivered Jeremiah from death in a deep and muddy water cistern (v.13), but there would be no deliverance for Zedekiah from the mire which he himself had created (v.22)

Verses 24-28: The Advice to Jeremiah

Rather than acting on the assurances given by Jeremiah that surrender to the Chaldeans would ensure his own safety and the preservation of Jerusalem (v.17), Zedekiah remained weak and fearful to the end. He was completely dominated by fear of his officials, and this was uppermost in his mind in the closing part of his interview with Jeremiah. Three things should be noted in the final verses of the chapter: the request for secrecy (vv.24-26); the compliance of Jeremiah (v.27); and the location of Jeremiah (v.28).

The request for secrecy (vv.24-26)

The discussion at this private interview was to remain secret: "Then said Zedekiah unto Jeremiah, Let no man know of these words, and thou shalt not die" (v.24). He explained that if the princes learned of their meeting they would want to know what had been said, and that Jeremiah would be threatened with death if he refused to tell them: "Declare unto us now what thou hast said unto the king, hide it not from us, and we will not put thee to death; also what the king said unto thee" (v.25). Quite clearly, Zedekiah was as suspicious of his officials as they were of him, and events certainly proved that they had been spying on him (v.27).

Zedekiah had a ready-made solution to the problem: Jeremiah was to say that the interview concerned his personal safety: "...thou shalt say unto them, I presented my supplication before the king, that he would not cause me to return to Jonathan's house, to die there" (v.26). This had certainly been true at the previous interview (37.20) and according to Laetsch it is implicit on this occasion as well. It will not escape notice that Zedekiah evidently wished to create the impression by this answer that it was Jeremiah who initiated the meeting with him, thus deflecting attention away from himself.

The compliance of Jeremiah (v.27)

"Then came all the princes unto Jeremiah, and asked him: and he told them according to all these words that the king had commanded. So they left off speaking with him; for the matter was not perceived." As it may be expected, Jeremiah has been criticised by commentators for complying with Zedekiah's in this way. One commentator (J. P. Hyatt) goes as far as to ask for indulgence for Jeremiah's "half-truth" and "white lie", of which Feinberg says, "This language is too strong", and continues, "It is better to realise that because the princes and their spies had no right to the information, Jeremiah was right in limiting himself to the one item of his not being consigned to the dungeon, which was unquestionably true".

The location of Jeremiah (v.28)

Jeremiah was returned to "the court of the prison", and remained there "until the day that Jerusalem was taken: and he was there when Jerusalem was taken". The fall of Jerusalem and capture of Zedekiah, together with Jeremiah's release from "the court of the prison" is described in the next chapter.

JEREMIAH 39

At the beginning of his ministry, some forty years previously, Jeremiah was told that the Lord would "call all the families of the kingdoms of the north…and they shall come, and they shall set every one his throne at the entering of the gates of Jerusalem, and against all the walls thereof round about" (1.15). At the same time, the prophet was told, "Thou therefore gird up thy loins, and arise, and speak unto them all that I command thee", and his faithful declaration of God's word had earned him, as predicted, the opposition of "the kings of Judah…the princes thereof…the priests thereof, and…the people of the land" (1.17-18). Following his warning, "Thus saith the Lord; If ye will not hearken to me, to walk in my law, which I have set before you…then will I make this house like Shiloh, and will make this city a curse to all nations of the earth" (26.4,6), priests, prophets and people had all clamoured for his death (26.8). But Jeremiah spoke "from the mouth of the Lord" (2 Chr 36.12), and the fall of Jerusalem described in the present chapter fully authenticated his prophecies: "the city was broken up. And all the princes of the king of Babylon came in, and sat in the middle gate" (vv.2-3).

There is never any doubt about the ultimate fulfilment of the Word of God. Years or centuries may intervene, but in the words of the Psalmist, "For ever, O Lord, thy word is settled in heaven" (Ps 119.89). Men may scoff at the Word of God and dispute its message, but "The Lord is not slack concerning his promise" (2 Pet 3.9).

Zedekiah had evidently hoped that with the approach of the Egyptian army, the withdrawal of the Chaldeans would be permanent (37.3,5), but as Jeremiah "had so forcibly pointed out, the inevitable hour could not be delayed indefinitely, and when the Egyptians decided not to go to the relief of Jerusalem, the Babylonians concentrated on breaching the walls and overthrowing the city" (Harrison). Nebuchadnezzar himself was not present: he had evidently made his headquarters at Riblah (v.5), on the river Orontes. Riblah lay some two hundred miles north of Jerusalem and some sixty-five miles north of Damascus.

The chapter may be divided as follows:

The Fall of Jerusalem (vv.1-3)
The Capture of Zedekiah (vv.4-7)
The Destruction of Jerusalem (v.8)
The Deportation of the People (vv.9-10)
The Deliverance of Jeremiah (vv.11-14)
The Preservation of Ebed-melech (vv.15-18).

Verses 1-3: The Fall of Jerusalem
"The long-suffering patience of God at last gives way to judgment: the

glory departs, and Jerusalem, whose name means 'the foundation of peace', or 'founded in peace', is delivered into the hands of the Gentiles. What other city on earth has had a history so full of pathos and tragedy, and which so dreadfully belies its name? Yet the prophetic word assures us that it shall eventually be established in peace, no more to be overthrown" (Ironside).

The fall of Jerusalem, the city having been weakened by the blockade without and the famine within (cp. 2 Kings 25.1-12 and Jer 52.4-16), took place after a siege of approximately eighteen months: "In the ninth year of Zedekiah king of Judah, in the tenth month, came Nebuchadrezzar king of Babylon and all his army against Jerusalem, and they besieged it. And in the eleventh year of Zedekiah, in the fourth month, the ninth day of the month, the city was broken up" (vv.1-2). According to Feinberg, scholars vary in computing the period: "either from January, 587 BC (the ninth year) to July, 586 BC (the eleventh year) (so Bewer) or from December, 589 BC, to June, 587 BC (so Cunliffe Jones)". Harrison, with Feinberg in agreement, states that "The siege had commenced in January, 588 BC, and apart from a brief respite in the summer, had continued until July, 587 BC, when all resistance collapsed". Since the Word of God does not give the actual calendar years, the matter can be left to the scholars. It is sufficient for us to know at which point in the reign of Zedekiah the siege commenced and concluded.

Having breached the city walls, the Babylonian princes took up position in the "middle gate" (v.3) which was either located "between the upper and lower divisions of the city" (Feinberg) or describes "the central gate of Jerusalem" where the "enemy generals established a military council" (Harrison). The members of the "military council" were "Nergal-sharezer, Samgar-nebo, Sarsechim, Rab-saris, Nergal-sharezer, Rab-mag, with all the residue of the princes of the king of Babylon" (v.3). Streane points out that "from the English it would appear that there are six princes mentioned by name", but continues by saying that "In fact however there are but four at the most, (*a*) Nergal-sharezer (*may Nergal protect the king*), (*b*) Samgar-nebo (*be gracious, O Nebo*), (*c*) Sarsechim, of whose name the meaning is still unknown, (*d*) another Nergal-sharezer. Rab-saris (*chief of the eunuchs*) and Rab-mag (*chief of the magi*) are the titles of those whose names they follow". It is not surprising that various other suggestions have been made in connection with the names given here. However, commentators are in general agreement that Nergal-sharezer (either the first or second man bearing the name) was Nebuchadnezzar's son-in-law, and succeeded him under the name of Neriglissar, having first killed Evil-merodach, Nebuchadnezzar's son, in a revolt. According to Harrison, "his name occurs in sixth-century BC Babylonian legal texts and other inscriptions". It should be noted that "Nebuzar-adan, the captain of the guard" (v.9) did not arrive in Jerusalem until a month later (52.12).

Verses 4-7: The Capture of Zedekiah

Zedekiah had been told, "I will give this city into the hand of the king of Babylon...And thou shalt not escape out of his hand, but shalt surely be taken, and delivered into his hand; and thine eyes shall behold the eyes of the king of Babylon, and he shall speak with thee mouth to mouth, and thou shalt go to Babylon" (34.2-3; cp. 32.3-5). It had also been predicted that Zedekiah would be taken "to Babylon to the land of the Chaldeans; yet shall he not see it, though he shall die there" (Ezek 12.13). The fulfilment of these "seemingly contradictory prophecies" (Laetsch) is described in these verses.

The king attempted to escape capture by the Babylonians by leaving Jerusalem at night. His departure from Jerusalem is described by Ezekiel: "And the prince that is among them shall bear upon his shoulder in the twilight, and shall go forth: they shall dig through the wall to carry out thereby: he shall cover his face, that he see not the ground with his eyes" (Ezek 12.12). With "all the men of war", he exited Jerusalem "by the way of the king's garden, by the gate betwixt the two walls: and he went out the way of the plain" (Jer 39.4). While the "two walls" cannot be identified with certainty, they were evidently part of the defence of the city (Is 22.11) and "connected Zion with the fortress known as Ophel (2 Chr 27.3; 33.14)" (Ellicott's Commentary). The gate in question was probably "the gate of the fountain" since this was evidently near to "the pool of Siloah by the king's garden" (Neh 3.15). The "way of the plain" is literally "the way of the Arabah" (JND margin), and refers to "the deep valley of Jordan north of the Dead Sea" which "seemingly offered the best escape route" (Harrison). It appears, therefore, that Zedekiah was making for Gilead, but other destinations have been proposed, including Egypt.

The attempted escape was unsuccessful: "the Chaldeans' army pursued after them, and overtook Zedekiah in the plains of Jericho: and when they had taken him, they brought him up to Nebuchadnezzar king of Babylon to Riblah in the land of Hamath, where he gave judgment upon him" (v.5). The book of Lamentations describes the capture of Zedekiah: "The breath of our nostrils, the anointed of the Lord, was taken in their pits, of whom we said, Under his shadow we shall live among the heathen" (Lam 4.20).

As Laetsch observes, "Nebuchadnezzar decided once for all to end any possibility of further rebellion". He "slew the sons of Zedekiah in Riblah before his eyes: also the king of Babylon slew all the nobles of Judah" (v.6). The very men who had so persistently opposed Jeremiah, accusing him of traitorous behaviour and consigning him to "the dungeon of Malchiah" (38.4-6), found to their cost that the prophet was right in saying, "Thus saith the Lord, He that remaineth in this city shall die by the sword...but he that goeth forth to the Chaldeans shall live; for he shall have his life for a prey, and shall live" (38.2). Nebuchadnezzar then dealt with the king of Judah: "Moreover he put out Zedekiah's eyes, and bound him with chains, to carry him to Babylon" (39.7). It has been said that having seen his sons and his nobles put to death, Zedekiah's eyes were put out "so the last memory of this world's light might remain a grief". Perhaps, blind and shackled, Zedekiah was taken to Babylon with the words of Jeremiah ringing in his ears, "Thus saith the Lord, the God of hosts, the God of Israel; If thou wilt assuredly go forth to the king of Babylon's princes, then thy soul shall live…But if thou wilt not go forth unto the king of Babylon's princes, then…thou shalt not escape out of their hand" (38.17-18). It is perilous either to ignore or to disobey the Word of God.

Verse 8: The Destruction of Jerusalem

Jerusalem was destroyed by fire as predicted, and its walls broken down: "And the Chaldeans burned the king's house, and the houses of the people, with fire, and brake down the walls of Jerusalem". The book of Lamentations personifies ruined Jerusalem, and she is heard to say, "From above hath he that sent fire into my bones, and it prevaileth against them: he hath spread a net for my feet, he hath turned me back: he hath made me desolate and faint all the day" (Lam 1.13). The city walls and gates remained in this state until Nehemiah, having been told that "the wall of Jerusalem also is broken down, and the gates therefore are burned with fire" (Neh 1.3), undertook the work of reconstruction.

Jeremiah had pleaded with Zedekiah to surrender to the Babylonians, not only in his own interests, but also in the interests of the city (38.17-18), and it has already been noted that the Chaldeans would execute the very judgment on idolatrous Jerusalem demanded by the Mosaic law: "Thou shalt surely smite the inhabitants of that (idolatrous) city with the edge of the sword…and shalt burn with fire the city, and all the spoil thereof every whit" (Deut 13.15-16). Jeremiah had said that the Chaldeans would "come and set fire on this city, and burn it with the houses, upon whose roofs they have offered incense unto Baal, and poured out drink offerings unto other gods, to provoke me to anger" (32.29).

Verses 9-10: The Deportation of the people

Having dealt with the leadership at Riblah, Nebuchadnezzar then dispatched Nebuzar-adan to Jerusalem. His assignment was to arrange the deportation of the people remaining in the city, together with all who had previously defected to the Chaldeans: "Then Nebuzar-adan the captain of the guard carried away captive into Babylon the remnant of the people that remained in the city, and those that fell away (cp. 38.19), that fell to him, with the rest of the people that remained" (v.9). Nebuzar-adan was the commander of the imperial guard. The words "captain of the guard" mean, literally, "the chief butcher", and is generally said to mean "chief of the executioners". The connection is clear! Feinberg calls this "an instance where the old name remained after the function had changed entirely". According to 52.30, "seven hundred forty and five persons" were deported at this time.

Nebuzar-adan, who was evidently authorised by Nebuchadnezzar to oversee the settlement of Judah, took steps to ensure that the land was not left desolate. He "left of the poor of the people, which had nothing, in the land of Judah, and gave them vineyards and fields at the same time" (v.10). Quite clearly, Nebuzar-adan did not expect any trouble from the "poor of the people". It has been suggested that that their gratitude on receiving "vineyards and fields" would effectively counter any thought of rebellion against their new masters.

Verses 11-14: The Deliverance of Jeremiah

What of Jeremiah at this time? The prophet was "in the court of the prison...when Jerusalem was taken" (38.28). At his call to service, he received the promise, "I am with thee, saith the Lord, to deliver thee" (1.19). In context, the promise refers to deliverance from hostile Judæans, but the Lord now takes steps to ensure the safety of His servant when Judah had been overrun by the Chaldeans.

There can be no doubt that these verses give a bare outline of his deliverance, referring only to Jeremiah's release from prison and delivery into the safekeeping of Gedaliah (vv.13-14). No reference is made in the current passage to the fact that between these two events, Jeremiah had been rounded up with the deportees, but liberated shortly afterwards at Ramah (40.1-5), whence he went "unto Gedaliah the son of Ahikam to Mizpah; and dwelt with him among the people that were left in the land" (40.6). Having been released from prison on the instructions of Nebuchadnezzar (vv.11-12), Jeremiah was evidently unrecognised by the Babylonian officials responsible for rounding up Jews for deportation, and was placed in chains ready for transportation to Babylon. The apparent discrepancy between the two accounts (39.11-14 and 40.1-6) can be reasonably explained in this way. Gedaliah was the son of Ahikam, who had befriended Jeremiah when his life was threatened during the reign of Jehoiakim (26.24), and there is good reason to believe that Shaphan, Ahikam's father, was scribe or secretary to King Josiah (2 Kings 22.8-10). Gedaliah, who was appointed governor over the cities of Judah by Nebuchadnezzar (40.5), evidently had a good spiritual pedigree!

It is of interest to notice Nebuchadnezzar's concern for Jeremiah's welfare: "Now Nebuchadrezzar king of Babylon gave charge concerning Jeremiah to Nebuzar-adan the captain of the guard, saying, Take him, and look well to him, and do him no harm; but do unto him even as he shall say unto thee" (vv.11-12). The Babylonian princes (v.13) therefore "sent, and took Jeremiah out of the court of the prison, and committed him unto Gedaliah the son of Ahikam the son of Shaphan, that he should carry him home: so he dwelt among the people" (v.14). Bearing in mind that throughout the siege, Jeremiah had counselled submission to Babylon (38.2,17), and that this had almost certainly been reported to the Babylonian authorities by those who had deserted the city (38.19), it is not entirely surprising that Nebuchadnezzar looked on him with favour. He probably regarded him as "a sympathiser" (Feinberg). Jeremiah was treated better by the invaders than he was by his own countrymen, illustrating the words of the Lord Jesus that "A prophet is not without honour, save in his own country, and in his own house" (Mt 13.57). Sadly, Harrison is right in saying that "It is not unknown for Christians to be treated with greater respect by the world than by the fellowship of believers".

Verses 15-18: The Preservation of Ebed-melech

If the previous verses (vv.11-14) show how the Lord preserved His servant, then the concluding verses of the chapter exhibit the Lord's concern for the man who rescued him from his imprisonment in the cistern (38.1-13).

"Now the word of the Lord came unto Jeremiah, while he was shut up in the court of the prison, saying, Go and speak to Ebed-melech the Ethiopian" (vv.15-16). While this message must have been imparted to Jeremiah shortly after his rescue by Ebed-melech and is therefore out of chronological order, it is usually suggested that it was included at this point, rather than at the time, to avoid interrupting the chain of events culminating in the capture of Jerusalem. While it is quite possible that the men of whom Ebed-melech was afraid were Jeremiah's enemies, who were undoubtedly angry that he had been lifted out of the cistern, the context suggests it was the conquering Babylonian army which caused his fear: "Thus saith the Lord of hosts, the God of Israel; Behold, I will bring my words upon this city for evil, and not for good; and they shall be accomplished in that day before thee. But I will deliver thee in that day, saith the Lord: and thou shalt not be given into the hand of the men of whom thou art afraid" (vv.16-17).

Laetsch has a nice piece in connection with the Lord's promise to preserve Ebed-melech: "The Lord provides not only for His chosen spokesman, as He had promised (1.8,19), He thinks with loving care for one who was not the protégé of a mighty ruler, but a poor, unknown friendless slave, harassed with dread fear as to his future. Ebed-melech had given more than a cup of cold water (Mk 9.41) to the prophet, and in keeping with His promises (Ps 37.40; 41.2; 97.10) the Lord was with him also in his hour of need....The Searcher of hearts saw that the wellspring of that daring rescue was not merely natural pity, but true faith in the Lord of justice and mercy. Through faith he had delivered Jeremiah, through faith he would be delivered from harm". Ebed-melech was thus reassured by the Lord: "I will surely deliver thee, and thou shalt not fall by the sword, but thy life shall be for a prey unto thee: because thou hast put thy trust in me, saith the Lord" (v.18).

JEREMIAH 40

This chapter marks the commencement of a new section in the book (chs.40-45) which contains prophecies and a record of events after the fall of Jerusalem. Chapters 40-42 are concerned with prophecies and details of events in Judah, chapters 43-44 with those in Egypt, and chapter 45 is addressed to Baruch, Jeremiah's secretary, who was taken with the prophet into Egypt (43.6). While chapter 45 is chronologically out of order, it is evidently included at this point in the book to emphasise the fulfilment of God's promise to preserve Baruch's life (45.5).

The opening words of the chapter are a fitting introduction to the whole section: "The word that came to Jeremiah from the Lord, after that Nebuzar-adan the captain of the guard had let him go from Ramah" (v.1). While the voice of Jeremiah is not heard again until chapter 42, the intervening passages describe the circumstances leading to the request of Johanan for the prophet's help in seeking the Lord's guidance (42.1-3).

The chapter may be divided as follows:

> Jeremiah's Release (vv.1-6)
> Gedaliah's Rule (vv.7-12)
> Johanan's Report (vv.13-16).

Verses 1-6: Jeremiah's Release

These verses amplify 39.11-14 which, as already noted, gives a bare outline of Jeremiah's deliverance from prison, referring only to his release and delivery into the safekeeping of Gedaliah (39.13-14). No reference is made in those verses to the fact that between these two events, and contrary to the instructions of Nebuchadrezzar (39.11-12), Jeremiah had been inadvertently rounded up with his fellow-countrymen and taken, with manacles on his hands, to Ramah in preparation for deportation. Ramah, some five miles north of Jerusalem "had been selected as a general staging-area from which the deportees would leave for Babylonia" (Harrison). The "very embarrassing error" (Harrison) of the Babylonian officials responsible for organising the deportation was recognised at Ramah by Nebuzar-adan, "the captain of the guard", and the prophet was released.

The details of Jeremiah's release (v.1) are now given, and attention is drawn to the following: the accuracy of God's word (vv.2-3); the alternatives before God's servant (v.4); and the advice to God's servant (vv.5-6).

The accuracy of God's word (vv.2-3)

At first glance, the words of Nebuzar-adan "sound curious in the mouth of a pagan Mesopotamian soldier" (Harrison), but there can be no doubt that this high-ranking official was well aware of Jeremiah's preaching: in fact Nebuzar-adan's words sound very much like those of Jeremiah himself:

"The Lord thy God hath pronounced this evil upon this place. Now the Lord hath brought it, and done according as he hath said: because ye have sinned against the Lord, and have not obeyed his voice, therefore this thing is come upon you". This is not at all unlikely, especially when it is remembered that a number of Jews had "fallen to the Chaldeans" (38.19), and that Jeremiah's reputation as a prophet had evidently reached the ears of Nebuchadrezzar himself (39.11-12). The fact that Jeremiah's preaching was recognised in this way by Nebuzar-adan probably does not "imply more than the belief of the polytheist, that each nation had its own guardian deity" (Ellicott's Commentary). However, it is worth remembering that one of the many features that distinguish the Lord, the true God, from idols, is His ability to predict the future accurately (cp. Is 41.21-23). Jeremiah's preaching had been generally rejected by his own people, but it had made an impression on their enemies, who had witnessed its fulfilment with their very eyes. The Lord's people today need have no doubt whatsoever that, for good or evil, "what he has promised he is able also to do" (Rom 4.21, JND).

The alternatives before God's servant (v.4)

In accordance with the instructions of Nebuchadrezzar (39.11-12), Jeremiah was given the opportunity of either proceeding to Babylon, where he would be favourably treated, or remaining in his native land: "And now, behold, I loose thee this day from the chains which were upon thine hand. If it seem good unto thee to come with me into Babylon, come; and I will look well unto thee: but if it seem ill unto thee to come with me into Babylon, forbear: behold, all the land is before thee: whither it seemeth good and convenient for thee to go, thither go". Harrison makes the thought-provoking statement that "When others were being taken unwillingly into captivity, Jeremiah was given compete freedom of choice by the enemy of Judah. The events of current history had vindicated his integrity completely, showing his opponents that he had indeed been proclaiming the whole counsel of God".

Centuries before, Moses chose "rather to suffer affliction with the people of God, than to enjoy the pleasures of sin for a season" (Heb 11.25). Jeremiah was given the option of Nebuzar-adan's personal patronage and protection in Babylon, with their attendant material comforts. This must have been a rather attractive proposition after the harrowing experiences through which he had passed during the course of his ministry. He had faced the stormy seas of verbal and physical attack, all of which he felt very deeply, and now he was offered peace and honour in Babylon. The alternative was to remain in poverty-stricken Judah, with its population reduced to a mere remnant, and no immediate prospect of escaping the shadow of mighty Babylon. The same alternatives face God's people today. Another Babylon beckons, and in many places the true children of God are in reduced circumstances.

The advice to God's servant (v.5-6)

On noting Jeremiah's apparent hesitation (v.5) not, it is suggested, over whether or not he should go to Babylon, but where he ought to go in Judah, Nebuzar-adan urged him to return to Gedaliah, the newly-appointed governor. "Go back also to Gedaliah…whom the king of Babylon hath made governor over the cities of Judah, and dwell with him among the people: or go wheresoever it seemeth convenient unto thee to go…Then went Jeremiah unto Gedaliah the son of Ahikam to Mizpah; and dwelt with him among the people that were left in the land." Feinberg quotes another commentator in saying: "Jeremiah chose to stay in the land he loved. This does not mean that he doubted his own message in 24.4-10. He loved his people in spite of their mistreatment, hatred, and threats on his life…His devotion to the land, and his conviction that it would be the scene of future blessing, influenced his decision to remain in it at this critical time". Jeremiah had no desire for the earthly glory and material rewards of Babylon. He evidently felt that his place was with the remnant of his people. Like the "great woman" of Shunem, Jeremiah answered, in effect, "I dwell among mine own people" (2 Kings 4.13). Local assemblies would be so much stronger today if the Lord's people adopted the same attitude!

Jeremiah left Ramah with food and an unspecified gift, indicating the high esteem in which he was held or, at the very least, some recompence for his arrival there with manacles on his wrists: "So the captain of the guard gave him victuals and a reward, and let him go". Either way, the manner in which he was treated by Nebuzar-adan stands in striking contrast with the treatment that he had received from his own countrymen, particularly in the last days of Jerusalem. It should be noted that Mizpah had become the administrative centre of Judah. Feinberg suggests that "the Babylonians did not care to have the Jews remaining in Jerusalem, their former capital". There is a difference of opinion over the location of Mizpah. Some place it four and a half miles north-west of Jerusalem, and others about eight miles north of the capital (Harrison).

Verses 7-12: Gedaliah's Rule

As already noted, Gedaliah, who had been was appointed "governor over the cities of Judah" by Nebuchadnezzar (v.5), was the son of Ahikam, who had befriended Jeremiah when his life was threatened during the reign of Jehoiakim (26.24). It has been pointed out that "the official title is significant. Jerusalem is treated as if it been blotted from the face of the earth, and required no superintendence" (Ellicott's Commentary). The appointment of Gedaliah reflected Nebuchadnezzar's loss of faith in the house of David. The selection of a governor of Davidic descent might have aroused the hopes of the colonists and exiles in Babylon for a speedy restoration of the royal house, strengthening any lingering thoughts of revolution and rebellion. Gedaliah's support for Jeremiah indicated that, like the prophet, he counselled submission to Nebuchadnezzar, and could therefore be relied upon to promote Babylon's interests in Judah. Laetsch makes the following observations: "In choosing Gedaliah, Nebuchadnezzar proved himself an eminent statesman. His plan was to rebuild Judah into a flourishing self-supporting Jewish commonwealth under Babylonian sovereignty and supervision, but enjoying home rule to a great extent, and complete freedom in industry and commerce, and particularly in religion. He knew that a satisfied people, having an opportunity to make a decent living, would be more willing to remain loyal to Babylon and at the same time to resist Egyptian efforts to annex Judah or to foment rebellion against Babylon among the Jews, than if he deprived them of all their liberties and reduce them to a state of virtual slavery". Sadly, Gedaliah's governorship was very brief: he was assassinated shortly after his appointment (41.1-2).

Nebuchadnezzar's confidence in Gedaliah was shared by his own countrymen: his appointment was recognised by the guerilla captains (vv.7-10) and by refugees from Judah in nearby countries (vv.11-12).

His recognition by the guerillas (vv.7-10)

"Now when all the captains of the forces which were in the fields, even they and their men, heard that the king of Babylon had made Gedaliah the son of Ahikam governor in the land, and had committed unto him men, and women, and children, and of the poor of the land, of them that were not carried away captive to Babylon; Then they came to Gedaliah to Mizpah" (vv.7-8). Feinberg describes "the captains of the forces which were in the fields" as "chiefs of the guerilla bands, who remained hidden while the Babylonian army was besieging" and who "waited the turn of events after the fall of the capital". Laetsch describes "the forces" as "small commandos, military bands, that had escaped capture or annihilation by the Babylonian armies". According to Harrison, "Halting guerilla activity was the first step towards political and economic stability", in which case it has to be said that the wisdom of Nebuchadnezzar in appointing Gedaliah became evident at once.

The names of "the captains of the forces" are given: "Ishmael the son of Nethaniah, and Johanan and Jonathan the sons of Kareah, and Seraiah the son of Tanhumeth, and the sons of Ephai the Netophathite (Netophah was a village near Bethlehem), and Jezaniah the son of a Maachathite (Maachah lay in Bashan, on the east side of Jordan), they and their men" (v.8). Variations occur between some names in this verse and their counterparts in 2 Kings 25.23. Ishmael was of royal descent (41.1) which may account for his part in the plot hatched by Baalis to overthrow Gedaliah (v.14). It is quite possible that he took strong exception to being passed over in favour of Gedaliah. Johanan, on the other hand, disclosed the assassination plot to Gedaliah (v.14).

True to his appointment as governor of Judah, Gedaliah urges the "captains of the forces" and their men to submit to the Chaldeans: "Fear not to serve the Chaldeans: dwell in the land, and serve the king of Babylon, and it shall be well with you" (v.9). In New Testament language, he counselled them to "be subject unto the higher powers" (Rom 13.1), and the words which follow, "do that which is good, and thou shalt have praise of the same" (Rom 13.3), approximate to Gedaliah's promise, "it shall be well with you". The Jews had nothing to fear from "the powers that be" (Rom 13.1) as long as they served the Chaldeans acceptably.

Gedaliah's responsibility as governor was to attend personally to the interests of the Chaldeans: "And as for me, behold, I dwell at Mizpah, to stand before the Chaldeans, who will come unto us" (v.10, JND). The Chaldean officials were expected to visit Judah from time to time "to receive reports of progress made and to deliver the imperial mandates" (Laetsch). It is not unlikely that another reason for these official visits was the collection of tribute. No doubt, like New Testament elders, Gedaliah, who would be required to "give account", wished to undertake his responsibilities "with joy, and not with grief" (Heb 13.17). With this in mind, he invited the "captains of the forces" and their men to act peaceably and "gather…wine, and summer fruits, and oil" (v.10). Streane points out that "Although, owing to the national troubles, no corn had been sown, yet the fruits spoken of would be produced as usual". Apparently Nebuchadnezzar had not ravaged the countryside, as many of his Assyrian predecessors had done during their campaigns. Since "Jerusalem fell in the middle of summer (39.2), the people had time to gather the late fruits of summer to sustain them during their first bleak winter in the land" (Feinberg). Laetsch puts it slightly differently: "They still had time to gather ample stores for the coming winter season. Do not let the blessing go to waste that God has offered to you as an evidence of His loving-kindness". This is worthy of current application! The "captains of the forces" and their men were also urged to dwell permanently in the cities which they had "taken", or "seized" (8610), during their guerilla activities.

His recognition by the fugitives (vv.11-12)

Similar provision was available to Jews scattered "in Moab, and among the Ammonites, and in Edom, and that were in all the countries" (v.11). Having heard of the appointment of Gedaliah, and having "returned out of all places whither they were driven", they too "gathered wine and summer fruits very much" (v.12). The appointment of Gedaliah evidently inspired confidence amongst all Jews remaining in the area, whether in Judah itself or in neighbouring countries, but they did not stay long in the land (43.5-7).

Verses 13-16: Johanan's Report

Although some semblance of peaceful conditions was appearing, new storm clouds were gathering. The Ammonite king, Baalis, was plotting the removal of Gedaliah and intended to achieve his aim through Ishmael, one of the "captains of the forces which were in the fields" (v.7). Ishmael appears to have acted as a "lone wolf" since information about his intentions was brought to Gedaliah by the other "captains", for whom Johanan evidently acted as spokesman, but to no avail. His warning was rejected (vv.13-14) and his wish was refused (vv.15-16).

His warning was rejected (vv.13-14)

"Moreover, Johanan the son of Kareah, and all the captains of the forces that were in the fields, came to Gedaliah to Mizpah, And said unto him, Dost thou certainly know that Baalis the king of the Ammonites hath sent Ishmael the son of Nethaniah to slay thee?". Baalis, the Ammonite king, is otherwise unknown, although according to Feinberg, a recent "excavation in Jordan has uncovered the Siran Bottle (dated in the period of 667-580 BC), which bears the name of a King Ba'lay, who has been identified with the Baalis of Jeremiah".

The reason for the animosity of Baalis is a matter of conjecture. Laetsch suggests that he had "hoped that Judah would fall an easy prey to his hunger for more territory and was sorely disappointed when Gedaliah was appointed governor, and a stable, firm government was about to be established". But, as Streane observes, "It is easier to see the motives of Ishmael than those of his instigator Baalis". As already noted, it is quite possible that Ishmael felt aggrieved that, although of royal birth, he had been set aside in favour of Gedaliah.

The representations by the "captains", led by Jonathan, fell on deaf ears: "But Gedaliah the son of Ahikam believed them not" (v.14). It does seem that "he was unable to accept the fact that others were less sincere than himself in his desire for national stability. His tragedy lay in his inability to make a critical assessment of situations and people alike. His degree of commitment to the welfare of his charges precluded the requisite amount of emotional detachment from his task" (Harrison). Such treachery seemed impossible to Gedaliah, a man of transparent integrity and fidelity. It should be said that the Lord Jesus was not swayed by appearances. Although "many believed in his name, when they saw the miracles which he did", He "did not commit himself unto them, because he knew all men, And needed not that any should testify of man: for he knew what was in man" (Jn 2.23-25). Appearances can be deceptive, and for this reason Paul gave Timothy some good advice: "Lay hands suddenly on no man", and continued, "Some men's sins are open beforehand, going before to judgment; and some men they follow after. Likewise also the good works of some are manifest beforehand; and they that are otherwise cannot be hid" (1 Tim 5.22, 24-25).

His wish was refused (vv.15-16)

Having failed at the first attempt, Johanan tried again to save Gedaliah from assassination: "Let me go, I pray thee, and I will slay Ishmael the son of Nethaniah, and no man shall know it" (v.15) Johanan realised that Gedaliah's leadership was necessary for the survival of the remnant in Judah, and foresaw what would happen in the event of Gedaliah's death: "wherefore should he slay thee, that all the Jews which are gathered unto thee should be scattered, and the remnant in Judah perish?" (v.15). But his second attempt was also unsuccessful: "But Gedaiah the son of Ahikam said unto Johanan the son of Kareah, Thou shalt not do this thing: for thou speakest falsely of Ishmael" (v.16).

Subsequent events proved that Johanan's fears were well-grounded (41.1-3). Gedaliah, for all his virtues, was too trusting and naïf to believe Johanan's warning. He took no steps to investigate and verify Johanan's report, or to protect himself from danger. As Feinberg pertinently observes, "Gedaliah was right in forbidding Johanan to assassinate Ishmael, but wrong in his estimate of Ishmael".

Since good leadership is essential for the spiritual safety of assemblies, it is not surprising that elders are also subject to attack. Amongst other things, Paul had this in mind when, having arrived at Miletus, "he sent to Ephesus, and called the elders of the church" (Acts 20.17). In view of coming crises, he gave wise counsel to the Ephesian elders: "Take heed therefore unto yourselves, and to all the flock...For I know this, that after my departing shall grievous wolves enter in among you, not sparing the flock. Also of your own selves shall men arise, speaking perverse things, to draw away disciples after them. Therefore watch, and remember, that by the space of three years I ceased not to warn every one night and day with tears" (Acts 20.28-31). Timothy was similarly exhorted: "Take heed unto thyself, and unto the doctrine; continue in them: for in doing this thou shalt both save thyself, and them that hear thee" (1 Tim 4.16).

Sadly, Johanan failed to "take heed" to himself, with disastrous results for the people in his care.

JEREMIAH 41

Johanan's worst fears were realised within a short space of time. He had warned Gedaliah that his life was in danger: "Dost thou certainly know that Baalis the king of the Ammonites hath sent Ishmael the son of Nethaniah to slay thee?" (40.14), and pointed out the consequences: "wherefore should he slay thee, that all the Jews which are gathered unto thee should be scattered, and the remnant in Judah perish?" (40.15). Now, in the current chapter, Gedaliah pays the price for wrongly accusing Johanan of speaking falsely about Ishmael (40.16).

The narrative may be divided with reference to the three places named in the chapter:

> The Atrocities at Mizpah (vv.1-10)
> The Deliverance at Gibeon (vv.11-15)
> The Halt near Bethlehem (vv.16-18).

Verses 1-10: The Atrocities at Mizpah

It now becomes clear that Johanan had not been misinformed about Ishmael, and had not misunderstood the effect of his murderous intentions. Attention is drawn to the following: the assassination of Gedaliah (vv.1-3); the massacre of the pilgrims (vv.4-9); and the abduction of the remnant (v.10).

The assassination of Gedaliah (vv.1-3)

The murder of Gedaliah took place in the "seventh month", without any reference being made to the year in question, and it is not surprising that this omission has led most commentators to the conclusion that the dastardly crime was committed three months after the fall of Jerusalem (39.2). It should be said, however, that this is not universally accepted, and that some commentators appeal to 52.30 in postulating a later date, but this does seem unlikely. The assassination narrative speaks for itself. "Now it came to pass in the seventh month, that Ishmael the son of Nethaniah the son of Elishama, of the seed royal, and the princes of the king, even ten men with him, came unto Gedaliah the son of Ahikam to Mizpah; and there they did eat bread together at Mizpah. Then arose Ishmael the son of Nethaniah, and the ten men that were with him, and smote Gedaliah the son of Ahikam the son of Shaphan with the sword, and slew him, whom the king of Babylon had made governor over the land. Ishmael also slew all the Jews that were with him, even with Gedaliah at Mizpah, and the Chaldeans that were found there, and the men of war." The conjunction "and" in the last cause of v.3 is omitted in the Hebrew text so that the words "the men of war" refer to the Chaldeans (Ellicott's Commentary).

In spite of Johanan's warning, Gedaliah had taken no precautions, and the plot was carried out smoothly. Quite possibly the visit purported to be one of courtesy and recognition. "The remaining representatives of the house of David (v.1) would show that they were ready to welcome the new Satrap" (Ellicott's Commentary). Ishmael made no distinction between Jews and Babylonians; he killed all the men present, including Gedaliah's Babylonian bodyguard (v.3). The death of such a large group of men at the hands of eleven assassins indicates that the victims were completely unsuspecting. The reference to "all the Jews" must be restricted to those who were present with Gedaliah at Mizpah. The plot to kill him was carried out while Ishmael and his confederates were enjoying Gedaliah's hospitality. Their true intentions were masked by pretended fellowship.

In the New Testament, Paul assured the believers at Thessalonica of the integrity of his motives: "For our exhortation was not of deceit, nor of uncleanness, nor in guile: But as we were allowed of God to be put in trust with the gospel, even so we speak; not as pleasing men, but God, which trieth our hearts. For neither at any time used we flattering words, as ye know, nor a cloke of covetousness; God is witness" (1 Thess 2.3-5). Centuries before, Solomon warned against deception as follows: "He that hateth dissembleth with his lips, and layeth up deceit within him; When he speaketh fair, believe him not: for there are seven abominations in his heart" (Prov 26.24-25). The Lord Jesus warned His disciples to beware of "false prophets" coming "in sheep's clothing, but inwardly they are ravening wolves" (Mt 7.15).

The massacre of the pilgrims (vv.4-9)

The murderous intentions of Ishmael continued unabated. No one escaped to report the assassination of Gedaliah so that when, two day's later, eighty men arrived from Shechem, Shiloh and Samaria in mourning, bringing offerings to the now ruined Temple, they did not suspect the intentions of Ishmael: "And it came to pass the second day after he had slain Gedaliah, and no man knew it, That there came certain from Shechem, from Shiloh, and from Samaria, even fourscore men, having their beards shaven, and their clothes rent, and having cut themselves, with offerings (meal offerings) and incense in their hand, to bring them to the house of the Lord" (vv.4-5).

Shechem, Shiloh and Samaria were all located in the former northern kingdom (Israel) which had been colonised, on the instructions of the king of Assyria, by "men from Babylon, and from Cuthah, and from Ava, and from Hamath, and from Sepharvaim" (2 Kings 17.24). The eighty men are not identified, but possibly they belonged to the remnant left in the land (2 Chr 34.9), who evidently desired to continue to worship at Jerusalem and to keep the appointed feasts. The Feast of Trumpets, the Day of Atonement, and the Feast of Tabernacles all took place in the seventh month (Lev 23.24,27,34). Their desire to worship the Lord at Jerusalem was accompanied by "bloodless sacrifices because no facilities were available for animal sacrifices" (Feinberg), and heathen mourning. Through

Moses, the Lord had made it clear that His people were not to be like the idolatrous world, and to ape its customs and practices: "Ye shall not round the corners of your heads, neither shalt thou mar the corners of thy beard. Ye shall not make any cuttings in your flesh for the dead, nor print any marks upon you: I am the Lord" (Lev 19.27-28); "Ye are the children of the Lord your God: ye shall not cut yourselves, nor make any baldness between your eyes for the dead" (Deut 14.1). Unconverted men and women today disfigure themselves in other ways, such as tattooing and body-piercing in various forms. They damage their bodies by smoking and drinking. These are practices which should not, in Paul's words, "be once named among you, as becometh saints" (Eph 5.3).

Joining them as they neared Mizpah, Ishmael showed every sign of sharing their sorrow, but on arrival there most of them shared the fate of Gedaliah: "And Ishmael the son of Nethaniah went forth from Mizpah to meet them, weeping all along as he went: and it came to pass, as he met them, he said unto them, Come to Gedaliah the son of Ahikam. And it was so, when they came into the midst of the city, that Ishmael the son of Nethaniah slew them, and cast them into the midst of the pit, he and the men that were with him" (vv.6-7). "Just as in the assassination of Gedaliah, Ishmael used the element of surprise. Here it enabled eleven men to slaughter seventy of the eighty pilgrims. The motive for the massacre is not entirely clear. It may have been done for plunder and to intimidate the remnant in Judah" (Feinberg).

Ishmael's "crocodile tears" remind us that "Satan himself is transformed into an angel of light" (2 Cor 11.14). With such dangers facing them today, the Lord's people must watch and pray, and not be "ignorant of his devices" (2 Cor 2.11).

There were, however, ten men who were able to buy their lives: "But ten men were found among them that said unto Ishmael, Slay us not: for we have treasures in the field, of wheat, and of barley, and of oil, and of honey. So he forbare, and slew them not among their brethren" (v.8). Streane explains that the expression "treasures in the field" refers to "hidden stores": "In the East it is to this day a common custom to use wells or cisterns for grain. In them the farmers store their crops of all kinds after the grain is threshed and winnowed. These cisterns are cool, perfectly dry, and tight. The top is hermetically sealed with plaster, and covered with a deep bed of earth…They would not answer in a wet country, but in these dry climates stores have been found quite fresh and sound many years after they were thus buried".

The pit mentioned into which the bodies were thrown is not elsewhere mentioned in Scripture, but it was presumably an old cistern, constructed centuries before for the storage of water by King Asa when he fortified Mizpah against a possible attack by Baasha (1 Kings 15.22; 2 Chr 16.6): "Now the pit wherein Ishmael had cast all the dead bodies of the men, whom he had slain because of Gedaliah, was it which Asa the king had made for fear of Baasha king of Israel: and Ishmael the son of Nethaniah filled it with them that were slain" (v.9). According to Ellicott's Commentary, the words "because of Gedaliah" are literally 'by the hand of Gedaliah', and refer to the usage of his name by Ishmael in beguiling the unsuspecting pilgrims.

The abduction of the remnant (v.10)

Ishmael's next move was to transport the remnant from Mizpah to Ammon. Johanan had stated that Ishmael had been commissioned by the king of Ammon to slay Gedaliah, and it is not therefore surprising that he makes for Ammonite territory with the king's daughters and all who remained at Mizpah: "Then Ishmael carried away captive all the residue of the people that were in Mizpah, even the king's daughters, and all the people that remained in Mizpah, whom Nebuzar-adan the captain of the guard had committed to Gedaliah the son of Ahikam: and Ishmael the son of Nethaniah carried them away captive, and departed to go over to the Ammonites". While, undoubtedly, he feared reprisals from the Chaldeans, he could have intended to "sell the remnant as slaves to the Ammonites" (Feinberg). Since Jeremiah was at Mizpah, he was evidently among the contingent carried off by Ishmael. In the words of Laetsch, "A dozen energetic gangsters, well armed, may easily hold several hundreds of unarmed men and women and children in panicky fear by threatening to kill everyone who would dare show the least sign of resistance".

The abduction of the Jews by Ishmael illustrates the way in which men with forceful characters can dominate others against their will. John describes Diotrephes in this way: "Diotrephes, who loveth to have the preeminence among them, receiveth us not...prating against us with malicious words: and not content therewith, neither doth he himself receive the brethren, and forbiddeth them that would, and casteth them out of the church" (3 Jn vv.9-10). The Lord Jesus described men like these as "thieves and robbers" whose business was "to steal, and to kill, and to destroy" (Jn 10.8,10). Paul described them as "grievous wolves...not sparing the flock" (Acts 20.29).

Verses 11-15: The Deliverance at Gibeon

But now the news was out, and Johanan and his fellow-captains pursued Ishmael, overtaking him at Gibeon. "But when Johanan the son of Kareah, and all the captains of the forces that were with him, heard of all the evil that Ishmael the son of Nethaniah had done, Then they took all the men, and went to fight with Ishmael the son of Nethaniah, and found him by the great waters that are in Gibeon. Now it came to pass, that when all the people which were with Ishmael saw Johanan the son of Kareah, and all the captains of the forces that were with him, then they were glad. So all the people that Ishmael had carried away captive from Mizpah cast about and returned, and went unto Johanan the son of Kareah" (vv.11-14).

According to Feinberg, Gibeon is only a mile from Mizpah, but it has been suggested that Ishmael may have taken a circuitous route to confuse his pursuers. According to Harrison, the great pool of Gibeon (v.12) is "probably a reference to the large, rock-hewn cistern found at el-Jib (cp. 2 Sam 2.13), dating from the early Iron Age. This pit had been excavated thirty-five feet down into the rock, with steps leading down into a tunnel a further forty feet to a water chamber".

Faced with a superior force, Ishmael and eight of his men made their escape: "But Ishmael the son of Nethaniah escaped from Johanan with eight men, and went to the Ammonites" (v.15). Possibly two of Ishmael's men had been slain during the rescue operation. While the remainder "went scot-free as far as the records go" (Laetsch) this does not mean that they escaped punishment. The prosperity of the wicked caused the Psalmist great concern: "When I thought to know this, it was too painful for me", but only "Until I went into the sanctuary of God; then understood I their end" (Ps 73.16-17).

Verses 16-18: The Halt near Bethlehem

These verses describe the preparation for departure to Egypt, which seemed to be the only recourse in the circumstances (v.18). The departure from Judah and the arrival in Egypt are described in chapters 42 and 43. While Johanan had exhibited good leadership in recovering the captives, this did not continue, and he proceeded to lead the people in the wrong direction. In this he followed Gideon who was used by the Lord to dispossess the Midianites, but who ended by leading the people into idolatry (Judg 8.27). Solomon did the same (1 Kings 11.1-8).

Leaders amongst the Lord's people today need to seek the His guidance for themselves before they attempt to guide His people, but Johanan made up his mind first, and then consulted the Lord (42.3). Sadly, the consultation was purely cosmetic (42.20). He had forgotten the advice of Solomon in his better days: "Trust in the Lord with all thine heart; and lean not unto thine own understanding. In all thy ways acknowledge him, and he shall direct thy paths" (Prov 3.5-6.).

The following should be noticed in these verses: the resolution to find refuge in Egypt (vv.16-17a); the rest on the way to Egypt (v.17b); and the reason for seeking refuge in Egypt (v.18).

The resolution to find refuge in Egypt (vv.16-17a)

"Then took Johanan the son of Kareah, and all the captains of the forces that were with him, all the remnant of the people whom he had recovered from Ishmael the son of Nethaniah, from Mizpah, after that he had slain Gedaliah the son of Ahikam, even mighty men of war, and the women, and the children, and the eunuchs, whom he had brought again from Gibeon: And they departed…to go to enter into Egypt."

The resolve of the leadership should be noted. Johanan and his colleagues had determined to remove the Lord's people from their national inheritance, where there was a measure of security, and take them to a place which would prove utterly insecure. This was nothing less than worldly wisdom. They were leading the Lord's people back to the very place from which God had originally delivered them. Moses chose "rather to suffer affliction with the people of God, than to enjoy the pleasures of sin for a season; Esteeming the reproach of Christ greater riches than the treasures in Egypt: for he had respect unto the recompence of the reward" (Heb 11.25-26). Egypt would prove a very unsuitable place for the remnant in Judah (43.8-13), and the world, with its pleasures, pastimes and entertainment, is a very unsuitable place for the Lord's people today, and their leaders must use great care in guiding "the flock of God" (1 Pet 5.2). They must emulate "the good shepherd" who "calleth his own sheep by name, and leadeth them out" (Jn 10.3).

The rest on the way to Egypt (v.17b)

From Gibeon, north of Jerusalem, Johanan and his company journeyed to Bethlehem, south of Jerusalem, *en route* for Egypt: "And they departed, and dwelt in the habitation of Chimham, which is by Bethlehem, to go to enter into Egypt". The contrast is significant: David was associated with Chimham in his return to Jerusalem (2 Sam 19.31-40), whereas Johanan is associated with Chimham's name in the return to Egypt!

The "habitation of Chimham" was apparently part of a grant of land by David to Chimham in appreciation of the services rendered by Barzillai the Gileadite, who refreshed David when he fled from Absalom (2 Sam 17.27-29). It seems that Chimham had built the place as a resting place for travellers. According to Streane, "the Hebrew word for 'habitation' (1628) occurs only here…The need for shelter led very early to the erection of rude and simple buildings of varying size, known as khans, which offered the wayfarer the protection of walls and a roof, and water, but little more…From immemorial antiquity it has been a favourite mode of benevolence to raise such places of shelter. The special utility of this khan lay in its being on the great caravan route to Egypt. Such was the inn, and in that very neighbourhood too, in which "there was no room" for the mother of our Lord and Joseph just before the Nativity (Lk 2.7)".

The reason for seeking refuge in Egypt (v.18)

The party was travelling to Egypt "Because of the Chaldeans: for they were afraid of them, because Ishmael the son of Nethaniah had slain Gedaliah the son of Ahikam, whom the king of Babylon made governor in the land". The murder of Gedaliah seemed certain to incur the wrath of the Chaldeans, and Egypt seemed their only refuge. As events were to prove, what seemed to be a sure refuge with far more advantages than Judah, proved to be disastrous, and served to confirm the words of

Solomon that "The fear of man bringeth a snare: but whoso putteth his trust in the Lord shall be safe" (Prov 29.25).

The following chapter will show that their intentions were far from the will of God. They had no need to fear (42.10-12) and as Feinberg points out, "Johanan was wrong in thinking flight to Egypt was the only solution to the problems of the remnant. Actually, it created other problems, and certainly it did not place them beyond the reach of Nebuchadnezzar". They lived to prove the veracity of God's word: "Cursed be the man that trusteth in man, and maketh flesh his arm, and whose heart departeth from the Lord. For he shall be like the heath in the desert, and shall not see when good cometh; but shall inhabit the parched places of the wilderness, in a salt land and not inhabited" (17.5-6).

JEREMIAH 42

Laetsch may not be far wrong in saying, "Perhaps the very next morning the leaders, together with the people, assembled before Jeremiah in order to receive an oracle from the Lord". The "remnant" (v.2), that is, those survivors who remained in Judah after the fall of Jerusalem, had already decided to leave their homeland, fearing retaliation by the Babylonians for the murder of Gedaliah (41.18). From their perspective Egypt appeared to be a safe haven, and they were already *en route* to Tahpanhes (43.7). While still evidently encamped near Bethlehem, they approached Jeremiah and ostensibly requested his help in obtaining guidance from the Lord, even though their decision had already been made. Their request for the Lord's guidance was cosmetic; they were actually seeking confirmation of their own plans.

This chapter may be divided into two major sections:

> The Request to Jeremiah (vv.1-6)
> The Reply by Jeremiah (vv.7-22).

Verses 1-6: The Request to Jeremiah

Attention is drawn in these verses to the request by the people (vv.1-3); the reply by Jeremiah (v.4); and the response of the people (vv.5-6).

The request by the people (vv.1-3)

At first glance, this seemed most commendable. The way in which the request was made carried every expectation of divine approval:

They were unanimous

"Then all the captains of the forces, and Johanan the son Kareah, and Jezaniah the son of Hoshaiah, and all the people from the least even unto the greatest, came near, And said unto Jeremiah the prophet, Let, we beseech thee, our supplication be accepted before thee" (vv.1-2). Unity amongst the Lord's people is vital. The assembly at Jerusalem "lifted up their voice to God with one accord" (Acts 4.24). It is so important to be "likeminded, having the same love, being of one accord, of one mind" (Phil 2.2).

They asked a man of God to pray for them

"...pray for us unto the Lord thy God, even for all this remnant" (v.2). They exhibited recognition and respect for Jeremiah. It could be said that they recognised that "The effectual fervent prayer of a righteous man availeth much" (James 5.16). However, Ironside makes the valid point that "It is always a bad sign when there is diffidence in approaching God; when the petitioner has more confidence in the prayers of a ministering servant than in his own. Unmistakably, it reveals the lack of communion with God which inspires confidence in the hour of need".

They recognised their own weakness

"...we are left but a few of many, as thine eyes do behold us" (v.2). Jehoshaphat recognised the weakness of Judah at the time of invasion in saying, "we have no might against this great company that cometh against us; neither know we what to do: but our eyes are upon thee" (2 Chr 20.12), and victory followed. Confession of personal weakness leads to divinely-given strength. The Apostle Paul recognised his own weakness in writing, "For this thing I besought the Lord thrice, that it (the 'thorn in the flesh') might depart from me. And he said unto me, My grace is sufficient for thee: for my strength is made perfect in weakness", leading Paul to say, "when I am weak, then am I strong" (2 Cor 12.8-10).

They sought divine guidance

"...pray for us...That the Lord thy God may shew us the way wherein we may walk, and the thing that we may do" (vv.2-3). Paul prayed that the believers at Colosse "might be filled with the knowledge of his will in all wisdom and spiritual understanding", and "walk worthy of the Lord unto all pleasing, being fruitful in every good work, and increasing in the knowledge of God" (Col 1.9-10).

For completeness, the response of the people to Jeremiah's reply should be included at this point.

They promised to obey the Lord's instructions

"Whether it be good, or whether it be evil, we will obey the voice of the Lord our God" (v.6).

All this would be quite splendid if they had been intent on "doing the will of God from the heart" (Eph 6.6). But, sadly, this was not the case: "ye dissembled in your hearts, when ye sent me unto the Lord your God, saying, Pray for us unto the Lord our God; and according unto all that the Lord our God shall say, so declare unto us, and we will do it" (v.20). Feinberg points out that although "most expositors consider their enquiry a hypocritical one", others "have suggested that if it had been such, the Lord would not have responded but would have exposed their hypocrisy". But this, surely, is exactly what He did ten days later (vv.7, 19-22). Very clearly, they earnestly wanted confirmation of their decision, not guidance from the Lord! "Self-interest has predominated once again, and now their concern is merely to know if God will approve their plan to migrate to Egypt. They are not seeking spiritual guidance in the usual sense of that term" (Harrison).

The reply by Jeremiah (v.4)

"Then Jeremiah the prophet said unto them, I have heard you; behold, I will pray unto the Lord your God according to your words; and it shall come to pass, that whatsoever thing the Lord shall answer you, I will declare it unto you; I will keep nothing back from you." "Jeremiah gently reminds the remnant that the Lord is their God, as well as his" (Feinberg). They had said to him: "pray for us unto the Lord *thy* God" (v.2), and he replied by saying, "I will pray unto the Lord *your* God" (v.4). Whereas in the past, Jeremiah was commanded, "pray not thou for this people" (7.16; 11.14), or "Pray not for this people" (14.11), this prohibition was no longer in force; divine judgment had been executed on Jerusalem and the people were no longer worshipping idols. Regrettably, this was to change once the people arrived in Egypt (44.7-8). Jeremiah's words, "I will keep nothing back from you", imply that he already knew that the answer might not be to their liking. Eli evidently thought the same when he said to Samuel, "What is the thing that the Lord hath said unto thee? I pray thee hide it not from me: God do so to thee, and more also, if thou hide any thing from me of all the things that he said unto thee" (1 Sam 3.17). At an early age, Samuel learned the importance of faithfully conveying God's word to others, even though they might find it unpalatable. Servants of God must not shun to "declare all the…counsel of God" (Acts 20.27).

The response of the people (vv.5-6)
    They declared their willingness to obey the word of the Lord, whatever it involved: "The Lord be a true and faithful witness between us, if we do not even according to all things for which the Lord *thy* God shall send thee to us" (v.5) and then "growing bolder" (Ironside), they used the term "the Lord *our* God" in declaring, "Whether it be good, or whether it be evil, we will obey the voice of the Lord our God, to whom we send thee; that it may be well with us, when we obey the voice of the Lord our God" (v.6). These were "good words and fair speeches" (Rom 16.18), and the Lord certainly took them at face value; He did prove to be "a true and faithful witness" when they disobeyed His word. He spelt out the consequences of disobedience at the time (vv.13-18) and later in Egypt (44.11-14). The Word of God cannot be disobeyed with impunity. The Lord's people today must be careful what they say and what they sing. Despite their profession, the Judæan "remnant" were only prepared to obey if it suited their plans (43.2). The Pulpit Commentary puts it very clearly indeed: "If we take counsel with God, we must consent to obey Him. Otherwise our prayer is a mockery; for God is not an Oracle, but an Authority. What He reveals is not merely hidden mystery, but obligations of duty. He guides us to His will. It is our place to follow the guidance and do what is thus not only declared, but commanded". Taken out of context, the words "we will obey…that it may be well with us, when we obey the voice of the Lord our God", make good reading, but not in the context of this chapter!

Verses 7-22: The Reply by Jeremiah
    "And it came to pass after ten days, that the word of the Lord came unto Jeremiah" (v.7). While the episode generally does the Lord's people here no credit, it must be said that at least they waited until the Lord answered

their request through Jeremiah. They might have set out for Egypt without delay! Saul made the mistake of acting before the arrival of Samuel and was told, "Thou hast done foolishly" (1 Sam 13.13). No reason is given for the delay of ten days before Jeremiah received the word of the Lord, but "we should learn that prayer does not fail because the response is not immediate. Whatever be the delay, we may be sure that to true prayer in Christ's Name the right answer will come at the right time. God is not dilatory. He will never wait beyond the best season for acting" (The Pulpit Commentary). Ezekiel waited for seven days before the word of the Lord came to him by the river Chebar (Ezek 3.15-16).

It should be carefully noted that Jeremiah, who doubtless "gave himself to prayer" (Meyer), said nothing until he had received the Lord's explicit word. Feinberg makes an excellent comment here: "This passage (vv.7-17) sheds light on the inspiration of the prophets. They did not confuse God's revelation with personal desires or judgments. They would not announce God's will until they knew it. Scripture always distinguishes between the subjective (the prophet's own thoughts) and the objective (the word of God) in all revelatory matters".

The balance of the chapter may be divided as follows: the alternatives (vv.8-18); and the accusation (vv.19-22).

The alternatives (vv.8-18)

"Then called he Johanan the son of Kareah, and all the captains of the forces which were with him, and all the people from the least even to the greatest (cp. v.1), And said unto them, Thus saith the Lord, the God of Israel, unto whom ye sent me to present your supplication before him" (vv.8-9). Jeremiah then spelt out the results of remaining in the land (vv.10-12); and removing from the land (vv.13-18).

Remaining in the land (vv.10-12)

"If ye will still abide in this land, then will I build you, and not pull you down, and I will plant you, and not pluck you up" (v.10). This should be compared with 1.10 and 24.6. The Lord would *prosper them*. Ironside has a nice thought here: "What riches of grace are here unfolded! On their part, no adequate sense of guilt; yet on His, such amazing compassion and loving-kindness. If they will but trust Him now in their weak, broken state - if they will rely upon His mighty arm and thus dwell in the land He had given them - if they will accept the chastisement, and bow to His Word, then He will build them up and care for them as a husbandman cares for his vintage".

It should be pointed out that when, as here, reference is made to divine repentance, "for I repent me of the evil that I have done unto you" (v.10), the Lord does not change His will, but He does deal with men according to their obedience or disobedience to His will. With the Lord, repentance is not a change of mind and will, but a response consistent with a change of conduct as in the case of Nineveh: "And God saw their works, that they turned from their evil way; and God repented of the evil, that he had said that he would do unto them; and he did it not" (Jonah 3.10). In this case, genuine obedience to His will would bring divine blessing, as opposed to the divine judgment executed in the fall of Jerusalem following blatant disobedience to His word.

Moreover, the Lord would *protect them*: "Be not afraid of the king of Babylon, of whom ye are afraid; be not afraid of him, saith the Lord: for I am with you to save you, and to deliver you from his hand. And I will shew mercies unto you, that he may have mercy upon you, and cause you to return to your own land" (vv.11-12). By remaining in the land, they were assured of the Lord's presence ("I am with you"), of His active help ("to save you"), and of His continuing mercy ("I will shew mercies unto you"). The words, "cause you to return to your own land", give some commentators difficulty, and one explanation is that the alteration of one vowel in the original text would give the rendering "cause you to *dwell* in your own land" (Streane), or "permit you to *remain* in your own land" (Harrison). However, the reader should beware of suggested alterations to the text in this way, and it is more likely that the Judæan remnant, *en route* to Egypt, were assured that the Lord would constrain the king of Babylon to allow them "to return each man to his own field and vineyard" (Ellicott's Commentary).

In many places today, assemblies are in a "weak, broken state" (Ironside), and for them the future seems decidedly uncertain. When national life was threatened, the Lord urged His people to turn to Him in genuine sorrow and repentance: "turn ye even to me with all your heart, and with fasting, and with weeping, and with mourning: And rend your heart, and not your garments, and turn unto the Lord your God: for he is gracious and merciful, slow to anger, and of great kindness, and repenteth him of the evil. Who knoweth if he will return and repent, and leave a blessing behind him?" (Joel 2.12-14). Rather than abandoning the local assembly, believers are called upon to "Be watchful, and strengthen the things which remain, that are ready to die" and to "hold fast, and repent" (Rev 3.2-3).

Removing from the land (vv.13-18)
To do this would be a case of willful disobedience, and incur certain judgment: "But if ye say, We *will not* dwell in this land, neither obey the voice of the Lord your God, Saying, No; but *we will* go into the land of Egypt, where we shall see no war, nor hear the sound of the trumpet, nor have hunger of bread; and there will we dwell…If ye wholly *set your faces* to enter into Egypt, and go to sojourn there; Then it shall come to pass, that the sword, which ye feared, shall overtake you there in the land of Egypt, and the famine, whereof ye were afraid, shall follow close after you there in Egypt; and there ye shall die" (vv.13-16).

Quite clearly, Jeremiah knew that the Judæan remnant found Egypt most attractive. It has been pointed out that although Nebuchadnezzar had defeated Egypt at the battle of Carchemish (605 BC), the country had not itself been the scene of military action. In Egypt, they anticipated "no war, nor…the sound of the trumpet" (v.14). Babylon was a long way from Egypt, and not, they thought, liable to invasion. Moreover, it was one of the granaries of the ancient world, and therefore they anticipated no "hunger of bread" (v.14). But God's people seemed to have forgotten that "their fathers, beginning by going to Egypt for bread, ended by sinking into most oppressive bondage" (The Pulpit Commentary). However great the advantages might appear, it was worse than folly to trust in Egypt, rather than in the Lord. Amongst other things it would bring them into an idolatrous land (43.12) where they would be exposed to evil and impurity of the worst kind. Not only so, it meant placing themselves in the very country from which they had been delivered on the basis of shed blood. This constitutes an important lesson for the Lord's people today. The New Testament states that the Lord Jesus "gave himself for our sins, that he might deliver us from this present evil world, according to the will of God and our Father" (Gal 1.4). The injunction, "Love not the world, neither the things that are in the world" (1 Jn 2.15), should never be forgotten.

Recourse to Egypt would provide no security for the Jewish remnant, anymore than the world does for God's people today: "So shall it be with all the men that set their faces to go into Egypt to sojourn there; they shall die by the sword, by the famine, and by the pestilence: and none of them shall remain or escape from the evil that I will bring upon them…and ye shall be an execration, and an astonishment, and a curse, and a reproach; and ye shall see this place no more" (vv.17-18). The very calamities they feared would overtake them in the very place where they expected safety. "The survivors of the Fall of Jerusalem and Judah would suffer the same fate in Egypt that had overtaken them because of their disobedience" (Feinberg).

The accusation (vv.19-22)

Having warned the people against emigrating to Egypt (vv.13-18), Jeremiah repeats the Lord's prohibition, and exposes their duplicity: "The Lord hath said concerning you, O ye remnant of Judah; Go ye not into Egypt: know certainly that I have admonished you (testified against you) this day. For ye dissembled in your hearts, when ye sent me unto the Lord your God, saying, Pray for us unto the Lord our God; and according unto all that the Lord our God shall say, so declare unto us, and we will do it" (vv.19-20). Their request for the Lord's guidance was nothing more than pretence. They had already made up their minds to seek refuge in Egypt.

The words, "ye dissembled in your hearts" ("ye deceived yourselves in your own souls", JND; with the marginal reading, "led astray by your own souls"), indicate that they had deceived themselves by thinking that since they could see no alternative, divine approval must rest on their settled plans to leave Judah for Egypt. They had said, "according unto all that the Lord our God shall say, so declare unto us, and we will do it" (v.20), but in reality they had no intention of doing otherwise than implementing their own decision. Jeremiah had done exactly what they asked: "And now I have this day declared it to you" (v.21). But his reply was not what they wanted. They had thought that they could secure the Lord's blessing on their plans. "All the time they had intended doing their own will in the hope that God's will would coincide with theirs" (Feinberg).

Some commentators, perhaps using a little imagination, suggest that at this point Jeremiah saw the downcast faces of his audience (Ellicott's Commentary refers to their "Looks and whispers") and, without waiting for their reply, he proceeded by saying, "but ye have not obeyed the voice of the Lord your God, nor any thing for the which he hath sent me unto you" (v.21). The prophet had no alternative but to pronounce the very judgments against which he had warned them earlier (vv.16-18): "Now therefore know certainly that ye shall die by the sword, by the famine, and by the pestilence, in the place whither ye *desire to go and to sojourn*" (v.22). As Harrison observes, "They have shown themselves no better than their disobedient forebears, and thus equally deserving of the same kind of punishment".

Harrison's final comment is worthy of special attention: "Far too many Christians also expect God to honour plans which are none of His making".

JEREMIAH 43

Since the "remnant of Judah" (42.15) had already decided to seek refuge in Egypt, although professing obedience to the Lord in whatever He directed (42.5-6), it is not surprising that their leaders quickly rounded on Jeremiah once he had rebuked their deceit, and warned them that their plans would only end in disaster (42.19-22). He had hardly finished speaking when Azariah, Johanan and "all the proud men" voiced their opposition to his message and accused him of speaking falsely (43.2). But the charge that they had "not obeyed the voice of the Lord" (42.21) was completely justified. They soon implemented their plans: "So they came into the land of Egypt: for they obeyed not the voice of the Lord: thus came they even to Tahpanhes" (v.7). The narrative in this chapter begins in Judah, and ends in Egypt.

The chapter may be divided as follows:

> The Indictment of Jeremiah (vv.1-3)
> The Intransigence of Johanan (vv.4-7)
> The Invasion by Nebuchadnezzar (vv.8-13).

Verses 1-3: The Indictment of Jeremiah

Attention is drawn in these verses to the integrity of the accused (v.1); and the insolence of the accusers (vv.2-3).

The integrity of the accused (v.1)

Jeremiah spoke "unto all the people all the words of the Lord their God, for which the Lord their God had sent him to them, even all these words". He had not forgotten the terms of his commission some forty years previously: "thou shalt go to all that I shall send thee, and whatsoever I command thee thou shalt speak" (1.7); "arise, and speak unto them all that I command thee" (1.17). He was told later, approximately halfway through his ministry, to "Stand in the court of the Lord's house, and speak unto all the cities of Judah…all the words that I command thee to speak unto them; diminish not a word" (26.2). Now, as his preaching neared its end, he faithfully conveyed the word of the Lord to a hostile audience: he was not "dismayed at their faces" (1.17), and Paul's words would have been most appropriate in the mouth of Jeremiah: "none of these things move me" (Acts 20.24). Like the apostle, he "kept the faith" (2 Tim 4.7) to the end of the journey. Unlike some of the Lord's servants who started well in His service, but failed later, Jeremiah never made shipwreck. He was certainly amongst those described by James: "Take, my brethren, the prophets, who have spoken in the name of the Lord, for an example of suffering affliction, and of patience. Behold, we count them happy which endure" (James 5.10-11).

The insolence of the accusers (vv.2-3)

The Lord's servant was indicted on two counts: they said that he had misled them (v.2); and they said that he had been manipulated (v.3).

They said that he had misled them

"Then spake Azariah the son of Hoshaiah, and Johanan the son of Kareah, and all the proud men, saying unto Jeremiah, Thou speakest falsely: the Lord our God hath not sent thee to say, Go not into Egypt, to sojourn there" (v.2). It should be noticed that no attempt was made to answer Jeremiah's arguments. Instead, they challenged his veracity. Laetsch calls this "the old trick of Satan" and refers to the serpent's words, "Yea, hath God said?" (Gen 3.1). Feinberg may well be right in suggesting that by accusing Jeremiah of lying, they attempted to divert attention from their own broken promise to obey the Lord's message.

It is noticeable in Scripture that when men are defeated in argument, they resort to false accusation. Stephen's opponents "were not able to resist the wisdom and the spirit by which he spake", and "suborned men, which said, We have heard him speak blasphemous words against Moses, and against God...And set up false witnesses, which said, This man ceaseth not to speak blasphemous words against this holy place, and the law" (Acts 6.10,11,13). The religious leaders used the same tactics against the Lord Jesus (Mt 26.59-60). The Lord's people must not expect unbelievers to be always open and above board when they oppose their Christian witness. Some people will use fair means or foul in endeavouring to confound or silence them.

The expression "all the proud men" refers to more than pride in the commonly-accepted meaning of the word. According to Gesenius, the word "proud" (2086) means pride "with the connected idea of insolence and impiety". Laetsch vividly describes "the proud men" as "insolent, arrogant bullies, loudmouthed ruffians that invariably get to the front in times of trouble and assume the leadership".

They said that he had been manipulated

"Baruch the son of Neriah setteth thee on against us, for to deliver us into the hand of the Chaldeans, that they might put us to death, and carry us away captives into Babylon" (v.3). They accused Baruch of "conniving to get Jeremiah to deliver the remnant to the Babylonians" (Feinberg). While it is true that Jeremiah was by this time quite an old man and therefore, in the minds of his accusers, possibly under the influence of Baruch, there was "not a scintilla of evidence" for the charge: "The prophet who would not trim his message for the king (38.14-23), would never have been manipulated by his secretary" (Feinberg).

Verses 4-7: The Intransigence of Johanan

Jeremiah had nothing further to say. He had delivered the message entrusted to him by the Lord, and faithfully pointed out the fearful consequences of disobedience, but to no avail: "So Johanan the son of Kareah, and all the captains of the forces, and all the people, obeyed not the voice of the Lord, to dwell in the land of Judah. But Johanan the son of Kareah, and all the captains of the forces, took all the remnant of Judah, that were returned from all nations, whither they had been driven, to dwell in the land of Judah; Even men, and women, and children, and the king's daughters, and every person that Nebuzar-adan the captain of the guard had left with Gedaliah the son of Ahikam the son of Shaphan, and Jeremiah the prophet, and Baruch the son of Neriah. So they came into the land of Egypt: for they obeyed not the voice of the Lord: thus came they even to Tahpanhes". According to Feinberg, Tahpanhes, or Tahapanes (2.16) was "a fortress city on the northern border of Lower Egypt, guarding the road to Syria. Pharaoh had a palace there. Located on the Pelusian branch of the Nile, Tahpanhes was known to the Greeks as Daphne. It is the modern Tell el-Defenneh". The town lies approximately twenty-seven miles south-west of Port Said. It is generally thought that the exiles would have been compelled to halt there in order to secure permission to take up residence in the country. It has to be said while the expression "*all* the remnant of Judah" (v.5) means exactly what it says, Jeremiah and Baruch, at the very least, must have been taken to Egypt against their will.

These verses are quite self-explanatory, and it should be carefully noted that they commence and conclude with the words, "they obeyed not the voice of the Lord" (vv.4,7). In this way they clearly proclaimed the emptiness of their declaration, "we will obey the voice of the Lord our God" (42.6). It cannot be over-emphasised that the Lord's people are to be "obedient children" (1 Pet 1.14), and that "to obey is better than sacrifice, and to hearken than the fat of rams" (1 Sam 15.22).

The words, "So they came into the land of Egypt" (v.7), should not escape notice. "Thus the descendants of Abraham returned to Egypt after nine hundred years…It carries the mind involuntarily back to the night much to be remembered, when with a high hand, and outstretched arm, God had delivered them from the yoke of Pharaoh…And now after nine hundred years they returned, a remnant of exiles, fleeing in fear and rebellion, the very act of their coming to Egypt one of definite disobedience to the most recent message of the prophet of God" (Campbell Morgan). Having reviewed what he calls the "curious tendency to go to Egypt" in Israel's history, beginning with Abraham, Campbell Morgan continues: "All this is illustrative of the same principle, the return of a great people, an emancipated and illuminated people, to the things from which they seemed to have emerged, which in themselves were things of disaster and destruction and evil". These solemn and thought-provoking words highlight the danger of returning in spirit and desire to this "present evil world" (Gal 1.4) for apparent safety and satisfaction. To do this is to ignore the Old Testament warning: "Woe to them that go down to Egypt for help;

and stay on horses, and trust in chariots, because they are many; and in horsemen, because they are very strong; but they look not unto the Holy One of Israel, neither seek the Lord!…Now the Egyptians are men, and not God; and their horses flesh, and not spirit. When the Lord shall stretch our his hand, both he that helpeth shall fall, and he that is holpen shall fall down, and they all shall fail ('perish', JND) together" (Is 31.1,3). This is precisely what would happen to the Judæan remnant in Egypt (Jer 44.11-14). The New Testament warns similarly: "Love not the world, neither the things that are in the world. If any man love the world, the love of the Father is not in him…And the world passeth away, and the lust thereof: but he that doeth the will of God abideth for ever" (1 Jn 2.15,17).

Verses 8-13: The Invasion by Nebuchadrezzar

On arrival at Tahpanhes, Jeremiah receives a further communication from the Lord. In the words of Campbell Morgan, "The word of God still comes…The word of Jehovah came to Jeremiah in the dark days. These days were yet darker. All his prophesying had now been fulfilled after forty years. The city was a ruin; the house of God was burned; the captives were carried away; those that remained were fleeing in abject fear to Egypt. At last they came to Tahpanhes, the frontier fortress of the forbidden ground. The word of Jehovah came to them there. God never leaves Himself without a witness". The "word of the Lord" (v.8) confirmed the earlier message that "the sword, which ye feared, shall overtake you there in the land of Egypt" (42.16).

These verses refer to: the sign (v.9); and the significance (vv.10-13).

The sign (v.9)

"Take great stones in thine hand, and hide them in the clay in the brickkiln, which is at the entry of Pharaoh's house in Tahpanhes, in the sight of the men of Judah." This, like the sign of the linen girdle (13.1-11) was an "acted oracle". According to Gesenius, the word rendered "clay" (4423) refers to "cement, so called from being spread or smoothed over". According to Streane, the words "hide them in the clay" mean "cover them over with mortar". It is thought that word rendered "brickkiln" (4404), which means "a place connected with bricks" (Streane), refers to a brick pavement at the entrance of Pharaoh's palace at Tahpanhes. It does seem unlikely that Pharaoh would have had a brick kiln on his doorstep, although Streane states that "such a thing…is far from impossible in that country and at that time". Others suggest that "Pharaoh's house" does not refer to his palace, but to "some kind of official building used by the king when he visited this frontier city" (Habel).

As Harrison points out, "Just how Jeremiah was to accomplish this task is not stated, but it was evidently to be in the nature of an acted parable". In the nineteenth century, Flinders Petrie excavated Tahpanhes and "cleared a paved area in front of the entrance to the royal dwelling, identifying it with the 'platform' mentioned in this verse" (Harrison). Campbell Morgan goes further and states that "A few years ago, Professor Flinders Petrie discovered at Tel Defenneh a large brickwork pavement with great stones buried underneath. Jeremiah's stones!" His next words are less dramatic, but even more important: "The word of God is for ever proclaiming a fact, and producing it". It is important to notice that Jeremiah was to hide the great stones in this way "in the sight of the men of Judah" (v.9), so that when the sign became a reality the Judæan remnant would know that the Lord was fulfilling His word. Only the Lord can declare "the end from the beginning, and from ancient times the things that are not yet done" (Is 46.10). The arrival of Nebuchadrezzar in Egypt (v.10) could not be attributed to the fortunes of war or to a quirk of fate, but to the determining will of God.

The significance (vv.10-13)

"And say unto them, Thus saith the Lord of hosts, the God of Israel; Behold, I will send and take Nebuchadrezzar the king of Babylon, my servant, and will set his throne upon these stones that I have hid; and he shall spread his royal pavilion over them" (v.10). The king of Babylon is called "my servant" for the same reason that Cyrus is called "my shepherd" (Is 44.28). Both potentates were used by the Lord in fulfilling His will. Laetsch compares "Mighty Nebuchadnezzar, a puppet in God's hand" with "Jeremiah, God's representative" and adds, "Of the two servants of God, Jeremiah, the prophet despised and rejected by his people, is by far the greater and more honourable".

There is no ambiguity about the prediction. Precise details are given here, with more to follow (vv.11-13). Nebuchadrezzar would not only invade Egypt, but the specific location of his throne is clearly identified. The word rendered "pavilion" (8237) occurs only here in the Bible, and its meaning is uncertain, with "canopy" or "carpet" being suggested. Streane favours the former with the translation, "his canopy shall be stretched". Ellicott's Commentary refers to an alternative view that the word refers to "the leather covering which was placed over the pavement on which the throne was set, upon which the criminal knelt as on a scaffold to receive the death-stroke of the executioner. So taken, the prediction assumes a more definite and terrible aspect. The king was to sit upon the stones which Jeremiah had hidden, not merely in his regal pomp, but in the character of an avenger executing the wrath of Jehovah against the rebellious".

Harrison makes the very helpful observation that "The meaning of the parable…is clear: Though the Judæan refugees have buried themselves in populous Egypt, they will be discovered and feel, as their compatriots had done, the weight of Babylonian might". The Jews had fled to Egypt in order to escape the Babylonians (41.17-18), but their flight would prove futile. Nebuchadrezzar would follow them: "And when he cometh, he shall smite the land of Egypt, and deliver such as are for death to death; and such as are for captivity to captivity; and such as are for the sword to the sword" (v.11). The "sword" here is the sword of the executioner. This, doubtless, included the Judæan remnant (44.11-14).

Idolatry is obnoxious to the Lord, whether practised amongst His people, or by foreign nations. Despite the witness of creation, where "the invisible things of him from the creation of the world are clearly seen, being understood by the things that are made, even his eternal power and Godhead", men "changed the glory of the uncorruptible God into an image made like to corruptible man, and to birds, and fourfooted beasts, and creeping things" (Rom 1.20,23). Egypt was no exception (44.8) and the Lord proclaims coming judgment on the land for that reason: "And I will kindle a fire in the houses of the gods of Egypt; and he shall burn them, and carry them away captives" (v.12).

The gods of Egypt would be utterly destroyed. Moreover, the invasion and its sequel would be accomplished with very little trouble to Nebuchadrezzar: "he shall array himself with the land of Egypt, as a shepherd putteth on his garment" (v.12). He would complete the task with as much ease as "the casual way in which a shepherd wraps himself in his garment" (Feinberg). Nebuchadrezzar would destroy the idol temples and triumphantly carry the idols themselves to Babylon, so asserting the superiority of the Babylonian gods. In ancient times it was the custom for conquering kings to carry off the idols of defeated foes. It will be remembered that Nebuchadrezzar had been allowed by the Lord to carry "part of the vessels of the house of God…into the land of Shinar to the house of his god" (Dan 1.2) which proved, he thought, the superiority of his god over Jehovah.

Nebuchadrezzar would return unscathed from Egypt, "he shall go forth from thence in peace" (v.12), having broken "the images of Beth-shemesh, that is in the land of Egypt", and burned "the houses of the gods of the Egyptians" (v.13). Beth-shemesh (known as Heliopolis to the Greeks, and On to the Egyptians), meaning "the temple of the sun", or "the home of the sun", should be distinguished from the places of the same name in Judah (Josh 15.10; 2 Kings 14.11), Issachar (Josh 19.22), and Naphtali (Josh 19.38). Feinberg writes that " 'The temple of the sun' is the modern Tell Husn, about six miles northeast of Cairo. The sun god was elaborately worshipped there in antiquity". The "images" (4676) at Beth-shemesh were evidently the sacred pillars or obelisks associated with Egyptian idolatry.

According to Harrison, "A fragmentary inscription records that Nebuchadnezzar actually invaded Egypt in 568/7 BC, when Amasis (570-526 BC) was pharaoh. The attack was more of a punitive expedition than a wholesale reduction of the land". Amasis succeeded Pharaoh-hophra (44.30), whose death would be a further sign of coming judgment on the Judæan remnant (44.29-30).

JEREMIAH 44

This chapter describes the last recorded encounter between the prophet and his fellow expatriates: "The word that came to Jeremiah concerning all the Jews which dwell in the land of Egypt, which dwell at Migdol, and at Tahpanhes, and at Noph, and in the country of Pathros" (v.1). It seems likely that this took place some months or years after their arrival in Egypt, since the Jews were "now settled in places far apart, ranging from Migdol and Tahpanhes at the mouth of the Nile, and Memphis (Hebrew, Noph) just short of the delta, to the land of Pathros several hundred miles further upriver" (Kidner). Memphis was the chief city of Lower or northern Egypt, and Pathros was the general description of Upper or southern Egypt.

It should be said, however, that other commentators, including Harrison, suggest that some of the Jewish colonies in Egypt antedated considerably the fall of Judah, and therefore conclude that, having arrived in Egypt, Jeremiah quickly, rather than after a period of time, denounced the refugees' indulgence in pagan religious practices. But whether an earlier or later date is assigned to the chapter, the fact remains that "their substitution of Egyptian for Canaanite paganism showed that they had completely failed to grasp the significance of the catastrophe which had overtaken Jerusalem" (Harrison).

Since Jews from all over Egypt, including Pathros in the south of the country, were present when Jeremiah was speaking (v.15), it has been suggested that the occasion was some kind of festival, possibly held at Tahpanhes, not, however, in honour of the Lord, but in honour of the heathen deity called in this chapter "the queen of heaven" (vv.17,18,19,25). The same goddess had been worshipped in Jerusalem (7.17-18). According to Feinberg, "The worship of this goddess was widespread in the ancient Near East". The reader is referred to comments made in connection with her identity when considering 7.18.

The chapter may be divided as follows:

> The Condemnation of Idolatry (vv.1-14)
> The Justification of Idolatry (vv.15-19)
> The Visitation upon Idolaters (vv.20-30).

Verses 1-14: The Condemnation of Idolatry
Judah had persisted in idolatry prior to the sack of Jerusalem (vv.1-6), but the solemn lessons from their recent history had gone unheeded (vv.7-10), leaving them exposed, like the inhabitants of Jerusalem, to divine judgment by sword, famine and pestilence (vv.11-14). This section of the chapter may therefore be summarised as follows: past provocation (vv.1-6); present practice (vv.7-10); and future punishment (vv.11-14).

Past provocation (vv.1-6)
    The message in these verses recalls the Lord's dealings with Judah and emphatically reminds the Jews in Egypt that their sins had incurred the wrath of God. Through Jeremiah, the Lord reminded the Judæan remnant of two well-attested facts.

Divine judgment and the reason
    "Ye have seen all the evil that I have brought upon Jerusalem, and upon all the cities of Judah; and, behold, this day they are a desolation, and no man dwelleth therein, Because of their wickedness which they have committed to provoke me to anger, in that they went to burn incense, and to serve other gods, whom they knew not, neither they, ye, nor your fathers" (vv.2-3). This had been clearly foretold by Jeremiah, and it was an inescapable fact that the destruction of Jerusalem and the cities of Judah was nothing less than divine judgment upon them.

Divine warning and the response
    "Howbeit I sent unto you all my servants the prophets, rising early and sending them" (v.4). This the last of eleven similar references in the book of Jeremiah (7.13,25; 11.7; 25.3,4; 26.5; 29.19; 32.33; 35.14-15). The Lord's appeal to His people, "Oh, do not this abominable thing that I hate" (v.4), expressed deep feeling. But there was no response: "But they hearkened not, nor inclined their ear to turn from their wickedness, to burn no incense unto other gods" (v.5). The Lord had spoken earnestly and untiringly to His people, but to no avail, and ultimately judgment fell: "Wherefore my fury and mine anger was poured forth, and was kindled in the cities of Judah and in the streets of Jerusalem; and they are wasted and desolate, as at this day" (v.6).
    As Kidner observes, "In its thorough, relentless way, this formidable passage is pacing over the ground that our Lord illuminated in a single flash...in Matthew 23.37-38: 'O Jerusalem, Jerusalem, thou that killest the prophets, and stonest them which are sent unto thee, how often would I have gathered thy children together, even as a hen gathereth her chickens under her wings, and ye would not! Behold, your house is left unto you desolate'".

Present practice (vv.7-10)
    The destruction and desolation of Jerusalem caused Jeremiah deep sorrow: "How doth the city sit solitary, that was full of people! how is she become as a widow! she that was great among the nations, and princess among the provinces, how is she become tributary!" (Lam 1.1). But there was no sorrow amongst the Jews in Egypt. Ignoring the lessons of recent national disaster, they persisted in idolatry (v.8). Attention is drawn to the following.

Idolatry endangers the future
    "Therefore now thus saith the Lord, the God of hosts, the God of Israel;

Wherefore commit ye this great evil against your souls, to cut off from you man and woman, child and suckling, out of Judah, to leave you none to remain?" (v.7). Continuance in idolatry damages its devotees to the extent that it threatens their very existence. The impotence and thoughtlessness of idolatry is stressed by the fact that they had turned to idols from none other than "the Lord, the God of hosts, the God of Israel", with all the majesty and strength that these titles convey. Idolatry in the lives of the Lord's people today, whatever form it may take, can cause only spiritual damage and endanger spiritual life. The injunction, "keep yourselves from idols" (1 Jn 5.21), has in view our ongoing devotion to "the true God" (1 Jn 5.20).

Idolatry incurs divine anger
   "...ye provoke me unto wrath with the works of your hands, burning incense unto other gods in the land of Egypt, whither ye be gone to dwell" (v.8). This is anger arising from divine jealousy: "For thou shalt worship no other god: for the Lord, whose name is Jealous, is a jealous God" (Ex 34.14). There are numerous references in the Old Testament to the Lord's jealousy, and examples occur in Deuteronomy 32.16,21; Psalm 78.58, and Ezekiel 8.3.

Idolatry destroys testimony
   "...that ye might cut yourselves off, and that ye might be a curse and a reproach among all the nations of the earth" (v.8). Moses warned Israel that the "plagues" and "sicknesses" of the land would cause the nations to ask, "Wherefore hath the Lord done thus unto this land? what meaneth the heat of this great anger?", with the reply: "Then men shall say, Because they have forsaken the covenant of the Lord God of their fathers" (Deut 29.24-25). Idolatry in the lives of the Lord's people exhibits total disregard for the injunction, "Walk in wisdom toward them that are without" (Col 4.5).

Idolatry exhibits refusal to learn from the past
   "Have ye forgotten the wickedness of your fathers, and the wickedness of the kings of Judah, and the wickedness of their wives, and your own wickedness, and the wickedness of your wives, which they have committed in the land of Judah, and in the streets of Jerusalem?" (v.9). The New Testament emphasises the lesson: "But with many of them God was not well pleased: for they were overthrown in the wilderness. Now these things were our examples, to the intent we should not lust after evil things, as they also lusted" (1 Cor 10.5-6). It is sadly true that people who fail to learn from their mistakes will almost inevitably repeat them.
   The references to the wives should be noted (cp. vv.15-19). In the words of Harrison, "The wives were being castigated for enticing their husbands into idolatry, a tradition which originated in Israelite life in the Solomonic period" (1 Kings 11.1-8).

Idolatry is rank disobedience

"They are not humbled even unto this day, neither have they feared, nor walked in my law, nor in my statutes, that I set before you and your fathers" (v.10). The determination of the Jews in Egypt to follow their own inclinations exhibited both pride and disobedience. This was the very antithesis of the Lord's requirement of His people to "walk humbly with thy God" (Micah 6.8). Pride is evidenced by self-assertiveness and self-will, leading to disobedience.

Future punishment (vv.11-14)

As a consequence of their idolatry, the Jews in Egypt would perish: "Behold, I will set my face against you for evil, and to cut off all Judah. And I will take the remnant of Judah, that have set their faces to go into the land of Egypt to sojourn there, and they shall all be consumed, and fall in the land of Egypt...For I will punish them that dwell in the land of Egypt, as I have punished Jerusalem, by the sword, by the famine, and by the pestilence: So that none of the remnant of Judah, which are gone into the land of Egypt to sojourn there, shall escape or remain...for none shall return but such as shall escape". The determination of the Jews to implement their will by emigrating to Egypt (v.12) would be met by the Lord's determination to execute His will. But "even in punishing the disobedient remnant, God will still allow a few survivors to trickle back to Judæa, thereby maintaining the connection between the people and the land" (Harrison). The escapees are later described as "a small number" (v.28). The words, "the land of Judah, to the which they have a desire to return to dwell there" (v.14), indicate that the exiles still cherished the hope of returning to their homeland.

Verses 15-19: The Justification of Idolatry

These verses have been described as "a most revealing glimpse of spiritual perversity, for in blaming all their troubles on the reformation (vv.17-18) instead of on the evils it had tried to root out, these people were turning the truth exactly upside down" (Kidner). In effect, they blamed the Lord for their troubles. Not once did they connect their trials with their sins. With this in mind, the following should be noticed: their refusal to listen to God's word (vv.15-17a); their reason for continuing in idolatry (vv.17b-18); and the role of both men and women (v.19).

Their refusal to listen to God's word (vv.15-17a)

Jeremiah was faced by united hostility: "Then all the men which knew that their wives had burned incense unto other gods, and all the women that stood by, a great multitude, even all the people that dwelt in the land of Egypt, in Pathros, answered Jeremiah, saying, As for the word that thou hast spoken unto us in the name of the Lord, we will not hearken unto thee. But we will certainly do whatsoever thing goeth forth out of our own mouth, to burn incense unto the queen of heaven, and to pour out drink-offerings unto her". The words, "whatsoever thing goeth forth out of our own mouth", or "every word that is gone forth out of our mouth" (JND), evidently refer to their vow to worship the "queen of heaven". With complete openness, and without any trace of shame, the people refused to forsake their idolatry. It could be said of this occasion, as it had been said previously, "Were they ashamed when they had committed abomination? nay, they were not at all ashamed, neither could they blush" (6.15; 8.12). They made no attempt at pretence, and were utterly resolute in their desire to continue their idolatrous practices. They were quite unlike Ezra, who cried, "O my God, I am ashamed and blush to lift up my face to thee, my God: for our iniquities are increased over our head, and our trespass is grown up unto the heavens" (Ezra 9.6). But in Egypt, the word of God was met with blank denial. Alas, it could not be said that the Jews received "with meekness the engrafted word" (James 1.21).

Their reason for continuing in idolatry (vv.17b-18)

The determination of the Jews to continue in their worship of "the queen of heaven" was fuelled by the conviction that their misfortunes were attributable to her wrath at the discontinuance of their offerings, whereas Jeremiah had cited Jerusalem's destruction as the consequence of their sin. They argued that they had "plenty of victuals, and were well, and saw no evil" (v.17) when they worshipped "the queen of heaven", and that it was only when this ceased that they were "consumed by the sword and by the famine" (v.18). The reference to the cessation of their offerings is probably an allusion to Josiah's reforms. "In short, the remnant claimed that idolatry had done more for them than the Lord whom Jeremiah represented. Nothing is more blinding than unbelief" (Feinberg).

Ironside makes the very pertinent observation that "The reasons given illustrate the grave danger of trusting in experience rather than going to the Word of God, in spite of all outward appearances…How plausible and specious was their sophistry! Yet are there not many who reason in similar ways now? It was the appeal to a momentary experience, instead of to the word of God - the only safe guide". Moses made it clear that judgment must not be clouded by religious deception (Deut 13.1-4). A plausible argument and compelling evidence (if "the sign or the wonder come to pass", Deut 13.2) must not obstruct obedience to the Word of God. Everything must be tested by the commandments of the Lord (Deut 13.4). The Word of God was the only court of appeal: "To the law and to the testimony: if they speak not according to this word, it is because there is no light in them" (Is 8.20). The great bulwark against all error is the maintenance of original teaching. Paul was obliged to remind the Galatians that "though we, or an angel from heaven, preach any other gospel unto you than that which we have preached unto you, let him be accursed" (Gal 1.8).

It should be noted that emphasis is placed upon the women in connection with this form of idolatry: "Then all the men which knew that *their wives* had burned incense unto other gods, and all *the women* that stood by, a great multitude" (v.15); "Then Jeremiah said unto all the people, to the men, and to *the women*" (v.20); "Moreover Jeremiah said unto all the people, and to all *the women*, Hear the word of the Lord, all Judah that are in the land of Egypt: Thus saith the Lord of hosts, the God of Israel, saying; Ye and *your wives* have both spoken with your mouths, and fulfilled with your hand" (vv.24-25). Ironside sums up the situation as follows: "Idolatry of the most degrading character had already been secretly practised by them; the women leading, and the men abetting, as formerly in the land (v.15)". It has been suggested that the women were prominent here because Astarte, "the queen of heaven", was the goddess of fertility.

The role of both men and women (v.19)

With perhaps a little imagination, it could be said that at this point the women stepped forward, and added: "And when we burned incense to the queen of heaven, and poured out drink offerings unto her, did we make her cakes to worship her, and pour out drink offerings unto her, *without our men?*". Prior to the captivity, entire families were involved in this idol-worship: "The children gather wood, and the fathers kindle the fire, and the women knead their dough, to make cakes to the queen of heaven, and to pour out drink-offerings unto other gods, that they may provoke me to anger" (7.18), and this evidently continued in Egypt. Streane points out that "the consent of the husband was necessary before the wife's vow could be binding (Num 30.6-7). Hence the women plead that they have their husband's approval in this worship and that therefore Jeremiah had no right to interfere". According to Streane, the "cakes" had an image of Astarte on them, said to be the likeness of the full moon. Ellicott's Commentary describes them as "crescent-shaped cakes".

Verses 20-30: The Visitation upon Idolaters

These verses constitute the very last recorded message of Jeremiah. The remaining chapters evidently contain prophecies dating from earlier years. It should be noted that Jeremiah answers their argument (vv.20-23); anticipates their unwavering disobedience (vv.24-25); and announces their judgment (vv.26-30).

He answers their argument (vv.20-23)

Jeremiah flatly denies their "twisted defence of idolatry" (Feinberg). They had asserted that their idolatry had proved beneficial: "for then we had plenty of victuals, and were well, and saw no evil" (v.17), to which the prophet replied that whilst the Lord had been completely aware of their evil practices, He had allowed them to continue in their idolatry until His longsuffering was exhausted: "The incense that ye burned in the cities of

Judah, and in the streets of Jerusalem, ye, and your fathers, your kings, and your princes, and the people of the land, did not the Lord remember them, and came it not into his mind? So that the Lord could no longer bear, because of the evil of your doings…therefore is your land a desolation, and an astonishment, and a curse, without an inhabitant, as at this day" (vv.21-22). It must be remembered that the Lord "is longsuffering…not willing that any should perish, but that all should come to repentance" (2 Pet 3.9).

These verses (vv.21-22) emphasise their sin of commission, whereas the following verse emphasises their sin of omission: "ye…have not obeyed the voice of the Lord, nor walked in his law, nor in his statutes, nor in his testimonies; therefore this evil is happened unto you, as at this day" (v.23). Divine judgment would not have been incurred had Judah obeyed what Harrison calls "the covenantal stipulations, here described as *law*, *statutes* and *testimonies*". Harrison continues by defining these as follows: "The first of these terms was reserved exclusively for divinely-revealed material through human intermediaries; the second, coming from a root meaning 'to engrave', referred to permanent rules of conduct prescribed by lawful authority and recorded for the guidance of individuals or society, while the third, derived from a root meaning 'to attest', 'to affirm', 'to admonish', was uniformly used to refer to the testimony of God".

He anticipates their unwavering disobedience (vv.24-25)

The Jews in Egypt were entrenched in their disobedience: "Ye and your wives have both spoken with your mouths, and fulfilled with your hand (Jeremiah was possibly referring the "cakes" in their hands at the time), saying, We will surely perform our vows that we have vowed, to burn incense to the queen of heaven, and to pour out drink offerings unto her" (v.25). Jeremiah saw no future change on their part: "ye will surely accomplish your vows, and surely perform your vows", or "Ye will certainly establish your vows, and entirely perform your vows" (v.25, JND). Feinberg suggests that "in a powerful expression of irony and revulsion" Jeremiah was telling "the remnant to proceed with fulfilling their godless vows".

He announces their judgment (vv.26-30)

These verses emphasise the certainty of coming judgment (vv.26-28), and give the sign of coming judgment (vv.29-30).

The certainty of coming judgment (vv.26-28)

Their disobedience would be appropriately rewarded by the Lord: "Behold, I have sworn by my great name, saith the Lord, that my name shall no more be named in the mouth of any man of Judah in all the land of Egypt, saying, the Lord God liveth" (v.26). While other suggestions have been made, it does seem that the explanation is given in the following verse: "Behold, I will watch over them for evil, and not for good: and all the men of Judah that are in the land of Egypt shall be consumed by the sword and by the famine, until there be an end of them" (v.27). No Jew there would be able to say, "the Lord God liveth", because, with the exception of a remnant that would return to Judah (v.28), they would all perish in Egypt. Both the surviving remnant, "easily numbered because they are so few" (Feinberg), and "all the remnant of Judah, that are gone into the land of Egypt to sojourn there", would prove the inerrancy of God's word. The survivors would live to bear witness to this, and so would the remainder when faced with death "by the sword and by the famine". All would "know whose words shall stand, mine, or theirs" (v.28). The people who had persisted in their idolatrous worship because, they alleged, the "queen of heaven" saw to it that they were abundantly blessed (v.17), would discover, all too late for the vast majority of them, that "Like as the Lord of hosts thought to do unto us, according to our ways, and according to our doings, so hath he dealt with us" (Zech 1.6). It is worth noting that verb rendered "watch over" (v.27) is earlier rendered "hasten" (1.12), meaning "watchful" (JND). The Lord never ceases to be both vigilant and diligent in connection with fulfilment of His word.

Since there were evidently large Jewish communities in Egypt in the centuries before Christ, it has been suggested that the Jews in Jeremiah's day repented on hearing the prophet's preaching and were spared from judgment, but this not an acceptable explanation. Jeremiah specifically states that divine judgment would be executed against them. According to Streane, "The many Jewish colonists afterwards living in Egypt were probably attracted thither in times subsequent to this…Ptolemy, after his capture of Jerusalem (320 BC), brought many Jews into Egypt as settlers, and gave those at Alexandria equal rights with the Macedonians (Josephus, *Ant. xii.i*)".

The sign of coming judgment (vv.29-30)

The death of Pharaoh-hophra (588-568 BC) would confirm the Lord's intention to punish the Jews in Egypt for their idolatry. Since it was this monarch who sent an army to help Zedekiah when Jerusalem was besieged (37.5), it can be inferred that the king of Egypt was favourably disposed towards the Jews. His death would therefore be a considerable blow to the Judæan remnant. Pharaoh-hophra would prove to be no better refuge than Zedekiah.

In this connection, it must be remembered that divine judgment would be inflicted on the Jews in Egypt through Nebuchadrezzar (43.10), and that the death of the Egyptian king would remind the Jews that the fulfilment of God's word was imminent: "And this shall be a sign unto you, saith the Lord, that I will punish you in this place, that ye may know that my words shall surely stand against you for evil: Thus saith the Lord; Behold, I will give Pharaoh-hophra king of Egypt into the hand of his enemies". The precise wording of this prediction should be noticed. It is not said that Pharaoh-hophra would be given into the hand of Nebuchadrezzar, but into "the hand of his enemies". History records that "Hophra was actually overthrown by Amasis, one of his officers, who revolted against him and then shared rule with him" (Feinberg). It is said that following a struggle between the two men, Pharaoh-hophra was strangled by Amasis, and that shortly after this event Nebuchadrezzar invaded Egypt. As always, the prophetic word in relation to past events was exactly fulfilled, just as it will be precisely fulfilled in relation to events which are still future.

It is not known whether Jeremiah lived to see the fulfilment of this prediction. The Scriptures are silent on matters of his welfare and movements after the events described in this chapter. It could be argued that at the end of many years of faithful service, he saw "his lifework thwarted, his life's purpose frustrated, his life's hopes dashed to the ground", and that "he had lived and laboured and hoped and prayed in vain!". Further, that "after his forty-three years of strenuous, tearful efforts, his people had deliberately left the land of Jehovah and the worship of Jehovah, and had chosen, instead, the Queen of Heaven!" (Laetsch). But Jeremiah had done far more than witness the final sad years of Judah's independence, and accompany them into exile while they were still practising rebellion and disobedience. If this were the outcome of his preaching, he might indeed have died a most unhappy man. But he had seen the glory of national restoration and renewal when the Lord's own word concerning the nation would be fulfilled, "I will put my law in their inward parts, and write it in their hearts; and will be their God, and they shall be my people" (31.33). Moreover, the city he last saw in ruins would "be built to the Lord" and would be "holy unto the Lord; it shall not be plucked up, nor thrown down any more for ever" (31.38,40). Jeremiah was no A-millennialist!

But were all those painful years in vain so far as Jeremiah personally was concerned? Meyer answers the question magnificently: "But how gladly did the prophet close his eyes upon the wreck that sin had wrought on the chosen people, and open them on the land where neither sin, nor death, nor the sight and sound of war break the perfect rest! What look of surprise and rapture must have settled upon the worn face, the expression of the last glad vision of the soul as it passed out from the body of corruption, worn and weary with the long conflict, to hear the 'Well done!' and welcome of God". Meyer's poetic licence cannot be far from the truth.

JEREMIAH 45

This chapter marks the end of the section in the book (chs.40-45) which records prophecies and describes events after the fall of Jerusalem. It has already been noted that while chapters 40-42 are concerned with prophecies and events in Judah, and chapters 43-44 with those afterwards in Egypt, chapter 45 contains the Lord's personal message to Baruch before any of these events took place. It was delivered to him by Jeremiah "in the fourth year of Jehoiakim the son of Josiah king of Judah" (v.1).

It must be stressed again that there is nothing haphazard about the structure of the prophecy of Jeremiah. Although, chronologically, chapter 45 should appear immediately after chapter 36, it is evidently placed after chapters 40-44 to emphasise the fulfilment of God's promise to preserve Baruch's life: "thy life will I give unto thee for a prey in all places whither thou goest" (v.5). Jehoiakim had ordered the arrest of "Baruch the scribe and Jeremiah the prophet: but the Lord hid them" (36.26), and although it is not specifically stated, Baruch was evidently in danger some years later after Jeremiah had warned the Judæan remnant against emigrating to Egypt (43.3). Both men were then taken into Egypt (43.6), and it is only then that the reader is made aware of the promise made to Baruch during the reign of Jehoiakim. In spite of various traditions, it is impossible to say whether Baruch was in Egypt when the predicted Babylonian invasion took place, and "all the men of Judah" were "consumed by the sword and by the famine" (44.27), but if this were the case then the promise made to him must have held good at that time as well.

But there is a second reason why the Lord's message to Baruch is placed here. Chapters 46-51 comprise the "foreign nations" section of the prophecy, and chapter 46 deals with Egypt. The chapter commences with events which took place in the same year as the delivery of the Lord's message to Baruch, that is, in "the fourth year of Jehoiakim" (45.1; 46.2) which, significantly, was also "the first year of Nebuchadrezzar king of Babylon" (25.1). In this connection, the reader is referred to comments made in introducing chapter 25. Having described the Babylonian defeat of the Egyptian army "by the river Euphrates in Carchemish" (46.2), chapter 46 continues by describing the then future Babylonian invasion of Egypt (46.13). It is often said that Nebuchadrezzar's victory at Carchemish changed the balance of world power, and that Babylon then became the undisputed master of the world. In view of these events, Baruch was told, "And seekest thou great things for thyself? seek them not: for, behold, I will bring evil upon all flesh" (v.5).

It should also be noted that in spite of the apparent rebuke (v.5), it might well be said of Baruch, as indeed of Ebed-melech (39.15-18), that "God is not unrighteous to forget your work and labour of love, which ye have shewed toward his name" (Heb 6.10).

This short chapter may be divided as follows:

The Lord's Awareness (vv.1-3)
The Lord's Answer (v.4)
The Lord's Advice (v.5a)
The Lord's Assurance (v.5b).

Verses 1-3: The Lord's Awareness

It can be said that the Lord was aware of the faithful service of Baruch (v.1); and of the deep sorrow of Baruch (vv.2-3).

He was aware of Baruch's faithful service (v.1)

"The word that Jeremiah the prophet spake unto Baruch (meaning 'blessed') the son of Neriah (meaning 'lamp of Jehovah', or 'the Lord is my lamp'), when he had written these words in a book at the mouth of Jeremiah."

Prior to this, the deeds of Jeremiah's property in Anathoth were committed to Baruch for safekeeping (32.12-14), from which it may deduced, together with other considerations, that he was "the confidant and closest friend of the prophet, a gracious gift of the Lord in view of the Lord's command to Jeremiah not to marry" (Feinberg). Baruch's diligence is seen particularly in the way in which he took dictation from Jeremiah, and read the resultant scriptures publicly in Jerusalem at Jeremiah's request: "Baruch wrote from the mouth of Jeremiah all the words of the Lord, which he had spoken unto him, upon a roll of a book…And Baruch the son of Neriah did according to all that Jeremiah the prophet commanded him, reading in the book the words of the Lord in the Lord's house" (36.4,8). He later answered the question, "How didst thou write all these words at his mouth?", by saying, "He pronounced all these words unto me with his mouth, and I wrote them with ink in the book" (36.17,18). Following the consignment of the pages of the book to the flames by Jehoiakim, Baruch was given "another roll" by the prophet, and he "wrote therein from the mouth of Jeremiah all the words of the book which Jehoiakim king of Judah had burned in the fire: and there were added besides unto them many like words" (36.32).

Baruch did not have the high profile of men like Jeremiah who were constantly in the public eye, but he undertook invaluable service for the Lord. His role in producing the Scriptures was of vast importance. So much depended on care and accuracy in their transmission, and Baruch was not found wanting. Unlike the case of Baruch, the Scriptures do not always name servants of God, but their "record is on high" (Job 16.19). In the New Testament, Paul refers not only to fellow-labourers by name, but to unnamed colleagues as well, adding in one place, "whose names are in the book of life" (Phil 4.3). The Lord, who "telleth the number of the stars;

he calleth them all by their names" (Ps 147.4), is thoroughly aware of the labours of every one of His servants.

He was aware of Baruch's deep sorrow (vv.2-3)

The Lord was aware of Baruch's state of mind, and addressed him personally: "Thus saith the Lord, the God of Israel, unto thee, O Baruch; Thou didst say, Woe is me now! for the Lord hath added grief to my sorrow; I fainted in my sighing, and I find no rest". This does not necessarily imply that Baruch had expressed his feelings publicly. Perhaps his grief and sorrow could be likened to that of the Lord Jesus who in healing the man "that was deaf, and had an impediment in his speech", looked up to heaven and "sighed" over the physical havoc caused by sin (Mk 7.32,34), and later "sighed deeply in his spirit" (Mk 8.12) when confronted with the unbelief of the Pharisees. In both cases the word "sighed" describes the deep grief of the Lord Jesus: in the first case, He "groaned" (JND), and in the second He answered the Pharisees "groaning deeply" (JND margin). The Lord's people today "have not an high priest which cannot be touched with the feeling of our infirmities; but was in all points tempted like was we are, yet without sin" (Heb 4.15). His awareness of His people's sorrow has been beautifully expressed by the hymn-writer:

> In every pang that rends the heart,
> The Man of sorrows bears a part;
> He knows and feels our every grief,
> And gives the suffering saint relief.
>   (M. Bruce)

Baruch's sorrow was evidently attributable to two connected reasons, the first giving rise to the second.

Sorrow for the nation

He was distressed because, in his own words, "the Lord hath added grief to my sorrow" (v.3), referring to his "sorrow" over the wretched condition of the nation. There can be no doubt that Baruch shared Jeremiah's distress as the prophet warned the unbelieving city again and again of coming judgment. It has been said that "The greatest weariness is not the result of hard work; it comes from distress of heart. It is trouble, not work, that breaks down the strong life to premature old age. The blessedness of the heavenly rest is that it is rest from sorrow as well as from toil" (The Pulpit Commentary).

One of the charges brought against Israel by the prophet Amos was the self-indulgence of the leadership who "drink wine in bowls, and anoint themselves with the chief ointments: but they are not grieved for the affliction of Joseph" (Amos 6.6). It is sadly possible for believers today to be so immersed in their own interests that they remain unmoved by the distressing conditions and erosion of spiritual life amongst the Lord's people, let alone by the appalling degeneration in society at large. Baruch was of the same spirit as the men in Jerusalem that "sigh and that cry for all the abominations that be done in the midst thereof" (Ezek 9.4).

Sorrow for himself

Bearing in mind the Lord's words, "seekest thou great things for thyself? seek them not" (v.5), it appears that Baruch experienced additional "grief" (v.3) for personal reasons. "In the approaching overthrow of the nation, all his cherished hopes of personal ambition were shattered. The most sanguine too often suffer the bitterest disappointments" (The Pulpit Commentary). Baruch evidently recognised that he himself was living under the shadow of the impending disaster predicted in the very scriptures dictated to him by Jeremiah. In the words of Laetsch, "Baruch realised with ever-greater clarity that during his lifetime he could look only for hardships, persecution, shame, poverty, destitution...Bitterly he lamented, because the Lord was adding grief to grief, and sorrow to sorrow, until life began to appear altogether intolerable".

Verse 4: The Lord's Answer

Before addressing Baruch's personal grief, the Lord reveals His own deep sorrow over the nation: "Thus shalt thou say unto him, The Lord saith thus; Behold, that which I have built will I break down, and that which I have planted I will pluck up, even this whole land". This could mean that, notwithstanding Baruch's grief, the Lord would not be diverted from His intention to remove Judah, even though He had established them in the first place. But while the Lord's determination to act in this way cannot be disputed, the phraseology implies His sorrow in dealing with Judah after this fashion. "Jeremiah has to remind Baruch of God's own sorrow at destroying that which He had laboured so hard to preserve", although "such a calamity was inevitable because of the wilful disobedience and apostasy of those chosen to exemplify a much higher calling" (Harrison). Some commentators, possibly in view of the terms of Jeremiah's commission (1.10) and the reference to "all flesh" (v.5), have concluded that the words "even this whole land" refer to the whole earth, but the immediate context suggests otherwise.

It should be remembered that the Lord "delighteth in mercy" (Micah 7.18), and that judgment is His "strange work" and a "strange act" (Is 28.21). The Lord has "no pleasure in the death of the wicked" (Ezek 33.11). On beholding Jerusalem, the Lord Jesus "wept over it" (Lk 19.41) in view of its coming destruction.

Verse 5a: The Lord's Advice

"And seeketh thou great things for thyself? seek them not: for, behold, I will bring evil upon all flesh, saith the Lord." The passage does not identify the "great things" which occupied Baruch's mind, and this is probably a deliberate omission. Had the information been disclosed, the scope for application would have been lessened. Similarly, Paul's "thorn in the flesh" (2 Cor 12.7) is unidentified, and the anonymity of the affliction is one of its important lessons.

Should, however, the reader wish to pursue the matter further, it may be worth remembering that Baruch was of noble birth, being the grandson of Maaseiah (32.12), who was governor of Jerusalem in the time of Josiah (2 Chr 34.8). Perhaps, therefore, he dreamed of high office. It is also worth noticing that Baruch's brother, Seraiah, became an official in the court of King Zedekiah (Jer 51.59). He is described as "a quiet prince" or "chief chamberlain" (JND). Both the NKJV and the RSV call him "the quartermaster". As Gordon S. Bissett (*Precious Seed*, August, 2005) observes, "By all accounts he held a position of some importance, with a measure of security in the precarious situation of the royal household". Bissett continues by saying that if this were the kind of advancement that Baruch secretly hoped for, then "Jeremiah's inspired message saved him from deportation to Babylon, for when King Zedekiah was ignominiously led off into captivity Seraiah went with him as part of the king's household!".

Looking at Baruch's "grief" from a different point of view, Ironside suggests that Baruch "had not received the recognition as Jehovah's servant and the amanuensis of Jeremiah that he looked for. Hence he faints in the day of adversity, because his strength is small".

Whatever the nature of Baruch's aspirations, the message is clear: he was not to seek position or recognition in a condemned world. Since the Lord would "bring evil upon all flesh", it was inappropriate for the Lord's servant to pursue his own interests in a society ripe for divine judgment. The New Testament emphasises the same lesson: "But this I say, brethren, the time is short: it remaineth, that both they that have wives be as though they had none; And they that weep, as though they wept not; and they that rejoice, as though they rejoiced not; and they that buy, as though they possessed not; And they that use this world, as not abusing it: for the fashion of this world passeth away" (1 Cor 7.29-31). The Lord's people are to "seek those things which are above, where Christ sitteth on the right hand of God"; they are to set their "affection on things above, not on things on the earth" (Col 3.1,2).

This is not to say that the Lord's people are to be devoid of ambition. Paul refers to spiritual ambition in the following passages: "Yea, so have I strived ('being ambitious', RV margin) to preach the gospel" (Rom 15.20); "Wherefore we labour, that, whether present or absent, we may be accepted of him", or "Wherefore also we make it our aim (margin 'are ambitious')…to be well-pleasing unto him" (2 Cor 5.9, RV); "study ('be ambitious', RV margin) to be quiet, and to do your own business" (1 Thess 4.11). These are excellent ambitions!

The Lord Jesus did not seek "great things" for Himself. He "pleased not himself" (Rom 15.3), and could say, "I came down from heaven, not to do mine own will, but the will of him that sent me" (Jn 6.38); "And he that sent me is with me: the Father hath not left me alone; for I do always those things that please him" (Jn 8.29).

Verse 5b: The Lord's Assurance

Ironside is surely right in saying that the Lord had for Baruch "a needed word, both of admonition and of comfort. His is no harsh, unkind rebuke; no hard and severe scourging. Knowing full well that Baruch was, after all, seeking to honour Him, however he might have, well-nigh unconsciously, permitted self to have a place, He ministers a needed word in tenderness and love". While Baruch was to abandon the pursuit of his cherished ambitions, for the Lord would "pluck up, even this whole land" (v.4) and "bring evil upon all flesh" (v.5), he is given assurance that his life would be spared: "thy life will I give unto thee for a prey in all places whither thou goest". His faithfulness would not pass unrewarded.

These words evidently point, not only to "a life of wandering and exile" (Ellicott's Commentary), but to the fact that Baruch would have to flee for his life. The words, "thy life will I give thee for a prey" occur, with slight variations, in 21.9; 38.2; 39.18. According to Feinberg, "Most English translations render the words literally, but the force of the idiom is lost". The word "prey" (7998) can be rendered "booty" and when dealing with the similar occurrence of the word in 21.9, Gesenius gives the rendering, "his life shall be to him for booty", with the explanation: 'he shall be preserved alive'. Ellicott's Commentary describes his preservation as "spoil rescued from the spoiler".

Jeremiah was given a similar promise at the commencement of his ministry: "I have made thee this day a defenced city...And they shall fight against thee; but they shall not prevail against thee; for I am with thee, saith the Lord, to deliver thee" (1.18-19). The Lord's people today can enjoy the peace of mind that this brings, knowing that He has said, "I will never leave thee, nor forsake thee. So that we may boldly say, The Lord is my helper, and I will not fear what man shall do unto me" (Heb 13.5-6). This does mean that believers are exempt from suffering, or even death, in the service of God, but that they are assured of His sustaining grace and help in the trials they experience. The Lord had given similar assurance to His earthly people: "When thou passest through the waters, I will be with thee; and through the rivers, they shall not overflow thee: when thou walkest through the fire, thou shalt not be burned; neither shall the flame kindle upon thee" (Is 43.2). While exemption from "the waters", "the rivers", and "the fire" is not promised, the Lord promises to be with them in the trials. How reassuring to know that "The eternal God is thy refuge, and underneath are the everlasting arms" (Deut 33.27).

JEREMIAH 46

The first verse of the chapter introduces a new section in the prophecy, and serves as an appropriate title for the chapters that follow: "The word of the Lord which came to Jeremiah the prophet against the Gentiles" (v.1). He was "ordained...a prophet unto the nations" (1.5).

Jeremiah chapters 46-51 comprise the "foreign nations" section of the prophecy, and describe the Lord's judgment on Egypt (46.1-26), Philistia (47.1-7), Moab (48.1-47), Ammon (49.1-6), Edom (49.7-22), Damascus (49.23-27), Kedar and Hazor (49.28-33), Elam (49.34-39), and Babylon (50.1-51.64). Passing reference is also made to Tyre and Zidon (47.4). Isaiah and Ezekiel also include a large "foreign nations" section. Attention is drawn to Isaiah chapters 13-23 (which deal with Babylon, Palestina, Moab, Damascus, Ethiopia, Egypt, Dumah, Arabia, Jerusalem and Tyre), and to Ezekiel chapters 25-32 (which are concerned with Ammon, Moab, Edom, Philistia, Tyre, Zidon, and Egypt). In some cases, representative cities are named, rather than nations in their entirety. Amos chapters 1-2 contains a much smaller section on the same subject. It should be noted that the section in Isaiah includes Judah and Jerusalem ("The burden of the valley of vision", 22.1-25), and that the section in Amos includes Judah and Israel (2.4-16), indicating that God's people had lost their distinctive character. Because they had become like the nations, they are treated as one of them. The people who should not have been "reckoned among the nations" (Num 23.9) had merged with the world. The ongoing warning to God's people is expressed in the New Testament: "And be not conformed to this world: but be ye transformed by the renewing of your mind, that ye may prove what is that good, and acceptable, and perfect, will of God" (Rom 12.2).

These chapters in Jeremiah, together with the appropriate chapters in Isaiah, Ezekiel and Amos, emphasise that the Lord is not a mere tribal deity. He is "the Judge of all the earth" (Gen 18.25). All men are accountable to Him. He will judge all nations. Chapters 46-51 are therefore of relevant interest; they are not to be regarded as isolated cases. The Lord remains in perfect control of national and international affairs; no nation is permitted to exceed the allotted place in His purposes or to avoid payment for its wickedness. Nebuchadnezzar learned that "the most High ruleth in the kingdom of men, and giveth it to whomsoever he will, and setteth up over it the basest of men" (Dan 4.17). It should also be remembered that nations rise and fall with reference to their treatment of God's earthly people: "I will bless them that bless thee, and curse him that curseth thee" (Gen 12.3).

The Lord's universal supremacy is frequently stressed in the Old Testament, and the following examples should be noted: "For the kingdom is the Lord's: and he is the governor among the nations" (Ps 22.28); "For the Lord most high is terrible; he is a great King over all the earth" (Ps

47.2). Jehoshaphat was very aware of this; it was in connection with an invasion by an alliance including "the children of Moab, and the children of Ammon" (2 Chr 20.1) that he said "O Lord God of our fathers, art not thou God in heaven? and rulest not thou over all the kingdoms of the heathen?" (2 Chr 20.6). Hezekiah "prayed before the Lord, and said, O Lord God of Israel…thou art the God, even thou alone, of all the kingdoms of the earth; thou hast made heaven and earth" (2 Kings 19.15). The New Testament describes God's "two witnesses" at the end-time as "the two olive trees and the two candlesticks ('lampstands', margin), standing before the Lord of the earth" (Rev 11.4, RV).

It is appropriate that the pronouncement against Egypt should be placed first in the "foreign nations" section of the prophecy. While Harrison is undoubtedly correct in saying that "Jeremiah commences with Egypt because Palestine had long been a sphere of Egyptian political influence", his later observation carries greater weight: "Pharaoh-necho had killed Josiah at Megiddo in 609 BC when he attempted to stop an Egyptian relief force from going to help the Assyrians in beleaguered Harran". Having slain Josiah (2 Kings 23.29-30; 2 Chr 35.20-24), Pharaho-necho then removed his son, Jehoahaz, from the throne of Judah, which he had occupied for only three months, imprisoned him at Riblah before taking him to Egypt, and replaced him by Jehoiakim (2 Kings 23.31-34; 2 Chr 36.1-4). It must be remembered that, having referred to the nations that "spoiled" His people, the Lord said, "he that toucheth you toucheth the apple of his eye" (Zech 2.8).

A further reason for placing Egypt first in this section of the book is that the defeat of her army marked an enormous shift in the balance of world power. Following the fall in 612 BC of the Assyrian Empire, which Egypt favoured against the rising power of Babylon, the defeat at Carchemish brought her military aspirations to an end and ushered in Babylonian supremacy, marking the beginning of "the times of the Gentiles" (Lk 21.24). It has already been noted that "the fourth year of Jehoiakim the son of Josiah king of Judah" (605 BC) was also "the first year of Nebuchadrezzar" (25.1), and the reader is again is referred to comments made in introducing chapter 25. It should be said that for four years (609-605 BC) "the Egyptian army was based on Carchemish, and Pharaoh dominated Syria and Palestine, setting up his puppet kings while Babylon's main force was preoccupied elsewhere. Then at last the Babylonian army fell upon the Egyptians in 605 BC, routing them utterly" (Kidner).

After the general introduction (v.1), the chapter may be divided as follows:

> Egypt's Defeat at Carchemish (vv.2-12)
> Egypt's Invasion by Nebuchadrezzar (vv.13-26)
> Israel's Restoration after Divine Discipline (vv.27-28).

The two parts into which the prophecy against Egypt is divided (vv.2-12; 13-26) were probably written at different times, and the introduction to the second message provides some confirmation of this view: "The word that the Lord spake to Jeremiah the prophet, how Nebuchadrezzar king of Babylon should come and smite the land of Egypt" (v.13). Streane must be right in saying that "As regards subject matter, however, the second follows naturally upon the first, the declaration of further subjugation upon the proclamation of the enemy's signal success at Carchemish".

Verses 2-12: Egypt's Defeat at Carchemish

While these verses describe an event that had already taken place (v.2), the rout of the Egyptian army had been predicted beforehand (vv.3-12). The section therefore records the fulfilment of the prophecy against Egypt, providing further confirmation of the inerrancy of the prophetic word. Attention is therefore drawn to the fulfilment of the prophecy (v.2); and to the details of the prophecy (vv.3-12).

The fulfilment of the prophecy (v.2)

The prophecy is "Against Egypt, against the army of Pharaoh-necho king of Egypt, which was by the river Euphrates in Carchemish, which Nebuchadrezzar king of Babylon smote in the fourth year of Jehoiakim the son of Josiah king of Judah". As a result, "the king of Egypt came not again any more out of his land: for the king of Babylon had taken from the river of Egypt unto the river Euphrates all that pertained to the king of Egypt" (2 Kings 24.7).

According to Streane, Carchemish was evidently not Cercesium, at the junction of the rivers Chebar and Euphrates, but was located considerably higher up the Euphrates. He quotes Professor Rawlinson who describes Carchemish as "the key to Syria on the east, and as commanding the ordinary passage of the Euphrates", adding that it was "the only great city in that quarter" and that its name means "the fort of Chemosh", the god of the Moabites (2 Kings 23.13). Feinberg states that it had been under the rule of the Hittites and Assyrians.

The details of the prophecy (vv.3-12)

The defeat of the Egyptian army is described in what have been called "two parallel poems" (Laetsch). In the first place the Egyptians were defeated in spite of their careful preparation (vv.3-6), and in the second in spite of their immense numbers (vv.7-11). The second "poem" heightens the ignominy of Egypt's collapse by recounting the presumptuous boast, "I will go up...I will destroy" (v.8).

Their intense preparation

"Order ye the buckler and shield, and draw near to battle. Harness the horses; and get up, ye horsemen, and stand forth with your helmets; furbish (polish) the spears, and put on the brigandines" (vv.3-4). The "buckler" was a small round shield, said to protect a lightly-armed soldier, whereas the "shield" was much larger and covered the entire body. It was sometimes carried by a shield-bearer. Chariots formed a very important element in Egyptian warfare. According to Streane, "helmets were not worn except actually in battle, and hence this command was equivalent to an order instantly to engage". "Brigandines" were coats of mail. After this flurry of instructions, the Egyptian army stood ready for battle.

But Carchemish witnessed their defeat: "Wherefore have I seen them dismayed and turned away back? and their mighty ones are beaten down, and are fled apace, and look not back: for fear was round about, saith the Lord" (v.5). According to Streane, "the Hebrew…expresses the inexplicable character of the sight. That so brilliant a host should be defeated! It is beyond comprehension". Feinberg suggests that the Egyptian's "fear" was nothing less than supernaturally-induced panic. With all their speed and power, the Egyptian army fell in battle: "Toward the north, hard by the river Euphrates, they have stumbled and fallen" (v.6, JND).

Their immense numbers

"Who is this that cometh up as a flood, whose waters are moved as the rivers? Egypt riseth up like a flood, and his waters are moved like the rivers" (vv.7-8a). The advance of the Egyptian army is likened to the annual flooding of the Nile, and to the branches of the Nile in the Delta region of Lower Egypt.

The Egyptians march into the war zone with confidence reminiscent of their ancestors when pursuing Israel (cp. Ex 15.9): "…he saith, I will go up, and will cover the earth; I will destroy the city and the inhabitants thereof" (v.8b), not knowing that they are being drawn into battle by the Lord: "Come up, ye horses; and rage (drive furiously), ye chariots; and let the mighty men come forth; the Ethiopians and the Libyans ('Cush and Phut', JND), that handle the shield; and the Lydians, that handle and bend the bow" (v.9). The Ethiopians, Libyans and Lydians are "mercenary troops, who formed from the days of Psammetichus the chief part of the Egyptian armies" (Streane). The Ethiopian and Libyan contingents formed the heavily-armed section of the army, whilst the Lydians were lightly-armed. All three are mentioned again as Egyptian mercenaries by Ezekiel (Ezek 30.5). The Libyans are evidently a different people from the modern state in North Africa. Nahum distinguishes "Put" ('Phut', JND) from "Lubim ('Libyans', JND)" (Nahum 3.9). Feinberg identifies Libya here as Somaliland. It is generally thought that the Lydians (or "Ludim", Gen 10.13) here were also an African people living west of Egypt, rather than the Asiatic people ("Lud") mentioned in Isaiah 66.19.

The defeat of the Egyptian armies at Carchemish was divinely inflicted. It has already been noted that the Lord calls Nebuchadrezzar (or Nebuchadnezzar) "my servant" (25.9; 27.6; 43.10). The Babylonian victory was no mere fortune of war: "For this is the day of the Lord God of hosts, a day of vengeance, that he may avenge him of his adversaries…for the Lord God of hosts hath a sacrifice in the north country by the river Euphrates" (v.10). In a different connection, although Nebuchadnezzar was also involved, Zephaniah refers to "the Lord's sacrifice" (Zeph 1.8). Further sacrifices of this nature are mentioned in Isaiah 34.6 and Ezekiel 39.17.

Streane suggests that the words "this is the day" (v.10) refer to the day determined by the Lord to inflict judgment rightly on Egypt on account, not only of "the undying memory of the bondage of old times, but of later troubles, such as that of Rehoboam's time (1 Kings 14.25-26), and those in much more recent days". The Egyptians who said, "I will go up, and will cover the earth; I will destroy the city and the inhabitants thereof" (v.8), are crushed and humiliated. "The Lord had picked a day for Egypt's downfall. And this was that day" (Habel).

In words that "have the tone of a triumphant irony" (Ellicott's Commentary), Egypt is advised to seek a remedy for her wounds: "Go up into Gilead, and take balm, O virgin, the daughter of Egypt: in vain shalt thou use many medicines; for thou shalt not be cured" (v.11). The "balm of Gilead" was highly esteemed for its healing powers (8.22), and it is said that Egypt was "full of physicians" (Homer, quoted by Feinberg) and "famous for her medical arts" (Pliny, quoted by Feinberg), but the wounds sustained by Egypt at Carchemish would prove to be incurable. "It proved, in fact, to be a blow from which the old Egyptian monarchy never recovered" (Ellicott's Commentary). The words, "O virgin, the daughter of Egypt" refer to the fact that, hitherto, it had remained unconquered.

The defeat of Egypt would be widely publicised: "The nations have heard of thy shame, and thy cry hath filled the land ('the earth', JND): for the mighty man hath stumbled against the mighty, and they are fallen both together" (v.12). "The report of the defeat and utter rout and confused fight that followed would be spread far and wide among the nations" (Ellicott's Commentary).

The Egyptians would have done well to have heeded the advice, "Let not him that girdeth on his harness boast himself as he that putteth it off" (1 Kings 20.11), and the Lord's people today must certainly remember the injunction, "Wherefore let him that thinketh he standeth take heed lest he fall" (1 Cor 10.12).

Verses 13-26: Egypt's Invasion by Nebuchadrezzar

The record of Egypt's defeat by Nebuchadrezzar (vv.2-12) is accompanied by a prediction of his invasion of Egypt: "The word that the Lord spake to Jeremiah the prophet, how Nebuchadrezzar king of Babylon should come and smite the land of Egypt" (v.13). According to Harrison, the expedition against Egypt took place in 568/7 BC. Some details of the invasion have already been given in 43.10-13, and the reader is referred to comments made in connection with those verses.

The course of the invasion is now described, and attention is drawn to the following: the dismay in Egypt (vv.14-17); the dominance of Nebuchadrezzar (v.18); the devastation of Egypt (vv.19-24); and the deliverance of the gods and kings of Egypt (vv.25-26).

The dismay in Egypt (vv.14-17)

With the approach of the Babylonian army, the alarm would be sounded throughout Egypt: "Declare ye in Egypt, and publish in Migdol, and publish in Noph (Memphis) and in Tahpanhes: say ye, Stand fast, and prepare thee; for the sword shall devour ('devoureth', JND: perhaps referring to the subjugation of neighbouring nations) round about thee" (v.14). But the army would be gripped by fear, and the mercenaries would return to their native countries: "Why are thy valiant men swept away? they stood not, because the Lord did drive them. He made many to fall, yea, one fell upon another: and they said, Arise, and let us go again to our own people, and to the land of our nativity, from the oppressing sword" (vv.15-16). It should be noted that the fear and panic in the Egyptian army was induced by the Lord. He ensured that His servant Nebuchadrezzar (43.10) would be successful in battle. Some commentators, following the Septuagint Version, espouse the rendering "why has Apis fled" (RSV), referring to the sacred bull of Egypt, but this is rejected by other expositors, particularly as "Apis was worshipped only in Memphis, and was in no sense representative of the gods or power of Egypt as the context demands" (Feinberg).

The defecting mercenaries have little time for Pharaoh, whom they describe as "a noise" because he had "passed the time appointed" (v.17). Harrison suggests that they scornfully regarded Pharaoh as a "loudmouth", regarding him as "a braggart who has missed his opportunity". The expression "time appointed" is probably best explained as "the opportune time when he might have averted disaster" (Unger).

The dominance of Nebuchadrezzar (v.18)

"As I live, saith the King, whose name is the Lord of hosts, Surely as Tabor is among the mountains, and as Carmel by the sea, so shall he come." Nebchadrezzar was king of Babylon, and Pharaoh (in this case, as above, Amasis) was king of Egypt, but the "Lord of hosts" was *the* King" (v.18). He rules over all! Both earthly potentates had vast resources at their disposal, but these paled into insignificance when compared with the resources of the "Lord of hosts" who, in the words of Nebuchadnezzar himself, "doeth according to his will in the army of heaven, and among the inhabitants of the earth: and none can stay his hand, or say unto him, What doest thou?" (Dan 4.35).

Amongst earthly kings, Nebuchadrezzar was dominant, and in taking the road to Egypt he would pass Tabor, looming above the plain of Esdraelon, and Carmel, looming above the Mediterranean. Both were "conspicuous in relation to the neighbouring terrain" (Harrison). In similar fashion, Nebuchadrezzar towered above other monarchs, including the king of Egypt.

The devastation of Egypt (vv.19-24)

As a result of the coming invasion, the Egyptians were to prepare for exile: "O thou daughter dwelling in Egypt, furnish thyself to go into captivity" (v.19a). The reasons follow.

Places would be lost

"Noph shall be waste and desolate without an inhabitant" (v.19b). Noph (Memphis) was the capital of Lower Egypt (northern Egypt).

Personnel would be lost

"Egypt is like a very fair heifer, but destruction cometh ('the gad-fly cometh', JND); it cometh out of the north. Also her hired men are in the midst of her like fatted bullocks; for they also are turned back, and are fled away together: they did not stand, because the day of their calamity was come upon them, and the time of their visitation" (vv.20-21). The country itself is described as "a very fair heifer", referring to the wealth and luxury she had enjoyed, but her peace was about to be disturbed by Nebuchadrezzar, who is likened to the "gad-fly" (7171; "destruction", AV), "an insect that stings oxen and drives them to madness" (Laetsch). Egypt's mercenaries ("hired men") are likened to "fatted bullocks" ready for slaughter. They are evidently well aware of the fact, and make their escape. Ellicott's Commentary describes them as "a drove of terrified cattle, fed to the full, driven to the slaughter-house". Perhaps it could be said of these soldiers, "The hireling fleeth, because he is an hireling" (Jn 10.13). According to Herodotus, Hophra (predecessor to Amasis) hired 30,000 mercenaries from Asia Minor, Charrans and Ionians, and settled them in the fertile lands above Bubastis in the Delta country.

Believers today are to "Put on the whole armour of God" in order to "be able to stand against the wiles of the devil", and to "withstand in the evil day, and having done all, to stand" (Eph 6.11,13). Paul urged the believers at Corinth to "stand fast in the faith, quit you like men, be strong" (1 Cor 16.13), and the believers at Philippi were to "stand fast in the Lord" (Phil 4.1). Having heard Timothy's report, the apostle rejoiced that the Lord's people at Thessalonica had not succumbed to pressure: "Therefore, brethren, we were comforted over you in all our affliction and distress by your faith: For now we live, if ye stand fast in the Lord" (1 Thess 3.7-8).

Protection would be lost

"The voice thereof shall go like a serpent; for they shall march with an army, and come against her with axes, as hewers of wood. They shall cut down her forest, saith the Lord, though it cannot be searched; because they are more than the grasshoppers (697; 'locusts', JND), and are innumerable" (vv.22-23). The voice of Egypt is likened to the sound of a frightened serpent when it is aroused from its lair by woodcutters. According to Feinberg, "The serpent figure is an ironic reference to one of the most noted of Egyptian deities, prominent even in royal insignia – the coiled uraeus". The density of Egypt's population, likened to a forest that "cannot be searched", would pose no problem to the axe-wielding Babylonian army that was so numerically strong that it is said to exceed a plague of locusts. All this would contribute to the shame and distress of Egypt: "The daughter of Egypt shall be confounded ('put to shame', JND, or 'disgraced', Streane); she shall be delivered into the hand of the people of the north" (v.24).

The deliverance of the gods and kings of Egypt (vv.25-26)
"The Lord of hosts, the God of Israel, saith; Behold, I will punish the multitude of No ('Amon of No', JND), and Pharaoh, and Egypt, with their gods, and their kings; even Pharaoh, and all them that trust in him: And I will deliver them into the hand of those that seek their lives, and into the hand of Nebuchadrezzar king of Babylon, and into the hand of his servants." No (Thebes) was the capital of Upper Egypt (southern Egypt), and Amon is said to be "the sun god, for centuries the chief god of the Egyptian pantheon, identified with Zeus by the Greeks" (Laetsch). The titles, "The Lord of hosts, the God of Israel", have particular significance in their current context: as "The Lord of hosts" He is perfectly able to accomplish His will, and as "the God of Israel" He is utterly superior to the gods of Egypt. The Lord abhors idolatry, whether amongst His own people or amongst pagan peoples. The "kings" (v.25) have been defined as "officials of royal blood" (Laetsch). The reference to all who trust in Pharaoh (v.25), and who would not escape the vengeance of Nebuchadrezzar (v.26), must include the Judæan remnant who had fled to Egypt for refuge, and this gives added significance to the title, "the God of Israel". The reader is referred to comments made in connection with 43.10 and 44.11-14.

The section concludes with the restoration of Egypt: "and afterward it shall be inhabited, as in the days of old, saith the Lord" (v.26b). According to Ezekiel, "the land of Egypt shall be desolate and waste…No foot of man shall pass through it, nor foot of beast shall pass through it, neither shall it be inhabited forty years…Yet thus saith the Lord God; At the end of forty years will I gather the Egyptians from the people whither they were scattered: And I will bring again the captivity of Egypt…and they shall be there a base kingdom. It shall be the basest of the kingdoms; neither shall it exalt itself any more above the nations" (Ezek 29.9,11,13-15). While "under Cyrus, forty years after Nebuchadnezzar's conquest, Egypt was liberated from the Babylonian yoke, she never regained her former greatness" (Unger). There can therefore be little doubt that the prophecy refers to the end-time, when Israel will "be the third with Egypt and with Assyria, even a blessing in the midst of the land: Whom the Lord of hosts shall bless, saying, Blessed be Egypt my people, and Assyria the work of my hands, and Israel mine inheritance" (Is 19.24-25). The predicted regathering of Egypt in the current passage should be compared with the closing words of the prophecies against Moab (48.47), Ammon (49.6), and Elam (49.39).

Verses 27-28: Israel's Restoration after Divine Discipline

These verses make a striking contrast with the portrayal of Egypt's defeat and destruction. "But fear not thou, O my servant Jacob, and be not dismayed, O Israel: for, behold, I will save thee from afar off, and thy seed from the land of their captivity; and Jacob shall return, and be in rest and at ease, and none shall make him afraid" (v.27). The prophecy envisages restoration to the land, not only from Egypt, but from all nations: "Fear thou not, O Jacob my servant, saith the Lord: for I am with thee; for I will make a full end of all the nations whither I have driven thee: but I will not make a full end of thee, but correct thee in measure; yet will I not leave thee wholly unpunished" (v.28). These verses substantially repeat 30.10-11, and the reader is referred to comments made at that point in the prophecy. There can be little doubt that the promise of national restoration and blessing is repeated here to encourage God's people in captivity. If a promise is made of recovery for Egypt (v.26), how much more for the Lord's people! It is worth repeating that while the Lord will not make a "full end" of His people, He will nevertheless correct them "in measure" and not leave them "wholly unpunished".

The Lord's people today must remember that while "the God of all grace" has called every believer "unto his eternal glory" (1 Pet 5.10), they must "all appear before the judgment seat of Christ; that every one may receive the things done in his body, according to that he hath done, whether it be good or bad" (2 Cor 5.10). In the matters of faithfulness and service, "Every man's work shall be made manifest…If any man's work abide which he hath built thereupon, he shall receive a reward. If any man's work shall be burned, he shall suffer loss: but he himself shall be saved; yet so as by fire" (1 Cor 3.13-15).

JEREMIAH 47

The second prophecy in the "foreign nations" section of the book concerns Philistia: "The word of the Lord that came to Jeremiah the prophet against the Philistines" (v.1).

While it is usually said that that these particular prophecies (chs.46-51) move from west to east, there is no apparent significance in the order of their occurrence, except that Babylon is placed last since she was used by the Lord to execute judgment on the nations previously named in these chapters. With the fall of Babylon, "the hammer of the whole earth" would be "cut asunder and broken!" (50.23). It is quite possible that the prophecy against Philistia follows the prediction of Egypt's downfall simply because the two nations occupied adjoining territory.

The Philistines were the perennial foes of Israel, and it is worth remembering some of the ways in which they attacked and harassed God's people in the past.

They filled wells: "For all the wells which his (Isaac's) father's servants had digged…the Philistines had stopped them, and filled them with earth" (Gen 26.15).

They exercised lordship: "Knowest thou not that the Philistines are rulers over us?" (Judg 15.11).

They prevented ascent: "After that thou shalt come to the hill of God, where is the garrison of the Philistines" (1 Sam 10.5).

They despatched spoilers: "And the spoilers came out of the camp of the Philistines in three companies" (1 Sam 13.17).

They prohibited weapons: "Now there was no smith found throughout all the land of Israel: for the Philistines said, Lest the Hebrews make them swords or spears" (1 Sam 13.19).

These tactics are still used by the spiritual opponents of the Lord's people. The Philistines have their counterpart today in the satanically led "principalities" and "powers" (Eph 6.12).

This brief prophecy concerning the Philistines is of absorbing interest, and the following should be noticed:

> The Time of the Prophecy (v.1)
> The Identity of the Invader (v.2a)
> The Immensity of the Invasion (v.2b)
> The Impact of the Invasion (v.3)
> The Inclusiveness of the Invasion (vv.4-5)
> The Irreversibility of the Invasion (vv.6-7).

Verse 1: The Time of the Prophecy

In view of the somewhat indefinite historical reference, "before that Pharaoh smote Gaza", it is difficult to assign a date to the prophecy. The attack on Gaza has been attributed either to Pharaoh-necho (609-594 BC), or to Pharaoh-hophra (588-568 BC). Those who favour Pharaoh-necho suggest that he attacked Gaza either about the time that he defeated Josiah at Megiddo (2 Kings 23.29), or later on his return to Egypt after his defeat by Nebuchadrezzar at Carchemish (46.2). Those who support the view that Pharaoh-hophra (44.30) was responsible suggest that he took Gaza in his campaign against Tyre and Sidon.

The absence of specific details in such instances as this indicates that the significance of the event lies elsewhere, and in this case it is the fact that the fall of Philistia was predicted, not only before it took place, but before an earlier defeat at the hand of a different enemy took place, emphasising yet again the inerrancy of Biblical prophecy.

Verse 2a: The Identity of the Invader

While it is true that the imagery of flood-water is used of the Egyptian armies (46.7-8), in the current passage reference is made to the Babylonians: "Behold, waters rise up out of the north". The expression "out of the north" is frequently used in the book with reference to Babylon, and occurs first in connection with the commissioning of the prophet: "Out of the north an evil shall break forth upon all the inhabitants of the land" (1.14). Jeremiah had predicted that the Lord would "send and take all the families of the north…and Nebuchadrezzar the king of Babylon, my servant, and will bring them against this land…and against all these nations round about, and will utterly destroy them, and make them an astonishment, and an hissing, and perpetual desolations" (25.9). The roster of the nations involved included "all the kings of the land of the Philistines, and Ashkelon, and Azzah (Gaza), and Ekron, and the remnant of Ashdod" (25.20). It also included "all the kings of Tyrus, and all the kings of Zidon" (25.22), and reference is made to these two maritime cities in v.4 of the present chapter.

Verse 2b: The Immensity of the Invasion

The invasion from the north is likened to "an overflowing flood" that would "overflow the land, and all that is therein; the city, and them that dwell therein". In the words of Harrison, "The image is that of a flood which will engulf the Philistine plain". The Assyrian invasion of Judah is similarly described: "behold, the Lord bringeth up upon them the waters of the river, strong and many, even the king of Assyria, and all his glory: and he shall come up over all his channels, and go over all his banks: And he shall pass through Judah; he shall overflow and go over" (Is 8.7-8). It is no small wonder that the Jeremiah adds, "then the men shall cry, and all the inhabitants of the land shall howl". Resistance would be impossible; nothing could halt an army of such vast proportions.

Verse 3: The Impact of the Invasion

The approach of the enemy would create such unnerving panic in the land that terror-stricken parents would be utterly paralysed by fear, and leave their children to the mercy of the invader: "At the noise of the stamping of the hoofs of his strong horses, at the rushing of his chariots, and at the rumbling of his wheels, the fathers shall not look back to their children for feebleness of hands". The imagery of a vast flood gives place to the noise of actual battle. "The prophet hears the agonized shrieks, the howls of despair; hears the noise of stamping hoofs, the rattling of the chariots, the rumbling of the wheels, as the enemy speeds onward in his victorious *Blitzkrieg*" (Laetsch).

Verses 4-5: The Inclusiveness of the Invasion

It is emphasised that the invasion would engulf the entire country. The coming catastrophe is described as "the day that cometh to spoil *all* the Philistines, and to cut off from Tyrus and Zidon every helper that remaineth: for the Lord will spoil the Philistines, the remnant of the country of Caphtor" (v.4). Zephaniah also describes the desolation of Philistia, and the occupation of her territory by Judah (Zeph 2.4-7).

The desolation of Philistia by the Babylonian hordes would adversely affect Tyre and Sidon. Laetsch suggests that this refers to the severance of any help that the Phoenician cities might have received against the Babylonians, and continues, "Unable to obtain any more mercenaries from Philistia, the proud, rich commercial cities (cp. Ezek 27.1-25) shall be humiliated (Ezek 26.1-21; 27.26-36)". It has been suggested that there was some form of alliance between Philistia and the two Phoenician cities, and that this is supported by the inclusion of "the Philistines with the inhabitants of Tyre" in the roster of nations allied in their determination to obliterate Israel (Ps 83.7). Attention is drawn to Ezekiel's prediction: "Behold, I will bring upon Tyrus Nebuchadrezzar king of Babylon, a king of kings, from the north, with horses, and with chariots, and with horsemen, and companies, and much people...By reason of the abundance of his horses their dust shall cover thee: thy walls shall shake at the noise of the horsemen, and of the wheels, and of the chariots, when he shall enter into thy gates" (Ezek 26 7,10).

The "island of Caphtor" (v.4, JND), with the marginal note, "or 'sea-coast'", is named as the original homeland of the Philistines and this is confirmed in the prophecy of Amos: "Have not I brought up Israel out of the land of Egypt? and the Philistines from Caphtor, and the Syrians from Kir?" (Amos 9.7). Caphtor is usually identified with Crete, although some scholars, including Streane, favour the coast of the Egyptian Delta. According to Feinberg, "Jeremiah sees Philistia as the remnant of the ancient Aegean civilization headed by Caphtor...Crete was probably the original home of the Philistines before their entrance to Palestine (Deut 2.23)". The name Palestine is derived from the word Philistine. The Philistines were settled in the land in patriarchal times (Gen 21.32,34; 26.1-18).

Further reference is made to the desolation of Philistia: "Baldness is come upon Gaza; Ashkelon is cut off (possibly meaning 'speechless') with the remnant of their valley: how long wilt thou cut thyself?" (v.5). The "baldness" of Gaza could refer to deep mourning. The shaven head was a sign of shame and humiliation (7.29; 16.6; 48.37; Micah 1.16), but it could also be "a metaphor for the city's destruction" (Feinberg). The expression, "the remnant of their valley", does not necessarily imply a deep valley. According to Gesenius, the word translated "valley" (6010) is used of "a low tract of land of wide extent", and probably refers to the plain of Philistia (commonly known as the *Shephelah*), in which case the expression, "the remnant", could well refer to the neighbourhood of Ashkelon. Some commentators follow the Septuagint Version and read "Anakim" in the place of "their valley", pointing out that the Anakims were associated with the Philistines before the conquest of Canaan (Josh 11.22), but Feinberg cites Keil and Delitzsch and J. Bright in saying that "there is insufficient evidence…to sustain the LXX reading here". Harrison calls the suggestion "pure conjecture". The people in the area evidently mutilated themselves, something forbidden to the Lord's people (Deut 14.1), in order, according to Laetsch, "to rouse the pity of their gods (cp. 1 Kings 18.28)". As Habel points out, "The rites of mourning performed by the Philistine cities would prove futile".

Verses 6-7: The Irreversibility of the Invasion

It is generally concluded that the cry, "O thou sword of the Lord, how long will it be ere thou be quiet? put up thyself into thy scabbard, rest, and be still" (v.6), comes from the lips of the Philistines, although Harrison suggests that "Jeremiah pleads for the divinely-wielded sword to cease its ravages". On reflection, it does appear unlikely that the Philistines should turn so quickly from their idolatrous practices, and call on the Lord for clemency. However, it has been pointed out that centuries before, after experiencing "the hand of the Lord" in judgment on their cities (1 Sam 5.6,9), the Philistines cried, "Send away the ark of the God of Israel, and let it go again to his own place, that it slay us not, and our people" (1 Sam 5.11). Just as on that occasion the Philistines had hoped to escape the further judgment by returning the Ark of the Covenant together with a "trespass offering" (1 Sam 6.2-8), so now they hoped "to escape Jehovah's judgment by pleading with Him to desist from punishing them" (Laetsch).

But divine judgment could not be averted, and the question (v.6) is answered by a counter-question: "How can it be quiet, seeing the Lord hath given it a charge against Ashkelon, and against the sea shore? there hath he appointed it" (v.7). According to Harrison, Ashkelon was sacked by Nebuchadnezzar in 604 BC for the way in which it resisted him, and its people were deported to Babylonia. This may account for the fact that the city is mentioned particularly here.

At Calvary, the "sword of the Lord" was used against the Lord Jesus: "Awake, O sword, against my shepherd, and against the man that is my fellow, saith the Lord of hosts: smite the shepherd, and the sheep shall be scattered: and I will turn mine hand upon the little ones" (Zech 13.7). The Lord Jesus quoted these words: "All ye shall be offended because of me this night: for it is written, I will smite the shepherd, and the sheep of the flock shall be scattered abroad" (Mt 26.31). The words, "*I* will smite the shepherd", emphasise that He was smitten under divine judgment.

> Jehovah bade His sword awake;
> O Christ, it woke 'gainst Thee!
> Thy blood the flaming blade must slake,
> Thy heart its sheath must be;
> All for my sake my peace to make,
> Now sleeps that sword for me.
>
> (Anne Ross Cousin)

JEREMIAH 48

The third prophecy in this section of the book concerns Moab: "Against Moab thus saith the Lord of hosts, the God of Israel" (v.1). The fact that the Lord is described as "the God of Israel" is perhaps to emphasise His utter superiority over Chemosh, the god of Moab.

Lying to the east of the Dead Sea, Moab comprised a high tableland between the rivers Arnon to the north and Zered to the south. Their northern and southern neighbours were Ammon and Edom respectively. The Moabites were descended from Lot (Gen 19.36-7) and have been described as "another of Israel's traditional enemies" (Habel). As a result of "the doctrine of Balaam" (Rev 2.14), Moabitish women were responsible for leading Israel into immorality and idolatry (Num 25.1-3; 31.16), and once Israel had occupied Canaan there was intermittent warfare between the two peoples (Judg 3.12-30; 1 Sam 14.47) until David made them tributaries (2 Sam 8.2,12). According to Harrison, "In the late eighth century (800-700 BC) Assyria conquered the Moabites, but when the empire collapsed, Moab regained its independence. It was again subdued by Nebuchadnezzar after 581 BC, and later came under Persian and Arab influence". The Moabites worshipped Chemosh (vv.7,13,46), but Ruth was ready to abandon these idolatrous practices; in cleaving to Naomi, her mother-in-law, and forsaking the land of her birth, she was led to say, "thy people shall be my people, and thy God my God" (Ruth 1.16).

Although the date of this prophecy cannot be determined with certainty, it is quite possible that it was delivered either during the reign of Jehoiakim or that of Zedekiah. It was following Jehoiakim's rebellion against Nebuchadnezzar that the Lord sent not only "bands of the Chaldees", but "bands of the Syrians...of the Moabites, and...of the children of Ammon...against Judah to destroy it" (2 Kings 24.2). It was early in the reign of Zedekiah that the kings of Edom, Moab, Ammon, Tyrus and Zidon were involved with him in a proposal to throw off the Babylonian yoke (Jer.27.1-11). While Jeremiah is not alone in pronouncing the doom of the Moabites, his prophecy against them is more extensive than others in the Old Testament, of which examples are found in Isaiah 15.1-16.13, Ezekiel 25.8-11, and Amos 2.1-3.

The chapter may be divided in the following way:

> The Cry of Moab (vv.1-6)
> The Condemnation of Moab (vv.7-39)
> The Conqueror of Moab (vv.40-46)
> The Coming Restoration of Moab (v.47).

Verses 1-6: The Cry of Moab

The destruction of Moab is vividly conveyed by a variety of words or phrases, amongst which the word "confounded" occurs twice in v.1, the expressions "let us cut it off" and "cut down" occur in v.2, and the words "crying" or "cry" occur three times in vv.3-5.

Moab would be confounded

"Woe unto Nebo! for it is spoiled: Kiriathaim is confounded and taken: Misgab is confounded and dismayed" (v.1). The words "spoiled" (7703) and "confounded" (3001) both signify destruction, "spoiled" meaning "to act violently with any one, to oppress, to destroy him…to lay waste" (Gesenius), and "confounded" meaning "put to shame" which, according to Gesenius, is poetic language for the overthrow of the cities named. Commentators are at pains to point out that Nebo here is not the mountain bearing that name (Deut 32.49; 34.1), but a city of Reuben (Num 32.38). According to the Moabite Stone, said to have been erected *circa* 840 BC and discovered at Dibon in AD 1868, Nebo was captured by King Mesha after his revolt against Israel following the death of Ahab. Kiriathaim is also named on the Moabite Stone and is said to be possibly "the modern El Quraiyat, some six miles north-west of Dibon in Jordan" (Harrison). Misgab, meaning "the height" or "the citadel" (Streane) is unidentified. It has been suggested that the name might be a common noun, and therefore be a general reference to any fortress.

Moab would be cut off

"There shall be no more praise of Moab (meaning, 'the glory of Moab is no more'): in Heshbon they have devised evil against it; come, and let us cut it off from being a nation" (v.2). The identity of the speakers here is not disclosed at this point in the prophecy, but the enemy evidently made their plans to conquer Moab at Heshbon, standing on the northern or Ammonite frontier of Moab, and once the capital of the Amorite kingdom of Sihon (Num 21.26; Deut 2.24). "Madmen" (v.2) is unidentified, but its inhabitants would be relentlessly hunted down: "the sword shall pursue thee". It is said that there is a play on the sound of the Hebrew words in the case of both Heshbon and Madmen. It is impossible to reproduce accurately the effect in English, but an approximation might be "they plotted in plot-town (Heshbon), and there will be silence in silent-town (Madmen)". The use of paronomasia is particularly noticeable in Micah 1.10-15.

Moab would cry out

"A voice of crying shall be from Horonaim" (v.3); "her little ones have caused a cry to be heard" (v.4); "for in the going down of Horonaim the enemies have heard a cry of destruction" (v.5). Isaiah describes the Moabites as "fugitives" in what can certainly be described as a parallel passage (Is 15.5).

While Horonaim is unidentified, its association with Luhith indicates that it was located on low ground, whereas Luhith was situated on a hill: "For in the going up of Luhith continual weeping shall go up; for in the going down of Horonaim the enemies have heard a cry of destruction" (v.5). Laetsch has probably captured the picture accurately in saying, "Up the hills and down the hills terrified men, excited women, shrieking children, hurry panic-stricken to reach the southern desert lands". Streane suggests, however, that the words "little ones" (v.4) might have been translated "abject ones", made so by distress, although Ellicott's Commentary states that the reference here is to cities, not to children. The only place of safety was "the southern desert lands" (Laetsch): "Flee, save your lives, and be like the heath in the wilderness" (v.6). According to Gesenius, the word "heath" (6176) is, properly, "naked", and means "needy", referring, in that sense, to a destitute man. However, there is evidently an allusion to a desert bush, either a juniper or, possibly, a tamarisk. The reader is referred to comments made in connection with 17.6 where "the man that trusteth in man" (17.5) is likened to "the heath in the desert".

Verses 7-39: The Condemnation of Moab

Four reasons are given for the destruction of Moab, and these may be summarised as follows: Moabite prosperity is condemned (vv.7-10); Moabite complacency is condemned (vv.11-13); Moabite strength is condemned (vv.14-25); and Moabite pride is condemned (vv.26-39).

Moabite prosperity is condemned (vv.7-10)

"For because thou hast trusted in thy works and in thy treasures, thou shalt also be taken" (v.7). The reference to Moab's "works" and "treasures" (cp. v.36), implies that materialism was one reason for her coming destruction, and this is a timely warning to God's people today: "But they that will be rich fall into temptation and a snare, and into many foolish and hurtful lusts, which drown men in destruction and perdition. For the love of money is the root of all evil: which while some coveted after, they have erred from the faith, and pierced themselves through with many sorrows" (1 Tim 6.9-10). The Lord Jesus warned against covetousness, saying that "a man's life consisteth not in the abundance of the things which he possesseth" (Lk 12.15) and illustrating His teaching by the parable of the rich fool, with its conclusion: "So is he that layeth up treasure for himself, and is not rich toward God" (Lk 12.21). The "rich fool" lost everything, and so would the Moabites: "And the spoiler shall come upon every city, and no city shall escape" (v.8). Everything in which they trusted would be destroyed, and their land, whether "the valley" (referring to the Jordan Valley, which touched Moab on the west) or "the plain" (referring to the plateau or tableland where most of the cities were located), would fall to the invader.

Their idolatry would not saved them. "Chemosh shall go forth into captivity with his priests and his princes together" (v.7). The priests and princes of Ammon would suffer the same fate (49.3). It is not without significance that Chemosh is mentioned in connection with Moab's materialism. No doubt the Moabites ascribed their prosperity to Chemosh. They are, in fact, described as "the people of Chemosh" (v.46; cp. Num 21.29). Sadly, Solomon erected a high place for Chemosh near Jerusalem (1 Kings 11.7) and it remained there until demolished by Josiah (2 Kings 23.13). How easily the people of God can be tempted to worship at the altars of materialism! In the hymn-writer's words:

> Jesus calls us from the worship
> Of the vain world's golden store,
> From each idol that would keep us;
> Saying, "Christian, love Me more".
>   (C. F. Alexander)

Chemosh was "a god that cannot save" (Is 45.20), and flight was the only option: "Give wings unto Moab, that it may flee and get away: for the cities thereof shall be desolate, without any to dwell therein" (v.9). As Streane observes, "If the *god* is powerless to prevent his own captivity, what chance is there for the *people?*". Streane also helps to resolve the problem surrounding the words "wings" (6731): "The word elsewhere in pure Hebrew means *a flower*, but in later Hebrew and in Chaldee has frequently the sense which it here bears. The sense is that nothing short of wings would enable the Moabites to escape before their enemies".

The oft-quoted verse, "Cursed be he that doeth the work of Jehovah negligently ('deceitfully', AV)" (v.10, JND), is used of the still unidentified destroyer. He was to do the work thoroughly: "cursed be he that keepeth back his sword from blood". The Lord describes the Assyrian as "the rod of mine anger, and the staff in their hand is mine indignation" (Is 10.5). The Lord expects His servants, whoever they may be, including Nebuchadnezzar (Jer 25.9; 27.6; 43.10) and Cyrus ("my shepherd", Is 44.28), to carry out their allotted tasks in human history.

Moabite complacency is condemned (vv.11-13)

Moab did not lie on the main invasion route, and because of her location she had been largely insulated from occupation and deportation. The Moabites had never experienced exile: "Moab hath been at ease from his youth, and he hath settled on his lees, and hath not been emptied from vessel to vessel, neither hath he gone into captivity: therefore his taste remained in him, and his scent is not changed" (v.11). The nation is compared to undisturbed vintage wine which had been allowed to rest on its sediment instead of being decanted from jar to jar. In ancient times, new wine was allowed to settle on its "lees", the sediment, until it had acquired the highest degree of flavour and strength. As Harrison points out, "The simile is particularly apposite because of the esteem in which Moabite vineyards were held (cp. Is 16.8-11)".

But Moab's complacency would be rudely interrupted. Whereas, in the past, the nation is likened to "an earthenware jar that is carefully tilted so as not to lose the sediment of the wine" (Feinberg), Moab would undergo some very rough treatment: "behold, the days come, saith the Lord, that I will send unto him wanderers, that shall cause him to wander, and shall empty his vessels, and break their bottles" (v.12), or "I will send unto him pourers that shall pour him off, and shall empty his vessels, and break in pieces his flagons" (JND). The words translated "wanderers" and "wander" (6808) mean "to incline" referring to "a vessel which is to be emptied" (Gesenius). The verse can be legitimately rendered, "I will send unto him tilters, that shall cause him to be tilted".

The second reference to Moab's idolatry in this chapter emphasises Moab's complete disillusion with Chemosh: "And Moab shall be ashamed of Chemosh, as the house of Israel was ashamed of Bethel their confidence" (v.13). Israel was urged to "seek not Bethel, nor enter into Gilgal, and pass not to Beersheba: for Gilgal shall surely go into captivity, and Bethel shall come to nought" (Amos 5.5). Just as the golden calf at Bethel (1 Kings 12.26-29) gave no protection against Shalmaneser (2 Kings 17.1-6), so Chemosh would give no protection against the enemies of Moab. In both cases, idolatry was disastrous. The Lord's people today can rejoice that their confidence is vested in the Lord Jesus whom John describes as "the true God" (1 Jn 5.20). They can say confidently, with Paul, "I am not ashamed: for I know whom I have believed, and am persuaded that he is able to keep that which I have committed unto him against that day" (2 Tim 1.12). Chemosh could keep nothing and nobody!

Moabite strength is condemned (vv.14-25)

This section of the chapter commences with the question, "How say ye, We are mighty and strong men for the war?" (v.14), and concludes with the statement, "The horn of Moab is cut off, and his arm is broken" (v.25). Reference is made in the intervening verses to the destruction of Moab's strength: "Moab is spoiled...his chosen young men are gone down to the slaughter" (v.15); "How is the strong staff broken" (v.17); "He shall destroy thy strong holds" (v.18). Moab's confident assertion of strength would prove to be an empty boast. Believers today must to heed the injunction, "let him that thinketh he standeth take heed lest he fall" (1 Cor 10.12). They are to be "strong in the Lord, and in the power of his might" (Eph 6.10), and "strong in the grace that is in Christ Jesus" (2 Tim 2.1). Attention is drawn to the following.

The end of Moab's strong soldiery (v.15)

"Moab is spoiled, and gone up out of her cities, and his chosen young men are gone down to the slaughter", or "Moab is laid waste, and they are gone up into her cities (or, 'her cities are gone up in smoke', margin), and his chosen young men are gone down to the slaughter" (RV). The "young men" of Damascus and Babylon would also be slaughtered (49.26; 50.30). Bearing in mind that "The glory of young men is their strength" (Prov 20.29), the loss of Moab's youth meant that the nation was enfeebled. This is the chilling reality in many assemblies today, and should lead every company of God's people to cry earnestly, "Give me children, or else I die" (Gen 30.1).

The fulfilment of the prophecy is assured by the identity of its Author. He is "the King, whose name is the Lord of hosts" (v.15). He proclaimed Himself in identical terms in connection with the invasion of Egypt (46.18) and the destruction of Babylon (51.57). Chemosh was powerless and without any resource. The Lord does not declare Himself to be "King of Israel", but to be "the King". He is the "King of nations" (10.7). His power is irresistible. Moab might say, "We are mighty and strong men for the war", but the Lord is "the living God, and an everlasting king: at his wrath the earth shall tremble, and the nations shall not be able to abide his indignation" (10.10). "The King" is above all kings. He is "the King eternal, immortal, invisible, the only wise God" (1 Tim 1.17), the "King of kings and Lord of lords" (1 Tim 6.15).

The end of Moab's strong government (vv.16-17)

"The calamity of Moab is near to come, and his affliction hasteneth fast. All ye that are about him, bemoan him; and all ye that know his name, say, How is the strong staff broken, and the beautiful rod!" The staff and rod symbolise authority and strength, both of which would cease under divine judgment.

The end of Moab's strong fortifications (vv.18-25)

"Thou daughter that dost inhabit Dibon, come down from thy glory, and sit in thirst; for the spoiler of Moab shall come upon thee, and he shall *destroy thy strong holds*" (v.18). The words "daughter that dost inhabit Dibon" are poetic language for the inhabitants of Dibon. According to Streane, Dibon was built on two hills, hence the words "come down from thy glory". Streane continues by explaining that "the picture is of the inhabitants driven forth from the city and about to be led away, but obliged meanwhile to sit on the ground hungry and thirsty and await their captor's pleasure". Dibon, the modern Diban, was four miles north of the Arnon and thirteen miles east of the Dead Sea.

Aroer (v.19) was located to the south-west of Dibon, and its significance here lay in its position near the Arnon, the perennial stream that flows into the Dead Sea, indicating that the news of Moab's utter destruction would reach the very border of the land. The news would be broken to the inhabitants of Aroer by the fugitives streaming out of Moab. When the question is asked, "What is done?" (v.19), the answer is given, possibly by the refugees themselves, but more likely by the prophet: "Moab is confounded; for it is broken down: howl and cry; tell ye it in Arnon, that Moab is spoiled" (v.20). It has been said that the expression "by the way" (v.19) refers to "an age-old trade and military route leading from the Gulf of Akabah to Damascus, a distance of three hundred miles…this highway passed through Aroer and Dibon" (Laetsch). This introduces a list of the towns involved (vv.21-24), showing the extent of the destruction. According to Feinberg, "The towns are listed from north to south" (following the progress of the invasion), and modern scholars state that "most of the places are unknown". Having mentioned Holon, Jahazah, Mephaath, Dibon, Nebo, Beth-diblathaim, Kiriathaim, Beth-gamul, Beth-meon, Kerioth and Bozrah, Jeremiah adds, "and upon all the cities of the land of Moab, far or near", with the conclusion, "The horn of Moab is cut off, and his arm is broken, saith the Lord" (vv.24-25). Moab would be totally deprived of strength and military power.

Moabite pride is condemned (vv.26-39)

These verses commence with the charge, "Make ye him drunken: for he magnified himself against the Lord" (v.26; cp. v.42), and conclude with Moab's shame and humiliation: "how hath Moab turned the back with shame! so shall Moab be a derision and a dismaying to all them about him" (v.39). At the heart of the passage lie the words, "We have heard the pride of Moab" (v.29). The sin of pride is therefore one of the principal reasons for Moab's downfall, and the solemn lesson should not escape God's people today. Through Jeremiah the Lord had said, "Let not the wise man glory in his wisdom, neither let the mighty man glory in his might, let not the rich man glory in his riches: But let him that glorieth glory in this, that he understandeth and knoweth me, that I am the Lord which exercise lovingkindness, judgment, and righteousness, in the earth: for in these things I delight, saith the Lord" (9.23-24). Pride is the first of the seven things that the Lord hates: "These six things doth the Lord hate: yea, seven are an abomination unto him: A proud look, a lying tongue, and hands that shed innocent blood, An heart that deviseth wicked imaginations, feet that be swift in running to mischief, A false witness that speaketh lies, and he that soweth discord among brethren" (Prov 6.16-19). Moab was to discover that "God resisteth the proud" (1 Pet 5.5). The following should be noted.

Pride treats others with contempt (vv.26-28)

"Make ye him drunken: for he magnified himself against the Lord: Moab also shall wallow in his vomit, and he also shall be in derision. For was not Israel a derision unto thee? was he found among thieves? for since thou spakest of him, thou skippedst for joy" (vv.26-27), or "Was he found among thieves, that as oft as thou didst speak of him, thou didst shake the head?" (JND). Streane explains this very clearly: "Thou couldest not, O Moab, have treated him with more contempt, hadst thou caught him in the act of stealing". It should be observed that the principal lesson here does not lie in the actual occasion on which Moab acted derisively, although this could have been at some time during the siege of Jerusalem, but in the fact that by speaking contemptuously of the Lord's people Moab had magnified themselves against the Lord Himself: "he that toucheth you toucheth the apple of his eye" (Zech 2.8). The law of sowing and reaping (Hos 8.7; Gal 6.7) would apply: the Moabites would be brought into derision in the same way that they had derided Israel. Moab would "reel and totter and finally fall down…into the filth and shame that he had brought upon himself by his haughty self exaltation against the Lord (v.26)", and be forced "to seek refuge in the most inaccessible places, in the caves and clefts of the mountains like the wild pigeon (v.28)" (Laetsch).

Pride is accompanied by boasting (vv.29-30)
"We have heard of the pride of Moab, (he is exceeding proud) his loftiness, and his arrogancy, and his pride, and the haughtiness of his heart. I know his wrath ('pride, haughtiness', Gesenius), saith the Lord; but it shall not be so; his lies shall not so effect it", or "his boastings have wrought nothing" (RV); "his pratings are vain: they do not as they say" (JND).

It has been suggested that in saying, "We have heard of the pride of Moab", both Isaiah (16.6) and Jeremiah (v.29) were "quoting freely a proverb concerning Moab's well-known pride" (Feinberg). The opportunity must be taken to notice that the current chapter should be read in conjunction with Isaiah chs.15 and 16, indicating "the early-date view of Isaiah" (Feinberg). Further references to Moab's pride are found in Isaiah 25.11 and Zephaniah 2.8-10.

Pride robs people of joy (vv.31-34)
Before noting the effect of pride on Moab itself, attention is drawn to the fact that the destruction of the nation brought no joy to the prophet: "Therefore will I howl for Moab, and I will cry out for all Moab; mine heart shall mourn for the men of Kir-heres" (v.31). The Lord takes "no pleasure in the death of the wicked; but that the wicked turn from his way and live" (Ezek 33.11), and His servants should be similarly minded. The Lord's people should never be heartless or vindictive. Kir-heres, or Kir-hareseth (Is 16.7), was "an ancient Moabite capital located sixteen miles south of the Arnon" (Harrison). It was evidently a strong city since it was the only Moabite city that survived the general demolition by Jehoshaphat and Jehoram (2 Kings 3.25).

Since the area was well known for its viticulture, divine judgment is expressed in language which is appropriate to the region: "O vine of Sibmah, I will weep for thee with the weeping of Jazer: thy plants ('branches', RV) are gone over the sea, they reach even to the sea of Jazer: the spoiler is fallen upon thy summer fruits and upon thy vintage" (v.32). What would happen at Sibmah would have already happened at Jazer (both places evidently lay in the vicinity of Heshbon). The renown of the vineyards of Sibmah was evidently known beyond the Dead Sea ("the sea"), and the vineyards themselves spread "even to the sea of Jazer", which is unidentified but which may refer to an inland lake or pool. The removal of joy is stressed further: "And joy and gladness is taken from the plentiful field, and from the land of Moab; and I have caused wine to fail from the winepresses: none shall tread with shouting; their shouting shall be no shouting" (v.33). There would be no harvest and no joy, and the cry, not now of joy but of despair, would sweep from place to place: "From the cry of Heshbon even unto Elealeh, and even unto Jahaz, have they uttered their voice, from Zoar even unto Horonaim, as an heifer of three years old" (v.34). The words "as an heifer of three years old" are not easily explained, and are evidently best treated as a proper name, Eglath-shelishijah (JND), although Ellicott's Commentary suggests that the epithet of the "third-year heifer", meaning a heifer not yet brought under the yoke, could indicate cities "as yet untaken by the foe". It is thought that Nimrim is "probably the wadi en-Numeirah, ten miles from the southern tip of the Dead Sea" (Harrison). The words, "the waters also of Nimrim shall be desolate" (v.34), probably indicate that the area would lie waste.

In the past there had been singing and shouting, but no longer (v.33). It is noteworthy that there is no reference of praise to God for His goodness to them. They were a proud people. The Psalmist rejoiced in the goodness of God, and gladly acknowledged His provision: "Thou hast put gladness in my heart, more than in the time that their corn and their wine increased" (Ps 4.7).

Pride ultimately brings humiliation (vv.35-39)

Attention has already been drawn to the impotence and emptiness of Moab's idolatry (vv.7,13). The prophet now emphasises that Chemosh would be deprived of her devotees: instead of offering "in the high places" and burning "incense to his gods" (v.35), Moab would be given to mourning. The Lord would "bring to end the hateful veneration of Chemosh" (Harrison): "Therefore mine heart shall sound for Moab like pipes, and mine heart shall sound like pipes for the men of Kir-heres: because the riches that he hath gotten are perished" (v.36). Gesenius explains that the word "pipes" (2485) refers to the flute, and according to Feinberg, this instrument was used particularly at funerals. This is supported in the New Testament: Matthew refers to the flute-players in the house of Jairus (Mt 9.23, JND). Moab's mourning is described in the verses which follow: "For every head shall be bald, and every beard clipped: upon all the hands shall be cuttings, and upon the loins sackcloth" (v.37). The reader is referred in this regard to comments made in connection with 16.6. The complete misery of the nation is further emphasised: "There shall be lamentation generally upon all the housetops of Moab, and in the streets thereof: for I have broken Moab like a vessel wherein is no pleasure, saith the Lord" (v.38).

The proud Moabites (v.29) would be engulfed with shame: "They shall howl, saying, How is it broken down! how hath Moab turned the back with shame! so shall Moab be a derision and a dismaying to all them about him" (v.39). Moab would be a sad spectacle to her neighbours. If they did continue to say, "We have heard the pride of Moab" (v.29), it would only be in derision. Moab would prove that the Lord "scorneth the scorners" (Prov 3.34), and that "Pride goeth before destruction, and an haughty spirit before a fall" (Prov 16.18).

Verses 40-46: The Conqueror of Moab

The Lord had said that He would bring "Nebuchadrezzar the king of Babylon, my servant...against this land (Judah), and against the inhabitants thereof, and against all these nations round about, and will utterly destroy them, and make them an astonishment, and an hissing, and perpetual desolations" (25.9). Jeremiah was then told to "Take the wine cup of this fury at my hand, and cause all the nations, to whom I send thee, to drink it", and the roster of the nations concerned included Moab (25.15,21). The hitherto unnamed invader in this chapter is therefore Nebuchadrezzar, and this is confirmed by the words, "he shall fly as an eagle, and shall spread his wings over Moab" (v.40), just as he would over Bozrah (49.22). The Babylonian Empire is likened to "a lion" with "eagle's wings" (Dan 7.4), and the Chaldeans are described as flying "as the eagle that hasteth to eat" (Hab 1.8). The matter is put beyond any doubt by Ezekiel who describes a "great eagle with great wings, longwinged, full of feathers, which had divers colours", and continues: "Know ye not what these things mean? tell them, Behold, the king of Babylon is come to Jerusalem" (Ezek 17.3,12). The eagle is symbolic of the speed of the conqueror.

There is no escape from the swooping eagle: "Kerioth (literally, 'the cities', JND margin) is taken, and the strong holds are surprised ('seized', JND), and the mighty men's hearts in Moab at that day shall be as the heart of a woman in her pangs (cp. 49.22,24; 50.43; 1 Thess 5.3). And Moab shall be destroyed from being a people, because he hath magnified himself against the Lord" (vv.41-42). As already noticed (vv.26-39), pride was the major sin of Moab. The inescapable and terrifying advance of the invader is further described: "Fear, and the pit, and the snare shall be upon thee, O inhabitant of Moab, saith the Lord. He that fleeth from the fear shall fall into the pit; and he that getteth up out of the pit shall be taken in the snare: for I will bring upon it, even upon Moab, the year of their visitation, saith the Lord" (vv.43-44).

The fleeing Moabites would make for Heshbon, which stood, as previously noted (v.2) on the northern or Ammonite frontier of the land, but any expectation of refuge and help there (perhaps from the Ammonites) would be cruelly dashed: "They that fled stood under the shadow of Heshbon, because of the force ('powerless', JND; 'without strength', RV): but a fire shall come forth out of Heshbon, and a flame from the midst of Sihon, and shall devour the corner of Moab, and the crown of the head of the tumultuous ones (the panic-stricken clamorous crowds of fugitives)" (v.45). The words, "because of the force" evidently refer, not the possession of strength, but to the lack of it. The implication is that Heshbon had already fallen to the invader (cp. v.2) and that the fugitives would be destroyed there. A centuries-old proverb, dating back to the time of Sihon, referred to the defeat of Moab: "Come into Heshbon, let the city of Sihon be built and prepared: For there is a fire gone out of Heshbon, a flame from the city of Sihon: it hath consumed Ar of Moab, and the Lords of the high places of Arnon" (Num 21.27-28). Now history would be repeated.

While Balaam predicted that "there shall come a Star out of Jacob, and a Sceptre shall rise out of Israel, and shall smite the corners of Moab, and destroy all the children of Sheth" (Num 24.17), the fulfilment of his prophecy lies still in the future, and should not be confused with the current passage. While "the corner of Moab" might refer to the corner of the beard, and "the crown of the head" to the hair on the crown of the head, it does seem the verse refers to something far more serious than singeing. The suggestion that "the corner of Moab" refers of the side of the body and "the crown of the head" to the skull should be considered. As Laetsch points out, "There is not much life left in anyone whose side and skull, the seat of the brain, have been consumed by fire". National life would certainly be extinguished: "Woe be unto thee, O Moab! the people of Chemosh perisheth: for thy sons are taken captives, and thy daughters captives" (v.46). According to Josephus, Nebuchadnezzar subjugated the Moabites and the Ammonites after his expedition against Coelosyria, some five years after the destruction of Jerusalem.

Verse 47: The Coming Restoration of Moab

Habakkuk cried, "in wrath remember mercy" (Hab 3.2). As Feinberg observes, "God's pity knows no end. Wrath is always His strange work in which He does not delight". The chapter concludes by anticipating better things for Moab: "Yet will I bring again the captivity of Moab in the latter days, saith the Lord". Similar promises of restoration are made in this section of the book in respect of Egypt (46.26), Ammon (49.6), and Elam (49.39). The competent authorities say that after the Moabites were exiled, they disappeared as a people, having been absorbed by neighbouring nations. But reference is made to Moab in connection with the invasion launched by the coming "king of the north" (Dan 11.40-41), and in connection with the millennial kingdom (Is 11.14). It has to be said, with Unger, "Where such a remnant is, or how the Lord is going to accomplish such a restoration, we do not know". But it has also to be said, again with Unger, that "We do know that He will fulfil His own Word in His own omniscient and omnipotent way".

Ellicott's Commentary suggests that the final words, "Thus far is the judgment of Moab", are a note made by the scribe, possibly Baruch, "to indicate the close of one section and the beginning of another".

JEREMIAH 49

Having addressed Egypt (ch.46), Philistia (ch.47) and Moab (ch.48), this chapter contains prophecies relating to five further nations:

Ammon (vv.1-6)
Edom (vv.7-22)
Damascus (vv.23-27)
Kedar and Hazor (vv.28-33)
Elam (vv.34-39).

Some commentators suggest that Kedar and Hazor are two separate nations, making six in all.

Verses 1-6: Ammon
The Ammonites were descended from Ben-ammi, the son of Lot by his younger daughter (Gen 19.38). Their territory lay to the east of the river Jordan and the Dead Sea, beyond the land occupied by the tribes of Reuben and Gad, and was situated between the rivers Jabbok in the north and Arnon in the south. The Moabites were their southern neighbours. The principal city was Rabbah (Rabath-Ammon), and the name Ammon survives in modern Amman, the capital of the Hashemite Kingdom of Jordan.

According to Streane, it seems likely that the Ammonites originally possessed the territory allocated to the tribe of Gad after the defeat of Sihon (Num 21.21-24), who had in all probability taken it from Ammon. Following the deportation of the tribes on the east of Jordan by Tiglath-pileser III, king of Assyria (2 Kings 15.29), the Ammonites repossessed the area formerly occupied by Gad. This explains the three questions with which the chapter commences (v.1). Reference is made in 2 Kings 24.2, Jeremiah 40.14 and Ezekiel 25.1-7 to the hostility of Ammon towards Judah at the end of the monarchy, but this does not appear to be the subject of the current passage.

The prophecy against Ammon may be divided as follows: the occupation by Ammon (v.1); the overthrow of Ammon (vv.2-5); and the restoration of Ammon (v.6).

The occupation by Ammon (v.1)
"Concerning the Ammonites, thus saith the Lord; Hath Israel no sons? hath he no heir? why then doth their king inherit Gad, and his people dwell in his cities?" (v.1), or "Hath Israel no sons? hath he no heir? Why is Malcam heir of Gad, and his people dwell in the cities thereof?" (JND), with a marginal note, "or, 'their king': but it may be another form of Milcom, the divinity of the Ammonites". Milcom was certainly the name or title of Ammon's national god (1 Kings 11.5,33), also called Molech in 1 Kings 11.7. According to Feinberg, the names Molech, Malcam and Milcom all

derive from *malkam*, meaning "their king". Although the northern tribes had been carried away by Tiglath-Pileser III, their territory still belonged to them and the promise, addressed to the mountains of Israel, will be ultimately fulfilled: "I will settle you after you old estates ('I will cause you to be inhabited as in your former times', JND), and will do better unto you than at your beginnings" (Ezek 36.11). The Lord is "jealous for his land" (Joel 2.18), and jealous for His "holy name" (Ezek 39.25). He will not permit a foreign god and its devotees to occupy land which belongs peculiarly to Him and to His people.

The overthrow of Ammon (vv.2-5)

The current position would be reversed: "then shall Israel be heir unto them that were his heirs, saith the Lord" (v.2). The complete fulfilment of this particular part of the prophecy awaits the dawn of the millennial age. In the meantime, divine judgment would fall on Ammon. The "alarm of war ('clamour of war', JND)" would "be heard in Rabbah of the Ammonites; and it shall be a desolate heap (8510)" (v.2). The same word (TEL) is employed today in Arabic for the sites of ancient ruined cities (Unger). The words "her daughters shall be burned with fire" (v.2) refer to the villages in the vicinity of Rabbah. Two further towns are mentioned: Heshbon (v.3), which is also known as a Moabite city (48.2), but as a frontier town it had probably changed hands more than once, and Ai (v.3), which has not been satisfactorily identified. It is not the town of the same name captured by Joshua (Josh 8.1-29).

The "daughters of Rabbah" (v.3), referring, as noted above, to the villages surrounding the capital city, are likened to panic-stricken people lamenting and running "to and fro by the hedges", or "enclosures of the vineyards" (Streane). Unger suggests that with the destruction of the towns, and the removal of both religious and administrative authority, they would be deprived of shelter and security: "for their king (referring again to Malcam, JND) shall go into captivity, and his priests and his princes together" (v.3). The nation would be left without religious leadership and stable government.

It is worth noting that a similar passage occurs in Amos 1.14-15 in connection with earlier atrocities committed by Ammon against the inhabitants of Gilead. Quite clearly even then, the Ammonites had designs on Israel's territory east of Jordan (Amos 1.13). Both passages (Amos 1.15; Jeremiah 49.3) announce coming captivity. Since "the king of the Ammonites" was amongst the conspirators against Babylon in the days of Zedekiah (27.3), there can be little doubt that Ammon was overthrown by Nebuchadnezzar: "And it shall come to pass, that the nation and kingdom which will not serve the same Nebuchadnezzar the king of Babylon...that nation will I punish, saith the Lord, with the sword, and with the famine, and with the pestilence, until I have consumed them by his hand" (27.8). According to Josephus, Nebuchadnezzar defeated Ammon in the fifth year after the destruction of Jerusalem (cited by Feinberg).

Like Moab (48.29) and Edom (49.17), Ammon was immensely proud of her position and her possessions: "Wherefore gloriest thou in the valleys, thy flowing valley, O backsliding daughter? that trusted in her treasures, saying, Who shall come unto me?" (v.4). "Living in an inaccessible country with mountains on three sides, Ammon considered herself beyond invasion. She was proud of her valleys made fertile by the Arnon waters" (Feinberg). Even so, the precise meaning of "thy flowing valley" perplexes the minds of commentators, and there is considerable support for the suggestion that the expression could refer, not to a valley flowing with water, but to ebbing strength, with the resultant rendering, "Thy valley shall flow down, O backsliding daughter" (JND). The expression, "O backsliding daughter", is perhaps best understood either with reference to the opportunity she had of worshipping the God of Israel, or to the fact that she trusted in her apparently invincible position, rather than in the Lord. Divine judgment was inevitable: "Behold, I will bring a fear upon thee, saith the Lord God of hosts, from all those that be about thee; and ye shall be driven out every man right forth; and none shall gather up him that wandereth" (v.5).

The restoration of Ammon (v.6)

"And afterward I will bring again the captivity of the children of Ammon, saith the Lord." As previously noted, similar promises of restoration are made in this section of the book in respect of Egypt (46.26), Moab (48.47), and Elam (49.39). In general terms, comments made in connection with restoration of Moab are equally applicable to Ammon.

Verses 7-22: Edom

The Edomites were descended from Esau (Gen 36.1-9). His name means "hairy" and although he was red at birth (Gen 25.25) the name "Edom", meaning "red", occurs first with reference to the "red pottage" served to him by his brother Jacob (Gen 25.30). He received his name from his supper! The Edomites were the implacable enemies of Israel, and, although Esau and Jacob had been partially reconciled, Esau's hatred had been transmitted to his posterity. It has been said that "we should beware of bequeathing bitterness to the next generation" (J. Hay).

After the death of his father Isaac, Esau and his family emigrated from Canaan and settled in mount Seir (Gen 36.8). The territory was previously occupied by the Horites (Gen 14.6), a tribe descended from Seir, and whose name means, literally, "rock dwellers". The area itself extended southwards from the Dead Sea to the Gulf of Aqaba. It is a remarkably mountainous district with lofty peaks and deep glens, but also with very productive plains. Reference is made to the topography of the land in the passage: "O thou that dwellest in the clefts of the rock, that holdest the height of the hill" (v.16).

It was the mountainous terrain of this country that gave the Edomites the security in which they boasted (v.16). Identical references in two Psalms confirm the strategic position of the Edomite city of Petra: "Who will bring me into the strong city? who will lead me into Edom?" (Ps.60.9; 108.10). The Hebrew word rendered "rock" (v.16) is SELA (5553), and its equivalent in Greek is *petra*. Amaziah "slew of Edom in the valley of salt ten thousand, and took *Selah* by war" (2 Kings 14.7). Petra was rediscovered by the western world in 1812 through a young Swiss, John Lewis Burchhardt, disguised as a sheikh. He described it as "a rose-red city, half as old as time". After the Babylonian conquest, Petra, was occupied by the Nabataeans, an Arabian tribe, and it seems likely that the city visited by Burchhardt was actually their work rather than that of the Edomites who preceded them. Petra, now in Jordan, is a great tourist attraction. A large part of the city, lying in a valley reached by a narrow ravine, was carved, not built, out of sandstone. Revolutionary construction methods were employed in creating the facades to their buildings hewn out of the rock. They started at the top, so that the weight of unhewn stone always rested on the ground.

The close relationship between the current passage and the prophecy of Obadiah should be noted: verses 9 and 14-16 are found, with slight differences, in Obadiah verses 5 and 1-4 respectively. Although some scholars would disagree, and support their view with cogent arguments, it does seem clear that the present passage gives adequate credence to a sixth century date for the prophecy of Obadiah, but this is not an issue in the current exposition. It is more important to notice that Edom's cardinal sin, after a long history of animosity against Israel, was its implacable and violent hatred of God's people at the overthrow of Jerusalem (Ps 137.7; Ob vv.10-14), and it is to this that Ezekiel particularly refers (Ezek 25.12-14; 35.1-15).

The following should be noted: Edom would be deprived of its assets (vv.7-11); Edom would be desolate through pride (vv.12-18); and Edom would be destroyed by an invader (vv.19-22).

Edom would be deprived of its assets (vv.7-11)

These verses may be summarised in the following way: Edom would be deprived of its wisdom (v.7), its associates (v.8), and its resources (vv.9-10).

It would be deprived of its wisdom (v.7)

"Is wisdom no more in Teman? is counsel perished from the prudent? is their wisdom vanished?". In the words of Ellicott's Commentary, "The form of the questions implies that all three are to be answered in the affirmative". Some commentators suggest that the questions imply that Edom could not see that destruction was imminent. Teman was the grandson of Esau (Gen 36.11), and "gave his name to a tribe living in northern Edom, and also to the territory which they inhabited. Teman was also used as a synonym for the entire land (Hab 3.3), whose inhabitants were renowned in antiquity for their wisdom" (Harrison). Teman was the home of Eliphaz

(Job 2.11). Believers today have something infinitely better than the "wisdom of words...the wisdom of the wise...the wisdom of this world" (1 Cor 1.17,19,20): in Christ they enjoy all "the treasures of wisdom and knowledge" (Col 2.3). He is made unto them "wisdom, and righteousness, and sanctification, and redemption" (1 Cor 1.30).

It would be deprived of its associates (v.8)

"Flee ye, turn back, dwell deep, O inhabitants of Dedan; for I will bring the calamity of Esau (used as a synonym for Edom) upon him, the time that I will visit him." According to Isaiah 21.13 the Dedanites were traders, perhaps trafficking between Edom and other countries. The words "dwell deep" refer to the recesses of the desert and the mountains. In view of the coming invasion, they were to retire as far as possible from Edom.

It would be deprived of its resources (vv.9-10)

"If grapegatherers come to thee, would they not leave some gleaning grapes? if thieves by night, they will destroy till they have enough." The parallel passage in Obadiah reads as follows: "If thieves came to thee, if robbers by night (how art thou cut off!) would they not have stolen till they had enough? if the grapegatherers came to thee, would they not leave some grapes?" (Ob v.5). Both robbers and reapers would have left something, but Edom would be completely cut off. There would be nothing left: "I have made Esau bare, I have uncovered his secret places, and he shall not be able to hide himself: his seed is spoiled, and his brethren, and his neighbours, and he is not". It has been suggested that the expression "I have made Esau bare" might have reference to the Edomite fortresses: in short, Edom has no hiding place, there is no escape from judgment.

Yet the Lord is just and merciful, and spares the innocent: "Leave thy fatherless children, I will preserve them alive; and let thy widows trust in me" (v.11). Ellicott's Commentary asks the question, "Were these words uttered in the stern irony of one who veils a threat in the form of a promise, as some have thought, or was there even in the case of Edom a mingling of pity for the helpless?", and answers: "The latter view seems truer to the prophet's character (48.36). If the sentence was passed which left the wives of Edom widows, and their children orphans, yet God had not forgotten that He was the God of the widow and the fatherless".

Edom would be desolate through pride (vv.12-18)

In considering these verses, the following should be noticed: the certainty of her desolation (vv.12-13); the call for her desolation (vv.14-15); the cause of her desolation (v.16); and the completeness of her desolation (vv.17-18).

The certainty of her desolation (vv.12-13)

"Behold, they whose judgment was not to drink of the cup have assuredly drunken; and art thou he that shall altogether go unpunished? thou shalt not go unpunished, but thou shalt surely drink of it" (v.12). For an explanation of the words "drink of the cup", the reader is referred to comments made in connection with Jeremiah 25.15-29. That particular passage concludes with the words, "For, lo, I begin to bring evil on the city which is called by my name, and should ye be utterly unpunished?" (25.29). Making "all the nations to drink" (25.17) is symbolic language for declaring the Lord's judgment on them. George Williams (*The Student's Commentary on the Holy Scriptures*) is therefore correct in saying, "The first part of verse 12 applies to Israel; the second part to Edom. If God's children must be punished for sin, how much more those who are not His children!" Bearing in mind the presence of Edomites at the sack of Jerusalem (Ps 137.7; Ob vv.10-14), some commentators suggest that this verse indicates a date of composition after 586 BC for this prophecy. It appears that Bozrah (v.13) is particularly mentioned because it was the capital of Edom in Jeremiah's time. It was midway between Petra and the Dead Sea, and its modern name is el-Buseirah (Feinberg). The inevitability of divine judgment is emphasised: "I have sworn by myself, saith the Lord, that Bozrah shall become a desolation, a reproach, a waste, and a curse; and all the cities thereof shall be perpetual wastes" (v.13).

The call for her desolation (vv.14-15)
   "I have heard a rumour from the Lord, and an ambassador is sent unto the heathen, saying, Gather ye together, and come against her, and rise up to the battle" (v.14). It has been pointed out that the word translated "ambassador" (6735) might be better rendered "messenger", as on other occasions in the Old Testament, "since no negotiations but only a command was in question" (Streane). The king of Babylon was assembling his army and summoning the nations to war against Edom. But the "most High ruleth in the kingdom of men" (Dan 4.17), and the Chaldean invasion was under His control: "For, lo, *I* will make thee small among the heathen, and despised among men" (v.15). The parallel passage in Obadiah makes it clear the Lord himself is speaking here: "Thus saith the Lord God *(Adonai Jehovah)* concerning Edom; We have heard a rumour from the Lord, and an ambassador is sent among the heathen, Arise ye, and let us rise up against her in battle. Behold, I have made thee small among the heathen: thou art greatly despised" (Ob vv.1-2).

The cause of her desolation (v.16)
   "Thy terribleness hath deceived thee, and the pride of thine heart, O thou that dwellest in the clefts of the rock, that holdest the height of the hill: though thou shouldest make thy nest as high as the eagle, I will bring thee down from thence, saith the Lord." The word translated "terribleness" (8606) occurs only here and evidently refers, not to any terror that she created in the minds of others, but to her terrible mistake in assuming

that she was impregnable (Streane). It is thought that while "thou that dwellest in the clefts of the rock (SELA)" refers to Petra, the chief fortress of Edom, the words "that holdest the height of the hill" refer to Bozrah (Streane). Obadiah gives added emphasis to Edom's pride: "The pride of thine heart hath deceived thee…whose habitation is high; that saith in his heart, Who shall bring me down to the ground? Though thou exalt thyself as the eagle, and though thou set thy nest among the stars, thence will I bring thee down, saith the Lord" (Ob vv.3-4). The opposite of pride is humble dependence upon the Lord, and its results are described by Isaiah: "But they that wait upon the Lord shall renew their strength; they shall mount up with wings as eagles" (Is 40.31). The New Testament stresses the lesson: "God resisteth the proud, and giveth grace to the humble. Humble yourselves therefore under the might hand of God, that he may exalt you in due time" (1 Pet 5.5-6). It has been rightly said that "God's way up, is down".

The completeness of her desolation (vv.17-18)

"Edom prided itself in its wisdom and its impregnable position (in the clefts of the rock), but God has decreed that it will be without inhabitants" (George Williams; *op cit*). The ruin of Edom would be irreversible. It would become "a desolation", and passers-by would look on with horror: "every one that goeth by it shall be astonished, and shall hiss at all the plagues thereof" (v.17). According to Gesenius, the word "hiss" (8319) is used here in mockery. Jerusalem was similarly treated (Lam 2.15). Edom's destruction is likened to that of Sodom and Gomorrah and their neighbouring cities, Admah and Zeboim (Gen 14.8; Deut 29.23): "no man shall abide there, neither shall a son of man dwell in it" (v.18). Similar language is used of Babylon (50.40). Isaiah describes Edom's ultimate state as "burning pitch" that would "not be quenched night nor day; the smoke thereof shall go up for ever" (Is 34.9-10). Joel states that it would become "a desolate wilderness" (Joel 3.19).

Edom would be destroyed by an invader (vv.19-22)

The invader is described as a lion ravaging and scattering a flock (vv.19-21), and as an eagle swooping on the prey (v.22). The enemy would be as strong as a lion, and as swift as an eagle.

As a lion

"Behold, he shall come up like a lion from the swelling of Jordan" (v.19). As a lion comes up from the thick growth of semi-tropical vegetation fringing the banks of Jordan, so the enemy would pounce upon Edom and its cities. The reader is referred to comments made in connection with Jeremiah 12.5, where it was noted that the expression, "the swelling of Jordan", refers to "its green and shady banks, beautifully clothed with willows, tamarisks and cane, where lions used to lie among the reeds"

(Gesenius). It should be noticed that while similar language is used in describing the overthrow of Babylon (50.44-46), there is no reason to doubt the authenticity of a reused descriptive passage. The language employed confirms that the invader is executing the will of the Lord Himself. Having said that "he (the invader) shall come up like a lion from the swelling of Jordan against the habitation of the strong (Edom)", the passage continues: "but *I* will suddenly make him run away from her ('from it', JND): and who is a chosen man, that *I* may appoint over her? for who is like *me*? and who will appoint *me* the time? and who is that shepherd that will stand before *me*?" (v.19). In the first place, as a lion scatters a flock, so the enemy would scatter the inhabitants of Edom: they would "run away". In the second place, the man who heads the invasion is the Lord's chosen servant: "and whoso is chosen, him will I appoint over her" (RV), referring undoubtedly to Nebuchadnezzar (or Nebuchadrezzar) "my servant" (25.9; 27.6; 43.10). In the third place, the Lord, who empowers Nebuchadnezzar, is both incomparable ("who is like *me*?") and in absolute control of events ("who will appoint *me* the time?"). In the fourth place, the Lord is irresistible: none in Edom can stand against Him.

Having said, "hear the counsel of the Lord", referring to His determined judgment "that he hath taken against Edom", and to "his purposes, that he hath purposed against the inhabitants of Teman", from which all the wisdom of Teman (v.7) could not deliver them, the statement is made: "Surely the least of the flock shall draw them out; surely he shall make their habitations desolate with them" (v.20). While it is not easy to ascertain the precise meaning of these words, there is considerable merit in Unger's suggestion that "the least of the flock" refers to "the weakest of the Chaldean armies". He refers to an earlier passage in the book which describes the invading Babylonian armies as "flocks" (6.3), and continues by suggesting that the Chaldeans would drag the Edomites into exile as a lion drags feeble sheep, leaving the land utterly devastated. The fall of Edom is described in strong poetic language: "The earth is moved at the noise of their fall, at the cry the noise thereof was heard in the Red sea" (v.21). According to Harrison, supported by others, the "Red sea" here refers to "a papyrus marsh in the swampy area between the Bitter Lakes and the Egyptian frontier post of Zilu" which "was drained when the Suez Canal was constructed". The reader, however, is advised to exercise considerable caution in accepting this suggestion, and to consider 1 Kings 9.26 for a better, and safer, explanation.

As an eagle

"Behold, he shall come up and fly as the eagle" (v.22). The reader is referred to comments made in connection with Jeremiah 48.40, where reference was made to Ezekiel 17.3,12; Daniel 7.4; Habakkuk 1.8. The eagle is symbolic of the speed with which the Babylonians, under Nebuchadnezzar, achieved their conquests. There would be no escape from the swooping eagle. The capital city, Bozrah, would fall and Edomite soldiers would writhe in pain: "and at that day shall the heart of the mighty men of Edom be as the heart of a woman in her pangs" (v.22).

No promise of restoration is held out for Edom. Unlike the prophecies concerning Moab (48.47) and Ammon (49.6), there is no message of hope and restoration here. "Dispersion, destruction and devastation would be the lot of Edom" (Feinberg).

Verses 23-27: Damascus

After dealing with the destruction of Edom to the south of Israel, the "foreign nations" section of the book (chs.46-51) directs attention to Damascus, the ancient capital of Syria in the north. The name of the city is evidently used for the nation: "the head of Syria is Damascus" (Is 7.8). Damascus was in southern Syria, and Hamath and Arpad lay approximately one hundred and two hundred miles respectively to the north of the capital.

Hamath and Arpad (or Arphad) fell to the Assyrians "prior to 738 BC (Is 10.9; 36.19; 37.13), while Damascus was overthrown in 731 BC (2 Kings 16.9). Hamath rebelled against Sargon II in 729 BC, but was subdued with little difficulty" (Harrison). However, all this was evidently past history at the time of Jeremiah's prophecy against Damascus, and little else is known of subsequent events. It is said that Damascus was conquered by Nebuchadnezzar in 605 BC, and according to The New Bible Commentary Revised, "notices in the Babylonian Chronicle record Nebuchadrezzar taking tribute from the area". It should be said, very clearly, that lack of knowledge should never be taken as ground for rejecting any part of Scripture.

The reason for the inclusion of Damascus at this point is not given here, but the reader is referred to Amos 1.3 in his connection, together with the fact that the Syrians mounted prolonged opposition to God's people, not only in the past, but also in Jeremiah's lifetime (2 Kings 24.2).

"Concerning Damascus. Hamath is confounded ('put to shame', JND) and Arpad: for they have heard evil tidings: they are fainthearted ('they are melted away', JND); there is sorrow on the sea; it cannot be quiet" (v.23). News of the enemy's approach would strike terror into the heart of one city after another. The reference to "the sea" is evidently figurative since "Syria had no seacoast in ancient times" (Feinberg), but the precise meaning of "there is sorrow on the sea; it cannot be quiet" is not easily ascertained. Various conjectural solutions have been proposed, including, "Their heart dissolves with worry, it cannot be still" (quoted by Feinberg) and "they are troubled like the sea" (RSV). Ironside refers to "the restlessness of the sobbing surf" as a picture of the inhabitants of Damascus who, "waxing feeble, sought to flee".

The oracle may be summarised by the following alliteration: Damascus is described as both "*fainthearted*" (v.23) and "*feeble*" (v.24) as a result of which she "turneth herself to *flee*" (v.24), being encompassed by "*fear*" (v.24). The fall of the city would mean that her young men would "*fall* in her streets" (v.26), and "*fire*" would consume the wall and the palaces (v.27). Some commentators suggest that the words, "the city of my joy" (v.25), belong to a citizen of Damascus as he laments the destruction of what was evidently a beautiful city, but it is possible that they are the words of the Lord Himself, who would bring destruction on Damascus: "I will kindle a fire in the wall of Damascus" (v.27). According to Laetsch, "The praises of Damascus' beauty have been sung throughout the ages". Attention is drawn to the apparent difficulty attaching to the words, "How is the city of praise *not* left" (v.25). Harrison suggests that this is a transcriptional error, but it seems more likely to be a lamentation over the fact that the city was not abandoned with the onset of danger. This is the view of Streane, and others: "How sad that she has not been forsaken by her inhabitants before her fall. This agrees both with the preceding verse, describing the paralysis that had taken possession of the people, and prevented them from saving themselves by flight, and also with the following words, which tell of the destruction to be wrought in the streets of the town".

The final words of the prophecy, "And I will kindle a fire in the wall of Damascus, and it shall consume the palaces of Ben-hadad" (v.27) should be compared with Amos 1.4. Ben-hadad is the name or title of several kings, among them the major Syrian antagonist of Israel (1 Kings 20.1; 2 Kings 6.24).

Verses 28-33: Kedar and Hazor

Not content with the conquest of urban communities, Nebuchadnezzar would turn his attention to at least some of the nomadic eastern tribes located in the north-western part of the Arabian desert. This oracle concerns "Kedar, and…the kingdoms of Hazor, which Nebuchadrezzar king of Babylon shall smite" (v.28). According to The Babylonian Chronicle, Nebuchadrezzar advanced on these kingdoms on 599 BC (Harrison). Attention is drawn to the two subsections (vv.28-29 and 30-33) into which this part of the chapter is divided.

The conquest of Kedar (vv.28-29)

Kedar was the son of Ishmael (Gen 25.13; 1 Chr 1.29) and although, as already noted, it was evidently an important tribe inhabiting the north-west of Arabia, it is often suggested that the name is used with reference to the Arabs generally. Support for the suggestion may be found in Isaiah 21.13-17. Isaiah also refers to the "villages that Kedar doth inhabit" (Is 42.11). The tribe bred sheep (v.29, cp. Is 60.7), traded with Tyre (Ezek 27.21), and were evidently skilled archers (Is 21.16-17). But their expertise with bow and arrow would avail nothing against the might of Babylon who would smite them (v.28) and plunder their possessions: "Their tents and their flocks shall they take away: they shall take to themselves their curtains, and all their vessels, and their camels; and they shall cry unto them, Fear is on every side" (v.29).

The conquest of Hazor (vv.30-33)

Hazor was not the well-known city of northern Canaan conquered by Joshua (Josh 11.1-13), but an unidentified place in the desert. It has been suggested that it may have been a collective name for villages occupied by semi-nomadic Arabs. Like the inhabitants of Dedan (v.8), the inhabitants of Hazor were advised to "dwell deep" (v.30) by seeking refuge in remote areas of the desert. The coming invasion by Nebuchadrezzar left them no other alternative. The king of Babylon had "taken counsel" and "conceived a purpose" against them (v.30), not purely on his own initiative, but as the Lord's servant, in response to divine direction: "Arise, get you up unto the wealthy nation ('the nation at ease', JND), that dwelleth without care, saith the Lord, which have neither gates nor bars, which dwell alone" (v.31). The description fits a nomadic camp-site, rather than an established city. Like Kedar, the people of Hazor would see their possessions plundered by the Babylonians: "their camels shall be a booty, and the multitude of their cattle a spoil" (v.32). The people themselves would be scattered "to every wind" (JND) and, like the inhabitants of Kedar who would experience "Terror on every side" (v.29, JND), they would face "calamity from all sides thereof" (v.32). The words, "them that in the utmost corners (v.32), or "have the corners of their beard cut off" (JND), may refer to a heathen practice in honour of Bacchus, the god of wine. The reader is referred to comments made in connection with 9.26, which refers to divine judgment on various peoples including "all that have the corners of their beard cut off" (JND).

Hazor would never recover from the divine judgment implemented by Nebuchadrezzar: "Hazor shall be a dwelling for dragons ('jackals', JND), and a desolation for ever: there shall no man abide there, nor any son of man dwell in it" (v.33).

The judgment upon of Hazor should be regarded as a divine warning against self-indulgence and carefree living. As Harrison observes, "The life of the Christian, who has been bought with a price (1 Cor 6.20; 7.23), must be spent in the service of God and man, not in selfish indulgence".

Verses 34-39: Elam

Elam, an ancient kingdom (Gen 14.1), lay "two hundred miles east of Babylon and west of the Tigris River" (Feinberg). It is said to have been co-extensive with the modern Iranian province of Khuzestan. Having been conquered by the Assyrians under Ashurbanipal about 640 BC (Ezra 4.9-10), Elam regained its independence after his death, and having been later united with Media, and then Persia, contributed to the overthrow of the Babylonian Empire in 540 BC. It has to be said, however, that this event does not form part of this prophecy. Elam's capital city was Susa (Shushan).

Unlike the preceding prophecies, this oracle is dated from the beginning of Zedekiah's reign in 597 BC (v.34), and although Nebuchadnezzar is not specifically mentioned here, reference being made to Elam's enemies in general (v.37), the Babylonian Chronicle apparently suggests that he that he attacked Elam in 595/4 BC, but no details are preserved. As Harrison observes, "the oracle refers to some event in Elamite history about which there is little information at the present". The event in question evidently aroused the "fierce anger" of the Lord (v.37), and could possibly be the role of Elam in the destruction of Jerusalem as predicted by Isaiah (Is 22.6). The date of the prophecy might give some weight to this suggestion. According to Motyer, "Elam…was throughout Isaiah's period an independent power allied to Babylon against Assyria". According to Ezekiel, the Elamites "caused…terror in the land of the living" (Ezek 32.24).

Like the men of Kedar, who were proficient archers (Is 21.17), the Elamites were also famed for the use of the bow (Is 22.6), and therefore the Lord's pronouncement against them is expressed in significant language: "I will break the bow of Elam, the chief of their might" (v.35). Elam could not resist the power of the Lord, of whom the Psalmist said, "he breaketh the bow, and cutteth the spear in sunder; he burneth the chariot in the fire" (Ps 46.9). Like Kedar and Hazor (vv.29,32), Elam would be overwhelmed from every direction, and scattered in every direction (v.36). Their destruction would be complete: "I will cause Elam to be dismayed before their enemies…I will bring evil upon them…I will send the sword after them, till I have consumed them…I will set my throne in Elam, and will destroy from thence the king and the princes, saith the Lord" (vv.37-38). The words, "I will set my throne in Elam", indicate that the Lord would sit in judgment upon the Elamites, executing His wrath against them through the depredations of Nebuchadnezzar's armies.

But this would not be the end of the nation: "But it shall come to pass in the latter days, that I will bring again the captivity of Elam, saith the Lord" (v.39). While it has been suggested that there may have been a partial fulfilment of this promise in the rise of the Persian Empire, the expression "the latter days" gives an "eschatological dimension" (Feinberg) to the prophecy. No reason is given for the restoration of Elam in the millennial age, but it might be worth considering that unlike the Edomites, with their implacable hatred for the Lord's people, the kings of Persia showed them considerable kindness.

At this point in his commentary, Derek Kidner looks back over the chapter and observes that "verse 35 singles out *the mainstay of their might* for the Lord's special attention". Kidner continues: "Elam relied on its archers (v.35), Ammon on its Molech (v.3), Edom on its cleverness and its crags (vv.7,16), Damascus on its fame (v.25), and Kedar on its remoteness and its mobility (vv.29,31). The list could be extended and modernised, or it could be summed up in the great saying of 9.23-24: 'Let not the wise man glory in his wisdom, neither let the mighty man glory in his might, let not the rich man glory in his riches: But let him that glorieth glory in this, that he understandeth and knoweth me, that I am the Lord which exercise lovingkindness, judgment, and righteousness in the earth: for in these things I delight, saith the Lord'."

JEREMIAH 50

The final prophecy in the "foreign nations" section of the book concerns Babylon. It comprises two long chapters (chs.50 and 51), and as Kidner observes, "Fittingly, the empire which struck the most devastating blow ever suffered by the kingdom of David, receives the longest series of oracles about her own future". Streane concurs with this: "This prophecy against Babylon forms an appropriate conclusion to the series. The nations immediately bordering upon Palestine have had their fate foretold, and then the more remote, but none the less is that Empire, which is to execute God's judgment upon them, destined in its turn to fall. And this, the climax of the prophecies against foreign nations, is marked by the grandeur of the images employed by the prophet". The man who was "ordained...a prophet unto the nations" (1.5), now delivers the final oracle in "The word of the Lord which came...against the Gentiles" (46.1).

While the words, "wrote in a book" (51.60), may suggest that the prophecy against Babylon is a compilation of several oracles spoken by Jeremiah against the city, its message was to be read in Babylon by Seraiah when he accompanied "Zedekiah the king of Judah into Babylon in the fourth year of his reign" (51.59). Bearing in mind that Zedekiah's eleven-year reign ended in 586 BC (some say 588 BC), the oracle was evidently delivered in 593 BC, some fifty-four years before the city's overthrow in 539 BC.

Hitherto, the numerous references in the book to the advance of a northern army have referred to Babylon, and examples are found in 1.14-15; 4.6; 6.1; 13.20; 25.9; 47.2. But now Babylon itself is to fall to a northern invader: "For out of the north there cometh up a nation against her" (v.3); "For, lo, I will raise and cause to come up against Babylon an assembly of great nations from the north country" (v.9); "Behold, a people shall come from the north, and a great nation, and many kings shall be raised up from the coasts of the earth" (v.41). The aggressor is identified in chapter 51: "the Lord hath raised up the spirit of the kings of the Medes" (v.11); "Prepare against her the nations with the kings of the Medes, the captains thereof, and all the rulers thereof, and all the land of his dominion" (v.28). According to The Wycliffe Bible Commentary, cited by Feinberg, the Medes were allied with Babylon in the destruction of Nineveh in 612 BC, but later they joined the Persians to defeat Babylon in 539 BC (Dan 5.28,30-31).

It is worth mentioning at this juncture that the violent destruction of Babylon described in chapters 50 and 51 did not evidently take place in 539 BC when the city was occupied by the invader without a battle and without extensive damage to the city. According to Kidner, Xerxes put down a rebellion there some fifty years later, "smashing its fortifications and pillaging its temples". But even so, "the city survived and recovered. Its eventual decline...was gradual, due largely to the building of a new capital, Seleucia on the Tigris, in 275 BC; but it still had inhabitants in the first century AD". As Feinberg observes, "But as with other predictive prophecies, if a fulfilment does not occur in one period, it is to be sought for in another and future one".

The current chapter comprises seven paragraphs dealing alternately with divine retribution upon Babylon (vv.1-3; 9-16; 21-32; 35-46), and the return of God's people to their homeland (vv.4-8; 17-20; 33-34). In connection with the former, the first of the four relevant paragraphs (vv.1-3) is a brief summary of coming judgment, the second and third paragraphs (vv.9-16; 21-32) are more detailed, stating the reasons for divine retribution (vv.11,28), and the fourth (vv.35-46) emphasises that Babylon's overthrow will be both comprehensive and irresistible. In connection with the repatriation of exiles from Babylon to Israel, Jeremiah deals with their return and the covenant (vv.4-8), their return and their pardon (vv.17-20), and their return and their Redeemer (vv.33-34).

Verses 1-3: The Retribution upon Babylon (1)
"The word that the Lord spake against Babylon and against the land of the Chaldeans by Jeremiah the prophet" (v.1). As already noted, the opening verses briefly summarise the details given in later sections of the chapter. Attention is drawn to:

The capture of the city (v.2a)
"Declare ye among the nations, and publish, and set up a standard; publish and conceal not: say, Babylon is taken." It has been said that "As long as Babylon ruled the world, fear silenced the tongue of the conquered nations. Now there is no longer any need of such fear" (Laetsch). The news of Babylon's fall would be broadcast far and wide. The expression "set up a standard" refers here, not to a rallying-point for an army, as elsewhere (4.6,21) but to the communication of news. A century or so before, Isaiah had described the advance by "Elam" and "Media" (Is 21.2) on Babylon, together with the return of the victorious army bearing tidings of victory: "Babylon is fallen, is fallen" (Is 21.9). Bearing in mind that at the time of Isaiah's prophecy many years were to pass before the fall of the city, the certainty of its accomplishment is stressed by the use of the present tense. Over fifty years were to elapse before the fulfilment of Jeremiah's prophecy regarding the fall of Babylon, but the same certainty remained. It should be noted that the conquest of historical Babylon presages the destruction of future Babylon, when the cry will be heard, "Babylon the great is fallen, is fallen" (Rev 18.2).

The confounding of the idols (v.2b)
"Bel is confounded, Merodach is broken in pieces; her idols are confounded, her images are broken in pieces", or "her images are put to shame, her idols are dismayed" (JND). Babylonia is described as "the land of graven images" and the people are said to be "mad upon their idols"

(v.38). But the Babylonian idols could not deliver the city from its conquerors, through whom the Lord would "do judgment upon the graven images of Babylon" (51.47). According to various authorities, when Babylon rose to power, its chief deity Marduk (the Merodach of the Old Testament) was invested with the characteristics of Bel, the counterpart of the Sumarian god Enil (or Enlil), and in the course of time the name Bel displaced Marduk in common use. The word "images" (JND) is used contemptuously, and means, literally, something rolled, referring to "the huge tree trunks or stone blocks that had to be formed into likenesses of Bel-Marduk and were placed on rollers to be put into position" (Laetsch).

The completeness of the desolation (v.3)
"For out of the north there cometh up a nation against her, which shall make her land desolate, and none shall dwell therein: they shall remove, they shall depart, both man and beast." As Streane observes, "The Medo-Persian Empire is meant. Media was north-west of Babylon". The destruction of Babylon is amplified in each of the subsequent paragraphs dealing with the Lord's judgment upon the city. In this connection, attention is drawn to vv.13,23,45, where specific reference is made to her desolation. It has already been pointed out that the total desolation of Babylon did not become an accomplished fact until a long period of time had elapsed.

Verses 4-8: The Return of Israel (1)
In this paragraph, Jeremiah deals with Israel's return and the covenant: "Come, and let us join ourselves to the Lord in a perpetual covenant that shall not be forgotten" (v.5). Attention is drawn to the following:

The time of the return (v.4a)
It would be "In those days, and in that time". Bearing in mind that this expression occurs again in v.20 where, clearly, the blessings of cleansing and pardon will not be enjoyed by God's earthly people until Messianic times, the complete fulfilment of vv.4-5 will evidently also take place in the future. This would account for the reference to both Israel and Judah, a united people (v.4), whereas the return to the land in the days of Zerubbabel and Ezra involved Judah only.

A problem arises in connection with the fulfilment, or partial fulfilment, of this prophecy prior to the time of Babylon's overthrow in 539 BC. It should be remembered that some fifty years lay between the delivery of these exhortations to flee the city and its overthrow at the hands of the Medes. Even so, there is no record in the Old Testament of exiles actually returning to Judah and Jerusalem prior to the expeditions led by Ezra and Zerubbabel, that is after the fall of Babylon, whereas chapters 50 and 51 contain exhortations to flee the city (50.8; 51.6,45) prior to its fall. It must be said that, in any case, there is not the slightest resemblance between the command to leave Babylon in order to escape its judgment, and the beneficent edict of Cyrus, initiated by the Lord himself (Ezra 1.1-3), so that the return described in the book of Ezra can hardly be regarded as the people's response to Jeremiah's exhortations!

One possible solution to this apparent problem is that while, almost certainly, the Jews would not have been permitted to leave Babylon for Judah prior to the fall of the city (cp. v.33), they could have left the city for other areas in Babylonia in order to escape the city's overthrow. It should also be said that when Babylon fell, there were some escapees who brought the news to Jerusalem (v.28).

The manner of the return (vv.4b-5)

The exiles would return weeping and seeking: "the children of Israel shall come, they and the children of Judah together, going and weeping: they shall go, and seek the Lord their God. They shall ask the way to Zion with their faces thitherward, saying, Come, and let us join ourselves to the Lord in a perpetual covenant that shall not be forgotten." The tears of the returning exiles could be tears of penitence or tears of joy, perhaps both. No longer would they worship Baal and the queen of heaven (7.18; 44.17), but would "seek the Lord their God". Commentators state that the word "thitherward" is better rendered "hitherward" (supported by the RV margin), with the comment that this indicates that the prophecy was written in Judah, and confirms Jeremiah's authorship.

The reference to the desire of the returning exiles to join themselves "to the Lord in a perpetual covenant that shall not be forgotten", evidently indicates that they had in mind the "new covenant" described in 31.31-34, of which the Lord said, "I will make an everlasting covenant with them, that I will not turn away from them, to do them good; but I will put my fear in their hearts, that they shall not depart from me" (32.40). In the days of Nehemiah, led by Levites, the people said, "And because of all this (past failure) we make a sure covenant, and write it; and our princes, Levites, and priests, seal unto it" (Neh 9.38). Alas, they did forget, and the record of their repeated failure is given in Nehemiah 13. While, as already stated, events that took place after the decree of Cyrus partly fulfilled the prophecy here, its complete fulfilment lies in the future.

The reason for their captivity (vv.6-7)

Their captivity in the first place is attributed to the national "shepherds", referring to the spiritual and political leadership of the nation, of which Jeremiah had said, "Woe be unto the pastors that destroy and scatter the sheep of my pasture! saith the Lord" (23.1). The Lord describes them as having been "lost sheep", whose shepherds "have caused them to go astray, they have turned them away on the mountains: they have gone from mountain to hill, they have forgotten their restingplace" (v.6), or "'caused them to go astray on the perverting mountains', alluding to the idolatrous high places" (JND margin). Kidner rightly describes God's people as "badly shepherded" and adds, referring to the words, "All that found them have devoured them" (v.7), "Spiritually too (to adopt the New Testament connotation of 'shepherd'), a badly pastured flock is soon astray, then swiftly preyed upon".

The forgotten "restingplace" (v.6), or "crouching place" (Streane), refers to the fold in which they should have lain. Israel's idolatry on the mountains and hills gave their enemies reason to justify their cruelty: "their adversaries said, We offend not, because they have sinned against the Lord, the habitation of justice, even the Lord, the hope of their fathers" (v.7). Some commentators take the view that Israel's true "restingplace" was the Lord Himself, "the Lord, the habitation of justice", in whom alone they could find rest and peace for their souls.

The initiative in their return (v.8)

The exhortation, "Remove out of the midst of Babylon, and go forth out of the land of the Chaldeans, and be as the he goats before the flocks", has been explained as follows: "Just as the male goats try to leave the enclosure first, so Judah ought to be at the forefront of captive peoples leaving Babylonia for home" (Harrison). As already noted, similar exhortations occur later in the oracle against Babylon: "Flee out of the midst of Babylon, and deliver every man his soul: be not cut off in her iniquity" (51.6); "My people, go ye out of the midst of her, and deliver ye every man his soul from the fierce anger of the Lord" (51.45). Ellicott's Commentary draws attention to the fact the Jeremiah "re-echoes almost the very words of Isaiah" (Is 48.20). At the end-time, after the fall of latter-day Babylon has been announced, the cry will be heard, "Come out of her, my people, that ye be not partakers of her sins, and that receive not of her plagues" (Rev 18.4).

Ellicott's Commentary points out that the advice here "is obviously in marked contrast with the counsels in 29.5-7 that the exiles should build houses and plant gardens, and seek the peace of the city and their conquerors. That was a wise and right counsel for the time, but it was for a time only; and when the hour of the fall of Babylon came they were to be as the he-goats (better, *rams*) of the flock, leading the captives of other nations in the work of liberation and of flight".

Verses 9-16: The Retribution upon Babylon (2)

These verses are an advance on the introductory summary (vv.1-3), and the following should be noted:

The strength of the invader (vv.9-10)

The description needs little amplification or comment. The invasion would be undertaken by "an assembly of great nations from the north country" (v.9). Further details are given later: "call together against her the kingdoms of Ararat, Minni, and Ashchenaz; appoint a captain against her; cause the horses to come up as the rough caterpillers. Prepare against her the nations with the kings of the Medes, the captains thereof, and all the rulers thereof, and all the land of his dominion" (51.27-28). The words "from thence she shall be taken" (v.9) are best understood in relation to the invader: he will come from "the north country". The success of the invasion is assured: "their arrows shall be as of a mighty expert man; none shall return in vain. And Chaldea shall be a spoil: all that spoil her shall be satisfied, saith the Lord" (vv.9-10). While, grammatically, the words "none shall return in vain" could refer either to the warrior or the arrow, Jeremiah is evidently referring here to the returning warrior.

The reason for the invasion (vv.11-14)

The fall of Babylon was no quirk of fate, and these verses give three reasons for her pending destruction.

They exulted in their conquest

"Because ye were glad, because ye rejoiced, O ye destroyers of mine heritage, because ye are grown fat as the heifer at grass, and bellow as bulls" (v.11), or "For ye rejoiced, for ye triumphed, ye plunderers of my heritage; for ye have been wanton as the heifer at grass (or, 'that treadeth out the corn', margin), and neighed as steeds" (JND). Streane suggests the word "leap" in the place of "grown fat", and continues: "The command not to muzzle the ox that trode out the corn (Deut 25.4) would bring about special playfulness on the part of animals thus unusually well fed". However, Harrison feels that the picture of "a calf threshing...does not suit the imagery of a frisky animal very well"! The overall picture is of Babylon's boastful and carefree satisfaction, failing to recognise that "the Lord of hosts" had said of His people, "he that toucheth you toucheth the apple of his eye" (Zech 2.8). As a result, "Your mother shall be sore confounded; she that bare you shall be ashamed" (v.12). Since Jeremiah is addressing the people of Babylon, he therefore depicts the city as their mother. Babylon's humiliation is described: "behold, she is become hindmost ('the last', margin) of the nations, a wilderness, a dry land, and a desert" (v.12, JND).

They were subject to divine wrath

"Because of the wrath of the Lord it shall not be inhabited, but it shall be wholly desolate: every one that goeth by Babylon shall be astonished, and hiss at all her plagues" (v.13). Men and women do well to remember that "God is angry with the wicked every day" (Ps 7.11). The word "hiss" (8319), signifies mockery. The "assembly of great nations from the north country" (v.9) would unconsciously implement divine judgment. "Powerful Babylon will be reduced to minor status in the Near East when God punishes her, and once more the passer-by will gasp in astonishment (cp. 18.16; 19.8, used of Judah and Jerusalem; 49.17, used of Edom)" (Harrison).

They had sinned against the Lord

"Put yourselves in array against Babylon round about: all ye that bend the bow, shoot at her, spare no arrows: for she hath sinned against the Lord" (v.14). Ellicott's Commentary explains that Babylon had "sinned against the Lord in her cruelty and luxury and tyranny against the righteous government of Jehovah".

The progress of the invasion (vv. 15-16)

Having referred to the archers, said to be descriptive of the light-armed troops that formed the strength of the Medo-Persian army (50.14; 51.3-4), Babylon gives "her hand" (50.15) evidently "in pledge of surrender, because she sees everywhere the uselessness of resistance" (Laetsch): "her ramparts are fallen, her walls are thrown down" (v.15, JND), not purely as the result of military power, but because of "the vengeance of the Lord". There is some difference of opinion in connection with the precise time at which this destruction took place, bearing in mind that the invader "entered the city beneath the walls by the river bed, after diverting the stream" (Streane), but it is quite possible that the reference here is to breaches in the wall rather than to their total demolition. The command, "take vengeance upon her; as she hath done, do unto her" (v.15) illustrates the New Testament teaching that "God is not mocked: for whatsoever a man soweth, that shall he also reap" (Gal 6.7). A similar command is given in v.29, and "the New Testament seer uses language very similar in referring to mystical Babylon (Rev 18.6)" (Ironside). Although the words, "Cut off the sower from Babylon, and him that handleth the sickle in the time of harvest" (v.16), could possibly refer to fields within the walls of the city, it seems more likely that Jeremiah is looking here to the effect of the invasion on "the rural population" who would "feel the woes and hardships of warfare even before the city dwellers. To a large extent these tillers of the soil were foreigners, deported from their homeland by Babylonian conquerors. They flee from Babylon back to their native lands, leaving the newly sown fields together with the harvest already reaped in the hands of the advancing enemy" (Laetsch).

Verses 17-20: The Return of Israel (2)

In this paragraph, Jeremiah deals with Israel's return and her cleansing. In v.6, the Lord's people are described as "lost sheep". Now, the nation is described as "a scattered sheep ('a hunted sheep', JND)" which "the lions have driven...away: first the king of Assyria hath devoured him; and last this Nebuchadrezzar king of Babylon hath broken his bones" (v.17). The mention of Assyria alludes to the defeat and exile of the northern kingdom, which began during the reign of Shalmaneser and was completed by Sargon II. Divine retribution had fallen upon Assyria: it would now fall upon Babylon: "Therefore thus saith the Lord of hosts, the God of Israel; Behold, I will punish the king of Babylon and his land, as I have punished the king of Assyria" (v.18).

There can be little doubt that while the return from captivity described in the book of Ezra faintly fulfilled vv.19-20, the final fulfilment of these verses will not place until the end-time. "And I will bring Israel again to his habitation, and he shall feed on Carmel and Bashan, and his soul shall be satisfied upon mount Ephraim and Gilead. In those days, and in that time, saith the Lord, the iniquity of Israel shall be sought for, and there shall be none; and the sins of Judah, and they shall not be found: for I will pardon them whom I reserve ('those whom I leave remaining', JND)" (vv.19-20). It has already been pointed out that both occurrences of the words "In those days, and in that time, saith the Lord" (vv.4,20) are best understood with reference to the future regathering of Israel.

Verses 21-32: The Retribution upon Babylon (3)

This paragraph gives further details of Babylon's destruction, and a further explanation of divine judgment upon Babylon. Babylon, described as "the hammer of the whole earth", was soon to be "cut asunder and broken" (v.23). The prophetic Scriptures constantly make it clear that the Lord both initiates and controls the rise and fall of nations. Hence the command to the northern invader, "Go up against the land...do according to all that I have commanded thee" (v.21), and the statements, "The Lord hath opened his armoury, and hath brought forth the weapons of his indignation: for this is the work of the Lord God of hosts in the land of the Chaldeans" (v.25); "Behold, I am against thee, O thou most proud, saith the Lord God of hosts: for thy day is come, the time that I will visit thee" (v.31). Divine judgment is far from arbitrary in character. It is called "the vengeance of the Lord our God, the vengeance of his temple" (v.28), and operates, as already noted (v.15), on the basis of the law of sowing and reaping: "according to all that she hath done, do unto her" (v.29). Attention is drawn to the absorbing details of the section.

The description of Babylon (vv.21-23)

It seems highly likely that Jeremiah, under divine inspiration, deliberately selected Merathaim and Pekod (v.21) for the meaning of their names. Older commentators (Streane, and Plumptre in Ellicott's Commentary) are less certain about the former, with Plumptre suggesting that "the prophet coined it as a descriptive word", although both accept the existence of Pekod, whereas .Harrison (a modern commentator) is quite clear: "*Merathaim* and *Pekod* (literally 'Double Rebellion' and 'Visitation') are sarcastic wordplays on specific Babylonian localities. The former is the *Mat Marratim* district of southern Babylonia, while the latter is the name for *Puqudu*, an eastern Babylonian people (cp. Ezek 23.23)". Darby has no doubt about the intention of Jeremiah: "Go up against the land of double rebellion (or 'apostasy', margin), against it, and against the inhabitants of visitation (or 'punishment', margin)". The significance of the two place names is now realised: "A sound of battle is in the land, and of great destruction. How is the hammer of the whole earth cut asunder and broken! how is Babylon become a desolation among the nations!" (vv.22-23). But God has a still more powerful hammer: "Is not my word like as a fire? saith the Lord; and like a hammer that breaketh the rock in pieces?" (23.29).

The downfall of Babylon (vv.24-27)

These verses emphasise that the capture of the city was unexpected and irreversible. In the first place, the enemy entered the city in a most unexpected way: "I have laid a snare for thee, and thou art also taken, O Babylon, and thou wast not aware: thou art found, and also caught, because thou hast striven against the Lord" (v.24). According to Ellicott's Commentary, "The two captures of Babylon by Cyrus and Darius both answered to this description. Cyrus turned aside the waters of the Euphrates into another channel, and entered by the river-bed, so that the city was taken before those who lived in the middle of the city knew that it was attacked. In the latter case the gates were opened to Darius by the treachery of the Babylonian general Zopyrus". The information given in Ellicott's Commentary is based on the historical accounts given by Herodotus. The same events are described in further detail in 51.31-32. Harrison refers to wording found on the Cyrus Cylinder which credits his easy victory to Marduk, but Jeremiah attributes Babylon's fall to the Lord whose interests had been opposed by Babylon: "The Lord hath opened his armoury, and hath brought forth the weapons of his indignation: for this is the work of the Lord God of hosts in the land of the Chaldeans" (v.25). The resources of Babylon, whether in possessions or in personnel, would be destroyed: "Come against her from the utmost border ('from every quarter', JND), open her storehouses: cast her up as heaps, and destroy her utterly: let nothing of her be left. Slay all her bullocks; let them go down to the slaughter" (vv.26-27). The stored provisions of the city would be piled up, like sheaves after harvest, and burnt. It is generally thought that the "bullocks" are either Babylon's captains or men of war, or "the youthful Babylonian warriors" (Harrison). The time in which the loss of Babylon's soldiery would take place is called "the time of their visitation" (v.27) which Streane defines as "the day of their calamity".

The declaration about Babylon (v.28)

"The voice of them that flee and escape out of the land of Babylon, to declare in Zion the vengeance of the Lord our God, the vengeance of his temple." Amongst other things, it was with his in mind that "the Lord...raised up the spirit of the kings of the Medes: for his device is against Babylon, to destroy it; because it is the vengeance of the Lord, the vengeance of his temple" (51.11). Feinberg rightly points out that chapters 50 and 51 "emphatically stress the truth of Matthew 25.31-46. The criterion by which God judges the nations is their treatment of His chosen people whom He has made the vehicle of salvation (cp. Jn 4.22), and placed at the centre of the consummation of human history (cp. Is 2.1-4)".

It does seem necessary to differentiate between the exiles in Babylon who are urged to flee the city before its overthrow (50.8; 51.6,45), and the exiles here who would bring the news to Jerusalem that the city had fallen. The escapees described here can hardly be identified with the exiles who returned in the days of Zerubbabel and Ezra.

Divine retribution upon the nation that had destroyed the Temple in Jerusalem serves to remind the Lord's people today that "If any man defile (corrupt) the temple of God, him shall God destroy (corrupt)" (1 Cor 3.17). The "temple of God" here is the local assembly: "Know ye not that ye are the temple of God (or 'temple of God'), and that the Spirit of God dwelleth in you?" (1 Cor 3.16). W. E. Vine's definition of the word "corrupt"' is worth quoting in full: "With the significance of destroying, it is used of marring a local church by leading it away from that condition of holiness of life and purity of doctrine in which it should abide...and of God's retributive destruction of the offender who is guilty of this sin" (*Expository Dictionary of Bible Words*). It should be added that the immediate context strongly suggests that Paul has in mind the "envying, and strife, and divisions" present in the assembly (1 Cor 3.3).

The denouncement of Babylon's pride (vv.29-32)
The details in these verses are quite self-explanatory. Verse 30 is repeated almost verbatim from 49.26 which describes the fate of Damascus. These verses (vv.29-32) emphasise the pride of Babylon: "according to all that she hath done, do unto her: for she hath been *proud* against the Lord, against the Holy One of Israel...Behold, I am against thee, O thou most *proud*, saith the Lord God of hosts...And the most *proud* shall stumble and fall, and none shall raise him up" (vv.29,31,32). The fall of Babylon illustrates the oft-quoted statement that "Pride goeth before destruction, and an haughty spirit before a fall" (Prov 16.18). The "proud look" is the first of seven things which the Lord hates (Prov 6.16-17), and "An high look, and a proud heart, and the plowing of the wicked, is sin" (Prov 21.4). The consequences of Babylonian pride should remind the Lord's people today that "God resisteth the proud, and giveth grace to the humble" (1 Pet 5.5).

Verses 33-34: The Return of Israel (3)
In this paragraph, Jeremiah deals with Israel's return and her Redeemer. In the Old Testament, the kinsman-redeemer (1350), a family member, usually a brother, undertook the responsibility of "redeeming" property (Lev 25.23-28), and persons (Lev 25.47-55). He was also responsible for redressing wrong, and in this capacity he was called the "avenger" or "the revenger of blood" (Num 35.12,21). The kinsman-redeemer is sometimes called the "kinsman" and sometimes the "redeemer", but the underlying Hebrew word (GOEL) remains the same. In the current passage, the

"Redeemer" (v.34) is the Lord Himself, and Job certainly understood this as a divine title: "I know that my redeemer liveth" (Job 19.25).

Feinberg puts it nicely in saying, "The Kinsman-Redeemer is voluntarily committed to champion Israel's cause. He brings peace to His own but unrest to His oppressors". Like the man who had sold himself unto "unto the stranger" (Lev 25.47), the Lord had to say of the nation, "Behold, for your iniquities have ye sold yourselves" (Is 50.1), and, in consequence, "The children of Israel and the children of Judah were oppressed together ('were together oppressed', JND): and all that took them captives held them fast; they refused to let them go" (v.33). This, no doubt, includes both the Assyrian and Babylonian captivities (v.17). Assyria had fallen, and now "the hammer of the whole earth" (v.23) was about to prove that Israel's "Redeemer" was infinitely stronger: "Their Redeemer is strong; the Lord of hosts is his name: he shall throughly plead their cause, that he may give rest to the land ('the earth', RV), and disquiet the inhabitants of Babylon" (v.34).

As in the case of the two previous paragraphs dealing with Israel (vv.4-8; 17-20) the complete fulfilment of this prophecy must lie in the future. Ultimately, "When the enemy shall come in like a flood, the Spirit of the Lord shall lift up a standard against him. And the Redeemer (1350) shall come to Zion" (Is 59.19-20). It should be remembered that the kinsman-redeemer must have the right to redeem, the ability to redeem, and the desire to redeem. In connection with our redemption, the Lord Jesus met these requirements in full: through His incarnation, He has become a "near kinsman" (Heb 2.16-17; 10.4-5); by reason of His perfect life, He had the ability to redeem: He was "in all points tempted like as we are, yet without sin" (Heb 4.15); He had the desire to redeem, and fulfilled that desire in going willingly to the cross to accomplish our redemption: He "*gave himself* for our sins" (Gal 1.4). It must also be said that the Lord Jesus came, lived, died and rose again to be Israel's Kinsman-Redeemer. Israel's "warfare" could never be "accomplished" unless "her iniquity is pardoned" (Is 40.2), and that can only take place because, as the nation will ultimately say, "the Lord hath laid on him the iniquity of us all" (Is 53.6).

Verses 35-46: The Retribution upon Babylon (4)

The chapter concludes by stressing again the totality of destruction. Attention is drawn to the following.

Judgment would be comprehensive (vv.35-38)

"A sword is upon the Chaldeans, saith the Lord, and upon the inhabitants of Babylon, and upon her princes, and upon her wise men (the rulers in civil and religious matters respectively). A sword is upon the liars ("more literally, *babblers*, utterers of random prophecies", Streane); and they shall dote ('become fools', JND): a sword is upon her mighty men; and they shall be dismayed. A sword is upon their horses, and upon their chariots, and upon all the mingled people (the foreigners employed as mercenaries) that are in the midst of her; and they shall become as women: a sword is upon her treasures; and they shall be robbed. A drought is upon her waters; and they shall be dried up: for it is the land of graven images, and they are mad upon their idols ('they are mad after frightful idols', JND)" (vv.35-38). Streane explains that the "drought" evidently "refers to the drying up of the many canals by which the water of the Euphrates was distributed throughout the whole country for drainage and irrigation, as well as for commercial purposes".

Judgment would be complete (vv.39-40)

A parallel is drawn between the total overthrow of Sodom and Gomorrah, and destruction of Babylon. The site would be inhabited by "the wild beasts of the desert with the wild beasts of the islands ('with jackals', JND: literally, 'the shriekers' leading others to suggest hyenas)…and the owls shall dwell therein", and as "God overthrew Sodom and Gomorrah and the neighbour cities thereof…so shall no man abide there, neither shall any son of man dwell therein". These verses should be compared with Isaiah 13.19-22. According to Laetsch the site of the city was excavated during 1910-1911, and the archeologist (Koldewey) reported that "the ruins of Babylon in many places were covered with forty to eighty feet of sand and rubble". Babylon did become "a wilderness, a dry land, and a desert" (v.12). Writing in 1906, Ironside who, unlike other careful and conservative commentators, strongly and extensively rejects any possibility of rebuilding, observes that "the silent mounds by the Euphrates are as distinct witness to the holiness of God as the salt plains by the Dead Sea".

At the end-time, an angel will cry "mightily with a strong voice, saying, Babylon the great is fallen, is fallen, and is become the habitation of devils, and the hold of every foul spirit, and a cage of every unclean and hateful bird" (Rev 18.1-2). "Babylon the great" will evidently become the "prison house of demons" (J. Allen; *What the Bible Teaches: Revelation*), and ornithologists are therefore assured that the "owls" in Jeremiah 50 are not described as "unclean and hateful" birds in Revelation 18! In any case, according to Gesenius, the word rendered "owls" (3284) actually refers to the ostrich.

Judgment would be cruel (vv.41-46)

"Behold, a people shall come from the north…They shall hold the bow and the lance: they are cruel, and will not shew mercy: their voice shall roar like the sea, and they shall ride upon horses, every one put in array, like a man to the battle, against thee, O daughter of Babylon. The king of Babylon hath heard the report of them, and his hands waxed feeble: anguish took hold of him, and pangs as of a woman in travail" (vv.41-43). These verses reproduce 6.22-24 with "Babylon" being substituted for "Zion" and "the king of Babylon" for "we". This is certainly not a coincidence. Babylon was soon to suffer all that she had inflicted on Jerusalem.

Similarly, vv.44-46 reproduce 49.19-21, substituting "Babylon" for "Edom", "the Chaldeans" for "Teman", and "among the nations" for "in the Red sea". While there can be little doubt that the lesson from the previous reproduction of earlier verses in the book is re-emphasised here, and Babylon would reap where she had sowed, Feinberg makes the pertinent observation that "since Edom's sins resemble Babylon's, God in righteousness must judge them similarly". The reader is referred to comments made in connection with 49.19-21 for an explanation of the imagery used in vv.44-46. The "lion" (v.44) is now Cyrus: it was Nebuchadnezzar in 49.19. Kidner draws attention to "the humbling fact that in the end there is little to choose between what awaits the pride of an empire and the pride of a clan - the only difference being in the reverberation of their respective falls: compare that of Edom, 'heard in (at) the Red Sea' (49.21), with that of Babylon, 'heard among the nations' (50.46)".

JEREMIAH 51

The prophecy against Babylon which commenced in chapter 50 continues in this chapter and concludes with instructions for the proclamation of Babylon's doom in the city itself. The two sections of the chapter may therefore be entitled:

> The Destruction of Babylon (vv.1-58)
> The Declaration in Babylon (vv.59-64).

Verses 1-58: The Destruction of Babylon

These verses expand and amplify information already given in the previous chapter, and one feature common to both passages is the relationship between Babylon's downfall and her treatment of God's people. While any attempted analysis of the current passage is likely to be arbitrary at best, it is suggested that these verses may be divided into nine paragraphs, of which the first eight (vv.1-6; 7-10; 11; 12-19; 20-24; 25-37; 38-46; 47-53), having described divine judgment upon Babylon, conclude with either the reason for her downfall (vv.5-6; 10; 11b; 15-19; 24; 34-37; 49-53) or, in one case, a command to the deportees from Judah to flee the city (vv.45-46). The reasons vary from paragraph to paragraph, but they are all related to the Lord's concern for His people and for (in the words of David) "the habitation of thy house, and the place where thine honour dwelleth" (Ps 26.8). The final paragraph (vv.54-58) summarises the downfall of Babylon.

The reasons for Babylon's downfall, with the command to flee the city, may be set out as follows:

> The Lord had not forsaken His people (vv.5-6)
> The Lord would vindicate His people in Babylon (v.10)
> The Lord would avenge the destruction of the Temple (v.11b)
> The Lord would display His superiority over idols (vv.15-19)
> The Lord would avenge the destruction of Zion (v.24)
> The Lord would avenge the cruelty towards His people (vv.34-37)
> The Lord would provide for the escape of His people (vv.45-46)
> The Lord would avenge the taunts against His people (vv.49-53).

The Lord had not forsaken His people (vv.1-6)

The judgment upon Babylon (vv.1-4) was evidence that the promises of God had not been rescinded. The people, personified by Zion, who cried, "The Lord hath forsaken me, and my Lord hath forgotten me" (Is 49.14), had not been forsaken (v.5). These verses describe the retribution upon Babylon (vv.1-4); and the reason for her downfall (vv.5-6).

The retribution described (vv.1-4)

The responsible invaders (the armies of the Medes and Persians) are called "a destroying wind" (v.1) and "fanners, that shall fan her, and shall empty her land" (v.2). Babylonia would be emptied like a threshing-floor: she would be destroyed as chaff winnowed from grain. According to the competent authorities, the words, "them that dwell in the midst of them" (v.1) is literally, "the heart of *Leb-kamai*" (JND margin), and it is generally said that this is an unexplained cipher for Chaldea. Jeremiah turns from a metaphor to a direct statement in saying, "Against him that bendeth let the archer bend his bow, and against him that lifteth himself up in his brigandine ('coat of mail', JND): and spare ye not her young men; destroy ye utterly all her host. Thus the slain shall fall in the land of the Chaldeans, and they that are thrust through in her streets" (vv.3-4). Some commentators suggest that the words, "Against him that bendeth let the archer bend his bow", refer throughout to the defenders, with the resulting translation, "Let not the archer bend his bow, and let none lift himself up in his coat of mail", meaning that resistance would be futile. However, this appears to require some alteration to the text, and it should be said that the words which follow indicate "that it is not the attacked but the attacking host that are addressed", whereupon the meaning becomes clear: "Although the Babylonians post themselves on the walls with their weapons and arrayed in armour, yet the archer is to attack them from without, and not one of the fighting men is to be spared" (Streane). This view is adequately confirmed in 50.29.

The reason explained (vv.5-6)
    "For Israel hath not been forsaken, nor Judah of his God, of the Lord of hosts; though their land was filled with sin against the Holy One of Israel" (v.5). Unger finds support from other commentators in stating that "Israel and Judah had not been forsaken by their God…because of His covenanted faithfulness to them, in spite of their unfaithfulness to Him". Ironside states this view very clearly: "Israel and Judah were under the rod of the Lord's chastening because of their sins, but nothing could alter His covenanted mercies to them". This conclusion rests on the assumption that the words "their land" refers to Israel.
    Other translations point rather to Chaldea as "the land" in question. "For Israel is not forsaken…*for* their land (margin, 'the land of the Chaldeans') is full of guilt against the Holy One of Israel" (JND); "For Israel and Judah have not been forsaken…*but* the land of the Chaldeans is full of guilt against the Holy One of Israel" (RSV). It must be said, however, that a footnote ("Hebrew 'their land'") makes it clear that the RSV rendering, "land of the Chaldeans", is an interpretation rather than a translation. Nevertheless, the use of the present tense could well confirm that Chaldea is in view, and this conclusion can be supported by regarding the reference to Israel and Judah (v.5) as a parenthesis, leaving "the connection of thought" (Streane) as follows: "And the slain shall fall in the land of the Chaldeans, and they that are thrust through

in her streets…for their land is full of guilt against the Holy One of Israel" (vv.4-5, JND).

The fact that "Israel hath not been forsaken, nor Judah of his God, of the Lord of hosts" is confirmed by the warning given to them: "Flee out of the midst of Babylon, and deliver every man his soul: be not cut off in her iniquity" (v.6). This is the second of three appeals to God's people to flee from Babylon (cp. 50.8; 51.45). The warning of coming judgment was confirmation that He had not abandoned His people in accordance with the promise, "though I make a full end of all nations whither I have scattered thee, yet will I not make a full end of thee" (30.11), which is virtually repeated in 46.28. It should be noted that a similar call is made to God's people to flee "Great Babylon" (Rev 18.2, JND) at the end-time: "Come out of her my people, that ye be not partakers of her sins, and that ye receive not of her plagues" (Rev 18.4).

The Lord would vindicate the remnant in Babylon (vv.7-10)

The pattern in the previous section is repeated: the retribution upon Babylon (vv.7-8); and the reason for her downfall (vv.9-10).

The retribution upon Babylon (vv.7-8)

"Babylon hath been a golden cup in the Lord's hand, that made all the earth drunken: the nations have drunken of her wine; therefore the nations are mad" (v.7). This is clearly explained by Streane who, having referred to 25.15-16, continues by pointing out that there "it was Jeremiah himself who was commanded to make the nations drink of the wine of God's wrath. Inasmuch, however, as Babylon was the means which God employed for their overthrow, she is here spoken of under the same figure, as having made all the nations drunk. She is called a golden cup from the splendour and glory which belonged to her as an empire". Babylon is called "the golden city" (Is 14.4). At the end-time, another Babylon, described as "the great whore that sitteth upon many waters", is depicted with "a golden cup in her hand full of abominations and filthiness of her fornication" (Rev 17.1,4). Like historical Babylon, which was to fall suddenly and be destroyed (v.8), the latter-day Babylon will follow suit (Rev 14.8; 18.2). In fact, it is stated that her fall would take place not only in "one day", but in "one hour" (Rev 18.8,10,17,19). Isaiah's proclamation of Babylon's fall (Is 21.9) preceded Jeremiah's announcement by over a century.

The reason for her downfall (vv.9-10)

Having been told, "howl for her; take balm for her pain, if so be she may be healed" (v.8b), the Jewish captives reply, "We would have healed Babylon, but she is not healed" (v.9). This is best explained with reference to the fact that the exiles in Babylon were instructed, amongst other things, to "seek the peace of the city whither I have caused you to be carried away captives, and pray unto the Lord for it: for in the peace thereof shall ye have peace" (29.7). Streane observes that "The terrible character of her fall is skillfully suggested by the prophet when he thus calls upon those who had suffered most grievously at her hands to have compassion upon the ills of their former oppressor". The judgment upon Babylon "is measureless as is the distance from heaven to earth" (Ellicott's Commentary): it "reacheth unto heaven, and is lifted up even to the skies" (v.9). A similar statement is made about the sins of "Babylon the great" (Rev 18.2): "her sins have reached unto heaven, and God hath remembered her iniquities" (Rev 18.5).

It should be noted that Babylon had evidently rejected the testimony of the Jewish exiles who "would have healed Babylon" and who were now left with the only course of abandoning the city: "forsake her, and let us go every one into his own country" (v.9). The Jews evidently spoke in the name of all the exiles in Babylon. The testimony of God's people in Babylon would be vindicated by divine judgment on the city, causing the exiles to say, "The Lord hath brought forth our righteousness ('righteousnesses', JND margin): come, and let us declare in Zion the work of the Lord our God" (v.10). The sense of "hath brought forth our righteousness" is "hath made known the justice of our cause (by thus delivering our enemy over to the sword)" (Streane). The way in which the Lord had accomplished this would be declared in Zion (v.10).

The Lord would avenge the destruction of the Temple (v.11)

Having said, "Make bright the arrows ('Sharpen the arrows', JND); gather the shields: the Lord hath raised up the spirit of the kings of the Medes: for his device ('purpose', JND) is against Babylon", the reason is given: "because it is the vengeance of the Lord, the vengeance of his temple". Attention is again drawn to:

The retribution upon Babylon (v.11a)

The identity of the northern invader is now revealed. Under divine compulsion, the Medes would prepare to invade Babylon. The words, "gather the shields" are, literally, "fill the shields" which has been explained as "fill...with arm or body" (JND margin). These large shields "covered the whole body, and the man literally filled them" (Ellicott's Commentary). According to Streane, "Media was a country lying north-west of Persia. It consisted in early times of a number of small tribes, whose leaders are here called 'kings'. It was the Medo-Persian Empire that succeeded by conquest to the dominions of Babylon".

The reason for her downfall (v.11b)

The self-explanatory statement, "it is the vengeance of the Lord, the vengeance of his temple", virtually repeats 50.28, and the reader is referred to comments made in connection with that passage. In the words of Kidner, Psalm 74 "recalls the savage shouts with which they (the Babylonians) went to work": "Thine enemies roar in the midst of thy congregations; they set up their ensigns for signs. A man was famous according as he had lifted up axes upon the thick trees. But now they break down the carved work thereof at once with axes and hammers. They have cast fire into thy sanctuary, they have defiled by casting down the dwelling place of thy name to the ground" (vv.4-7).

The Lord would display His superiority over idols (vv.12-19)

The pattern in previous paragraphs is discernible here: having described the overthrow of Babylon with all its security and wealth (vv.12-14), Jeremiah proclaims the utter superiority of "the Lord of hosts" (v.14) over the gods of Babylon (vv.15-19), saying, "They are vanity, the work of errors: in the time of their visitation they shall perish" (v.18).

The retribution upon Babylon (vv.12-14)

These verses may be summarised by the words, "thine end is come" (v.13). The besiegers, rather than the besieged are described: "Set up the standard upon ('towards', JND) the walls of Babylon, make the watch strong, set up the watchmen, prepare the ambushes" (v.12). According to Ellicott's Commentary, "The 'standards' are the banners or signals that direct an attack on a given point on the walls. The 'watch' and 'watchmen' are the scouts and sentinels placed to give notice of any attempt at a sally on the part of the besieged. The 'ambush' may indicate generally any sudden attack, or, more specifically, the stratagem of a feigned flight, like that employed by Joshua in the attack on Ai (Josh 8.14-16; cp Judg 20.32-35)".

The fall of Babylon was certain, and the fact that Jeremiah penned these words at least fifty years before the event did not alter that certainty in the slightest degree. With the picture before him of the besieged city fifty years hence, Jeremiah could confidently say, "the Lord hath both devised and done that which he spake against the inhabitants of Babylon" (v.12). The security of the city (v.13) would prove unavailing. Ellicott's Commentary, having quoted the inscribed words of Nebuchadnezzar: "I made water to flow all around in this immense dyke of earth. I carried an aqueduct across these great waters that are like unto the depths of the sea", continues: "The channels which were cut for the waters of the Euphrates seemed at once intended for a line of defence against attack, and for irrigation and navigation". But Babylon's carefully planned defences would not prevent its fall. The words, "thine end is come, and the measure of thy covetousness" (v.13), evidently mean, bearing in mind that Babylon's "covetousness" refers to her abundant "treasures" (v.13), that the allotted time of her prosperity had come to an end. This could not be averted: "The Lord of hosts hath sworn by himself, saying, Surely I will fill thee with men, as with caterpillars; and they shall lift up a shout against thee" (v.14). The invaders would swarm over her like locusts (3218), and shout (1959) like men treading grapes in the wine-press, "the received symbol of conquest and destruction (Is 63.2-3)" (Ellicott's Commentary).

The reason for her downfall (vv.15-19)

These verses, which contrast the vanity of idol-worshippers with the superlative inheritance of the Lord's people, are also found, with a few minor differences, in 10.12-16, and are restated here to emphasise the ability of the "Lord of hosts" (v.14), with all His infinite power, to overthrow Babylon and expose the impotence of her gods. Nebuchadnezzar may have boasted in the city's defences, but this was no obstacle to the Lord who "hath made the earth by his power" and "hath established the world by his wisdom, and hath stretched out the heaven by his understanding" (v.15).

As Streane rightly points out, in the earlier passage the words "form a natural sequence with that which precedes, assuring the Israelites that they need not fear the power of false gods, while here they are quoted by the prophet as the solemn declaration to the Chaldeans that their idols will prove worthless in the day of their calamity". The idols of Babylon, like all pagan idols, had "no breath in them" (v.17), but "The portion of Jacob is not like them; for he is the former of all things: and Israel is the rod of his inheritance: the Lord of hosts is his name" (v.19). The reader is now referred to comments made in connection with 10.12-16.

The Lord would avenge the destruction of Zion (vv.20-24)

Once again, attention is drawn to retribution upon Babylon and the reason for her downfall.

The retribution upon Babylon (vv.20-23)

Divine judgment on Babylon is clearly proclaimed (v.24), but commentators are divided over the identity of the military power described as "my battle axe ('maul', JND, or 'mace') and weapons of war" (v.20). The passage has been explained in three ways.

The first explanation identifies the Lord's "battle axe" as Israel and does so for the reason that having described God's people as "the rod (referring to a measuring rod) of his inheritance" (v.19), the passage proceeds without an obvious break by saying, "Thou art my battle axe and weapons of war: for with thee will I break in pieces the nations, and with thee will I destroy kingdoms" (v.20). Ironside espouses this explanation: "This people He had formed for Himself. He would use them as His battle-axe and weapon of war. With them He would break in pieces the nations and destroy the kingdoms of their oppressors. All classes must learn that the Lord hath chosen Jacob; for with them, not the warrior only, but the people in every walk of life, must be broken, and His word fulfilled which declared, 'And I will render unto Babylon and to all the inhabitants of Chaldea all their evil that they have done in your sight, saith the Lord' (vv.21-24)". If this explanation is accepted, then the passage must refer to events that still lie in the future, since the Lord did not use His people in the downfall of Babylon in 539 BC. On these grounds, Ironside's explanation does not appear to be correct.

The second explanation is that the Lord's "battle axe and weapons of war" is Cyrus, king of Persia, of whom it was said over a century previously, "Thus saith the Lord to his anointed, to Cyrus, whose right hand I have holden, to subdue nations before him; and I will loose the loins of kings, to open before him the two leaved gates; and the gates shall not be shut; I will go before thee, and make the crooked places straight: I will break in pieces the gates of brass, and cut in sunder the bars of iron" (Is 45.1-2). On the basis of this explanation, Babylon, described as "the hammer of the whole earth" (50.23), would be broken by an even mightier weapon. Feinberg understands the passage in this way: "This passage underscores the great power of Persia. Ten times the phrase 'with you' (AV 'with thee') falls like hammer blows (vv.20-23). The Hebrew verb…indicates a violent and intense shattering". This view is worthy of careful consideration.

The third explanation which, it is suggested, carries more contextual weight than the preceding views, identifies the Lord's "battle axe" as Babylon itself, and does so on the assumption that vv.20-23 refer to her prowess at the time of writing, some fifty years before her overthrow. Streane is quite convinced that this is the case: "there can be little doubt that Babylon is the subject of the address in this and the succeeding verse. Compare 50.23, where she is likened to a hammer. It is clear from the tense of the oft-repeated verb in the original that she is thought of as still in the height of her power, and in the midst of her oppressive treatment of the nations of the earth". This is not without precedent: the conquests and downfall of Assyria are similarly described (Is 10.5-19). In the words of Kidner, vv.20-23 refer to Babylon's "role", and v.24 to her "requital". Unger writes similarly: "Babylon had served as the Lord's agent of judgment (vv.20b-23; cp. 27.4-11), but now her own judgment was impending (v.24)". The way in which the chapter proceeds appears to confirm this conclusion. Having described the way in which all obstacles would be mercilessly crushed (vv.20-23), the Lord proclaims judgment on Babylon: "Behold, I am against thee, O destroying mountain, saith the Lord, which destroyest all the earth" (v.25). "Babylon's irrevocable destruction will be God's recompense for past iniquity" (Harrison).

The reason for her downfall (v.24)

While the identity of the Lord's "battle axe and weapons of war" may not be resolved to the satisfaction of all, there is no doubt about the primary reason for Babylon's downfall: "And I will render unto Babylon, and to all the inhabitants of Chaldea all their evil that they have done in Zion in your sight, saith the Lord". The exiles who had witnessed the demolition of Jerusalem are assured that the perpetrators would not go unpunished.

The promise made to Abraham would be fulfilled: "I will bless them that bless thee, and curse him that curseth thee" (Gen 12.3).

The Lord would avenge the cruelty towards His people (vv.25-37)

The observable pattern in previous sections of the chapter is present here. The retribution upon Babylon is described in vv.25-33 and the reason for her downfall is given in vv.34-37.

The retribution upon Babylon (vv.25-33)

The "destroying mountain" would become "a burnt mountain" (v.25). It has been rightly said that Babylon was located on a plain and that the expression "destroying kingdom" is "a metaphor for a powerful kingdom" (Feinberg). This is well-supported by Daniel 2.25,44-45. Feinberg continues, "But Babylon will become as an extinct volcano - 'a burned-out mountain'. She will never be rebuilt": "And they shall not take of thee a stone for a corner, nor a stone for foundations; but thou shalt be desolate for ever, saith the Lord" (v.26). As Kidner observes, "The picture changes from Babylon as a weapon to Babylon as a destroying mountain (vv.25-26) - in fact, as a volcano which not only spews out destruction, but ends by blowing itself to bits".

Conservative scholars and commentators divide on the literality of "Babylon the great" (Rev 18.2), and not all would agree with Ironside: "Words could not be plainer to declare Babylon's absolute destruction. Not only shall the city itself never be rebuilt, but the very stones should not be used, as in the case of many another fallen capital, for the rebuilding of any other place. As an accursed thing, her foundations should be held in perpetual abhorrence and her site given up to continual desolation. Nor can the words, by any process of reasoning, be legitimately made to refer to a future overthrow immediately before the Millennium. For over two millenniums already the wastes of Babylon have been a testimony to the sure word of God. It will be so for ever". While the statement in v.26, and statements elsewhere in chapters 50 and 51, seem quite clear and unambiguous, other commentators argue the contrary case with good logic and equal vehemence!

The downfall of Babylon would be accomplished by an alliance of nations under the Median standard. "Set ye up a standard in the land, blow the trumpet among the nations, prepare the nations against her, call together against her the kingdoms of Ararat, Minni, and Ashchenaz; appoint a captain against her; cause the horses to come up as the rough caterpillars. Prepare against her the nations with the kings of the Medes, the captains thereof, and all the rulers thereof, and all the land of his dominion" (vv.27-28). The words "appoint a captain against her" and "all the land of his dominion" indicate that this was no disorganised rabble. The invasion would be under unified command, and led by the king of the Medes and Persians. Feinberg calls the "kingdoms of Ararat, Minni, and Ashchenaz", the "people north

of Babylon, who were conquered by the Medes early in the sixth century
BC". It is said that Ararat and Minni were the central or southern and the
western parts respectively of modern Armenia, and that Ashchenaz refers
to the nearby Scythians. Feinberg points out that in modern Hebrew
Ashkenaz denotes Germany and Ashkenazi signifies a German Jew. The
invading horde is likened to "the rough caterpillars", or "the bristly
caterpillars" (JND). Other authorities have "the bristly locusts" which,
according to Ellicott's Commentary, "describes the insect in its third stage
of growth, when the wings are not yet unfolded from their cases, and
when they are most destructive in their ravages". As always, God's figures
of speech cannot be bettered!

The invasion would bring the numbing effect of fear upon the land
and city: "And the land shall tremble and sorrow: for every purpose of
the Lord shall be performed against Babylon, to make the land of
Babylon a desolation without an inhabitant. The mighty men of Babylon
have forborn to fight, they have remained in their holds: their might
hath failed; they became as women" (vv.29-30). The panic in Babylon is
described: having said that that "they (the besiegers) have burned her
dwellingplaces; her bars are broken" (v.30b), the couriers and
messengers are depicted running from one to another in conveying
the news to the king: "One post shall run to meet another, and one
messenger to meet another, to shew the king of Babylon that his city is
taken at one end ('from end to end', JND), And that the passages are
stopped, and the reeds ('reedy places', JND) they have burned with
fire, and the men of war are affrighted" (vv.31-32). The picture is painted
in some detail in Ellicott's Commentary and makes fascinating reading:
the invaders "begin by setting the houses on fire and breaking open
the gates that led from the river to the streets of the city, while the
panic-stricken people fled to their citadel in despair". The "passages"
were "probably the ferries across the Euphrates, by which one part of
the city was in communication with the other...Besides these there
was one bridge over the Euphrates in the middle and a tunnel under it
(Herod. i.186)...The word for 'reeds' is elsewhere (Is 14.23; 41.18; Ex
7.19; 8.5) translated 'pools' (or 'ponds'). Here it probably refers to the
great pool constructed by Nitocris as a reservoir or dock. This was
probably left dry by the diversion of the river into another channel,
and the reeds which grew in it, perhaps also the flood-gates of the
canals, and the ships that were in dock, were burned by the Persians.
The very pools were the scene of a conflagration".

The situation is summed up as follows: "For thus saith the Lord of hosts,
the God of Israel; The daughter of Babylon is like a threshingfloor, it is
time to thresh her: yet a little while, and the time of her harvest shall
come" (v.33). The "harvest" is evidently the accumulated wealth of Babylon
which would be "harvested" by the invader, and the "threshingfloor" is
the city itself which would be trodden under foot.

The reason for her downfall (vv.34-37)

The downfall of the city and nation would be the Lord's answer to Zion's complaint against Babylon. Zion, or Jerusalem, is personified in saying: "Nebuchadrezzar the king of Babylon hath devoured me, he hath crushed me, he hath made me an empty vessel, he hath swallowed me up like a dragon, he hath filled his belly with my delicates (delicacies), he hath cast me out. The violence done to me and to my flesh be upon Babylon, shall the inhabitant of Zion say; and my blood upon the inhabitants of Chaldea, shall Jerusalem say. Therefore thus saith the Lord; Behold, I will plead thy cause, and take vengeance for thee" (vv.34-36). The way in which Nebuchadrezzar had "devoured" Zion is described in 52.4-30. The city had been spoiled until it was an "empty vessel" (v.34). According to Streane, the word translated "dragon" (v.34; 8577) denotes "any great monster", including the crocodile. It has been suggested that the "delicates" (v.34) are the corn, wine, oil and fruits of the land.

Bearing in mind that "he that toucheth you toucheth the apple of his eye" (Zech 2.8), the Lord would recompense Babylon: "I will dry up her sea, and make her springs dry. And Babylon shall become heaps, a dwelling-place for dragons ('jackals', JND), an astonishment, and an hissing, without an inhabitant" (vv.36-37). While some commentators give "sea" and "springs" a figurative meaning, and refer to the "sea" of confluent nations and the "springs" of wealth that fed her greatness, it seems better to take the these expressions literally. Accordingly, others understand the "sea" and the "springs" with reference to "the Euphrates, or to the sea-like alluvial plan, intersected by canals and streams in which the city stood, often flooded by the river, so that it became an actual sea (Herod. i.184)" (Ellicott's Commentary). Bearing in mind that the word "springs" is actually in the singular, the reference could be to "the great lake or reservoir, four hundred and twenty furlongs in circumference, made by queen Nitocris (Herod. i.185)" (Streane).

There is no doubting the literality of the "heaps" (v.37) or "piles of ruins" (Unger), and it is not without significance that the terms used to describe ruined Babylon are also used to describe ruined Jerusalem (9.11; 19.8; 25.9,18), emphasising the law of retribution. With characteristic forthrightness, Ironside makes the point that "this utter desolation is to follow, not some future overthrow, but the sack of the city resulting from the turning aside of the waters in which her inhabitants trusted".

The Lord would provide for the escape of His people (vv.38-46)

Having described the desolation of Babylon (vv.36-37), and before resuming the description (vv.42-44), together with a further appeal for God's people to flee the city (vv.45-46), Jeremiah describes the scene of revelry that preceded its capture (vv.38-41). These verses may therefore be divided as follows: the retribution upon Babylon (vv.38-44); and the warning to flee the city (vv.45-46).

The retribution upon Babylon (vv.38-44)

It is for good reason that Streane observes that it was "while they are exulting over the spoil which they had won from the conquered nations" that God "destroyed them at unawares", adding that "this found a signal fulfilment in the capture of Babylon during a feast". While vv.38-41 refer to Babylonian feasts in general (v.39), there can be little doubt that the passage anticipates Belshazzar's "great feast to a thousand of his Lords", when the king and his guests quaffed wine from "the golden vessels that were taken out of the temple of the house of God which was a Jerusalem", and "praised the gods of gold, and of silver, of brass, of iron, of wood, and of stone" (Dan 5.1-4). Jeremiah describes the noise and the drunkenness at the feast: "They shall roar together like lions: they shall yell as lions' whelps. In their heat I will make their feasts (carousals, or drinking bouts), and I will make them drunken, that they may rejoice, and sleep a perpetual sleep, and not wake, saith the Lord" (vv.38-39). In the words of Ellicott's Commentary, "When the revellers are hot with wine and lust (cp. Hos 7.4-7), Jehovah would call them to a banquet of another kind. The wine cup which He would give them would be that of His wrath (cp. 25.16-17), and their drunken joy should end in eternal sleep. So Herodotus (i.191) narrates that when Cyrus took the city by his stratagem the inhabitants were keeping a feast with their wonted revelry and license". It was on the night of Belshazzar's feast that the king was slain, and "Darius the Median took the kingdom" (Dan 5.30-31).

The inhabitants of Babylon are described as animals ("lambs...rams...he goats") taken to the slaughter-house (v.40), and although the word "surprised" (8610) means "to seize" or "take hold of", the element of surprise, to the extent of incredulity, over Babylon's downfall is certainly present in the words: "How is Sheshach taken! and how is the praise of the whole earth surprised! how is Babylon become an astonishment among the nations!" (v.41). Similar incredulity was expressed over the sack of Jerusalem: "The kings of the earth, and all the inhabitants of the world, would not have believed that the adversary and the enemy should have entered into the gates of Jerusalem" (Lam 4.12). The destruction of latter-day Babylon will elicit sorrow and surprise (Rev 18.9-10, 15-19). The name "Sheshach" (v.41) occurs in 25.26, and the reader is referred to comments made there in this connection. It should be noted that Zion, the very city sacked by Nebuchadnezzar, will be called "the joy of the whole earth" (Ps 48.2).

Having described the circumstances in which Babylon would fall to the invader, Jeremiah refers to the irresistible progress of the invasion by likening it to the inundation of the Euphrates. The enemy hordes would pour in like a flood, with resulting devastation: "The sea is come upon Babylon: she is covered with the multitude of the waves thereof. Her cities are a desolation, a dry land, and a wilderness, a land wherein no man dwelleth, neither doth any son of man pass thereby" (vv.42-43). The Egyptian armies are similarly described: "Who is this that cometh up as a flood, whose waters are moved as the rivers? Egypt riseth up like a flood, and his waters are moved like the rivers" (46.7-8). "The prophet seems to dwell with a stern delight on the seeming paradox that the sea with which Babylon is to be overflowed, the floods of invaders and destroyers, shall leave her cities and plains drier and more sandy than before" (Ellicott's Commentary).

The god of Babylon and the wall of Babylon would both prove incapable of saving her from the invader: "And I will punish Bel in Babylon, and I will bring forth out of his mouth that which he hath swallowed up: and the nations shall not flow any more unto him: yea, the wall of Babylon shall fall" (v.44). Bel is mentioned in 50.2, and the reader is referred to comments made in connection with that verse. It was evidently the custom of the Babylonians to place looted treasures in the temple of Bel. The Chaldean imputed "his power unto his god" (Hab 1.11). Nebuchadnezzar carried "part of the vessels of the house of God…into the land of Shinar to the house of his god; and he brought the vessels into the treasure house of his god" (Dan 1.2), and in doing this he proclaimed that Bel was superior to the God of Israel. But Bel would be compelled to disgorge his amassed wealth! "Cyrus the king brought forth the vessels of the house of the Lord, which Nebuchadnezzar had brought forth out of Jerusalem, and had put them in the house of his gods; Even those did Cyrus king of Persia bring forth by the hand of Mithredath the treasurer, and numbered them unto Sheshbazzar, the prince of Judah" (Ezra 1.7-8). Bel was evidently recognised, not only as the god of Babylon, but as the god of the Babylonian Empire: the nations subject to Babylon are said to have flowed "unto him". Nebuchadnezzar certainly took steps to unify the various "people, nations…languages" which made up his empire, under one religion, and one common object of worship, by erecting an image in the plain of Dura, and commanding his herald to say: "To you it is commanded, O people, nations and languages…fall down and worship the golden image that Nebuchadnezzar the king hath set up" (Dan 3.4-5).

According to Ellicott's Commentary, the name Bel was incorporated in the names given to the two great walls of Babylon: Imgur-Bel (meaning 'Bel protects') and Nimetti-Bel (meaning 'the dwelling of Bel'). The walls "were thus specially consecrated to him as their tutelary deity". But the wall of Babylon would fall. Walls present no problem to the Lord. Ask the inhabitants of Jericho!

The warning to flee the city (vv.45-46)
"My people, go ye out of the midst of her, and deliver ye every man his soul from the fierce anger of the Lord" (v.45). As previously noted this is the third of three similar appeals (cp. 50.8; 51.6). Having been told who would ultimately be responsible for the downfall of Babylon, God's people were not to be terrified by persistent rumours and internal conflicts: "And let not your heart faint, neither fear ye for the rumour that shall be heard

in the land; for a rumour shall come one year, and after that in another year shall come a rumour, and violence in the land, ruler against ruler" (v.46, RV). Once again, Ellicott's Commentary provides information not easily available to the ordinary reader: "It lies in the nature of the case that the final catastrophe of the city would be preceded by a period of uncertainty and suspense. Men would hear of the union of the Medes and Persians under Cyrus, of the murder of Evil-Merodach by Neriglissar, of the death of Neriglissar in fighting against the enemy (555 BC). The child-king, whom Berosus calls Laborosoarchord, was dethroned by his nobles after a few months, and was succeeded by the father of the Belshazzar of Daniel 5.1, the Labynetus of Herodotus, whose true name was Nabo-nahid. The whole empire was in the throes of dissolution". This recitation of ancient history ends with the comment: "The words present a singular parallel to those which speak of 'wars and rumours of wars' in Matthew 24.6-7; Luke 21.9".

The Lord would avenge the taunts against His people (vv.47-53)

For the last time in this chapter, attention is drawn to the retribution upon Babylon (vv.47-48) and the reason for her downfall (vv.49-53). The overthrow of Babylon would be the Lord's answer to the way in which His people had suffered reproach in Babylon on account of His supposed inability to preserve them from captivity (v.51).

The retribution upon Babylon (vv.47-48)

These verses are quite self-explanatory: "Therefore, behold, the days come, that I will do judgment upon the graven images of Babylon: and her whole land shall be confounded, and all her slain shall fall in the midst of her" (v.47). However confusing the rumours (v.46), with more than one "false dawn", God's people could rightly infer from them that the day of vengeance was at hand. Isaiah describes the fate of "the graven images of Babylon": "Bel boweth down, Nebo stoopeth, their idols were upon the beasts, and upon the cattle…They stoop, they bown down together; they could not deliver the burden, but themselves are gone into captivity" (Is 46.1-2). Babylon's impotent idols would be exposed for what they were - just "graven images", and no more! The fall of Babylon to the northern invader would bring joy to heaven and earth: "Then the heaven and the earth, and all that is therein, shall sing for Babylon: for the spoilers shall come unto her from the north, saith the Lord" (Jer 51.48). The fall of latter-day Babylon will be similarly celebrated: "Rejoice over her, thou heaven, and ye holy apostles and prophets; for God hath avenged you on her" (Rev 18.20).

The reason for her downfall (vv.49-53)

This is clearly stated: "As Babylon hath caused the slain of Israel to fall, so at Babylon shall fall the slain of all the earth" (v.49). The AV rendering, "of all the earth", points to "other nations from all parts of the earth who are mingled with her people" (Ellicott's Commentary), but it should be said that the RV reads "the slain of all the land" as "giving more emphatically the law of retribution" (Ellicott's Commentary). The Jewish escapees from Babylon are told to "remember the Lord afar off, and let Jerusalem come into your mind" as they witnessed Babylon's overthrow (v.50). Quite evidently ruined Jerusalem was constantly in their minds. Over the years of their captivity they had said, "We are put to shame, for we have heard reproach; confusion hath covered our face: for strangers are come into the sanctuaries of Jehovah's house" (v.51, JND). This translation gives weight to Streane's explanation that "The exiles speak, while in exile, and lament the reproaches that are cast in their teeth for worshipping a God who will not defend His people from misfortune, and His temple from sacrilege". Their cry in this way would be answered: "Wherefore, behold, the days come, saith the Lord, that I will do judgment upon her graven images (the images of the very gods thought to be superior to the Lord): and through all her land the wounded shall groan. Though Babylon should mount up to heaven, and though she should fortify the height of her strength ('Even if Babylon reaches the sky and fortifies her lofty stronghold', NIV), yet from me shall spoilers come unto her, saith the Lord" (vv.52-53). The words, "Though Babylon should mount up to heaven" (v.53) recall the intentions of her first builders: "Go to, let us build us a city and a tower, whose top may reach unto heaven" (Gen 11.4).

The concluding summary of Babylon's downfall (vv.54-58)

These verses draw attention to the cry of Babylon (v.54); the requital of Babylon (vv.55-56); the impotence of Babylon (v.57); and the destruction of Babylon (v.58).

The cry of Babylon (v.54)

"A sound of a cry cometh from Babylon, and great destruction from the land of the Chaldeans." Like the "voice of crying...from Horonaim", Babylon's cry will result from her "spoiling and great destruction" (48.3). The destruction of latter-day Babylon will be accompanied by profound grief on the part of "the kings of the earth...the merchants of earth...And every shipmaster, and all the company in ships, and sailors, and as many as trade by sea" (Rev 18.9,11,17).

The requital of Babylon (vv.55-56)

The cry is uttered: "Because the Lord hath spoiled Babylon, and destroyed out of her the great voice; when her waves do roar like great waters, a noise of their voice is uttered: Because the spoiler is come upon her, even upon Babylon, and her mighty men are taken, every one of their bows is broken: for the Lord God of recompences shall surely requite". This is helpfully explained in Ellicott's Commentary: "The 'great voice' which Jehovah 'destroys' or 'makes to cease' is the stir and tumult of life that surged, as it were, through the city (Is 17.12-13). The "waves" are those of the "sea" of the legions of her conqueror (see v.42), and they 'roar' while the voices that were heard before are hushed in the silence of death". The Lord is called "the Lord God of recompences" (v.56). In this capacity, he has already said: "I will render unto Babylon and to all the inhabitants of Chaldea all the evil that they have done in Zion in your sight" (v.24). Believers today can rest with assurance that they can leave the recompense for harm and injustice perpetrated against them with the Lord (Rom 12.19; 2 Thess 1.6).

The impotence of Babylon (v.57)
    "And I will make drunk her princes, and her wise men, her captains, and her rulers, and her mighty men: and they shall sleep a perpetual sleep, and not wake, saith the King, whose name is the Lord of hosts." The imagery of v.39 is repeated here. Far from sinking into the usual drunken sleep after a carousal, the nobility of Babylon would enter the perpetual sleep of death. However, in this case, they would be drunk with the wine of divine wrath. Daniel addressed Belshazzar with the words, "O thou king" (Dan 5.18), but the Babylonian monarch was shortly to lose his life at the instigation of "the King, whose name is the Lord of hosts". Behind the hosts of invading Medes and Persians stood the "Lord of hosts".

The destruction of Babylon (v.58)
    "Thus saith the Lord of hosts; The broad walls of Babylon shall be utterly broken ('laid bare', JND, with a marginal note: "or 'undermined' "), and her high gates shall be burned with fire; and the people shall labour in vain, and the folk in the fire, and they shall be weary." The city walls were immense: "Under Nebuchadnezzar, Babylon was surrounded with a double wall of defensive fortifications which according to Herodotus (i.178ff.), enclosed an area of 200 square miles" (Harrison). The historian Herodotus states that "the outer wall of the city was 200 royal cubits (about 373 feet/ 115 metres) high, while it was fifty cubits wide" (Streane). While these measurements have been challenged on the grounds of exaggeration, there can be no doubt that they were vast, and it is known that "the thickness of the wall allowed four chariots to run abreast" (Feinberg). According to Herodotus, "In the circuit of the wall are a hundred gates, all brass, with brazen lintels and side-posts". But, as Ironside observes, "the labour of the people to make it the grandest city in all the world would thus end in vanity". The words, "and the people shall labour in vain, and the folk in the fire ('so that the peoples will have laboured in vain, and the nations for the fire', JND), and they shall be weary", are paralleled by those of Habakkuk: "Behold, is it not of the Lord of hosts that the people shall labour in the very fire, and the people shall weary themselves for very vanity?" (Hab 2.13). Ellicott's Commentary explains that both passages refer

to "the stately edifices which had been raised with so much toil by the slave-labour of Nebuchadnezzar's subjects and captives". But all to no avail. Babylon would be destroyed.

Verses 59-64: The Declaration in Babylon
The contents of the prophecy against Babylon were written in a book by Jeremiah and committed to Seraiah, son of Neriah, who was given instructions to read the book when he visited the city with Zedekiah, king of Judah. Attention is drawn to the identity of the messenger (v.59); the declaration of the message (vv.60-62); and the illustration of the message (vv.63-64).

The identity of the messenger (v.59)
"The word which Jeremiah the prophet commanded Seraiah the son of Neriah, the son of Maaseiah, when he went with Zedekiah the king of Judah into Babylon in the fourth year of his reign. And this Seraiah was a quiet prince", or "chief chamberlain" (JND). It is generally thought that Zedekiah visited Babylon in the fourth year of his reign (594-593 BC) either in an attempt to clear himself of complicity in a revolt against Nebuchadnezzar or, more likely, to allay suspicions at Babylon over the visit to Jerusalem by envoys from Edom, Moab, Ammon, Tyre, and Zidon (27.3), which also took place in the fourth year of Zedekiah's reign (28.1). This is the only place in Scripture where the visit by Zedekiah to Babylon is recorded. According to Feinberg, Seraiah was "the staff officer responsible for looking after the comfort of the king of Judah whenever he stopped for the night". He was evidently the brother of Baruch (32.12).

Commentators rightly point out that in the fourth year of Zedekiah's reign Jeremiah both urged submission to Babylon (27.1-11) and pronounced the city's doom. "He counselled submission for the present, because resistance was premature, and would prove futile. He looked forward to the time when the law of retribution would be fulfilled in Babylon as it had been fulfilled in Jerusalem" (Ellicott's Commentary).

The declaration of the message (vv.60-62)
"So Jeremiah wrote in a book all the evil that should come upon Babylon, even all these words that are written against Babylon. And Jeremiah said to Seraiah, When thou comest to Babylon, and shalt see, and shalt read all these words; Then shalt thou say, O Lord, thou hast spoken against this place, to cut it off, that none shall remain in it, neither man nor beast, but that it shall be desolate for ever." The prophecy against Babylon was evidently written, literally, "in one book" (Streane), or upon one parchment. It has been suggested that when the time came to cast the scroll into the Euphrates (v.63), its consignment to the river in one piece would illustrate the complete overthrow of Babylon.

It seems hardly likely that the book was to be read to the Babylonians since that would have inevitably placed Seraiah in great danger. Streane is probably correct in saying that "the words are nevertheless to be pronounced in the presence of Jewish witnesses, who could in after days testify that thus, long before the overthrow of Babylon, these words had been read in the midst of the very city where they were to take effect".

The illustration of the message (vv.63-64)

"And it shall be, when thou hast made an end of reading this book, that thou shalt bind a stone to it, and cast it into the midst of Euphrates: And thou shalt say, Thus shall Babylon sink, and shall not rise from the evil that I will bring upon her: and they shall be weary." The symbolic act needs no explanation. The stone was tied to the scroll in order that it might sink at once, and thus prefigure the destruction of the city. The ruin of Babylon would be irretrievable. The final words of Jeremiah so far as this narrative is concerned, "and they shall be weary", repeat the closing words of the prophecy itself (v.58), and Ellicott's Commentary makes the rather attractive suggestion that "Seraiah was to repeat the last words of the prediction (v.58), and, as they passed his lips, was to fling the roll into the river. That submersion was typical of the end of the futile labour and weariness of the men of the doomed city". According to Harrison, "Massoretic scribes apparently copied the word rendered 'and they shall be weary' (AV, RV) from the end of v.58 when vv.59 to 64 were inserted. It can be omitted, with LXX, RSV and NEB". The explanation in Ellicott's Commentary is preferable!

Similar symbolism is used in describing what Ellicott's Commentary calls "the destruction of the mystical Babylon": "And a mighty angel took up a stone like a great millstone, and cast it into the sea, saying, Thus with violence shall that great city Babylon be thrown down, and shall be found no more at all" (Rev 18.21). This raises the question of the role of Babylon at the end-time, and it must be said that the clear and unambiguous statements made by Jeremiah in chapters 50 and 51 lead to the conclusion that the city will not be rebuilt. It is sometimes argued that this conclusion cannot be justified since the city was not destroyed as Sodom and Gomorrah (50.40), but the verse in question refers to the total obliteration of those cities rather than the way in which this was accomplished. Nevertheless, Babylon will reappear on the world stage (Rev chs.17 and 18) and will exercise immense power and influence before her swift destruction. It hardly seems tenable to argue that the "great city" described in Revelation 17.18 differs from the "great city" described in Revelation 18.18-19, and this could lead to the conclusion that if the description in chapter 17 is couched in figurative language then the description in chapter 18 must be regarded in the same way. Very clearly, there can be no doubt about the re-emergence of Babylon, but not all prophetic students agree on the form in which it will appear. If the prophetic role of Babylon is *literal,* then the city must be rebuilt: if *figurative* and standing for a religious power controlling politics and commerce, then rebuilding is not essential since it stands for a world *system*.

Feinberg, who evidently does not expect Babylon to be rebuilt, avers that "The reason…that the apostle John is not speaking of literal historical Babylon" is: "First he uses the word 'mystery' with reference to Babylon. This conveys the force of a mystical Babylon. Second, Revelation is fond of using proper nouns figuratively: Jezebel (2.20); the key of David (3.7); Jerusalem (the new) comes down out of heaven (21.2,10); Sodom and Egypt (11.8); Gog and Magog (20.8, not the same geographical area as of Ezekiel 38,39); Babylon (chs.17,18), not the city of Mesopotamia, which was situated on a plain [cp. 17.9])".

The debate will continue, with the sobering thought that ultimately one of the two views will be proved right, and the other wrong!

The final words of the chapter, "Thus far are the words of Jeremiah" (v.64), were written, in all probability, by the writer of the concluding chapter. It is "commonly understood to be a compiler's note, added to separate chapter 51 from chapter 52, which parallels passages in 2 Kings" (Feinberg). It is quite possible that the editor was Baruch.

JEREMIAH 52

Commentators are in general agreement that this chapter is a historical supplement to the book of Jeremiah, and while it has been suggested that its purpose is "to show how Jeremiah's prophecies were fulfilled in contrast to those of the false prophets" (Feinberg), it has to be said that the fall of Jerusalem and the capture of Zedekiah, with some of the attendant events, had already been recorded by the prophet (39.1-10). It was therefore already proven that, unlike the false prophets, Jeremiah was a man who had "stood in the counsel of the Lord, and hath perceived and heard his word" (23.18).

It is therefore suggested that the purpose of this appendix is rather to demonstrate that although Nebuchadnezzar, "the hammer of the whole earth" (50.23), had crushed Jerusalem, removed its king, destroyed its Temple and deported its inhabitants, the Lord had not forgotten the house of David, even though its surviving representative had been in exile for thirty-seven years. Against a most sombre background (vv.1-30), "Evil-merodach king of Babylon in the first year of his reign lifted up the head of Jehoiachin king of Judah, and brought him forth out of prison, And spake kindly unto him, and set his throne above the throne of the kings that were with him in Babylon" (vv.31-32).

This information is not without significance. Jehoiachin (also known as Coniah and Jeconiah) is found in Matthew's genealogy of the Lord Jesus Christ, where his name is shown as Jechonias (Mt 1.12). Matthew's purpose, under divine inspiration, was to establish the *legal* right of the Lord Jesus to the throne of David, and the royal line was preserved through the turbulent days of the exile and beyond, until Christ was born. There can be no doubt that through the centuries, Satanic attempts had been made to extinguish "the house and lineage of David" (Lk 2.4), notably through Athaliah (2 Chr 22.10), and the imprisonment of Jehoiachin may also be regarded in this way. Joash was preserved (2 Chr 22.11-12) from death at the hands of Athaliah, and Jehoiachin was preserved in Babylon. The purposes of God cannot be frustrated.

Jeremiah certainly saw the fulfilment of the majority of events narrated in vv.1-30, and if he actually wrote vv.31-34, he must have lived for some twenty-five years after them. But bearing in mind the concluding words of chapter 51, "Thus far are the words of Jeremiah" (v.64), and the fact that the prophet would have probably been between eighty-five and ninety years old had he personally recorded Jehoiachin's release from prison, it seems likely that chapter 52 was added by another hand, possibly, as already noted, that of Baruch. As Feinberg observes, "Since chapter 52 agrees so closely with 2 Kings 24.18-25.30, in all probability it was taken from the same source as the historical document".

This chapter may be divided as follows:

The Detainment of Zedekiah (vv.1-11)
The Destruction of Jerusalem (vv.12-16)
The Dismantling of the Temple (vv.17-23)
The Death of Judah's Officials (vv.24-27)
The Deportations to Babylon (vv.28-30)
The Deliverance of Jehoiachin (vv.31-34).

Verses 1-11: The Detainment of Zedekiah

"Zedekiah was one and twenty years old when began to reign, and he reigned eleven years in Jerusalem. And his mother's name was Hamutal, the daughter of Jeremiah of Libnah. And he did that which was evil in the eyes of the Lord, according to all that Jehoiakim had done. For through the anger of the Lord it came to pass in Jerusalem and Judah, till he had cast them out from his presence, that Zedekiah rebelled against the king of Babylon" (vv.1-3). These verses in their entirety parallel those in 2 Kings 24.18-25.7, and vv.4-11 also parallel those in Jeremiah 39.1-7. There are minor differences in the details given in all three passages, including some spellings, but these are quite inconsequential, and the information in them is completely harmonious.

Hamutal (v.1) was the wife of Josiah and mother of Jehoahaz and Zedekiah (2 Kings 23.31; 24.18). Zedekiah's rebellion against the king of Babylon (2 Kings 24.20; 2 Chr 36.13), involving help from Egypt (Jer 37.5-7), was short-lived and brought the armies of Babylon for the third time (2 Kings 24.1,11; 25.1) to the gates of Jerusalem. Kidner, having referred to Jeremiah chapters 34,37,38, describes Zedekiah "as 'a double-minded man…unstable in all his ways' (James 1.8), tragically unfit for his role as Nebuchadnezzar's deputy, set between the hammer of Babylon and the anvil of his own people. Timid though he was, he is held responsible for the downward path he trod: breaking faith first with God (v.2), then with his overlord (v.3b) and finally with the slaves whom he liberated and heartlessly took back again (34.8,16,21)".

The king of Babylon would not tolerate the rebellion of his vassal-king in Jerusalem, and took steps to deal with the situation. The record is quite self-explanatory: "And it came to pass in the ninth year of his reign, in the tenth month, in the tenth day of the month, that Nebuchadrezzar king of Babylon came, he and all his army, against Jerusalem, and pitched against it, and built forts (moveable towers, sometimes with battering rams) against it round about. So the city was besieged unto the eleventh year of king Zedekiah. And in the fourth month, in the ninth day of the month, the famine was sore in the city, so that there was no bread for the people of the land. Then the city was broken up, and all the men of war fled, and went forth out of the city by night by the way of the gate between the two walls, which was by the king's garden; (now the Chaldeans were by the

city round about:) and they went by the way of the plain. But the army of
the Chaldeans pursued after the king, and overtook Zedekiah in the plains
of Jericho; and all his army was scattered from him. Then they took the
king, and carried him up unto the king of Babylon to Riblah in the land of
Hamath; where he gave judgment upon him. And the king of Babylon
slew the sons of Zedekiah before his eyes: he slew also all the princes of
Judah in Riblah. Then he put out the eyes of Zedekiah; and the king of
Babylon bound him in chains, and carried him to Babylon, and put him in
prison till the day of his death" (vv.4-11). It is noteworthy that the Lord
informed Ezekiel, in Babylonia, on the very day, that the siege had
commenced: "Again in the ninth year, in the tenth month, in the tenth day
of the month, the word of the Lord came unto me saying, Son of man,
write thee the name of the day, even of this same day: the king of Babylon
set himself against Jerusalem this same day" (Ezek 24.1-2). The Lord is
light years ahead of modern telecommunications!

Since these verses substantially reproduce those in 39.1-7, the reader is
referred to comments made in connection with that passage. The fact that
the current passage alone states that Zedekiah was "put…in prison ("house
of the wards", AV margin) till the day of his death" (v.11), may indicate that
it was written at a later date than 2 Kings 25.7. Ellicott's Commentary draws
attention to the fact that the word rendered "prison" (v.11) is unusual,
and may be rendered "house of visitation", possibly implying "either stricter
custody, or more severe punishment in addition to imprisonment…The
Septuagint renders it by 'house of the mill' as though Zedekiah, after he
had been blinded, had been made to do slave-work like that of Samson".
Zedekiah learnt that it was indeed "an evil thing and bitter" to have forsaken
the Lord (2.19).

Verses 12-16: The Destruction of Jerusalem

"Now in the fifth month, in the tenth day of the month, which was the
nineteenth year of Nebuchadrezzar king of Babylon, came Nebuzaradan,
captain of the guard, which served the king of Babylon, into Jerusalem,
And burned the house of the Lord, and the king's house; and all the houses
of Jerusalem, and all the houses of the great men, burned he with fire:
And all the army of the Chaldeans, that were with the captain of the guard,
brake down all the walls of Jerusalem round about. Then Nebuzaradan
the captain of the guard carried away captive certain of the poor of the
people, and the residue of the people that remained in the city, and those
that fell away, that fell to the king of Babylon, and the rest of the multitude.
But Nebuzaradan the captain of the guard left certain of the poor of the
land for vinedressers and for husbandmen." There can be little doubt that
it was the conqueror's intention to ruin Jerusalem beyond repair, but events
were to prove that God thought otherwise. Events in the "fourth month"
(v.6) and the "fifth month" (v.12) were later commemorated by fasts (Zech
8.19). (The two other fasts mentioned in this verse, in the seventh and

tenth months, commemorated the murder of Gedaliah (41.1-2) and the siege of Jerusalem (52.4) respectively.)

These verses parallel those in 2 Kings 25.8-12 and Jeremiah 39.8-10. The reader is referred to comments made in connection with the latter passage. For the second time, there are minor differences in the details given in all three passages but, again, these are quite inconsequential, and the information in them is completely harmonious. The fact that 2 Kings 25.8 reads, "in the fifth month, on the *seventh* day of the month" as opposed to "the fifth month, in the *tenth* day of the month" (v.12) may be explained as follows: "It is easy to allow such a margin of time between the arrival of Nebuzar-adan in the neighbourhood of Jerusalem and his actual entry upon the work which he had been sent to do" (Streane).

Verses 17-23: The Dismantling of the Temple

Having described the demolition of the city and the marshalling of the captives, the passage records the methodical removal of everything of value remaining in the Temple after it had been plundered some ten years before (2 Kings 24.13). As Kidner points out, Jeremiah had "rebuked the optimists who promised a rapid return of those treasures, bidding them to pray instead that God would spare the rest of the vessels. He held out little hope for it (for they were in no mood to pray), but he did predict the vessels' return in God's good time (27.18-22)".

The narrative makes dismal reading, and it is particularly sad to note that large items were smashed to make transportation easier: "Also the pillars of brass that were in the house of the Lord, and the bases, and the brasen sea that was in the house of the Lord, the Chaldeans brake, and carried all the brass of them to Babylon. The caldrons also, and the shovels, and the snuffers, and the bowls, and the spoons, and all the vessels of brass wherewith they ministered, took they away. And the basons, and the firepans, and the bowls, and the caldrons, and the candlesticks, and the spoons, and the cups; that which was of gold in gold, and that which was of silver in silver, took the captain of the guard away ('whatever was of gold the captain of the guard took away as gold, and what was of silver, as silver', The Amplified Old Testament). The two pillars, one sea, and twelve brasen bulls that were under the bases, which king Solomon had made in the house of the Lord: the brass of all these vessels was without weight. And concerning the pillars, the height of one pillar was eighteen cubits; and a fillet of twelve cubits did compass it; and the thickness thereof was four fingers: it was hollow. And a chapter (capital) of brass was upon it; and the height of one chapter was five cubits, with network and pomegranates upon the chapters round about, all of brass. The second pillar also and the pomegranates were like unto these. And there were ninety and six pomegranates on a side; and all the pomegranates upon the network were an hundred round about".

The "brasen sea (bronze sea)" (v.17), with its "twelve brasen bulls" (v.20), is described in 1 Kings 7.23-26, and the two pillars in 1 Kings 7.15-22.

These verses parallel those in 2 Kings 25.13-17. The current chapter gives greater detail in connection with the Temple furniture carried to Babylon, and a more detailed description of the "two pillars". According to 2 Kings 25.17, "the height of the chapiter" was "three cubits; and the wreathen work, and pomegranates upon the chapiter round about, all of brass: and like unto these had the second pillar with wreathen work". Streane draws attention to "an apparent discrepancy between the number of pomegranates as given here and in 1 Kings 7.20" and continues, "It is possible that the account here may not be inconsistent with the existence of such a double row upon each chapiter, though it certainly does not suggest it, or again, one of the rows may have been removed before this period, leaving one hundred on each chapiter, probably twenty-four on each side…and one at each corner".

As already noticed, Jeremiah had predicted the return of the Temple vessels (27.22), and Kidner refers to this quite delightfully: "If the present was a dark moment, there was the promise to hold on to; and the very thoroughness of the operation - depressingly businesslike - was to wear a different aspect one day, when the royal treasurer not only produced these sacred objects but 'counted them out to Sheshbazzar the prince of Judah' in their thousands (Ezra 1.7-11)". It must be said that "Babylon" is still intent on robbing the children of God of their treasures. It is therefore heartening to read that "All these did Sheshbazzar bring up with them of the captivity that were brought up from Babylon unto Jerusalem" (Ezra 1.11). Sheshbazzar was made a steward of the Temple treasure. In a unique way, the apostles were "stewards of the mysteries of God" (1 Cor 4.1): but, like Timothy, the Lord's people are called upon to "keep the entrusted deposit" (1 Tim 6.20, JND). At the end of his life, Paul could say, "I have kept the faith" (2 Tim 4.7). Various types of vessels were committed to Sheshbazzar, and God still commits various gifts to His people. It would be good if it could be said that all the Lord's people today are "good stewards of the manifold grace of God" (1 Pet 4.10).

Verses 24-27: The Death of Judah's Officials

The men who had been prominent in resisting Nebuchadnezzar, and in the defence of the city were executed, together with sixty "people of the land" who were possibly "leading men whose homes were in the country parts" (Streane), although Harrison suggests that if they were "actually peasants, these men may have been executed representatively for the survivors": "And the captain of the guard took Seraiah the chief priest, and Zephaniah the second priest, and the three keepers of the door: He took also out of the city an eunuch, which had the charge of the men of war; and seven men of them that were near the king's person (literally, 'that saw the king's face'), which were found in the city; and the principal scribe of the host, who mustered the people of the land; and threescore men of the people of the land, that were found in the midst of the city. So Nebuzar-adan the captain of the guard took them, and brought them to the king of Babylon to Riblah. And the king of Babylon smote them, and put them to death in Riblah in the land of Hamath. Thus Judah was carried away captive out of his own land".

These verses are paralleled in 2 Kings 25.18-21. The two passages are mutually complementary with the exception that the current passage refers to "seven men of them that were near the king's person" (v.25) as opposed to "five men of them that were in the king's presence" (2 Kings 25.19). The difference is thus far unexplained. Seraiah (v.24) was the grandson of the high priest Hilkiah (1 Chr 6.13-14), who had discovered the lost book of the law in the reign of Josiah (2 Kings 22.8). His son was Jehozadak (1 Chr 6.14-15), and his grandson was Jeshua (Ezra 3.2), the high priest at the return from exile. "So the family line survived his violent death, and another branch of it would produce the great Ezra, a century hence (Ezra 7.1-5)" (Kidner). Zephaniah (v.24) seems to be the priest mentioned in Jeremiah 29.24-29 and 37.3. On two occasions he had been sent by Zedekiah to consult Jeremiah over the siege of Jerusalem (21.1; 37.3), and now, with others, he had to pay the price of refusing to surrender to Babylon as advised by the prophet.

Verses 28-30: The Deportations to Babylon

These verses detail the total number of captives carried away from Jerusalem on three occasions: "This is the people whom Nebuchadrezzar carried away captive: in the seventh year three thousand Jews and three and twenty: In the eighteenth year of Nebuchadrezzar he carried away captive from Jerusalem eight hundred thirty and two persons: In the three and twentieth year of Nebuchadrezzar Nebuzar-adan the captain of the guard carried away captive of the Jews seven hundred forty and five persons: all the persons were four thousand and six hundred".

Kidner points out that "there are some minor puzzles here over dates, since the seventh and eighteenth years of Nebuchadrezzar appear in 2 Kings 24.12; 25.8 as his eighth and nineteenth", but goes on to say that "these reflect the two ways of dating the king's reign: either from his actual accession (autumn 605 BC) or, in Babylonian reckoning, from his formal enthronement in the new year (spring 604 BC). Three deportations are recorded.

In Nebuchadrezzar's seventh year (v.28)

His "seventh year" would therefore be 598/597 BC, following Babylonian reckoning. At this time, the date of Jehoiachin's surrender, 3023 Jews were transported to Babylon, but this is vastly different from the figures given in the relevant historical passage: "And he carried away...ten thousand captives, and all the craftsmen and smiths...And all the men of might,

even seven thousand, and craftsmen and smiths a thousand, all that were
strong and apt for war, even them the king of Babylon brought captive to
Babylon" (2 Kings 24.14,16). Older commentators, perhaps surprisingly,
espouse the suggestion that "seventh year" should probably read
"seventeenth year" (on the basis that in the Hebrew text *tenth* has dropped
out before *seventh*), which would then make the passage refer to the time
of Jerusalem's siege and to the captivity of people from country areas.
This explanation, based on words having "dropped out", is hardly
satisfactory, and may be viewed with justifiable apprehension. The contrary
explanation, espoused by more recent commentators, is that the figures
given in 2 Kings 24 are "probably round numbers including all the people
deported", whereas the figure of 3023 given in the current passage refers
to "an exact count of adult males" (J. Bright, quoted by Kidner). This seems
far more satisfactory! This deportation included Ezekiel (Ezek 1.1-2) and,
of course, Jehoiachin himself (v.31).

In Nebuchadrezzar's eighteenth year (v.29)

His "eighteenth year" would therefore be 587/586 BC, following
Babylonian reckoning. This relates to the fall of Jerusalem, and "probably
counts only adult males. And possibly only people taken from the urban
population of Jerusalem" (J. Bright, quoted by Kidner). Ellicott's
Commentary is probably correct in saying that "The comparatively small
number indicates the ravages of the sword, the pestilence, and the famine
to which Jeremiah so often refers. The captives were probably the scanty
remnant of the defenders of the city, and the deportation that by Nebuzar-
adan narrated in v.15".

In Nebuchadrezzar's twenty-third year (v.30)

His "twenty-third year" would therefore be 582/81 BC. This is the only record
of a deportation at this time, and it has been suggested that it was "a punitive
measure after the assassination of the governor Gedaliah (41.1-2)" (Habel).

It should be pointed out that there is no reference to a general
deportation during the reign of Jehoiakim. Some were taken to Babylon
at this time, but evidently only young men were involved "in whom was
no blemish, but well favoured, and skilful in all wisdom, and cunning in
knowledge, and understanding science, and such as had ability in them to
stand in the king's palace, and whom they might teach the learning and
the tongue of the Chaldeans" (Dan 1.4).

Verses 31-34: The Deliverance of Jehoiachin

"And it came to pass in the seven and thirtieth year of the captivity of
Jehoiachin king of Judah, in the twelfth month, in the five and twentieth
day of the month, that Evil-merodach king of Babylon in the first year of
his reign lifted up the head of Jehoiachin king of Judah, and brought him
forth out of prison, And spake kindly unto him, and set his throne above

the throne of the kings that were with him in Babylon, And changed his prison garments: and he did continually eat bread before him all the days of his life. And for his diet, there was a continual diet given him of the king of Babylon, every day a portion, until the day of his death, all the days of his life."

These verses are paralleled in 2 Kings 25.27-30. The two passages are mutually complementary with the exception that the current passage refers to "the five and twentieth day of the month" (v.31) as opposed to "the seven and twentieth day of the month" (2 Kings 25.27). The difference is thus far unexplained, but it is quite possible that there might have been two days between the promulgation of the royal decree and its implementation. Evil-merodach (or, to give him his Babylonian name, Amel-Marduk) was the son of Nebuchadnezzar, and reigned from 562 BC to 560 BC. He was assassinated by his brother-in-law Neriglissar, who succeeded him. Neriglissar is known as Nergal-sharezer (39.3,13).

It is said of Jehoiachin (Coniah), who is described as "Jeconiah, the captive" (1 Chr 3.17, RV), "Thus saith the Lord, Write ye this man childless, a man that shall not prosper in his days: for no man of his seed shall prosper, sitting upon the throne of David, and ruling any more in Judah" (22.30). Jehoiachin actually had seven sons (1 Chr 3.17-18, RV), but it has been pointed out that the "verse does not say that he is to be absolutely childless, but only that he is to be legally counted so, no son or descendant succeeding to him" (Orelli). E. W. Bullinger concurs: not "no sons", but "no sons to sit on the throne of David". His grandson, Zerubbabel, became governor of Judah (Hag 1.1), but neither he nor any of his descendants ever ruled as king. Jehoiachin's uncle, Zedekiah, reigned after him, but died before him (vv.10-11), and Jehoiachin was therefore the last of the Judæan kings.

The book of Jeremiah therefore ends, not only with God's promised punishment upon His apostate and idolatrous people, but with the hope of restoration. In the words of Unger, "In the restoration of the long-chastised, covenant-breaking king to his suzerain's favour, there can be detected the future restoration of the covenant-breaking people of Judah. Hence the book of Jeremiah - in a sense a book of doom and gloom, and necessarily so - ends on a note of glorious hope, a hope that flashed periodically throughout the book like the brilliant sunlight of God's grace, bursting every now and then through the scurrying storm clouds of human sin and its judgment, to call His erring people back to His arms of love".

LAMENTATIONS

J. M. Riddle

CONTENTS

Page

INTRODUCTION

In introducing the book of Lamentations, notice should be taken of its Subject; its Style; its Structure; its Standpoint; and its Significance.

The Subject of the Book

Whilst the book of Lamentations is anonymous, there is no reason to assign its authorship to anyone other than Jeremiah. In fact, the earliest extant translation, the Septuagint, ascribes it to him in a note prefixed to the first chapter: "And it came to pass, after Israel was taken captive, and Jerusalem made desolate, that Jeremiah sat weeping, and lamented with this lamentation over Jerusalem, and said...", which the Vulgate expands by adding the phrase, "...with a bitter spirit sighing and wailing". It has been said that while the book of Jeremiah contains warning, the book of Lamentations contains mourning. However, tears most certainly flowed in the prophecy of Jeremiah (9.1; 13.17; 14.17), and they continue to flow in Lamentations (2.11,18; 3.48,49).

The entire book is concerned with the destruction of Jerusalem and its aftermath. Some thirty-five years previously, Jeremiah had "lamented for Josiah", and, according to the chronicler, "all the singing men and the singing women spake of Josiah in their lamentations to this day, and made them an ordinance in Israel: and, behold, they are written in the lamentations" (2 Chr 35.25). This has led some to suggest that this refers to the book of Lamentations, but even a cursory examination of its text will show that it rather refers to events described in Jeremiah chapters 39 and 52. As Streane points out, "That the book could not have been written long after this time is clear from the graphic manner in which the horrors of the siege are portrayed".

Our English Bibles give the name of the book as "Lamentations", which corresponds with its name in the Latin Vulgate, but according to Streane and other scholars, the title of the book in the Hebrew canon is EKA (349) meaning "ah", "how", "alas". This is "in accordance with Jewish custom to name a book of the Bible by a conspicuous word at or near its beginning" (Streane). In fact, chapters 1, 2 and 4 all commence in the same way. This gives character to the book from the very outset as it expresses deep grief over the destruction of Jerusalem and the slaughter of its inhabitants. At the same time, it draws attention to the national sin which brought about these calamities. For Jeremiah, this was the real cause of Judah's downfall.

Lamentations is found in the third division of the Hebrew Scriptures (cp. Lk 24.44). It is therefore regarded as amongst the poetical books of the Canon. It appears in a section called *Megilloth*, or Rolls, so called because each of the five books in the section was written on a roll for reading at Jewish festivals as follows: the Song of Songs at Passover; Ruth at the Feast of Weeks, or Pentecost; Ecclesiastes at the Feast of Tabernacles;

Esther at the Feast of Purim; and Lamentations at the anniversary of the destruction of Jerusalem.

The Style of the Book

Attention is drawn to the method of its arrangement, and the meaning of its arrangement.

The method of its arrangement

The book consists of five poems, all of which are elegies, or dirges, each poem occupying one of the five chapters. Four of the poems are in acrostic form, that is each verse commences with a consecutive letter of the Hebrew alphabet. Chapters 1, 2 and 4 are each made up of twenty-two verses corresponding to the twenty-two letters in the Hebrew alphabet. In each case, the first verse begins with *Aleph,* the second with *Beth,* the third with *Gimel*, and so on until the twenty-second letter which is *Tau.* The only difference in this respect between the three chapters is that chapters 1 and 2 contain twenty-two verses of three lines each, and chapter 4 contains twenty-two verses of two lines each.

Chapter 3 also follows the Hebrew alphabet, but with a difference. There are sixty-six verses of one line each, and in this case the first three verses each begin with *Aleph*, the second three verses with *Beth,* the third three verses with *Gimel*, and so on until the end of the Hebrew alphabet. Scholars point out that in the second, third and fourth chapters, the order of two letters is reversed, and that on each occasion it is the same pair (*Ayin* and *Pe*, the sixteenth and seventeenth letters respectively) which are transposed in this way. This has not been satisfactorily explained.

Ironside makes a most helpful comparison between the use of the Hebrew alphabet in Psalm 119, and its use in chapters 1-4 of Lamentations: "In Psalm 119 we have twenty-two divisions of eight verses each, similarly arranged, as even the ordinary English Bible shows. There, every letter of the alphabet (which represents the whole compass of man's speech) is used in the praise of the perfect law of the Lord. In Lamentations, every letter is required to express the sorrows following upon the neglect and breaking of that law".

Chapter 5 comprises twenty-two verses, but there the correspondence ends: the chapter does not follow the acrostic pattern of its predecessors. Ellicott's Commentary suggests, among other things, "that the writer found himself too overwhelmed by emotion to keep within the limits of the artificial plan he had before prescribed to himself". In the words of Bullinger, "Lamentation is resolved into a prayer, and the acrostic arrangement gives way before the outburst of emotion".

The meaning of its arrangement

Amongst several suggestions, it has been said that the acrostic arrangement was employed to aid memory, and there seems no good reason to doubt this. The Holy Spirit wished to impress clearly upon the nation the straits to which it had been reduced, the need for repentance, the prospect of hope. "If, as seems probable, the *Lamentations* were intended to be sung, as in fact they were sung by those who mourned then, or in later times, for the destruction of Jerusalem, then it is obvious that the task of the learner would be much easier with this mnemonic help than without it" (Ellicott's Commentary).

The Structure of the Book

In the words of J. Sidlow Baxter, "The structure of this quintuple poem is remarkable. These five elegies are not unconnected digits: they belong together, and make one complete poetic quintuplet...The two *outer* poemettes – the first and fifth, correspond. The two *inner* ones – the second and fourth, correspond. The *middle* one – the third, which is the most elaborate in conception and the most finished in execution, is three times the size of the others, and stands at the centre like a great throne draped with mourning".

Following this analysis, it is observable that the first and fifth elegies narrate the city's destruction and attendant events, with the first emphasising the plight of God's people and the fifth leading to their prayer. The second and fourth elegies emphasise that these distressing conditions are the result of divine anger: this is described in the second elegy, and fully justified in the fourth. The third elegy, which has been likened to a mountain peak jutting out of the mists into the sunshine, contains a message of hope in a book of tears. Hope lies at the centre of the book.

However, each elegy does appear to have its own outstanding feature.

Chapter 1. This could be entitled, *The Lonely Widow.*
In this connection, attention is drawn to the following: "she hath none to comfort her" (v.2); "she had no comforter" (v.9); "the comforter that should relieve my soul is far from me" (v.16); "there is none to comfort her" (v.17); "there is none to comfort me" (v.21).

Chapter 2. This could be entitled, *The Angry God.*
The word "anger" occurs six times in the chapter: "How hath the Lord covered the daughter of Zion with a cloud in his anger...and remembered not his footstool in the day of his anger!" (v.1); "his fierce anger" (v.3); "the indignation of his anger" (v.6); "thou hast slain them in the day on thine anger" (v.21); "the day of the Lords anger" (v.22).

Chapter 3. This could be entitled, *The Confident Prophet.*
The word "hope" occurs five times in the chapter, and although the first occurrence (v.18) does not convey confidence at all, thereafter the word is used positively: "This I recall to my mind, therefore have I hope"

(v.21); "therefore will I hope in him" (v.24); "It is good that a man should both hope and quietly wait for the salvation of the Lord" (v.26); "He putteth his mouth in the dust; if so there may be hope" (v.29). There is emphasis on hope in a chapter of tears.

Chapter 4. This could be entitled, *The City Streets.*
The prophet draws attention to rubble "in the top of every street" (v.1); to the "desolate in the streets" (v.5); to the Nazarites "in the streets" (v.8); to the prophets and priests "in the streets (v.14); to danger "in our streets" (v.18).

Chapter 5. This could be entitled, *The Earnest Appeal.*
The chapter has been described as "a prayer that the lamenting remnant might be delivered from its distress, and restored to prosperity" (Harrison).

The Standpoint of the Book

There is no trace of elation, only deep sorrow. Jeremiah did not enjoy the fact that his ministry had been vindicated. The prophet was deeply distressed over the destruction of Jerusalem. He had wept prospectively; now he weeps retrospectively, which serves to recall that a greater than Jeremiah "beheld the city, and wept (sobbed) over it, Saying...the days shall come upon thee, that thine enemies shall cast a trench about thee, and compass thee round, and keep thee in on every side, and shall lay thee even with the ground, and thy children within thee; and they shall not leave in thee one stone upon another; because thou knewest not the time of thy visitation" (Lk 19.41-44), later adding, "O Jerusalem, Jerusalem, thou that killest the prophets, and stonest them which are sent unto thee, how often would I have gathered thy children together, even as a hen gathereth her chickens under her wings, and ye would not! Behold, your house is left unto you desolate" (Mt 23.37-38).

But Jeremiah's grief was not his alone. Isaiah writes, in another connection, that "In all their affliction, he (Jehovah) was afflicted" (Is 63.9) The same God who, in Christ, wept over Jerusalem in Luke 19, wept over Jerusalem in Lamentations. The sorrows of Jerusalem did not leave Him unmoved. "It is of the Lord's mercies that we are not consumed, because his compassions fail not....For the Lord will not cast off for ever: But though he cause grief, yet will he have compassion according to the multitude of his mercies. For he doth not afflict willingly nor grieve the children of men" (3.22, 31-33). "He loves that which He is obliged to smite, and is obliged to smite that which He loves" (Darby).

The Significance of the Book

It is quite inconceivable that God should include a book of dirges in His Word for no other reason than an expression of regret. The oft-quoted words, "For whatsoever things were written aforetime were written for our learning, that we through patience and comfort of the scriptures might have hope" (Rom 15.4), certainly include Lamentations. It has already been said that hope lies at the centre of the book, and while Lamentations constitutes a warning of the inevitable consequences of sin and apostasy, it teaches that repentance brings hope: "And I said, My strength and my hope is perished from the Lord: Remembering mine affliction and my misery, the wormwood and the gall. My soul hath them still in remembrance, and is humbled in me. This I recall to my mind, therefore have I hope" (3.18-21).

LAMENTATIONS 1

In the first of the five elegies which comprise the book of Lamentations, Jerusalem is depicted as a lonely widow. She is almost immediately described in this way: "how is she become as a widow...she hath none to comfort her" (vv.1-2), and her loneliness is a prominent feature as the poem proceeds (vv.9,16,17,21).

Streane draws attention to "the general subject running through this first chapter" and notes that "Verses 1-11 lament the sufferings which Jerusalem is now undergoing, while twice in the course of this portion (vv.9,11) the city itself breaks out into a wail of distress, and thus leads up to the second division of the chapter, vv.12-22, where the city itself is the speaker". According to Ellicott's Commentary, "Each verse is divided into three lines, each line beginning, in the Hebrew, with the same letter".

The chapter may be divided as follows:

> Her Desolation is Described (vv.1-11): "O Lord, behold my affliction" (v.9)
> Her Desolation is Divinely-determined (vv.12-17): "The Lord hath afflicted me" (v.12)
> Her Desolation is Deserved (vv.18-22): "The Lord is righteous; for I have rebelled" (v.18).

Verses 1-11: Her Desolation is Described

This section of the chapter may be further divided in the following way:

> The downfall of the city (v.1)
> The distress of the city (v.2)
> The despair of the city (vv.3-11).

The downfall of the city (v.1)

Three things are emphasised.

Her population had gone

"How doth the city sit solitary, that was full of people!" Jerusalem was bereft of inhabitants. The departure of the captives had left the city so denuded of people that "the foxes walk upon it" (5.18).

Her position had gone

"How is she become as a widow! she that was great among the nations", or "She that was great among the nations is become as a widow" (JND). It has been suggested that this refers to the loss of her king or to the loss of friends in general, but it seems more likely that Jeremiah speaks here of the loss of the Lord Himself. At the coming restoration of the nation it will be said, "Thou...shalt not remember the reproach of thy widowhood any more. For thy Maker is thine husband; the Lord of hosts is his name" (Is 54.4-5).

Her prestige had gone
"She that was…princess among the provinces, how is she become tributary!" It cannot be without significance that the word "princess" (8282/ 8283) appears in the Old Testament as Sarah, Abraham's wife, and that she was to be "a mother of nations; kings of people shall be of her" (Gen 17.16). In replying to the letter written to him by Rehum, Shimshai and their colleagues, Artaxerxes acknowledged that "There have been mighty kings also over Jerusalem, which have ruled over all countries beyond the river; and toll, tribute, and custom, was paid unto them" (Ezra 4.20). The city which once had such immense influence, and received "toll, tribute, and custom", is now herself a vassal. Earthly potentates found this astonishing: "The kings of the earth, and all the inhabitants of the world, would not have believed that the adversary and the enemy should have entered into the gates of Jerusalem" (4.12).

Each local assembly should seriously consider the solemn lessons conveyed by the opening verse of this chapter. Disobedience and departure will yield the same sad results in local testimony, and while reduced numbers in fellowship do not necessarily indicate spiritual decline, it is certainly not unknown for unspiritual conduct, sometimes seen in bitter and heated divisions amongst local believers, to have a decidedly adverse effect on a hitherto "good report" among "them that are without" (Col 4.5).

The distress of the city (v.2)
"She weepeth sore in the night, and her tears are on her cheeks: among all her lovers she hath none to comfort her: all her friends have dealt treacherously with her, they are become her enemies." It has been said that "the intensity of the sorrow is emphasised by the fact that the tears do not cease even in the time which commonly brings rest and repose to mourners" (Ellicott's Commentary).

At this point in the lamentation, Jeremiah emphasises the distress of Jerusalem over the treachery of the people among whom she had sought friendship, and upon whom she had relied for help. They had both failed her and had turned against her. The "lovers" and "friends" are the nations with which Judah had been in alliance, including Egypt (Jer 2.36) and those nations whose ambassadors had come to Jerusalem during the reign of Zedekiah (Jer 27.1-3). (The reader is referred to comments made in this connection with the use of Jehoiakim's name in Jeremiah 27.) The terms used to describe Jerusalem's pagan neighbours may well include the way in which God's people had worshipped their gods. Jeremiah refers to the pagan deities as "lovers" (Jer 3.1; 4.30), and Hosea deals extensively with the recourse of God's people to idolatry with the inevitable judgment that must follow: "And I will visit upon her the days of Baalim, wherein she burned incense to them, and she decked herself with her earrings and her jewels, and she went after her lovers, and forgat me, saith the Lord" (Hos 2.13).

Compromise brought Jerusalem no help in the day of crisis. The Lord used the very people with whom she was once allied (Jer 27.1-3) to execute judgment upon her: "And the Lord sent against him (Jehoiakim) bands of the Chaldees, and bands of the Syrians, and bands of the Moabites, and bands of the children of Ammon, and sent them against Judah to destroy it, according to the word of the Lord, which he spake by his servants the prophets" (2 Kings 24.2). The Edomites (Jer 27.3) were present at the destruction of Jerusalem, crying "Rase it, rase it, even to the foundation thereof" (Ps 137.7).

The Word of God warns believers against compromise (2 Cor 6.14-18; 1 Jn 2.15-17). In this connection, the use of the words "lovers" and "friends" recalls New Testament teaching: "Ye adulterers and adulteresses, know ye not that the friendship of the world is enmity with God? whosoever therefore will be a friend of the world is the enemy of God" (James 4.4).

The despair of the city (vv.3-11)

Jerusalem despaired over her immense loss: "O Lord, behold my affliction" (v.9); "see, O Lord, and consider; for I am become vile" (v.11), and it is a salutary lesson to note what her compromise enabled the enemy to accomplish. "Lovers" and "friends" become "enemies" (v.2), "persecutors" (v.3), and "adversaries" (v.5). She had become prey to the very people in whom she had formerly trusted, and had "no rest" (v.3), "no pasture" (v.6), and "no comforter" (v.9). The following, with their spiritual lessons, should be carefully noted.

Loss of liberty (v.3)

"Judah is gone into captivity, because of affliction, and because of great servitude: she dwelleth among the heathen, she findeth no rest: all her persecutors overtook her between the straits." According to Ellicott's Commentary, "The Hebrew admits...the rendering 'from affliction', and so the words speak of the forcible deportation of the people from misery at home to a yet worse misery in Babylon as the land of their exile". This does seem preferable to the alternative explanation that "the long sufferings of the Jews at the hands of Egypt and Chaldæa had induced many of them to go voluntarily to dwell in other lands" (Streane). Harrison helpfully explains the expression, "all her persecutors overtook her between ('within', JND) the straits", as follows: "All resistance collapsed when the refugees were overtaken and captured in the narrow defiles around Jerusalem. This leads to the larger figurative sense of the distress or extremity overtaking a person which the word METSAR (straits, AV) normally implies". Even in exile the captives had found no rest: they had survived, but only to see the fulfilment of God's word that "among these nations shalt thou find no ease, neither shall the sole of thy foot have rest: but the Lord shall give thee there a trembling heart, and failing of eyes, and sorrow of mind" (Deut 28.65). No one, saint or sinner, can sin against the Lord with impunity.

Loss of fellowship (v.4)

"The ways (roads) of Zion do mourn, because none come to the solemn feasts: all her gates are desolate (they are no longer thronged by the worshippers): her priests sigh, her virgins are afflicted, and she is in bitterness." The poetic language here includes mourning by inanimate objects ("ways" and "gates") as well by "her priests" and "her virgins". The name "Zion" first occurs in 2 Samuel 5.7 and evidently became known as "the city of David" (cp. 1 Kings 8.1). It is known as "the city of the great King" (Ps 48.2), a title which will be most appropriate in the millennial age when "the ransomed of the Lord shall return, and come to Zion with songs, and everlasting joy upon their heads: they shall obtain joy and gladness, and sorrow and sighing shall flee away" (Is 35.10). But here it is a place were the "priests sigh" because there are no worshippers, and the "virgins are afflicted" because "the young women who survived are grieved at the loss of prospective husbands and children" (Harrison).

All this is a far cry from the past when David said, "I was glad when they said unto me, Let us go into the house of the Lord. Our feet shall stand within thy gates, O Jerusalem. Jerusalem is builded as a city that is compact together: Whither the tribes go up" (Ps 122.1-4). Sin and disobedience ruin fellowship with God, and fellowship with one another.

Loss of dominance (v.5)

"Her adversaries are the chief, her enemies prosper", or "Her adversaries have become the head, her enemies prosper" (JND). Jerusalem is in captivity to her enemies, recalling the tragic statement, "Knowest thou not that the Philistines are rulers over us?" (Judg 15.11). The word "chief" (7218) is rendered "head" in Deuteronomy 28.44, "where this is foretold as the result of Israel's obstinacy" (Streane). The word "prosper" (7951) means safe or secure (Gesenius), and is used of those that love Jerusalem: "they shall prosper that love thee" (Ps 122.6).

The sad reversal is explained: "for the Lord hath afflicted her for the multitude of her transgressions: her children are gone into captivity before the enemy". Instead of enjoying divinely-given peace and security, the Lord's people were dominated by the very nations who should have been subject to them. Their peace had given place to captivity, and they were being driven "before the enemy" as either cattle (Streane) or slaves (Ellicott's Commentary) are driven. A believer who falls into sin and disobedience will not be able to say, "And this is victory that overcometh the world, even our faith" (1 Jn 5.4).

Loss of beauty (v.6a)

"And from the daughter of Zion all her beauty is departed", or "And from the daughter of Zion all her splendour is departed" (JND). According to Gesenius the word "beauty" (1926) means "ornament, adorning, decoration". The city had been denuded of all that made her glorious and unique, with resulting mockery from passers by: "Is this the city that men call The perfection of beauty (a different word), The joy of the whole earth?" (2.15). Alas, the word "Ichabod", meaning "The glory is departed" (1 Sam 4.21), has to be written today over many companies of God's people.

Loss of leadership (v.6b)

"Her princes are become like harts that find no pasture, and they are gone without strength before the pursuer." Ellicott's Commentary is undoubtedly correct in saying, "Probably a reference to the flight and capture of Zedekiah (2 Kings 25.5; Jer 39.5), who, with his sons and princes, fell into the hands of the Chaldeans like fainting and stricken deer". The very men should have led, fed and protected the Lord's "beautiful flock" (Jer 13.20) were culpably weak and feeble. Their failure to care for the nation was the direct result of their self-indulgence and total failure to act responsibly. The Lord Jesus described Himself as "the good shepherd" who "giveth his life for the sheep" (Jn 10.11). He has set the pattern for His "under-shepherds" whose work it is to "Feed (tend) the flock of God...taking the oversight thereof, not by constraint, but willingly; not for filthy lucre, but of a ready mind" (1 Pet 5.2).

Loss of enjoyment (v.7a)

"Jerusalem remembered in the days of her affliction and of her miseries all her pleasant things that she had in the days of old, when her people fell into the hand of the enemy, and none did help her", or "In the days of her affliction and of her wanderings, since her people fell into the hand of an adversary, and none did help her, Jerusalem remembereth all her precious things which she had in the days of old" (JND). According to Streane, the word "miseries" (4788) "is a rare one, and means compulsory wanderings, persecutions", an explanation confirmed by Gesenius. Jerusalem looks back to better days, and believers today are sometimes obliged to sing:

> Where is the blessedness I knew
> When first I saw the Lord?
> Where is the soul-refreshing view
> Of Jesus and His Word?
>
> What peaceful hours I once enjoyed!
> How sweet their memory still!
> But they have left an aching void
> The world can never fill.
> (William Cowper)

Loss of respect (vv. 7b-8)

"The adversaries saw her, and did mock at her sabbaths. Jerusalem hath grievously sinned; therefore she is removed: all that honoured her despise her, because they have seen her nakedness", or "the adversaries have seen her, they mock at her ruin ('at her desolations', RV). Jerusalem hath grievously sinned; therefore is she removed as an impurity" (JND). The difference in translation turns upon the meaning of the word "sabbaths" (AV). This is the only occurrence of the word (4868), which evidently means "ceasings" (RV margin). Her desolation had earned her, not pity, but loss of respect by the nations that once held her in high esteem. Jerusalem was painfully aware of her disgrace: "yea, she sigheth, and turneth backward".

The Lord Jesus warned His disciples that loss of distinctiveness would endanger their testimony: "Ye are the salt of the earth: but if the salt have lost his savour, wherewith shall it be salted? it is thenceforth good for nothing, but to be cast out, and to be trodden under foot of men" (Mt 5.13).

Loss of purity (v. 9)

"Her filthiness is in her skirts; she remembereth ('remembered', JND) not her last end." Not only is "The picture of pollution...pushed to its most loathsome extreme. The very skirts of the garment are defiled" (Ellicott's Commentary), but Jerusalem had given no thought to the consequences of her sin. She had completely ignored the inevitability of divine judgment, something that caused Moses despair: "For they are a nation void of counsel, neither is there any understanding in them. O that they were wise, that they understood this, that they would consider their latter end!" (Deut 32.28-29).

Jerusalem's "last end" is described: "she came down wonderfully (in a way that was beyond belief): she had no comforter", leading to her wail of distress, "O Lord, behold my affliction: for the enemy hath magnified himself". The Lord's people must never forget that "God is not mocked: for whatsoever a man soweth, that shall he also reap" (Gal 6.7).

Loss of sacred treasures (v. 10)

"The adversary hath spread out his hand upon all her pleasant things: for she hath seen that the heathen entered into her sanctuary, whom thou didst command that they should not enter into thy congregation." This prohibition refers in the first place to the Ammonites and Moabites (Deut 23.3), but it is evidently extended here to include all pagan peoples. Unless they were members of the priesthood, even the children of Israel were excluded from the most sacred precincts of the Temple. The words "pleasant things", literally "desirable things" (YLT), evidently refer to the Temple treasures. According to Harrison, the expression translates a rare word found only in the plural, meaning "valuables", and occurring in this sense in vv.7 and 11. Harrison continues: "In the attack of 587

BC, the Babylonians stripped the Temple of all its costly ornamentation and removed the most valuable of the cultic objects to Babylon (cp. Jer 52.17-23)".

Loss of personal possessions (v.11a)

"All her people sigh, they seek bread; they have given their pleasant things (4622) for meat to relieve (or "revive": literally "to bring back") the soul." According to Ellicott's Commentary, the present tense here is used "either as painting the sufferings of the past with the vividness of the historic present, or because the sufferings still continued even after the capture of the city". Harrison opts for the former: "The allusion to treasures in v.11 is to the inhabitants of Jerusalem selling their prized possessions in order to purchase food, reflecting conditions which obtained just before the collapse of resistance in 587 BC. Such actions were necessary to prolong life".

This dreadful list of losses concludes with a second wail of distress: "see, O Lord, and consider; for I am become vile" (v.11b). This serves to introduce a change of speaker for the remainder of the dirge.

Verses 12-17: Her Desolation is Divinely-appointed

Jerusalem herself now becomes the speaker and bewails her position, but since the words that she uses are put into her mouth by Jeremiah, there can be no doubt that they articulate the deep emotion of the "weeping prophet" himself. He has already referred to the "tears...on her cheeks" (v.2), but now sorrow is intensified: "For these things I weep; mine eye, mine eye runneth down with water" (v.16). Like the Apostle Paul, Jeremiah had "great heaviness" and "continual sorrow" in his heart (Rom 9.2).

While the desolation of Jerusalem has already been attributed to the Lord (v.5), it is in these verses that this is particularly emphasised: "the Lord hath afflicted me" (v.12); "the Lord hath delivered me into their hands" (v.14); "The Lord hath trodden under foot all my mighty men" (v.15); "the Lord hath trodden the virgin...as in a winepress" (v.15); "the Lord hath commanded concerning Jacob" (v.17).

Attention is drawn to the following:

> There was no comparison with her sufferings (v.12)
> There was no escape from her sufferings (vv.13-15)
> There was no comforter in her sufferings (vv.16-17).

There was no comparison with her sufferings (v.12)

"Is it nothing to you, all ye that pass by? behold, and see if there be any sorrow like unto my sorrow, which is done unto me, wherewith the Lord hath afflicted me in the day of his fierce anger." Having considered the Septuagint and Vulgate renderings, Ellicott's Commentary concludes that "The Authorised Version, however, has most to commend it", and continues, "What the mourning city felt most keenly was that her unparalleled sufferings were met with unparalleled indifference".

While, in context, these words refer to the suffering of Jerusalem, they cannot fail to remind believers of the sufferings of the Lord Jesus at Calvary where "sitting down they watched him there", and "they that passed by reviled him, wagging their heads" (Mt 27.36,39). Ironside points out that "The sins of Judah drew down that fierce anger upon their heads. It was the just recompense for their departure from the Lord. But when He, the holy Sufferer of Calvary, bowed His head beneath the overwhelming flood of God's wrath, it was for sins not His own; but He who knew no sin was made sin for us, that we might be made the righteousness of God in Him".

There was no escape from her sufferings (vv.13-15)

The Lord had visited his people in judgment in four ways: as a consuming fire (v.13a); a spread net (v.13b); a binding yoke (v.14); and a crushing foot (v.15).

As a consuming fire (v.13a)

"From above hath he sent fire into my bones, and it prevaileth against them." While judgment on Jerusalem had been executed by the Chaldeans under Nebuchadnezzar, it was nevertheless "From above". The invaders served the purpose of God. According to Gesenius, the word "prevaileth" (7287) has the meaning "to subdue, to rule over". Gesenius translates as follows: "From on high he hath sent fire into my bones and it ravageth in them". Jeremiah experienced what he called "a burning fire shut up in my bones" (Jer 20.9), but for very different reasons from those here.

As a spread net (v.13b)

"He hath spread a net for my feet, he hath turned me back: he hath made me desolate and faint all the day." Although the Chaldeans are described as fishermen catching nations "in their net" (Hab 1.15), the word here (7568) refers to a land-based net, and occurs, for example in Psalm 9.15; 31.4; 57.6. "The fire burns into the innermost recesses of the city, and the net prevents anyone from escaping" (Harrison).

As a binding yoke (v.14)

"The yoke of my transgressions is bound by his hand: they are wreathed, and come up upon my neck: he hath made my strength to fall ('fail', JND), the Lord hath delivered me into their hands, from whom I am not able to rise up." The word "wreathed" (8276) means twisted together. Jerusalem's transgressions are likened to a yoke on the neck of a beast of burden. The Lord Jesus describes His "yoke" quite differently: "Take my yoke upon you, and learn of me…For my yoke is easy, and my burden is light" (Mt 11.29-30).

As a crushing foot (v.15)

"The Lord hath trodden under foot all my mighty men in the midst of me: he hath called an assembly against me to crush my young men: the Lord hath trodden the virgin, the daughter of Judah, as in a winepress." This familiar figure of speech is employed in both Old and New Testaments: "I have trodden the winepress alone" (Is 63.3); "the great winepress of the wrath of God" (Rev 14.19); "he treadeth the winepress of the fierceness and wrath of Almighty God" (Rev 19.15). "The virgin daughter of Judah" (JND) describes the nation that was once "the virgin pure and undefiled, a daughter loved by the Lord" (Laetsch). The adjective "mighty" ("mighty men") is elsewhere used of "bulls" (Ps 22.12; Is 34.7), but "stands here for the heroes of Judah who fell, not in open battle, but ignominiously 'in the midst' of the captured city" (Ellicott's Commentary). The word "assembly" (4150), often translated "feasts", is commonly used for proclaiming a religious festival (Lev 23.2,4,37,44), but here "the festival is proclaimed, not for Jerusalem, but against her, and is to be kept by those who exult in the slaughter of her youthful warriors" (Ellicott's Commentary).

There was no comforter in her sufferings (vv.16-17)

"For these things I weep; mine eye, mine eye runneth down with water, because the comforter that should relieve my soul is far from me." As Jensen observes, "If that absent comforter was God, as some interpret the text, the words prepare the reader for the captive's prayer to God recorded in vv.20-22". It has been pointed out that the repetition ("mine eye, mine eye") is quite in Jeremiah's style (cp. Jer 4.19; 6.14; 8.11; 22.29; 23.25). The hands of Zion are extended either in supplication, or in lamentation and despair. She was alone, desolate, and without any to give succour: "my children are desolate, because the enemy prevailed. Zion spreadeth forth her hands, and there is none to comfort her: the Lord hath commanded concerning Jacob, that his adversaries should be round about him", or "Jehovah hath given his adversaries round about charge against Jacob" (JND margin). "The neighbouring nations look upon Jerusalem at once with hatred, and, as the last words express, with contempt" (Streane). The word "menstruous" (5079) is elsewhere rendered "filthiness" (2 Chr 29.5; Ezra 9.11) in connection with Israel's idolatry.

The terrible losses enumerated in vv.3-11, together with the unparalleled distress described in vv.12-17, convey the clear lessons that God cannot continue to bless His people when they rebel against Him, and that He is obliged to deal with their sin. It should be said, in Jeremiah's words, that "though he cause grief, yet will he have compassion according to the multitude of his mercies. For he doth not afflict willingly nor grieve the children of men" (3.32-33). The withdrawal of divine blessing is designed to bring confession and repentance on the part of God's people. An earlier prophet made this clear: "And I also have given you cleanness of teeth in all your cities, and want of bread in all your places; yet have ye not returned unto me, saith the Lord" (Amos 4.6), and four further judgments are described, each of them followed by the words, "Yet have ye not returned unto me, saith the Lord" (Amos 4.8,9,10,11).

In the concluding verses of the chapter Jerusalem acknowledges the enormity of her sin, and this leads to hope for the future.

Verses 18-22: Her Desolation is Deserved

This is clearly recognised: "I have rebelled against his commandment" (v.18); "I have grievously rebelled" (v.20). In this connection, attention is drawn to the following:

> Her acknowledgement (vv.18-19)
> Her anguish (vv.20-21a)
> Her anticipation (vv.21b-22).

Her acknowledgement (vv.18-19)

"The Lord is righteous; for I have rebelled against his commandment", or "I have rebelled against his mouth" (JND margin)" (v.18a). Zion publicly confesses that the consequences of her rebellion are thoroughly deserved: "hear, I pray you, all people ('all ye peoples', JND), and behold my sorrow: my virgins and my young men are gone into captivity. I called for my lovers, but they deceived me: my priests and mine elders gave up the ghost in the city, while they sought their meat to relieve their souls ('revive their soul', JND)" (vv.18b-19). The words of the dying thief would have been most appropriate in her mouth: "we receive the due reward of our deeds" (Lk 23.41). If repentance does not follow disobedience, it is vain to look elsewhere for help when trouble comes. Jeremiah has already pointed out that "among all her lovers she hath none to comfort her; all her friends have dealt treacherously with her" (v.2).

Her anguish (vv.20-21a)

Jerusalem's lamentation is now expressed in a heart-rending cry: "Behold, O Lord; for I am in distress: my bowels are troubled; mine heart is turned within me; for I have grievously rebelled: abroad the sword bereaveth, at home there is as death" (v.20). Streane defines "bowels" as "the vital parts (specially the heart), as the seat of the emotions". There was no escape either outside the city ("abroad"), or within the city ("at home"). Ellicott's Commentary points out that the reading "at home there is *as* death" suggests that "It is not death pure and simple...but the...starvation, disease, exhaustion, which were all deadly...in their working". There was no sympathy from her enemies, rather hilarity: "They have heard that I sigh: there is none to comfort me: all mine enemies have heard of my trouble; they are glad that thou hast done it" (v.21a).

Her anticipation (vv.21b-22)

These verses introduce a faint glimmer of hope: "thou wilt bring the day that thou hast called, and they shall be like unto me" (v.21b). While Streane suggests that this means that the day of Judah's punishment will be shared by others, it seems more likely that "the day" refers to the punishment of her exulting foes: "Let all their wickedness come before thee; and do unto them, as thou hast done unto me for all my transgressions: for my sighs are many, and my heart is faint". Isaiah speaks similarly of judgment upon Assyria (Is 10.12-16). The words "do unto them, as thou hast done unto me" bespeak, not revenge, but righteous judgment.

LAMENTATIONS 2

The outstanding feature of this chapter is the anger of God. The word "anger" (639) occurs six times in the passage: "How hath the Lord covered the daughter of Zion with a cloud in his *anger*…and remembered not his footstool in the day of his *anger*!" (v.1); "He hath cut off in his fierce *anger* all the horn of Israel" (v.3); "the Lord hath…despised, in the indignation of his *anger* the king and the priest" (v.6); "thou hast slain them in the day of thine *anger*; thou hast killed, and not pitied" (v.21); "in the day of the Lord's *anger* none escaped nor remained" (v.22). Reference is also made to "his wrath" (v.2) and "his fury" (v.4). The intensity of God's anger is emphasised by the repetition of the words "swallowed up" or "swallowed her up" (vv.2,5,16). The same word (1104) is translated "destroying" in v.8.

In chapter 1 the "enemies…persecutors…adversaries" (vv.2,3,5,) were the Chaldaeans and Judah's near neighbours, whereas in the current chapter, the "adversary" and "enemy" is the Lord himself: "He hath bent his bow like an enemy: he stood with his right hand as an adversary…The Lord was as an enemy" (vv.4-5). Ironside draws attention to the expressions, "*like* an enemy…*as* an adversary…*as* an enemy", and continues, "An *enemy* He never was, though their conduct compelled Him to act as if He were". The words "he hath" and "the Lord hath" occur frequently in vv.1-9. In fact, it would not be inappropriate to write over the chapter the words, "they rebelled, and vexed his holy Spirit: therefore he was turned to be their enemy, and he fought against them" (Is 63.10).

The elegy may be divided as follows:

> The Destruction of the City (vv.1-9a)
> The Despair of the People (vv.9b-12)
> The Distress of the Prophet (vv.13-14)
> The Derision of the Enemies (vv.15-17)
> The Desperation of the Cry (vv.18-22).

Verses 1-9a: The Destruction of the City
As Harrison points out, "This lament describes in considerably greater detail the nature of the calamity which has descended upon the southern kingdom. Its vividness and vitality bear the obvious marks of an eye-witness". These verses give a comprehensive picture of the destruction of Zion and with it the entire nation. Divine judgment had totally encompassed God's people and had destroyed: their city (v.1); their kingdom (v.2); their strength (vv.3-5); their religious life (vv.6-7); and their security (vv.8-9a).

Their city had been destroyed (v.1)
"How hath the Lord covered the daughter of Zion with a cloud in his

anger, and cast down from heaven unto the earth the beauty of Israel, and remembered not his footstool in the day of his anger!". The expression, "the daughter of Zion", refers, not to the people who lived there, but to the place itself. Its meaning can be conveyed by the title "Daughter-Zion" (Harrison). The city is darkened by the thunder-cloud of divine judgment in the same way that Tehaphnehes would be "darkened, when I shall break there the yokes of Egypt…a cloud shall cover her, and her daughters shall go into captivity" (Ezek 30.18). An entirely different cloud had once accompanied the children of Israel: "And the angel of God, which went before the camp of Israel, removed and went behind them; and the pillar of the cloud went from before their face, and stood behind them: And it came between the camp of the Egyptians and the camp of Israel; and it was a cloud and darkness to them, but it gave light by night to these" (Ex 14.19-20). That cloud was the emblem of the Lord's presence and blessing, but the cloud here is the emblem of divine anger. When His wrath has run its full course, and He "shall have washed away the filth of the daughters of Zion…the Lord will create upon every dwelling place of mount Zion, and upon her assemblies, a cloud and smoke by day, and the shining of a flaming fire by night: for upon all the glory shall be a defence" (Is 4.4-5).

The words, "cast down from heaven unto the earth", simply mean that that the city which had once enjoyed so much divine favour was now reduced to the level of other cities. The expression, "the beauty of Israel", is a clear allusion to the words of the psalmist: "Great is the Lord, and greatly to be praised in the city of our God, in the mountain of his holiness. Beautiful for situation, the joy of the whole earth, is mount Zion…the city of the great King" (Ps 48.1-2). The fact that the city is called "the beauty of *Israel*" is not without significance, bearing in mind that the name "Israel" means "prince with God", or "ruling with God". But far from "ruling with God" the city was in the hands of a foreign power, obliging Jeremiah to say, "Servants have ruled over us: there is none that doth deliver us out of their hand" (Lam 5.8). The words "his footstool" suggest that Jerusalem was the place where the Lord could rest with pleasure (cp. 1 Chr 28.2; Ps 99.5), but their sin meant that He had "trodden the virgin, the daughter of Judah, as in a winepress" (1.15). The Lord's "footstool" had become the place where He trampled upon His disobedient people.

The description of the city in this way is the first of a series of references to divinely-instituted things: "The Lord…remembered not *his* footstool" (v.1); "he hath destroyed *his* strong holds" (v.5); "he hath…taken away *his* tabernacle" (v.6); "The Lord hath cast off *his* altar" (v.7); "he hath abhorred *his* sanctuary" (v.7). In the words of J. N. Darby, "He no longer respects what He has set up. It is a solemn thing when Jehovah is forced to reject that which He acknowledges as His own. But it must be so if His Name is only a means of falsifying the testimony of what He is". The Lord fulfilled His own solemn promise: "But go ye now unto *my* place which was in Shiloh, where I set *my* name at the first, and see what I did to it for the wickedness of my people Israel…Therefore will I do unto this house, which is called by *my* name, wherein ye trust, and unto the place which I gave to you and to your fathers, as I have done to Shiloh" (Jer 7.12,14). The Lord's letter to Ephesus clearly proves that He continues to remove what He has established, if it fails to fulfill its original purpose: "I have somewhat against thee, because thou hast left thy first love. Remember therefore from whence thou art fallen, and repent, and do the first works; or else I will come unto thee quickly, and will remove thy candlestick out of his place, except thou repent" (Rev 2.4-5). God does not bless His people "for old time's sake". Current blessing demands current spirituality. God is not duty bound to maintain something if His people have turned it into a farce.

Their kingdom had been destroyed (v.2)

It had been "swallowed up…thrown down…polluted". Having seen the destruction of the Egyptian army, Moses said, "Thou stretchedst out thy right hand, the earth swallowed them" (Ex 15.12), but now, centuries later, Jeremiah exclaims, "The Lord hath swallowed up all the habitations of Jacob, and hath not pitied: he hath thrown down in his wrath the strong holds of the daughter of Judah; he hath brought them down to the ground: he hath polluted the kingdom and the princes thereof" (cp. v.5). Her enemies claimed that this was something that they had accomplished (v.16), not knowing that they were but instruments in the hand of God. While the word "habitations" (4999) may have a general meaning, it is used of places "where shepherds lived with their flocks (cp. Jer 25.37; Amos 1.2) and so would imply the open village areas of Judaea. These undefended settlements are then contrasted with the fortified towns in the next phrase" (Harrison).

The terms, "habitations of *Jacob*" and "strong holds of…*Judah*", are not without significance. The name Jacob emphasises the grace of God. It has been nicely said that while "Jacob" suggests the depths to which the grace of God will go to reach a man, "Israel" suggests the heights to which the grace of God will take that same man (J. G. Bellett). The nation which had benefited so much from the grace of God had despised His provision for them. Judah means "praise", and it is therefore significant that one result of the nation's sin is "mourning and lamentation" (v.5). The Lord Jesus made it clear that obedience and joy go hand in hand (Jn 15.10-11). The word "polluted" (2490) is elsewhere rendered "profaned": "thou hast profaned his crown, by casting it to the ground" (Ps 89.39), leading to the conclusion that "The term involves the thought that it had been a consecrated thing. It had become unclean, first through the sins, and then through the defeat and degradation, of its rulers" (Ellicott's Commentary).

Their strength had been destroyed (vv.3-5)

"He hath cut off in his fierce anger all the horn of Israel" (v.3). The word "horn" is "often used metaphorically to signify strength and honour, since horns are the chief weapons and ornaments of the animals which possess them" (Cruden's Concordance). The Apostle John "beheld, and, lo, in the midst of the throne…stood a Lamb, as it had been slain, having seven horns and seven eyes, which are the seven Spirits of God sent forth into all the earth" (Rev 5.6). The Lamb is omnipotent, omniscient and omnipresent.

Sadly, strength no longer belonged to Israel, but rather to her enemies: "he hath set up the horn of thine adversaries" (v.17). It could no longer be said of God's people, "thou art the glory of their strength: and in thy favour our horn shall be exalted" (Ps 89.17), although the nation will ultimately sing, "He also exalteth the horn of his people, the praise of all his saints; even of the children of Israel, a people near unto him. Praise ye the Lord" (Ps 148.14). At the Red Sea the Lord had exerted His strength on behalf of His people: "Thy right hand, O Lord, is become glorious in power: thy right hand, O Lord, hath dashed in pieces the enemy" (Ex 15.6), but now He exerts His strength against them: "He hath drawn back his right hand from before the enemy…he stood with his right hand as an adversary" (vv.3-4).

When the Temple was dedicated, God signified His approval by fire: "Now when Solomon had made an end of praying, the fire came down from heaven, and consumed the burnt offering and the sacrifices; and the glory of the Lord filled the house" (2 Chr 7.1). But now God's people witnessed His judicial fire: "he burned against Jacob like a flaming fire, which devoureth round about…he stood…and slew all that were pleasant to the eye ('all that was pleasant to the eye', JND) in the tabernacle of the daughter of Zion: he poured out his fury like fire" (vv.3-4). The destruction included "not only warriors and youths, but everything dear and precious" (Ellicott's Commentary). The word "tabernacle" ('tent', JND) refers here, not to the Temple, but to the city itself as the dwelling place of the people collectively described as "the daughter of Zion" (v.4).

Wholesale destruction had taken place throughout the land, including the fortified cities ('strong holds', AV): "The Lord was as an enemy: he hath swallowed up Israel, he hath swallowed up all her palaces: he hath destroyed his strong holds, and hath increased in the daughter of Judah mourning and lamentation" (v.5).

It should be said that the Lord did not deal with His people in this way without repeated warning: "Since the day that your fathers came forth out of the land of Egypt unto this day I have even sent unto you all my servants the prophets, daily rising up early and sending them" (Jer 7.25). The Lord makes this statement, with variations, on eleven occasions during Jeremiah's preaching. He testified against Israel's sin, but His warnings went unheeded. The Lord's people today must not think that they are in any way exempted from His displeasure when they rebel against Him.

Their religious life had been destroyed (vv.6-7)

Harrison evidently considers that the words, "he hath violently taken away his tabernacle, as if it were of a garden" (v.6), describe the destruction of the Temple: "because of national wickedness, the holy structure is demolished as though it were merely a worthless garden shed". However, according to Gesenius, the word "tabernacle" (7900) means "a hedge", leading to the conclusion that Jeremiah refers here rather to the withdrawal of divine protection, leaving the city and the Temple vulnerable. Their destruction meant the end of "the solemn feasts and sabbaths" (v.6). The requirement for all the men in Israel to come "Three times in a year" to "the place which he shall choose" (Deut 16.16) could no longer be fulfilled: "he hath destroyed his places of the assembly ('his place of assembly', JND): the Lord hath caused the solemn feasts and sabbaths to be forgotten in Zion" (v.6). At the end-time, the Lord will "gather them that are sorrowful for the solemn assembly…to whom the reproach of it was a burden" (Zeph 3.18). The solemn words, "the Lord…hath despised in the indignation of his anger the king and the priest" (v.6), are a fearful commentary on the total lack of integrity in the men who led the nation. In the millennial reign, the Lord Jesus, "the man whose name is The BRANCH…shall bear the glory, and shall sit and rule upon his throne; and he shall be a priest upon his throne: and the counsel of peace shall be between them both" (Zech 6.12-13).

In describing the pillage and desecration of the Temple and its associated buildings, particular mention is made of the altar: "The Lord hath cast off his altar, he hath abhorred his sanctuary, he hath given up into the hand of the enemy the walls of her palaces; they have made a noise in the house of the Lord, as in the day of a solemn feast" (v.7). The altar was at the heart of national life and was the basis of their relationship with God. It is therefore of no little significance than when the first contingent of exiles returned from Babylonia, "they set the altar upon his bases…and they offered burnt offerings thereon unto the Lord" (Ezra 3.3). Harrison makes a telling observation in connection with the rejection of the altar here: "More significant, however, is the implication that no amount of ritualistic procedure could avert divine judgment from a people guilty of the continued rejection of covenant love". The palace walls belonged to other buildings in the Temple complex, including the royal palace, which took longer than the Temple to construct (1 Kings 6.38; 7.1). The building that once rang with the hallelujahs of God's people now rang with the triumphant shouts of pagan conquerors.

Their security had been destroyed (vv.8-9a)

"The Lord hath purposed to destroy the wall of the daughter of Zion: he hath stretched out a line, he hath not withdrawn his hand from destroying: therefore he made the rampart and the wall to lament; they languished together. Her gates are sunk into the ground; he hath destroyed and broken her bars." It has been said that the walls were to keep out those who should not be in, and the gates were to give access to those who should be in! Some 140 years later, Nehemiah was told that "the wall of Jerusalem also is broken down, and the gates thereof are burned with fire" (Neh 1.3). If Jeremiah lamented the destruction of the wall and gates of Jerusalem in his day, then Nehemiah "sat down and wept, and mourned certain days, and fasted, and prayed before the God of heaven" (Neh 1.4).

National disobedience had left Jerusalem without protection and without a dividing line between the city and its surroundings. Walls are an emblem of salvation: "salvation will God appoint for walls and bulwarks" (Is 26.1); "thou shalt call thy walls Salvation" (Is 60.18), and it is vital to the spiritual welfare of the Lord's people that the doctrines of salvation are in place in personal and assembly life. Sadly, there appears to be little division between the professing church and the world, and Paul's injunction is relevant: "Take heed unto thyself, and unto the doctrine; continue in them: for in doing this thou shalt both *save* thyself, and them that hear thee" (1 Tim 4.16), but in many places the wall has been destroyed. Disobedience had robbed Jerusalem of counsel. The gates were places where administration and business were conducted. The city gate was recognised as an open court of justice where civil and criminal cases were investigated by the elders (cp. Deut 16.18-20; Ruth 4.1). The Lord's people must ensure that nothing deprives them of the teaching and guidance of God's Word. It is their only court of appeal in all matters of doctrine and practice. But in many places, the gates "are sunk into the ground", which is another way of saying that they had completely disappeared. Since in the millennial age it will be said, "but thou shalt call...thy gates Praise" (Is 60.18), the destruction of the gates should suffice to remind the Lord's people that disobedience also robs them of joy and thanksgiving.

Verses 9b-12: The Despair of the People
God's anger was felt by five classes of people: the king and the princes (v.9b); the prophets (v.9c); the elders (v.10a); the virgins (v.10b); and the children (vv.11-12).

The king and the princes (v.9b)
There was no *leadership*: the kings and princes were *scattered*: "her king and her princes are among the Gentiles: the law is no more". While the priests took responsibility in religious matters, the king and court officials administered the civil law. The Lord's people had become "as sheep that have no shepherd" (2 Chr 18.16). The king of Judah is described as "The breath of our nostrils, the anointed of the Lord...of whom we said, Under his shadow we shall live among the heathen" (4.20), but events had dashed their hopes and aspirations in this direction. Sadly, the leadership had reaped the consequences of failing to act responsibly in implementing the law of God in national life. The New Testament assigns great importance

to spiritual shepherds: "Take heed therefore unto yourselves, and to all the flock, over the which ('wherein', JND) the Holy Ghost hath made you overseers" (Acts 20.28).

The prophets (v.9c)

There was no *message*: the prophets were *sightless*: "her prophets also find no vision from the Lord". They professed to have the word of the Lord, but they were "prophets of the deceit of their own heart" (Jer 23.26). Further censure follows: "Thy prophets have seen vain and foolish things for thee: and they have not discovered thine iniquity, to turn away thy captivity; but have seen for thee false burdens and causes of banishment" (v.14). Jude describes apostate teachers as "clouds…without water" (Jude v.12), where apparent promise leads only to disappointment. The overthrow of Jerusalem and attendant events had silenced the false prophets, with all their hopes of peace and prosperity, leading Asaph to say, "We see not our signs: there is no more any prophet: neither is there among us any that knoweth how long" (Ps 74.9). Disobedience will silence the voice of God. Bearing in mind the evil practised by Eli's family, it is not at all surprising that "the word of the Lord was precious (rare) in those days; there was no open vision" (1 Sam 3.1).

The elders (v.10a)

There was no *counsel*, the elders were *silent*: "The elders of the daughter of Zion sit upon the ground, and keep silence: they have cast up dust upon their heads; they have girded themselves with sackcloth". Each city, including Jerusalem, evidently had its own elders who exercised control over local affairs (cp. Deut 19.12; 21.2; 1 Sam 16.4; 2 Kings 10.1). With the desolation of the land, "the elders had no civil duties to perform, and were reduced to grief-stricken impotence by the calamity of the exile" (Harrison). Placing dust on the head and wearing sackcloth (made from goat's hair, and black in colour) were signs of mourning. Believers today are reminded that they must "Obey them that have the rule over you ('your leaders', JND), and submit yourselves: for they watch for your souls, as they that must give account; that they may do it (the work) with joy, and not with grief: for that is unprofitable for you" (Heb 13.17). Mourning elders are not unknown today.

The virgins (v.10b)

There was no *prospect*, the virgins were *sad*: "the virgins of Jerusalem hang down their heads to the ground". Ellicott's Commentary, possibly referring to Psalm 45.14; 68.25; Jeremiah 31.13, explains this as follows: "The maidens, who had once joined with timbrels and dances in festive processions, walk to and fro with downcast eyes". For an alternative suggestion, however, the reader is referred to comments made in connection with 1.4.

The children (vv.11-12)

There was no *future*: the children *swoon*. When Jeremiah turned his attention to the children, his grief knew no bounds: "Mine eyes do fail with tears, my bowels are troubled (cp. 1.20), my liver is poured upon the earth, for the destruction of the daughter of my people" (v.11). The word "liver" (3516), meaning "heavy" (Harrison), is well named since it is the heaviest organ of the human body. The liver, heart and bowels are "thought of as the centre of all intense emotions, both of joy or sorrow" (Ellicott's Commentary). The prophet was deeply stirred "because the children and the sucklings swoon in the streets of the city. They say to their mothers, Where is corn and wine? when they swooned as the wounded in the streets of the city, when their soul was poured out into their mothers' bosom". "Even while they were crawling among the rubble, searching for scraps of food, they collapsed in their tracks and died. In their extremity the children sought the kind of security which they had known as infants, and in this helpless posture they expired from hunger" (Harrison). Instead of feeding in their mother's bosom, they died in their mother's bosom. Jeremiah returns to these harrowing scenes in vv.19-21; 4.4,10. This tragic picture contrasts vividly with Zechariah's description of millennial Jerusalem, which will "be full of boys and girls playing in the streets thereof" (Zech 8.5).

The suffering of infants and young children may appear at first glance to present a moral dilemma, but Harrison is most helpful here: "Although it is theoretically possible to regard them as innocent, they were nevertheless a formal and recognised part of an iniquitous, apostate nation. Like all children, their destiny was deeply involved with that of their parents, who showed little if any signs of rearing their offspring in the ethical and spiritual traditions of the covenant…The callous indifference of the wanton, selfish parents to the destiny of their offspring shows the depth of depravity to which the Judæans had sunk. Instead of bringing up their children in the fear and nurture of the Lord, they had sold them in emotional and spiritual bondage to Baal". He adds, "Christian parents have an important responsibility in the matter of instilling Christian spiritual values in the children, while the latter in turn must be obedient and considerate (cp. Eph 6.1; Col 3.20; 1 Tim 5.4)".

Verses 13-14: The Distress of the Prophet

With these ineradicable scenes in his mind, Jeremiah cries out in deep distress: "What thing shall I take to witness for thee? what thing shall I liken to thee, O daughter of Jerusalem? what shall I equal to thee, that I may comfort thee, O virgin daughter of Zion? for thy breach is great like the sea: who can heal thee?" (v.13). Divine judgment had burst upon Zion like the sea forcing its way through a protective wall, and her consequent suffering was incomparable.

A major share of responsibility for the catastrophe which had overtaken Jerusalem is laid at the doors of the false prophets. Instead of exposing the sin of God's people in transgressing the covenant, and urging them to turn to Him in repentance, they had proclaimed peace and coming prosperity: "Thy prophets have seen vain and foolish things for thee: and they have not discovered thine iniquity, to turn away thy captivity; but have seen for thee false burdens and causes of banishment" (v.14), or "Thy prophets have seen vanity and folly for thee; and they have not revealed thine iniquity, to turn away thy captivity; but have seen for thee burdens of falsehood and causes of expulsion" (JND). Jeremiah was already aware of this: "For they have healed the hurt of the daughter of my people slightly, saying, Peace, peace; when there is no peace" (Jer 8.11); "Then said I, Ah, Lord God! behold, the prophets say unto them, Ye shall not see the sword, neither shall ye have famine; but I will give you assured peace in this place" (Jer 14.13).

The dire results of such teaching are clearly described in this chapter. There is terrible danger in telling people what they wish to hear, and centuries later, Paul warned Timothy that "the time will come when they will not endure the sound doctrine; but, having itching ears, will heap to themselves teachers after their own lusts; and will turn away their ears from the truth, and turn aside unto fables" (2 Tim 4.3-4, RV). The spiritual consequences are no less real than the terrible legacy of false prophecy in the Old Testament. But there was another result.

Verses 15-17: The Derision of the Enemies

In these verses Jeremiah draws attention to three features in the enemies of God's people: their sarcasm (v.15); their satisfaction (v.16); and their strength (v.17).

Their sarcasm (v.15)

Their contempt is thinly veiled: "All that pass by clap their hands at thee; they hiss and wag their head at the daughter of Jerusalem, saying, Is this the city that men call The perfection of beauty, The joy of the whole earth?" (v.15). The Lord had fulfilled His word in this respect: "I will make this city desolate, and an hissing; every one that passeth thereby shall be astonished and hiss because of all the plagues thereof" (Jer 19.8). The city described as being "Beautiful for situation, the joy of the whole earth" (Ps 48.2) was anything but beautiful; it was a heap of smoking ruins.

The taunts of the enemies here serve to remind the Lord's people today of the necessity for good conduct in order that "the word of God be not blasphemed" (Titus 2.5), and that "he that is of the contrary part might be ashamed, having no evil thing to say of you (Titus 2.8). Although Paul is referring particularly to the conduct of younger widows, it remains that all believers should "give none occasion to the adversary to speak reproachfully" (1 Tim 5.14).

Their satisfaction (v.16)

As Harrison observes, "The long-smouldering resentment of Judah's enemies could now be given full expression over her helpless, prostrate form": "All thine enemies have opened their mouth against thee: they hiss and gnash the teeth: they say, We have swallowed her up: certainly this is the day that we looked for; we have found, we have seen it". Needless to say, the spiritual forces ranged against the children of God today wish to achieve the same result. Bearing in mind the ongoing hostility of Satan, Paul urged the believers at Corinth to be mindful of his desire to "get an advantage of us" adding, "for we are not ignorant of his devices" (2 Cor 2.11).

Their strength (v.17)

"He hath caused thine enemy to rejoice over thee, he hath set up the horn of thine adversaries." While Jerusalem's enemies had exerted their strength, their ability to do this was divinely-given: "The Lord hath done that which he had devised; he hath fulfilled his word that he had commanded in the days of old: he hath thrown down, and hath not pitied". Through Zechariah, the Lord reminded His people that "my words and my statutes, which I commanded my servants the prophets, did they not take hold of ('overtake', JND) your fathers?" (Zech 1.6). It should be remembered that the oft-quoted statement, "my word…shall not return unto me void" (Is 55.11), is applicable to divine judgment as well as to divine blessing. Although the Lord's people should never underestimate the arch-enemy's strength, they can rejoice that "a stronger than he" has "come upon him" (Lk 11.22), and, in the words of the Apostle John, that "greater is he that is in you, than he that is in the world" (1 Jn 4.4).

Verses 18-22: The Desperation of the Cry

In the closing section of the dirge, Jeremiah calls upon the stricken and distraught city, describing the people collectively, to cry to the Lord in her distress. These verses may be divided as follows: how they were to pray (vv.18-19); and what they were to say (vv.20-22).

How they were to pray (vv.18-19)

"Their heart cried unto the Lord, O wall of the daughter of Zion, let tears run down like a river day and night" (v.18). While Harrison considers that the words, "O wall of the daughter of Zion", are in apposition to "the Lord", making the Lord himself the wall, and finds support for this in Zechariah 2.5, consideration should also be given to the alternative explanation that "His people, here prefigured as a broken wall", were "to pray the kind of prayer they ought to pray in such a state" (Unger). Support for this suggestion lies in the way in which the past tense, "Their heart cried unto the Lord", gives place to the present tense, "let tears run down like a river day and night". The people who had already "cried unto the Lord", were urged to continue to do so with renewed vigour and deepening distress. The necessary alteration in punctuation to support this explanation is supplied in the following: "Their heart cried unto the Lord. O wall of the daughter of Zion, let tears run down like a torrent day and night" (JND).

They were to continue to pray with reality. Well over a century before, the Lord had said, "this people draw near me with their mouth, and with their lips do honour me, but have removed their heart far from me" (Is 29.13), but pretence had already given place to reality, and Jeremiah called for even deeper sorrow. The wall of the city is personified and urged to weep day and night, which implies, since the wall was broken down, that the people were to pray from broken hearts, something so well known to David: "The sacrifices of God are a broken spirit: a broken and a contrite heart, O God, thou wilt not despise" (Ps 51.17). The people who had neglected to "let judgment run down as waters, and righteousness as a mighty stream" (Amos 5.24), were to "let tears run down like a river" because their failure had brought divine judgment upon them. Moreover, this was to be no passing phase: their sorrow was to be deeply rooted and deeply felt; it was to be expressed "day and night", and they were urged, "give thyself no rest; let not the apple of thine eye cease. Arise, cry out in the night: in the beginning of the watches (18.00 to 22.00, 22.00 to 02.00, and 02.00 to dawn) pour out thine heart like water before the face of the Lord: lift up thy hands toward him for the life of thy young children, that faint for hunger in the top of every street" (vv.18-19). The word rendered "apple" (1323) is, literally, "daughter" and is usually translated in this way. It stands for the pupil of the eye, said to be the most sensitive part of the human body.

What they were to say (vv.20-22)

These verses, which describe the awful carnage in the city, covering all age groups, are a desperate plea for mercy and pity in which personified Zion calls upon the Lord to remember the suffering of His own people: "Behold, O Lord, and consider to whom thou hast done this" (v.20). The horrifying picture that follows needs no explanation: "Shall the women eat their fruit, and children of a span long? shall the priest and the prophet be slain in the sanctuary of the Lord? The young and the old lie on the ground in the streets: my virgins and my young men are fallen by the sword" (vv.20-21). It should be noted that these verses, far from expressing reproach and recrimination, are an acknowledgement of divine righteousness: "thou hast slain them in the day of thine anger; thou hast killed and not pitied. Thou hast called as in a solemn day my terrors round about, so that in the day of the Lord's anger none escaped nor remained: those that I have swaddled and brought up hath mine enemy consumed" (vv.21-22). The expression, "the day of the Lord's anger ('Jehovah's anger', JND)" emphasises that what had taken place was the result of "a prolonged violation of the covenant relationship" (Harrison). Although the Lord had "hewed them by the prophets", and "slain them by the words of my mouth...they like men have transgressed the covenant" (Hos 6.5-7). In consequence, having "sown the wind", they had reaped "the whirlwind" (Hos 8.7).

Zion's prayer and confession, with all its profound sorrow and anguish over her unimaginable suffering, is not an end in itself. It forms the basis on which there can be future blessing: "And I said, My strength and my hope is perished from the Lord: Remembering mine affliction and my misery, the wormwood and the gall. My soul hath them still in remembrance, and is humbled in me. This I recall to my mind, therefore have I hope" (3.18-21). Hope lies at the centre of the third elegiac poem.

LAMENTATIONS 3

The reader is reminded that in common with the first two and the fourth chapters of the book, this chapter follows the Hebrew alphabet, with a difference that its first three verses each begin with *Aleph*, its second three verses with *Beth,* its third three verses with *Gimel*, and so on until the end of the Hebrew alphabet. Attention has already been drawn to the fact that in this chapter, together with the preceding and succeeding chapters, the order of the sixteenth and seventeenth letters of the Hebrew alphabet is reversed, for which, apparently, no satisfactory explanation has yet been given.

The outstanding feature of this chapter is its message of hope. While the word "hope" occurs five times in the passage (vv.18,21,24,26,29), it should be noted that, according to Strong's Exhaustive Concordance, four different words are used in the Hebrew text, and attention will be drawn to these variations as the exposition proceeds. Although the first occurrence (v.18) refers to the disappearance of hope, this sad experience, evidently in Jeremiah's own life, did not become permanent, and four positive statements follow: "Remember thou mine affliction and my wandering, the wormwood and the gall. My soul hath them constantly in remembrance, and is humbled in me. - This I recall to heart, therefore have I *hope*" (vv.19-21, JND); "The Lord is my portion, saith my soul; therefore will I *hope* in him" (v.24); "It is good that a man should both *hope* and quietly wait for the salvation of the Lord" (v.26); "He putteth his mouth in the dust; if so be there may be *hope*" (v.29). The chapter, with particular reference to vv.18-29, has been likened to a mountain peak jutting out of the mists into the sunshine.

It has been suggested that in vv.1-24, with their repetition of "I...me...my", Jeremiah is putting words into the mouth of Jerusalem, in the same way that he personified the city in 1.9b,11b,12-22. On the basis of this interpretation, it is Jerusalem that cries, "I am the man that hath seen affliction by the rod of his wrath" (v.1), and the voice of the city continues to be heard in the verses that follow. However, the suggestion that Jeremiah is either speaking representatively, or identifying himself with the people, is perhaps questionable in view of his cry, "I was a derision to all my people; and their song all the day" (v.14). It is noticeable that, unlike the earlier confession of transgressions, rebellion and unfaithfulness by personified Jerusalem (1.14,18,19), no mention is made of transgression and rebellion in the current chapter while Jeremiah is speaking in the first person. It is not until he appeals to the nation that sin is mentioned: "Let us lift up our heart with our hands unto God in the heavens. We have transgressed and have rebelled: thou hast not pardoned" (vv.41-42). This strongly suggests that in vv.1-36 Jeremiah is relating his own experiences (vv.1-24) together with the lessons he had learned in them (vv.25-36), not purely for the historical record, but to point the way forward for God's people. He knew from his own experience the necessity for humility and recourse to God, and calls the nation to confession and repentance.

Bearing this in mind, the chapter may be divided into five main paragraphs:

> His Acceptance of God's Will (vv.1-21)
> His Appreciation of God's Character (vv.22-36)
> His Appeal to the Nation (vv.37-47)
> His Approach to God (vv.48-51)
> His Adversity and Adversaries (vv.52-66).

Verses 1-21: His Acceptance of God's Will

There are two major parts in this section of the chapter: the recollection of his experiences (vv.1-18); and the reason for his experiences (vv.19-21).

The recollection of his experiences (vv.1-18)

As suggested above, these verses evidently relate Jeremiah's own experiences, and he concludes, using the past tense, "And thou hast removed my soul far off from peace: I forgat prosperity. And I said, My strength and my *hope* is perished from the Lord" (vv.17-18). According to Gesenius, the word "hope" (8431) means "expectation". The chapter therefore commences dismally, and this particular section ends with the prophet at his lowest ebb; the fact that he had to say, "I was a derision to all my people; and their song all the day" (v.14), was bad enough, but to discover, as he thought, that even the Lord was against him, was infinitely worse: "Even when I cry and shout, he shutteth out my prayer" (v.8, JND).

There is certainly an affinity between Jeremiah's protests at God's dealings with him during the course of his ministry, and his recollections in the current verses. Indeed, his past language was even more startling at times: "Why is my pain perpetual, and my wound incurable, which refuseth to be healed? wilt thou be altogether unto me as a liar, and as waters that fail?" (Jer 15.18); "O Lord, thou hast deceived me, and I was deceived" (Jer 20.7). Very clearly, there were occasions in his lifetime when the Lord's servant bitterly resented the way in which he had been exposed to such rejection and opprobrium, and now, in his own words, "My soul hath them still in remembrance" (v.20).

While the following analysis can only be described as rather arbitrary, it represents an attempt to capture the leading thoughts in Jeremiah's mind as he recalls the way in which the Lord had dealt with him.

There was no explanation for him

"I am the man that hath seen affliction by the rod of his wrath. He hath led me, and brought me into darkness, but not into light" (vv.1-2). While it has to be said that that the opening words (v.1) would be

particularly appropriate if Jeremiah were articulating the cry of
Jerusalem, nevertheless they can rightly be taken as his personal cry.
Job used similar language: "Let him take his rod away from me, and let
not his fear terrify me" (Job 9.34). In the words of Laetsch: "In his deep
sorrow the prophet sees and feels only the rod of God's wrath. His way
is wrapped in dense darkness, he cannot understand God's judgments".
Jeremiah's "darkness", describing his perplexity as well as his misery,
can be discerned in his bitter complaint, "Wherefore came I forth out
of the womb to see labour and sorrow, that my days should be consumed
with shame?" (Jer 20.18). Job spoke similarly: "When I looked for good,
then evil came unto me: and when I waited for light, there came
darkness" (Job 30.26).

There was no relief for him
     "Surely against me is he turned; he turneth his hand against me all the
day" (v.3), or "Surely against me hath he turned again and again his hand
all the day" (JND). "No matter what he began, God's hand was against
him, frustrating every plan" (Laetsch). Jeremiah uses a mixture of
metaphors in describing his unrelieved suffering. "My flesh and my skin
hath he made old ('wasted away', JND); he hath broken my bones. He
hath builded against me, and compassed me with gall and travail. He hath
set me in dark places, as they that be dead of old" (vv.4-6). According to
Streane, "The flesh, skin, and bones are taken as comprising the whole
man, the former two denoting the softer portions, the last the harder,
which must be fractured, in order to destroy it".
     While some suggest that the words, "He hath builded against me" (v.5),
allude to the construction of siege mounds or ramparts against a city, and
thus vividly recall the Chaldean siege of Jerusalem, there seems to be no
etymological reason to understand the word "builded" in this way. Jeremiah
felt surrounded with "gall", a poisonous bitter herb, and therefore signifying
bitterness, and "travail" (8513), meaning "labour, toil, weariness"
(Gesenius). Streane suggests that the expression "dark places" (v.6) is used
as "an equivalent for misery, as light for happiness", and the words which
complete the sentence, "as they that be dead of old", or "as those that
have been long dead" (JND), imply that there was, it seemed, no return
from the misery described in this way.

There was no escape for him
     "He hath hedged me about, that I cannot get out: he hath made my
chain heavy" (v.7). The word "hedged" (1443), later translated "inclosed"
(v.9), refers to an insurmountable wall. Changing the metaphor, Jeremiah
then likened his impediment to a heavy chain (literally, "brass"). There
was no possibility of escape, a sentiment shared by Job: "He hath fenced
up (1443) my way that I cannot pass, and he hath set darkness in my paths"
(Job 19.8). He could see no way of extricating himself from his

circumstances, and received no answer to his cry for deliverance: "when I cry and shout, he shutteth out my prayer" (v.8).

In referring again to the wall which prevented his escape (v.5), Jeremiah emphasises that it seemed impregnable: it was built of "hewn stone" (v.9). It was "carefully prepared, fitting close together, a well-made, strong wall" (Laetsch), and "when he turns aside into by-paths, they are turned and twisted in labyrinthine confusion, and lead nowhither" (Ellicott's Commentary): "he hath made my paths crooked" (v.9). The Apostle Paul describes the same situation: "We are troubled on every side, yet not distressed; we are perplexed ('without a way'), but not in despair ('not utterly without a way')" (2 Cor 4.8). While Paul's reassurance in the circumstances is expressed immediately, Jeremiah waits a little longer before revealing his confidence (vv.19-36).

There was no warning for him
"He was unto me as a bear lying in wait, and as a lion in secret places. He hath turned aside my ways, and pulled me in pieces: he hath made me desolate" (vv.10-11). Ellicott's Commentary explains this as follows: "The terror caused by the lion turns the traveller from his path, and there is no other; and then comes the attack by which he is torn in pieces". According to Ellicott's Commentary, the words "hath made me desolate" are better rendered "hath made me astonied", conveying "the stupefaction of terror". Then, changing the metaphor yet again, from a beast of prey to that of a hunter, "He hath bent his bow, and set me as a mark for the arrow. He hath caused the arrows of his quiver (literally, in poetic language, 'the sons of his quiver') to enter into my reins" (vv.12-13). The "arrow" is a metaphor for persecution and tribulation (cp. Job 6.4; Ps 38.2).

There was no regard for him
"The personal experience of the prophet breaks through the succession of imagery. The arrows that pierced to the quick were the taunts of the mockers who derided him" (Ellicott's Commentary): "I was a derision to all my people; and their song all the day" (v.14). This evidently refers to Jeremiah's consignment to the stocks by Pasher the son of Immer: "O Lord, thou hast deceived me, and I was deceived: thou art stronger than I, and hast prevailed: I am in *derision* daily, every one mocketh me. For since I spake, I cried out, I cried violence and spoil; because the word of the Lord was made a reproach unto me, and a *derision*, daily" (Jer 20.7-8).

There was no joy for him
"He hath filled me with bitterness (literally, 'bitternesses'), he hath made me drunken with wormwood" (v.15). His sorrows here have been called "the bitter herbs of life", and they had filled him to the extent that it was as if "he had been made drunk with wormwood" (Ellicott's Commentary). The prophet then turns from drinking to eating: "He

hath also broken my teeth with gravel stones, he hath covered me with ashes" (v.16). Jeremiah likens his sorrows to bread made from gritty sand instead of flour. Sorrow had invaded every part of his life; there was no pleasure for him in any direction. Alternatively, since the word "covered" (3728), found only here, could mean "pressed down" (Streane), it has been suggested that the "gravel stones" could possibly refer to the grit which filled his mouth when, metaphorically he was pressed down into the ashes. Whatever the correct explanation, the expression signifies deep humiliation and sorrow.

There was no hope for him

"And thou hast removed my soul far off from peace: I forgat prosperity" (v.17). The meaning of the word "removed' (2186) is to "thrust away" (Gesenius), leading to the translation, "thou hast rejected my soul" (Streane). With this, the sorrow of the mourning prophet verges on utter despair: "And I said, My strength and my *hope* is perished from the Lord" (v.18). The Psalmist used similar language: "For thou art the God of my strength: why dost thou cast me off? why go I mourning because of the oppression of the enemy?" (Ps 43.2).

In short, the prophet bitterly complained at the stigma involved in faithfulness to God; his prayer appeared to fall on deaf ears (v.8), and he felt utterly rejected (v.18). The alternative explanation, that Jeremiah speaks as the voice of Jerusalem, is not without its merits but, as already noted, in view of the prophet's past recriminatory language (cp. Jer 15.18; 20.7), it is not unreasonable to conclude that he is expressing his deep personal feelings.

While the Lord's people today may not complain at "the offence of the cross" (Gal 5.11), they are sometimes "pressed out of measure, above strength" (2 Cor 1.8) in other ways and, unlike the Apostle Paul in Asia, find difficulty in understanding their circumstances. Painful illnesses and incapacity, premature bereavement, family problems, redundancy, and pressing assembly difficulties, all exert pressure and tax endurance to the extent that faithful and godly believers can be left in perplexity. Prayer apparently remains unanswered (v.8) and divine help is apparently not forthcoming (v.18). While believers are hardly likely to express their feelings in the same way as Jeremiah, their hearts are often torn with anguish and sorrow. But encouragement follows, and from this low point in his experience Jeremiah begins to re-examine the circumstances through which he has passed, and despondency and despair give place to hope. Having recollected his experiences (vv.1-18), he now traces the divine hand in them, tacitly saying, "It is good for me that I have been afflicted" (Ps 119.71).

The reason for his experiences (vv.19-21)

While commentators suggest that the words, "Remembering mine affliction and my misery, the wormwood and the gall" (v.19), are best taken as an imperative, resulting in the translation, "Remember thou mine affliction and my wandering, the wormwood and the gall" (JND), it nevertheless makes good sense to follow the AV rendering. The prophet recapitulates his adversity in vv.1-18, and continues, "My soul hath them still in remembrance, and is humbled in me" (v.20). This marks an important change in his perception. Whereas, at the time, he found it impossible to explain his experiences and bitterly resented them, he had come to realise that, rather than complaining at the apparent injustice of his sufferings, he must humbly accept the Lord's will. Since, in his own words, the Lord "doth not afflict willingly nor grieve the children of men" (v.33), his afflictions must therefore have a purpose, leading him to say, "This I recall to my mind, therefore have I hope (3176)" (v.21). The word "hope" here and in v.24 signifies "to wait with hope" (Young's Concordance).

Jeremiah had passed through stormy seas (vv.1-18), but not to his detriment (vv.19-21), as the following verses (vv.22-36) make abundantly clear. Before proceeding, the following should be noted.

Jeremiah remembered his experiences

The lessons learned in untoward circumstances remained with him. Centuries later, the Apostle Paul wrote: "I have learned, in whatsoever state I am…to be content. I know both how to be abased, and I know how to abound: every where and in all things, I am instructed both to be full and to be hungry, both to abound and to suffer need" (Phil 4.11-12).

Jeremiah related his experiences

While, undoubtedly, Jeremiah's experiences were for his personal benefit, they also enabled him to speak with moral authority when counselling his fellow-countrymen. In saying, "Let us search and try our ways, and turn again to the Lord" (v.40), Jeremiah was urging something that he had done himself. In response to Jeremiah's complaint to Him about his situation some years before, the Lord had said, "If thou return, then will I bring thee again, and thou shalt stand before me: and if thou take forth the precious from the vile, thou shalt be as my mouth" (Jer 15.19). It is worth remembering that lessons learned under the hand of God in personal life can be of immense help to fellow-believers. The Apostle Paul furnishes an example of this in saying, "And whether we be afflicted, it is for your consolation and salvation, which is effectual in the enduring of the same sufferings which we also suffer: or whether we be comforted, it is for your consolation and salvation" (2 Cor 1.6).

Jeremiah profited from his experiences

He learned that the Lord had no intention of destroying or damaging him by the circumstances through which he passed, but rather that through them, his spiritual life would be enhanced. The verses that follow (vv.22-

36) leave no doubt about the matter. The New Testament is equally clear: "And ye have forgotten the exhortation which speaketh unto you as unto children (sons), My son, despise not thou chastening of the Lord, nor faint when thou art rebuked of him…For they (our fathers) verily for a few days chastened us after their own pleasure (as seemed good to them); but he for our profit, that we might be partakers of his holiness" (Heb 12.5,10).

Verses 22-36: His Appreciation of God's Character

Having related his own experiences, and the lessons learned in them, Jeremiah now enlarges on the subject of hope. Having humbled himself "under the mighty hand of God" (1 Pet 5.6), the Lord's servant is completely transformed: bitter complaint gives place to exultant hope! Jeremiah now re-interprets his experiences, and sees them quite differently. God had not been dealing with him in an arbitrary way; He had Jeremiah's spiritual welfare in mind all the time! The transition from v.20 to v.21 can be expressed in the words of the psalmist: "Why art thou cast down, O my soul? and why art thou disquieted in me? hope thou in God: for I shall yet praise him for the help of his countenance" (Ps 42.5). It could be said that Jeremiah now follows the psalmist in turning from his circumstances to the Lord. A familiar hymn encourages believers to follow suit:

> O soul, are you weary and troubled?
> No light in the darkness you see?
> There's light for a look at the Saviour,
> And life more abundant and free!
>
> Turn your eyes upon Jesus,
> Look full in His wonderful face;
> And the things of earth will grow strangely dim
> In the light of His glory and grace.
>
> (H. H. Lemmel)

The following should be noted: the mercy of God engendered hope (vv.22-23a); the faithfulness of God engendered hope (v.23b); the sufficiency of God engendered hope (v.24); the salvation of God engendered hope (vv.25-26); the discipline of God engendered hope (vv.27-33); and the justice of the God engendered hope (vv.34-36). It can only be concluded that the Lord is by no means intent on consuming His people, but rather on displaying His compassion towards them.

Hope rests in the mercy of God (vv.22-23a)

"It is of the Lord's mercies ('loving-kindness', JND) that we are not consumed, because his compassions fail not." There was no cessation of God's affection for His people; His compassions "fail not". The nation had not been extinguished. The Lord could have completely finished with Israel. But they were His people: He loved them "with an everlasting love" (Jer 31.3). This is expressed elsewhere, with particular reference to the northern kingdom: "Is Ephraim my dear son? is he a pleasant child? for since I spake against him, I do earnestly remember him still: therefore my bowels are troubled for him; I will surely have mercy upon him, saith the Lord" (Jer 31.20); "How shall I give thee up, Ephraim? how shall I deliver thee, Israel? how shall I make thee as Admah? how shall I set thee as Zeboim? mine heart is turned within me, my repentings are kindled together" (Hos 11.8). Every believer can exclaim with David, "He hath not dealt with us after our sins; nor rewarded us according to our iniquities" (Ps 103.10).

Moreover, the Lord never fails. No wonder the Psalmist says, "My voice shalt thou hear in the morning, O Lord; in the morning will I direct my prayer unto thee, and will look up" (Ps 5.3). Believers often begin the day quite differently: the weather looks uncertain, jobs clamour for attention, another hectic day looms, somebody in the family is ill.... It all looks like a bad start to a bad day! Jeremiah bids the Lord's people to pause and look in a different direction: "His compassions...are new every morning". But it is more than that – the God of infinite resource and provision never ceases to surprise us! As the hymn-writer puts it:

> Grace taught my wandering feet
> To tread the heavenly road;
> And new supplies each hour I meet
> While pressing on to God.
> (P. Doddridge)

Hope rests in the faithfulness of God (v.23b)

"Great is thy faithfulness." This must refer, in context, to the Lord's faithfulness to His covenant: "I am the Lord, I change not; therefore ye sons of Jacob are not consumed" (Mal 3.6). At the same time, it is a statement of complete confidence in God's daily faithfulness to His people. Jeremiah himself had every reason to extol the faithfulness of God. At the beginning of his ministry he had been told that although the kings of Judah, the princes, the priests and the people would all oppose him, he would enjoy the Lord's presence and preservation (Jer 1.18-19). The word of God had proved true on both counts. Jeremiah had been discredited, derided and persecuted. Throughout his lifetime, everything and everybody was against him, and the pressure on him intensified as the years proceeded. As already noted, there were times when God's servant could not understand why he had been allowed him to face so much adversity. It is very easy to say, "Great is thy faithfulness", when everything is congenial and pleasant, but Jeremiah makes the statement after many difficult years and, at the time of writing, in most uncongenial circumstances! He knew that, despite appearances, the Lord had not, and would not, fail him, neither would He renege on His covenant mercies to Israel.

The prophet Habakkuk expresses this beautifully: "Although the fig tree shall not blossom, neither shall fruit be in the vines; the labour of the olive shall fail, and the fields shall yield no meat; the flock shall be cut off from the fold, and there shall be no herd in the stalls: Yet will I rejoice in the Lord, I will joy in the God of my salvation" (Hab 3.17-18). In similar vein, Job, having lost his health, and his wealth, and his friends, and his family, was still able to say, "Though he slay me, yet will I trust in him" (Job 13.15). The Lord's people today do well to ask themselves whether in similar circumstances, shorn of all the trappings of life, they too would be able to say, with conviction, "great is thy faithfulness...I will joy in the God of my salvation...yet will I trust in him".

Hope rests in the sufficiency of God (v.24)

The man who said, "Thou hast removed my soul far off from peace: I forgat prosperity...My strength and my hope is perished from the Lord" (vv.17-18), now says, "The Lord is my portion, saith my soul; therefore will I hope (3176) in him". The depths of his despair have given place to the heights of joy and glad anticipation.

After the conquest of Canaan, the land was divided amongst the tribes. Each tribe had its allocation, and was given "coasts" and "borders". No doubt the lines were fairly drawn, but of necessity, each "lot" had limits and boundaries. But there are no limits here: "The Lord is my portion". What can believers today possibly say about their "portion" in view of the statement, "if children, then heirs; heirs of God, and joint-heirs with Christ" (Rom 8.17)? As part of the present "portion" of His people, believers are reminded that "his divine power hath given unto us all things that pertain unto life and godliness" (2 Pet 1.3).

Hope rests in the salvation of God (vv.25-26)

The man who said, "Also when I cry and shout, he shutteth out my prayer" (v.8), now says, "The Lord is good unto them that wait for him, to the soul that seeketh him. It is good that a man should both hope and quietly wait for the salvation of the Lord". According to Young's Concordance, the word "hope" here means "to stay", evidently in the sense of patiently waiting. Jeremiah no longer "cried" and "shouted", but looked patiently for salvation as in the anticipation of divine intervention on behalf of his people. Similarly, the Lord's people today look patiently for divine intervention, but of a different kind: "Cast not away therefore your confidence, which hath great recompence of reward. For ye have need of patience, that, after ye have done the will of God, ye might receive the promise. For yet a little while, and he that shall come will come, and will not tarry" (Heb 10.35-37); "Be patient therefore, brethren, unto the coming of the Lord…Be ye also patient; stablish your hearts: for the coming of the Lord draweth nigh" (James 5.7-8).

Hope rests in the discipline of God (vv.27-33)

In this connection the following should be noticed, always bearing in mind that divine discipline does not necessarily imply punishment because of sin, but rather spiritual training.

The purpose of discipline (vv.27-30)

God disciplines His people with the object of using them in His service: "It is good for a man that he bear the yoke in his youth" (v.27). Jeremiah evidently refers here to his experiences described in vv.1-18. Streane comments helpfully: youth "is the time when passions are strongest and therefore most need the discipline, which, if established in its seat then, will hold sway throughout life. The words by no means imply that the writer was young at the time…Rather he is looking back through a long life of trouble and the experience which he has gained in the course of it". This agrees with Ellicott's Commentary: "It may fairly be contended…that the tone of the maxim is that of one who looks back from the experience of age on the passionate complaints of earlier years". It is generally said that vv.28-30 are best taken as hortatory: "Let him sit alone and keep silence because he (the Lord) hath laid it (the yoke) upon him. Let him put his mouth in the dust; if so there may be hope. Let him give his cheek to him that smiteth him; let him be filled full with reproach" (RV). It is most interesting, at the very least, to notice that word "hope" here (8615) is used in connection with the "*line* of scarlet thread…the scarlet *line* in the window" (Josh 2.18,21), from which it might be inferred that the word indicates expectation.

In connection with the "yoke" (v.27), Unger comments: "The way out is not to fight against the yoke, as would a young bull that is unaccustomed to it (Jer 31.18; Acts 9.5), but to submit to it, as would a man who was used to it from his youth". The way forward is to accept the yoke with humility and submission, and this is expounded in the New Testament: "Now no chastening for the present seemeth to be joyous, but grievous (as Jeremiah had proved): nevertheless afterward it yieldeth the peaceable fruit of righteousness unto them which are exercised thereby" (Heb 12.11). The "peaceable fruit of righteousness" is one way of describing the benefit of the yoke described by the Lord Jesus: "Come unto me, all ye that labour and are heavy laden, and I will give you rest. Take my yoke upon you, and learn of me; for I am meek and lowly in heart: and ye shall find rest unto your souls. For my yoke is easy, and my burden is light" (Mt 11.28-30).

The period of discipline (v.31)

While God disciplines, it is only for a limited duration: "For the Lord will not cast off for ever". He withdraws His chastening hand once its purpose has been accomplished, recalling the words of Peter: "Wherein ye greatly rejoice, though now *for a season,* if need be, ye are in heaviness through manifold temptations" (1 Pet 1.6).

The tenderness in discipline (vv.32-33)
   While God disciplines, it is not at the expense of His love: "But though he cause grief, yet will he have compassion according to the multitude of his mercies. For he doth not afflict willingly nor grieve the children of men", recalling not only that divine discipline is "for a season", but that it is also "if need be" (1 Pet 1.6). Adversity and difficulty are only necessary as the Lord sees fit.

> My times are in Thy hand,
> Why should I doubt or fear?
> My Father's hand will never cause
> His child a needless tear.
> (W. F. Lloyd)

Hope rests in the justice of God (vv.34-36)
   The fact that "he doth not afflict willingly" (v.33) is proved by the fact that He disapproves of unrighteousness: "To crush under his feet all the prisoners of the earth, To turn aside the right of a man before the face of the most High, To subvert a man in his cause, the Lord approveth not". Commentators point out that, in the first case, Jeremiah refers to the cruel treatment of prisoners of war, something that he would have witnessed at the hands of the Chaldeans; in the second, to unrighteous decisions at law; and in the third, to defrauding a man of his legal rights. Whilst God always afflicts righteously, men afflict unrighteously.

Verses 37-47: His Appeal to the Nation
   Thus far in the elegy, Jeremiah has spoken of his own experiences, and drawn conclusions from them. He now applies his conclusions and gives counsel. He knew from experience the necessity for humility and calling upon God, and now he calls the nation to repentance. In appealing to the people to return to the Lord, the prophet calls for four conditions: recognition of His righteousness (vv.37-39); self-examination (v.40); absolute sincerity (v.41); and confession of sin (vv.42-47).

They must recognise God's righteousness (vv.37-39)
   "Who is he that saith, and it cometh to pass, when the Lord commanded it not?" (v.37). This emphasises that what had happened to Judah and Jerusalem was ordained by God. While the city had been overthrown by the Chaldeans, that "bitter and hasty nation" (Hab 1.6) had been raised up for that very purpose. Nebuchadrezzar was God's servant (Jer 25.9). The Lord reminds His people, moreover, that the execution of His will involves

calamity as well as blessing: "Out of the mouth of the most High proceedeth not evil and good?" (v.38). It hardly needs to be said that the meaning of "evil" here (7451) is not "sin" but "sorrow... wretchedness... adversity... afflictions... calamities" (Scofield). Since God always acts justly, no just complaint can be leveled against Him: "Wherefore doth a living man complain, a man for the punishment of his sins?" (v.39). The expression, "a living man", has been variously explained, and perhaps the best suggestion begins with Jeremiah's own words, "It is of the Lord's mercies that we are not consumed" (v.22), leading to the following: "Why doth a man whose life is spared him...complain of sufferings, which, however unjust as far as those who cause them are concerned, are, in relation to the sufferer, the just punishment of his own sins?" (Ellicott's Commentary).

The necessity for self-examination (v.40)

In view of the fact that their afflictions were, in the language of the dying thief, "the due reward of our deeds" (Lk 23.41), Jeremiah identifies himself with God's people in saying, "Let us search and try our ways, and turn again to the Lord", thus following the example of the psalmist: "I thought on my ways, and turned my feet unto thy testimonies" (Ps 119.59). There is a vast difference between self-occupation and self-examination, and the latter remains necessary, particularly with reference to partaking of the emblems at the Lord's Supper: "Let a man examine himself, and so let him eat" (1 Cor 11.28).

The necessity for absolute sincerity (v.41)

Well over a century before it had been said, "this people draw near me with their mouth, and with their lips do honour me, but have removed their heart far from me" (Is 29.13), and the insincerity of God's people at the time of Isaiah's ministry was still present when the Lord Jesus was on earth (Mt 15.8). The cry, "Let us lift up our heart with our hands unto God in the heavens", is echoed in the New Testament with reference to the assembly prayer meeting, "I will therefore that men pray every where, lifting up holy hands, without wrath and doubting" (1 Tim 2.8). The external form was to be matched by inward reality. In the words of Laetsch, "Let us not be satisfied with lifting up our hands, with the uplifted hands let us lift our hearts in sincere repentant prayer".

The necessity for confession of sin (vv.42-47)

The fact that God's people had not lifted up their hearts with their hands becomes apparent: "We have transgressed and have rebelled: thou hast not pardoned. Thou hast covered with anger ('Thou hast covered thyself with anger', JND), and persecuted us: thou hast slain, thou hast not pitied. Thou hast covered thyself with a cloud, that our prayer should not pass through" (vv.42-44). There had been no pardon because there had been no genuine repentance, and for that very reason their prayers had not been heard, recalling the words of the psalmist: "If I regard iniquity in my heart, the Lord will not hear me" (Ps 66.18). In fact, God's people had become so resolute in their sin, that on three occasions in his earlier ministry Jeremiah had been told that it would be vain for him to intercede on their behalf (Jer 7.16; 11.14; 14.11). The inevitable judgment had now fallen: "Thou hast made us as the offscouring and refuse in the midst of the people ('the peoples', JND). All our enemies have opened their mouths against us. Fear and a snare ('the pit', JND) is come upon us, desolation and destruction ('devastation and ruin', JND)" (vv.45-47). It is striking that while Judah and Jerusalem were regarded as "the offscouring (or 'sweepings…anything vile', Gesenius) and refuse" among the nations because of their disobedience, Paul and his fellow-labourers were treated as "the filth of the world, and…the offscouring of all things" (1 Cor 4.13) because of their obedience to the will of God!

Verses 48-51: His Approach to God
    The condition of the people under divine judgment caused the prophet deep sorrow, and at this point in his lament Jeremiah becomes again the "weeping prophet" (cp. 1.16; 2.11). It could be said that Jeremiah wept for his people (v.48); wept towards God (vv.49-50); and wept from his heart (v.51).

He wept for his people (v.48)
    "Mine eye runneth down with rivers of water for the destruction of the daughter of my people." The expression, "the destruction of the daughter of *my* people", should be noticed. Jeremiah did not distance himself from God's people or view them dispassionately; he did not enjoy the fact that his ministry had been vindicated. Rather, he felt their affliction deeply. Paul was similarly affected: "Therefore watch, and remember, that by the space of three years I ceased not to warn every one night and day with tears" (Acts 20.31); the parchment on which the first epistle to the assembly at Corinth was written was stained with his tears (2 Cor 2.4). Solomon said, "he that is glad at calamities shall not be unpunished" (Prov 17.5). "We cannot take pride, satisfaction, or credit from having escaped. Nor should one believer ever delight in the fall of another believer" (A. J. Higgins; *What the Bible Teaches: Proverbs*).

He wept toward God (vv.49-50)
    "Mine eye trickleth ('poureth', JND) down, and ceaseth not, without any intermission, Till the Lord look down, and behold from heaven." His tears were an appeal to God for mercy. The note of expectation should be observed: not, "*so that* the Lord might look down", but "*till* the Lord look down, and behold from heaven".

He wept from his heart (v.51)

These were not "crocodile tears": "Mine eye affecteth mine heart because of all the daughters of *my* city". While the expression, "the daughters of my city" could refer to "the villages, daughter towns of Jerusalem" (Streane), it seems more likely the prophet has in mind the young women whose suffering he has already lamented (cp. 1.4,18; 2.10,21). As already noted, Jeremiah did not view the ruined city and its distressed inhabitants dispassionately. What he saw touched him deeply. If the hands and hearts of God's people were to be in unison (v.41), then their eyes and heart are to follow suit. The Lord Jesus "saw the multitudes" and was "moved with compassion on them, because they fainted, and were scattered abroad, as sheep having no shepherd" (Mt 9.36). He, above all, could rightly say, "Mine eye affecteth mine heart".

Verses 52-66: His Adversity and his Adversaries

The concluding verses of the chapter are not without difficulty for the expositor. Very clearly, the prophet is addressing the Lord (vv.55, 58,59,61,64), but the capacity in which he does this can be understood in two different ways: either personally, in which case he looks back over his own experiences (vv.52-54), extols the faithfulness of the Lord in delivering him (vv.55-58), and calls upon the Lord to deal with his enemies (vv.59-66), or representatively, in which case he "speaks for the Israelites generally in their hour of suffering, especially of the godly" (Streane). It should be said that Streane gives both views without stating his preference. Laetsch espouses the latter view, stating, amongst other things, that the expression "in the dungeon" (v.53) cannot refer to the imprisonment of Jeremiah (Jer 38.4-6) since "there was no water flowing over his head" which "would have meant a swift death". However, since the prophet clearly used metaphorical language in vv.1-16, it is quite reasonable to conclude that he does so again here in describing his actual experiences in "the dungeon…that was in the court of the prison" (Jer 38.6).

Having said this, it has to be decided why Jeremiah refers here to his experiences at that particular time. Attention has been drawn to the prominence of "hope" in this elegy. It begins with hope born out of adversity, and now ends similarly. Jeremiah had been delivered from both mental anguish (vv.1-21) and physical harm (vv.52-58), and his experiences in this way are an example of the way in which the Lord can deliver His people when, like the prophet himself, they call upon Him (vv.55-58). In the first case the prophet enjoyed divine help *in* his circumstances, and in the second he enjoyed divine deliverance *from* his circumstances. Attention is drawn to his deliverance from death" (vv.52-58): "O Lord…thou hast redeemed my life" (v.58); and the destruction of his enemies (vv.59-66).

His deliverance from death (vv.52-58)

Jeremiah evidently refers to the relentless attempts of the princes to silence him: "Mine enemies chased me sore, like a bird, without cause. They have cut off my life in the dungeon, and cast a stone upon me" (vv.52-53). Having consigned him to prison "in the house of Jonathan the scribe" (Jer 37.15), the princes then put pressure on Zedekiah to authorise his consignment to the dungeon of Malchiah where, they hoped, he would die (Jer 38.4-6). While Laetsch insists that the words, "cast a stone upon me", mean "threw stones at me", rather than "to place a stone on the pit", others aver that the latter is quite admissible. As already noted, Laetsch's suggestion that Jeremiah cannot be referring to his experience in the dungeon, since he sank "in the mire" rather than being submerged in water (v.54), is hardly viable. As Streane observes, "Whether the reference be to the prophet as an individual or not, this must be merely a figure to express intense misery".

The intervention of Ebed-melech may well be in view in Jeremiah's account of his deliverance: "I called upon thy name, O Lord, out of the low dungeon. Thou hast heard my voice: hide not thine ear at my breathing, at my cry. Thou drewest near in the day that I called upon thee: thou saidst, Fear not. O Lord, thou hast pleaded the causes of my soul; thou hast redeemed my life" (vv.55-58). Jeremiah recognised that the Lord Himself had initiated his deliverance. Such language would be appropriate in the mouth of any believer. The word "redeemed" (1350) refers to the work of the "kinsman-redeemer" (cp. Lev 25.25, 47-55).

The destruction of his enemies (vv.59-66)

Having given thanks for his deliverance through the intervention of Ebed-melech, Jeremiah turns his attention to the men who had consigned him to the dungeon. These verses are quite self-explanatory: "O Lord, thou hast seen my wrong: judge thou my cause. Thou hast seen all their vengeance and all their imaginations against me. Thou hast heard their reproach, O Lord, and all their imaginations against me; The lips of those that rose up against me, and their device against me all the day. Behold their sitting down, and their rising up; I am their musick" (vv.59-63). According to Gesenius, the word "musick" (4485) means "a song, specially in mockery, a satire". Jeremiah had become the subject of their taunt-song.

Commentators who see in these verses the cry of the nation interpret the final request (vv.64-66) as her desire for the punishment of her "traditional enemies" (Kidner). It must be said, however, that the language of Jeremiah here is consistent with his earlier request for divine judgment on those who said, "Come, and let us devise devices against Jeremiah…and let us smite him with the tongue, and let us not give heed to any of his words", to which he cried, "forgive not their iniquity, neither blot out their sin from thy sight, but let them be overthrown before thee; deal thus with them in the time of thine anger" (Jer 18.18,23). Those who oppose the will of God and oppress His servants will not escape divine judgment: "Render unto them a recompence, O Lord, according to the work of their hands. Give them sorrow of heart, thy curse unto them. Persecute and destroy them in anger from under the heavens of the Lord". Of the Lord's people today it can be said, "it is a righteous thing with God to recompense tribulation to them that trouble you", to which Paul adds, "And to you who are troubled rest with us". While the Lord's people are so often "troubled" now, they will "rest" then, but those who "know not God, and that obey not the gospel of our Lord Jesus Christ" will "be punished with everlasting destruction from the presence of the Lord, and from the glory of his power" (2 Thess 1.6-9).

LAMENTATIONS 4

Like chapters 1 and 2, this chapter comprises twenty-two verses corresponding to the twenty-two letters of the Hebrew alphabet, with the difference that, whereas in chapters 1 and 2 each verse is composed of three lines, in chapter 4 each verse is composed of two lines.

The destruction of Jerusalem had been greeted with derision: "All that pass by clap their hands at thee; they hiss and wag their head at the daughter of Jerusalem, saying, Is this the city that men call The perfection of beauty, The joy of the whole earth?" (2.15). The passers-by made no attempt to even thinly veil their sarcasm. How utterly dreadful that God's people should have incurred His anger to the extent that He left them exposed to such mockery and opprobrium! It is incumbent upon the Lord's people to live and act in a manner which ensures "that the name of God and his doctrine be not blasphemed" (1 Tim 6.1). David gave "great occasion to the enemies of the Lord to blaspheme" (2 Sam 12.14). It would be sad beyond words should His people today do the same.

This chapter, which records Jeremiah's fourth elegy, is devoted to a tour of the city streets, once thronged by eager pilgrims who exclaimed, "Let us go into the house of the Lord. Our feet shall stand within thy gates, O Jerusalem. Jerusalem is builded as a city that is compact together: Whither the tribes go up, the tribes of the Lord, unto the testimony of Israel, to give thanks unto the name of the Lord" (Ps 122.1-4). But the streets of Jerusalem now mirrored the city's desolation and the reduced circumstances of its inhabitants. The beauty and joy of Jerusalem had given place to ugliness and sorrow.

There are five references in the chapter to the city streets (vv.1,5,8,14,18), and these may be used to divide the elegy as follows:

> The Rubble in the Streets (vv.1-2)
> The Poor in the Streets (vv.3-6)
> The Nazarites in the Streets (vv.7-10)
> The Blind in the Streets (vv.11-16)
> The Danger in the Streets (vv.17-20); it should be said that the word (7339) used in v.18 could also mean "an open place", or "forum" (Gesenius)
> The chapter concludes with: The Judgment upon Edom (vv.21-22).

Verses 1-2: The Rubble in the Streets

Glory had gone: "How is the gold become dim! how is the most fine gold changed! the stones of the sanctuary are poured out in the top of every street. The precious sons of Zion, comparable to fine gold, how are they esteemed as earthen pitchers, the work of the hands of the potter!" Attention is drawn to the place (v.1); and to the people (v.2).

The place (v.1)

Jeremiah evidently refers here to the Temple, although some commentators suggest that that "the expressions are metaphorically used for the people themselves" (Streane). Some support for this suggestion may be found in the fact that the children of Jerusalem "faint for hunger in the top of every street" (2.19). The references to "gold" and "the most fine gold" do, however, recall the construction of the Temple by Solomon, who "overlaid the house within with pure gold: and he made a partition by the chains of gold before the oracle; and he overlaid it with gold. And the whole house he overlaid with gold, until he had finished all the house: also the whole altar that was by the oracle he overlaid with gold" (1 Kings 6.21-22). Nebuchadnezzar destroyed this magnificent building: "And all the vessels of the house of God, great and small, and the treasures of the house of the Lord....he brought to Babylon. And they burnt the house of God" (2 Chr 36.18-19). This was only allowed to take place after "the Lord God of their fathers" had "sent to them by his messengers, rising up betimes, and sending; because he had compassion on his people, and on his dwelling place", but His mercy and longsuffering were totally rejected: "But they mocked the messengers of God, and despised his words, and misused his prophets, until the wrath of the Lord arose against his people, till there was no remedy" (2 Chr 36.15-16). Following their disobedience and rebellion, "the gold" had "become dim" and "the sanctuary" had been dismantled. The rubble was in the streets for all to see.

The lesson must not be ignored. The passage emphasises two features of the Temple: its gold, which symbolises divine glory, and its function as a sanctuary, which stresses divine sanctity. Both had gone. In the New Testament, the "house of God" is "the church of the living God" (1 Tim 3.15), referring to the local assembly. It is a place where the glory of Christ must be revered and displayed: a place where people say, with Thomas, "My Lord and my God" (Jn 20.28). It is therefore a place of sanctity and holiness: "Know ye not that ye are the temple of God, and that the Spirit of God dwelleth in you? If any man defile the temple of God, him shall God destroy; for the temple of God is holy, which temple ye are" (1 Cor 3.16-17). But, alas, "How is the gold become dim!" The glory and dignity of Christ has become dimmed in the appreciation of many by over-familiarity. "My Lord and my God" has become the "Sweet Jesus" of modern so-called hymnology. In some places the "temple of God" has completely lost its divinely-ordained character.

The people (v.2)

The people were precious to God as well. They are described as "The precious sons of Zion, comparable to fine gold". But disobedience and rebellion had cheapened the people of God, and changed their character. According to Unger, "a potter was one of the lowliest of the common labourers, a worker whose products were so trifling in value that they could be replaced with little expenditure". The words, "the work of the hands of the potter", are therefore a very sad commentary on the state of God's people. Instead of reflecting their divinely-given position as "a peculiar treasure unto me above all people" (Ex 19.5), they had become nothing more than ordinary people. Like Samson, they had "become weak...like any other man" (Judg 16.17).

It should surely be the desire of each child of God today to be "a vessel unto honour, sanctified, and meet for the master's use, and prepared unto every good work" (2 Tim 2.21).

Verses 3-6: The Poor in the Streets

Prosperity had gone: "They that did feed delicately are desolate in the streets; they that were brought up in scarlet embrace dunghills" (v.5). This section of the chapter describes the terrible result of famine. The jackals were kinder to their young than the mothers of Jerusalem were to theirs "Even the sea monsters ('jackals', JND) draw out the breast, they give suck to their young ones: the daughter of my people is become cruel, like the ostriches in the wilderness. The tongue of the sucking child cleaveth to the roof of his mouth for thirst: the young children ask bread, and no man breaketh it unto them" (vv.3-4). The reference to the ostriches is explained in the book of Job: "the ostrich...Which leaveth her eggs in the earth, and warmeth them in dust, And forgetteth that the foot may crush them, or that the wild beast may break them. She is hardened against her young ones, as though they were not hers" (Job 39.13-16). It should be the prayer of every assembly that there will be men and women who will break the bread of life to children. "Unspeakably sad is the state of God's people when their assemblies are not like nurseries where new-born babes and young saints can find nourishing food such as is suitable for them" (Ironside).

Jeremiah observes that the people in the streets of Jerusalem were once well fed (v.5a); and once well clothed (v.5b).

They were once well fed (v.5a)

"They that did feed delicately" were "desolate in the streets". According to Unger, the words, "They that did feed delicately", mean that "they that used to feed on delicacies". Today, healthy eating is all the rage! But spiritual healthy eating is even more important, and Jeremiah himself is a prime example: "Thy words were found, and I did eat them; and thy word was unto me the joy and rejoicing of mine heart" (Jer 15.16). Like Timothy, the Lord's people need to be "nourished up in the words of faith and of good doctrine" (1 Tim 4.6). The Epistle to the Hebrews describes a sad situation: "For when for the time ye ought to be teachers, ye have need that one teach you again which be the first principles of the oracles of God" (Heb 5.12). These believers had been saved sufficiently long to be teachers, but, sadly, they seemed to have forgotten the very teaching that they should have imparted to others. Tragically, there are believers today who once feasted on the Word of God, and frequented places where it was taught, but are now "desolate in the streets". The overall lesson of these verses must not be forgotten; sin and disobedience had brought God's people to these reduced circumstances, and sin and disobedience will deprive the Lord's people today of their spiritual food.

They were once well clothed (v.5b)

"They that were brought up in scarlet embrace dunghills." They did this, according to Streane, "for want of a better couch". Scarlet attire (8144) was evidently worn by well-dressed people. David called on the "daughters of Israel" to "weep over Saul, who clothed you in scarlet, with other delights" (2 Sam 1.24), and the "virtuous woman" was "not afraid of the snow for her household: for all her household are clothed with scarlet" (Prov 31.21). According to Ellicott's Commentary, the words "brought up" are, literally, "that were carried (as children are carried)", and scarlet "stands for the shawls or garments of the rich, dyed, as they were, in the Tyrian purple or crimson".

The Lord's people should make it clear that they are "clothed…with the garments of salvation" and "covered…with the robe of righteousness" (Is 61.10). As noted, scarlet was associated with the upper classes, and those who once wore the attire of the noble and the rich, were scavenging on the city refuse tips. It is appalling to see men and women searching for food in rubbish bins today, and it is equally appalling when believers scavenge on the rubbish dumps of this world. The Lord's people are to display the features of the "royal priesthood" (1 Pet 2.9) and, like Mephibosheth, "eat continually at the king's table" (2 Sam 9.13).

The lingering judgment of God upon His people is contrasted with the instantaneous removal of Sodom: "the punishment of the iniquity of the daughter of my people is greater than the punishment of the sin of Sodom, that was overthrown as in a moment, and no hands stayed on her" (v.6). The overthrow of Sodom was accomplished without human aid: "the Lord rained upon Sodom and upon Gomorrah brimstone and fire from the Lord out of heaven" (Gen 19.24).

Verses 7-10: The Nazarites in the Streets

Beauty had gone: the once striking Nazarites were now unrecognisable: "they are not known in the streets" (v.8). It should be said that some commentators suggest that since the word translated "Nazarite" (5139), meaning "one separated", is elsewhere translated "separate" (Gen 49.26) or "separated" (Deut 33.16), it has here the meaning of "princes", since they are separated as a class from their fellow-countrymen. But this seems rather tortuous, and Ellicott's Commentary is surely correct in saying that "There is no reason…for abandoning the rendering of the Authorised Version". Ellicott's Commentary continues by saying that the "reference to the Nazarites in Amos 2.11-12 shows that they were prominent as a body during the history of the monarchy". The vow of the Nazarite, or "Nazirite", is described in detail in Numbers 6. Attention is drawn to two most important lessons: that separation to God is beautiful (v.7); and that identification with the world is pitiful (v.8).

Separation to God is beautiful (v.7)

It is important to remember that the Nazarite vow involved devotion to the Lord: it was "unto the Lord" (Num 6.2,5,6,8,12,21). The strength of the Nazarite's devotion enabled him to abstain from three things: "He shall separate himself from wine and strong drink…All the days of the vow of his separation there shall no rasor come upon his head…All the days that he separateth himself unto the Lord he shall come at no dead body" (Num 6.3,5,6). The vow involved separation from things which were in themselves quite legitimate, but which were to have no place in the life of a man or woman (Num 6.2) who was separated to the Lord. The Nazarite behaved differently: he (or she) did not conform. Believers of whom it can be truly said, "the consecration of his God is upon his head" (Num 6.7), may well encounter ridicule, sometimes, sadly, from fellow believers who regard them as being rather odd. But this is not the divine assessment of people who "separate themselves unto the Lord". He describes them quite differently.

He speaks about their purity

"Her Nazarites were purer than snow, they were whiter than milk." Men and women who "separate themselves unto the Lord" (Num 6.2) are "partakers of the divine nature, having escaped the corruption that is in the world through lust" (2 Pet 1.4).

He speaks about their health

"They were more ruddy (119) in body than rubies." Gesenius inclines to the view that "rubies" (6443) could be translated "red coral". This recalls the picture of health that greeted Samuel when David appeared: "Now he was ruddy (132), and withal of a beautiful countenance" (1 Sam 16.12). David is also described as "ruddy (132), and of a fair countenance" (1 Sam 17.42). Men and women who "separate themselves unto the Lord" enjoy prosperity of soul (3 Jn v.2).

He speaks about their beauty

"Their polishing was of sapphire." The word "polishing" appears to mean "cut and polished", leading Streane to say that "their well-shaped figures suggested a carefully cut precious stone". Sapphire, the heavenly colour (Ex 24.10; Ezek 1.26), points to a heavenly demeanour, deportment, and manner of life. Men and women who "separate themselves unto the Lord" can rightly say, "let the beauty of the Lord our God be upon us" (Ps 90.17).

Identification with the world is pitiful (v.8)

The Nazarites were no longer recognised in the streets. They had changed immeasurably, something that should remind the Lord's people that sin and disobedience will deprive them of spiritual beauty. The fact that even the Nazarites were not exempt from the dreadful conditions in Jerusalem suggests that they too were party to the sins which had brought divine judgment.

Once "whiter than milk", their visage had become "blacker than a coal", or "darker than blackness" (JND). This evidently refers to the effect of famine: "our skin was black like an oven because of the terrible famine" (5.10). The Lord's people must beware lest they too become "blacker than a coal", not because spiritual nourishment is unavailable, but because they fail to draw on the rich provision of God whose "divine power hath given unto us all things that pertain unto life and godliness" (2 Pet 1.3).

Once "more ruddy in body than rubies", now "their skin cleaveth to their bones". How different to the description of the man described by the psalmist: "The righteous shall flourish like the palm tree: he shall grow like a cedar in Lebanon....they shall be fat and flourishing" (Ps 92.12,14)!

Once "their polishing was of sapphire", now their skin had become "withered" and resembled "a stick". In the words of Unger, "They were a picture of walking famine, with their skin shrunk over their bones and become dry as wood".

The verses which follow enlarge on the famine conditions: "They that be slain with the sword are better than they that be slain with hunger: for these pine away, stricken through for want of the fruits of the field" (v.9). This needs no explanation: those that died quickly by the sword experienced less suffering than those who died slowly through famine and hunger. Worse follows: "The hands of the pitiful women have sodden their own children: they were their meat in the destruction of the daughter of my people" (v.10). Streane points out that the words "pitiful women" mean not "full of pity", but "much to be pitied". As Unger observes, "The horror of the siege is portrayed with awesome pathos" with women "boiling their own children (cp. 2.20; 2 Kings 6.29; Jer 19.9), reduced by frightful straits to the spectre of cannibalism (Deut 28.53-57)".

Verses 11-16: The Blind in the Streets

Authority had gone: the prophet and the priest were silent. "For the sins of her prophets, and the iniquities of her priests, that have shed the blood of the just in the midst of her, They have wandered as blind men in the streets" (vv.13-14). Attention is drawn to their role in the fall of Jerusalem (vv.11-14); and their rejection by the people of Jerusalem (vv.15-16).

Their role in the fall of Jerusalem (vv.11-14)

It is not without significance that the prophets and priests are mentioned in connection with the reason for the desolation and suffering of Jerusalem. This lies at the heart of the elegy: "The Lord hath accomplished his fury; he hath poured out his fierce anger, and hath kindled a fire in Zion, and it hath devoured the foundations thereof" (v.11). Its destruction had caused astonishment (v.12). Jerusalem's neighbours had referred to the former beauty of Jerusalem (2.15), but they evidently also regarded it as impregnable, perhaps in view of the marvellous deliverance in the days of Hezekiah (2 Chr 32.21-22), which is a salutary reminder that there is no strength in reputation alone. The Lord Jesus said of the church in Sardis, "thou hast a name that thou livest, and art dead" (Rev 3.1). The fact that reference is next made to the sins of the prophets and priests emphasises that failure to communicate the Word of God faithfully, and failure to approach God with sincerity, must bring disaster to the most illustrious assembly.

As already noted, the major responsibility for this tragedy is laid firmly at the door of the men who had failed to give good spiritual leadership to the nation: "The kings of the earth, and all the inhabitants of the world, would not have believed that the adversary and the enemy should enter into the gates of Jerusalem. It is for the sins of her prophets, and the iniquities of her priests, who have shed the blood of the righteous in the midst of her" (vv.12-13, JND). The RV reads similarly. Prophets and priests played a key role in the life of the nation. The prophet represented God to the people, and the priest represented the people to God, but there was now no word from God through the prophets, who in any case had spoken "a vision of their own heart, and not out of the mouth of the Lord" (Jer 23.16), nor worship of God by the priests, who in any case were so spiritually obtuse that they had said, "Where is the Lord?" (Jer 2.8). Prophet and priest were alike impotent: "they have wandered ('staggered', Gesenius) as blind men in the streets" (v.14). They could not discern God's will. Nothing had changed in over a hundred years, for the Lord had said through Isaiah, "His watchmen are blind: they are all ignorant, they are all dumb dogs, they cannot bark; sleeping, lying down, loving to slumber" (Is 56.10).

The enormity of their crimes is conveyed by the words, "they have polluted themselves with blood, so that men could not touch their garments" (v.14), referring to their injustice and heinous crimes. These men evidently followed in the steps of the northern priests, of whom it is said, "as troops of robbers wait for a man, so the company of priests murder in the way by consent: for they commit lewdness" (Hos 6.9). The New Testament warns against spiritual bloodshed: "But if ye bite and devour one another, take heed that ye be not consumed one of another" (Gal 5.15).

Their rejection by the people of Jerusalem (vv.15-16)

The prophets and priests were held in such low esteem that those that met them in the streets "cried unto them, Depart ye; it is unclean; depart,

depart, touch not" (v.15). People "warned them off with the leper's cry, *Unclean, unclean!* (Lev 13.45)…corresponding with the cry which in the case of leprosy the afflicted man was himself to raise" (Streane).

But even worse, their evil reputation reached the ears of the heathen. God's people had such a bad name that "when they fled away and wandered, they said among the heathen, They shall no more sojourn there" (v.15). They would be "like vagabonds, for no nation would permit them to settle down" (Laetsch). They were no longer regarded by the Lord, and they were not respected by men: "The anger of the Lord hath divided ('hath dispersed', JND margin) them; he will no more regard them: they respected not the persons of the priests, they favoured not the elders" (v.16). Centuries later, Paul censured the Jews for bringing God's name into disrepute: "For the name of God is blasphemed among the Gentiles through you" (Rom 2.24). How necessary it is for the Lord's people to "Walk in wisdom toward them that are without" (Col 4.5), and to "give none occasion to the adversary to speak reproachfully" (1 Tim 5.14).

Verses 17-20: The Danger in the Streets

Liberty had gone: "They hunt our steps, that we cannot go in our streets" (v.18). Peter counsels his readers to be "sober, be vigilant; because your adversary the devil, as a roaring lion, walketh about, seeking whom he may devour: Whom resist stedfast in the faith, knowing that the same afflictions are accomplished in your brethren that are in the world" (1 Pet 5.8-9). It is one thing, however, for God's people to contend with an enemy in the world: it is quite another for them to contend with an enemy in their midst. The New Testament is not silent in this connection. Paul warned the Ephesian elders that after his departure "shall grievous wolves enter in among you, not sparing the flock. Also of your own selves shall men arise, speaking perverse things, to draw away disciples after them" (Acts 20.29-30). Further passages on the subject are found in Galatians 2.4; 2 Peter 2.1; Jude v.4. Attention is drawn to the following: the failure of Egypt (v.17); the freedom lost (v.18); and the flight from the city (vv.19-20).

The failure of Egypt (v.17)

The "nation that could not save us" (v.17) was evidently Egypt. "Then Pharaoh's army was come forth out of Egypt: and when the Chaldeans that besieged Jerusalem heard tidings of them, they departed from Jerusalem. Then came the word of the Lord unto the prophet Jeremiah, saying, Thus saith the Lord, the God of Israel; Thus shall ye say to the king of Judah…Behold, Pharaoh's army, which is come forth to help you, shall return to Egypt into their own land. And the Chaldeans shall come again, and fight against this city, and take it, and burn it with fire" (Jer 37.5-8). Jerusalem had to cry, "And as for us, our eyes yet failed for our vain help".

It was a case of "Hope deferred maketh the heart sick" (Prov 13.12). The lesson is so clear: look to the world for help, and it will bring disappointment and ruin.

The freedom lost (v.18)

The words, "They hunt our steps, that we cannot go in our streets: our end is near, our days are fulfilled; for our end is come" (v.18), are explained in the following way by Streane: "This expresses either the definite danger which existed in the more exposed parts of the city, from the towers advanced gradually nearer to the walls by the besiegers, in which they lay in wait and let fly at the citizens, or in general it denotes the constant dread which beset their hearts under the figure of game for which the hunter lies in wait". Since, however, Jeremiah is evidently referring to current conditions in Jerusalem, he may be describing "the stringent controls exercised by the Babylonian conquerors over those who were allowed to remain in the land under the governorship of Gedaliah. The Babylonians were determined to forestall any possible future uprisings in Judah" (Harrison). Very clearly, the people of Jerusalem could not even move about freely in the streets of their own city, which has its counterpart in early New Testament assembly life, of which Paul wrote, "I went up again to Jerusalem…And that because of false brethren unawares brought in, who came in privily to spy out our liberty which we have in Christ Jesus, that they might bring us into bondage" (Gal 2.1,4).

The flight from the city (vv.19-20)

Enemy activity extended beyond the city walls: "Our persecutors are swifter than the eagles of the heaven: they pursued us upon the mountains, they laid wait for us in the wilderness" (v.19). The choice of words is exact: the enemy is likened to "the eagles of the heaven", and in explaining the parable of the "great eagle with great wings, longwinged, full of feathers, which had divers colours", the Lord said, "Know ye not what these things mean? tell them, Behold, the king of Babylon is come to Jerusalem" (Ezek 17.3,12). When Zedekiah and his "men of war" attempted to flee, "the Chaldeans' army pursued after them, and overtook Zedekiah in the plains of Jericho" (Jer 39.4-5).

Reference is evidently made to this in v.20: "The breath of our nostrils, the anointed of the Lord (Zedekiah, the anointed king), was taken in their pits (or 'snares'), of whom we said, Under his shadow we shall live among the heathen". Judah obviously pinned their hopes on Zedekiah. He was "The breath of (their) nostrils". As Streane observes, "We are to remember that whatever may have been his personal weaknesses (and he was weak rather than vicious), he was the one on whom the whole of the people's hopes depended for the continuance of their national life". All of which proves how inadvisable it is to rely on men. The people who had said, "Under his shadow we shall live among the heathen", would have been far better to have remembered that "He that dwelleth in the secret place of the most High shall abide under the shadow of the Almighty" (Ps 91.1).

Verses 21-22: Judgment upon Edom

The elegy concludes with a message for Edom, the people of whom the psalmist said, "Remember, O Lord, the children of Edom in the day of Jerusalem; who said, Rase it, rase it, even to the foundation thereof" (Ps 137.7). The same Psalm continues with reference to Babylon: "O daughter of Babylon, who art to be destroyed; happy shall he be, that rewardeth thee as thou hast served us" (v.8). Edom had a history of perpetual hatred for God's people: "For three transgressions of Edom, and for four, I will not turn away the punishment thereof; because he did pursue his brother with the sword, and did cast off all pity, and his anger did tear perpetually, and he kept his wrath for ever" (Amos 1.11). Edom's "wrath" was vented upon God's people at the destruction of Jerusalem, causing Obadiah to say, "thou shouldest not have looked on the day of thy brother in the day that he became a stranger; neither shouldest thou have rejoiced over the children of Judah in the day of their destruction; neither shouldest thou have spoken proudly in the day of distress….thou shouldest not have looked on their affliction in the day of their calamity…Neither shouldest thou have stood in the crossway, to cut off those of his that did escape" (Ob vv.12-14).

Undoubtedly, it was Edom's hatred of his brother-nation at the destruction of Jerusalem that led Jeremiah, under the guidance of the Holy Spirit, to refer to him at the conclusion of this elegy: "Rejoice and be glad, O daughter of Edom, that dwellest in the land of Uz; the cup also shall pass through unto thee: thou shalt be drunken, and shalt make thyself naked" (v.21). Edom is told to enjoy her triumph while she can: it would be short-lived, and she would soon drink from "the cup" of God's wrath, with consequent "drunkenness" and "nakedness", which "is a figurative way of saying, 'thou shalt be exposed in the eyes of the world to the contempt which attends upon disaster'" (Streane). Uz (cp. Job 1.1) appears to have been in the region of Edom, possibly extending to the eastern boundary of Egypt. Laetsch calls Uz the "border state" of Edom.

The concluding statement, "The punishment of thine iniquity is accomplished, O daughter of Zion; he will no more carry thee away into captivity" (v.22), had an interim fulfilment in that there was no further deportation for some 400 years, but it remains "a prophecy transcending the Roman Diaspora of AD 70 and yet awaiting fulfilment in Israel's final regathering for Kingdom blessing (Amos 9.15)" (Unger). There is a striking similarity between Jeremiah's language here and that of Isaiah: "Speak ye comfortably to Jerusalem, and cry unto her, that her warfare is accomplished, that her iniquity is pardoned" (Is 40.2). The Pulpit Commentary calls Jeremiah's words "a gleam of prophetic hope" and continues, "From doleful lamentations the poet is able to look forward and see the end of the sad desolation of Jerusalem".

While, in the interim, divine judgment fell on Edom at the hand of the Babylonians some five years after the fall of Jerusalem, with Antigonus, a general of Alexander the Great, crushing Edom in 312 BC, the Maccabees almost wiping out the Edomites in 2 BC, and the last remnant of Edom perishing during the Roman siege of Jerusalem, the book of Obadiah points to a future revival of Edomite power (Ob vv.17-21). But "the house of Jacob shall be a fire, and the house of Joseph a flame, and the house of Esau ('Esau is Edom', Gen 36.8) for stubble...and there shall not be any remaining of the house of Esau; for the Lord hath spoken it".

LAMENTATIONS 5

While this chapter comprises twenty-two verses, and the English reader might therefore have expected further correspondence with the letters of the Hebrew alphabet, the final elegy does not follow the structure of previous laments. As noted in the introduction, Ellicott's Commentary suggests that at this point "the writer found himself too overwhelmed by emotion to keep within the limits of the artificial plan he had before prescribed to himself". Morrish's New and Concise Bible Dictionary reads similarly: in previous chapters, "all had been confessed, and hope in God had been expressed", and now "an affecting appeal is made to God". The chapter commences and concludes with an appeal: "Remember, O Lord, what is come upon us...Turn thou us unto thee, O Lord, and we shall be turned; renew our days as of old" (vv.1,21).

The chapter may be divided with reference to three words occurring in the text: "*Remember*, O Lord" (v.1); "Thou, O Lord, *remainest*" (v.19); "O Lord...*renew* our days as of old" (v.21), leading to the following analysis:

> Confession of Sin (vv.1-18)
> Confidence in the Lord (v.19)
> Cry for Restoration (vv.20-22).

Verses 1-18: Confession of Sin

In these verses Jeremiah describes the sad condition of God's people. They are a synopsis of the preceding chapters, and form the basis of the appeal to God for mercy. It might be helpful at this juncture to make some general observations.

These verses are not a complaint, but a confession

This is made very clear indeed: "woe unto us, that we have sinned!" (v.16). The consequences of their sin are set out in detail. It is a painful confession, and recalls the oft-quoted words of the New Testament teaching: "If we confess our sins, he is faithful and just to forgive us our sins" (1 Jn 1.9), where, let it be carefully noted, John does not say, "If we confess our sin", but "If we confess our sins". The very process of detailed confession to God brings true sorrow and thorough-going repentance, which are pre-requisites for forgiveness. In David's words, "The sacrifices of God are a broken spirit: a broken and a contrite heart, O God, thou wilt not despise" (Ps 51.17).

These verses demonstrate God's faithfulness to His word

Deuteronomy 28 sets out the "blessings" (v.2) and the "curses" (v.15) following obedience and disobedience respectively. The "curses" (vv.15-68) are introduced with the words, "If thou wilt not hearken unto the voice of the Lord thy God...that all these curses shall come upon thee, and overtake thee" (v.15), including the despoliation of the nation by an invader: "The Lord shall bring a nation against thee from far, from the end of the earth, as swift as the eagle flieth (cp. 4.19)...A nation of fierce countenance, which shall not regard the person of the old, nor shew favour to the young: And he shall eat the fruit of thy cattle, and the fruit of thy land...And he shall besiege thee in all thy gates...And thou shalt eat the fruit of thine own body" (vv.49-53). Jeremiah now recounts the fulfilment of Moses' warning.

This serves to emphasise that it is perilous to ignore the word of God. Zechariah made this very plain indeed: "But my words and my statutes, which I commanded my servants the prophets, did they not take hold of (overtake) your fathers? and they returned and said, Like as the Lord of hosts thought to do unto us, according to our ways, and according to our doings, so hath he dealt with us" (Zech 1.6). Zechariah vividly describes the inescapable power of God's word in the vision of the "flying roll" (Zech 5.1-4).

These verses describe the weakness of God's people before their enemies

This is conveyed by the words, "consider, and behold our reproach" (v.1), which are best understood with reference to earlier passages in the book: "All that pass by clap their hands at thee; they hiss and wag their head at the daughter of Jerusalem, saying, Is this the city that men call The perfection of beauty, The joy of the whole earth?" (2.15); "The kings of the earth, and all the inhabitants of the world, would not have believed that the adversary and the enemy should have entered into the gates of Jerusalem" (4.12). The words of Asaph may be used to sum up the situation: "We are become a reproach to our neighbours, a scorn and derision to them that are round about us...Wherefore should the heathen say, Where is their God?" (Ps 79.4,10). How important it is for the Lord's people to live and act in a manner which gives "none occasion to the adversary to speak reproachfully" (1 Tim 5.14).

As to Lamentations 5, the "reproach" so deeply felt by God's people arose from their reduced circumstances, including loss of possessions (vv.2-4); loss of power (vv.5-10); loss of people (vv.11-13); and loss of the place (vv.14-18).

Loss of possessions (vv.2-4)

"Our inheritance is turned to strangers, our houses to aliens. We are orphans and fatherless, our mothers are as widows. We have drunken our water for money; our wood is sold unto us." The words, "our inheritance...our houses...our mothers...our water...our wood", should be noted. God's people had lost the joy, the liberty and the benefits of their inheritance. The Lord had given them "a land of hills and valleys, and drinketh water of the rain of heaven: A land which the Lord thy God careth for: the eyes of the Lord thy God are always upon it, from the beginning of the year even unto the end of the year" (Deut 11.11-12). But now they had to say, "Our inheritance is turned to strangers" (v.2). The words, "our mothers are as widows" suggest that "their husbands, though living, were carried into exile, and they were as destitute as though they had been deprived of them by death" (Ellicott's Commentary). The same meaning attaches to the words, "We are orphans and fatherless".

The New Testament refers to the believer's inheritance today. It is described in one place as "an inheritance incorruptible, and undefiled, and that fadeth not away, reserved in heaven for you" (1 Pet 1.4), but in another place reference is made to the believer's current inheritance, for God has already "blessed us with all spiritual blessings in heavenly places in Christ" (Eph 1.3). Although He has made abundant provision for the spiritual welfare of His children in bestowing upon them "all things that pertain unto life and godliness" (2 Pet 1.3), sin and disobedience will dissipate their peace and joy. While the confession in the current chapter makes sad reading indeed, God's people, for whom Jeremiah speaks representatively, were at least thoroughly aware of their low straits, unlike Samson who "wist not that the Lord was departed from him" (Judg 16.20). The Lord's words, "Remember therefore from whence thou art fallen, and repent, and do the first works" (Rev 2.5), are salutary advice to every wayward believer, let alone to every wayward assembly.

The details in these verses are an eloquent reminder that the enemy will intrude into every aspect of a believer's life. He will intrude into his domestic life: "our houses to aliens" (v.2); into his family life: "We are orphans and fatherless" (v.3); into his resources: their water and their wood were no longer freely available (v.4). Erstwhile Christian homes have been invaded by alien influences; Christian families have been destroyed by immorality and divorce; many believers who once enjoyed the liberty of gathering according to the Scriptures now find themselves in bondage to man-made arrangements. The enemy has not changed; he will still take every opportunity to deprive God's people of their enjoyment of divinely-imparted blessings and privileges. As Ironside points out, those "who here complain that they have drunken their water for money, had foolishly forsaken Him who is 'the Fountain of living waters' (of which all might drink freely), and had hewed out for themselves cisterns that could hold no water (Jer 2.13)".

Loss of power (vv.5-10)

This is demonstrated in various ways. Joshua had said that "One man of you shall chase a thousand: for the Lord your God, he it is that fighteth for you, as he hath promised you", but he went on to say, "Take good heed therefore unto yourselves, that ye love the Lord your God", and if they failed to do this, then "as all good things are come upon you, which the Lord your God promised you; so shall the Lord bring upon you all evil

things, until he have destroyed you from off this good land which the
Lord your God hath given you" (Josh 23.10,11,15). The book of
Lamentations proves that Joshua, like Moses before him, was not mistaken.

Their servitude to the invader brought loss of power
   "Our necks are under persecution ('our pursuers are on our necks',
JND): we labour and have no rest" (v.5). Jeremiah uses the figure of a
toiling slave to describe Israel, thus fulfilling the prediction of Moses,
"Therefore thou shalt serve thine enemies which the Lord shall send against
thee...and he shall put a yoke of iron upon thy neck" (Deut 28.48). The
"yoke of iron" had been placed on the necks of God's people and their
near-neighbours by Nebuchadnezzar, although his conquests had been
initiated by the Lord Himself: "For thus saith the Lord of hosts, the God of
Israel; I have put a yoke of iron upon the neck of all these nations, that the
may serve Nebuchadnezzar king of Babylon" (Jer 28.14). It is quite possible
that Jeremiah alludes here to "the ancient practice of a victor placing his
foot on the neck of a prostrate enemy to symbolise complete subjugation
(cp. Josh 10.24; Is 51.23)" (Harrison).
   It is worth pointing out that the Tekoite nobles were not subject to a
"yoke of iron", but neither did they "put...their necks to the work of
their Lord" (Neh 3.5), as opposed to Priscilla and Aquila, who were
willing to expose themselves to risk, leading Paul to say of them, "who
have for my life laid down ('staked' or 'hazarded') their own necks
('neck', JND)" (Rom 16.4).
   The tolerance of sin in a believer's life will be accompanied by
lessening resistance to temptation. Even children of God can become
enslaved to evil habits and practices. Sin is a hard taskmaster: "we labour,
and have no rest" (v.5). Before he confessed his sin and enjoyed God's
forgiveness, David had "no rest": "When I kept silence, my bones waxed
old through my roaring all the day long. For day and night thy hand
was heavy upon me: my moisture is turned into the drought of summer.
Selah" (Ps 32.3-4).

The compromise of the fathers brought loss of power
   "We have given the hand to the Egyptians, and to the Assyrians, to be
satisfied with bread" (v.6). According to Laetsch, the expression "given the
hand" signified the "pledge of surrender" (Jer 50.15). God's people had
made an agreement with the Egyptians and Assyrians to supply food. This
may refer to past alliances on the part of the kings of Judah. Ahaz, for one,
sent "unto the kings of Assyria to help him" (2 Chr 28.16) and Zedekiah,
for another, sought help from Egypt (Ezek 17.15), but without any beneficial
result. The northern kingdom also sought help from Egypt and Assyria
(Hos 7.11), and paid the price for acting in this way (Hos 9.3). How sad
that God's people found it necessary to go elsewhere for nourishment,
and it is equally sad when believers today seek satisfaction in worldly

pursuits, instead of being "nourished up in the words of faith and of good doctrine" (1 Tim 4.6), commodities that the world can never supply.

Harrison suggests that Jeremiah refers here to "the desperate plight of the remnant under Gedaliah, which had become so critical that they would gladly ally with either Egypt or Assyria (named here as a surrogate for Babylonia) if it would ensure their survival". While this suggestion is worthy of consideration, it overlooks the apparent connection with the following verse (v.7), namely, that the compromise of past generations in this way, as indicated above, had exerted a baneful influence on their successors. While this would not always be the case, since a time would come when "they shall say no more, The fathers have eaten a sour grape, and the children's teeth are set on edge" (Jer 31.29), Jeremiah was obliged to say in the present circumstances, "Our fathers have sinned, and are not; and we have borne their iniquities" (v.7). The fathers had no thought for succeeding generations, and believers today must never forget that their actions too have far-reaching consequences. Who would have thought that Israel's sin at the foot of Mount Sinai (Ex 32.8) would be imitated centuries later by Jeroboam, the son of Nebat (1 Kings 12.28)? Every generation of believers should be deeply concerned about the kind of spiritual legacy it will leave for others. It is so important to build well for the future. Short term methods - for example, entertainment instead of Bible teaching, and compromise with the world rather than fidelity to the Scriptures - will often produce short term results numerically and in interest, whereas building for the long term may sometimes look rather pedestrian, and appear to produce very little immediate result, but time will prove its lasting value.

The rule of servants over them brought loss of power

"Servants have ruled over us: there is none that doth deliver us out of their hand" (v.8). Had Jeremiah named Nebuchadnezzar, or his captain, Nebuzar-adan, the people might have pleaded some excuse, but "servants"! God's people were so weak, that even servants could dominate them. In the words of Agur, "For three things the earth is disquieted, and for four which it cannot bear: For a servant when he reigneth" (Prov 30.21-22), and in the words of Solomon, "I have seen servants upon horses, and princes walking as servants upon the earth" (Eccl 10.7). God's people had become spiritual Canaanites: "Cursed be Canaan; a servant of servants shall he be unto his brethren" (Gen 9.25).

The fear of ambush brought loss of power

"We gat our bread with the peril of our lives because of the sword of the wilderness" (v.9). According to Streane, this refers to "the bands of wild Arabs (Bedaween), seeking opportunities for the plunder of those who venture from the shelter of the city to reap the harvest". God's people were not sufficiently strong to withstand and rout people who were intent on robbing them. It is for precisely this reason that the New Testament requires an assembly overseer to hold "fast the faithful word as he hath been taught, that he may be able by sound doctrine both to exhort and to convince the gainsayers. For there are many unruly and vain talkers and deceivers, specially they of the circumcision: Whose mouths must be stopped, who subvert whole houses, teaching things which they ought not, for filthy lucre's sake" (Titus 1.9-11).

The ravages of famine brought loss of power
"Our skin was black like an oven because of the terrible famine" (v.10), or "Our skin gloweth like an oven, because of the burning heat of the famine" (JND). According to Ellicott's Commentary, "The words paint the hot fever of hunger rather than the livid paleness of exhaustion".

Loss of people (vv.11-13)
Men and women, old and young, were affected. In the New Testament, Paul reminded Timothy that an assembly is a spiritual family: "Rebuke not an elder, but intreat him as a father; and the younger men as brethren; The elder women as mothers; the younger as sisters, with all purity" (1 Tim 5.1-2). Although not in the same order, the current passage refers to all four categories mentioned by the apostle.

"They ravished the women in Zion" (v.11a)
Leaving aside, in the interests of delicacy, the precise details of this horrifying aspect of war and conquest, it can be said generally that there was no respect or honour for the older women. In the assembly, believers should treat "the older sisters as they would their own mother" (A. Leckie). In sending greetings to believers at Rome, Paul included "Mary, who bestowed much labour on us…the beloved Persis, which laboured much in the Lord…Rufus…and his mother and mine" (Rom 16.6,12-13). Sadly, there is a tendency in some places for the younger generation either to forget, or worse, to ride roughshod over, older believers, with scant regard for their wishes or their feelings.

"They ravished…the maids in the cities of Judah" (v.11b)
Again, without recourse to detail, the opportunity is taken to emphasise that in the assembly, to use Paul's language, younger women are to be treated "as sisters, with all purity", that is, "as sisters, and no more" (A. Leckie).

"Princes are hanged up by their hand: the faces of elders were not honoured" (v.12)
While the words, "hanged up by their hand", might refer to the "hand" of the enemy, it seems more likely that they describe the spectacle of princes "suspended in mid-air with their hands bound together", possibly humiliated in this way by "the 'slaves' who had risen to power (v.8)"

(Harrison). Streane interprets this differently in saying, "The reference probably is not to death by crucifixion, but to subsequent impalement in order to expose to the utmost ignominy". One way or the other, there was no respect for leadership, represented by the "princes", or for experience, represented by the "elders", all of which are far removed from Paul's instructions, "Rebuke not an elder, but intreat him as a father". Good leadership, and wisdom born of experience, is so often swept aside by powerful and purposeful groups of younger people, or others, who think they know better. Paul taught differently: "And we beseech you, brethren, to know (recognise) them which labour among you, and are over you (take the lead among you) in the Lord, and admonish you; And to esteem them very highly in love for their work's sake" (1 Thess 5.12-13).

"They took the young men to grind, and the children ('youths', JND) fell under the wood" (v.13)

The potential of the young men was abused. As Streane points out, "the general sense of the verse is that as rank and advanced age was no safeguard, neither did the tenderness of age secure against the most oppressive and menial of labours".

In assembly life, great care must be taken in handling younger believers. The Shepherd-King will "gather the lambs with his arm, and carry them in his bosom" (Is 40.11). While "It is good for a man that he bear the yoke in his youth" (3.27), all too often younger men have been exposed prematurely to the stresses and strains of assembly life, with disastrous results. The concept of a "brethren's meeting" where all, however young, are party to discussion and debate on assembly affairs, is most unwise at its mildest, and sheer folly at its worst. It is equally sad when younger believers, not to mention those who are older, are bought body, mind, and soul, by their careers and employment, with resulting neglect and impairment of their spiritual potential, not to mention spiritual loss to the assembly.

Loss of the place (vv.14-18)

The city, once throbbing with life and vitality, "is desolate, the foxes walk upon it" (v.18). Foxes walked where men once walked. On a technical note, Gesenius favours the word "foxes" (7776), but points out that "The name of foxes appears to have been commonly used as also including jackals by the Hebrews, like the other orientals…and these are apparently the animals intended". Jeremiah's dismal picture of Zion is a far cry from the glowing description given in Psalm 48 which, while anticipating millennial conditions, must also describe the past glories of the city: "Walk about Zion, and go round about her: tell the towers thereof. Mark ye well her bulwarks, consider her palaces; that ye may tell it to the generation following" (Ps 48.12-13). The bustling and secure city had been transformed into a heap of empty ruins, and, alas, many once bustling and strong assemblies have also been reduced to ruins, and for the same reason: "Woe unto us, that we have sinned!" (v.16).

Jeremiah describes four things which had happened to the place where the Lord had "put his name" (Deut 12.5), all of which serve to warn the Lord's people today.

There was no counsel in the gate
"The elders have ceased from the gate" (v.14a). The city gates were the places where advice was sought and counsel given. They were the administrative centre of city life (Deut 21.19-20; Ruth 4.1; Prov 31.23). The local assembly should be a place where spiritual advice and counsel are given.

There was no joy in the heart
"The young men (have ceased) from their musick. The joy of our heart is ceased; our dance is turned into mourning" (vv.14b-15). Sin will turn joy into sadness. The assembly should be a place where believers "rejoice in the Lord" (Phil 3.1).

There was no crown on the head
"The crown is fallen from our head" (v.16). The words of Job explain this statement: "He hath stripped me of my glory, and taken the crown from my head" (Job 19.9). Streane puts it succinctly: "honour is brought to the dust". The assembly should be a place where the saints display the dignity of their calling. Believers should resemble "the children of a king" (Judg 8.18).

There was no light in the eye
"For this (what follows in v.18) our heart is faint; for these things our eyes are dim" (v.17). One again, Job explains: "Mine eye also is dim by reason of sorrow" (Job 17.7), and Jeremiah follows suit: "Mine eyes do fail with tears" (Lam 2.11). The assembly should be a place where the eyes of the saints gleam with anticipation as they say, "Thine eyes shall see the king in his beauty: they shall behold the land that is very far off" (Is 33.17).

Verse 19: Confidence in the Lord
The book of Lamentations commenced with reference to Israel's "lovers" and "friends" (1.2); "I called for my lovers, but they deceived me" (1.19). They had proved totally unreliable in time of crisis. Now, at the end of the book, Jeremiah turns to the unchanging God: "Thou, O Lord, remainest ('sittest', JND margin) for ever; thy throne from generation to generation". The use of "Jehovah" ("LORD", AV), is immensely significant. Jeremiah refers to the God of Israel as the covenant-keeping God, implying expectation that He would not abandon His people. The throne of Judah

had fallen, but God's throne remained, and would do so for ever. John saw "a throne...set in heaven" (Rev 4.2).

Unlike the thrones of some European potentates such as King Constantine of Greece, King Carol of Romania, King Peter of Yugoslavia, and King Zog of Albania, God's throne cannot be toppled. Habakkuk asks the rhetorical question, "Art thou not from everlasting, O Lord my God, mine Holy One?" (Hab 1.12), and the psalmist beautifully contrasts the impermanence of creation with the permanence of the Creator: "Of old hast thou laid the foundation of the earth: and the heavens are the work of thine hands. They shall perish, but thou shalt endure: yea, all of them shall wax old like a garment; as a vesture shalt thou change them, and they shall be changed: But thou art the same, and thy years shall have no end" (Ps 102.25-27). In the language of another psalm, "The Lord shall reign for ever, even thy God, O Zion, unto all generations. Praise ye the Lord" (Ps 146.10). As Albert Barnes points out, "There shall be no change of dynasty as there is in human governments; but the same King shall reign from age to age".

Jerusalem had proved, to its awful cost, that on earth, "there is none that doth deliver" (v.8). Only the Lord could deliver them, and Jeremiah acknowledges His strength, stability and permanence. Confession of sin leads to contemplation of God's might and majesty. In this respect, the prophet follows the psalmist: "I will lift up mine eyes unto the hills, from whence cometh my help. My help cometh from the Lord, which made heaven and earth" (Ps 121.1-2); "Unto thee lift I up mine eyes, O thou that dwellest in the heavens" (Ps 123.1).

Verses 20-22: Cry for Restoration

The circumstances of God's people led them to the conclusion that the Lord had forgotten and forsaken them: "Wherefore dost thou forget us for ever, and forsake us so long time?" (v.20). The Lord, who "remainest for ever" (v.19) appeared to have forsaken them "for ever". There appeared to be no hope for them. This was, of course, not the case. Over a century before, "Zion said, The Lord hath forsaken me, and my Lord hath forgotten me" with the reply, "Can a woman forget her sucking child, that she should not have compassion on the son of her womb? yea, they may forget, yet will I not forget thee. Behold, I have graven thee upon the palms of my hands; thy walls are continually before me" (Is 49.14-16). This had not changed in the intervening period: "For the Lord will not cast off for ever: But though he cause grief, yet will he have compassion according to the multitude of his mercies" (Lam 3.31-32).

But this did not seem to be the case at the time, and from the depths of their despair, with all the apparent hopelessness of their case, the cry is uttered: "Turn thou us unto thee, O Lord, and we shall be turned; renew our days as of old" (v.21). The cry is a confession of their own utter weakness, with fervent prayer to God for His help in strengthening their spiritual resolve to serve Him. The words, "renew our days as of old" are reminiscent of the early days of their national history of which the Lord had said, "I remember thee, the kindness of thy youth, the love of thine espousals, when thou wentest after me in the wilderness, in a land that was not sown. Israel was holiness unto the Lord, and the firstfruits of his increase" (Jer 2.2-3). For the assembly at Ephesus, the "days as of old" were the believers' "first love" (Rev 2.4).

The prophet is deeply conscious that their restoration depended completely upon God. "Turn thou us unto thee, O Lord, and we shall be turned; renew our days as of old" (v.21). These words are evidently taken from Jeremiah 31.18, and the reader is referred to comments made at that point in this commentary. Restoration is a divine work. In this connection, David's oft-quoted words, "He restoreth my soul" (Ps 23.3), come readily to mind. He also said, "Create in me a clean heart, O God; and renew a right spirit within me" (Ps 51.10). Asaph also recognised that restoration was a divine work: "Turn us again, O God, and cause thy face to shine; and we shall be saved" (Ps 80.3). In the New Testament, Timothy was told to instruct "those who oppose, if God perhaps may sometime give them repentance to acknowledgement of the truth" (2 Tim 2.25, JND).

The Scriptures emphasise that when Israel's restoration takes place, it will not be on the basis of her merit, but solely on the basis of God's grace and glory: "Therefore say unto the house of Israel, Thus saith the Lord God; I do not this for your sakes, O house of Israel, but for mine holy name's sake, which ye have profaned among the heathen, whither ye went....Not for your sakes do I this, saith the Lord God, be it known unto you" (Ezek 36.22,32). The prophet Micah is equally clear: "Who is a God like unto thee, that pardoneth iniquity, and passeth by the transgression of the remnant of his heritage? he retaineth not his anger for ever, because he delighteth in mercy. He will turn again; he will have compassion upon us; he will subdue our iniquities; and thou wilt cast all their sins into the depths of the sea" (Micah 7.18-19).

But Jeremiah takes nothing for granted. The cry for restoration and renewal is made in full recognition of God's anger: "Or is it that thou hast utterly rejected us? Wouldest thou be exceeding wroth against us?" (v.22, JND). This is supported by Streane who reads, "Unless thou hast utterly rejected us; unless thou art very wroth against us", and continues by saying that "the whole sentence is an hypothesis not to be accepted as fact, and to express this, there should be a note of interrogation after *us* in both parts of the verse". He concludes, "God's anger cannot last for ever, and thus there is yet hope". However, the Lord's people must never presume on the restoring grace of God. Jeremiah was all too conscious of God's hatred for sin, but nevertheless, the book does conclude with the language of hope.

Ellicott's Commentary points out, with others, that "in synagogue use and in many manuscripts, verse 21 is repeated after verse 22, so that the book may not end with words of so terrible a significance". However, this device seems quite unnecessary in view of the actual meaning of v.22. It could be said of this chapter that Jeremiah had put his "mouth in the dust: if so be there may be hope" (3.29). Ironside rightly points out that "The day of Judah's lamentations will never be truly over until the Sun of Righteousness shall arise with healing in His wings, to dry their every tear, and to restore them to the land promised to Abraham for an inheritance for ever...Then Jerusalem's mourning will be accomplished; her warfare will be ended!".